The 1939 BALTIMORE Elite Giants

Edited by Frederick C. Bush, Thomas Kern,
and Bill Nowlin

Associate editors – Len Levin and Carl Riechers

Society for American Baseball Research, Inc.
Phoenix, AZ

The 1939 Baltimore Elite Giants
Edited by Frederick C. Bush, Thomas Kern, and Bill Nowlin
Associate editors Len Levin and Carl Riechers

Design: Gilly Rosenthol

Front cover photograph is in the public domain, as are numerous images throughout this book.
Back cover photograph courtesy of David Stinson and Bernard McKenna.

978-1-960819-25-3 (paperback)
978-1-960819-24-6 (ebook)
Library of Congress Control Number: 2024909308

Cronkite School at ASU
555 N. Central Ave. #416
Phoenix, AZ 85004
Phone: (602) 496-1460

Web: www.sabr.org
Facebook: Society for American Baseball Research
Twitter: @SABR

The 1939 BALTIMORE Elite Giants

CONTENTS

Dedicated to Frederick "Rick" Bush

PREFACE AND ACKNOWLEDGMENTS

This history of the 1939 Baltimore Elite Giants is the seventh in a series of SABR books about the great Negro League teams of the first half of the twentieth century. The story begins with Tom Wilson, who established the team in Nashville in 1921. They had been previously known as the Nashville Standard Giants, a semipro team that Wilson founded in 1918. Wilson was a local businessman, transplanted from Atlanta, with a love for baseball. The idea of a competitive Black team in the South around the time that the Negro National League was forming farther north under the aegis of Rube Foster appealed to Wilson. But as much as he was loyal to Nashville, his entrepreneurial instincts and wish for financial success led him to relocate the franchise from time to time in search of greener pastures.

Columbus and Washington, DC, became way stations for Wilson as he moved the team in search of a sizable and stable fan base that Nashville's Black population did not offer. Eventually, in 1938, after a poor showing in Washington, he found what he was looking for – a receptive environment for his Elites – and moved the team one more time, to Baltimore, less than 50 miles up the road. The following year, 1939, the Baltimore Elite Giants struck pay dirt and won the Negro National League championship in a four-team playoff, besting first the Newark Eagles and then the juggernaut Homestead Grays. They remained in Baltimore for the duration of their existence, until the team folded in 1950.

This book provides a detailed account of the Elite Giants and an array of essays about the players and team officials behind them that resulted in Baltimore's 1939 crown. A complete season timeline, the story of Oriole Park, where the Elites often played, the historical context of the time, and articles about some of standout games are also included. They offer a backdrop for Tom Wilson's bio and player narratives ranging from the young Roy Campanella and the likes of Biz Mackey, Burnis "Wild Bill" Wright, Henry Kimbro, and player-manager Felton Snow to those serving as the supporting cast.

In addition to the players with bios published in this book, over a dozen additional players were identified in *The Negro Leagues Book*, published in 1994 edited by Dick Clark and Larry Lester, as well as in James A. Riley's extensive work, *The Biographical Encyclopedia of The Negro Baseball Leagues*, as having appeared at some point with the Elite Giants in 1939. Seamheads has captured few if any details on these players in

a 1939 Elite Giants uniform; the transient nature of players led to their ephemeral appearances on the roster or even just the occasional bench warming at best in any given year. To quote the late Rick Bush, "[I]t has been inevitable that we find one or more players who cannot be identified or about whom we can find no evidence of their participation in the year on which the book is focused. The following individuals have been omitted from this book for such reasons." But while the surmised place of these players in Baltimore in 1939 remains uncertain, they merit brief attention and the hope that a future researcher will unearth more details about their lives and baseball careers.

I.V. ("Vet" or "Ed") Barnes. Seamheads lists Vet (nicknamed Schoolboy or Ed) Barnes as having played for the Kansas City Monarchs in 1937 and 1938. There are no records (yet) for any time with the Elite Giants in 1939. He was born on December 23, 1911, in Silver Creek, Mississippi, and died on May 13, 1974, in Vallejo, California. Alternatively, Ed Barnes is listed by Riley as having played for the Monarchs in 1937-1938 and then for Baltimore in 1939-1940.[1]

Charles Green "Wooger" Beverly (a.k.a. Beverie). Beverly ostensibly played some third base for the Elite Giants in 1939.[2] His career, ranging from 1925 to 1939, otherwise had him as a left-handed pitcher primarily for the Kansas City Monarchs, but also for the Birmingham Black Barons, Cleveland Stars, Pittsburgh Crawfords, Philadelphia Stars, and Newark Eagles. A so-so record of 17-21 and a career batting average of .179 framed his itinerant career, of which portions of eight seasons are documented. Barnes was born in Walker County, Texas, on May 6, 1900, and died in Sealy, Texas, on March 20, 1981.

George Britt. Britt had an extensive career in the Negro Leagues, dating from 1917 and lasting into the early 1940s. He played for 10 teams, including the precursor to the Elite Giants in Baltimore, the Baltimore Black Sox, from 1923 to 1926. A pitcher who also caught and served as a utility player, Britt was a serviceable right-hander with a decent curve. According to Riley, he was nicknamed "Chippy" because that is what he called everyone else.[3] His longest tenure was with the Homestead Grays; sandwiched on either side of his supposed time with the Elite Giants in 1939, he played for the Washington Black Senators and Grays. He was born in Lexington, Kentucky, on

July 6, 1895, and died in Erie, Pennsylvania, in January 1981 at the age of 85.

Jimmy Direaux. Pitcher, third baseman, outfielder. Records show Direaux having pitched for Baltimore in 1938, but no carryover is immediately documented for the 1939 season. Luke suggests that Direaux, along with Andy Porter and Schoolboy Griffith, jumped to the Mexican Leagues that season for better pay.[4] In fact, Direaux spent most of his career in Mexico, playing stateside only for the Elite Giants both in Washington and Baltimore. Direaux was born in Pasadena, California in 1916, and a record of his death has not yet been found.

Al Johnson. A brief career for the Washington Black Senators and the Elite Giants in 1939 and 1940,[5] with an earlier appearance with the Washington Elite Giants in 1936, Johnson was a pitcher, but nothing else is known about him.

Francis Matthews. Seamheads identifies first baseman-outfielder Fran Matthews as a Newark Eagles lifer in the late 1930s and early 1940s with time off for military service, but Riley suggests he played for Baltimore, even sparingly, in 1939. Matthews was born in Cambridge, Massachusetts, on November 2, 1916, attended Boston University before his baseball career began, and died in Los Angeles on August 24, 1999, at the age of 82. He was deemed a promising player in his early years, but his career might have been affected by being hit by Monte Irvin with a throw from third base.[6]

John "Lefty" Phillips. Born in Nashville in 1918, death date unknown. Information on Phillips is scarce, although Seamheads shows him appearing in five games over the 1939 and 1940 seasons with Baltimore for a total of 5⅔ innings pitched and an ERA of 12.71.

Andrew Porter. Andy "Pullman" Porter was considered one of the big three with Baltimore in 1938 alongside Jonas Gaines and Bill Byrd. However, according to Luke, in 1939 he opted to take his talents to Mexico with teammates Jimmy Direaux and Schoolboy Griffith.[7] The tall right-hander had a 15-year career split between the Negro Leagues and Mexico, playing in the latter for at least four seasons. He returned to Baltimore in the early 1940s and finished his career with the Indianapolis Clowns. Porter lived to be 100; he was born in Sweet Home, Arkansas, on March 7, 1910, and died in Los Angeles on July 1, 2010.

Sarah "Mutt" Roberts. Riley lists Roberts as a pitcher for the Philadelphia Stars in 1937-1938 before appearing with the Elite Giants in 1939. No records otherwise have been found.[8]

Clarence Williams. Records for Clarence Williams, a pitcher and outfielder, are scarce. Riley suggests he played three seasons, first for the Washington Black Senators in 1938 and in 1939 and 1940 for Baltimore.[9] Seamheads found him in one Elite Giants box score in 1939, going 0-for-2. No other information on him is readily available.

G. Williams. Shown as a utility player for Baltimore in 1939 by Riley; no other details are readily available.[10]

M. Williams. Not much is known about this right-handed pitcher who ostensibly played for Baltimore briefly in 1939 and then for the Newark Eagles during the World War II years.[11]

Woodrow Wilson "Willie" Williams. Seamheads lists a contemporary as "Lilly" but no Willie Williams. Riley's records show Willie or "Woody," a left-handed pitcher, as having played from 1933 to 1941 including time with the Elite Giants, in Washington in 1937 and then with the Baltimore club in 1938-1940 before ending his career with the Birmingham Black Barons in 1941.[12]

Jim Willis. With the monikers "Cannonball" and "Bullet Jim" to underscore his lethal fastball, Willis played for four iterations of the Elite Giants from Nashville to Columbus to Washington and Baltimore. Seamheads shows him with a career 32-49 record and at least two appearances for Baltimore in 1939. He was born in Sewanee, Tennessee, on February 28, 1908, but had no date of death listed.[13]

Zollie Wright. Born on September 17, 1909, in Milford, Texas, Wright, a right-handed-batting right fielder, played for nearly a decade in the 1930s for a handful of teams, including the Elite Giants franchise beginning with the Columbus version and then Washington (where he earned a 1936 selection to the East-West All-Star Game) and Baltimore. He ended his career with stints with the New York Black Yankees (in 1939 and 1940) and the Philadelphia Stars (1941). The Black Yankees and Elite Giants exchanged players from time to time in the late 1930s; perhaps Wright surfaced for a time in Baltimore in 1939. He died in Philadelphia on April 12, 1976.[14]

This book and those in the series that have preceded it has been made possible by the 30 SABR members who have collaboratively and diligently researched and written each article. A difficult task in compiling a book like this continues to be the collection of photos of as many as possible of those portrayed in it. Some of the more obscure players pose challenges and we are grateful for the efforts of those who have been able to help in finding visual representations.

It is important to take a moment and note the passing of Frederick C. "Rick" Bush, editor of so many of SABR's baseball compilations. He died in 2023, having already invested much time and effort in planning and organizing this book. He set an example and tone for all who have contributed to books like these, for which we are thankful. He will be missed.

We express our thanks to the tireless efforts of our fact-checker Carl Riechers and copy editor Len Levin. They have served in these capacities in earlier books in the series and are consummate professionals at what they do. Finally, it is fitting to paraphrase how Rick Bush might have concluded this Preface and Acknowledgments, noting that another book in this series is already in the works – the 1945 Cleveland Buckeyes. For now, enjoy yet another window on Black Baseball's past – the 1939 Baltimore Elite Giants.

—Thomas Kern

NOTES

1   James A. Riley, *Biographical Encyclopedia of the Negro Baseball Leagues* (New York: Carroll & Graf Publishers, Inc., 1994), 58.

2   Riley, 82.

3   Riley, 109-110.

4   Bob Luke, *The Baltimore Elite Giants* (Baltimore: The Johns Hopkins University Press, 2009), 43.

5   Riley, 429.

6   Riley, 521-522.

7   Luke, 43.

8   Riley, 669.

9   Riley, 848.

10   Riley, 849.

11   Riley, 858.

12   Riley, 864.

13   Riley, 865.

14   Riley, 884.

IN 1939

BY MALCOLM ALLEN

In 1939 the minor-league Baltimore Orioles, winners of seven consecutive International League pennants from 1919 to 1925, endured a losing season under first-year manager Rogers Hornsby, the 43-year-old future Hall of Famer. Still, without a successful Orioles season to celebrate, the achievements by the other hometown team, the Elite Giants, did not seem to offer solace and the team's 1939 Negro National League championship drew little attention in the city's leading newspaper.[1] When the *Baltimore Sun* selected Maryland's top sports standouts at year end, both were from Frederick County: New York Yankees rookie Charlie Keller, and Challedon, the Preakness Stakes winner and American Horse of the Year.[2]

Although the Yankees won their fourth straight World Series, it would be a mistake to think that little had changed for the champions in pinstripes, or baseball itself, in 1939. Lou Gehrig's streak of 2,130 consecutive games played ended on May 2. Seven weeks later Gehrig was diagnosed with amyotrophic lateral sclerosis (ALS). On the Fourth of July at Yankee Stadium, the player nicknamed the Iron Horse delivered his iconic "Today, I consider myself the luckiest man on the face of the earth" speech.

On June 12, 1939, the National Baseball Hall of Fame opened in Cooperstown, New York. Ten of the original 13 inductees were introduced to the crowd (Ty Cobb arrived late; Willie Keeler and Christy Mathewson had already died) and Commissioner Kenesaw Mountain Landis remarked, "I should like to dedicate this museum to all America, to lovers of good sportsmanship, healthy bodies and keen minds. For those are the principles of baseball."[3]

A *New York Times* headline the next day read, "Baseball Pageant Thrills 10,000 at Game's 100th Birthday Party."[4] The US Post Office issued a 3-cent "Centennial of Baseball" stamp.[5] The truth expressed in Harrington "Kit" Crissey's 1976 *Baseball Research Journal* piece – "Serious baseball research has refuted the earlier contention that Abner Doubleday laid out the first baseball diamond at Cooperstown, N.Y. in 1839 while a cadet at the U.S. Military Academy" – had not yet taken root.[6]

The inaugural Little League game was played on June 6, 1939, in Williamsport, Pennsylvania. (Lundy Lumber defeated Lycoming Dairy, 23-8.)[7] On May 17 baseball was broadcast on TV for the first time, with Princeton defeating Columbia University, 2-1, in an "Ivy League" (the title did not become official until 1954) clash. "The players were best described by observers as appearing 'like white fliers' running across the screen," the *Times* reported. "It was impossible for the single camera to include both the pitcher's box and home plate at the same time. When the ball flashed across the grass it was a comet-like white pinpoint. The umpires in the dark uniforms stood out more vividly than did the players in white suits."[8]

Television sets had been available to American consumers only since May 1, the day after RCA introduced them at the opening of the World's Fair in New York City. By the end of the year, only a few hundred US homes had TVs.[9]

The first major-league games were televised on August 26, 1939, a Brooklyn Dodgers-Cincinnati Reds doubleheader. Empire State Building-based station W2XBS (later WNBC) sent two cameras to capture the action at Ebbets Field, and viewers up to 50 miles away could tune in. Contrasting the telecast to the springtime Princeton-Columbia contest, the *Times* observed, "It was apparent that considerable progress had been made in the technical requirements and apparatus for this sort of outdoor pick up, where the action is fast. At times it was possible to grasp a fleeting glimpse of the ball as it sped from the pitcher's hand toward home plate."[10]

The NCAA basketball tournament also debuted in 1939. Eight teams competed in the first edition of what eventually came to be called March Madness, with contests in Philadelphia, San Francisco, and Evanston, Illinois. The University of Oregon prevailed by defeating Ohio State, 46-33. Future major-league second baseman Ford "Moon" Mullen was a reserve for the victorious Webfoots.

In college football, the Agricultural and Mechanical College of Texas (now Texas A&M) went undefeated, and 20-year-old Jackie Robinson more than lived up to the hype that accompanied his arrival at the University of California, Los Angeles.[11] But the Heisman Trophy went to University of Iowa quarterback Nile Kinnick, who shared Associated Press Athlete of the Year recognition with Alice Marble, the winner of tennis's singles, doubles, and mixed doubles competitions at both Wimbledon and the US National Championships. (Bobby Riggs, 21, won the men's singles events at each tournament).

In the National Football League, the Green Bay Packers shut out the New York Giants, 27-0, to secure their fifth championship in 11 years under coach Curly Lambeau. Arguably no athlete was more popular than the Brown Bomber, boxing's Joe Louis. The Detroit resident defended his heavyweight championship four times, including an 11th-round knockout of Bob Pastor at Briggs Stadium on September 20 that *The Ring* magazine proclaimed the "Fight of the Year."

When *Time* magazine named its Best Song of the [Twentieth] Century in 1999, the choice was Billie Holiday's "Strange Fruit," which was recorded on April 20, 1939. In

Manhattan's Sheridan Square that spring, Holiday performed the song nightly at Café Society. "The music is very beautiful and Miss Holiday sings this piece with extraordinary power," remarked NAACP executive secretary Walter White.[12] After Holiday's recording was released, *Variety* described it as "Anti-Lynch Propaganda in Swingtime, on a Disc."[13]

Originally a 1937 poem by New York City English teacher Abel Meeropol (under his pseudonym Lewis Allan), "Strange Fruit" was inspired by a photograph of two African American teens hanging from a tree after they were lynched in Indiana. "I wrote Strange Fruit because I hate lynching, and I hate injustice, and I hate the people who perpetuate it," Meeropol explained.[14]

The number of lynchings in the United States had declined steadily, and sharply, over the previous half-century.[15] Yet, as the *Baltimore Afro-American* newspaper noted on January 6, 1940, "Tuskegee reports three lynchings in 1939, and the NAACP records five. ... The main thing we want to point out is that three lynchings are three too many. Even one unpunished lynching is a horror from which civilized people should shrink."[16]

In Arlington, Tennessee – the same state where the Negro National League's Elite Giants had gathered for spring training – an African American sharecropper lost his life because he asked for a receipt on April 28, 1939.[17] When a record number of Blacks voted in Miami's mayoral primary in May, they were met by 50 carloads of Ku Klux Klan members that burned 25 crosses.[18]

In Baltimore, Mayor Howard W. Jackson was reelected to his third consecutive (and fourth overall) term without incident. However, when the African American associate pastor of Orchard Street Methodist Church attempted to move his family into a home on Baker Street in April, the *Sun* reported, "A crowd of boys brushed past the police guard stationed there and dragged out several pieces of furniture to the street and smashed them. A crowd of almost 1,000 people participated in the melee and fists were swung freely."[19] Later that spring, the *Sun* described a new technique that Baltimore's police commissioner approved for the city's predominantly Black Western district: "A flying squad of five policemen surrounds a tavern catering to Negro trade, orders all the patrons to line up and then 'frisks' them for concealed weapons."[20]

In Washington, DC, African American singer Marian Anderson attracted a crowd estimated at 75,000 on Easter Sunday.[21] Although the 52-year-old contralto had entertained audiences across Europe and the United States for years, her concert took place on the steps of the Lincoln Memorial because the Daughters of the American Revolution had denied her permission to sing at the DAR's historic Constitution Hall, citing an unwritten "Whites only" policy. One of the thousands of DAR members who resigned in protest was Eleanor Roosevelt, the wife of President Franklin D. Roosevelt. That summer, the first lady appeared at the NAACP convention to present Anderson the Spingarn Medal.[22]

In retrospect, many historians cite 1939 as the end of the decade-long Great Depression, though it was hardly a smooth transition.[23] On the first day of 1940, the Associated Press re-

ported, "The Stock Market underwent the shock of tremendous and confusing events in 1939 – events, perhaps, eventually of more far-reaching import than the economic collapse of 1929. The price wheel turned the full circle, from boom to bust and back to boom again."[24]

On December 31, 1939, the *Sun* published an Institute of Public Opinion piece that noted, "First and foremost in the minds of Americans at the year's end is the outbreak of war last September between England and France on one side and Germany on the other – an event which has been foreseen and dreaded by the average American for the last several years."[25] Although the United States remained officially neutral in the conflict that later escalated into World War II, Germany's September 1 invasion of Poland was overwhelmingly opposed by most US citizens, who supported the French and British 84 percent to 2 percent, according to a Gallup poll that appeared on the same page of the newspaper. (The Soviet Union's incursion into Finland at the end of November – ordered by Josef Stalin, *Time's* Man of the Year for 1939 – was even less popular, with Americans backing the Finns, 88 percent to 1 percent.)[26]

Yet, the United States was one of three countries (along with Cuba and Canada) that had refused to allow entry to more than 900 passengers – most of them Jews fleeing persecution in Führer Adolf Hitler's Nazi Germany – aboard the *M.S. St. Louis* that spring.[27] Instead, they were forced to return to Europe, where more than a quarter of them were likely murdered in the Holocaust.[28] Their story became the subject of the 1976 feature film *Voyage of the Damned* (based on a 1974 book with the same title).

As for the movies released during the Elite Giants' Negro National League championship year, Michael Glitz opined in a 2008 Huffington Post article, "Film buffs have declared 1939 as the greatest year for movies so many times that it's seen as historical fact, rather than just a widely accepted opinion."[29] (*Hollywood's Golden Year, 1939,* and *1939: Hollywood's Greatest Year* are each titles of books.) Although *Mr. Smith Goes to Washington* and one of the most successful films of all time, *Gone with the Wind*, were released after the baseball season, another future cinema classic had its Baltimore premiere about three miles south of Oriole Park in August 1939. "The strangest thing about 'the Wizard of Oz,' now at the Century, is that it resembles a color cartoon by Walt Disney," reported *Sun* reviewer Donald Kirkley. "It seems at times to have been drawn, rather than enacted on solid stages by living people. One of the greatest technical achievements in screen history, the film is something for grownups, as well as children, to marvel at."[30]

The film version of John Steinbeck's 1937 book *Of Mice and Men* was also released in 1939 while the new novel that would earn him the Pulitzer Prize, *The Grapes of Wrath*, topped the *New York Times* Best Seller List throughout the Elite Giants' campaign.[31]

Those who preferred comic books were introduced to Batman in the spring of 1939.[32] Shortly after, another *Action Comics* sensation from the previous year gained his own series with the publication of the inaugural *Superman* issue.[33]

Although the *Sun* and *The Sporting News* ignored the 1939 Baltimore Elite Giants' heroics, that fall, Ric Roberts of the *Atlanta Daily World* proclaimed the Elites "the greatest race baseball team in the business."[34] Their triumph was chronicled by Black newspapers like the *Baltimore Afro-American*, the *New Journal and Guide* of Norfolk, Virginia, the *New York Amsterdam News*, the *Chicago Defender*, and the *Kansas City Call*. The *Pittsburgh Courier*'s Bandy Dixon – conceding that coverage of the Elite Giants' September 24 championship clincher had been "pushed to the background by the hysteria encircling" Louis's knockout of Pastor four days earlier – penned a 300-word column on October 7 headlined, "Belated Plaudits for the Title Coup of the Elite Giants."[35] Now, for their success during a year dominated by transformative events, enduring icons, and memorable feats, it is fitting that the members of the 1939 Baltimore Elite Giants receive further overdue recognition.

NOTES

1   Although the dearth of Elite Giants' coverage was not mentioned specifically, in 2022 the *Baltimore Sun* Editorial Board published a lengthy apology for news coverage and editorial opinions that "sharpened, preserved and furthered the structural racism that still subjugates Black Marylanders" throughout the first 185 years of the newspaper's history. *Baltimore Sun* Editorial Board, "We are Deeply and Profoundly Sorry: For Decades, the Baltimore Sun Promoted Policies that Oppressed Black Marylanders; We are Working to Make Amends," *Baltimore Sun*, February 18, 2022, https://www.baltimoresun.com/2022/02/18/we-are-deeply-and-profoundly-sorry-for-decades-the-baltimore-sun-promoted-policies-that-oppressed-black-marylanders-we-are-working-to-make-amends/ (accessed January 28, 2024).

2   "Keller and Challedon Bring Fame to State for Sports Feats in 1939," *Baltimore Sun*, December 31, 1939: S3.

3   Arthur J. Daley, "Baseball Pageant Thrills 10,000 at Game's 100th Birthday Party," *New York Times*, June 13, 1939: 1.

4   Daley.

5   Gordon T. Trotter, "Centennial of Baseball," https://postalmuseum.si.edu/exhibition/about-us-stamps-bureau-period-1894-1939-commemorative-issues-1938-1939/baseball (accessed January 20, 2024).

6   Harrington "Kit" Crissey, "Abner Doubleday Would Have Been Proud," 1976 *Baseball Research Journal*), https://sabr.org/journal/article/abner-doubleday-would-have-been-proud/ (accessed January 20, 2024).

7   "History of Little League," https://www.littleleague.org/who-we-are/history/ (accessed January 20, 2024).

8   "First Television of Baseball Seen," *New York Times*, May 18, 1939: 29.

9   "The History of Television (Or, How Did This Get So Big?)," https://www.cs.cornell.edu/~pjs54/Teaching/AutomaticLifestyle-S02/Projects/Vlku/history.html (accessed January 20, 2024).

10 "Games Are Televised," *New York Times*, August 27, 1939: S4.

11 Andy Wittry, "Jackie Robinson's Football Career at UCLA Hinted at Greatness to Come," NCAA.com, April 14, 2023, https://www.ncaa.com/news/football/article/2022-04-14/jackie-robinsons-football-career-ucla-hinted-greatness-come (accessed January 20, 2024).

12 "Night Club Singer Waxes First Song About Lynching," *New Journal and Guide* (Norfolk, Virginia), June 17, 1939: 16.

13 "Anti-Lynch Propaganda in Swingtime, on a Disc," *Variety* (Los Angeles), May 10, 1939: (Volume 134, Issue 9): 40.

14 Aida Amoako, "Strange Fruit: The Most Shocking Song of All Time?" BBC.com, April 17, 2019, https://www.bbc.com/culture/article/20190415-strange-fruit-the-most-shocking-song-of-all-time (accessed January 14, 2024).

15 From 1882 to 1968, the Tuskegee Institute recorded 4,742 lynchings in the United States, with 72.6 percent of the victims African Americans. The average number of annual lynchings by decade declined from 154 in the 1890s, to 88.8 in the 1900s, 62.2 in the 1910s, 31.5 in the 1920s, and 12.8 in the 1930s. The last year in which a double-digit number of victims was counted was 1935. http://law2.umkc.edu/faculty/projects/ftrials/shipp/lynchingyear.html (accessed January 14, 2024).

16 "Three Too Many Lynchings" *Baltimore Afro-American*, January 6, 1940: 4.

17 "Jesse Lee Bond," *Lynching Sites Project, Memphis*, https://lynchingsitesmem.org/lynching/jesse-lee-bond# (accessed January 20, 2024).

18 Associated Press, "Miami Negroes Ignore Klan Threat and Cast Record Vote," *Baltimore Sun*, May 3, 1939: 2.

19 "Fists Fly Freely in Racial Clash," *Baltimore Sun*, April 16, 1939: 3.

20 "Police Flying Squad Seeks to Reduce Cutting Affrays," *Baltimore Sun*, June 5, 1939: 18.

21 Edward T. Folliard, "Ickes Introduces Contralto at Lincoln Memorial," *Washington Post*, April 10, 1939: 1.

22 Since 1914 the NAACP has presented the Spingarn Medal in most years to an African American for outstanding achievements. As of 2023, Jackie Robinson (1956) and Henry Aaron (1976) were the only baseball players to receive it. Obie S. McCollum, "5,000 See Mrs. Roosevelt Present NAACP Medal to Marian Anderson," *Baltimore Afro-American*, July 8, 1939: 1.

23 In 2021 the Harvard Business School published Alberto Cavallo, Sophus A. Reinert, and Federica Gabrieli's "The Global Great Depression, 1929-1939," https://www.hbs.edu/faculty/Pages/item.aspx?num=61531 (accessed January 21, 2024). Other examples of 1939 being cited as the end of the Great Depression include Charles P. Kindleberger, *The World in Depression 1929-1939* (University of California Press, 2013) and "The Great Depression and New Deal, 1929-1939," *PBS Learning Media*, https://ny.pbslearningmedia.org/collection/us-history-collection/era/the-great-depression-and-new-deal-19291939/ (accessed January 21, 2024).

24 Associated Press, "Stocks Confined Throughout Year," *Baltimore Sun*, January 1, 1940: 10.

25 Institute of Public Opinion, "Foreign Affairs Crowd Domestic Issues Out of National Limelight," *Baltimore Sun*, December 31, 1939: 8.

26 George Gallup, "Gallup Poll: – Reds Anger U.S.," *Baltimore Sun*, December 31, 1939: 8.

27 "Voyage of the St. Louis," *Holocaust Encyclopedia*, https://encyclopedia.ushmm.org/content/en/article/voyage-of-the-st-louis (accessed January 21, 2024).

28 Scott Miller and Sarah Oglivie, *Refuge Denied: The St. Louis Passengers and the Holocaust* (Madison: University of Wisconsin Press, 2010), 174-175.

29 Michael Glitz, "DVDs: 1939 – The Best Year for Movies … Ever!" Huffington Post, February 15, 2008, https://www.huffpost.com/entry/dvds-1939-the-best-year-f_b_86897 (accessed January 27, 2024).

30 Donald Kirkley, "A Film Version, with Music, of L. Frank Baum's 'The Wizard of Oz' Shown Here," *Baltimore Sun*, August 18, 1939: 10.

31 "Adult New York Times Best Seller Lists for 1939," Hawes Publications, https://www.hawes.com/1939/1939.htm (accessed January 27, 2024).

32 Alex Zalban, "When 'Is' Batman's Birthday, Actually?" MTV.com, March 28, 2014, https://www.mtv.com/news/xxfa1g/batman-75th-anniversary-birthday-date (last accessed January 27, 2024).

33 "Superman (1939 first series) Comic Books," https://www.mycomicshop.com/search?TID=22601073 (accessed January 27, 2024).

34 Ric Roberts, "Atlanta Is the No. 1 Ungrateful Sports Town of the Nation," *Atlanta Daily World*, October 1, 1939: 8.

35 Bandy Dixon, "Belated Plaudits for the Title Coup of the Elite Giants," *Pittsburgh Courier*, October 7, 1939: 17.

A HISTORY OF THE 1939 BALTIMORE ELITE GIANTS

FROM NASHVILLE TO NEGRO NATIONAL LEAGUE II CHAMPIONS

BY BOB LUKE

By 1939 the Elite Giants had earned the moniker "The well-traveled Elite Giants." The team's arrival in Baltimore in the spring of 1938 marked the end of a long search for a dependable fan base and financial stability. Seventeen years earlier, at a January 7, 1921, meeting of team officials in the Elite (pronounced "EE-lite) Pool Room in Nashville, Tennessee, 38-year-old president and owner Thomas T. "Smiling Tom" Wilson had renamed the Nashville Standard Giants, a semipro team he had founded in 1918, the Nashville Elite Giants. The name "Giants" indicated, in the vernacular of the day, that it was a "colored" team.[1] Wilson promised Nashville residents the team "will be the fastest Colored club in the south next season."[2]

Nashville and the Negro Southern League

The team was one of 10 teams in the Negro Southern League in 1921. Teams returning from 1920, the league's first season, were the Birmingham Black Barons, Knoxville Giants, Montgomery Grey Sox, and New Orleans Caulfield Ads. New teams, in addition to the Elites, were the Memphis Red Sox, Mobile Braves, Chattanooga Tigers, Atlanta Black Crackers, Bessemer Alabama Stars, and Gadsden Alabama Giants.[3]

Opening Day on April 25, 1921, began with a festive occasion that Wilson continued to invoke at opening days in the years to come. The club's directors led a parade consisting of a brass band and automobiles carrying members of both teams – the Elites and the Memphis Red Sox. A community leader threw out the ceremonial first pitch.[4] The highlight of the Elites' maiden season was a 17-game winning streak in July and August on their way to copping the pennant in the newly organized 1921 version of the NSL, which was considered a "minor league" of the African American leagues. Rube Foster's recently created Negro National League was the preeminent Black league of the day.

Pitching led the way. Three no-hitters, one by Wild Bill Nesbitt and two by rookie Darltie Cooper, brother of Hall of Fame pitcher Andy Cooper, highlighted the team's inaugural season. Cooper finished the season with a 14-8 record, while Frenchy Gibson led all Elite moundsmen with a 15-6 record. Full of confidence and bravado after receiving the championship silver cup, Wilson announced, "The Nashville club will play any team anywhere."[5]

While it is unknown if any team accepted Wilson's challenge, the Elites started the 1922 season in fine fettle. They swept five straight games from the Louisville Cardinals, a new addition to the NSL. Wilson expanded a strong pitching staff with the addition of Ralph "Square" Moore from the New Orleans Crescents and two outfielders, Will Holt and George "Jew Baby" Bennett. Wilson named third baseman Felton Leroy Stratton as manager. Stratton could also play any position and wielded a decent bat as was evidenced by his six hits in a doubleheader win over the Birmingham Black Barons. Newly acquired shortstop Hooty Phillips, a baserunner extraordinaire, beat many a catcher's throw to second and third base.[6] By early June, Nashville led the NSL with a 20-15 record.[7] By July 30, they led the pack by three games and finished in first place for the first half of the season. However, Wilson's men did not have a chance to defend their previous season's championship, since the entire NSL folded in early August due in part to mismanagement and lack of baseball experience on the part of some team owners. The Elites and several other teams continued as independent ballclubs.[8]

The ensuing three seasons (1923-1925) saw fragmentation again characterizing the NSL. Team owners had decided to split the 1923 season into a first and second half, but the league once again dissolved, this time before the second half began. Several teams went under for financial reasons. Two teams, the Birmingham Black Barons and the Memphis Red Sox, cast their lots with the Negro National League. The Nashville Elite Giants survived by barnstorming through the 1924 and '25 seasons.

The 1926 season saw another resurrection of the NSL. Wilson's Nashville Elite Giants joined seven other teams, each of which put up a $500 franchise fee and $70 "for promotional purposes."[9] Always on the lookout for capable players, Wilson dispatched his right-hand man and club secretary, Vernon "Fat Baby" Green, on a tour of several Northern states in early June. Green had been a catcher on the 1921 Elites but found his talent lay more in administration than playing, and he served as Wilson's aide-de-camp for more than 20 years.[10] He returned with four players – pitcher Clarence White, catcher Russell Bailey, outfielder William Mc Neal, and shortstop Joe Cates.[11] The new players did little to improve the Giants' performance, and the team languished in sixth place as the season ended. In two games of note, the renamed Chattanooga White Sox beat the Elites behind the pitching of a 20-year-old rookie named Satchel Paige.[12]

In 1927 the Elites started on a more promising note. Wilson had again revamped the roster, and only four players remained from the 1926 team. Wilson acquired Joe Hewitt from the Chicago American Giants in the NNL "at great expense" to replace Felton Stratton as manager.[13] Stratton remained with the team as a player and returned to the hot corner. Hewitt turned to managing as his 17-year career as a stellar infielder was coming to an end. Wilson acquired several players from other NSL teams, notably pitcher Jim "Cannonball" Willis and catcher Red Charleston. The *Nashville Banner* predicted that the team would be "strong."[14]

The paper's prediction proved true for the first half of the season, in which the Elites were "generally declared to be the winner" amid conflicting newspaper accounts of games won and lost. Results for the second half of the season were not published. The Elites, however, won a championship that year, capturing the Negro Dixie Series title. Their first-half win entitled the Elites to represent the NSL against the Dallas Black Sox, champions of the Black Texas League. The Elites beat the Texans, 5-4, in the series' final game before a wildly cheering crowd at Sulphur Dell. The Negro Dixie Series mirrored that of the annual post-season matchup between the champions of the White Southern Association and the Texas League (also White).[15]

A Move to the Negro National League

Eager to improve his team's performance and prestige, Wilson attended the 1928 annual NNL winter meetings, held as usual in January in Chicago, in hopes of joining the league, which was deemed to be the "major league" of Black baseball. He came away with a promise that the Elites would be considered an associate member of the league and that full membership would be granted should the Memphis Red Sox drop out. Games with associate members did not count in the standings, and associate members could not compete for the pennant. Memphis stayed in the NNL, and Wilson returned to Nashville only to see the NSL disintegrate once again.[16] The Elites, as an associate member of the NNL, played independent ball that year, and they continued to do so during the 1929 and '30 seasons.[17]

One of the 1930 games, played on May 14 in Nashville's Wilson Park against the NNL's Kansas City Monarchs, was notable for two reasons: 1) It drew one of the largest crowds in recent memory, and 2) it was the first night game ever played in Nashville. Floodlights at first and third base and two in the outfield provided the illumination. The Monarchs prevailed, 4-3. Wilson Park, built by Tom Wilson in 1928, had a capacity of 8,000 spectators and afforded the team the ability to schedule

The 1939 Baltimore Elite Giants at Oriole Park. Back row: Sammy Hughes, Wild Bill Wright, Bill Byrd, Eddie Dixon, Hoss Walker, Bill Hoskins, Willie Hubert, Emery Adams. Front row: Jonas Gaines, Boogie Wolf Childress, Red Moore, Felton Snow, Tom Butts, Roy Campanella, Henry Kimbro, Tom Glover.

games independent of the White minor leagues' Nashville Vols' schedule. Games for which the crowd was expected to exceed 8,000 continued to be played at Sulphur Dell.[18]

The year 1930 also marked Wilson's first foray to California. The California Winter League accepted his application to field a team he called the Elite Giants. This was not the Nashville Elite Giants but rather a handpicked aggregation of the top "colored" players. They included St. Louis Stars shortstop Willie Wells and first baseman-outfielder Mule Suttles, "The Race Babe Ruth"; pitcher Satchel Paige; outfielder Norman "Turkey" Stearnes from the Detroit Stars; and third baseman Judy Johnson from Pittsburgh's Homestead Grays – all eventual Hall of Famers. Wilson claimed the Elites "will be the most popular on the Coast." Whether or not the team was the most popular, it was certainly the best. They won the 1930-31 CWL championship. It would not be their last.[19]

The Moves Begin

At the same time, the Elites were finally granted full membership in the NNL for the 1931 season. Wilson's NNL membership, however, was for Cleveland, not Nashville. He moved the Elites franchise to the City by the Lake, where the team played as the Cleveland Cubs. Notable Cubs players included Satchel Paige and a 19-year-old rookie infielder named Ray Dandridge, who had quit the floundering Detroit Stars due to that team's financial difficulties. After a short stint with the Cubs, Dandridge starred in the Negro Leagues for 16 seasons and gained induction into the Hall of Fame in 1987.[20]

Wilson rarely left Nashville, where he had a number of business interests, so he relied on Vernon Green to oversee all games. One game, however, brought Wilson to Cleveland. In a July game against Louisville, Paige, in a fit of pique, threw a ball at umpire Baby King and cussed him out. King ejected Paige, prompting Cubs manager Joe Hewitt to call the Cubs off the field. Green and Louisville manager Columbus Ewing managed to quell tempers so the game could continue. The incident added fuel to the criticism that Black baseball had descended into a state of rowdyism brought on by a lack of interest on the part of managers and owners. Hearing about the fracas, Wilson arrived in Louisville, where he fined Hewitt and suspended him for five games. The *Chicago Defender* complimented Wilson's actions as "the right step in the direction of restoring the game to its former high plane."[21]

While no standings were published, incomplete records show the Cubs were credited with a 24-22 record for the portion of the season during which the team was in business. The Great Depression was in full swing and practically all of Black baseball felt its sting. The NNL disbanded, the Cubs folded, Paige signed with the Pittsburgh Crawfords, and Wilson took the remaining Elites back to Nashville for play in the NSL for the rest of the 1931 season.[22]

While many of the Elites' best players had migrated to Cleveland, fortune smiled on those left behind and perhaps others who made up the '31 Nashville Elite Giants based in Nashville. Wilson now presided over two teams; one in the NNL II and one in the NSL. The two teams faced each other at least once in late April for a doubleheader. The Cubs easily took both games, 7-1 and 5-0.[23] By the end of June, the Nashville team led the NSL, and its resurgence was highlighted by an 11-game winning streak. By July, however, its lead had been cut to one game over the once-again-renamed Chattanooga Lookouts. In the end, the Nashville Elites squeaked by the Memphis Red Sox to take the first-half pennant by a mere 3 percentage points.[24] The Elites went on to win the second-half flag as well, thus earning the right to play the Monroe Monarchs, champions of the Texas-Louisiana League. The Elite Giants lost the series in seven games. The *Chicago Defender* called the series "one of the most heated battles that has ever been played in the South."[25]

A New Negro Southern League

While the Elite Giants were tearing up the CWL out West, a new Negro Southern League consisting of six teams was organized, with Wilson's Nashville Elite Giants among the member franchises. Wilson was elected league treasurer. Reuben B. Jackson, his friend, physician, fellow frequent NSL officer, and Nashville resident, was elected vice president. To contain costs, the NSL limited the number of teams to six, with each team carrying 13 players (including the manager).[26]

As the Depression continued to take its toll, teams that once belonged to the defunct Negro National League either folded or sought new affiliations. Wilson consolidated the Elite Giants into one team in the NSL for the 1932 season. That season the powerhouse Chicago American Giants joined the NSL. Chicago and Nashville finished the season as the top two NSL teams and faced off in the Dixie Series, which was broadcast over the radio by both NBC and CBS. The American Giants, behind the likes of future Hall of Famers Willie Foster (half-brother of Rube Foster) and Turkey Stearnes, a Nashville native best known for his play with the Detroit Stars, won the seventh and deciding game at Wilson Park, 3-2. Shortly thereafter, Wilson took an all-star Black team to the West Coast for another championship season in the CWL.[27]

While the Elite Giants continued their mastery of the CWL, six of Black baseball's most prominent moguls met in January 1933 in Chicago to reconstitute the Negro National League, known initially as The National Association of Baseball Clubs but later renamed the Negro National League II (NNL2). The Elite Giants, based in Nashville at the time, finally achieved full membership.[28]

In their first season as full NNL2 members, Wilson's Nashville nine finished third in the first-half standings but picked up their play and claimed the second-half title. This qualified the Elite Giants to face the Crescent Stars of New Orleans in the Negro Dixie Series. Considerable prestige was at stake as the winner of the series was to be crowned the best team in the South. The honor went to the Crescents but not without controversy sparked by faulty newspaper reporting.

New Orleans won the first three games before an appreciative home crowd of over 11,000 spectators who cheered Nashville's star pitcher Cannonball Willis's offerings and those of his relievers "being swatted to all corners of the lot."[29] The teams then traveled to Nashville for the final four games. A *Chicago Defender* article of September 23, 1933, credited the Elites with winning both ends of the opening doubleheader, thereby narrowing the Crescents' lead to 3-2. H.D. English, secretary of the Stars club, took issue with the account. He accused the sportswriter for the Elites of being asleep during the doubleheader and asserted that the Crescents had won the double bill, 2-1 and 7-4, making them victorious in the series, five games to two. "I am wondering," English continued, "just what the Nashville fans will say as they sat there and saw the Giants lose."[30]

As the Dixie Series was underway, Wilson once again assembled a team of Negro League stars to take to California. His latest squad, now named the Royal Elite Giants, once more came out on top of the CWL, giving Wilson's teams four pennants in four seasons. The pitching of Satchel Paige and Cannonball Willis foiled the bats of many opponents. Willis had been a mainstay of the Nashville team from 1927 to 1934 and was one of the few Nashville Elites to travel west in the winters. The bats of sluggers Mule Suttles, Turkey Stearnes, and Wild Bill Wright complemented the slick fielding of shortstop Willie Wells and Elite infielders Sammy T. Hughes at second base and Felton Snow at third as the Royal Elite Giants rolled to another CWL pennant to the tune of a 34-5 record.[31]

Elites Back in the Negro National League

As the Depression continued, owners expressed more interest in minimizing travel costs by placing teams in Eastern cities, which were closer to one another than those in the Midwest and South. In January 1934, the NNL2 owners met in Philadelphia rather than Chicago and emerged with a few new member teams that gave the league a decidedly Eastern flavor. The league comprised the Philadelphia Stars, Pittsburgh Crawfords, Chicago American Giants, Newark Dodgers (soon to become the Newark Eagles), Nashville Elite Giants, Baltimore Black Sox, Philadelphia Bacharach Giants, and Cleveland Red Sox. The Elite Giants, heavy preseason favorites "to be among the big threats," were strengthened by the addition of pitcher Walter "Steel Arm" Davis and manager Candy Jim Taylor, recognized as one of the game's smartest managers. The Elites ended up being less than the big threat envisioned by Wilson to claim the NNL2 pennant; Seamheads shows the team finishing in fifth place.[32]

Yet another change was in store for the Elites in 1935. No longer the Nashville Elite Giants, they were slated to become the Detroit Elite Giants, a location that would put them closer to other teams in the league. A White Detroit businessman, John Roesing, who was assumed to be the owner of a lease for Roesing Stadium in the nearby village of Hamtramck, welcomed the team and promised to make all necessary repairs to bring the park up to date. "Well, I'm glad that's over," a relieved Wilson

sighed once the negotiations had concluded. The trouble was that Roesing had unknowingly lost his lease on the park by nonpayment of taxes. By an action of the Hamtramck City Council, the lease was now in the hands of the Detroit Lumber Company and the city of Hamtramck, and a full schedule of semipro games in the ballpark for a local White team already had been arranged. Upon hearing the news, just a week before Opening Day, a not-so-relieved Wilson quickly relocated the team to Columbus, Ohio, in time for Opening Day against the New York Cubans on May 16, 1935. The Columbus Elite Giants finished third in the NNL2 standings, just .003 percentage point ahead of the Philadelphia Stars.[33]

Dissatisfied with Columbus, Wilson again sought greener pastures. The nation's capital caught his eye. Washington was only 40 miles from Baltimore, and both cities had large and growing Black populations. In an effort to tap both markets, Wilson decided that the now Washington Elite Giants would play their day games in DC and split their night games between the two cities. The team boasted an impressive roster.[34] Jim "Shifty" West at first base had proved to be a consistent .300-plus hitter the last two seasons and delighted fans with his fancy glove work. Sammy T. Hughes was considered the league's premier second baseman and was a solid hitter with speed on the bases. Team captain and sometimes manager Felton "Skipper" Snow, who held down the hot corner, owned a rifle of an arm, respectable batting averages, and a knack for stealing bases. Snow managed the team through most of the 1940s.

Bowlegged Leroy Morney, who had been with the Elites for two seasons, was seen "as a master shortstop" and completed the infield. The outfield consisted of Wild Bill Wright, who hit the long ball from both sides of the plate, had a strong if not always accurate arm, and was considered the fastest Negro League player; Zollie Wright, who was no relation to Wild Bill, usually batted cleanup and manned right field; and Homer "Goose" Curry, an adequate outfielder who played four season for the Elites, started in left. The Elites featured a strong pitching rotation of Schoolboy Bob Griffith, Andy Porter, Jim Willis, and Tom Glover, a hard-throwing sophomore.

Of particular note was the addition of Biz Mackey, a 2006 inductee into the Hall of Fame, to the lineup at the catcher's spot. The "old man" of the team at age 38, Mackey, acquired in a trade with the Philadelphia Stars, kept runners hugging their bases, hit with power, and would mentor a 15-year-old rookie catcher named Roy Campanella when he joined the team in 1937. Campanella, a native of Philadelphia, was the only player on the '37 team born north of the Mason-Dixon Line. The rookie learned well but didn't find the mentoring easy. "Biz," he said, "didn't want me to do just one or two things good. He wanted me to do everything good. ... There were times when Biz made me cry with his constant dogging. But nobody ever had a better teacher."[35]

With this lineup, manager Candy Jim Taylor, who had been an exceptional third baseman before embarking on a successful managerial career, including the past two seasons with the Elite Giants, predicted that the team "will be a first division club."[36]

Taylor's prediction proved true for the 1936 season's first half but not until a decisive game with the Philadelphia Stars, postponed in June, was finally played in September. The Giants won and were belatedly recognized as the league's first-half winner. They fared less well in the second half by losing the title to the Pittsburgh Crawfords.[37] Often the winners of the first half and second half faced off in a NNL2 championship series, but for unknown reasons no such series was played this season. William Augustus "Gus" Greenlee, a Pittsburgh tavern owner and Black community leader, in his capacity as NNL president and, not incidentally, owner of the Crawfords, ruled that the title belonged to the Craws as they had best record for the entire season; a .593 winning percentage against .460 for the second-place Elites.[38]

The bus that carried the Elites south for spring training in March of 1937 held essentially the same roster as the year before with two notable additions. 20-year-old Jimmy Direaux, a right-handed pitcher and a Los Angeles native, came to Wilson's attention by striking out 108 batters in a six-game stretch for the semipro Arizona Broncos, an accomplishment featured in *Ripley's Believe It or Not*. He ended up spending two unremarkable seasons with the Elites before jumping to the Mexican League. Henry "Kimmie" Kimbro, a 25-year-old outfielder, was the second acquisition. An all-around exceptional player, he remained with the Elites for 11 seasons, an unusually long tenure with a single team in the Negro Leagues. Biz Mackey replaced Taylor as manager while Campanella, still in high school, played occasionally. Douglass O. Smith, a booking agent with the power to arrange Negro League games at certain ballparks in return for a fee, put a dent in Baltimore's segregation policies by securing the city's best stadium, Oriole Park, for Elites' night games. The ballpark had been closed to "colored" teams for years.[39]

The 1937 Washington Elites came out of the gate in fine fashion. By the end of May they were in first place in the six-team league. By the end of July, they maintained their lead by downing the New York Black Yankees in a doubleheader. But it was downhill for the rest of the season. Wilson's nine fell to fifth place at season's end with a 23-36-3 record, thereby dashing early-season hopes for a pennant.[40]

Baltimore

Not only was Washington's record a disappointment, but its finances were as well. Wilson once again searched for a city that would adequately support the Elites. He decided on Baltimore. "Last year," he lamented at the 1938 annual owners' winter meeting, "we lost money with the club operating from Washington. I sincerely feel Baltimore is far superior to Washington as a baseball town." But there was a hitch. Wilson wanted to play in Oriole Park, home park of the Independent League Baltimore Orioles, but to do so he'd have to again go through Smith, which would cut into the team's finances.[41] Wilson's reluctance to work with Smith, together with the objections that White citizens voiced to Oriole Park officials about the "noise and fanfare" generated by night games the previous season, resulted in Bugle Field becoming the Elites' home park for the 1938 season.[42]

Wilson's optimism about Baltimore was buoyed by the efforts of Richard Powell who had many contacts in the city. He talked up the Elites to Black leaders and community groups. Powell gained the backing of Baltimore's chapter of the Frontiers Club of America, composed of leading businessmen, which supported minority group leaders striving to ameliorate racial, social, and civic issues. He also gained the support of Leon Hardwick, the *Baltimore Afro-American*'s sports editor. Hardwick promised to run frequent articles about the team, many of which Powell wrote on his second-hand typewriter. Powell also arranged for some players to stay in private homes, including his own, where they could enjoy home-cooked meals. Others stayed at the Clark Boarding House and ate at segregated restaurants. His biggest financial contribution was to lease Bugle Field for the Elites from its owner, the Gallagher Realty Company, saving Wilson the usual 10 to 15 percent fee charged by booking agents.[43]

Baseball was the main attraction at Bugle Field, but it was not the only one. The ballpark was a haven where people could relax and have a good time without the stress generated by Baltimore's culture of segregation and discrimination. Frederick Lonesome, a frequent spectator, recalled, "You didn't have to have a lot of money to enjoy yourself, and you didn't have to be afraid." Gambling was enjoyed by many. Lonesome recalled "seeing coins and dollar bills change hands as people bet on what the batter would do, like make a hit or get an out." Home-brewed whiskey, either gin or rye, sold for $3.00 a pint; a beer cost 20 cents. Candy, hot dogs, peanuts, and ice cream were plentiful. Many dressed to the nines and brought picnic baskets.[44]

The now Baltimore Elite Giants, the youngest team in the league the previous year, started 5-6 but began to find their footing. The *Pittsburgh Courier* lauded their "speedy pace" in the second half by trouncing the Homestead Grays 8-4 in a late July game,[45] They finished in fifth place, but a writer for the *Courier* hailed the soon to be Baltimore Elite Giants as pennant contenders for the coming 1938 season.[46]

Such hopes were dashed early. By the second week of June 1938, the Elites found themselves in fourth place in the NNL2 with a 5-6 record. By the end of the first half, on July 4, the team had slipped a notch to fifth place. Second-half standings were muddled because of inconsistent scorekeeping and some teams not reporting the outcomes of their games. Greenlee and Cum Posey, owners of the Pittsburgh Crawfords and Homestead Grays respectively, filled the void by listing the second-half order of finish as follows: the Grays in first place followed by the Philadelphia Stars, Pittsburgh Crawfords, Baltimore Elite Giants, Newark Eagles, and New York Black Yankees. How the two men arrived at their findings is not known, but they gave the league championship to the Grays, who had won the first half with a 26-6 record.[47] In spite of the Elites' disappointing record, Wilson saw enough bright spots to keep the team in

Kimbro in action, arriving at home plate. Courtesy John W. Mosley Photograph Collection, Charles L. Blockson Afro-American Collection, Temple University Libraries.

Baltimore. For one thing, the box office had been good to him. In addition to that, Hughes, Wright, and Mackey had been elected to the East squad for the East-West All-Star Game, held at Comiskey Park on August 21.

The Elites fared better in 1939 despite the fact that three starting pitchers, Andy Porter, Schoolboy Griffith, and Jimmy Direaux, had cast their lots with the Mexican League before spring training had started in Nashville. A bit of good news was that booking agents Ed Gottlieb and Smith persuaded the owners of Oriole Park, with 2,000 more seats than Bugle Field, to allow the Giants to play several doubleheaders there. Wilson paid their fee, banking on the possibility of more spectators than Bugle Field could accommodate. The first game at Oriole Park was an Opening Day doubleheader on Sunday, May 19, against the Grays. The Elites took a double drubbing, 7-1 and 11-0. Wilson's roster shook off their inglorious start and managed to

place third in the first half of the season while the Grays again easily took first place.[48]

As the second half got underway, a second competition – the Jacob Ruppert Memorial Cup Tournament – was introduced in late June. In a rare acknowledgement of the Negro leagues by a major-league organization, Ed Barrow, former general manager and recently appointed president of the New York Yankees, selected five NNL2 four-team doubleheaders to be played in Yankee Stadium as Ruppert Cup games. The winner of the most games would be awarded a trophy and $500. The games honored Col. Jacob Ruppert, the Yankees' owner and president from 1915 until his death on January 13, 1939, a four-term congressman, and the owner of Ruppert Brewery. Ruppert had opened Yankee Stadium to Negro League teams on July 5, 1930, when the New York Lincoln Giants and the Baltimore Black Sox played a doubleheader. As Barrow introduced the Ruppert Cup, he said, "Negro baseball can build its own structure right alongside the majors. Given sufficient opportunity to show their ability, the colored stars will undoubtedly attract thousands of fans and supporters who will help them in their fight to reach the pinnacle of organized baseball."[49]

Whether the prospect of winning the Ruppert Cup built a fire under the Elites is not known, but their second-half performance showed marked improvement. They took three straight from the Philadelphia Stars to start the second half. Wilson again changed personnel as he acquired five players from the Atlanta Black Crackers, a move the Chicago *Defender* described as "the biggest switch in players to be heralded in many seasons." To make room for the new men, Wilson sold Mackey to the Newark Eagles and West to the Philadelphia Stars. The new Elites were James "Red" Moore, a fancy fielding and good hitting first baseman; two pitchers, Ed Dixon and Felix Evans; catcher Oscar Boone, who could back up Campanella now that he was the starting backstop; and the pick of the litter, shortstop Tommy "Pee Wee" Butts, who stayed with the Elites until 1951 (save for jumping to the Mexican League for the 1943 season).[50] Lennie Pearson, the longtime first baseman of the Newark Eagles, said of him, "Butts was a tremendous shortstop and pesky hitter. He could go behind second better than any man I ever saw." Pearson said that Butts's "love of life" kept him out of the majors: "[H]e loved life, and when I say he loved life, I mean he loved life, especially women. After a game, Butts had a tendency to go out on the town."[51]

The "switch" in personnel helped. The Elites played above .500 ball for the rest of the season to edge the Grays for the second-half NNL2 championship. This year, instead of pairing the winners of the first and second halves for the NNL2 championship, the owners decided on two five-game series to determine which teams would contend for the title. Perhaps the additional revenue that would come from the extra games influenced their decision. Based on total wins for the season, the first-place Homestead Grays were paired against the fourth-place Philadelphia Stars, while the second-place Newark Eagles took on the third-place Elites. The Grays and Elites each won their series to advance to the five-game championship series. Campanella provided the best performance by a hitter in a single game. In Game Four of the championship series, played at Philadelphia's Parkside Field, Campanella, a Philly native, thrilled the home crowd by leading his mates to 10-5 win with a home run, a double, and two singles.[52] Campy's heroics helped the Giants tie the series at 2-2. The final and deciding game was scheduled for September 24 in Yankee Stadium.

Two Championships and Controversy

Not only would the NNL2 championship be up for grabs on the 24th, but the winner of that game would also claim the Ruppert Cup trophy. Nearly 10,000 spectators saw southpaw Elite pitcher Jonas "Lefty" Gaines shut out the power-laden Grays for seven innings before loading the bases in the eighth with consecutive two-out walks to Grays power hitters Josh Gibson, Buck Leonard, and Vic Harris. Gaines gave way

to Bubber Hubert, a journeyman right-hander, who retired Grays pitcher Thomas "Big Train" Parker on a popout to protect the Elites' 2-0 lead. Hubert held the Grays scoreless in the ninth inning.

The Giants had scored both of their runs in the seventh. Bill Hoskins, an outfielder in his second year with the Elites, drove in Wild Bill Wright, who had doubled, with a line-drive single to left field. Campanella soon followed with a single through the box that brought Hoskins, known for his speed on the bases, across the plate for the team's second tally.[53]

Gaines had shut down some of the league's leading hitters. In a list published by Cum Posey at the end of the 1939 season, five of the top 16 batters were Grays. Josh Gibson finished the season banging the ball at a .402 clip, while Sam Bankhead hit .378, Buck Leonard batted .363, Ray Brown finished at .316, and Henry Spearman hit .315. The Elites' Bill Wright ranked 10th with a .365 average. Amid postgame speeches by several dignitaries, Tom Wilson, with a broad smile across his face, celebrated winning the NNL2 championship and hoisted the Ruppert Cup trophy for all to see.[54]

The press had no question about who the champions were. "Climaxing an uphill campaign in a blaze of glory, the … Giants won the Negro National League baseball championship and the Jacob Ruppert Trophy," wrote the *Baltimore Afro-American* in a September 30, 1939, article. A July 6, 1940, *Chicago Defender* article referred to the Elites as "champions of 1939."

The Grays had no problem with the Elites winning the Ruppert Cup, but they did hotly contest the Elites winning the NNL2 championship. Buck Leonard spoke for many when he claimed the Grays should wear the crown because they had won the most games during the season.[55] In later years, Grays ownership still seemed unsure about how to present their team's 1939 season: The team's stationery for 1947 did not include 1939 as one of their many championship years, but their envelopes for 1949 did.[56] Playoff results show that in 1939 the itinerant Elite Giants had two championships to savor.

SOURCES

In addition to the sources cited in the Notes, the author is thankful for interviews with Frederick Lonesome, Barbara Powell Golden, and Gary Ashwill, and for access to the Art Carter Papers, Box 170-16, Folder 1, Manuscript Division, at the Moorland-Spingarn Research Center, Howard University, Washington, DC.

NOTES

1   An exception was the New York Giants, which were founded in 1883 and renamed from the Gothams to the Giants in 1885.

2   "Organize Nashville Elite Giants," *Chicago Defender*, January 8, 1921. Thomas Aiello, "The Southern Against the South: The Chicago Conspiracy in the 1932 Negro Southern Baseball League," *Journal of Illinois State Historical Society*, 1989, Vol. 102, No. 1, Spring, 2009, 10.

3   "Organize Nashville Elite Giants," *Chicago Defender*, January 8, 1921.

4   William J. Plott, *The Negro Southern League: A Baseball History*, 1920-1951 (Jefferson, North Carolina: McFarland & Co., 2015), 25.

5   Richard Schweid, "Club Built Against All Odds," *Nashville Tennessean*, September 2, 1987; "Elite Giants Win Seventeen Straight," *Nashville Banner*, August 15, 1921; "Elite Giants Win Southern Championship," *Chicago Defender*, October 1, 1921; www.negrosouthernleagueMuseumresearchcenter.org. Accessed March 21, 2023; James A. Riley, *The Biographical Encyclopedia of Negro Baseball Leagues* (New York: Carroll and Graf Publishers, 1994), 192.

6   Plott, 25, 36.

7   "The Southern League," *Chicago Defender*, June 3, 1922.

8   Plott, 41; Riley, 247.

9   Plott, 49.

10 Riley, 336.

11 "Elite Giants Obtain Four New Players," *Nashville Banner*, June 9, 1926.

12 "White Sox Outfit at Top Negro Loop," *Chattanooga Daily Times*, July 7, 1926; "Elite Giants Defeated by Chattanooga," *Nashville Banner*, September 6, 1926.

13 "Elite Giants to Be Strong This Season," *Nashville Banner*, April 8, 1927.

14 "Elite Giants to be Strong This Season"; Riley, 166.

15 Plott, 74-75; Riley, 379; "Elites Capture Negro Dixie Title," *Nashville Banner*, September 12, 1927.

16 Plott, 76.

17 "Elites Opener Is May 4 With Black Barons," *Chicago Defender*, April 12, 1929; Plott, 76-80. Gary Ashwill email to author.

18 "Large Crowd Sees First Night Game," *Nashville Banner*, May 15, 1930.

19 "Tom Wilson to Enter Strong Club in Coast Winter League," *Chicago Defender*, September 13, 1930; James Newton, "Nashville Elites Win Coast Baseball Flag," *Chicago Defender*, March 7, 1931.

20 https://www.seamheads.com/NegroLgs/player.php?playerID=dandrorray, accessed May 9, 2023; Riley, 209; Bill Gibson, "Hear Me Talkin' to You," *Baltimore Afro-American*, September 9, 1933.

21 Seamheads.com – Cleveland Cubs 1931; "Thomas Wilson, Owner of Cleveland Cubs, Fines and Suspends Mgr. Joe Hewitt," *Chicago Defender*, August 1, 1931.

22 Riley, 179.

23 "Elite Giants Drop 2 Games to Cleveland," *Chicago Defender*, April 25, 1931.

24 "Around the Diamond," *Chicago Defender*, June 13, 1931; "Elites Lead Dixie League," *Pittsburgh Courier*, July 18, 1931.

25 "Monroe Holds Record for Ball Titles," *Chicago Defender*, August 29, 1931; "The Southern League Meets January 23rd," *Chicago Defender*, January 16, 1932.

26 "Negro Southern League Organized," *Nashville Banner*, March 15, 1931; Aiello, 12.

27 R.R. Jackson, "Giants, Elites Prep for Dixie Title Series," *Pittsburgh Courier*, August 27, 1932; Luther Carmichael, "Chicago Giants Swamp Nashville in Dixie Championship Game," *Atlanta Daily World*, September 23, 1932; "Chicago Drubs Elite Giants," *Nashville Banner*, October 3, 1932.

28 Al Monroe, "Six Clubs in New League," *Chicago Defender*, January 14, 1933.

29 "New Orleans Leads Title Series," *Chicago Defender*, September 16, 1933.

30 "Nashville Wins 2, Cops Third Place," *Pittsburgh Courier*, July 15, 1933; "Nashville Giants in Negro Dixie Series," *Nashville Banner*, September 9, 1933; "Dispute Halts Southern Play-Off," *Chicago Defender*, September 23, 1933; H.D. English, "Here's More About Southern Playoff," *Chicago Defender*, September 30, 1933. English simply said the unsigned article the *Defender* had run on September 23 was incorrect, and that all those present at the game saw the second game played to its conclusion, editorializing further that "[a]rticles going to papers that have tried to help baseball, such as The Chicago Defender, should be exact and correct."

31 Riley, 865; James Newton, "Nashville 9 Enters West Coast League," *Chicago Defender*, September 23, 1933; James Newton, "Nashville Again Winner on Coast," *Chicago Defender*, February 10, 1934; Jim Taylor, "Elite Giants Victor in Winter Loop Race," *Chicago Defender*, February 16, 1935.

32 "League Season to Open Here May 12," *Chicago Defender*, May 17, 1934; "Baseball Men Meet in Philly," *Baltimore Afro-American*, February 10, 1934; "Elite Giants Have Roesink Stadium for Detroit Park," *Baltimore Afro-American*, March 25, 1935. For final standings, see https://www.seamheads.com/NegroLgs/year.php?yearID=1934&lgID=NN2&tab=standings.

33 "Elite Giants Have Roesink Stadium"; "Detroit Has Team, But No Place to Play," *Baltimore Afro-American*, May 11, 1935; Dan Burley, "The Sports Round-Up, "*Philadelphia Tribune*, May 16, 1935; John Holway, *The Complete Book of Baseball's Negro Leagues: The Other Half of Baseball History* (Fern Park, Florida: Hastings House Publishers, 2001), 316. The final standings are per Seamheads.com as of August 2023.

34 "Lewis Wins From Ed Simms," *Baltimore Afro-American*, May 14, 1936.

35 Roy Campanella, *It's Good to Be Alive* (New York: Little, Brown & Co., 1959), 58-59 as cited in Luke, 34.

36 Candy Jim Taylor, "Nashville Elites Play as Washington's Home Team," *Chicago Defender*, April 18, 1936.

37 Seamheads has Pittsburgh as first-half champions and the Elites as second-half champs.

38 Cum Posey, "Posey's Points," *Pittsburgh Courier*, September 26, 1936; "Nashville Seeks Title in Belated Ball Finale," *Chicago Defender*, May 1, 1937; Riley, 764-765, 628-629.

39 "Tom Wilson Signs Young Pitching Star," *Pittsburgh Courier*, February 27, 1937; "Elites to Use Oriole Park," *Baltimore Afro-American*, April 10, 1937; Riley, 462-463.

40 https://www.seamheads.com/NegroLgs/team.php?yearID=1937&teamID=WEG&LGOrd=1, accessed May 16, 2023. "Washington Sweeps Yank Series: Leads Loop," *Pittsburgh Courier*, July 24, 1937; "Standings," *Pittsburgh Courier*, May 29, 1937.

41 "May Transfer Elite Giants From Washington to Balto," *Baltimore Afro-American*, February 5, 1938.

42 "Baltimore Elites Down to Work," *Baltimore Afro-American*, April 2, 1938.

43 "Vernon Green Succumbs to Heart Attack in Baltimore," *Baltimore Afro-American*, June 4, 1949; Riley, 639; Barbara Powell Golden (daughter of Richard Powell) interview, April 27, 2006 as cited in Bob Luke, *The Baltimore Elite Giants: Sport and Society in the Age of Negro League Baseball* (Baltimore: The Johns Hopkins University Press, 2009), 160.

44 Interview with Frederick Lonesome, October 10, 2006. As cited in Luke, 30.

45 "Washington Wins from Grays: Keeps League Lead," *Pittsburgh Courier*, July 31, 1937.

46 "Baltimore Elites to Be Real Pennant Contenders," *Pittsburgh Courier*, April 2, 1938. Final season standings are as reported by Seamheads in 2023. "Posey's Points," September 26, 1936, and "Nashville Seeks Title in Belated Ball Finale," May 1, 1937, both cite the Elites winning the first half and the Crawfords the second.

47 Gus Greenlee and Cum Posey, "NNL Turns in Report," *Baltimore Afro-American*, September 10, 1938, 23 as cited in Luke, 41.

48 "Homestead Grays Hand Double Beating to Baltimore," *Chicago Defender*, May 20, 1919, as cited in Luke, 41-47.

49 https://baseballhall.org/hall-of-famers/ruppert-jacob, Accessed May 27, 2023. "Ed Barrow, President of N.Y. Yankees, Donates Trophy to Negro Nat'l League," *Pittsburgh Courier*, June 3, 1939.

50 "Five Atlanta Players Signed by Baltimore," *Chicago Defender*, July 22, 1939; Riley, 139. Neither Dixon nor Evans appears on the roster as presented by Seamheads.

51 John Holway, *Voices from the Great Black Baseball Leagues* (New York: Dodd Mead & Co., 1975), 328.

52 https://retrosheet.org/NegroLeagues/boxesetc/1939/B09230HOM1939.htm.

53 "Elite Giants Win National League Championship," *Baltimore Afro-American*, September 30, 1939; Riley, 394.

54 "Baltimore Whips Homestead Grays for Title," *Chicago Defender*, September 30, 1939. "Elite Giants Win National League Championship, *Baltimore Afro-American*, September 30, 1939; "Wright Gains NNL Batting Crown," *Baltimore Afro-American*, September 30, 1939; Riley, 299, 398, 603.

55 Buck Leonard and James A. Riley, *Buck Leonard: The Black Lou Gehrig* (New York: Carroll Publishers, 1995), 112, as cited in Luke, 51.

56 Art Carter Papers, Box 170-16, Folder 1, Manuscript Division, Moorland-Spingarn Research Center, Howard University, Washington, DC, as cited in Luke, 50.

EMERY ADAMS

BY RICHARD BOGOVICH

Emery Adams pitched during 11 years in the top Negro Leagues, from 1932 to 1947, with military service during World War II explaining one break in his statistical record. Two earlier gaps seemingly resulted from run-ins with the law, but a jury acquitted him of the serious charge that might have cost him the entire 1936 season. His most common nickname was Ace, which he was given before the 1940 season,[1] yet he really didn't achieve like an ace during nine years in top leagues. Still, in his prime with the second-place Baltimore Elite Giants of 1940 and 1941, no other hurler excelled for them in both seasons.[2] As of December 2023, all five of his career shutouts occurred in those two years, as did 17 of his 24 complete games. Also, fans voted him onto a roster for the East-West All-Star Game in August of 1940 (though he didn't play).[3] What's more, the pinnacle of his career might have come shortly after that season, when he sparkled for multiple scoreless innings as the starting pitcher in the Negro Leagues' sixth North-South Classic all-star game.[4]

Emery Adams was born in the vicinity of Collierville, Tennessee, on October 10, 1911, according to his 1940 military registration card. Collierville is about 20 miles from Memphis. Based partly on the censuses from 1900 to 1920, his parents were farmers named Sam and Polly. Sam's entry in the 1900 census stated that he was born in South Carolina during 1845 and thus 16 years prior to the Civil War. He was presumably a slave well into his teens. Sam would have been 66 when Emery was born. Polly was much younger, reportedly born in 1870 in Mississippi.

Emery Adams.

The 1910 census indicated that it was the second marriage for both of Emery's parents. In early 1899, a Memphis newspaper noted that a "Colored" couple, Sam Adams and Polly Williams, had obtained a license to be married.[5] However, her death record and Emery's 1948 certificate of marriage, among other documents accessible via genealogical websites, identified Polly's maiden name as Butler. Emery apparently had at least five half-siblings born before 1900 and was the youngest of at least four children born to Sam and Polly. In the 1910 census, Polly was reported to have given birth to five children, of whom four were still living.

In the 1920 census, Emery and his two brothers, ages 12 and 13, were all reported as attending school. In the 1940 census, it was stated that Emery had completed one year of high school. A history of Collierville focusing on civil rights noted that a school for Black children opened in Collierville during the 1920s.[6] It was rarely mentioned in Memphis's daily newspapers, but the "Collierville Industrial School, a negro institution," existed by the summer of 1923, if not earlier.[7] It was called the Collierville Industrial Junior High in an article five years later, about its students' participation in the "eighteenth annual negro Tri-State Fair."[8]

Census records show the township's population in 1920 and 1930 hovered around 1,000.[9] During that decade, farming operations in the Collierville area began to shift dramatically, as boll weevil beetles began to devastate cotton crops. Over just a few years, up to 1929, the number of dairies in Collierville jumped from a handful to several hundred.[10] Sam Adams was identified as a farmer up to the time he died.

The elder Adams's Certificate of Death, accessible via genealogical websites, indicates that he died in nearby Germantown on February 9, 1929. In the following year's census the Adams household comprised Polly, Emery, and one of his brothers. Polly was still listed as a farmer, while Emery's occupation was farm helper.

Emery Adams got married on July 8, 1930, in the county of his birth. The marriage license reported his bride's name as Emma Bell Hull. They were husband and wife for no more than six years. The couple apparently had one child together, a girl named Virginia, also known as Annie Virginia. She was reportedly born September 1, 1933.[11]

However, Emery's obituary noted that he was also survived by a son, Emery Jr. Two Social Security records agree that Junior's birthday was August 8, but one showed 1932 and the other 1933. Though Emery Jr. was likely older than Virginia, he was born to a different mother, Lula M. Craft. Because her mother was also named Lula, Junior's mother was often called Mary or Mattie instead. She and Emery Senior might never have married one another.[12]

Emery Adams turned 20 years old during the autumn of 1931, and six months later he was pitching for the Memphis Red Sox of the Negro Southern League. Though it seems very likely that he had considerable baseball experience prior to 1932, there might be no records in existence documenting any of that. The Red Sox received decent coverage in newspapers during 1931, but dailies in that city rarely mentioned any Black semipro or amateur teams.[13] Among more than 30 players on the Red Sox at some point during 1931, none was named Adams.[14]

The NSL was generally considered Black baseball's top minor league for much of its existence, but for the 1932 season it is considered to have been a "major league," a status officially recognized by Major League Baseball in 2020.[15] For just that one season, the NSL included two prominent Northern teams, the Chicago American Giants and the Indianapolis ABCs, plus a short-lived club in Columbus, Ohio. In fact, in the second game of a preseason doubleheader at home on April 17, Adams shut out Chicago, 3-0, in a game limited to five innings so the visitors could catch a train. He gave up just two singles, walked one batter, and struck out four.[16]

Emery Adams made his regular-season debut as a pro on May 1, 1932, in a doubleheader against the first-place Monroe (Louisiana) Monarchs. He was 20 years old. He started the seven-inning second game, and in the bottom of the third frame his team gave him a 3-0 lead. The only other scoring was a pair of runs by Monroe in the top of the fifth. Details of that inning aren't available, except that Adams retired just one batter before being replaced by a reliever. He struck out two Monarchs and yielded only two hits, but his three walks may have contributed to Monroe's threat in that fifth frame. (Also, each of Memphis' middle infielders made an error at some point, and the home team's catcher was charged with a passed ball.) Adams did contribute a little on offense: Though he was hitless in one at-bat, he stole a base and scored a run.[17]

As the 1932 season unfolded, only Harry Cunningham and player-manager Goose Curry logged more innings than Adams as starting pitchers for Memphis, based on seamheads.com data as of 2024. He started 10 of 11 games, completed four, and had a 4-3 record.[18] He was on the wrong end of a shutout at least twice, in May and in July.[19]

Memphis's stats in the Seamheads database jump to 1937 because the NSL reverted to minor-league status after 1932. In 1937 the Red Sox joined the Negro American League. However, from 1933 to 1936, William J. Plott's painstaking history of the NSL listed Emery Adams on the club's roster only in 1935, though in 1936 the club did have a pitcher named Adams (first name unrecorded) during April, if not later.[20] The 1933-1934 and 1936 gaps in Adams's personal record might be explained by Memphis newspaper reports about legal action against a local man (or men) named Emery Adams.

On February 6, 1933, "Emery Adams, negro," was prosecuted for "assault to murder, because of a fusillade of shots fired at W.B. Sandlin, marshal of Germantown, Dec. 21." In the end, he "pleaded guilty to assault to commit second degree murder, not more than three years at the penal farm."[21] Though Adams was mentioned often during 1935 as a member of the Memphis Red Sox, that name instead showed up in local legal news in 1936, from April 25 into October. A companion of Adams received a

10-year prison sentence for the shooting death of another Black man named Martin Hill, but Adams himself, "who was jointly accused of the crime, was found not guilty by a jury in Judge Tom W. Harsh's criminal court."[22] Assuming this relieved defendant was the Red Sox pitcher, then he celebrated his freedom the following month by getting married. His wife was the former Floyd Myers (an uncommon first name for a woman, but the November 22 marital record accessible via genealogical websites isn't the only place it was rendered that way).

"Statistically, the 1935 season was the worst ever" for the NSL, Plott insisted, because "results of any kind were found for only 33 league games." Plott said Bill Howard was the winning pitcher in all seven Memphis wins he'd located, but on June 30, Adams had an impressive victory in the second game of a doubleheader (following a win by Howard): He shut out the Claybrook (Arkansas) Tigers in a seven-inning contest, 1-0. Overall, Memphis did well enough to qualify for a postseason playoff series, which it lost to Claybrook.[23]

Adams pitched a few times against Claybrook in September. On September 1 Claybrook took both games of a doubleheader "to claim the National semipro championship," as reported by the *Chicago Defender*. In defeat, "Adams, the Memphis hurler, had a fair day on the hill, tossing the apple by the batters for strikeouts in usual manner."[24]

Coverage later in the month indicates the doubleheader was part of a seven-game series to determine the NSL championship. Adams relieved in both games of a doubleheader in Claybrook on September 8, which the teams split.[25] The teams had each won three games by September 15, when nearly 3,000 fans in Memphis attended the finale, which the home team lost, 5-2.[26]

Another mystery relating to Adams during the 1935 season was whether he was the Bill Adams who was with Claybrook briefly. If so, he was in the front row of a team photo that season.[27] "Bill" was a secondary nickname for Emery Adams, though possibly not otherwise in print prior to 1941.[28]

Regardless, September ended on a high note for Adams, when he pitched in the very first North-South Classic all-star game. It was played on September 29, at Memphis's Russwood Park before 3,800 fans. Adams pitched the final two innings for the South, against a lineup that included future Hall of Famers Cool Papa Bell leading off and Oscar Charleston batting cleanup. Adams allowed just one hit and was the only hurler on either team not to yield a run.[29]

On April 15, 1936, a preview of a game against the Monroe Monarchs mentioned Adams as one of two Memphis pitchers. On April 26 Adams was Memphis's reliever against a Black team visiting from Omaha.[30] It was two mornings earlier when the aforementioned Martin Hill, a Black man residing in Germantown, was shot to death by an unknown person. At some point within a month Adams and a companion were formally accused, but clearly not prior to his team's game on the 26th.[31] Though he was found not guilty in October, Adams may have been jailed for about half of that year due to the serious nature of the charge.[32]

As noted previously, for the 1937 season the Memphis Red Sox switched from the NSL to the NAL. Adams hurled a complete-game 7-6 victory at home against the Chicago American Giants on Opening Day, May 9. That gave the Red Sox a split of a doubleheader.[33]

As of 2024 the Seamheads database had data for 20 Memphis games in 1937, only one of which was a victory by Adams (in four appearances). However, in addition to that Opening Day win, brief newspaper coverage indicates he had a complete-game win vs. Indianapolis on May 17 and beat the St. Louis Stars later that month.[34] Also not documented in Seamheads is a game in August when he helped beat Birmingham by swatting a 10th-inning double (although he didn't pitch).[35]

A preview of a game late that month said "Adam [*sic*] hurled for the New Orleans Black Pelicans before joining Memphis." Unclear was whether that meant before he first joined Memphis in 1932, or before he rejoined the club much more recently.[36] Regardless, searches for a pitcher named Adams on that club prior to mid-1937 were fruitless.

To date, the Seamheads database shows just one game in 1938 for Adams, a four-inning relief outing for the Red Sox. In fact, that game was a preseason exhibition at home on April 3, a 7-3 loss to the Homestead Grays. The *Atlanta Daily World* printed a batter-by-batter account, though it wasn't clear in which middle inning Adams entered the game. He was mentioned again in a preview on April 16, but might not have been with the Red Sox during the regular season.[37] One distinct possibility is that he was injured. Another explanation is that he was making steady money at another job: Memphis's 1938 and 1939 city directories show him as employed by the Memphis Power and Light Company.

In any case, in 1939 Emery Adams played his first games in the second Negro National League, as a member of the Baltimore Elite Giants. As of 2024 the Seamheads database has documented five games pitched by Adams during that regular season, including two victories, plus a playoff loss. Using different criteria, the timeline for SABR's book on the 1939 Elite Giants identified 19 games for Adams from May through August (though at least six were nonleague contests).[38]

A high point for Adams during the season's first half was in June 12 in Indianapolis, against the Homestead Grays, reportedly the league's preseason favorite. It certainly helped that the famous Josh Gibson was unavailable due to a bruised hip, "but Adams, ace right-hander for the Giants, refused to allow the Champs a chance to get a line on his famed smoke ball." He struck out 11 Grays on the way to a 7-3 win for Baltimore.[39]

Not long before the NNL playoffs, Adams notched a complete-game win at home against the New York Cubans on August 27. It was the seven-inning nightcap of a doubleheader, and the final score was 8-4.[40] He then started the first game of a best-of-five playoff series against the Newark Eagles on September 6, at the opposition's Ruppert Stadium. After the top of the fourth inning, Adams and his teammates led 5-0, but Newark scored eight runs by the end of the sixth inning and

Emery Adams throwing.

ultimately won, 8-6.[41] The Seamheads entry for this game shows Adams having retired one batter in the sixth before exiting. He was charged with giving up seven runs, five earned. There's no record of Adams playing in the championship series against the Grays, but on September 24 the Elites became the NNL champs.[42] Though Adams pitched a half-dozen more seasons in the NNL, there's no indication that he ever appeared in another playoff game.

In the 1940 census, Emery and Floyd Adams were living in Memphis in the home of her mother, at 2563 Spottswood Avenue, near a very large railroad yard. Adams earned his nickname of Ace that year. The Seamheads database shows him as having won 12 games and lost five for the Elite Giants.

In June he tossed a 6-0 shutout against the Philadelphia Stars in a doubleheader's seven-inning nightcap, and his nine-inning shutout against the New York Cubans about a week into September won the Ruppert Memorial Cup for the Elites again.[43] In between those two high points, he was the only Baltimore pitcher named to the East team's roster for the East-West Classic in August, though he didn't play.[44]

The peak of Adams' career might have come shortly after the 1940 season. At New Orleans' Pelican Stadium on October 1, he sparkled for multiple scoreless innings as the starting pitcher in the Negro Leagues' sixth North-South Classic all-star game, though sources disagree on whether he pitched the first four or five innings. Regardless, the game wasn't decided until the ninth, when his North teammates scored once to break a 1-1 tie.[45]

Adams was on the Cienfuegos club in Cuba's winter league during 1940-1941, but he couldn't approximate his success of recent months. In 14 games, he had a record of 2-6.[46] In fact, a passenger list accessible via genealogical websites shows Memphis resident Emery Adams (born October 10, 1911) as having sailed from Havana to Miami on January 2, 1941. At least three Cienfuegos teammates made the same trip on January 20.

The 1941 season was the second of Adams's career for which the Seamheads database has documented considerable success. Though data is available for fewer games, his winning percentage with a record of 7-3 for Baltimore was comparable to that of 1940, with three shutouts documented in 1941 compared with two the prior season. One 1941 shutout was pitched on July 12 against the Newark Eagles and another on September 1 against the Black Yankees.[47]

Adams's 1942 season was largely unremarkable until a five-game "do-or-die series" with the Philadelphia Stars at the end of the season, which found the Elites hanging onto pennant hopes. Adams lost games in relief on September 6 and 7, and thus ended Baltimore's season.[48]

During spring training in 1943, the Baltimore Afro-American's sports editor, Art Carter, reported that Adams was "on the market as trade material." And by early May he'd been purchased by the Black Yankees.[49] Adams had at least four awful starts before the end of June, in which he pitched no more than five innings yet gave up 7 to 13 runs, Not surprisingly, he was called upon to pitch much less from July onward, but instead was frequently in New York's lineups as an outfielder. The Philadelphia Stars borrowed him as their starting pitcher on September 12, but he was back in New York's outfield within 10 days.[50] In fact, it was reported on September 20 that his batting average of .350 was the best among the Black Yankees.[51]

Less than three months into 1944, Emery Adams' life took a dramatic shift. US Army enlistment records accessible online show him having started military service on March 27. The military registration card he'd completed back in 1940 included a handwritten note specifying that he received an honorable discharge on September 9, 1944. Vaguely, the stated reason was "a lack of adaptability for military service."[52] If Adams played a little pro ball in the weeks after his discharge, it might have gone unreported.

Adams returned to the Black Yankees for the 1945 season, but was rarely used as a pitcher. In February of 1946, Adams was to be on a team projected to tour the Pacific for three months, playing against military ballclubs. The announced leader as Joe Lillard, a Black halfback for the NFL's Chicago Cardinals in 1932 and 1933, who'd helmed such a tour in Asia a year earlier. Very shortly after the 1946 trip was announced, it was "postponed indefinitely."[53] Adams then saw minimal action that season with New York, and likewise in 1947. That was apparently the extent of his pro career.

In 1948 Adams married for (at least) the third time. A Delaware certificate of marriage accessible via genealogical websites shows him marrying Irene Geter of New York City on March 21. The document presumably had a few details wrong (e.g., he'd been single, it was his first marriage, and he was born in Delaware), but his birthdate matched. In the 1950 census, the couple was living near a relative of hers in New York City, and he was employed as an inspector at a television factory.

Emery and Irene presumably divorced by mid-1952, because in October of that year she was identified by her maiden name, Geter, in a newspaper article detailing how she was swindled out of thousands of dollars a few months after a personal-injury lawsuit. In June, attorneys won her $40,000 for a leg amputation that resulted from a bus accident, and after their fees and court expenses, she took home $15,000. A con man cheated her out of that entire amount, though police did catch him.[54]

Emery Adams died "suddenly" in New York on January 22, 1955. His obituary published in Memphis mentioned that he was survived by daughter Virginia and son Emery Junior. There was no mention of any spouse, and his two surviving grandchildren were unnamed. (Of course, his daughter and son could have had additional children after his death.) He was survived by a sister and three brothers, all of whom were named with their places of residence. The funeral director was back in Collierville.[55]

Almost 60 years after his death, Adams was reportedly the central figure in an auction of a "Negro League game-used uniform," which had "E. Adams" written in marker near the manufacturers' tag. Grey Flannel Auctions of Scottsdale, Arizona, attributed it to Adams, and dated it in the mid-1930s. However, the tag identified the producer of this Memphis Pros jersey as Lawson-Cavette, a Memphis sporting-goods firm that had changed its name from Lawson-Getz during the summer of 1948. This would seem to indicate that for at least one season after leaving the Black Yankees, Adams went back home to play more baseball. At the time, he couldn't possibly have imagined that this jersey would have been purchased at the end of 2014 for $1,420.[56]

SOURCES

Information about Adams's personal life is from Ancestry.com (Library Edition) and FamilySearch.org.

Except when contemporary coverage of games is cited in endnotes, the sources for his statistics and individual game performances are the Seamheads database, starting at https://www.seamheads.com/NegroLgs/player.php?playerID=adams01eme and the Retrosheet website, starting at https://www.seamheads.com/NegroLgs/player.php?playerID=adams01eme.

NOTES

1   For example, he was called "Ace" in the preseason article, "Elites to Open Against Stars," Baltimore Afro-American, May 11, 1940: 21.

2 See https://www.seamheads.com/NegroLgs/player. php?playerID=adams01eme. In 1940 and 1941, Adams was the only pitcher to start more than six games each season for Baltimore, as of research up to 2024.

3 "Homers May Decide East-West Classic," *Chicago Defender*, August 17, 1940: 24. See also https://retrosheet.org/NegroLeagues/boxe-setc/1940/B08180ASW1940.htm.

4 See https://retrosheet.org/NegroLeagues/boxesetc/1940/ B10010SAS1940.htm.

5 "Licensed to Wed," *Memphis Commercial Appeal*, February 18, 1899: 7.

6 Collierville Community Justice, "We Can't Understand Collierville's Present Without Understanding Collierville's Past," https://www. colliervillejustice.org/history. This history reported no race-related incidents in the twentieth century until the mid-1960s.

7 "County Fighting Malaria," *Memphis Commercial Appeal*, August 30, 1923: 8.

8 "Negro Fair Promises Best Show Yet Held," *Memphis Commercial Appeal*, October 25, 1928: 14. The school was occasionally mentioned in articles published by Black newspapers, such as "Popular Teacher Bids Farewell to Classroom as Cupid Beckons," *Atlanta Daily World*, September 21, 1936: 3.

9 See https://www2.census.gov/prod2/decennial/docu-ments/33973538v1ch09.pdf at page 1022.

10 Town of Collierville, "Collierville the Dairy Town," https://www. colliervilletn.gov/government/town-departments/morton-museum/ exhibitions/collierville-the-dairy-town.

11 In particular, see "Death Notices," *Memphis Press-Scimitar*, January 26, 1955: 30. Emma's Certificate of Death in 1953, which identified her by widower husband's surname of Allen, said she was the daughter of Jim Hull and Rosie Green. She was using her mother's surname in the 1940 census and was Mrs. Allen by the 1950 census, both of which included daughter Virginia in her household. As of 2024, an Ancestry.com family tree for Emma B. Hull identified three of her children, namely Willie Mae Franklin, Rosie Lee Gray, and Roscoe Lindsey. The latter's obituary in 1981 reported that he was survived by Willie Mae Franklin and Rosie Lee, plus a third married sister, Mrs. Annie Virginia Beard. See "Deaths," *Memphis Commercial Appeal*, August 21, 1981: 16. The Beard family tree on Ancestry.com identified Adams as her maiden name and said she had been born in Germantown on September 1, 1933, information that quite possibly came from the woman herself.

12 "Death Notices," *Memphis Press-Scimitar*, January 26, 1955: 30. See also two Social Security Applications and Claims Index entries for Emery Adams Jr., accessible via genealogical websites. In the 1940 census near Memphis, he is presumably "Emory Byas," 6-year-old brother of Katy May Byas, son of 23-year-old Mary Byas, and grandson of 55-year-old Lula Craft, the head of that household. Another half-sister's obituary mentioned being survived by two brothers, "Emery Adams and Charles Byas." See "Mary G. Williams," *Michigan Chronicle* (Detroit), October 22, 1997: D-6.

13 For example, when the Red Sox scheduled an exhibition game against the Chisca Hotel Bears, one Memphis paper said the latter was "probably the best negro amateur club in the city." However, there seems to be no record of any Memphis daily actually reporting on any of that team's games. See "Red Sox to Play Bears," *Memphis Commercial Appeal*, May 19, 1931: 15. (It's likely the game wasn't played that day, based on "Chicks, Barons Rained Out; Kelly vs. Edwards Today," *Memphis Commercial Appeal*, May 20, 1931: 16). For a rare example of a Black amateur game that received publicity

as well as some coverage in Memphis dailies that year, see "Negro Barbes Lose," *Memphis Commercial Appeal*, September 15, 1931: 15.

14 William J. Plott, *The Negro Southern League: A Baseball History, 1920-1951* (Jefferson, North Carolina: McFarland & Company, Inc., 2015), 217.

15 Anthony Castrovince, "MLB adds Negro Leagues to Official Records," December 16, 2020, https://www.mlb.com/news/negro-leagues-given-major-league-status-for-baseball-records-stats.

16 "Red Sox Win Two More from Chicago; Open Season Friday," *Memphis Commercial Appeal*, April 18, 1932: 9.

17 "Red Sox Win Two Games from Monroe; End Series Today."

18 See https://www.seamheads.com/NegroLgs/player. php?playerID=adams01eme; click on "MRS" next to 1932 for the team's record.

19 Holsey Drake, "Montgomery Had a Word for Memphis Reds," *Atlanta Daily World*, May 15, 1932: 5. "Memphis Red Sox 9 Split 2 with Monroe," *Memphis Commercial Appeal*, August 1, 1932: 7. The latter shutout ended 1-0.

20 Plott, 222, 224, 225-226, and 227. "Red Sox Play Monroe," *Memphis Commercial Appeal*, April 15, 1936: 19. "Memphians Down Omaha Negro Club," *Memphis Commercial Appeal*, April 27, 1936: 13.

21 "Auto Theft Trials Will Open Tomorrow," *Memphis Commercial Appeal*, February 5, 1933: 20. "News in the Courts," *Memphis Commercial Appeal*, February 7, 1933: 16.

22 "News of the Courts," *Memphis Commercial Appeal*, May 27, 1936: 25. News of the Courts," *Memphis Commercial Appeal*, June 18, 1936: 27. "Negro Sent to Prison," *Memphis Commercial Appeal*, October 23, 1936: 21.

23 Plott, 133-134. "Claybrook Loses Pair to Memphis," *Memphis Commercial Appeal*, July 1, 1935: 14.

24 Robert Ratcliffe, "Arkansas 9 Cops Semi-Pro Baseball Title," *Chicago Defender*, September 7, 1935: 14.

25 "Negro Red Sox Split Two," *Memphis Commercial Appeal*, September 9, 1935: 11.

26 "Clay Brooks in 5 to 2 Victory," *Chicago Defender*, September 21, 1935: 15. This article identified all dates, locations, and results of the series, though it didn't report the final scores. The *Defender* might have provided the most detailed coverage, but it left readers with a minor mystery. "The Red Sox were forced to use two pitchers," that weekly noted, the second of whom was Howard. "Five errors by [Red] Longley, Sox second baseman, and wild pitching by Adams accounted for three of the Tiger scores," the paper added. However, the line score's battery for Memphis instead listed its starting pitcher as R. Jones, not Adams. One possibility is that Jones did start and Memphis used two *relievers*, not just two pitchers all told. However, player-manager Ruben Jones wasn't known at all as a pitcher, so the inclusion of him in the battery was most likely just a mistake.

27 For the 1935 Claybrook Tigers' photo that included a Bill Adams, see http://arkbaseball.com/tiki-index.php?page=Claybrook+Tigers.

28 Adams was called Bill in "Stars Wopped by Elites," *Philadelphia Tribune*, July 10, 1941: 1.

29 See https://retrosheet.org/NegroLeagues/boxesetc/1935/ B09290SAS1935.htm, though it doesn't appear to align completely with the box score that accompanied the brief account, "North Downs South in All-Star Battle," *Commercial Appeal*, September 30, 1935: 13.

30 "Red Sox Play Monroe," *Memphis Commercial Appeal*, April 15, 1936: 19. "Memphians Down Omaha Negro Club," *Memphis Commercial Appeal*, April 27, 1936: 13.

31 "Negro Slain," *Commercial Appeal*, April 25, 1936: 5. "News of the Courts," *Memphis Commercial Appeal*, May 27, 1936: 25.

32 "Negro Sent to Prison," *Memphis Commercial Appeal*, October 23, 1936: 21.

33 "Red Sox Split Two with Chicago Team," *Memphis Commercial Appeal*, May 10, 1937: 11.

34 "Memphis Red Sox Win," *Memphis Commercial Appeal*, May 18, 1937: 16. "Memphis Is Too Much for St. Louis 9," *Chicago Defender*, May 29, 1937: 13.

35 "Memphis Wins," *Chicago Defender*, August 14, 1937: 22.

36 "Negro Teams Meet Monday," *Decatur* (Illinois) *Daily Review*, August 28, 1937: 15.

37 "Josh Gibson Two Home Runs Wellmaker's Hurling Beats Memphis Red Sox, 7 To 3," *Atlanta Daily World*, April 5, 1938: 5. Sam R. Brown, "Philly Stars Meet Redsox," *Pittsburgh Courier*, April 16, 1938: 16.

38 Bill Nowlin, "1939 Baltimore Elite Giants Timeline," *The 1939 Baltimore Elite Giants* (Phoenix: SABR, 2024).

39 "Grays Bow 7-3 to Baltimore With Gibson Out of Line-up," *Indianapolis Recorder*, June 17, 1939: 14.

40 Ralph F. Boyd, "Elites and Cubans Split Twin Bill," *Baltimore Afro-American*, September 2, 1939: 23.

41 "Mule Suttles Slugs Hard," *Newark Evening News*, September 7, 1939.

42 "Elites Win, 2-0, in Colored Final," *New York Daily News*, September 25, 1939: 40. Adams did remain with the Elites after the Newark series, having started an exhibition game midway through the championship series. See John G. Palmer, "Bushwicks, Met. Champions, Win From Negro League Champs, 3 to [sic]," *Brooklyn Citizen*, September 20, 1939: 6. To complete that headline, the score was 3-1. Palmer reported Adams's first name as Cliff.

43 "Box Scores," *Philadelphia Tribune*, June 13, 1940: 11. "Grays Win Over Memphis, 3-1," *New York Daily News* September 9, 1940: 40. For details about the Ruppert Cup, see a few paragraphs into an article by the National Baseball Hall of Fame and Museum's Library Associate Bill Francis, "Negro Leagues Photos Now Available Online through Pastime," https://baseballhall.org/discover/negro-leagues-photos-now-available-on-pastime.

44 See Note 3.

45 See https://retrosheet.org/NegroLeagues/boxesetc/1940/B10010SAS1940.htm (which shows Adams as having stolen a base). At least one article said Adams pitched five innings. See Hayward Jackson, "Mackey's Single Helps North Beat South, 2-1," *Pittsburgh Courier*, October 12, 1940: 18. At least one box score also showed he pitched five innings. See "North Wins 2-1 Game From South in N. Orleans," *Chicago Defender*, October 12, 1940: 24. However, the box score accompanying the latter incorrectly called Adams the winning pitcher, while omitting that actual pitcher of record, Baltimore teammate Bud Barbee. At least one preview of this game stated, incorrectly, that Adams had earlier started that summer's East-West Classic, but he didn't pitch in it at all. Contrast https://retrosheet.org/NegroLeagues/boxesetc/1940/B0818oASW1940.htm with

46 Hayward Jackson, "North-South Baseball Classic for Crescent City October 1," *Atlanta Daily World*, September 21, 1940: 5.

46 Jorge S. Figueredo, *Cuban Baseball: A Statistical History, 1878-1961* (Jefferson, North Carolina: McFarland & Company, 2003), 239.

47 Details relating to the two shutouts are available via https://www.retrosheet.org/NegroLeagues/boxesetc/1941/Padame1011941.htm. In contrast to Adams's Seamheads line for 1941, the Retrosheet list for Adams in 1941 currently shows him with only two shutouts and only five regular-season wins (plus an exhibition win against the Birmingham Black Barons on August 11). Conversely, Retrosheet shows him with two regular-season losses plus two in exhibition games.

48 "Elite Hurlers Face Tough Task in Philly Series," *Baltimore Afro-American*, September 5, 1942: 25. "Grays Win NNL Flag; Elites Split," *Baltimore Afro-American*, September 8, 1942: 19. See also the September 6 and 7 entries at https://www.retrosheet.org/NegroLeagues/boxesetc/1942/Padame1011942.htm.

49 Art Carter, "Adds to Elites' Problems as Camp Opens," *Baltimore Afro-American*, April 17, 1943: 24. "Baseball Bits," *Baltimore Afro-American*, May 8, 1943: 26. The latter article called him "John (Ace) Adams."

50 See his Pitching Log outings of May 15, May 25, June 20, and June 24 at https://www.retrosheet.org/NegroLeagues/boxesetc/A/Padame101.htm. His Batting Log is also accessible there. According to a profile posted online by the Center for Negro League Baseball Research, citing author John Holway, Adams also lost a game for Philadelphia in 1940, in addition to 1943. However, no such game has been logged by Seamheads or Retrosheet. See Dr. Layton Revel, "Forgotten Heroes: Roy 'Red' Parnell," 2018, at http://www.cnlbr.org/Portals/0/Hero/Roy_Parnell%202019-10.pdf .

51 "Black Yanks Here for Tilt Tomorrow With Memphis Nine," *Muskogee* (Oklahoma) *Times-Democrat*, September 20, 1943: 11.

52 A little more specifically, it's possible he was labeled with some sort of "personality disorder," as was another veteran of that war as described in a published case, at https://www.va.gov/vetapp08/files2/0816194.txt.

53 "Joe Lillard to Take Negro Ball Club on USO-Camp Show Tour," *Cleveland Call and Post*, February 2, 1946: 8B. "Delay Star Nine's Overseas Tour," *Baltimore Afro-American*, February 2, 1946: 22.

54 "Woman Swindled – 15Gs," *New York Amsterdam News*, October 25, 1952: 1.

55 "Dead," *Memphis Commercial Appeal*, January 26, 1955: 23. His obituary in Memphis dailies (see Notes 11 and 12) spelled his first name as "Emory." His daughter was identified as "Mrs. Virginia Moore" but attempts to determine the first name of her husband then have been unsuccessful. However, in 2008, she became the widow of long-time Memphis resident George Beard Sr.; see "Deaths," *Memphis Commercial Appeal*, November 6, 2008: DSA4. Around 1970, Emery Junior was married to the former Alma Jean Arnold, according to Perry O. Withers, "50th Wedding Anniversary," *Tri-State Defender* (Memphis), August 1, 1970: 8.

56 See https://greyflannelauctions.com/Mid_1930s_Memphis_Pros_Negro_League_Game_Used_Unif-LOT33011.aspx. It's quite possible the Memphis Pros baseball club was never mentioned in local newspapers.

OSCAR BOONE

BY FREDERICK C. BUSH

Baseball teams rely on their stars and regulars to make the greatest impact. Of course, backups also play important roles, giving starters a rest and filling in when injuries occur. Oscar Boone assumed the role of second-string catcher behind future Hall of Famer Roy Campanella for the Baltimore Elite Giants in 1939 after Biz Mackey (who also became a HOF enshrinee) was shipped out to the Newark Eagles in midseason. Unfortunately for Boone, he did not see much playing time during his brief tenure with Baltimore, and he was left off both the team's playoff and World Series rosters.

The short stint with the Elite Giants was typical of a life in which Boone pursued diverse vocations, different women, and employment with various semipro and professional baseball clubs. After Boone's playing career and third marriage both ended, his wanderlust merged with alcoholism and contributed to his violent demise at the youthful age of 47.

Oscar Boone was born on March 28, 1911, in Cameron, Texas, to Jesse and Willie (Hammonds) Boone. Jesse, a farmer, and Willie had married on December 26, 1909, but their union turned out to be short-lived, and Oscar was their only child. Willie Boone's mother, Malinda (Williams) Hammonds,[1] and brother, Bradford Hammonds Jr., lived with the Boones at the time of the 1910 census; oddly, Malinda, was listed as a "hired woman" rather than a relative.

After Jesse and Willie Boone divorced, Oscar lived with Malinda in the town of Mart, about 48 miles north of Cameron and 18 miles east of Waco.[2] Oscar's illiterate 62-year-old grandmother, who was twice widowed and had suffered the death of 12 of her children, now worked as a "common laborer" while raising him. His uncle, Bradford Jr., worked in the city of Ranger, 183 miles northwest of Mart, and inadvertently was counted twice in the 1920 census as he split his time between residences in both places. Bradford Jr. met an untimely death by gunshot in Ranger on January 4, 1931, while Oscar was in the US Army.[3] Both of Oscar's parents eventually remarried, but there is no evidence that they played any further role in his upbringing or adult life.

Boone no doubt saw the Army as a way out of the poverty and negative circumstances that had afflicted the members of his immediate family. The 1930 census shows that he was stationed at Fort Huachuca, Arizona. At the time, this installation was

Oscar Boone.

home to the 10th Cavalry "Buffalo Soldiers," the Army's famed all-Black cavalry corps, of which Boone was a member.[4] Boone carried on the tradition of the Buffalo Soldiers as outstanding riders, which was evidenced by the fact that "Pvt. Boone, F troop, on Mouse" had placed second in "jumping for privates" in the 10th Cavalry horse show on June 16, 1930.[5]

In addition to riding pursuits, Boone also honed his baseball skills as a member of Fort Huachuca's segregated all-Black team. At 5-feet-8 and 170 pounds, the fact that Boone became a catcher by trade in the Negro Leagues and semipro ball is rather surprising. During his time as a member of the Fort Huachuca team in 1930 and 1931, he split his playing time between third base and shortstop.[6] On August 10, 1930, Boone had a stellar day with a 4-for-5 line at the plate that included two solo home runs as well as five putouts and five assists at shortstop. His performance went for naught, though, as the Nogales Internationals scored two runs in the ninth to edge Fort Huachuca, 6-5.[7]

Boone was honorably discharged from the Army on August 31, 1936. He moved to San Angelo, Texas, which was home to Fort Concho, a deactivated Army post that also once had housed the 10th Cavalry's Buffalo Soldiers in the late nineteenth century.[8] Boone found employment at the Cactus Hotel, and he joined the San Angelo Black Sheepherders baseball team in 1938.

Although the Black Sheepherders were a semipro squad, Boone found himself among several people who, like him, were to become members of teams in the major Negro Leagues. In fact, manager Ruben Jones had already skippered the Birmingham Black Barons in 1927 and went on to take the reins of the Memphis Red Sox in 1940. One teammate, Norman "Bobby" Robinson, who also joined the Baltimore Elite Giants in 1939, later became best known for a consequence that resulted from an injury he suffered. In 1948 Robinson was the starting center fielder for Birmingham until he stepped into a hole and broke a leg. His injury opened the door for a 17-year-old phenom, Willie Mays, to take over his job in center field.[9]

In late June, the Black Sheepherders briefly assumed an identity as a team from the state of Kansas as the squad attempted to qualify for the fourth annual National Baseball Congress World Series to be held in Wichita. The *Emporia Gazette* explained:

The Sheepherder team is originally from San Angeles [sic], Texas, and is qualifying through the Kansas semi-pro tournament at Wichita for the National Semi-pro baseball tourney because the Texas program bars colored teams. The team was sent to Emporia by Frank Kice, state baseball commissioner. The Sheepherders finished in third place in the 1936 Kansas Semi-pro tournament and are reported to have an even better ball club this year.[10]

On July 1, at Emporia's Summers Field, the Kansas City Black Sheepherders, as the press often called them, defeated the Emporia Bakers, 9-2, in an exhibition game prior to the state tournament at Wichita.[11]

The Sheepherders started the tournament with a bang as they steamrolled Oswego, 13-1,[12] and Wellington, 19-1, with Boone going 4-for-5 at the plate and scoring four runs in the latter contest.[13] Although the Sheepherders "established themselves as one of the hardest hitting clubs in the tourney,"[14] the team's pitching was also dominant. On July 19, with Boone as his catcher, Schoolboy Walker struck out 15 batters, including 11 in a row at one point, in a 9-2 triumph over the Topeka Barber-Wreckers.[15]

In its July 21 edition, the *Wichita Eagle* noted, "This is the first year in the history of the tournament when a negro club has been one of the potential champions. A win tonight for the Sheepherders would make them prohibitive favorites to enter the championship game to decide the 1938 title."[16] It was not to be, however, as the Wichita Water Company dealt the Sheepherders an 8-1 defeat on July 23 to qualify for the championship game against the Solomon Candy squad; the Watermen defeated Solomon to recapture the tournament title they had last held in 1935.[17] The Sheepherders played Chanute for third place but lost that game as well, dashing any hope they had of qualifying for the NBC World Series.[18]

The Sheepherders reverted to their San Angelo identity and barnstormed back to Texas. On July 26 they took out their frustrations against the Seminole (Oklahoma) Redbirds in a 14-5 victory that ended the locals' eight-game winning streak. The local press contrasted the play of the two teams, noting, "In a tilt that saw the negro team take advantage of every possible play, the Redbirds plodded along giving a fair showing that looked almost weak in comparison with the sparkling game of the Sheepherders."[19] Boone went 3-for-5 and scored one of San Angelo's runs. The Sheepherders had battered starting pitcher Leroy Witcher, having arrived too early in the week to face Oklahoma A&M student and Redbirds hurler Allie Reynolds,[20] who became a six-time World Series champion with the New York Yankees.

Boone's performance with San Angelo resulted in a position with the Negro American League's Atlanta Black Crackers at the outset of the 1939 season. The Black Crackers held spring training in Atlanta, which gave the press and fans a close-up look at the players. In late March, columnist Lucius "Melancholy" Jones raved, "Catcher Oscar Boone, the 200-pound mask and mitt

man from San Angelo, Texas, had fans watching the workout on the BTWHS athletic field spellbound with his sensational first day's form."[21] The *Atlanta Daily World* profiled Boone in its "A Cracker a Day" series on April 22 and described him as "a quiet unassuming chap with plenty of courage and natural ability."[22] The paper added that Boone "has been playing professionally for 6 years from New York to Texas and knows what the game is all about."[23]

Although Boone had to battle through some minor injuries he suffered in spring exhibition games, he was still one of the team's top performers. On April 25, he was batting .518, which was second only to right fielder Donald Reeves' .552 mark.[24] Boone and Reeves' performances were the highlights, however, as the team itself scuffled and lost most of its preseason games. Then, in early May, it was reported that "[a]fter more than a month's training, the Atlanta Black Crackers, whose franchise has been moved to Indianapolis, Ind., in the negro American league [sic], will meet the Cleveland Bears at Ponce de Leon park tonight starting at 8 o'clock."[25]

Despite the purported move to Indianapolis, which was an attempt to create financial stability for the franchise, the Atlanta Black Crackers-Indianapolis ABCs team of 1939 continued to use Atlanta's Ponce de Leon Park as its home field. As a result, the NAL expelled the Black Crackers from the league at its midseason meetings. John H. Harden, the team's owner, protested the NAL's decision, stating that "the Indianapolis park was not available for rental on June 18, the day set aside by the league for him to open there."[26] He also "inferred that the Indianapolis ball park officials had told him that he wouldn't be able to rent the place at all for games during the season."[27]

Harden's protests effected no change, and the Black Crackers ended their abbreviated season with a 6-10 record in NAL play and were 7-19 against all Negro League opponents. The team's expulsion from the NAL also cost Boone and first baseman Red Moore spots on the West All-Stars team for the annual East-West Game that was scheduled to be played on August 6 at Chicago's Comiskey Park.[28] Moore had led the Black Crackers with a .434 batting average in 15 NAL games while Boone had been second with a .358 average in 16 games. More importantly, Atlanta's players now had to find employment with new teams for the remainder of the 1939 season.

On July 22 the *Chicago Defender* reported that the Baltimore Elite Giants had sold first baseman Jim West to the Philadelphia Stars and catcher Biz Mackey to the Newark Eagles. In a follow-up move by Baltimore, the paper reported that "[t]he Elites will get five players from the Atlanta Crackers. The five are: 'Red' Moore, first baseman; Tom Butts, shortstop; Ed Dixon, pitcher; Felix Evans, pitcher, and Oscar Brown [sic], catcher."[29]

As the backup to Campanella, Boone found himself relegated to playing mostly in exhibition games.[30] He appeared in only three NNL2 games and managed a lone pinch-hit RBI single in a losing cause against the Newark Eagles in the first game of a July 23 doubleheader at Washington's Griffith Stadium.[31] Although Boone had played at an all-star level with Atlanta, his .143 batting average in his limited league appearances for Baltimore resulted in his being left off the team's postseason rosters against the Newark Eagles and Homestead Grays. It was an unfortunate ending to a season that had started out so promisingly for Boone's baseball career.

Another event that occurred during Boone's time in Atlanta, which may or may not have been happier than his brief tenure with the Elite Giants, was his marriage to Josie Goodwin. However, the origins of the bride as well as her fate, or the fate of her union with Boone, remain unsolved mysteries.[32] When Boone filled out a World War II draft registration card in October 1940, he was back at his job with the Cactus Hotel in San Angelo and listed his cousin, Margie Simpson, as his contact person.

Before returning to Texas late in 1940, Boone had spent the early part of spring training with the Birmingham Black Barons and then had played for the Ethiopian Clowns most of the year.[33] Legendary manager Candy Jim Taylor led the Black Barons that season and, while he did not retain Boone in Birmingham, he brought him north to the Windy City the following year when he took over as skipper of the Chicago American Giants.

Although the Clowns were renowned for the use of stereotyped "African" names and the antics they performed to entertain crowds, the team's players were seasoned professionals who also played for other Negro League teams over the course of their careers. After the Clowns swept a doubleheader from the American Giants, the *Chicago Defender* wrote:

> The Ethiopian Clowns of Miami, Fla., Hunter Campbell, manager, put on their shadow ball stunt and some other things which gave the slim crowd a good laugh – and then the visitors put on an exhibition of ball playing worth going miles to see. They trimmed the Giants in a double bill, 4 to 2 in nine innings and 8 to 3 in seven.
>
> Although the players all use Ethiopian names, the Defender learned that the boys know their baseball. Their victory in a series with the Crawfords on the spring training tour was no fluke.[34]

The *Defender* also noted that "Oscar Boone caught the first encounter," and the box score indicates that his "Ethiopian name" was "Tarzan." Three of his former 1939 Black Crackers teammates – Spencer Davis, Eddie Dixon, and Felix "Chin" Evans – were members of the 1940 Ethiopian Clowns as well.[35]

The barnstorming Clowns were such a formidable foe that, at one point from July to early August, the team won 27 consecutive games.[36] Team owner Syd Pollock decided that the Clowns would play a return engagement in the prestigious *Denver Post* Tournament to vie for the $10,000 prize. The team had participated in the tournament for the first time in 1939 and had finished in fifth place.[37]

The Clowns opened the tourney in style as they clobbered the Lead-Deadwood (South Dakota) team, 15-1. However, the tables were turned in the next game against the 1939 champion Champlin Refiners from Enid (Oklahoma) as the Clowns suffered a 9-1 defeat. The team recovered from that thumping to emerge victorious over Englewood (Colorado), 6-5, and the Coors Brewers (Oklahoma), 8-6, as it tried to reach the final round.[38]

The Clowns' next match was against the Mt. Pleasant (Texas) team in what the *Denver Post* called "one of the wildest and most exciting games in the history of the Little World Series."[39] Boone, as Tarzan, struck a pinch-hit RBI single in the bottom of the ninth that tied the score, 6-6, but Mt. Pleasant came back with four runs in the top of the 10th inning to win, 10-6. The loss eliminated the Clowns from the tourney, and the team had to settle for a sixth-place finish.[40]

Before the 1941 baseball season, Boone embarked upon another short-term marriage as he wed Bessie Clark on April 1. Once again, there are gaps in public records about his bride, and her exact origins and fate remain unknown. The couple was wed in Schleicher County, which lies directly south of Tom Green County, where San Angelo is located. Divorce proceedings began in February 1942 and were finalized in September 1942.[41] Although the reason for the brevity of Boone's second marriage is unknown, one of two possible scenarios seems likely: 1) Immediately after the wedding, Boone went north to play for the Chicago American Giants, and it is possible that his new bride was unhappy with this arrangement; or 2) Boone had trouble staying faithful as may be evidenced by the fact that he married Maybelle Carson in Dallas on October 19, 1942, which was only one month after his divorce from Clark was final.[42]

Whatever the circumstances of Boone's personal life entailed, Candy Jim Taylor lured him to Chicago to split the catching duties with Pepper Bassett in 1941.[43] Boone regained the batting form he had displayed in Atlanta in 1939 as he batted .367 in NAL games that year while Bassett hit at only a .214 clip. Even so, Bassett was a well-known and popular veteran who had initially gained fame as "the Rocking-Chair Catcher," and he was voted to be the starting backstop for the West team in that season's East-West All-Star Game; the lesser-known Boone finished fifth in the voting for the West's catchers.[44] As for the team, the American Giants finished dead last in the six-team NAL with a league record of 16-29-2 and an overall ledger of 18-31-2.

After the 1941 season, Boone's baseball career began to wind down. In the spring of 1942, newspapers from different parts of the country gave contradictory accounts of his whereabouts: one had him back with the Sheepherders, another claimed that he was to play in a single exhibition game for the Baltimore Elite Giants, while a third claimed he was returning to the Chicago American Giants.[45] Despite these varied reports, San Angelo's 1942 city directory lists Boone as a bartender at the Harlem Inn, and there is no evidence of his participation in any baseball games that year.

Documentation does exist, however, for his marriage to Maybelle Carson in October 1942. Maybelle's maiden name was Callahan, and she was the widow of George W. Carson, with whom she had one daughter, Maenelle. The Carsons lived on Third Street within a block of Boone's cousin, Maggie Simpson. Since Boone had been living with Simpson when he filled out his World War II draft registration in 1940, he may have been acquainted with the Carson family for some time. Whatever intrigue may or may not have existed between Oscar Boone and Maybelle Carson, their marriage is the best-documented of Boone's three unions, and both their fates are known.

In 1943, the couple moved to Tucson, Arizona, about 57 miles northwest of Fort Huachuca. Boone apparently was unable to settle in one place for long, whether by nature, necessity, or both. He continued to travel, and he played in occasional semipro ballgames while looking for other work.[46] At the time of the 1950 census, Boone was working for a railroad in La Platte, Nebraska, and lived in the workers' camp while Maybelle remained in Tucson. Boone followed this lifestyle for the remainder of his days as Maybelle, after learning of Oscar's death, reported to authorities that the couple had divorced in 1953 and that Oscar had been "bumming around riding freight trains and working here and there ever since."[47]

Boone had been working and renting a room in Eloy, Arizona, 55 miles northwest of Tucson, when his life reached its tragic and violent end on October 12, 1958. A brief article in Tucson's *Arizona Daily Star* reported that Boone's body had been found "in a dry wash under a railroad bridge east of Eloy."[48] Deputy Cotton Doss of the Pinal County Sheriff's Office had received a call regarding a dead body. He discovered Boone "lying partly on his right side [and] face down in the sand" and noted that "[h]is head was hit on the side of the face and on the back of [the] head two or more times."[49] Boone was identified via his Social Security card, which was found in a small wallet on his person, and a police arrest card with a photo of Boone from an incident that had occurred earlier that year.

Boone had gained a reputation in Eloy as "a heavy drinker of wine," and a post-mortem blood test showed that he had been heavily intoxicated at the time he was killed, leading the sheriff's investigators to assert, "Also[,] after finding out how much alcohol Boone had in his body[,] he may have and probably was passed out when he was murdered, the blood alcohol test showed 0.56%."[50]

Investigators pursued numerous theories and interviewed several suspects. Of particular interest initially was a man named C.J. Wright, whom Boone had stabbed that January in the assault that had occasioned his arrest. Wright was alleged to have made threats that he would retaliate against Boone, but all his acquaintances averred that he had moved to Phoenix after being released from the hospital. One investigator stated that "the location of the murder and [modus operandi] makes me believe it is the type of crime most common among the Indians of this area." However, none of the "several Indian suspects" who were questioned could be placed at the scene of the crime. The investigation stalled and the lead investigator on the case conceded in a one-week follow-up report, "We have had no real leads in this case[,] but we have checked out several rumors all this week but to no avail."[51]

News of Boone's death quickly reached Maybelle in Tucson, likely through a mutual acquaintance, and she phoned the sheriff's office in Eloy to inform them that Oscar was her ex-husband. She also saw to it that Oscar was buried in the US Military Veterans section of the Eloy Park Memorial Cemetery. Maybelle Boone died in Tucson on November 24, 1967, and is interred in San Antonio, Texas.[52] The Boones had no children together, but Maybelle was survived by her daughter, Maenelle (Carson) Fleming, who also lived in Tucson.

SOURCES

Except where otherwise indicated, all player statistics and team records were taken from Seamheads.com.

Ancestry.com was consulted for US Census information, military records, and birth, marriage, and death records.

Oscar Boone's murder report, autopsy results, and blood test results were obtained from the Pinal County Sheriff's Office via a Freedom of Information Act (FOIA) request.

NOTES

1   Oscar Boone's family tree is complex and difficult to trace; however, sufficient documentation exists to confirm that Malinda Williams was Oscar's maternal grandmother. Malinda apparently had been once widowed before she embarked upon her second marriage to Bradford Hammonds with whom she had Willie (Oscar's mother), Bradford Jr., and a daughter named Laura before her second husband also died. After Bradford Hammonds Sr.'s death, Malinda again reverted to her maiden name, Williams, in official records; Bradford Jr.'s death certificate confirms Malinda's maiden name to have been Williams. Malinda and her parents were from Alabama and, given her approximate birth year of 1858 and the fact that she could neither read nor write (per multiple censuses), it is quite possible that they were former slaves who had obtained freedom after the Civil War. Whether or not that was the case, Malinda's life was filled with hardships. In addition to being twice widowed, the 1910 census states that she had given birth to 16 children, only four of whom still were living at that time.

2   On Ancestry.com, Boone is listed as "Asken Bearns" in the 1920 US Census; this is the result of both the census-taker's sloppy handwriting and the reliance on modern computer programs to read handwritten documents. A closer inspection of the original scanned census document showed that "Asken Bearns" might be "Oscar Boone," and additional research into Boone's family history established that this was indeed the fact.

3   Bradford Hammonds Jr.'s death certificate does not indicate whether his death was a homicide, suicide, or an accidental shooting.

4   U.S. Army, "History of Fort Huachuca," https://home.army.mil/huachuca/index.php/about/history, accessed July 1, 2023.

5   "Fort Huachuca," *Arizona Daily Star* (Tucson), June 19, 1930: 8.

6   "Internationals Win Their 22nd Consecutive Victory," *Arizona Daily Star*, August 4, 1930: 7; "Rails Outclass Fort Huachuca Soldiers, 14 to 3," *Arizona Daily Star*, July 6, 1931: 7.

7   "Internationals Triumph Over Soldiers," *Arizona Daily Star*, August 11, 1930: 6.

8   "Fort Concho, National Historic Landmark," https://fortconcho.com/, accessed July 1, 2023.

9   Bob LeMoine, "Bobby Robinson," SABR Biography Project, https://sabr.org/bioproj/person/bobby-robinson/#_edn12, accessed July 1, 2023.

10   "Bakers to Play Fast Colored Team Friday/Game with Texas Sheepherders to Start at 6:10 at Summers Field," *Emporia* (Kansas) *Gazette*, June 30, 1938: 13.

11   "Bakers Beaten by Texans, to Face Abilene/Game at Summers Field Sunday – Sheepherders Win by 9 to 2," *Emporia Gazette*, July 2, 1938: 7.

12   "Herders Look Good in Winning," *Wichita Eagle*, July 12, 1938: 6.

13   "Sheepherders in Slugging Form," *Wichita Eagle*, July 13, 1938: 9.

14   "Sheepherders in Slugging Form."

15   "Sheepherders in Two Big Innings Trounce Topeka," *Wichita Eagle*, July 20, 1938: 12: "Just Among Us Folk," *San Angelo Evening Standard*, July 20, 1938: 10.

16   "Two Featured Games Will Feature 'Old Timers' Tonight," *Wichita Eagle*, July 21, 1938: 8.

17   "Watermen Move into Finals of State Tourney," *Wichita Eagle*, July 24, 1938: 11; "Tonight Is Final Night at Tourney," *Wichita Eagle*, July 24, 1938: 11.

18   "Only One Kansas Team Assured of National Chance," *Wichita Eagle*, July 26, 1938: 7.

19   "Negro Team Ends Birds' Eight-Game Streak, 14-5/Allie Reynolds Will Get Starting Call for Cushing Contest Here Friday," *Seminole Producer*, July 27, 1938: 6. Oklahoma A&M University was renamed Oklahoma State University in 1958.

20   Royse Parr, "Allie Reynolds," SABR Biography Project, https://sabr.org/bioproj/person/allie-reynolds/, accessed July 1, 2023.

21   Lucius "Melancholy" Jones, "Slants on Sports/Donald Reeves Arrives, Ready to Don Crax Uniform; Oscar Boone, New 200 Pound Catcher, Thrills Crowd," *Atlanta Daily World*, March 25, 1939: 5. Either Boone had temporarily bulked up or Jones overestimated/overstated his weight: Boone's WWII draft registration, filled out in October 1940, listed his weight as 170 pounds. The abbreviation "BTWHS" denotes Booker T. Washington High School in Atlanta.

22   "A Cracker a Day," *Atlanta Daily World*, April 22, 1939: 5.

23   "A Cracker a Day." The claim about Boone playing in New York is in reference to his brief stint as a second-string catcher with the Mohawk Giants of Schenectady, New York, as that team made a swing through the South in April 1938. See "Mohawk Giants Schedule Eight Games in South," *Glens Falls* (New York) *Post Star*, April 6, 1938: 9; however, there is no evidence that Boone spent any time with the team in New York state.

24   Lucius "Melancholy" Jones, "Slants on Sports/Catcher Oscar Boone Had All but Stolen Donald Reeves' Batting Lead Through Sunday's Game," *Atlanta Daily World*, April 25, 1939: A5.

25   "Black Crackers to Play Tonight," *Atlanta Constitution*, May 8, 1939: 13.

26   Lucius "Melancholy" Jones, "Black Crax Out of Negro American League!/Slants on Sports/Atlanta Baseball at Crossroads After League Expels Black Crackers; Harden Charges Club Was 'Railroaded,'" *Atlanta Daily World*, June 26, 1939: 5.

27   Jones, "Black Crax Out of Negro American League!"

28   "East-West Officials Lament Red Moore's Fate: Seventh Annual Sepia All-Star Game to be 'Rubber' Tilt/Red Moore, Oscar Boone Miss Chance to Play in Colorful East-West Classic in Comiskey Park, Chicago, August 6," *Atlanta Daily World*, July 6, 1939: 5.

29   "Mackey to Philly – Five Atlanta Players Signed by Baltimore," *Chicago Defender* (National Edition), July 22, 1939: 8.

30   See, for example: "All-Stars Drop Hot Game to Elite Giants Team 7-1," *Poughkeepsie* (New York) *Eagle-News*, July 13, 1939: 8; "Easton East Penn Club Beats Colored Team, 8-7," *Allentown* (Pennsylvania) *Morning Call*, July 20, 2023: 16; "Schwartz Repulses Baltimore Elite Giants, 3 to 2," *Central New Jersey Home News* (New Brunswick), August 15, 1939: 10.

31   "Ex-Black Crax Keep Baltimore in League Lead/Red Moore Bats 1.000 as Elites Win 4-1; Drop Opening Tilt 4-2/Oscar Boone's Pinch Single Scores Run in First Game, but Rally Falls Short; Pea-Eye Butts Plays in Both Tilts," *Atlanta Daily World*, July 29, 1939: 5.

32   Boone's birth year and place of birth as listed on the 1940 census do not match up with the facts, but this is hardly an unusual occurrence in census documents. Much of the information jibes with Boone's background, and his occupation was listed as "Ball Player." Additionally, no other man named Oscar Boone can be found in the area at that time; thus, it appears that Boone was the man who was married to Josie Goodwin. Frustratingly, neither Josie herself nor any of her family members can currently be found in any additional census or other official documents. The couple may have divorced, or one of them may have decided to leave the other without a legal divorce; another possibility is that Josie Goodwin Boone died.

33   Marion E. Jackson, "Birmingham Takes On Baltimore Sunday," *Atlanta Daily World*, April 17, 1940: 5; Eulus L. Nance, "Ethiopian Clowns, Atlanta All-Stars at BTWHS Today/Donald Reeves, Oscar Boone to Be Seen in Game Here This Week," *Atlanta Daily World*, April 27, 1940: 6.

34   "Ethiopians Win Two from American Giants," *Chicago Defender* (National Edition), June 8, 1940: 24.

35   Lucius "Melancholy" Jones, "Slants on Sports/Erstwhile 'Name' Stars of Atlanta Black Crackers Now Making Headlines for Major Clubs of Negro American, National Leagues," *Atlanta Daily World*, July 23, 1940: 5.

36   "Ethiopians Win 27 Straight; Eye Denver Go/Chin Evans, Oscar Boone, Spencer Davis in $10,000 Diamond Meet," *Atlanta Daily World*, August 6, 1940: 5.

37   Jay Sanford, *The Denver Post Tournament: A Chronicle of America's First Integrated Professional Baseball Event* (Cleveland: Society for American Baseball Research, 2003), 90.

38   "Ethiopian Clowns Win Three, Lose One in $10,000 Denver Tourney," *Phoenix Index*, August 17, 1940: 6.

39   "Mt. Pleasant Trips Clowns, 10-6, in Tenth," *Denver Post*, August 11, 1940: 5-1, 5-3.

40   Sanford, 90.

41   Boone's last name was misspelled as "Boome" in the official marriage record; however, there was no individual by that name, nor was there any other man named Oscar Boone who lacked a middle name that lived anywhere close to the San Angelo area. However, there were two women named Bessie Clark in the vicinity. One, also with no middle name (as in the marriage record), was listed as "Mulatto," and, given the time and the place (Texas), must have been Boone's bride, while the other also had the middle initial "B" and was iden-

tified as "White." The "B" in Bessie B. Clark's name did not stand for "Boone" as the initial can be found in her name prior to the date of Boone's marriage; additional public records for Bessie B. Clark also indicate that she was a different person. For information about Oscar Boone and Bessie Clark's 1942 divorce, see: "51st District Court (Civil Docket)," *San Angelo Daily Standard*, February 13, 1942: 7, and "Double Divorce Decree Granted as Total Rises," *San Angelo Standard-Times*, September 23, 1942: 3.

42 Maybelle Carson did not escape misspellings of her name in official documents. Alternate spellings found are Mable, Mabel, Maebelle, Mae Bell, and Mabelle.

43 "American Giants to Use Chicago White Sox Stadium This Season/ Donald Reeves, Shug Cornelius, Oscar Boone with Taylor Crew," *Atlanta Daily World*, May 5, 1941: 5.

44 "Expect 50,000 at East-West Game Sun. July 27: Looks Like Paige Will Face 'Impo' Barnhill, New York Cubans Ace," *Chicago Defender* (National Edition), July 19, 1941: 24.

45 "Black Herders and Forth Worth Panthers Tangle," *San Angelo Standard-Times*, April 5, 1942: 14; "Cuban Stars, Equal of White Majors, Noted Baseball Scribes Say," *Atlanta Daily World*, April 15, 1942: 5; "Chicago and Monarchs in Double Bill/American Giants Have Improved Team for League Opener," *Michigan Chronicle* (Detroit), May 9, 1942: 16.

46 "Black Eagles Nudge San Angelo, 4 to 2," *Abilene Reporter-News*, August 25, 1947: 2.

47 "Oscar Boone Murder Case Report," Pinal County (Arizona) Sheriff's Office, October 12, 1958.

48 "Dead Body Found Near Eloy Bridge," *Arizona Daily Star*, October 13, 1958: 14.

49 "Oscar Boone Murder Case Report."

50 "Oscar Boone Murder Case Report."

51 "Oscar Boone Murder Case Report."

52 "Boone, Maybelle C.," *Arizona Daily Star*, November 26, 1967: 53.

TOM BUTTS

BY MALCOLM ALLEN

Tom Butts stood 5-feet-8 and weighed just 142 pounds, but his size was not the reason he acquired the nickname Pee Wee. Rather, the strong-armed shortstop's defensive prowess reminded observers of his White contemporary, Pee Wee Reese.[1] "I'd compare Butts with Reese or [Phil] Rizzuto or anyone I've seen in the big leagues," opined Roy Campanella, a former teammate of both Butts and Reese. "Butts could do everything. He just didn't get the opportunity to do it in the majors."[2]

Butts, known as "Pea Eye" in his hometown, was one of the Negro Leagues' outstanding shortstops, selected for East-West All-Star Games in eight years between 1942 and 1953.[3] During his 11 seasons with the Baltimore Elite Giants, the club won the 1939 Negro National League II (NNL2) championship, and the 1949 Negro American League (NAL) title.

Thomas Lee Butts was born on August 27, 1919, in Sparta, Georgia. His parents, Asbury and Mollie (Eagle) Butts, already had a son, Robert. Sparta, about 100 miles southeast of Atlanta in Hancock County, had fewer than 2,000 residents, and Asbury labored on a farm. Asbury's grandfather Berry had been enslaved in the same county.[4] By the 1930 census, Tom's family, including his younger sisters, Anna and Christine, had moved to Atlanta, where his father worked at a packing plant.

In the summer of 1935, the *Atlanta Daily World* noticed the 15-year-old Butts with the semipro Atlanta Red Caps. The newspaper noted, "Butts … played a sensational brand of ball at second sack and time and time again brought the fans to their feet in wild acclaim for some startling catch or throw."[5] Years later, after Butts made his mark in professional baseball, the paper recalled his teen gridiron exploits, reminding its readers, "His feats in football, according to the story tellers, were in the class of John Bunyan, Johnny Appleseed, Achilles, Alexander and other unbeatables of fact and fiction."[6]

In 1935, Butts' last year at David T. Howard Junior High School, he was named Atlanta's second team All-City quarterback. (Howard's coach and athletic director, "Chicken" Charlie Clark, had pitched in the Negro Leagues.[7]) Butts' brother, Robert, a center at Booker T. Washington High School (BTWHS), made the first team.[8]

Shortstop Tom Butts. Courtesy SABR Rucker Archive.

The taller Robert – 5-feet-11, according to military records – was an outfielder when he and Tom played baseball for the 1936 Red Caps.[9] That fall, the brothers were football teammates at BTWHS. "Pea Eye" was Tom's nickname, but the local press occasionally confused the two brothers for one another.

Pea Eye remained a football star at BTWHS, leading the Bulldogs to the 1937 Southeastern Inter-Scholastic championship as a sophomore.[10] One of his performances earned him praise as "a coach's dream" and "the canny little triple-threated field general."[11] His future was in professional baseball, though.

After his hometown Atlanta Black Crackers started ed slowly in 1938, he joined the NAL club in June.

On July 1, the *Daily World* hailed Tom Butts, 18, as "one of the most discussed youngsters in the game," noting, "He was called the greatest shortstop to appear in Memphis thus far in 1938. He made impossible chances look quite easy."[12]

Butts recalled years later how his teammates reacted after one opposing player knocked him down with a hard slide: "That started a rhubarb because they all wanted to protect me. I was sort of the prize star, and I was younger, too."[13]

During an August sweep of the league's first-half champion Memphis Red Sox, the *Daily World* reported, "In the opening game, (Butts) tripled to left center to score Red Moore and injected more life and spirit in the Atlanta team. During the same series, he made a perfect throw to [Joe] Greene at the plate to nab [Cowan] Hyde and cut off a run."[14]

Atlanta won 11 consecutive games to clinch the NAL's second-half title.[15] The first two games of the best-of-seven championship series were to be played in Memphis, the third in Birmingham, Alabama, and Game Four was scheduled to be "Butts' Night" in Atlanta.[16]

Atlanta lost the opener, 6-1, but Butts scored their only run and notched one of their five hits against Ted Radcliffe.[17] After the Black Crackers lost the second contest, 11-6, bad weather canceled the September 20 game in Birmingham.[18] Because the (White) Atlanta Crackers were hosting the Class A-1 Southern Association finals, Ponce de Leon Park was unavailable on Wednesday and Thursday, and a high-school football game was booked there on Friday.[19] The NAL playoffs were postponed until a Sunday doubleheader, but the *Daily World* noted, "Plans for Butts' Day are still going along smoothly and his classmates at

Booker Washington high are rallying behind the idea to make the young phenom supremely happy."[20]

On Friday afternoon, Butts quarterbacked BTWHS to a 28-6 victory over Tuskegee High.[21] However, the same page of the newspaper that described the action reported that the NAL championship series would not resume. It was noted that "[t]he Red Sox feel that they cannot win in Atlanta and that they won't be treated 'right.' Thus they disbanded and are scattered to the wind by the decree of their owner."[22] To recover some revenue, the Black Crackers swept an otherwise meaningless twin bill from the Birmingham Black Barons.[23] At the NAL meeting in December, the Red Sox were officially declared the champions.[24]

The following spring, journalist Ric Roberts observed, "Watching [Butts], you get the idea that before your very eyes cavorts a real ball player. 5,000 youngsters come and go for every single Butts."[25]

The Black Crackers agreed to have a second "home" city in 1939 – closer to most of their Midwest-based NAL opponents. As part of the deal, they would play as the Indianapolis ABC's.[26] But while the team was on the season-opening road trip, club owner John Harden learned that they would not be permitted to use the ballpark in Indianapolis, so he shifted operations back to Atlanta before the June 14 home opener.[27] A June 21 headline read "Black Crax No Longer Indianapolis ABC's."[28] But the June 26 *Daily World* reported, "Black Crax Out of Negro American League." At the NAL's midseason meeting, a majority of the other owners voted to expel Harden's team for failing to play as the ABC's.[29]

Less than two weeks later, the Baltimore Elite Giants of the NNL2 announced that they had acquired Butts and four of his teammates: first baseman Moore, catcher Oscar Boone, and pitchers Ed Dixon and Felix Evans.[30] "We got on the train to Baltimore that night, and that was one of the biggest thrills I ever had," Butts said. "Big town, big buildings – at the time Atlanta didn't have anything like that."[31]

On July 9 at Oriole Park, Butts debuted in the Elites' doubleheader sweep of the Philadelphia Stars.[32] He recalled that he made three throwing errors and admitted feeling nervous to manager-third baseman Felton Snow. "[Snow] said, "Aw, come on, "Cool Breeze" – that's where I got the name of Cool Breeze, right there – 'don't be nervous, you can do it.' He gave me a big lift there."[33]

Butts roomed with Roy Campanella, a 17-year-old catcher whom he called "Pooch." "[Campanella] was a talker," Butts said. "You know, you just can't go to sleep. ... He would talk me to sleep."[34]

When the Elite Giants played in the Deep South in early August, an Atlanta paper explained, "Butts is not on the present road trip. His leg is in a cast[,] and he is with Negro National League President (and Elites owner) Tom Wilson's home in Nashville. ... The classy young shortstop was injured in sliding in a game against a white team last week."[35]

Butts was back in action by August 13, when he went 3-for-5 with a stolen base in Baltimore's 11-1 victory over the New York Cubans at Yankee Stadium.[36] Yankee Stadium "looked like a hotel from the outside, it didn't look like a baseball park," he said. "But after all these bad fields, that was a good one. And after that, every time they said New York, I was ready."[37]

The Elites qualified for the NNL2's semifinal playoffs and beat the Newark Eagles, three games to one. Baltimore advanced to the championship series but dropped the opener, 2-1, to the Homestead Grays in Philadelphia. The Grays' second run scored when Butts juggled a potential first-inning-ending double-play grounder off the bat of Buck Leonard and recorded just one out.[38] The Elites won the next three contests and finished off the Grays with a 2-0 victory at Yankee Stadium on September 24. Butts batted .333 (5-for-15) in the series. After he posed alongside the Ruppert Cup trophy with his teammates, he appeared in the game between NNL2 players and White minor leaguers later that afternoon.[39]

Baltimore placed second behind the Grays in 1940. In 55 official NNL2 games, Butts hit .284, with 44 runs scored and 34 RBIs. His 4-for-4 performance in the second game of a July 28 doubleheader at Yankee Stadium helped the Elites defeat the Grays, 15-6, and evidenced his development as a hitter.[40] Butts credited veteran George Scales, who had returned to the Elites that season. "The more you swing, the less you hit the ball. You just get on base, walk, anything," he recalled Scales saying. "I choked up on my bat, cut down on my swing, and started to get those hits."[41]

Scales also helped the shortstop to improve his defense. Butts explained, "George Scales was a great teacher ... a little hard on you, but if you'd listen you could learn a lot. I used to have trouble coming in on slow balls. ... He drilled me until I finally caught on to it."[42]

Prior to the 1941 campaign, one writer observed, "Tommy Butts ... was rated the top shortfielder in the league on the All-NNL team for 1940. ... He has a magnificent pair of hands, a great arm and is improving constantly as a hitter."[43] That summer, he was called Pee Wee for the first time in print.[44] It was an homage to future Hall of Famer Pee Wee Reese, who was in his first season as a full-time Brooklyn Dodgers starter.[45]

Although Butts batted just .185 in 59 official games in 1941, he edged out the New York Cubans' Horacio Martínez as the first-team shortstop on Cum Posey's 18th annual All-American baseball team. "Butts can now be placed in a class with Jake Stevens [sic], [Dick] Lundy, [Willie] Wells and other greats," Posey wrote.[46]

Following a fight between fans after the Elites' 1942 home opener that caused minor damage to Oriole Park, the team lost access to the facility, and Bugle Field became their primary home ballpark.[47] "The infield was so rotted that shortstop Pee Wee Butts once took a bad hop between the eyes, called time, picked up the ball and heaved it over the left-field fence," noted a *Baltimore Sun* retrospective.[48] Butts said, "I used to go out myself and look for bad spots before I'd start playing. The ground was pretty bad, just a little too sandy."[49]

Butts helped the Elite Giants beat the Grays, 1-0, at Bugle Field on July 10. His seventh-inning RBI single off Roy Partlow produced the only score, and his ninth-inning throw cut down the potential tying run at home plate. With two runners on and one out, a drive by the Grays' Ray Brown hit a high-tension wire above the diamond and caromed to Baltimore center fielder Henry Kimbro. Butts' relay to catcher Bob Clarke nailed Josh Gibson attempting to score from second base, and Baltimore sealed the victory one batter later.[50]

When right-hander Leon Day of the visiting Newark Eagles struck out 18 Elites on July 31, 1942, Butts' leadoff single was the only hit allowed by the future Hall of Famer.[51] That summer Commissioner Kenesaw Mountain Landis insisted that the White majors had no rule prohibiting teams from signing Black players. Detroit-based sportswriter Russ Cowans had already named Butts among the 10 Negro Leaguers (and others) who could help big-league teams.[52] Grays manager Vic Harris also included Butts on his list of NNL2 stars who could likely succeed in the majors.[53] The *New York Daily News* reported, "[Butts] is another Pee Wee Reese – except that he hits better. He gets the ball away fast and has a terrific whip, sometimes throwing men out from behind third base."[54] Butts was an East squad reserve for the prestigious East-West All-Star Game at Comiskey Park, but he did not see action.[55]

Heading into a pair of season-ending doubleheaders against Philadelphia, the Elites had a chance to win the NNL2 pennant and meet the NAL champion Kansas City Monarchs in the revived Negro World Series. But Baltimore split both twin bills and finished behind the Grays.[56] The Elites' chances were hampered by the absence of Campanella, who had jumped to a team in Mexico.[57]

When Campanella remained in the Mexican League in 1943, Butts joined him in the Industriales de Monterrey's lineup. The team finished with a league-best 53-37 record. Butts teamed with Cuban second baseman Herberto Blanco up the middle and batted .248 with one homer and nine steals in 80 games.

In 1944 Butts and Campanella were both back with the Elite Giants. As the East-West All-Star Game approached, Sam Lacy of the *Baltimore Afro-American* wrote, "The brilliant Tommy Butts of the Baltimore Elite Giants can easily be the choice for the shortstop berth, mainly because he is just about the cleanest fielding infielder in Negro baseball at the moment and, too, because there is no better sacrifice man around than the Georgia cracker-jack."[58] (Three years later, Lacy reported, "Pee Wee Butts hates to be called Tommy."[59]) With 46,247 in attendance at Comiskey Park on August 13, Butts started and went 0-for-2 in the East's 7-4 defeat.[60]

After the Grays retained their NNL2 championship. Butts went to the Puerto Rican Winter League in 1944-45 and hit .237 in 76 at-bats with the Indios de Mayagüez.[61]

During training camp before Baltimore's 1945 campaign. Butts underwent an appendectomy.[62] He soon returned to action,

but he was not selected for the East-West All-Star Game for the only time in a seven-season (1944-1950) span. The Elites also failed to dethrone the Grays. That fall the Elites increased their winning streak against the White Baltimore Orioles of the International League to six consecutive games. Butts keyed a 3-1 victory with a first-inning RBI triple against Walt Masterson, a righty with big-league experience whom the Orioles had brought in to pitch the October 7 contest.[63]

Sixteen days later, the Brooklyn Dodgers signed Negro League infielder Jackie Robinson to a minor-league contract. Although Robinson received most of the headlines for his play with their International League affiliate in Montreal in 1946, Brooklyn also signed three other African Americans that offseason. Pitcher Johnny Wright spent the bulk of the season with Class-C Trois-Rivieres, Québec, while Campanella and right-hander Don Newcombe played for the Dodgers' Class-B farm club in Nashua, New Hampshire.

The Newark Eagles, featuring future Hall of Famers Larry Doby and Monte Irvin, won the 1946 NNL2 pennant and Negro World Series. Butts earned a return to the East-West All-Star Game with his best season to that point: .315 with 7 triples in a league-leading 64 games. That fall the *Afro-American* said an exhibition against a team of major-league all-stars would be "Kimbro-Butts Day," noting, "Baltimoreans will do a long-delayed honor to the Elites' most diligent pair of workmen."[64]

In 1947 Butts produced his personal best slash line: .351/.391/.459 in 59 games. "I never was a curve ball hitter, but

Tom Butts making a play.

if someone tried to sneak a fast ball, I'd get a little hit," was how he described his approach. "They always said I hit high balls. They said I hit them off my cap bill."[65] He was elected to start the East-West All-Star Game and went 0-for-2 in front of 48,112 and "a galaxy of major league scouts" in attendance at Comiskey Park.[66]

Butts played winter ball in Cuba for the Alacranes del Almendares in 1947-48.[67] "Adolph Luque in Cuba rated Butts even better than Rizzuto," recalled Lennie Pearson, another Negro Leaguer who played in the Cuban circuit. Pearson added, "He could go behind second base better than any man I ever saw in my life."[68] Butts also impressed former major-league catcher and coach Mike González, the manager of the champion Leones del Habana. The *Baltimore Afro-American* reported, "Gonzales [*sic*] said that Butts is the 'best I've ever seen' and the old National Leaguer has seen most of the top flight performers."[69]

Although the Negro Leagues had lost more players to the formerly segregated majors by the summer of 1948, Philadelphia Stars manager Oscar Charleston opined, "There is still plenty of big league material left, like Tommy Butts."[70] One of the circuit's budding stars was Butts' double-play partner, second baseman Junior Gilliam, who had joined the Elite Giants as a 17-year-old in 1946. "I don't know what kind of credit Junior Gilliam might give anybody, but Butts worked with him just like he was his own son and developed him into one of the top infielders in the Negro National League," remarked one opponent, Chico Renfroe.[71]

"Gilliam was a quiet guy, but when he got on the field he had more pep than you'd think he had. He could make a team go. ... He was really a baseball nut," said Butts. Although he insisted that Scales deserved recognition for making Gilliam a switch-hitter and second baseman, Butts acknowledged. "[Gilliam] was a little younger than I was, and the fellows told me to keep my eye on him, don't let him go running around."[72]

During Butts and Gilliam's second full season as a keystone duo in 1948, Lacy wrote, "Both are timely hitters if not great hitters. Both are fast, aggressive base-runners and offer serious threats to the opposition whenever they're on the base-paths. Between them, they have four of the best hands in baseball and their throwing arms, particularly Butts's, are not to be toyed with."[73] Baltimore advanced to the NNL2 championship series but lost to Homestead.

In June, Butts had been suspended for 10 days and fined $100 by NNL2 President John H. Johnson after an uncharacteristic incident at Yankee Stadium on May 30, 1948.[74] After Butts' liner to left field was caught on one hop by New York Cubans left fielder Cleveland Clark, umpire Julio Hernández ruled it a clean catch. Incensed, Butts struck the umpire twice – knocking him down – and jumped on him. "This marks the first time [Butts] has ever been in a dispute with an umpire," reported the *Afro-American*. "A quiet personality, he seldom takes issue with an umpire's decisions, despite the fact that teammates say there any many occasions when he would be justified in doing so."[75]

There is no evidence that the incident hampered Butts' major-league prospects.[76] That summer Lacy wrote, "Had he been fortunate enough to possess about 10 more pounds, Butts would have been one of the first NNL players sought by the major league outfit. But with only 146 pounds on his frame – wringing wet – Butts is much too small to serve effectively as a major league shortstop. This, to the writer's way of thinking, and this alone has kept him from being a big league player today."[77]

In the 80-game 1948-1949 Puerto Rican Winter League campaign. Butts hit .312 with 61 runs scored for the Cangrejeros de Santurce.[78] That team also lost in the championship series.

The NNL2 ceased operations before the 1949 season, but the Elite Giants joined the NAL and carried on. Before the Chicago White Sox signed White infielder Jim Baumer to a $50,000 "bonus baby" contract on June 2, White Sox GM Frank Lane inquired about Butts.[79] Another report said a Triple-A Pacific Coast League club expressed interest but signed Parnell Woods instead because the Elite Giants wanted too much money.[80] Butts remained with Baltimore, started another East-West All-Star Game, and led the circuit's shortstops in fielding.[81] Unlike many of his contemporaries, who left their gloves on the field when their team was at bat, Lacy noted, "Butts ... is superstitious, he ... carts it all the way to the front of his dugout."[82]

The Elite Giants swept the Chicago American Giants in four games to win the 1949 NAL title. The clinching 4-2 victory at Comiskey Park was scoreless until the top of the sixth inning, when Butts led off with an opposite-field single and scored on Lennie Pearson's double.[83]

After hitting just .221 in 280 at-bats for Santurce in winter ball, Butts returned to Baltimore in 1950 for what proved to be his final season with the Elite Giants. Bugle Field had been demolished, so Opening Day marked the first game between two Black teams at Memorial Stadium. Butts walked and scored twice against Philadelphia, including the decisive run in the bottom of the ninth on Gilliam's RBI.[84] Butts was elected an East-West All-Star Game starter again, but his Elite Giants career ended on September 3 when he was one of four players suspended by manager Kimbro before the club's home finale. Although their teammates had voted to accept business manager Dick Powell's proposal to remain on salary through Labor Day, Butts and three others refused to dress unless they received a percentage of the gate instead.[85]

Butts played for the Winnipeg Buffaloes of the semipro Manitoba-Dakota (ManDak) League in 1951. The team, managed by future Hall of Famer Willie Wells, was defeated in the circuit's championship series. "I didn't want to go back, it was too cold up there," Butts said.[86]

In 1952 three former Elite Giants – Butts, pitcher Al Wilmore, and second baseman Fleming Reedy – became the Philadelphia Athletics organization's first African American players.[87] Butts and Wilmore were signed by scout Judy Johnson.[88] After spring training in Savannah, Georgia, the trio was assigned to the Lincoln (Nebraska) A's in the Class-A Western League. (Reedy lasted 11 seasons in the minors, but arm problems derailed

Wilmore.) Butts hit just .170 in 47 games. When Lincoln tried to demote him to Class B that summer, Butts returned to the NAL instead. Later, he explained that he could tell his skills were slipping, and he did not think it would be fair to block a younger player.[89] Butts joined the Birmingham Black Barons and saw action in the 1952 NAL championship series, won by the Indianapolis Clowns club that featured 18-year-old shortstop Henry Aaron.[90]

Gilliam debuted with the Brooklyn Dodgers in 1953 and won the National League Rookie of the Year Award. "It broke Butts up when Gilliam went up to the big leagues and he didn't," said Pearson. "He wasn't too old for the majors. But he loved life, and when I say he loved life, I mean he loved life, especially women. After a game, Butts had a tendency to go off on the town, while Gilliam would stay around and listen to the old-timers talk and soak up that knowledge of baseball."[91]

Although Butts was voted a starter for one final East-West All-Star Game that summer, when the Black Barons played in Atlanta, the *Daily World* observed, "Good living, good time, good pay have taken their toll on Butts. He is now in the twilight of a brilliant career. ... The shuddering hardships of barnstorming competition have wrecked the splendid promise."[92]

In 1954 Butts saw action with the Black Barons and the Memphis Red Sox. In 1955 he appeared in 28 games in the Class-B Big State League, batting .265 for the Texas City Texans. Three of Butts' former Baltimore teammates contributed to the Brooklyn Dodgers team that won its only World Series that fall. Pitcher Joe Black won his only decision before he was traded in June, Gilliam started at second base, and Campanella was the NL MVP.

A 1960 Atlanta directory listed Butts as a helper for a metal fabrication company. He married Dorothy Butler, a Baltimorean, and fathered four children: Jean, Thomas, Retta, and Norma.[93]

When Negro Leagues historian John Holway interviewed him in 1970, Butts said attending an old-timers' game in Atlanta the previous year had been "a big thrill."[94] Butts described reuniting with Johnny Logan, a former Puerto Rican League teammate who told him that he still appeared to be in shape. "Yeah, I'm in shape, but I can't do anything now," he replied. Butts also shared how he had visited Campanella in New York since a January 1958 car accident had left his old roommate paralyzed.[95]

Tom Butts was 53 when he died on December 30, 1972, in Atlanta. He is buried in the city's South-View Cemetery, the final resting place for many prominent African Americans, including civil rights icons Julian Bond and John Lewis, sports greats Henry Aaron and Walt Bellamy, and Martin Luther King Sr.

Joe Black named Butts the first-team shortstop on his all-time Black all-star team in 1969.[96] Later, Black reflected, "Players like Leon Day, Pee Wee Butts, Larry Doby, Josh Gibson, Buck Leonard, those guys could play. ... They had credentials for the Hall of Fame."[97] When Black uttered those words in 1992, only Gibson and Leonard had been enshrined in Cooperstown, but Butts was the only player he named who had not been so honored as of 2024.

"If I'd been 10 years younger, I think I could have made the major leagues," Butts told Holway. "If the doors had opened up a little earlier, I think I'd have done pretty good."[98]

SOURCES

In addition to sources cited in the Notes, the author consulted www.ancestry.com, www.baseball-reference.com, www.retrosheet.org, https://sabr.org/bioproject, and https://seamheads.com/blog/.

Tom Butts' Puerto Rican Winter League statistics are from https://beisbol101.com/jugador/tommy-butts/

NOTES

1　Tom Holcomb, "'We Were Trailblazers for Jackie Robinson,'" *Atlanta Constitution*, June 27, 1997: E7.

2　John Holway, *Voices from the Great Black Baseball Leagues* (New York: Da Capo Press, Inc., 1992), 327.

3　In addition to Butts' four East-West All-Star Game seasons (1944, both 1946 contests, 1947, 1948) reflected by Baseball Reference in March 2023, he was a reserve – but did not play – in the 1942 contest. Butts also started East-West All-Star Games in 1949, 1950, and 1953, but the post-1948 Negro Leagues were not retroactively deemed major leagues.

4　In a 1937 "Ex-Slave Interview" for the Federal Writers Project, Berry's sister Carrie said her family had labored on Ben Bass's plantation. (According to military records, Bass's Confederate Army unit surrendered with General Robert E. Lee's forces at Appomattox Court House in Virginia in 1865.) After gaining their freedom, Carrie described how they initially remained there as low-wage workers before moving from farm to farm as renters. Aunt Carrie Mason, "Ex-Slave Interview" written by Estelle G. Burke, Federal Writers' Project July 7, 1937, https://www.ancestry.com/discoveryui-content/view/6227:1944?ssrc=pt&tid=171658784&pid=362378020616. (Subscription service, last accessed February 26, 2023).

5　Sam McKibben, "Atlanta Red Caps Take 5-1 Slugging," *Atlanta Daily World*, July 27, 1935: 5.

6　Marion E. Jackson, "Sports of the World," *Atlanta Daily World*, June 19, 1953: 7.

7　Ric Roberts, "'Chicken' Charlie Clark Affords Real Story for Ambitious Young Men," *Atlanta Daily World*, August 9, 1936: 2.

8　Sam McKibben, "McKibben Lists All City Prep Eleven," *Atlanta Daily World*, December 8, 1935: 5.

9　Sam McKibben, "Semi-pro Outfits to Commence Activities," *Atlanta Daily World*, May 4, 1936: 5.

10　"'Pea-Eye' Butts Will Be Honored by BTWHS Folk," *Atlanta Daily World*, September 16, 1938: 5.

11　Lucius Jones, "Atlanta Preps Wins Brilliant 'Intersectional' Tilt, 29-13," *Atlanta Daily World*, December 5, 1937: 1.

12　"BTWHS Grid Star, Butts, Newest Black Crax Phenom," *Atlanta Daily World*, July 1, 1938: 5.

13　Holway, 331.

14   "'Pea-Eye' Butts Will Be Honored by BTWHS Folk."

15   "Black Crackers Clinch Second Half Pennant," *Atlanta Daily World*, September 9, 1938: 11.

16   "Butts Night to Honor Black Crax Star," *Atlanta Daily World*, September 18, 1938: 8.

17   "Memphis Leads in Playoff for Championship," *Chicago Defender*, September 24, 1938: 8.

18   Scott News Syndicate, "Bad Weather Prevents Third Game," *Atlanta Daily World*, September 21, 1938: 5.

19   Roy White, "Purples Meet Monroe Aggies Friday Night," *Atlanta Constitution*, September 21, 1938: 10.

20   "Black Crackers to Face Memphis at Ponce de Leon Sunday, Sept. 25," *Atlanta Daily World*, September 21, 1938: 5.

21   "4,000 See BTWHS Rip Tuskegee High, 28-6," *Atlanta Daily World*, September 24, 1938: 5.

22   "Sunday Set Aside as Day to Help Our Black Crax Boys," *Atlanta Daily World*, September 24, 1938: 5.

23   "Black Crax Nip Black Barons in Pair, 5-3, 4-3," *Atlanta Daily World*, September 26, 1938: 5.

24   "Memphis Gets 1938 American League Pennant," *Chicago Defender*, December 17, 1938: 9.

25   Ric Roberts, "Shortstop Thomas Butts," *Atlanta Daily World*, March 24, 1939: 5.

26   Louisville was the initial city the Black Crackers agreed to represent, but they settled on Indianapolis after securing the use of a ballpark in Louisville became an issue. Scott News Syndicate, "Atlanta Changed Hands," *Atlanta Daily Work*, May 10, 1939: 5.

27   Lucius Jones, "Black Crax Win, 2-0; Show Again 3 P.M.," *Atlanta Daily World*, June 15, 1939: 5.

28   "Black Crax No Longer Indianapolis ABC's," *Atlanta Daily World*, June 21, 1939: 5.

29   Lucius "Melancholy" Jones, "Black Crax Out of Negro American League," *Atlanta Daily World*, June 26, 1939: 5.

30   "Five Atlanta Players Signed by Baltimore," *Chicago Defender*, July 22, 1939: 8.

31   Holway, 332.

32   "Elites Take Lead in Second Half," *Afro-American*, July 15, 1939: 21.

33   Holway, 332.

34   Holway, 329.

35   Holway, 332.

36   "Metropolitan Teams Bow in Double Bill," *Norfolk* (Virginia) *New Journal and Guide*, August 19, 1939: 19.

37   Holway, 333.

38   "Partlow Bests Byrd as Grays Win Opener, 2-1," *Baltimore Afro-American*, September 23, 1939: 1.

39   "Baltimore Whips Homestead Grays for Title," *Chicago Defender*, September 30, 1939: 9.

40   Art Carter, "Elites, Grays Split Double-Header," *Baltimore Afro-American*, August 3, 1940: 19.

41   Holway, 333.

42   Holway, 333.

43   Ed Perry, "Cash Lures Big League Overlords," *Norfolk New Journal and Guide*, April 19, 1941: 13.

44   "Baltimore Elites Only Club to Beat Bushies Twice, Play," *New York Amsterdam Star-News*, July 19, 1941: 18.

45   Holcomb, "'We Were Trailblazers for Jackie Robinson.'"

46   Cum Posey, "Posey's 18th All-American Baseball Team," *Pittsburgh Courier*, October 25, 1941: 17.

47   Robert V. Leffler Jr., "The History of Black Baseball in Baltimore from 1913 to 1951," master's thesis, Morgan State University, 1974: 87. Cited in Bob Luke, *The Baltimore Elite Giants* (Baltimore: The Johns Hopkins University Press, 2009), 70.

48   Bill Glauber, "Elite Giants: The Pride of Baltimore Baseball History," *Baltimore Sun*, April 29, 1990: 1A.

49   Holway, 332.

50   Art Carter, "Gaines Hurls 4-Hit Ball as Grays Are Blanked, 1-0," *Afro-American*, July 11, 1942: 22.

51   "Elites Drop 3 Straight as Grays Take Twin Bill," *Baltimore Afro-American*, August 1, 1942: 23.

52   Russ J. Cowans, "Sports Chatter," *Michigan Chronicle* (Detroit), June 6, 1942: 16.

53   Ric Roberts, "Vic Harris Says Build Own Baseball Leagues," *Baltimore Afro-American*, August 8, 1942: 23.

54   Lester Rose, "Major Prospects," *New York Daily News*, August 16, 1942: 34.

55   "Negro East-West Game Today May Attract 40,000," *Chicago Tribune*, August 16, 1942: B2. Another account published the previous day suggested that Butts could see action. Associated Negro Press, "Pea Eye Butts May Get Try," *Phoenix Index*, August 15, 1942: 6.

56   "Grays Win NNL Flag; Play K.C.'s," *Baltimore Afro-American*, September 12, 1942: 23.

57   "Roy Campanella Jumps Elite Giants; Said to be Playing in Mexico," *Philadelphia Tribune*, September 12, 1942: 14.

58   Sam Lacy, "Looking 'Em Over," *Baltimore Afro-American*, August 5, 1944: 18.

59   Sam Lacy, "From A to Z," *Baltimore Afro-American*, September 13, 1947: 12.

60   Harold Jackson, "46,000 See West Win All-Star Classic, 7-4," *Baltimore Afro-American*, August 19, 1944: 18.

61   "Tommy Butts," Béisbol 101, https://beisbol101.com/jugador/tommy-butts/ (last accessed March 13, 2023).

62   "Baltimore-Black Yankees at Stadium Sunday," *New York Amsterdam News*, May 19, 1945: 8B.

63   The article describes Butts' hit as a triple, but it is recorded as a double in the box score. "Orioles Humbled 3-1, 4-3 by Balto. Elite Giants," *Baltimore Afro-American*, October 13, 1945: 22.

64   Sam Lacy, "Looking 'Em Over," *Baltimore Afro-American*, October 12, 1946: 17.

65   Holway, 333.

66   "West's 5-2 Win Makes It 3 in a Row Over the East," *Norfolk New Journal and Guide*, August 2, 1947: 14.

67   "Negro Leaguers in Cuban Winter League," Center for Negro League Baseball Research, http://www.cnlbr.org/Portals/0/RL/Negro%20Leaguers%20in%20Cuban%20Winter%20League.pdf (last accessed March 18, 2023).

68   Holway, 327.

69 "Giants Seek Local Player, Bid Aspirants to Try Out," *Baltimore Afro-American*, April 17, 1948: 27.

70 Norvin (Rip) Collins, "Still 'Plenty of Negro Baseball Prospects," *Wilmington* (Delaware) *Journal-Every Evening* July 14, 1948: 28.

71 Holway, 328.

72 Holway, 335.

73 Sam Lacy, "NNL's Keystone Kuties Bonded by Close Friendship," *Baltimore Afro-American*, September 4, 1948: 8.

74 Scott News Syndicate, "Negro National League Meeting Set for June 23," *Atlanta Daily World*, June 12, 1948: 5.

75 Sam Lacy, "Butts Suspended, Fined $100 for Fight," *Baltimore Afro-American*, June 5, 1948: 9.

76 In an August 2023 note to the author Frederick Bush added that Philadelphia Stars catcher Bill Cash likely didn't make it into what was then considered Organized Baseball because of his run-in with an umpire in Leon Day's Opening Day no-hitter earlier that season. Owners like Effa Manley and reporters like Wendell Smith were convinced that such behavior was detrimental to a player's chances at playing in the minors or majors.

77 Lacy, "NNL's Keystone Kuties Bonded by Close Friendship."

78 "Tommy Butts."

79 Sam Lacy, "From A to Z," *Baltimore Afro-American*, June 11, 1949: C4.

80 The article identifies the PCL team as the San Diego Padres, but Woods signed with Oakland Oaks. Wendell Smith, "Louis Made Writers Look Good," *Pittsburgh Courier*, June 18, 1949: 22.

81 "Lenny Pigg Officially Designated Champion Batter of the NAL," *Chicago Defender*, December 24, 1949: 14.

82 Sam Lacy, "From A to Z," *Baltimore Afro-American*, September 10, 1949: 16.

83 R.S. Simmons, "Elite Giants Sweep Series for American League Championship," *Atlanta Daily World*, September 28, 1949: 5.

84 "10,000 Watch Elites Open NAL Season," *Baltimore Afro-American*, May 13, 1950: 18.

85 The players suspended with Butts were John Coleman, Ed Finney, and Al Wilmore. "Ban 4 Elites After Strike," *Baltimore Afro-American*, September 9, 1950: 17.

86 Holway, 337.

87 Bill Bowens, "Three Former Elite Giants Crack Tradition in Georgia," *Baltimore Afro-American*, April 19, 1952: 16.

88 Al Cartwright, "Judy Johnson Catches Two for A's," *Wilmington Journal-Every Evening*, March 7, 1952: 21.

89 Holway, 337.

90 "Flags Fly and So Do Fists at Negro League World Series," *Philadelphia Tribune*, October 7, 1952: 10.

91 Holway, 328.

92 Jackson, "Sports of the World."

93 "Funeral Notices," *Atlanta Constitution*, January 5, 1973: 6C.

94 Holway, 328.

95 Holway, 328.

96 Joe Black, "Ex-Dodger Joe Black Picks All-time All Star Black Team," *Chicago Defender*, August 9, 1969: 45.

97 Tom Haudricourt, "Negro League Players Get Overdue Tribute," *Milwaukee Sentinel*, June 19, 1992: 6B.

98 Holway, 329.

BILL BYRD

BY THOMAS KERN

"I had a gift. That's about all there was to it."
– Bill Byrd[1]

A Negro League ballplayer had no greater testimonial to his individual play than selection to the annual East-West All-Star Game. Of those who were pitchers, only three appeared in seven or more games. Leon Day led the way with nine, followed by Hilton Smith with seven. Bill Byrd also pitched in seven and was selected for two more games, one of which he appeared in as a pinch-hitter and the other in which he was not called on to play. Day and Smith are Baseball Hall of Famers. However, while devotees of Black baseball of the day knew how good Byrd was, playing outside the limelight of the showcase teams in the Negro Leagues has obscured his greatness. The fact is that Byrd's career certainly showed him to be Hall of Fame-worthy as well, and his story underscores that claim.

The Byrd family was a part of the Great Migration, living in Canton, Georgia, where William was born on July 15, 1907, and then relocating to Columbus, Ohio, for a better life when he was 12 years old. Not much is known about Byrd's parents, Robert and Ovelle (Blake). Byrd himself completed the National Baseball Hall of Fame's player profile form in 1973 and listed eight years of elementary education in both Canton, Georgia, and Riley, Alabama (the latter an apparent way station for the Byrd family on their way to Ohio).[2] Byrd lists no high school in Ohio, but a later newspaper reference ties him to East High School in Columbus.[3]

Byrd later reminisced about his love for baseball as a kid. "I never had training, never had a teacher," he told historian John Holway.[4] Another biography of Byrd sheds light on his youthful penchant for the game: "According to legend, Bill honed his baseball skills by throwing rocks and hitting rocks with a tree limb that he had fashioned into a baseball bat.[5] Simply put, his development as a ballplayer came on the sandlots.

Byrd's connection to Columbus gave him exposure to the higher levels of Black baseball. Byrd played on a team called the Columbus Turfs in 1932, a member of the Negro Southern League. In his history of the NSL, William J. Plott noted:

> The Columbus Turf Team was announced as a new league member in early July. The Ohio team was to play its first game on Saturday, July 16, at Neil Park [in Columbus], the home of the city's white American Association Team. ... It was reported that the Turf Club, sometimes called the Turf Stars, was bringing "colored professional baseball to Columbus" for the first time in ten years.[6]

Some of the players on the roster that season alongside Byrd were Satchel Paige, Dennis Gilchrist, C.B. "Clarence" Griffin, John Kerner, Alphonso "Duke" Lattimore, Sam Warmack, and Roy Williams; however, actual box scores have not yet been found.[7]

The Turfs' play in the NSL may offer insight into how Byrd eventually became known to Tom Wilson, owner of the Nashville Elite Giants, the franchise for which Byrd would play nearly all of his career.

The Elite Giants are very much the story of Wilson, their founder and longtime owner. Wilson was born in Atlanta in the late 1880s. (His birth year is disputed.) His family moved to Nashville to further their education and became doctors. Because of their successful careers, the Wilsons became part of the Black middle class, from which the young Wilson benefited in terms of the social standing and financial wherewithal that came with it.[8] Wilson's business acumen and entrepreneurial pursuits included baseball, and he formed the Nashville Standard Giants in 1920.

Plott's history of the NSL lists a team called the Nashville White Sox as a charter member of the league in 1920, run and managed by Marshall Garrett, one of Wilson's business partners. In 1921 the Nashville franchise became the Elite Giants, previously Wilson's Standard Giants. The NSL struggled early to find its footing. After its first four seasons, the league suspended play in 1924 and 1925, and again in 1928 and 1930. Through 1931, when the league did operate, Nashville won the title four times. In 1930 Wilson orchestrated the Elite Giants' elevation to the top-tier Negro National League. That team, however, struggled at the gate and finished poorly, and Wilson, always looking for a more viable financial setting, relocated the team north to Cleveland as the Cubs in 1931. A history of "Black Baseball in Depression Cleveland" noted that "Wilson more than likely moved his club from Nashville to Cleveland in an attempt to make a profit off the black population in Cleveland by way of the numbers game."[9] Although this might have been true, the larger African American population in Cleveland in 1930 was probably greater justification for the relocation (72,000 in Cleveland vs. 43,200 in Nashville, providing a bigger population to draw on for Elite games.)[10]

With the demise of the first, Rube Foster-founded NNL in 1931, the NSL ascended to "major" league status as the only premier Black Ball league left standing at the time. Wilson brought the team back to Nashville for the 1932 NSL season, and his squad, which won the league's second-half championship, participated in the so-called Dixie Series against the first-half champion Chicago American Giants. The American Giants prevailed over Nashville in seven games. The Elite Giants remained in the NSL for two more years, but with the ongoing economic uncertainty at the height of the Depression, Wilson moved the franchise again. At first, he took his team to Detroit[11] in 1935 to join the new Negro National League II (NNL2). However, after he was unable to arrange a lease on Hamtramck Field, he abruptly relocated to greener pastures in Columbus early that season.

Meanwhile, after his stint with the Turfs in 1932, the now 25-year-old Byrd surfaced on Columbus's first entry in the NNL2 in the league's 1933 inaugural year. The Blue Birds[12] had been one of five affiliate teams in 1931, the last season of the first NNL, and now were a charter member of the reconstituted NNL2. However, the franchise struggled, so Gus Greenlee, president of the league, "moved the Columbus ball club to Cleveland [as the Giants] in hopes of making a profit."[13] A comparison of the rosters of both teams shows several of the Blue Birds making the move to Cleveland.

Records for Byrd in 1933 list 13 appearances as a pitcher with the Blue Birds (including 11 starts with a 3-8 record), but no records are available with him on the Cleveland squad that finished the season and then folded.

Ted "Double Duty" Radcliffe and Roosevelt Davis were Byrd's teammates on the 1933 Blue Birds, and Byrd credited Davis with teaching him how to throw the spitter.[14] Byrd bounced around Depression baseball in his early professional years, and "[a]fter the Blue Birds folded that autumn, he went to the last place Cleveland Red Sox."[15] In 1934 the NNL2 tried to resuscitate a presence in Cleveland under what might have been league-appointed ownership of Prentice Byrd (no relation to Bill Byrd) and Dr. E.L. Langrum. The new owners hired Negro League veteran Bobby Williams as manager.[16]

The migration of Blue Birds/Giants players to the new Red Sox team saw Byrd joining "several of his Blue Bird teammates (Ameal Brooks, Roosevelt Davis, Kermit Dial, Dennis Gilchrist, Clarence Griffin, Wilson "Frog" Redus, and Roy Williams) on the new team.[17] The second iteration of Cleveland's entry in the league fared as poorly as the Cleveland Giants had, and it too was one and done in the league after playing to a 3-22 record. Byrd's 2-8 record for the NNL's cellar-dwelling team, along with an ERA of 6.90, was lackluster at best, but his adopted hometown of Columbus offered him another shot in 1935 with the arrival of the Elite Giants from Nashville via Detroit.

It is uncertain whether Wilson and his protégés remembered Byrd from the 1932 NSL season, but his modest beginning with the Columbus Elite Giants in 1935, in which he played alongside a reasonably stable lineup from the prior year, offered a foundation for his future success with that itinerant franchise.

And itinerant they continued to be, playing only one year in Columbus. In 1936 Wilson moved the team again, this time to Washington, DC, having arranged a deal with Washington

Senators owner Clark Griffith to lease Griffith Stadium for the Elite Giants' use. Manager Candy Jim Taylor, in a guest column for the *Pittsburgh Courier* in the spring of 1936, captured the move:

> The Nashville Elite Giants, to be known as the Washington Elites for the 1936 season, started training Saturday. ... Tom

Right-hander Bill Byrd. Courtesy SABR Rucker Archive.

Wilson, owner of the Elite Giants, has been in baseball for about 20 years and for the last few years his club has been in the Negro National League. He promised Washington fans the same kind of club that he has put on the field in the last few years, and from the looks of things now it will be a first division club. ... The pitching staff looks to be the best in the league. Bob Griffith, the schoolboy wonder heads the staff. [Andy] Porter the speed ball wonder, sick most of last season, is reported to be in fine shape, Byrd, the big side arm boy from Columbus, Jim Willis, the only veteran on the staff, seems to be ready for a great season. [Tom] Glover, southpaw with the club for a while last year will be back. Of the new men, Red Howard, from Memphis ... will round out the rotation. Biz Mackey, the old warhorse ... will be number one man behind the bat with his ability to handle pitchers.[18]

Having been promised a first-division team, Washington fans witnessed a slow start by the Elite Giants, but the team won the second-half crown, only to lose to the Pittsburgh Crawfords in the playoffs. Byrd, Jim Willis, and Bob Griffith anchored the Elite Giants' rotation, with Byrd tossing the most innings and finishing with a 9-4 record and a 3.38 ERA. The other members of Taylor's pitching staff did not fare as well (the team's ERA was a voluminous 4.88), and the Washington squad did not play .500 ball.

The Elite Giants reprised their time in Washington with a second season in 1937. Managed now by Mackey, Washington finished 23-36 in league play, a distant fifth to the champion Homestead Grays. Byrd had three batterymates – Mackey, Nish Williams, and 15-year-old Roy Campanella. Records for the year show that Byrd regressed on the mound. The team's two subpar years in Washington did not do much to build fan support or a financial grounding for the team and it was no surprise that Wilson found justification to relocate once again. In fact, the team played some of its schedule at Oriole Park in Baltimore after Wilson was unable to reach an agreement with Griffith on hosting a full slate of games at Griffith Stadium. In early 1938 the *Baltimore Afro-American* reported:

It is almost a certainty that the Elite Giants, for the last two years representatives of Washington, DC, in the Negro National League, will be transferred to Baltimore this season. [According to Tom Wilson, Elite Giants owner] "Only a slight hitch remains to be ironed out [regarding stadium usage]. ... Last year we lost money from operating from Washington. I sincerely feel Baltimore far superior to Washington as a baseball town. ... It has been a long time since Baltimore has had a regular league team and I feel the people there need one and will support one."[19]

Wilson and his partners "at last found adequate community support" in Baltimore.[20] The city had a sizable African American population (growing from 142,000 in 1930 to 225,000 in 1950 and to nearly a third of the population). The team's ballpark (Bugle Field) was situated in an East Baltimore working-class neighborhood, not far from the Old West neighborhood in the

west-central part of town that middle-class Blacks called home.[21] According to Luke, "Baltimore, with its large and growing black population and large black middle class, was just the kind of city Wilson needed for his baseball team."[22]

The now Baltimore Elite Giants performed promisingly in their new setting. Managed by George Scales, Baltimore finished third, well behind the Grays and Philadelphia Stars. There was some debate about the final standings, but this was often the case as the NNL2 had limited resources to maintain accurate records. Baltimore assembled a core team that year with players who populated the roster over the next few years: a pitching rotation of Byrd, Andy Porter, School Boy Griffith, and Jonas Gaines; a lineup with veterans Henry Kimbo, Burnis "Wild Bill" Wright, and Bill Hoskins in the outfield; James West, Sammy Hughes, Felton Snow, and Hoss Walker in the infield; and the tandem of veteran Mackey and the young Campanella behind the plate. Despite finishing well behind league-leading Homestead with its future Hall of Famers Josh Gibson, Buck Leonard, and Ray Brown, "Tom Wilson decided to keep the Elites in Baltimore. The box office had been good to him even if the team's won-loss record had disappointed."[23]

The 1939 season finally put the Elites on the Black baseball map. The team returned substantially the same lineup as in 1938, but with Felton Snow as manager and Andy Porter and School Boy Griffith having left for Mexico. Midseason pickup Pee Wee Butts was a plus and the rotation of Byrd, Gaines, Willie Hubert, Emery Adams, and Tom Glover was good enough to keep the team competitive. It was an atypical year for the league as the first- and second-half champion Grays and Elites did not play in a championship series. Instead, the top four teams engaged in a playoff. After the Grays defeated Philadelphia and Baltimore survived Newark, the winners played a five-game series. Byrd, the team's regular-season workhorse with the most wins, won Game Four of the series with the Grays despite giving up 15 hits (including three singles and a homer to Josh Gibson) in a 10-5 outcome that tied the series at two games apiece and set the stage for the winner-take-all Game Five. Baltimore won the game, 2-0, behind the pitching of Gaines and Hubert.[24] The *Baltimore Afro-American* averred, "Climaxing an uphill campaign in a blaze of glory, the Baltimore Elite Giants won the Negro National League baseball championship ... by turning back the Homestead Grays."[25]

Except for a one-year sojourn to Venezuela, Byrd centered his offseason play in a single Caribbean destination, Puerto Rico. Byrd journeyed to Puerto Rico for three successive winters (1939-1940, 1940-1941, and 1941-1942). The Puerto Rico Winter League had been inaugurated the year before Byrd's first appearance and became what now is "the longest continually running winter league in the Western Hemisphere."[26] Each owner in the six-team league was "determined to win the all-important inaugural winter league championship, and they set about to staff their rosters with the best players they could find. There was a flurry of activity over the summer of 1938 as the owners went on a recruiting campaign from New York to Caracas, with briefcases full of money."[27] And Negro League ballplayers were prime recruits. Despite competition from Cuba, with its longstanding winter play, "the owners were able to attract several Negro Leaguers to their first season, including George Scales, Dick Seay, Jimmy Crutchfield," and others.[28]

The Puerto Rico Winter League's success in its first year led to a more lucrative recruitment of Negro League ballplayers in 1939-1940. Signings included Satchel Paige, Ray Brown, Leon Day, Josh Gibson, Dick Seay, Roy Partlow, and Bill Byrd.[29] How Byrd surfaced in Puerto Rico is unclear, but the Negro League fraternity was such that those signed in Puerto Rico often informed their team owners about other players to consider for their squads. Byrd ended up on Santurce that winter with fellow Negro Leaguers Josh Gibson, who managed the team, and Dick Seay.[30]

Byrd tossed a blistering 229 innings in the league his first year and pitched to a record of 15-10 record with a 1.97 ERA.[31] Santurce finished at 26-29, with Byrd starting nearly half of the Crabbers' games, and finished fourth in the eight-team league.[32]

January 7, 1940, marked a game for the ages between two Negro League hurlers battling under Caribbean skies. Leon Day, pitching for Aguadilla, was Byrd's mound opponent. Aguadilla scored one run in the first and Santurce countered with one in the fourth. Then "Byrd and Day settled down to a long Sunday afternoon in the sun. The goose eggs piled up inning after inning until the sun set in the west and the umpire called the game on account of darkness. The final score of the 18-inning game was 1-1, and Leon Day had struck out 19 batters over the course of the day."[33]

The financial attraction of Puerto Rico, Mexico, and Venezuela in these years was compounded by the inability of the Negro National and American Leagues to pay their players well and "to standardize and enforce the contracts and agreements between owner and player which were often easily broken at the convenience of either party."[34] The difference in wages between the Negro Leagues and the Caribbean was a big deal. Ed Harris of the *Philadelphia Tribune* "viewed player jumps as inevitable, as some players were not even 'getting the wages they would on WPA [Works Progress Administration].'"[35] Wendell Smith of the *Pittsburgh Courier* noted that "[b]all players are always going to go where they make the most money. Right now, Mexico [and Puerto Rico] is the place. Efforts to stop this have been unsuccessful and will be until the moguls here get together and organize a league with a solid foundation."[36] Chester Washington, also of the *Courier*, noted "that in this so-called Land of Opportunity how tragic it was that the greatest home run hitter in the game today – Josh Gibson – had to leave his native America to make a lucrative living in far-away Venezuela just because the Negro League can't afford to pay him the salary he's worth and the major leagues bar him because he is black."[37]

Immediately after his time in the Puerto Rican Winter League in 1939-1940, Byrd was enticed to play for Venezuela's Centauros de Maracaibo. Records for the 13-15-game season that

spring are sparse, but it is known that Josh Gibson, Luis Aparico Sr., and Pedro "Perucho" Cepeda also played for the Centauros. Other Negro Leaguers were lured to Venezuela, including Satchel Paige, Ray Dandridge, and Leon Day. Apparently, Byrd's time in Venezuela also served as a honeymoon for him and his new wife, Hazel, as they both embarked upon a second marriage.[38]

When Bill Byrd returned to the United States after his time in Venezuela, he was asked why he had chosen to go to South America to play ball. He responded, "They treat you better down there. They pay your way down. Get you an apartment and pay you pretty well. ... They roll out the red carpet for you."[39] This was a common reaction. As Negro League historian Leslie Heaphy has noted, "Whether the Negro League players traveled south during the summer or winter they went because baseball was popular, they loved the game, they needed the extra money, and Latin American fans looked up them as heroes."[40]

The increasing exodus of many star players to Puerto Rico and Mexico led to a ban issued by Negro League owners in 1940:

> Aware of the potential for disaster during 1940, the two league presidents [J.B. Martin (NAL) and Tom Wilson (NNL)] agreed that any player jumping to a foreign locale would be suspended for three years, and all league clubs would be barred from playing independent teams using or competing against the suspended players.[41]

El Maestro,[42] as Byrd was called in Puerto Rico, had to pitch in the Winter League without his spitter, his bread-and-butter pitch. It was outlawed. Gene Benson, a fellow Negro Leaguer and Byrd's occasional winter season roommate, remarked to Holway that without the spitter, "I didn't see no difference. He still blinded us – he threw the ball right past us. He had everything else he needed: threw a hard, good curveball. Shoot, very few teams beat Bill."[43] Even so, Buck Leonard remarked that Byrd would occasionally try to get away with throwing it: "Byrd was cutting heads right and left with that spitter. ... Byrd would throw a high pitch over the batter's head and while everyone watched the ball, Bill hastily put his fingers to his mouth."[44]

Much is made of the 6-foot-1 right-hander as a spitballer. According to Luke, "Byrd chewed slippery elm; a soft greenish bark, to help his ball do tricks.[45] However, Byrd recounted to Holway:

> I threw almost everything: knuckler, slow knuckler, fast knuckler, curve, slider. I had good control ... a good fastball overhand. I'd get a guy set up and then throw it. ... [And Byrd insisted] I hated the spitter ... they made me throw it. ... [Candy Jim Taylor told him] if you're gonna throw it, fake it." The fear that Byrd *might* use his spitter ... made his other pitches more effective.[46]

Since Byrd had been banned by the NNL2, Baltimore was without his talents in 1940,[47] but the Elites managed to finish second, 3½ games behind the Homestead Grays in the six-team league. Meanwhile, Byrd made his way back to Puerto Rico for a second season, this time with Caguas. The Caguas owners broke the bank that winter to sign Negro League talent, and their investment paid dividends. Caguas won the first-half championship and Santurce the second half to set the stage for a seven-game championship series that ended up being a back-and-forth affair. Byrd lost 1-0 to Santurce's Ray Brown in Game One, but Caguas won Game Two. A week later, Byrd beat Brown and then Santurce took Game Four. When the series resumed several days later, Byrd was again on the short end of a duel with Brown in Game Five, but Roy Campanella bailed out Caguas to take Game Six the next day. Game Seven immediately followed Game Six and Byrd and Brown dueled for a third time. In the finale Byrd turned in a 6-2 complete-game win to capture the series for Caguas.[48]

The presence of Byrd and his peers in Puerto Rico and Mexico adversely impacted the NNL2 and NAL, which missed many of their marquee players in 1940. By early 1941, the owners reconsidered their position to ban players who journeyed south, and according to the *New York Age*:

> [The] … smart play the owners made was lifting the ban imposed on star players who had "jumped" the country for more lucrative jobs in Mexico, Porto Rico, and Venezuela. These players, whose ranks include some of the biggest names in Negro baseball, will now be allowed to return to the league upon payment of a $100 fine. Since nearly all the team owners are thirsting for the return of such drawing cards as Josh Gibson and Satchel Paige, they will probably be willing to pay the fines for the players of their choice.[49]

For the Baltimore Elite Giants, despite a decent 1940 season, getting Byrd back (he agreed to pay the $100 fine imposed by the league) made a difference as the Grays and Elites outpaced the rest of the NNL2 in 1941.[50]

Byrd played one more year in Puerto Rico, 1941-1942, again for Caguas. The team could not repeat its 1940-1941 championship season and finished tied for fifth despite Byrd's 10 wins. His Puerto Rican swan song ended with his selection to the league's North All-Star team, his second all-star designation after similar recognition the year before.[51]

Byrd's return to the NNL2 after his one-year ban was a remarkable one. Deservedly chosen for that year's All-Star Game, he compiled a 9-3 record with an ERA of 2.23 against league competition. The Elites lost the first-half pennant to their nemesis, the Grays. Although Baltimore finished ahead of Homestead in the second half, the team now trailed the New York Cubans and missed out on the playoffs. Byrd's battery-mate, Roy Campanella, had a breakout year for Baltimore that provided a hint of things to come in his career. Byrd's season was punctuated by a 3-2 win against the Memphis Red Sox in July in which he threw no-hit ball through the first eight innings and, purportedly, a three-strikeout "immaculate inning"

in the third, fanning the three Red Sox batters he faced with the minimum nine pitches.[52]

In what was a recurring theme in the 1940s, the Grays again bested the second-place Elite Giants in 1942. Over the next five years, from 1943 to 1947, Baltimore finished fifth, fourth, third, second, and fourth, well behind perennial pennant winners Homestead, and then Newark in 1946 and the New York Cubans in 1947. During those years, Byrd toiled in workmanlike fashion for the Elites, in a rotation that variously included Andy Porter, Jonas Gaines, Tom Glover, Bill Harvey, Bill Burns, and a young Joe Black.

In 1942 Byrd famously beaned Newark Eagles player-manager Willie Wells. The *Courier* wrote:

> The Jersey team had some … bad luck in the eighth when their player manager Willie Wells, was struck in the temple by a pitched ball from the hand of Bill Byrd, who relieved Porter on the mound. Wells suffered a slight concussion, but soon regained consciousness in the dressing room.[53]

The story is worth recounting because the incident allegedly led to Wells visiting a local construction site before his next game to obtain and modify a hard hat for use when batting.[54] Thus, Wells became the first Negro League player to use a batting helmet.

Ironically, one of Byrd's worst years in that stretch was 1944, the year in which he was chosen for both All-Star games. In 1945 Wild Bill Wright returned from his extended time in Mexico and along with Henry Kimbro, Roy Campanella, Bill Hoskins, and Norman "Bobby" Robinson, made for a solid lineup, with the team finishing second in league batting.

Even in his later 30s, Byrd still had gas in the tank. His league win totals from 1942 to 1947 were 10, 10, 6, 11, 4, and 8. With NNL2 play amounting to around 60 games per season, Byrd's career totals, if adjusted to a 162-game schedule, would have averaged 19 to 20 wins per season.

Negro League all-star teams commonly barnstormed against White teams after the regular season ended. In fact, "the Black and White all-stars met regularly in Baltimore [and elsewhere] to make some extra money barnstorming every Friday and Sunday until the weather got too cold. 'We had a good draw, white and black [Byrd said]. We all had a good time, no arguments, no fussing, nothing like that. Just nice baseball, friendly. I enjoyed playing them.'"[55] In 1945 Byrd played for Mackey's All-Stars in a five-game series against the White Charlie Dressen's All-Stars. The latter included the likes of Ralph Branca, Virgil Trucks, Red Barrett, and Eddie Stanky. Alongside Byrd were Don Newcombe, Roy Partlow, Monte Irvin, Roy Campanella, Johnny Davis, and Willie Wells.[56]

In 1947 the breaking of the color barrier was the beginning of the end for the Negro Leagues. "Official" statistics from the Howe News Bureau are available for numerous seasons after 1948, but cannot be fully corroborated by box scores. A new problem arose in that "players like Bill Byrd and Henry

Kimbro were two of the many Negro League players who were considered to be too old to be viable candidates to be signed by 'organized' baseball. Byrd and Kimbro's decision was real easy – return to the Baltimore Elite Giants because they didn't have any other real options."[57] Byrd pitched well for Baltimore in 1947,[58] a season marked by Tom Wilson's death and the transfer of Elite Giants ownership to Vernon Green. Bob Romby was the ace of the staff and, along with Byrd, the rotation included Jonas Gaines, Amos Watson, and Joe Black. Kimbro was the league's premier hitter. Baltimore finished in third place behind the New York Cubans and Newark Eagles.

Byrd was 10-4 with a 1.75 ERA in NNL2 games in 1948, belying his 40 years. Baltimore won the first-half championship in the last year of the NNL2 but lost to second-half Homestead for a chance to play NAL winner Birmingham in the final Negro League World Series. In the best-of-five series with the Grays, Elites manager Hoss Walker opted to open with Lefty Gaines over Byrd. Gaines lasted 3⅔ innings, giving up five runs in the eventual 6-0 defeat to Homestead. Byrd pitched 5⅓ innings to mop up the game, giving up three hits and a single tally in the top of the ninth. Two days later, on September 16, the Grays captured Game Two – also at Bugle Field – by a 6-2 score, with Joe Black taking the loss for the Elites. The two teams played to a 4-4 tie in Game Three the next day; the game was suspended because of Baltimore's 11:15 P.M. curfew. Byrd came back two days later to pitch a complete-game 11-3 win. However, the league subsequently declared the 4-4 game to be a forfeit by Baltimore since the team had used stalling tactics in the ninth inning that were intended to ensure that any Grays tallies in that inning would not be counted. The forfeit gave the Grays the series.[59]

L to R: Henry Kimbro, Bill Byrd, Felton Snow, and George Scales. Courtesy John W. Mosley Photograph Collection, Charles L. Blockson Afro-American Collection, Temple University Libraries.

The 1949 season offered the shrinking Negro League fan base glimpses of the Byrd of yesteryear as he pitched to a 12-3 record with a 3.50 ERA.[60] The Elites were now a member franchise of the NAL as the NNL2 had folded after the 1948 season. Baltimore won the second-half championship and played the first-half champion Chicago American Giants for the league crown. Baltimore swept Chicago in four games, with Byrd starting Game One and pitching a 9-1 win.[61]

Byrd's final year, 1950, saw him play sparingly for the Elites. The organized Black leagues were slowly imploding with fan interest moving to the American and National Leagues and their minor-league systems, which now incorporated the next generation of Black ballplayers. Not long into the season, Baltimore's owner Richard Powell (now in charge after Vernon Green's death) released Byrd, who for the rest of the season became player-manager for an independent team in Baltimore, the Negro League All Stars.[62]

Toward the end of his career, Byrd showed up in a few box scores for other teams, notably the Philadelphia Stars. Why Byrd was with the Stars in June 1944 on the winning end of a 13-0, three-hit, seven-strikeout complete game against the NAL Cincinnati Clowns is uncertain. The *Philadelphia Inquirer* referenced Byrd in the story "as a right hander from the Baltimore Elite Giants."[63]

Byrd was selected for the East-West All-Star Classic nine times, pitching in seven, pinch-hitting in one, and appearing on the roster in another. He first appeared in 1936 (August 23 in Chicago's Comiskey Park) as a Washington Elite Giant, pitching the middle three innings in a winning cause for the East, 10-2, striking out four and giving up an unearned run.

Byrd was selected for and started both games in 1939, a testimony to his superlative season for Baltimore. In Game One in Chicago (August 6), he pitched three innings with a strikeout, a walk, and two hits allowed. He left the game with a 2-0 lead, but Roy Partlow gave up three runs in the late innings as the East lost the game 4-2. Three weeks later at Yankee Stadium (August 27), Byrd gave up a run in three innings and left the game ahead, 5-1, in a game that the East won, 10-2.

Byrd missed out on the 1940 all-star game due to the ban on players who had started the season in Venezuela. In 1941 he pitched a scoreless ninth as the East won, 8-3, at Comiskey Park on July 27. In 1942 the *Cleveland Call Post* listed the East and West rosters, noting four Elite Giants: Gaines, Byrd, Kimbro, and Wright. Only Wright and Gaines entered the game.[64]

In 1944's August 13 contest in Chicago, Byrd shut out the West in his two innings pitched (the eighth and ninth) but it was mop-up duty as the East lost, 7-4. In 1945 Byrd pinch-hit for the Grays' Roy Welmaker in the ninth, was walked by Kansas City's Booker McDaniel, and scored one of the East's five runs that inning, but that was not enough in a 9-6 loss.[65] Byrd's turn as a pinch-hitter was no fluke. Holway recounted, "Like many other black pitchers, Bill was a threat at bat as well. He pitched righthanded but batted left or right. The left side was his strong side. ... Byrd played in the outfield between starts."[66]

The 1946 games marked Byrd's last selections to the East-West Classic (despite another lackluster regular season in which he finished 4-7 with a 4.48 ERA). In Washington on August 15, Byrd threw the middle three innings. He entered the game to stop a West rally, and the East mounted a comeback to win, 6-3, with Byrd as the winning pitcher. In his worst stint in All-Star play, Byrd pitched 1⅓ innings at Comiskey Park three days later and gave up all four runs the West scored in its 4-1 triumph.[67]

Byrd's All-Star legacy had him tied for second with most games pitched (7); tied for the most wins with two along with Dan Bankhead and Satchel Paige; third with most innings pitched (16 over seven games), and fifth-most strikeouts at 10.[68]

The collapse of the Negro Leagues on the heels of the gradual integration of the National and American Leagues and their minor leagues foreclosed any further baseball pursuits for Byrd (now in his 40s) save for the occasional semipro game. He found work in Philadelphia at General Electric as a stockman and retired in his 60.[69] After a prolonged bout with cancer, Byrd died at the age of 83 at the Medical College of Pennsylvania in Philadelphia.[70]

The *Baltimore Sun*'s Bill Glauber captured the essence of Bill Byrd, his career, and legacy, writing, "Bill Byrd was a pitcher who threw spitballs and a pioneer who helped pave the way for the integration of baseball. Others were more charismatic, and brought greater talent to the game, but Byrd was a seemingly indestructible master who became the symbol of the Baltimore Elite Giants during a Negro League career that spanned two decades." One of the winningest pitchers in Negro League history, "he also will be remembered as a teacher of future major-leaguers Roy Campanella, Jim Gilliam, and Joe Black."[71] So important was Byrd held in the esteem of younger ballplayers that he was known as "Daddy."[72]

Byrd finished his career with a 108-69 record (.610) with a 3.34 ERA in Negro League play. According to one statistical analysis, Byrd is the best pitcher of the Negro League's final decade not currently enshrined in Cooperstown:

> Byrd's lifetime winning percentage was in excess of .600 from 1932 to 1950, during which he had only one losing season. His career WAR of 33.4 through 1948 is higher than that of four other Negro League Hall of Fame pitchers, including contemporaries Leon Day and Hilton Smith. ... According to Seamheads, he accumulated the ninth highest number of wins of any pitcher in official American Negro League games, even though Byrd often pitched for lesser teams. As his teammate Roy Campanella put it when arguing for Byrd's admission to the Hall of Fame, "He was a good pitcher, and he was good for a long time."[73]

Byrd's 12-3 1949 season which, while not official yet,[74] further augments his career numbers. Holway's examination of Byrd led him to consider Byrd "Cy Young"-worthy in 1942, 1948, and 1949 (Holway's George Stovey award). Byrd was a finalist in the 2006 voting for the Negro League class inducted that year.[75] Others may deservedly have been chosen for the Hall before him, but greater awareness of his career as the Elite Giants' rotation anchor speaks to his ultimate merit. Asked about his career and whether he was bitter over not having a chance to play in the White major leagues, Byrd said, "No. Well, I did the best I could."[76]

SOURCES

Except where otherwise noted, all cited statistics are from Seamheads.com.

NOTES

1   Bill Glauber, "Bill Byrd, Negro Leaguer, Dies at 83/Baltimore Pitcher Trained Big Leaguers," *Baltimore Sun*, January 7, 1991.

2   Baseball Hall of Fame player profile, received January 1973, included in the National Baseball Hall of Fame's player file.

3   "Byrd to Play Here Friday," *Columbus Dispatch*, May 31, 1945.

4   John Holway, "The Original Baltimore Byrd," *Baseball Research Journal* 19 (1990): 24.

5   Dr. Layton Revel, "Forgotten Heroes: Bill Byrd," http://www.cnlbr.org/Portals/0/Hero/422255%20Center%20for%20Negro%20League%20Baseball_Bill%20Byrd.pdf, accessed July 6, 2023.

6   William J. Plott, *The Negro Southern League: A Baseball History, 1920–1951* (Jefferson, North Carolina: McFarland & Company, 2015), 98.

7   Revel, 4.

8   Andrea Williams, "Tom Wilson, Black Baseball and Nashville's Connection to the Negro Leagues," nashvillescene.com, 3. Last accessed on May 29, 2023.

9   Thomas E. Pfundstein, "Black Baseball in Cleveland, 1920–1950," Unpublished MA thesis, John Carroll University, 1996. Special thanks to the Cuyahoga County Public Library for their help in confirming this source.

10 See these websites that provide the estimated African American population in Nashville and Cleveland, respectively: Black Bottom | Tennessee Encyclopedia and AFRICAN AMERICANS | Encyclopedia of Cleveland History | Case Western Reserve University.

11 *California Eagle*, March 29, 1935: 7. The article states that "The Negro Baseball association has its plans all set now for the season. The roster will be the Philadelphia Stars, Chicago American Giants, Newark Dodgers, New York Cubans, Brooklyn Eagles, Pittsburg Crawfords, and the Detroit Elite Giants."

12 Perhaps a derivative name from the Columbus Red Birds of the American Association, which was similarly organized in 1931.

13 "Black Baseball in Cleveland," 13.

14 Holway, 24. This same accolade is due Davis for his tutoring of Chet Brewer, who also threw a spitter.

15 Holway, 24.

16 "Black Baseball in Cleveland," 16.

17 Revel, 6.

18 Candy Jim Taylor, "Mackey to Catch for Crack D.C. Ball Club," *Pittsburgh Courier*, April 18, 1936: 15.

19 "May Transfer Elite Giants from Washington to Balto," *Baltimore Afro-American*, February 5, 1938.

20 Bob Luke, *The Baltimore Elite Giants* (Baltimore: The Johns Hopkins University Press, 2009), 16.

21 Luke, 18-19.

22 Luke, 23.

23 Luke, 42.

24 Luke 43-51. Also "Homestead Grays, Elites Divide Pair," *Chicago Defender*, September 23, 1939: 8.

25 As quoted in Luke, 51-52.

26 William F. McNeil, *Black Baseball Out of Season: Pay for Play Outside the Negro Leagues* (Jefferson, North Carolina: McFarland & Co., 2007), 117.

27 McNeil, 117.

28 McNeil, 117.

29 McNeil, 121.

30 Winter League rules capped international players at no more than three for each team.

31 Thomas E. Van Hyning, *The Santurce Crabbers: Sixty Seasons of Puerto Rican Winter League Ball* (Jefferson, North Carolina: McFarland & Co., 1999), 214.

32 Van Hyning, 201.

33 McNeil, 120.

34 Neil Lanctot, *Negro League Baseball: The Rise and Ruin of a Black Institution* (Philadelphia: University of Pennsylvania Press, 2004), 90.

35 Lanctot, 91.

36 Wendell Smith, "Smitty's Sports Spurts," *Pittsburgh Courier*, April 5, 1941: 17.

37 Chester Washington, "Sez Ches," *Pittsburgh Courier*, May 18, 1940: 16.

38 Holway, 26.

39 Revel, 21.

40 Leslie A. Heaphy, *The Negro Leagues, 1869-1960* (Jefferson, North Carolina: McFarland & Co., 2003), 168.

41 Lanctot, 90.

42 Heaphy, 169.

43 Holway, 23.

44 Holway, 24.

45 Luke, 37-38.

46 Holway, 24.

47 The Elite Giants also lost Wild Bill Wright and Tom Glover to Mexico; see Luke, 59.

48 Van Hyning 13-14.

49 Buster Miller, "The Sports Parade," *New York Age*, March 22, 1941: 11.

50 Luke, 63.

51 McNeil, 123.

52 "Elites Shade Memphis Red Sox," *Baltimore Afro-American*, July 26, 1941: 19. See also Revel, 21.

53 "12,000 Witness Stadium Classic," *Pittsburgh Courier*, July 11, 1942: 16.

54 James A. Riley, *Dandy, Day, and the Devil* (Cocoa, Florida: TK Publishers, 1987), 112.

55 Holway, 26.

56 McNeil, 105.

57 Revel, 31.

58 Byrd was Baltimore's Opening Day starter that year, pitching a complete-game victory in a 20-4 defeat of the Philadelphia Stars on May 3 in Philadelphia. Luke, 105.

59 Baltimore's papers covered the series in detail. "Elite Giants Bow, 6-0, to Homestead Grays," *Baltimore Sun*, September 15, 1948: 23. "Homestead Nine Beats Elites Again in Playoff," *Baltimore Sun*, September 17, 1948: 17. "Grays and Elites Play 4-4 Tie in Series Game," *Baltimore Sun*, September 18, 1948: 11. "Elites Test Homestead," *Baltimore Evening Sun*, September 18, 1948: 9. "Elites Top Homestead in Playoff Test, 11-3," *Baltimore Sun*, September 20, 1948: 13. "League Upholds Grays Protest," *Baltimore Sun*, September 21, 1948: 20. "Elites Lose by Forfeit," *Baltimore Evening Sun*, September 21, 1948: 27.

60 "Official 1949 NAL Pitching Records," Center for Negro League Baseball Research, http://www.cnlbr.org/Portals/0/Stats/NAL%20 1949/NAL1949.pdf, accessed July 11, 2023.

61 "Elites Take NAL Title in Four Straight," *Chicago Defender*, October 1, 1949: 15.

62 Luke, 128.

63 "Stars Defeat Clowns 13-0," *Philadelphia Inquirer*, June 6, 1944: 40.

64 "Satch Paige, Josh Gibson at Stadium on August 18," *Cleveland Call Post*, August 15, 1942.

65 Larry Lester, *Black Baseball's National Showcase: The East-West All-Star Game, 1933-1953* (Lincoln: University of Nebraska Press, 2001), 230.

66 Holway, 24.

67 Lester, 82, 125, 130, 155, 186, 216, 230, 249, 255.

68 Lester, 479-480.

69 Holway, 27.

70 "William (Bill) Byrd; Pitcher, 83," *New York Times*, January 9, 1991: D21.

71 Bill Glauber, "Bill Byrd, Negro Leaguer, Dies at 83 Baltimore Pitcher Trained Big Leaguers," *Baltimore Sun*, January 7, 1991.

72 Roy Campanella, *It's Good to Be Alive* (Lincoln: University of Nebraska Press, 1995), 66.

73 Steven R. Greenes, *Negro Leaguers in the Hall of Fame: The Case for Inducting 24 Overlooked Ballplayers* (Jefferson, North Carolina: McFarland & Co., 2020), 146-47.

74 Official Negro League statistics as of 2023 reflected only certain leagues/seasons from 1920 to 1948 as being "major league."

75 Greenes, 149.

76 Holway, 27.

ROY CAMPANELLA

BY RICK SWAINE

Roy Campanella was the sixth acknowledged Black player to appear in the major leagues in the twentieth century, debuting with the Brooklyn Dodgers a year after Jackie Robinson broke the color barrier. Campanella went on to become the second Black player, after Robinson, to win a major-league Most Valuable Player award, and eventually became the second Black Hall of Famer, again following in Robinson's footsteps. Campanella, however, holds the distinction of being the first Black player to capture two MVP awards, and at the time of his death in June 1993 he was the only Black player to own three MVP trophies.

Campanella spent his entire big-league career with the Dodgers, taking over as their regular catcher during the 1948 campaign and serving in that capacity through 1957, the franchise's last season in Brooklyn. In those years the Dodgers won five National League pennants and a world championship. Prejudice and tragedy limited his major-league career to a mere 10 seasons, the color of his skin delaying his debut until he was 26 years old, and an automobile accident prematurely ending his playing days at the age of 35.

In fact, Campanella made the fewest major-league plate appearances of any Hall of Fame position player. Yet statistical guru Bill James rated him the third-best catcher of all time behind top-ranked Yogi Berra and runner-up Johnny Bench, ahead of such stalwarts as Mickey Cochrane, Carlton Fisk, Bill Dickey, and Gabby Hartnett.

Baseball-Reference.com lists Campanella's height at 5-feet-9 and his playing weight at 190 pounds, which may have been close to the truth when he started out. The 1954 *Baseball Almanac* and the 1955 *Who's Who in Baseball* list him at 205 pounds, which was still probably a generously low estimate considering that Campy himself pegged his weight at 215 to 220 pounds shortly before he signed with the Dodgers. Roger Kahn, author of *The Boys of Summer*, likened Campanella to a little sumo wrestler.[1] Despite his roly-poly appearance, the squatty catcher was extremely muscular with massive arms and a bulky torso. At the plate he was a dead pull hitter with a distinct uppercut. He was graceful behind the dish, supplementing surprising agility with a cannon-like arm. He was considered an astute handler of pitchers, both White and Black – knowing when to provide encouragement and when to provide a good kick in the butt.

Roy was also tough as nails. As a Negro Leaguer, he purportedly caught four games in one day – an early doubleheader in Cincinnati and a twi-nighter in Middletown, Ohio.[2] And he claimed to have caught three doubleheaders in one day in winter ball.[3] He endured repeated injuries to his fingers, hands, and legs – occupational hazards of working behind the bat – but in his last appearance he established a since-broken National League record for durability by catching at least 100 games in nine straight seasons, a remarkable achievement prior to the new generation of catcher's mitts that allow receivers to protect their throwing hand by catching one-handed.

The popular catcher was often described as gentle, unassuming, jovial, and full of life. He was a cheerleader, almost childlike in his enthusiasm. Although Campy and Jackie Robinson were teammates for nine years when there were only a handful of other Black major leaguers, they were not particularly close. In fact, there were even a few well-publicized feuds over the years. Robinson was sometimes frustrated with Campanella's reluctance to help carry the banner for their race. "There's a little Uncle Tom in Roy," he once remarked.[4]

Despite their differences, however, Campy deeply respected Jackie and fully appreciated the sacrifices he'd made. "Jackie made things easy for us," he said. "[Because of him] I'm just another guy playing baseball."[5]

Roy Campanella was born on November 19, 1921, in Philadelphia. He had no known middle name. At the time of Roy's birth his family lived in the Germantown section of the city, but they moved to an integrated section in the northern part of the city known as Nicetown when Roy was 7 years old. He was the product of an interracial marriage, an African-American mother and a father of Sicilian descent – something of a novelty in those days. He attended Gillespie Junior High and Simon Gratz High School, although he left high school before graduating. Growing up, the light-complexioned youngster was tauntingly called "half-breed" by kids of both races, which helped him develop into a pretty good scrapper. In fact, he briefly fought as a Golden Gloves boxer. Roy, the baby of the family, had three older siblings. His brother, Lawrence, about 10 years older, wasn't around very much when Roy was growing up. His sisters, Gladys and Doris, were both excellent female athletes.

John Campanella, Roy's father, made his living selling vegetables and fish out of a truck and later operated a grocery store while Roy's mother, Ida, ran the household. Growing up in the middle of the Depression, Roy had to work as a youngster. He helped his father, sold newspapers, shined shoes, and had a milk route as a teenager.

Through high school Roy attended integrated schools and played for integrated football, basketball, and baseball teams. Blacks were in the minority, but he was invariably chosen as the team captain, whatever the sport. Though he participated in other sports, baseball was his passion. He watched many a game at nearby Shibe Park from the top of an adjacent building. By the time he entered high school, he'd abandoned his early aspirations to be an architect and was determined to be a professional baseball player.

Gradually word of his prowess on the diamond spread. While in high school, he was reportedly offered an opportunity to work out with the Phillies, but the club rescinded the invitation when they discovered he was Black.

At the tender age of 15 in 1937, Campanella began his professional baseball career with a top-notch semipro team, the Bacharach Giants. Mama Campanella didn't want her baby to play pro ball with grown men, but when they promised to pay him more for a weekend of catching than his father made in a week, a compromise was reached. Despite his youth, Campanella performed so impressively for the Bacharach Giants that the Washington Elite Giants of the Negro National League soon signed him to spell veteran receiver and manager Biz Mackey on weekends. Roy was an indifferent student to begin with, but after he spent his summer vacation barnstorming with the Elite Giants, schoolwork could no longer hold his attention. After he turned 16, Roy quit school to play full time for the renamed Baltimore Elite Giants. In 1939 the precocious 17-year-old youngster took over the regular catching chores after Mackey was traded to the Newark Eagles in mid-season and helped lead the Giants to playoff victories over the Eagles and Homestead Grays. His hitting improved and he began showing more power in 1940, and was soon challenging the legendary Josh Gibson's status as the best catcher in Negro baseball. While still a teenager, he caught the entire 1941 Negro League East-West All-Star Game for the East, winning MVP honors for his excellent defensive work.

Campanella had married a Nicetown girl, Bernice Ray, in 1939 and they had two girls. With three dependents his draft status was 3-A when World War II broke out, so he was never called for active duty, although he was required to work in war-related industry for a time.

During the 1942 Negro League season, Campanella jumped to the Monterrey Sultans of the Mexican League after a contract dispute with the Elite Giants. He remained in Mexico for the 1943 season before returning to Baltimore for the 1944 and 1945 campaigns. Though he regained his All-Star status, he deferred to Josh Gibson in the 1944 game, playing a few innings at third base. But he was back behind the plate for the 1945 Classic.

In October 1945 Campanella caught for a Black all-star team organized by Effa Manley against a squad of major leaguers managed by Charlie Dressen in a five-game exhibition series at Ebbets Field. Dressen, a Dodgers coach at the time, approached Campanella during the series to arrange a meeting with Dodgers general manager and part-owner Branch Rickey later that month. Campanella spent four hours listening to Rickey, whom he later described as "the talkingest man I ever did see," and politely declined when Rickey asked if he was interested in playing in the Brooklyn organization.[6] Campy thought he was being recruited for the Brooklyn Brown Dodgers, a new Negro

League outfit that Rickey was supposedly starting. A few days later, however, he ran into Jackie Robinson in a Harlem hotel. After Robinson confidentially told him he'd already signed with the Dodgers, Campy realized that Rickey had been talking about a career in Organized Baseball for him. Afraid that he'd blown his shot at the big leagues, he fired off a telegram to Rickey indicating his interest in playing for the Dodgers just before leaving on a barnstorming tour through South America.

The 1946 spring-training season was already under way by the time Campanella returned from South America and

Teenage catcher Roy Campanella with the Elites. Courtesy John W. Mosley Photograph Collection, Charles L. Blockson Afro-American Collection, Temple University Libraries.

reported to the Dodgers office in Brooklyn. The Dodgers didn't quite know what to do with him or pitcher Don Newcombe, another Negro League star they'd signed. Robinson and former Homestead Grays hurler Johnny Wright were already slated for Montreal, and most of the organization's other minor-league franchises were located in the South or the Midwest. They tried to send Campanella and Newcombe to Danville of the Class-B Illinois-Indiana-Iowa (Three I) League, but the circuit wouldn't accept Black players. The Dodgers then checked with their Nashua, New Hampshire, farm club in the New England League, a lesser regarded Class-B circuit, where young general manager Buzzie Bavasi welcomed the opportunity to add two such talented Black players to their roster.

Like most of the first generation of Black players to cross the color line, Campanella took a steep pay cut to enter Organized Baseball and was forced to start at a level far below his ability. A top star in the Negro leagues, he found himself competing against a bunch of inexperienced kids, most of whom would never rise above Class-A ball. Furthermore, he would be making

Roy Campanella. *Courtesy National Baseball Hall of Fame and Library.*

only $185 a month for six months in the minors rather than the $600 a month he'd been earning with the Baltimore Elite Giants.

With Nashua in 1946, Campanella hit .290 and drove in 96 runs to win the New England League MVP award. Early in the season, Nashua manager Walter Alston, who doubled as the club's first baseman, asked Campy to take over the team for him if he ever got tossed out of a game. His reasoning was that Roy was older than most of the players and they respected and liked him. Sure enough, in a June contest Alston was ejected in the sixth inning and Campy became the first Black man to manage in Organized Baseball. Moreover, his strategic move resulted in a comeback victory when he called on the hard-hitting Newcombe to pinch-hit and was rewarded with a clutch home run.

Roy's experience in Nashua also changed his parents' life. Fences around the New England League were virtually unreachable, and a local poultry farmer offered 100 baby chicks for every Nashua home run. At the end of the season, Campy collected 1,400 chicks as reward for his 14 homers (a team-leading 13 in the regular season and one in the playoffs). He had them shipped to his father, who promptly began a farming business on the outskirts of Philadelphia.

Campanella went to spring training with the Dodgers in Havana before the 1947 season. He was listed on the Montreal roster, along with Robinson, Newcombe, and Roy Partlow, a left-handed pitcher. Robinson, of course, was promoted to the Dodgers, Newcombe was sent back to Nashua, and Partlow was released, leaving Campanella the only Black player in the International League. That season, while Robinson was burning up the basepaths as the first Black player in the majors in the twentieth century, Campanella starred in the International League. Veteran catcher Paul Richards, managing the Buffalo Bisons called him "the best catcher in the business – major or minor leagues."[7] With his extensive Negro League experience and an excellent Triple-A season under his belt, the 26-year-old receiver was ready for major-league duty.

Unfortunately, the Brooklyn Dodgers weren't yet ready for him. Brooklyn's regular catcher was Bruce Edwards, who in 1947 posted an excellent .295 batting mark, drove in 80 runs, and finished fourth in National League MVP balloting, the highest ranking of any Dodger. In addition, Edwards was a fine defensive backstop and was almost two years younger than Campy.

According to popular legend, Rickey wanted Campanella to break the racial barrier in the American Association, the Midwestern Triple-A circuit, before he became established with the Dodgers. Therefore, he attempted to conceal Campanella's skills from the press by carrying him on the preseason roster as an outfield candidate – a position for which Campanella was clearly ill-suited. A less Machiavellian, but plausible, explanation might be that Rickey didn't want to cause dissension or put too much pressure on Campanella by competing with the popular Edwards. Whatever the reason, the Dodgers brought Campanella to camp as an outfielder and even tried him out at third base.

But Edwards had injured his arm in the offseason, and it failed to come around in the spring of 1948. Manager Leo Durocher, back in command of the Dodgers after a year's suspension, fully appreciated Campanella's talents and wanted to insert him behind the plate in place of the injured Edwards. But Rickey did not want to put the rookie catcher's skills on display. The issue apparently became a source of friction between Durocher and Rickey.

Though Campanella broke camp with the Dodgers, the plan was to send him down to their St. Paul American Association farm club when rosters had to be trimmed to 25 players on May 15. He made his big-league debut against the New York Giants at the Polo Grounds on Opening Day. Gil Hodges, who hadn't made the move to first base yet, started behind the plate in place of Edwards, but went out for a pinch-hitter in the top of the seventh. In the bottom half of the inning, Campanella took over behind the plate with the Dodgers down 6-5. With ace reliever Hugh Casey on the mound, the Giants went scoreless for the final three innings while the Dodgers scored two runs to win the game. Campanella got to the plate in the top of the eighth inning and was promptly drilled by Giants reliever Ken Trinkle – the type of welcome that many more Black hitters would receive in the early days of baseball's integration era.

Campanella made his second big-league appearance three days later, replacing Hodges to finish up a 10-2 Phillies blowout. Then on April 27, after a pair of losses, Durocher defied Rickey and started Campy at catcher in Boston. He went hitless but acquitted himself well behind the plate. Though Brooklyn lost, wildman Rex Barney held the Braves to three runs with Campanella calling the pitches. Rickey was reportedly incensed and ordered Durocher not to use Campanella behind the plate again. This time Durocher complied. Campy warmed the bench until he was farmed out to St. Paul on May 15.

The American Association's first Black player broke the league's color barrier with a disastrous performance, going hitless and fanning twice in four at-bats, and making an error on a pickoff attempt. But he was soon terrorizing the opposition. In 35 games, Campy batted .325, slammed 13 homers, and drove in 39 runs, forcing the struggling Dodgers to recall him.

When Campanella joined the Dodgers' lineup on July 2, 1948, the defending National League champions had lost five straight and were languishing in sixth place with a 27-34 record. From that point on they won 57 while losing 36, a .613 pace – better than the .595 overall winning percentage posted by the pennant-winning Braves. Even more remarkable was the fact that the Dodgers won 50 of the 73 games that Campanella started after his recall, an incredible .685 mark. His installation behind the plate was the last in a series of moves orchestrated by Durocher to turn the club around. Three days earlier Gil Hodges, who had acquitted himself well behind the plate filling in for the injured Edwards, was shifted to first base, allowing Jackie Robinson to move over to his natural second-base position. Unfortunately for Durocher, he didn't stay around long enough

to enjoy the results, as he left the Dodgers to take over the reins of the New York Giants a week after Campanella's recall.

For his rookie year, Campanella batted .258 with 9 homers in 83 games and led National League catchers in percentage of runners caught stealing. He even garnered eight points in the MVP voting despite playing only half the season.

In 1949 Campanella hit .287 with 22 home runs and 82 runs batted in, cementing his hold on the Dodgers' first-string catching job. During the campaign, Don Newcombe was called up from the minors, combining with Campanella to form the major leagues' first Black battery. The pair had developed an excellent rapport at Nashua three years earlier and, under Roy's expert handling, the volatile young flamethrower quickly became the ace of the staff. Both Campanella and Newcombe made the 1949 National League All-Star squad, joining Robinson and Cleveland's Larry Doby in becoming baseball's first Black All-Stars. Campanella replaced starting catcher Andy Seminick in the fourth inning and went the rest of the way, beginning a streak in which he would catch every All-Star inning for the National League until Smoky Burgess relieved him in the eighth inning of the 1954 contest. Campanella also displayed his toughness later in the 1949 season when, after a beaning by Bill Werle of the Pirates, he rejected the doctor's recommendation to take a few days off and rejoined the lineup the next day.

Campanella upped his homer total to 31 in 1950 and batted .281, firmly establishing himself as the best catcher in the National League, if not all of major-league baseball. He caught all 14 innings in that summer's All-Star Game. In September he suffered a compound fracture from a foul tip off his right thumb and missed starting 11 consecutive games behind the plate – the Dodgers dropping seven of them. Campy's absence probably cost Brooklyn the pennant as they ended up losing to the Phillies on the last day of the season to finish two games off the pace.

In spring training before the 1951 season, Campy took another foul tip on his right thumb that chipped the bone and forced him to play in pain all year. Later, a beaning by Turk Lown of the Cubs sent him to the hospital for five days with a concussion and he experienced dizziness for weeks thereafter. Nevertheless, he batted a career-high .325 with 33 homers and 108 runs batted in, and finished third in the league in doubles, slugging, and OPS. On the last day of the regular season, which ended in a tie between the Dodgers and the New York Giants, Campanella aggravated a leg injury he had received in a collision at home plate a few days earlier. He gamely struggled through the first game of the three-game playoff series, but realized he was hurting the team and sat out the last two contests. It's widely believed that if Campanella had been behind the plate for the third game, he would have been able to nurse his pal Newcombe through the ninth inning – and Bobby Thomson would never have come to the plate to hit his historic pennant-winning home run. In MVP voting Campanella beat out Stan Musial of the Cardinals for the National League award. In the American League Yogi Berra of the Yankees captured his first MVP award. It was the first year in history that catchers won the annual award in both leagues.

Campanella followed his brilliant 1951 campaign with a disappointing performance in 1952. After he had endured numerous minor injuries early in the season, a foul tip chipped a bone in his left elbow in July. He played with the injury for 10 days before his arm had to be placed in a cast for nearly two weeks. His season average fell to .269 and he hit only 22 home runs. In the Dodgers' seven-game World Series loss to the Yankees, he managed only six singles.

In 1953 Campanella reported to spring training in great shape and stayed remarkably healthy through the season. And what a great season it was! He batted .312 and his 41 home runs and league-leading 142 RBIs established all-time highs for major-league catchers that stood until 1970. Campanella's home-run total was the third-highest in the league and he ranked third in slugging and fourth in OPS as he led the Dodgers to their second straight National League pennant. But in the first game of the World Series, Allie Reynolds of the Yankees hit him on the hand with a pitch and he was unable to properly grip the bat through the club's second straight Series defeat. His second National League MVP award, however, was a foregone conclusion.

In spring training before the 1954 campaign, Campanella injured his left wrist and hand when he slid awkwardly trying to break up a double play. The bone on the heel of his hand was fractured and pieces that chipped off were impinging on the nerve. Surgery was recommended, but Campanella tried to play with the painful condition. He finally agreed to an operation in early May. Initial estimates put the recovery time at eight to 10 weeks, but Campy returned to action in less than a month. Numbness in the hand bothered him all year, however, resulting in a dismal .207 batting average with 19 homers. Campanella's value to the Dodgers, even at less than full strength, was demonstrated by the fact that the club posted a .623 winning percentage for the 106 games he started, compared with .542 without him. At season's end, the Dodgers trailed the Giants by five games. Insult was added to injury when their crosstown rivals defeated the Cleveland Indians to capture the world-championship banner that had proved so elusive to the Dodgers. After the season Campanella submitted to further surgery on the hand to remove scar tissue and repair nerve damage.

It was feared that Campanella's hand injuries could mean the end of his career, or at least drastically curb his productivity. But the 33-year-old veteran made a miraculous comeback in 1955. At midseason he was leading the league in hitting when he was hit on the left kneecap by a foul tip that broke a bone spur loose from his patella. The knee was in a cast for more than two weeks and he missed his first All-Star Game since 1949, although he was picked for the team. Nevertheless, Campy was still challenging for the batting title late in the season, when the rigors of catching every day caused his hands to start bothering him again and his hitting fell off. He still finished with a .318

batting average, slammed 32 home runs, and knocked in 107 runs, despite sitting out more than 30 games. He again drove the Dodgers to the National League pennant, and led them to victory over the Yankees in the World Series. In National League MVP balloting he prevailed for a third time. In the American League, Yogi Berra also captured his third MVP trophy. Four years after Campy and Yogi became the first catchers to win MVP honors in the same season, they became the second and last duo to accomplish the feat (through the 2022 season).

But thousands of games behind the bat had taken a toll, and Campanella's 1956 season was ruined by more hand problems. His twice-operated-on glove hand, which had begun tormenting him again late the previous year, still ached. Then he broke his thumb when he slammed his right hand against the hitter's bat while attempting a pickoff throw to first, an injury that bothered him all year. He ended the campaign with a .219 batting average, but still managed 20 homers as the Dodgers captured their last pennant in Brooklyn. In the World Series, another seven-game loss to the Yankees, he hit only .182 with no homers and seven strikeouts.

Campanella decided to undergo another operation after the 1956 campaign to relieve the pain in his left hand, but the Dodgers insisted that he go on their offseason exhibition tour of Japan first, which drastically cut into his recovery time. With his hands still troubling him in 1957, he missed more than 50 games and hit .242 while belting just 13 home runs, and failed to make the All-Star squad for the first time since his rookie year. Brooklyn fell to third place in the National League amid persistent rumors of a move to the West Coast. Shortly after the Dodgers' last game, it was officially announced that the franchise would relocate to Los Angeles for the 1958 season.

Campy loved playing in Brooklyn and like most of the Dodger veterans hated the prospect of moving. But his hands were feeling better than they had in years and he was starting to warm up to the idea of taking aim at the 295-foot left-field fence of the Los Angeles Coliseum, an oval-shaped football stadium that would serve as the club's makeshift home field.

But in January 1958, just before he was due to report for spring training, Campanella was permanently disabled in a traffic accident. He had successfully invested in a liquor store in central Harlem, called Roy Campanella Choice Wines and Liquors, earlier in his career and worked there in the offseason. He normally left for home in the early afternoon, but on that fateful day he'd stayed in town to plug a YMCA fund-raising drive on a local television show. The appearance was canceled, but he stayed to help close up the liquor store before leaving for his home in Glen Cove, on the North Shore of Long Island. The Chevy station wagon Campy normally drove was in the shop for repairs, and he was driving a much lighter rental car when he lost control of the vehicle on an icy street. He hit a telephone pole and the car flipped over, pinning him under the steering wheel. Roy's neck was broken and his spinal cord was severely damaged, paralyzing him from the chest down.

Roy Campanella, once the best catcher in the National League, if not all of major-league baseball, would spend the rest of his life in a wheelchair.

The Dodgers continued to pay Campanella his salary while he was hospitalized for surgery and rehabilitation for almost a year after the accident. Though he never got a chance to play for the Dodgers in Los Angeles, a crowd of 93,103 fans, the largest in baseball history to that date, jammed the Los Angeles Coliseum on May 7, 1959, for a benefit exhibition game between the Yankees and Dodgers – a tribute to the former Brooklyn great.

Campanella's personal life began to unravel in the wake of his accident. His teenage marriage to Bernice Ray had quickly ended in divorce. With Roy away so much of the time, traveling the Negro League circuit or playing winter ball in the Caribbean, Bernice continued to live with her parents and the couple had gradually drifted apart. In 1945 Roy married Ruthe Willis, a fine athlete herself. They had two sons and a daughter together and Ruthe's son from a previous marriage also lived with them.

But Ruthe was unable to adjust to Roy's physical disability. In 1960 she sued for a legal separation; a messy affair that kept the city's tabloid press busy. In 1963 Ruthe suffered a fatal heart attack at the age of 40 before a divorce was finalized. On May 5, 1964, Roy married Roxie Doles, who remained at his side for the remainder of his life.

After enduring years of therapy, Campanella regained some use of his arms. He eventually was able to feed himself, shake hands, and even sign autographs with the aid of a device strapped to his arm, though he remained dependent on his wheelchair for mobility. Through it all he managed to maintain the positive, upbeat attitude that was his trademark and became a universal symbol of courage. In 1969, the same year he was inducted into the Hall of Fame, he received the Bronze Medallion from the City of New York, the highest honor the city confers upon civilians, awarded for exceptional citizenship and outstanding achievement. Three years later the Dodgers retired his uniform number 39 along with Robinson's number 42 and Sandy Koufax's 32.

Though Campanella stayed in New York, continuing to operate his liquor store and hosting a radio sports program called "Campy's Corner," he remained a part of the Dodgers family. He worked in public relations, helped with scouting, and served as a special instructor and adviser at the club's Vero Beach spring-training facility. In 1978 he moved to Los Angeles and took a job as assistant to the Dodgers' director of community relations, Don Newcombe, his former teammate and longtime friend.

On June 26, 1993, Campanella succumbed to a heart attack in Woodland Hills, California. He lived to be 71, far exceeding the normal life expectancy for someone in his condition. In 2006 he was honored with a US postage stamp bearing his image, and later that year the Dodgers announced the creation of the Roy Campanella Award, to be given annually to the Dodger who best exemplifies Campanella's spirit and leadership.

Roy Campanella's lifetime batting average for 10 major-league seasons was .276 and he hit 242 home runs while driving in 856 runs in 1,215 games. His 1953 totals of 41 homers and 142 RBIs stood as single-season highs for a catcher until Johnny Bench hit 45 homers and drove in 148 runs in 1970. Bench, however, played a 162-game schedule rather than the 154 contests played in 1953, and had 86 more at-bats than Campanella.

Campanella shone just as brightly on defense. Sportswriters often referred to him as "The Cat" because of his feline-like quickness blocking stray pitches or pouncing on bunts in front of home plate. He led National League catchers five times in percentage of runners caught stealing, and his career rate of 57 percent is the best all-time among catchers who appeared in more than 100 games.

But the most revealing statistic is the three Most Valuable Player awards Campanella earned in his all-too-brief career. When he was honored for the third time, in 1955, Stan Musial was the only other National Leaguer to have accomplished the feat, while Joe DiMaggio, Jimmie Foxx, and Yogi Berra were the only American Leaguers to have done so. Since then, only the names of Mickey Mantle, Mike Schmidt, Barry Bonds, Álex Rodríguez, and Albert Pujols have been added to the exclusive list.

Nonetheless, Campanella's career is sprinkled with what-ifs. It's fair to say that, even with the premature end to his career, Campy's third place ranking on Bill James's catchers list might have been higher if he hadn't been denied the opportunity to play in the major leagues at an earlier age. It's also probably realistic to assume that he wouldn't have had to wait six years after gaining eligibility to be elected to the Hall of Fame.

If circumstances had been right, Campanella could have been the first Black player in the big leagues. Back in 1943, he had been invited to Forbes Field to work out for the Pittsburgh Pirates, but team president William Benswanger succumbed to peer pressure and canceled the tryout.

And if not for the accident, Campanella might well have become the major league's first Black manager. Before joining the Dodgers, he managed the Caracas club in the Venezuelan Winter League for a few seasons. In 1946 the 25-year-old skipper's charges included Newcombe, Sam Jethroe, Harry Simpson, and Luis Aparicio, Sr., father of the Hall of Fame shortstop. Before his accident the Dodgers had already approached Campanella about a future coaching or managing in the minor leagues after his career ended.

In his autobiography *It's Good to Be Alive*, Campanella reminisced about the happiest days of his life in Brooklyn: "That's where I wanted to finish my playing career. I got my wish all right, but in a much different way."[8]

SOURCES

This article was adapted from the author's book *The Black Stars Who Made Baseball Whole: The Jackie Robinson Generation in the Major Leagues* (Jefferson, North Carolina: McFarland, 2004).

In addition to the sources cited in the Notes, the author consulted Baseball-Reference.com and a number of other sources, including:

Campanella, Roy II, "Roy Campanella" in *Cult Baseball Players*, Danny Peary, ed. (New York: Simon and Schuster, 1990), 251-9.

Golenbock, Peter, *Bums: An Oral History of the Brooklyn Dodgers* (New York: Putnam's, 1984).

James, Bill, *The New Bill James Historical Baseball Abstract* (New York: Simon and Schuster, 2001).

Peterson, Robert W., *Only the Ball Was White* (Englewood Cliffs, New Jersey: Carol Publishing, 1970).

The Sporting News, March 24, 1948, 22.

Clark, Dick, and Larry Lester, *The Negro Leagues Book.* (SABR, 1994, statistical section)

NOTES

1   Roger Kahn, *The Boys of Summer* (New York: Harper and Row, 1971), 327.

2   Larry Moffi and Jonathan Kronstadt, *Crossing the Line: Black Major Leaguers, 1947-1959* (Jefferson, North Carolina: McFarland, 1994), 28.

3   Kahn, 327.

4   Kahn, 327.

5   Moffi and Kronstadt, 27.

6   Roy Campanella, *It's Good to Be Alive* (New York: Dell, 1959), 109.

7   Jules Tygiel, *Baseball's Great Experiment: Jackie Robinson and His Legacy* (New York: Oxford University Press, 1997), 223.

8   Roy Campanella, 11.

LEON "BOOGIE WOLF" CHILDRESS

BY JOHN HAYNES

Leon "Boogie Wolf" Childress is one of many obscure "ghost players" of the Negro Leagues, a player skilled enough to make it onto the rosters and even into group photographs of some very good teams, but never earning regular playing time or appearing in any statistical record.

Leon was born on June 23, 1910, in Nashville, Tennessee, where he would spend most of his life. Nettie Johnson is listed as his mother, but 1930 census data notes that he was adopted and the only child in the household. His education ended after the sixth grade, and he took up work as a "boat-black" in a shoe shop with his father, Ike.[1]

In his early years, Childress was more accomplished on the football field than on the baseball diamond. In 1931 he joined the "other" Nashville Elite Giants, a semipro football team. The Elite Giants football team played their home games at Wilson Park and were an extension of Tom Wilson's baseball team. In 1932 Wilson and his business partners Dr. R.B. Jackson and Vernon Green created the Negro Southern Football League. That December, Jackson declared that the Elite Giants were "mythical" national champions due to their record. Leon Childress was listed as an "All-Southern" End on the roster.[2] One of Leon's teammates on the Elite Giants was running back Wild Bill Wright, a young outfielder on the baseball team of the same name and at the beginning of a career that spanned two decades.[3]

Where he began his baseball career is a bit foggier. "Childress" was a fairly common surname, with an infielder-pitcher named Childress appearing on the roster of the Little Rock Stars in 1933,[4] a Guthrie Childress pitching for the Claybrook, Arkansas Tigers at the same time,[5] and a set of Childress brothers playing in Texas for the San Angelo Black Sheepherders.[6]

In 1935 Leon Childress moved north and made the roster of the Cincinnati Tigers, a team formed by a local hero and Olympic gold medalist in track and field, DeHart Hubbard.[7] Hubbard formed the Tigers in 1934 with a core of young players from the "Class A" league in the city and augmented the team with solid backups like Childress and his football teammate Charles "Dusty" Decker. The Tigers played in the Negro Southern League and the integrated Indiana-Ohio League for their first few years of existence before later joining the Negro American League.

On a barnstorming trip out west on June 28, 1936, Childress stepped in for starting catcher Josh Johnson in the second game of a doubleheader against the famed integrated Bismarck Churchills, going hitless but scoring a run in a 5-4 victory.[8] On July 12 and 13, Childress was loaned to the Saskatoon Gems for a series against the Tigers along with Porter Moss, Ewing Russell, Jerry Gibson, and Sonny Harris. Childress had only one hit in eight at-bats for the Gems as the Tigers swept all three games.[9] Aside from photographs, the accounts of these appearances are the only evidence of his time in Cincinnati. When the Tigers joined the Negro American League in 1937, Childress was no longer on the club and disappeared from high-level baseball again.

In 1939 Childress appears to have been captured by John Mosley in two separate photos of the Philadelphia Stars but did not appear in any documented games and was possibly released before the regular season began.[10]

By the summer, Childress was in uniform with the Baltimore Elite Giants, backing up Roy Campanella and appearing in a team photo at Oriole Park next to recent acquisition Red Moore.[11] Childress is not credited with any league appearances but "the recruit from Nashville" remained on the team for "emergency duty behind the plate" through the end of the season.[12] It may be reasonable to speculate that while his playing time was limited, Childress's value to the team was indispensable in other duties to include driving the bus, managing equipment, and catching in the bullpen. After the Elites won the Jacob Ruppert Cup, the team posed for a photograph at Yankee Stadium with the trophy. Childress is clearly visible in the photo between Emery "Ace" Adams and Wild Bill Wright.[13] One of his only documented appearances for the Elites occurred a few days earlier on September 20, when he went 0-for-3 at the plate and committed an error and two passed balls in a 3-1 loss to the Brooklyn Bushwicks.[14]

Out of a big-league job in 1940, Childress returned home to Nashville and fell back to earth. In September he was arrested and charged with loitering, vagrancy, and a lottery violation.[15] It should be noted, however, that in the Jim Crow South, vagrancy was a trumped-up charge aimed at punishing Black people for being unemployed or homeless. This practice stretched back to the

Leon "Boogie Wolf" Childress.

post-Reconstruction days, with laws in many places coming off the books only in recent years.[16]

That fall, Childress registered for the military draft, a year before the United States' entry into World War II. His residence is listed at Eighth Street, the same address listed in his arrest report. His occupation was described as "unemployed."

Childress's activities in 1941 are unknown, but in 1942 he reappeared in the spotlight. On New Year's Day, he returned to the gridiron and played end and quarterback for the Nashville Pros against the Southern All-Stars in the second annual "Steel Bowl" game in Birmingham, Alabama. The Pros were an independent club that came into the matchup advertised as winners of 29 of their last 30 games, while their opponent was made up of college stars from several Black colleges in the region.[17] Childress was part of a "desperate passing attack that netted two touchdowns" in the last minutes of a 26-13 loss.[18]

In the spring of 1942, Childress returned to the baseball diamond. The Louisville and Nashville railroad company sponsored an independent team called the Nashville L&N Stars, often shortened to just "Nashville Stars" and sometimes referred to as the "Railroaders" in the press. Childress joined the club as their starting catcher and manager. In May 1942 the *Nashville Tennessean* reported that Childress and teammate Jim Willis were leaving for the Army,[19] but he was still managing and playing on August 12 when the Stars traveled to Cincinnati for a doubleheader against the Clowns.[20]

In 1943 Childress took over the managerial reins of the Nashville Black Vols, a separate club from the Stars.[21] Childress was no longer playing regularly but was described by the *Atlanta Daily World* as a "good hitter and fence buster."[22] In an uncommon stance of a Negro League team operating a minor-league affiliate, the Black Vols were owned by Elite Giants magnate Tom Wilson, who regularly shuttled players between the two clubs. In February 1944, his draft number was called, but he was designated as 4F, or physically unfit for service.[23]

Childress was still on the roster for the Black Vols in 1945 as they joined the resurrected Negro Southern League but was replaced as skipper by veteran Bill Perkins. The Black Vols finished behind the Atlanta Black Crackers in both halves of the season and went through at least three other managers – Bill Perkins, Granville Lyons, and Judge "Dusty" Owens. Childress split catching duties with Perkins throughout the season and appeared on the mound at least once. Box scores and complete statistics have yet to be found for any of the NSL's games in 1945.[24] In 1946 Childress was no longer with Nashville (now rebranded as the Cubs) and presumably out of professional baseball for good.

On May 10, 1948, he married Frances Mattie Mayberry of Williamson, Tennessee. Childress took a job as a mail handler for the post office, where he worked for at least a decade, according to census records. He remained active in the Nashville baseball scene into the 1960s on the coaching staff of the amateur Elite Giants in the Capital City League. In 1962 he was named to the staff of the league's all-star team.[25]

Just six years later, on September 21, 1968, Childress was reportedly at a bus stop in Nashville when he was approached by police officers and violently arrested for vagrancy. After he questioned why he was being arrested, he was beaten at the police station and denied medical care, resulting in permanent hearing loss. Childress filed a $50,000 lawsuit against Nashville police officer William B. McCullough, who was later fired and charged for a separate incident in which he allegedly beat a suspect in an alleyway.[26] The result of the suit was never published.

On July 30, 1976, at 66 years old, Leon Childress died in an unnamed Nashville hospital of an undisclosed illness. He was survived by his wife, Frances; six children; and nine grandchildren.[27] Frances died in 2002 at 80 years old. Perhaps Childress's lineage is best defined on the football field: His son Jerome played football for Tennessee State University, and his grandsons Ahmad and Gary played for Alabama and Clemson respectively.[28] Another grandson, O.J. Childress, played linebacker in the NFL for the Giants.[29] Boogie Wolf Childress may not have been a household name outside of his hometown, but his contributions and legacy as an athlete, manager, husband, and father reverberate through generations.

SOURCES

In addition to the sources cited in the Notes, the author used Ancestry.com to gather biographical data including birth, death, marriage, and military service information.

NOTES

1 While listed as "boat-black" in census data, this may have been a typographical error. His actual job title was likely a "bootblack," a profession frequently held by older male children at the time.

2 "Nashville Elite Giants Claim National Pro Football Title," *Nashville Banner*, December 24, 1932: 15.

3 "Elite Giants to Engage Soldiers," *Nashville Banner*, December 4, 1932: 14.

4 William Plott, *The Negro Southern League: A Baseball History, 1920-1951* (Jefferson, North Carolina: McFarland & Company Inc., 2015), 222.

5 "Claybrook's Tigers Show Form in Win," *Chicago Defender*, August 5, 1933: 9.

6 "Black Hubbers Meet 2 Teams at Local Park," *Lubbock* (Texas) *Morning Avalanche*, June 19, 1937: 2.

7 Childress is identified in team photographs with the Tigers as both "Wolf" and "Wolf Childers" – a common shortening and misspelling that appeared to follow him throughout his career. Phil Dixon and Patrick Hannigan, *The Negro Baseball Leagues, 1867-1955: A Photographic History* (Mattituck, New York: Amereon House, 1992), 164.

8 "Bismarck, Cincinnati Tigers Split Week-End Series," *Bismarck* (North Dakota) *Tribune*, June 29, 1936: 8.

9 "Gems Drop Both Games," *Saskatoon* (Saskatchewan) *Star-Phoenix*, July 16, 1936: 10.

10   In Mosley's photographs of the Philadelphia Stars, the club is wearing the Baseball Centennial patch that was worn across all of baseball for a single season, dating the photo to 1939. John Mosley, "Philadelphia Stars Player," Temple University Digital Collections, https://digital.library.temple.edu/digital/collection/p15037coll17/id/213/rec/32, accessed December 13, 2023.

11   Childress is simply identified as "Wolf C" in handwriting on the photograph. Bill Stetka, "Celebrating Negro Leagues Day in Maryland," MLB.com, https://www.mlb.com/news/featured/celebrating-negro-leagues-day-in-maryland, accessed December 13, 2023.

12   "Elites to Play Grays for Championship," *Baltimore Afro-American,* September 16, 1939: 23.

13   In this photograph, Childress is simply identified by his nickname of "Boogie Wolf." Bob Luke, *The Baltimore Elite Giants: Sport and Society in the Age of Negro League Baseball* (Baltimore: Johns Hopkins University Press, 2009), 51.

14   "Bushwicks Nip Elite Giants in Arclight Finale," *Brooklyn Daily Eagle,* September 21, 1939: 21.

15   "Lottery Violation," *Nashville Tennessean,* September 15, 1940: 10.

16   Charles Gallagher and Cameron Lippard, *Race and Racism in the United States: An Encyclopedia of the American Mosaic* (Santa Barbara, California: Greenwood, 2014), 145.

17   "Football," *Birmingham News,* December 30, 1941: 17.

18   Childress was identified by "Wolf Childers" in some accounts of this game. "Steel Bowl Result," *Chicago Defender,* January 10, 1942: 22.

19   "Castleman May Forgo Pro Career," *Nashville Tennessean* May 17, 1942: 39.

20   "Clowns Card Double Bill," *Cincinnati Post*, August 12, 1942: 12.

21   The Black Vols were renamed the Cubs in 1946 and had a rare meeting with the Stars in August of 1946. Childress was on neither club at the time. "Nashville Cubs, Stars Tangle in Twin Bill," *Nashville Tennessean,* August 30, 1946: 36.

22   J.C. Chunn, "Nashville Black Vols and Atlanta Black Crackers Meet Tonight at Ponce De Leon," *Atlanta Daily World,* June 24, 1943: 5.

23   "Board 9 Lists Classifications," *Nashville Banner,* February 17, 1944: 2.

24   Plott, *The Negro Southern League*, 230.

25   "Capital Stars Feature Searcy vs. Tri-State," *Nashville Tennessean,* July 20, 1962: 17.

26   "Nashville Man Seeks 50,000 in Damage Suit," *Elizabethton* (Tennessee) *Star,* September 23, 1969: 1.

27   "Childress, Leon (Boogie Wolf)," *Nashville Tennessean,* August 1, 1976: 70.

28   Chip Cirillo, "All Everything," *Nashville Tennessean,* August 14, 1999: 27.

29   "O.J. Childress Stats, Height, Weight, Position, Draft, College," Pro Football Reference, https://www.pro-football-reference.com/players/C/ChilO.20.htm, accessed December 16, 2023.

HOMER "GOOSE" CURRY

BY W.H. JOHNSON

He was a baseball man in the purest and most complimentary sense of the term, at various times in his professional career playing as a pitcher and an outfielder, along with a few occasions at second base, and finally working as a manager over a 26-year professional span. "He was a good contact hitter, had good speed, and was an adequate fielder … had a shrewd baseball mind," wrote James Riley in his magnum opus, the *Biographical Encyclopedia of The Negro Baseball Leagues*,[1] but that description is too bland to measure Goose Curry's long baseball life.

Homer Curry was born in Mexia, Texas, about 30 miles east of Waco, on May 19, 1905. He was the third child of five and the third son of parents Ben and Myrtie (Rhodes) Curry. His father farmed a family plot of land in the area.[2] By that time, as well, Texas was developing what became a rich baseball tradition. Waco had produced Andrew "Rube" Foster, the father of the first Negro National League in 1920. Other notable alumni from the region included Louis Santop, pitcher Cyclone Joe Williams, and Crush Holloway. That impressive roster was augmented by a legion of leagues and city teams that equaled their White contemporaries in both talent and local enthusiasm.

Although there is not much documentation of Curry's early life, given his professional success, it is almost certain that he not only played the game in central Texas, but played it well. While he completed only the fifth grade in school,

Homer "Goose: Curry. Courtesy John W. Mosley Photograph Collection, Charles L. Blockson Afro-American Collection, Temple University Libraries.

he was clearly a gifted athlete.[3] His baseball anonymity expired in 1928, when at age 23 he joined the Cleveland Tigers and hit .352 as a pitcher and occasional outfielder. The Tigers were Cleveland's entry in the Negro National League that year, but their ownership was somewhat unstable and the team finished last with a 20-59 record.[4] It was likely the paucity of talent on the squad that created an opportunity for the young Texan to crack into the big leagues.

At 6-feet-2 and 180 pounds, Curry was a natural power hitter, and his OPS+ of 131 clearly established his baseball bona fides, despite his relatively young age of 23. He batted left-handed

and pitched right-handed. On the mound, Curry threw 125⅔ innings that rookie year but allowed an ERA of 4.66, and his ERA+ left him just below league average.

From Cleveland, Curry moved on to work for the Memphis Red Sox beginning in 1929. He remained with the team through 1930, pitching and playing the field, then returned for the 1932 and 1937 seasons, and again in 1949-1950 and 1953-1955 in the surviving Negro American League. In Memphis in 1930, he was named one of the two regular starting pitchers, but the results were not optimal. There is some question as to his actual won-lost record that season, with various sources listing it at either 4-3 or 5-3, but his ability in the field, as a two-way player, largely ensured him of a spot on the roster.

There is not a great deal of information available about Curry's wife. Marie (Miles) Curry was born in west Tennessee in approximately 1906, and Curry likely met her during his time in Memphis. While they never had children, they had a lifelong marriage. The relationship fostered a bond between player and city that also lasted until Curry's death.

Curry was, as some biographers have described utility players in the early days of the organized Negro leagues, a bit of a figurative baseball tumbleweed, moving from town to town and team to team in search of a roster spot and a paycheck. In 1932 he spent time with Memphis as player and manager, and by then was locally acknowledged as a terrific outfielder. For 1933 he moved to the Nashville Elite Giants. He played well there and earned a number of favorable mentions in the press. One 1933 article referred to him as "fleet footed … the class of the league when it comes to the outfield."[5] In 1936 the team moved to the mid-Atlantic region of the country, between Washington D.C. and Baltimore, and Curry made the move as well. That season he played well enough to lead all outfielders in voting for the 1936 East-West All Star Game in Chicago. Still, despite garnering more votes than luminous contemporaries like Cool Papa Bell and Jimmie Crutchfield, Curry did not appear in the game.[6]

But there were other, unfortunately memorable moments as well. As historian Brent Kelley wrote about one particular one in his 1995 book *Voices From the Negro Leagues*, relating an anecdote from Henry Kimbro: "[Luis Tiant, he of an incredibly deceptive screwball] was pitching for the Cuban Stars, Fred McCreary was umpiring, Goose Curry was the hitter. Tiant went up and down and grunted and threw the ball and Goose Curry swung and said 'Jesus Christ! Man, how'd I miss it?!' Fred McCreary said, 'I oughtta call you out. That man throwed to first base.'"[7] There is no record of the play in the newspapers, but Kimbro swore it to be true.

Curry took the helm as player-manager for Memphis for part of the 1937 season, yet even with the new responsibilities, he excelled at the plate. That year his OPS of .952 equated to an OPS+ of 160, his career high. He spent 1938 with the New York Black Yankees. At age 33, he was credited with seven league appearances as an outfielder with New York, pitching in three

as well, but his OPS+ declined to 111. The following year, 1939, he was primarily an outfielder, and he split time between New York and the Baltimore Elite Giants, batting .343 and posting a terrific OPS+ of 151 for the full season.[8] Curry's bona fides as a hitter were unquestioned. His fielding prowess, though, was even more exciting.

In one particularly memorable game in 1939, Josh Gibson launched what appeared to be at least a triple, perhaps even home run number 60 for the year, in Pittsburgh:

"It was a beautiful fly," the *Pittsburgh Courier* reported, "and the fast-stepping Josh had rounded second and was heading toward third before the ball hit the fence. It looked like a sure homer. But suddenly someone flashed into the picture back there between the fence and the ball. It was the New York Black Yankees' fleet outfielder, Homer 'Goose' Curry. He galloped back there like a wild colt on a rampage. ... His speed made him collide with the fence. He hit the wall and bounced away

Goose Curry with the Philadelphia Stars in the 1940s. Courtesy National Baseball Hall of Fame and Library.

like a rubber ball. Then he straightened up and leaped in the air. The ball dropped near the fence and landed in Curry's glove. It bounced out of his mitt. It was a dramatic moment. Then he made a second dive for the bounding sphere in an attempt to retrieve it. His snatch was sure. He grabbed it and held tight. It was a great catch. We've seen many a big league game out at the Pirates park, but never a more thrilling catch than 'Goose' Curry's. … It terminated a Homestead rally and the Grays' goose was 'cooked.'"[9]

That year, 1939, as well, Curry was selected as a coach for the East team in the East-West All Star Game.[10] Overall the year was a grand success for the outfielder. He did not pitch at all that season for Baltimore, at least in league play, but his two appearances in the outfield earned him a permanent spot in the championship lore of the city.

The 1940 season was split between the Black Yankees and the Elite Giants after Curry was sold to Baltimore in midseason.[11] Curry remained with the Elites through 1941. Between those two seasons, Curry did make a trip to the West Coast for winter ball. His 1940 draft registration card confirms that he was residing in Los Angeles at that time, working for Tom Wilson and the Elite Giants, but also married to wife Marie, who was still in Memphis.[12] Curry was spending the winter of 1940-41 playing in the California Winter League on the Baltimore squad alongside Henry Kimbro, Biz Mackey, and Felton Snow, among others. Although other winter leagues, such as the one in Puerto Rico, had robbed the California variant of some of its baseball luster, it was still a terrifically competitive environment. In nine league games, Curry was credited with three doubles and a home run in 29 at-bats and posted a .379 average for the interim season.[13]

Back on the diamond in 1941, Curry played mostly in the outfield, and logged a .304 average and an OPS+ of 133. Even at his advancing age (36), he reached what became career highs in plate appearances (255) and at-bats (214), and swiped seven bases as well. In February 1942 Curry changed professional lanes and accepted the job as manager of the Philadelphia Stars.[14] According to the *Baltimore Afro-American*, "Curry is popular throughout the league and best known for his scrappy, enthusiastic leadership." According to news reports, the only reason that Baltimore owner Tom Wilson agreed to the transaction was that Stars owner Ed Bolden promised to name Curry the manager as well as outfielder.[15]

Curry was the player-manager of the Stars from 1942 to 1947. In 1942, at age 37, he batted .285. Curry was seen as a successful manager, even if the records do not support that claim with much vigor. He was also unafraid of conflict. As Riley wrote:

As the Stars' playing manager in 1946, he was involved in a brouhaha during the Newark Eagles' ace Leon Day's opening day no-hitter against his club. The incident began when the umpire called the Eagles' Larry Doby safe on a close play at the plate. Stars' catcher Bill Cash was infuriated and knocked the arbiter to the ground. Curry, who was already moving in from his position in right field to voice his objection to the call, arrived in time to kick the felled umpire while he was still on the ground. A riot ensued, with fans spilling out of the stands, necessitating the use of mounted police to clear the field.[16]

Overall, Curry is credited with a 203-207-11 record over his six seasons managing the Stars, and the fact that Ed Bolden continued to rehire Curry each year is testament to the confidence Curry earned from players and peers. But managers are hired to be fired, says the conventional wisdom of generations of writers, and in December 1947, Bolden fired Curry. That none other than the legendary Oscar Charleston took his place did not particularly ease the blow.[17]

Curry's formal time in the recognized Negro leagues (including the first and second National Leagues, the American League, and the Southern) ended after that 1947 season. He was a lifetime .301 hitter with a career OPS of .825 and an OPS+ of 124. In contrast with James Riley's introduction of the player earlier, Goose Curry was much more than a "good contact hitter" with "good speed." He was a lethal hitter for the greater part of 20 years, and in his age-42 season, as player-manager of the Stars, he logged 8 hits in 17 at-bats. He could pitch, but not at the same level as he slugged. His career ERA+ of 81 was 19 percent below the league averages of his time, and his lifetime won-lost record of 26-39 was similarly pedestrian.

When the second Negro National League folded after the 1948 season, Curry headed back south, managing and playing for the Atlanta Black Crackers.[18] Proving that he was not yet too old to swing a bat, not quite ready for the rocking chair, Curry impressed the locals in a May 1949 game against Chattanooga with a dramatic ninth-inning grand slam that produced a 7-6 Atlanta win.[19] As if that were not sufficient, Curry also homered in the nightcap as his contribution to the 3-1 win and the doubleheader sweep.

Curry spent the succeeding years managing several teams throughout the South, including the Memphis Red Sox, the Louisville Black Colonels, the Birmingham Black Barons, and again the Memphis Red Sox (now of the four-team Negro American League).[20] In 1956, his final season in the Negro Leagues, he managed the West team in the East-West Game.[21] After his playing days ended, Curry did some scouting and coaching for the Memphis Red Sox and never strayed too far from the game.[22]

On March 30, 1974, Homer Curry died following a long illness, two months before his 69th birthday.[23] He is buried at the Mount Carmel Cemetery in Memphis.[24]

SOURCES

All baseball statistics are derived from various web pages on the Seamheads.com site.

NOTES

1   James A. Riley, *The Biographical Encyclopedia of The Negro Baseball Leagues* (New York: Carroll & Graf, 1994), 220.

2   1920 United States Federal Census: Texas/Limestone (County)/ Justice Precinct 4/District 0090, https://www.ancestry.com/imageviewer/collections/6061/images/4392085_00204?pId=112958570

3   1940 U.S. Census/Memphis City/Ward 51/Block 19 (April 1940). https://www.ancestry.com/discoveryui-content/view/38243281:2442 ?tid=&pid=&queryId=c386cf307dd641b156ba2927238dbbe2&_phsrc= hebr2&_phstart=successSource.

4   "Cleveland Tigers (Baseball), in the Encyclopedia of Cleveland History curated by Case Western Reserve University. Online: https://case.edu/ech/articles/c/cleveland-tigers-baseball.

5   "Memphis Tops Southern Ball League," *Chicago Defender* (National edition), May 20, 1933: 8.

6   Larry Lester. *Black Baseball's National Showcase* (Lincoln: University of Nebraska Press, 2001), 93.

7   Brent P. Kelley, *Voices from the Negro Leagues* (Jefferson, North Carolina: McFarland & Co., 1998), 59.

8   "Black Yanks Leave for Carolinas: New Faces on Harlem Ball Club," *Chicago Defender*, April 15, 1939.

9   Chester L. Washington, "'Sez Ches': Josh Caught in the Act," *Pittsburgh Courier*, May 20, 1939: 16.

10 "The East Pits Its Best Against West Again Sunday: Teams Are Bolstered for Game; East's Second Sacker from Beale Avenue," *Chicago Defender*, August 26, 1939: 9.

11 J. Blow, "Western League Gets Satchel Paige: Baltim're Gets Bud Barbee, 'Goose' Curry; Manleys Lose Paige after June Meeting of Two Negro Leagues," *New York Amsterdam News*, June 29, 1940.

12 Homer Curry, United States form D.S.S. Form 1, dtd. October 16, 1940.

13 "California Winter League (1940-1941)," Center for Negro League Baseball Research (CNLBR), online: http://www.cnlbr.org/Portals /0/Stats/CWL/1940s/California%20Winter%20League%20 (1940-41).pdf.

14 "Curry New Manager of Philly Stars," *Baltimore Afro-American*, February 21, 1942: 23.

15 "Philly Stars Manager," *Chicago Defender*, July 25, 1942: 20.

16 Riley, 220.

17 Dusty Ballard, "Oscar Charleston Signed to Manage Stars for 1948 Season: Goose Curry Receives Unconditional Release," *Philadelphia Tribune*, December 23, 1947: 11.

18 "Black Crax Work Overtime for Opener Against Black Yankees," *Atlanta Daily World*, March 21, 1948: 7.

19 "Black Crackers Beat Choo Choos on Curry's 9th Inning Homerun," *Atlanta Daily World*, May 26, 1948: 5.

20 Russ J. Cowans. "The Goose Made a Mistake," *Chicago Defender*, September 1, 1956: 18.

21 "Curry, Steele NAL Managers," *Baltimore Afro-American*, July 28, 1956: 15.

22 "Birmingham Giants in Tryouts," *Chicago Daily Defender*, March 15, 1956: 21.

23 "Goose Curry Dies," *Northwest Arkansas Times* (Fayetteville), April 4, 1974: 2.

24 "Homer Curry," Find-a-grave online: https://www.findagrave.com/memorial/255315864/ homer-curry#source.

EDDIE LEE DIXON

BY MARGARET M. GRIPSHOVER

Eddie Lee Dixon was born on May 16, 1916, in Bonifay, Florida, in the Florida panhandle region, approximately 100 miles northeast of Pensacola, where Dixon spent most of his formative years. Except for his years in the Negro Leagues and while serving in the US Army during World War II, Dixon spent his entire life in Florida.

Dixon's family had roots in Georgia and North Carolina before settling in the Florida panhandle. Dixon's grandfather and father worked primarily in turpentine factories. The family's heritage of toiling in the pine tree products industry was prophetic given that Dixon's baseball career was built around two products that are related to turpentine distilling – rosin bags and pine tar.

Dixon grew up in a large household filled with siblings, half-siblings, extended family members, and boarders. He had three sisters and two brothers, none of whom played organized sports. He was the eldest of John and Gertrude Dixon's three sons. "Eddie Lee" was his official given name. But he was not the only "Ed" in the family. His second-youngest brother was Edward Julian Dixon. When Eddie Lee was a child, his family left Bonifay and moved 100 miles west to Pensacola, where he would spend the bulk of his adult life.

Eddie Lee Dixon with the 1939 Elites.

Dixon attended high school in Pensacola. Newspaper coverage of African American high-school sports in those years was scant, but if Dixon played high-school baseball, it was likely at the segregated Booker T. Washington Colored High School in West Pensacola. Washington Colored High had an interscholastic baseball team as early as 1931.[1] If Dixon didn't play baseball in high school, he could have gained some experience with one of several Pensacola city-league or semipro nines in the region including the Pensacola Beach Combers, Pensacola Black Sox, and the St. Joseph Athletics.[2]

Did Dixon play collegiate baseball before signing his first professional baseball contract? According to *Atlanta Daily World* sports columnist Chico Renfroe, Dixon, along with Roy Lee "Jack" Thornton, Chip "Tiny" Smith, Henry Thomas "Red" Hadley, Bill Cooper, and James "Sleeky" Reese, all played for the Morris Brown College Wolverines before turning pro with the Atlanta Black Crackers.[3] Morris Brown College was founded in Atlanta in 1881 and fielded a baseball team as early as 1897.[4] During the 1930s, Morris Brown College's diamond also served as the home field for some Atlanta Black Crackers games.[5] Details regarding Dixon's days as a Morris Brown College Wolverine are minimal and conflicting. For example, at the end

of the 1938 baseball season, it was reported that he was enrolled at Morris Brown College.[6] But according to the 1940 Census and his Army records, Dixon's education was limited to four years of high school. It is likely that Dixon did attend Morris Brown and possibly played baseball there, but it is unlikely that he was a college graduate.

In the spring of 1938, while working at a Civilian Conservation Corps (CCC) camp in Florida, Dixon was recruited by the Atlanta Black Crackers.[7] Many of the CCC camps had baseball teams that crossed bats with local nines, but published accounts of these games are scarce.[8] Dixon may have been scouted during the Black Crackers' spring-training stop in Orlando, Florida, in April 1938.[9] It is unlikely that Dixon enjoyed nearly instant success as a pitcher in the NAL in 1938 without some prior amateur or semipro experience. But according to Dixon's Black Crackers teammate James "Red" Moore, Dixon was a "surprise ace," and "someone no one had heard of who came in throwing the ball hard and striking people out."[10] In 1920, before Dixon was old enough to play professional baseball, the Pensacola Giants played their first season in the Negro Southern League.[11] It was rare for newspapers to include the names of any of the players let alone include line or box scores. There is no doubt that Dixon was pitching somewhere in Florida prior to his debut in professional baseball, but the lack of published accounts of those performances leaves a blank page in his résumé.

Dixon's 1938 spring-training camp debut with the Atlanta Black Crackers in Columbus, Georgia, drew favorable reviews, like this one:

"Among the pitchers, 'Bullet Joe' Dixon looks best. His fast curves and explosive speed had the U.S. Army team shut out, 15-0, when he retired to the shower at the close of the sixth inning Wednesday afternoon. He fanned 12 men and had such gilt-edge control that not one man was able to work him for a base on balls. Invariably he never threw more than two balls to any batter and gave up just one lone hit. He certainly looked impressive."[12]

When the Black Crackers left Columbus for more preseason competition in Atlanta, Dixon continued to impress as both a starter and as a reliever in spite of the lack of offensive and/or defensive support from his teammates. At the end of April 1938, Dixon was on the short end of the Black Crackers' 8-4 loss to the Homestead Grays, the 1937 National Negro League champions, but the rookie Dixon was not entirely to blame. As

Daily World sportswriter Lucius Jones noted, "Dixon, Atlanta starting hurler, worked seven innings, giving up six hits and five runs, but five errors were made behind him and three of the runs were unearned."[13] The rookie right-hander from Pensacola enjoyed his first taste of victory in a Black Crackers' uniform on May 12, 1938 when Atlanta defeated the Birmingham Black Barons, 2-0, at home at Ponce de Leon Park in their opening game as members of the NAL. Atlanta manager Nish Williams tapped Telosh Howard as his starter against Birmingham's Charles Blackmon. Williams's decision to pull Howard in the seventh inning and send the rookie Dixon to the mound was an unpopular decision with the hometown crowd. According to *Daily World* sportswriter Ric Roberts:

"Manager Nish Williams … motioned Howard to the showers and gave the ball to 'Bullet' Dixon. This gesture was against the second-guesses of the entire throng of 2,500 paying guests who would have retained Howard in the face of the latter's smart elbowing to that point. As things turned out, Manager Williams did himself a masterpiece in this business of substitution. All Dixon did with his lightening-fast [*sic*] curves and fireball was retire the next 8 consecutive batters and personally run down Owens in a chase off third base. Dixon fanned the hard hitting [David] Whatley and Blackmon on burning fast ball pitching.[14]

After Dixon's dazzling debut against the Black Barons in mid-May, he fell to earth like a spent bottle rocket. He pitched in relief in two losing efforts against Birmingham during which he "got the real fire baptism in his four innings during which his offerings were combed for 8 clean hits."[15] The early reviews were in. Dixon had potential but not necessarily as a starter, and he was as green as grass.

"[Dixon's] burning fast ball was invincible Thursday afternoon as he sat 8 batters down in a row, giving no hits and no bases on balls," an Atlanta scribe wrote. "The management thinks the rookie from Pensacola, Fla., may get somewhere in 1938 but they can't rush him too fast. He still has to learn 'how to pitch.' Right now he's throwing them past the hitters on sheer power. When he collects his share of cunning all of the American League clubs will hate to see him in there.[16]

The first half of the Black Crackers' 1938 season was less than stellar, and Dixon's star was not yet shining. Ric Roberts assessed the team at midseason in July with this lament: "Old Misfortune took a full stock at the best year Atlanta ever knew. The team started to down grade and there came arguments and misunderstandings. Man after man was given the gate and new ones added."[17]

Roberts may have been a little premature in predicting the terminal condition of the Black Crackers' 1938 season. Dixon and his teammates eventually found their grooves and helped Atlanta salvage what could have been a disastrous year. Their fortunes also improved when Gabby Kemp replaced Nish Williams as manager.[18] Dixon started to live up to his nickname – "Bullet Dixon," with his fiery fastball that neutralized opposing players' bats. For example, in a game at the end of July, Dixon notched 13 strikeouts as the Black Crackers vanquished the Fort Benning nine 11-2.[19] In mid-August, Dixon's record in 1938 mirrored the score against Fort Benning: 11 wins and 2 losses, albeit only a handful of those games were played against Negro League opponents.[20] According to Seamheads, when the regular season closed in mid-September, Dixon appeared in 23 games for the Black Crackers and chalked up five wins against three losses.[21]

By the end of September 1938, the Black Crackers had won the NAL second-half crown and were on a collision course with the Memphis Red Sox for the NAL championship. The playoffs were marred by controversy over the legitimacy of the teams' overall records, a potential tie with the Chicago American Giants, and league bureaucracy. But in the end it was determined that Atlanta would play Memphis for the championship.[22] It was the first time an Atlanta Negro League baseball team won a pennant.[23] Memphis dealt the Black Crackers a case of the blues by winning the first two games, 6-1 and 11-6.[24] Atlanta's Felix "Chin" Evans took the first loss on the chin, but Dixon did not pitch. In the second game of the series, Dixon came in as a reliever and walked four and struck out one. But Dixon's dinger was not enough to lift Atlanta over the Red Sox, and the Black Crackers found themselves 0-2. The series then shifted to Rickwood Field in Birmingham, Alabama, when the Black Crackers were unable to secure dates at Ponce de Leon Park due to the White Atlanta Crackers playing their playoff games at the same time.[25] But the final battle at Rickwood was scratched. The Black Crackers failed to show up in Birmingham and forfeited the games to the Memphis Red Sox.[26] The Black Crackers defaulted the championship to the Memphis Red Sox.[27] Ultimately, a disagreement over the distribution of gate receipts resulted in the abandonment of the series.[28] But perhaps the Black Crackers had other things on their minds. Just days after their twin losses to the Red Sox, at least four of the Black Crackers, including Dixon, Kemp, Evans, and Tommy "Pea Eye" Butts, tried out for football at Atlanta's Morris Brown College and Morehouse College.[29] If Dixon desired to trade in his pitcher's glove for a halfback's helmet and gallop on the gridiron for the Morris Brown Wolverines, it was not to be.[30] Only Evans, who was a football and baseball standout for the Morehouse College Maroon Tigers, made the cut.[31] Just a few weeks later, Dixon was back to work on the mound, barnstorming for the Atlanta Black Crackers in a losing effort against the Miami Ethiopian Clowns, a team he would play for in less than two years.[32] In the end, Dixon's 1938 season with Atlanta added up to a 5-3 record on the mound and a 2.92 ERA. He appeared in at least 23 games and led the Black Crackers with 55 strikeouts.

Dixon's 1939 season was bookended with lows and highs. He began the season with the Atlanta Black Crackers. He left Pensacola for Atlanta in early March for the team's spring workouts at Booker T. Washington High School.[33] Traveling with Dixon were two other pitchers, Lawrence "Tee" Mitchell, and a burly right-hander named "Johnson," whose name did not appear on the Black Crackers' roster for the season opener in late April.[34] Prospects for the Black Crackers were high given the previous season's second-half NAL title. Hopes were similarly lofty for Dixon, who was touted as "one of the finest pitchers in the country and, with a few runs … can really 'go to bed.'"[35] Dixon was also touted for his ability to keep baserunners honest because "Dixon insists on respect and gets it."[36] Before the start of the 1939 season, *Daily World* sports scribe Ric Roberts touted Dixon as "about the steadiest hurler on the Cracker staff in 1938," and he was "destined to become one of the greatest pitchers" and that Dixon was "ready to go all the time with no hint of arm trouble ever affecting his condition."[37] In a preseason interview with Roberts, Dixon named the Kansas City Monarchs as the "hardest American League team to beat" and Ted "Double Duty" Radcliffe as "the toughest batter in the league to fool or get out."[38] Dixon told Roberts that Oklahoma City was the "greatest baseball town in the country," and that the "biggest thrill" of his career to date was "when he pitched the Crax to a 9-2 victory over the Kansas City Monarchs in their own lot."[39] Roberts' prognostications for Dixon's career, and for the hurler's prospects for the immediate future, however, did not prove to be particularly accurate. Just days after his interview with Roberts, Dixon had a "disastrous day" on the mound in Chattanooga, Tennessee, for the Black Crackers, bearing the brunt of a 6-3 loss to the Baltimore Elite Giants in a game strewn with errors by the Crackers.[40] Dixon, who was described as a "chunky righthanded hurler," saw seven innings of shutout ball spoiled by Atlanta's bumbling defense.[41] It was a rough start for Dixon's 1939 season with the Black Crackers. Within a week of the loss to the Elite Giants in Chattanooga, Dixon and the Atlanta nine were hammered at home, 11-1, by the Homestead Grays at Ponce de Leon Park.[42] Dixon came into the game in relief of Black Crackers rookie southpaw Henry Clay "Lefty" Richburg.[43] Richburg gave up three runs in the first inning.[44] Dixon fared no better. He gifted the Grays with eight notches on the scoreboard, four of which came in the form of a grand slam off the bat of Buck Leonard, who came to the plate after Dixon intentionally walked Josh Gibson to load the bases.[45] In giving Gibson a pass, opined a sportswriter, "Pitcher Dixon then lived to realize his mistake. He worked on Buck Leonard, crack first-sacker of the Grays, with a fast one that he made just a trifle too good. The massive keystone man [*sic*] lifted it all the way to the last tier of the signboards in right field, then jogged around the bases to score behind Whatley, [Sam] Bankhead and Gibson. When the drive first left Leonard's huge mace, it looked for all the world that it would clear the park fence and land on the railroad tracks. But it fell a few feet short, denting the giant New Yorker ginger ale sign."[46]

Despite the hype about Dixon in 1938 by Atlanta sportswriters, his 1939 season did not meet those expectations. In early April, during an exhibition game loss to the Birmingham Acipco nine, Dixon took the mound in relief of rookie Richburg, who just sewed up three innings of scoreless ball. Dixon was not sharp, and according to Lucius Jones, "Dixon fared much worse, being touched for half of Birmingham's runs, but it was generally known that his arm had not come around at that time."[47] Jones speculated that "[i]t might take hotter weather to

restore the boy's 'smoke.'"[48] Even before Opening Day, signs of Dixon's arm problems were beginning to surface. The concerns about Dixon's desire to throw only heat rather than develop a full menu of pitching options were first raised in the spring of 1938, and proved quite prescient.[49] The fire behind all that smoke was already in need of kindling by Dixon after just one season in the Negro Leagues. Dixon's repertoire was limited to a blazing fastball, a serviceable curve, and a 'dinky' slider.[50] It was clear that Dixon had the ability to hurl the heat, but he never did quite grasp "how to pitch."[51]

Dixon started the 1939 season with the Black Crackers and had a brief layover with the peripatetic Crackers in Indianapolis before safely landing in Baltimore to pitch for the Elite Giants in the second half of the 1939 season. For the nanosecond he spent in Indy, Dixon was touted to local fans as having a "baffling curve with burning speed."[52] By May, the Crackers had lost 10 of their 14 starts.[53] At the end of April, Dixon's fellow Pensacolian, rookie flinger Henry "Lefty" Richburg, was the losing pitcher of record in an 8-5 defeat in which Dixon, who was the "chief bright feature of the contest," was stepping in at first base for an ailing Red Moore.[54] A few days later, Dixon returned to the mound only to suffer a humiliating 11-0 shutout loss to the swats of Mule Suttles and his Newark Eagles.[55] And as if things couldn't get any worse for Atlanta's bottom line, after their loss to Newark, the Crackers' team bus was involved in an accident and several players were injured while on their way to North Carolina for a tilt with the Raleigh Grays.[56] Dixon was fortunate. He was not hurt in the bus mishap and moved on with the hobbled team to Missouri where he rose to the occasion by pitching the Crackers to a 9-6 win over the St. Louis Stars and hitting what was likely the only home run in his NAL career.[57] Dixon was not known for his prowess at the plate, but he did manage to accrue a middling .246 career batting average.[58]

In the early summer of 1939, the Black Crackers' season was about to implode. Crackers owner John H. Harden faced deepening financial issues that he blamed on a combination of the difficulties in enticing Northern nines to trek to Atlanta to spin the turnstiles and increased transportation costs that were eating into the team's bottom line.[59] The bus accident did more than hurt some players – it helped to crash the Crackers as a business enterprise. It was becoming more challenging for Harden, who operated a service station in Atlanta, to cover team expenses and payroll.[60] After a brief failed flirtation with Indianapolis, the Black Crackers reclaimed their Atlanta identity and returned to the road in June with Dixon picking up victories against the Cleveland Bears and Memphis Red Sox, the latter in which he struck out eight and had a "'fog' ball" that was "cracking like a buggy whip."[61]

By mid-July, the Black Crackers exited the Negro American League and Harden had a fire sale on his players.[62] The greatest beneficiaries of Harden's financial hardships were the Baltimore Elite Giants, who scooped up Dixon, Butts, Evans, Moore, and Oscar Boone from the ashes.[63] It was a fortunate landing for Dixon and his fellow former Crackers. The Elite Giants were in need of pitchers and defensive players and their deal for five cast-offs from the Crackers ultimately helped them capture the 1939 crown for the second half of the Negro National League season.[64] It was hoped that Dixon would play a key role in meeting Baltimore's expectations.[65] It was thought that Dixon and the new additions to the Elite Giants roster were "really clicking" and were just the "sparkplug" that was needed to help Baltimore overcome their listless performances on the front end of the season and vie for the second-half crown.[66] The Elite Giants did indeed benefit from the infusion of talent from the Black Crackers but Dixon's direct contributions to Baltimore winning the second half of the season and ultimately claiming the NNL championship were minimal or nonexistent. His name did not appear in any box scores leading up to the series and he was not the starting pitcher in any of the championship games between the Elite Giants and the Homestead Grays. In the weeks leading up to the final series, he was rarely mentioned in game results, and toward the end of August, one newspaper published a list of the Elites' roster and placed Dixon last among all Baltimore's pitchers.[67] In the days leading up to the first game of the series, the *Baltimore Afro-American* did not include Dixon in a list of potential starters for the Elites but did name him as a member of the bullpen.[68] And on the eve of the opening game, the *Afro-American* did not even list Dixon among the six Baltimore pitchers in a "probable line-up."[69]

Dixon's contributions to Baltimore's 1939 NNL championship games are unclear. It is possible that he made some appearances in relief, but he was not a starter. Why didn't the once highly touted fireballer Dixon not get the call? Likely his arm was toast even before the championship series started.[70] "Bullet" Dixon was shooting blanks. He appeared in just eight games for the Black Crackers and rang up a 4.88 ERA. Dixon's stats are absent from 1939 Elite Giants totals on Seamheads. com. Dixon's waning effectiveness in 1939 would be confirmed when his NNL career abruptly ended in the spring of 1940. In the end, the Elite Giants defeated the Homestead Grays and received the Jacob Ruppert Memorial trophy in Yankee Stadium from Bill "Bojangles" Robinson, who said as he passed the hardware to the victors, "I hope I may live to see Colored players in both of the major leagues."[71] In 1947, two years prior to his death, Bill Robinson's wish was granted when Jackie Robinson started for the Brooklyn Dodgers and Larry Doby signed with the Cleveland Indians.

Despite his lack of contributions to the Elite Giants' 1939 championship season, and the questions regarding the soundness of his arm, on March 31, 1940, Dixon reported to Baltimore's spring-training camp in New Orleans.[72] In the spring of 1940, Dixon's name appeared at the end of a list of Baltimore's available pitchers.[73] His arm fell asleep in the fall of 1939, but it woke up from a long winter's nap in the spring of 1940. In April he made an effective relief appearance during a 13-2 drubbing by the New York Black Yankees, holding the opposition to two hits in three innings.[74] Dixon's performance drew comparisons to his days as a "fireball wizard" for the Atlanta Black Crackers, but

the magic proved momentary.[75] On April 7 he was the second of three hurlers used by the Elite Giants in a spring-training game against the Memphis Red Sox at Pelican Stadium, and he struggled.[76] He manned the mound for 2⅔ innings, copping one strikeout and while gifting six runs to Memphis in a 15-1 loss.[77] The following day, Dixon, along with manager Felton Snow and three Elites teammates; William "Big Bill" Hoskins," Sammy Hughes, and Woodrow "Woody" Williams, were enumerated in New Orleans by the US Census Bureau. Although the enumerator made several errors and corrections on Dixon's 1940 Census page, all five were boarding at Washington R. Butler's Hotel Theresa on South Rampart Street. Given the area's connections to baseball and Black enterprises, it is not surprising that at least five members of the Elite Giants chose the Hotel Theresa as their New Orleans spring-training base. When Dixon and his fellow Elite Giants resided at the Hotel Theresa, South Rampart Street was situated in the "'main stem' or center of Negro sporting and business endeavors."[78]

Dixon's season with the 1940 Baltimore Elite Giants appears to have ended not long before it started. By the end of April, his name was no longer routinely mentioned as part of Baltimore's hurling staff, and when it did appear as a member of the Elite Giants, he was usually the last name on the list of veteran pitchers.[79] Dixon was absent from Baltimore's roster from May through early June with the exception of his name being mistakenly included as "Tom Dixon," one of the "top-notch hurlers who helped carry the Elite Giants to the title last year."[80] The last time Dixon appeared in a possible lineup for the Elite Giants was on July 17, 1940, when he was named as part of Baltimore's roster in a game against the Lloyd A.C. nine of Chester, Pennsylvania.[81] Dixon never had a chance to take the mound. The game was rained out.[82] Dixon's career with the Elite Giants ended with a thud. He made just one appearance on the hill for Baltimore in 1940 and was dinged for six runs in 2⅔ innings of work.

Dixon's departure from the Elite Giants in July 1940 went unnoticed by the press but he did briefly continue his baseball career with another team, promoter Syd Pollock's traveling Miami Ethiopian Clowns.[83] Dixon joined the Clowns and found himself barnstorming with former Atlanta Black Cracker teammates Spencer Davis, Evans, and Boone.[84] Dixon's tenure with the Ethiopian Clowns is difficult to assess given that the Clowns played under pseudonyms that masked their identities with such stage names as "Selassie," "Wahoo," and even "Tarzan."[85] Although some Ethiopian Clowns players' stage names have been decoded, Dixon's has not. But given the likely poor state of his arm, and that he made little or no impact on the Elite Giants' 1940 season from spring training through the early summer, it is likely that Dixon's professional baseball career ended in the summer of 1940 by clowning with the Miami squad.

On October 16, 1940, Dixon registered for the draft in Pensacola. He was 24 years old and described as a "Negro," with brown eyes, black hair, with a "Light" complexion. He stood 5-feet 6-inches tall and weighed 167 pounds. Dixon was employed at Farrow's Café and Pure Oil Service Station in Pensacola that was owned by Dixon's sister's husband and his sister's mother-in-law. In the summer of 1942, Dixon married Jimmie Lee Harris in Pensacola. The following year, during World War II, he enlisted in the US Army at Camp Blanding in Starke, Florida. At the time of his enlistment, he stated that his education was limited to "4 years of high school," and made no mention of attending college. This is consistent with the education attainment information he provided in the 1940 and 1950 Censuses, which conflicts with newspaper accounts of his enrollment at Morris Brown College in Atlanta. Dixon served in the Army Quartermaster Corps. After completing his service, he was discharged at the rank of sergeant and returned to Pensacola and answered a different call – the siren sound of the baseball diamond.

This time it was to local Pensacola semi-pro leagues. In 1946 he managed the Pensacola Pepsi-Cola All-Stars.[86] The Pepsi-Cola team was organized in 1945 after being mothballed for several years during World War II and was much improved by the addition of veterans who were also good ballplayers.[87] Dixon had at least one familiar face on the roster, Henry Richburg, with whom he played on the Black Crackers during Richburg's brief residency with the Atlanta team in 1939.[88] Richburg was in his second season with the Pepsi-Colas when he reunited with Dixon.[89] The All-Stars were a local semipro club. Their opponents included the Birmingham Stars and the Mobile Prichard Athletics.[90] After their stint with the All-Stars, Dixon and Richburg migrated to the Pensacola Sea Gulls in 1951.[91] While managing the Sea Gulls, Dixon exchanged his manager's cap for a player's bat and managed to hit at least one homer for the Gulls in the spring of 1951, a rare feat for Dixon, who was not known for his prowess at the plate.[92] After Dixon moved on from the Sea Gulls, at least one of the Gulls graduated from the local semipros to a career in the major leagues – shortstop Johnny Lewis, who played for and later became the first African American coach for the St. Louis Cardinals.[93] Two years later, Dixon managed a different local aggregation, the Gulf Power softball team.[94] Dixon's shift to softball from baseball reflected changes to the Pensacola sports landscape. By the early 1950s, softball leagues were gaining in popularity and local games were drawing as many as 60,000 fans per season.[95] By 1955, there were three "Negro softball leagues" in the city.[96] That same year, interest in Pensacola softball leagues was described as "summer madness," with 855 players on 59 slow-pitch and fast-pitch teams.[97] No doubt that softball's expansion came at the expense of men's baseball leagues, both semipro and amateur. Dixon's baseball managerial acumen, however, was easily transferred to softball, and his squad won the first half of the Commercial League 1953 season.[98] Dixon's diamond days ended with the Gulf Power softball team. After 1953, his name no longer appeared in local baseball or softball reporting.

After he returned to civilian life in the mid-1940s. Dixon and his wife lived with his in-laws' extended-family household in Pensacola through the early 1950s. When not on a local diamond,

Dixon's day job was as a grocery warehouse worker, while his wife, Jimmie Lee, owned the Dixon Smoke Shop. Dixon also earned extra money when he enlisted in the Army Reserve in 1947 and retained his World War II rank of sergeant.[99]

After Dixon's father died in 1956, he and Jimmie Lee left Pensacola for Fort Lauderdale, Florida. Dixon found work in construction and his wife became an elementary-school teacher. There were no published reports of his participation in any locally organized sports. But his personal life was changing. In 1961 Dixon's mother, Gertrude Richardson, died in Pensacola, and he became a father when his only child, Carl Dixon, was born.

Eddie Lee Dixon died on July 8, 1993, in Fort Lauderdale "after a brief illness."[100] His death notices were carried in Pensacola and Fort Lauderdale newspapers.[101] According to his obituary, he was survived by his wife, son, one grandson, three sisters, three brothers, and one adopted sister.[102] The obituary gave his name as "Eddie L. 'Mount' Dixon," although the meaning of the nickname was not explained. Nor was there any mention of his baseball career in either of his death notices. Dixon was credited, however, with involvement in several community groups and was a "faithful member" of the Mt. Olive Baptist Church where he served as a chaplain and as a member of the choir.[103] Dixon was buried in the Forest Lawn Memorial Gardens Central in Fort Lauderdale with a marker honoring his World War II Army service.

Acknowledgment

The author would like to express her heartfelt appreciation for the wisdom, good humor, generosity, encouragement, and expert editing of the late Frederick C. Bush, who assisted with the early research for this chapter.

SOURCES

Unless otherwise indicated, all Negro League statistics and records were sourced from Seamheads.com and baseball-reference.com. Ancestry.com was used to access census, birth, death, marriage, military, immigration, and other genealogical and public records.

NOTES

1   "Negro High School Plays Here Today," *Pensacola Journal*, April 30, 1931: 2.

2   "Crack Negro Teams Will Clash Today," *Pensacola Journal*, May 6, 1934: 11; "Negro Ball Club Is Off for Jax," *Pensacola Journal*, July 9, 1934: 3; "Negro Clubs Battle Today," *Pensacola Journal*, August 12, 1934: 10.

3   Chico Renfroe, "Sports of the World," *Atlanta Daily World*, March 3, 1991: 8.

4   "What the Negro Is Doing," *Atlanta Constitution*, April 25, 1897: 8.

5   William J. Plott, *The Negro Southern League: A Baseball History, 1920-1951* (Jefferson, North Carolina: McFarland & Company, 2015), 8.

6   Ric Roberts, "Kemp, Dixon, Evans in Local Grid Try-Outs," *Atlanta Daily World*, September 23, 1938: 5.

7   Ric Roberts, "A Black Cracker a Day," *Atlanta Daily World*, April 16, 1939: 8.

8   Jerrell H. Shofner, "Roosevelt's 'Tree Army': The Civilian Conservation Corps in Florida," *Florida Historical Quarterly*, Apr. 1987, Vol. 65, No. 4, pp. 433-456.

9   "Atlanta Negro Team Plays Here Monday," *Orlando Evening Star*, April 16, 1938: 5; "Black Crackers to Play Sunday," *Atlanta Journal*, April 22, 1938: 15.

10   Todd Halcomb, "Year of the Black Crackers," *Atlanta Constitution*, June 27, 1997: E7.

11   Plott, 10.

12   "Donald Reeves, 'Bullet Joe' Dixon in Impressive Form at Columbus Camp," *Atlanta Daily World*, April 15, 1938: 5.

13   Lucius Jones, "Black Crackers Beaten in Final Game with Homestead Grays Tuesday, 8-4," *Atlanta Daily World*, April 27, 1938: 5.

14   Ric Roberts, "Crackers Win Opener," *Atlanta Daily World*, May 13, 1938: 1.

15   "Black Crackers Gain Odd Game in Baron Series by Winning First Game, 7 to 3," *Atlanta Daily World*, May 16, 1938: 5.

16   "Ex-Black Baron Pitchers Mitchell and 'Red' Howard Want Chance at Ex-Mates," *Atlanta Daily World*, May 14, 1938: 5.

17   Ric Roberts, "Most Promising Black Cracker Year Turns Out to Be Most Lamentable," *Atlanta Daily World*, July 6, 1938: 5.

18   "Black Crackers Hold 'Moore Day,'" *Atlanta Journal*, July 31, 1938: 16.

19   Allen Edward Joyce, *The Atlanta Black Crackers*, thesis, Emory University, 1975: 60.

20   "Atlanta Crackers Play Chairs Thursday Night," *Sheboygan (Wisconsin) Press*, August 3, 1938: 10.

21   Presumably using different criteria, Ric Roberts reported Dixon appearing in 31 games with a record of 16-4. See Roberts, April 16, 1939: 8.

22   "American Giants Split," *Chicago Tribune*, September 6, 1938: 25; Joyce, 65-66.

23   "Black Crackers Win Second Half," *Atlanta Journal*, September 18, 1938: 18.

24   "Memphis Leads in Playoff for Championship," *Chicago Defender*, September 24, 1938: 8.

25   "Red Sox Take Second from Black Crackers," *Atlanta Daily World*, September 20, 1938: 5; "Red Sox Win Another," *Memphis Commercial Appeal*, September 20, 1938: 13.

26   Sam Brown, "Memphis Red Sox to Meet Atlanta This Sunday," *Atlanta Daily World*, March 24, 1938: 5.

27   "Black Crackers Play Birmingham Sunday," *Atlanta Constitution*, September 24, 1938: 22.

28   Todd Holcomb, "Year of the Black Crackers," *Atlanta Constitution*, June 27, 1997: E7.

29   Ric Roberts, "Kemp, Dixon, Evans in Local Grid Try-Outs," *Atlanta Daily World*, September 23, 1938: 5.

30   Ric Roberts, "Red Sox Take Second from Black Crackers."

31   Chico Renfroe, "Sports of the World," *Atlanta Daily World*, February 9, 1990: 5.

32   "Clowns Shut Out Atlanta Club, 5-0," *Miami News*, October 5, 1938: 8.

33   Ric Roberts, "Atlanta Black Crax Regard Promising Baseball Campaign," *Atlanta Daily World*, March 7, 1939: 5; Lucius Jones, "Slant on Sports," *Atlanta Daily World*, March 21, 1939: 5.

34   Lucius Jones, "Slant on Sports," *Atlanta Daily World*, March 16, 1939: 5; "Black Crackers Play Here Soon," *Macon (Georgia) News*, April 25, 1939: 14.

35   Lucius Jones, March 21, 1939: 5.

36   Lucius Jones, "Slant on Sports," *Atlanta Daily World*, March 22, 1939: 5.

37   Ric Roberts, April 16, 1939: 8.

38   Ric Roberts, April 16, 1939: 8.

39   Ric Roberts, April 16, 1939: 8.

40   Lucius Jones, "Slants on Sports," *Atlanta Daily World*, April 18, 1939: 5.

41   Lucius Jones, April 18, 1939: 5.

42   Lucius Jones, "Champions Trim Black Crax, 11-1," *Atlanta Daily World*, April 22, 1939: 5.

43   Henry Richburg, like Dixon, lived in Pensacola. The surname errors may have resulted from confusing Henry Richburg with Lance Richbourg, also from Florida, who played eight seasons in the White majors between 1921 and 1932, including stints with Philadelphia Phillies, Washington Nationals, the Boston Braves, and the Chicago Cubs. According to Baseball-Reference.com, Henry Richbourg [sic] appeared in three games for the Black Crackers in 1939, twice as a starter, and was charged with one official loss. His hefty 8.64 ERA did nothing to enhance his résumé and helps to explain his very brief tenure in the Negro Leagues. But Richburg continued to play baseball after exiting the Atlanta bullpen. After World War II, Richburg and Dixon reunited and played for the Pensacola Sea Gulls during the early 1950s.

44   Lucius Jones, "Champions Trim Black Crax, 11-1," *Atlanta Daily World*, April 22, 1939: 5.

45   "Champions Trim Black Crax, 11-1."

46   "Champions Trim Black Crax, 11-1."

47   Lucius Jones, "Black Crax Seek Second Straight Victory," *Atlanta Daily World*, April 8, 1939: 5.

48   "Black Crax Seek Second Straight Victory."

49   "Ex-Black Baron Pitchers Mitchell and 'Red' Howard Want Chance at Ex-Mates," *Atlanta Daily World*, May 14, 1938: 5.

50   James A. Riley, *The Biographical Encyclopedia of the Negro Baseball Leagues* (New York: Carroll & Graf Publishers, Inc., 1994), 238.

51   "Ex-Black Baron Pitchers Mitchell and 'Red' Howard Want Chance at Ex-Mates."

52   "Meet the Boys," *Indianapolis Recorder*, April 20, 1939: 14.

53   Lucius Jones, "Slants on Sports," *Atlanta Daily World*, May 1, 1939: 5.

54   "Slants on Sports," May 1, 1939: 5.

55   "Suttles Pounds Ball Hard as ABC's Fall to Newark," *Pittsburgh Courier*, May 6, 1939: 15.

56   "Negro Teams Play," *Raleigh (North Carolina) News and Observer*, May 6, 1939: 6.

57   Black Crax Win First League Contest 9-6," *Atlanta Daily World*, May 16, 1939: 5.

58   Riley, 238.

59   Joyce, *The Atlanta Black Crackers*, 73.

60　Riley, 353.

61　"Black Crackers Play Memphis," *Atlanta Journal*, June 18, 1939: 15; Lucius Jones, "Atlanta, Memphis Play Twin Bill Today," *Atlanta Daily World*, June 18, 1939: 8.

62　Joyce, *The Atlanta Black Crackers*, 74.

63　"Elites Training in New Orleans," *New York Amsterdam News,* April 20, 1940: 18.

64　"Five Atlanta Players Signed by Baltimore," *Chicago Defender*, July 22, 1939: 8.

65　"Elites, Cubans on 4-Team Twin Bill," *Pittsburgh Courier*, August 5, 1939: 18.

66　Lucius Jones, "Donald Reeves Signs with Chicago Ball Club," *Atlanta Daily World*, August 6, 1939: 8; "Beating the Gun," *Phoenix* (Arizona) *Index,* August 19, 1939: 3.

67　"So You'll Know Them," *Warren* (Pennsylvania) *Times-Mirror,* August 23, 1939: 8.

68　"10,000 Expected When Elites Meet Eagles Sunday," *Baltimore Afro-American*, September 9, 1939: 23; Art Carter, "From the Bench," *Baltimore Afro-American*, September 9, 1939: 23; "Elites to Play Grays for Championship," *Baltimore Afro-American*, September 16, 1939: 23.

69　"Elites to Play Grays for Championship."

70　Todd Holcomb, "Year of the Black Crackers," *Atlanta Constitution*, June 27, 1997: E7.

71　Al Baker, "Sport," *Boston Guardian,* September 30, 1939: 7.

72　Cum Posey, "Posey's Points," *Pittsburgh Courier,* April 13, 1940: 16.

73　Posey.

74　"New York Black Yanks Rout Baltimore Elite Giants 13-2," *Phoenix Index*, April 6, 1940: 5.

75　"New York Black Yanks Rout Baltimore Elite Giants 13-2."

76　"Negro Ball Clubs Split Twin Bill Before 5000 Fans," *New Orleans States*, April 9, 1940: 23.

77　"Negro Ball Clubs Split Twin Bill Before 5000 Fans."

78　John E. Rousseau, "'Ramp Is Gone … Ain't What It Used to Be,' Declares Old Timer," *Louisiana Weekly* (New Orleans), March 13, 1965: 4.

79　Cum Posey, "Posey's Points," *Pittsburgh Courier*, April 13, 1940: 16.

80　"Elite Giants and Lloyd A.C. in Rubber Game this Evening," *Chester* (Pennsylvania) *Times*, June 7, 1940: 18.

81　"National Negro League Champions Here This Evening," *Chester Times*, July 17, 1940: 12.

82　"Larry File Day at Lloyd Baseball Park Tomorrow Night," *Chester Times*, July 18, 1940: 22.

83　Leslie A. Heaphy, *The Negro Leagues, 1869-1960* (Jefferson, North Carolina: McFarland & Company, Inc., 2003), 146.

84　Lucius Jones, "Slants on Sports," *Atlanta Daily World*, July 23, 1940: 5.

85　Robert Peterson, *Only the Ball Was White* (New York: Gramercy Books, 1970), 204.

86　"All-Stars to Meet Mobile Nine Today," *Pensacola Journal*, September 13, 1946: 2.

87　"Pepsi-Cola Nine to Meet Clowns Thursday," *Pensacola Journal*, April 9, 1945: 3; "Negro All-Stars Play Birmingham," *Pensacola News-Journal*, September 1, 1946: 15.

88　"All-Stars to Meet Mobile Nine Today."

89　"Negro Nine to Play Mobile Today," *Pensacola Journal*, August 20, 1945: 3.

90　"All-Stars to Meet Mobile Nine Today"; "Pepsi-Colas Play Mobile Nine Tonight," *Pensacola Journal,* September 18, 1946: 2.

91　"Sea Gulls Down Mobile Bear Nine," *Pensacola Journal*, May 21, 1951: 2.

92　"Sea Gulls Down Mobile Bear Nine."

93　"Before Jackie Robinson: Playing Ball for the Fun of It," *Pensacola News Journal*, July 30, 1989: C-1, C-10.

94　Gulf Power Plays All-Stars Friday," *Pensacola Journal*, June 17, 1953: 10.

95　"City Softball Leagues Start 'Biggest Year' Monday Night," *Pensacola Journal*, May 1, 1955: 13.

96　"Negro Softball Meeting Tonight," *Pensacola Journal*, March 24, 1955: 16.

97　"City Softball Leagues Start 'Biggest Year' Monday Night."

98　Gulf Power Plays All-Stars Friday," *Pensacola Journal*, June 17, 1953: 10.

99　"11 Vets Enlist in Army Reserves," *Pensacola News-Journal*, March 30, 1947: 14.

100　"Death Notices," *Pensacola News Journal*, July 12, 1993: 10; Obituaries," *South Florida Sun-Sentinel* (Fort Lauderdale), July 13, 1993: 4B.

101　"Death Notices," *Pensacola News Journal*, July 12, 1993: 10.

102　"Obituaries," *South Florida Sun-Sentinel*, July 13, 1993: 4B.

103　"Obituaries."

JONAS GAINES

BY ALAN COHEN

The discussions continue to this day. What would have happened if those denied the opportunity had been given the chance to play at the highest level of baseball before 1947? We have had glimpses of such players, often long past their prime.

In 1951, in a barnstorming game in Alabama, Jonas Gaines took the mound and played on a team with AL/NL Black players, some of whom, like Willie Mays were young, others, like Roy Campanella, his contemporaries, each of whom had been given the opportunity to play in the AL/NL majors. Gaines never pitched in the AL/NL majors, but after this game, he continued to pitch another six seasons in a professional career that extended over 21 years (1937-1957 with a full season and parts of two others off for military service) and that had him travel from the deep South, to the urban North, to Mexico, Cuba, and Venezuela, to the Northern border of the United States, to the Canadian provinces, to the Land of the Rising Sun, to the small towns near the Texas-New Mexico border.

Jonas George Gaines was born on January 9, 1915, in New Roads, Louisiana. He came from a large family. His parents were Willie and Minerva Baptiste Gaines. She had been born in 1879 and lived to the age of 96. Jonas had four sisters, Angeline, Reva, Julia (born in 1902), and Odette, and three brothers, Leon, Alonzo, and Lionel.

While attending Southern University in Baton Rouge, Louisiana, Jonas spent his summers pitching for the Colored YMCA Tigers team in Bogalusa, Louisiana, hurling a no-hitter on July 16, 1933, at Laurel, Mississippi, when he was only 18 years old.[1] The following spring, after pitching another no-hitter for the Bogalusa team, the left-hander traveled to Valley City, North Dakota. On May 13, in his first start for Valley City he pitched still another no-hitter, defeating New Rockford, 3-0.[2]

As Charles Hancock, a Valley City teammate, recalled in 1973, "We were looking for a big guy when Gaines got off the train (in Valley City), and he wasn't. But when we got back to the hotel, he showed me some clippings from the *New Orleans Picayune*. He had pitched five no-hit games. (Gaines was 18 at the time). We played in Valley City the next Sunday, and he went out and pitched another no-hitter."[3]

Gaines was still pitching for Valley City in 1935, and on June 26 was matched up against Satchel Paige who was pitching for Bismarck. Gaines lost a 6-1 decision and Paige struck out 17 and allowed two hits.[4]

Gaines returned to Louisiana in 1936 and pitched for Baton Rouge on April 12, losing a 3-0 decision to the Colored YMCA Tigers.[5] But he soon headed back to North Dakota. He first

pitched for the team in Page, and then he signed on with Bismarck, the defending national semipro champions. Such was the ongoing life of travel for the young Black pitcher. Pitching for Bismarck, he defeated Minot, 12-4, on June 22.[6] He followed that up on July 3 by winning a one-sided game against the Aztecas, 18-4, and had two hits to help his own cause.[7] At one point in the season, Bismarck put together a streak of 21 consecutive wins. The streak ended against the House of David on August 10 as Gaines lost a 3-2 decision.[8]

By 1937, the left-handed 5-foot-10 155-pound Gaines was with the Newark Eagles. Per Seamheads.com, the 22-year-old[9] appeared in five games and was 1-1 with an 8.27 ERA. He also pitched with the Washington Elite Giants, losing his two appearances.

The Elite Giants called at least three cities home during their time in the Negro National League, and in 1938 were playing as the Nashville Elite Giants (they were also known as the Baltimore Elite Giants that season) when they barnstormed against the Red Bank Pirates in New Jersey on August 30. Gaines authored a three-hitter that night and won, 3-1. The only Red Bank run came on a fourth-inning homer by former big-leaguer Al Cuccinello.[10] Seamheads.com, which does not reflect exhibitions and includes only games for which there are box scores, has Gaines appearing in just four games in 1938, going 0-1. On June 17 at Toledo, in a game for which there is no box score, he was the first of a parade of pitchers to be hammered by the Homestead Grays, the Elites losing 14-6. In the first inning he surrendered home runs to Ray Brown and Josh Gibson.[11] Records are incomplete for 1938, but he appears to have been winless that season with at least two losses.

On June 10, 1939, Gaines defeated Homestead, 4-2, in the first game of a doubleheader at Forbes Field. On July 2 the Elites faced the New York Black Yankees in the second game of a four-team doubleheader at Yankee Stadium. Gaines pitched a 4-0 shutout.[12] But again in 1939, there was a fair amount of barnstorming, and Gaines victimized the Brooklyn Bushwicks, 9-0, on August 18 under the lights at Dexter Park. He allowed only three hits.[13]

During Gaines's time with the Elites, his battery partner was often Roy Campanella. In 1939 Campanella, though only 17 years old, was in his third season with the Elites. The two paired up against the Homestead Grays at Dexter Park on September 4, but Roy Partlow hit a grand slam in the second inning, and the Grays won 5-3.[14]

After the season there were two rounds of playoff games. In the first round, Baltimore faced Newark in a best-of-five series.

Gaines was handed the ball on September 9 and defeated the Eagles, 11-3 in Philadelphia. The win evened the series at 1-1, and the Elites went on to subdue Newark in four games, sweeping a doubleheader in Baltimore the next day.

Baltimore faced the Homestead Grays for the NNL championship. Gaines pitched his team to a win in the second game of the series, 7-5, at Oriole Park in Baltimore before 2,800 fans on September 17.[15] A week later, at Yankee Stadium, he hurled his team to a 2-0 win, allowing three hits in 7⅔ innings, to clinch the league championship.[16] There was no Negro League World Series between the Negro American and National Leagues in 1939.

More than 80 years later, records are still incomplete, but Gaines appears to have won, including all appearances (regular season, postseason, all-star, and barnstorming), 10 games in 1939.

In 1940 Gaines played briefly for Los Azules de Veracruz in the Mexican League and spent most of the season with the Mexico City Reds, for whom he went 8-3 as they finished second in the league.

In 1941 he was back with Baltimore. The Elite Giants were matched up against the Bushwicks on July 20, and Gaines yielded four runs in the first inning. Thereafter, he dominated, allowing five hits over the last eight innings, and his team, led by Campanella, came back to win, 7-4.[17]

Not much Negro League baseball was played at Detroit's Briggs Stadium over the years, but on August 3, 1941, Gaines, in front of 27,949 fans, bested the Grays, 6-0. He allowed only four hits and only one runner made it as far as third base.[18] It was the first game involving Black players at Briggs Stadium since 1921.[19] Gaines's record for 1941 was 5-3 with a 2.39 ERA.

In spring training for the 1942 season, the Elite Giants ventured to New Orleans on April 12, where they faced the New York Cubans. Gaines did not yield a hit in the four innings he pitched. He was relieved by Bill Harvey, who completed the combined no-hitter, pitching the final three innings of the seven-inning game, with the Elite Giants winning 4-0 to close out a doubleheader sweep.[20]

Later in 1942, Gaines returned to Detroit and on June 14 he faced Dave Barnhill of the New York Cubans in a pitchers' duel. Gaines pitched eight innings, allowing a pair of tainted runs. A fielding gem by Cuban Heberto Blanco robbed Gaines of a hit in the sixth inning.[21] The Cubans won the game in the 12th inning, 4-2, scoring a pair of runs off Andy Porter. The culprit was Dave "Showboat" Thomas, whose double with two mates on base scored the winning runs.[22]

Gaines suffered his first loss of the 1942 season when, in front of 12,000 fans at Yankee Stadium in the second game of a doubleheader on June 21, he yielded a two-out ninth-inning single to familiar nemesis Thomas, which brought home the winning run in a 3-2 game.[23]

Gaines won five games in 1942, including a 1-0 shutout of the Homestead Grays at Baltimore's Bugle Field on July 3. He scattered four hits and yielded seven walks (three to Josh Gibson). He had seven strikeouts.

Three images of pitcher Jonas Gaines.

He was the starting pitcher in the annual East-West Game at Comiskey Park on August 16. He pitched three innings and allowed one run on one hit. The East won the game in the late innings, 5-2. When Gaines completed his Hall of Fame questionnaire in July 1972, he declared this appearance his outstanding achievement in baseball.[24] It was the first of two East-West appearances for Gaines in 1942. The second game was played two days later at Cleveland Stadium. Gaines pitched scoreless ball in the fourth and fifth innings as the East won, 9-2. The win went to starting pitcher Gene Smith of the New York Black Yankees.

In 1942 the drive for the integration of the big leagues intensified, although it would be another five years before the color line was broken at the major-league level. Gaines was considered a good candidate for the "big leagues." Lester Rose, in the *New York Daily News*, noted that Gaines "has a swell curve and change of pace. Usual lefty deliveries just break away, but on an overhand throw, Gaines' delivery dips, and on sidearm, it rises."[25] He was 27 years old at the time, but never got the call to the big leagues.

Gaines served in the US Army Quartermaster Corps from May 13, 1943, through December 15, 1945, attaining the rank of sergeant. In 1943 he was initially stationed at Fort Lewis in Tacoma, Washington, and hurled for its baseball squad, which was managed by Philadelphia Phillies outfielder Morrie Arnovich. On July 3, 1943, his Army company moved to Bend, Oregon, where Gaines was instrumental in organizing the baseball team.[26]

In 1944 Gaines was with the 320th Quartermaster Service Battalion at Fort Dix in New Jersey.[27] Gaines made the most of weekend passes, hurling for the Elite Giants in 1944. He recorded four wins, losing only once, in 10 appearances. On June 11 he appeared in front of 25,500 fans in Detroit and led Baltimore to an 8-5 complete-game win. Still in the service in 1945, he had only two opportunities to pitch for the Elite Giants, both in September. On September 3, against the Homestead Grays at Washington's Griffith Stadium, he pitched nine innings, allowing four hits, but the game was tied, 2-2, and extra innings were needed. The Grays pushed across a run in the 12th inning to win, 3-2. In a postseason exhibition at the Polo Grounds, he lost a 5-2 decision to Don Newcombe of the Newark Eagles in Newcombe's last Negro League game. Newcombe, along with Jackie Robinson and Roy Campanella, signed with Branch Rickey's Dodgers after the 1945 season.

Gaines rejoined the Elite Giants at the beginning of the 1946 season. On June 13 he sparkled, yielding only three hits in a 2-0 win over the Philadelphia Stars in the second game of a doubleheader at Shibe Park.[28] It was his third of four wins in the first half of the season. At Griffith Stadium on July 10, his mates staged a come-from-behind win with two ninth-inning runs as the Elite Giants defeated Philadelphia, 3-2, as 15,000 fans looked on.[29]

Gaines ended the season with three consecutive wins, and then traveled to Cuba, appearing in seven games for Almendares in the Cuban Winter League and posting a 1-1 record.

After the color line was broken in the previously segregated major leagues, Gaines remained on the outside looking in. He returned to the Baltimore Elite Giants in 1947. He won seven games against five losses (per Retrosheet), and his ERA was 3.68 (per Seamheads). His first win of the season came in the first game of a doubleheader against Philadelphia on June 22. Although he allowed only six hits, three Elite errors helped Philadelphia to score seven times. That was not nearly enough as the Elites scored 13 times for an easy win.[30]

The continued unrecognized status of the Negro Leagues was being discussed more frequently, and the name of Gaines entered the conversation. Writer Marion E. Jackson noted that when organized White Baseball recognized the Cuban Winter League as an unclassified minor league,

No move has been made to give the American Negro League and National League even a mention. Here is the paradox of baseball. Henry Kimbro, Jonas Gaines, and Lenny Pearson are members of organized baseball. Yet they are paradoxes as they are playing for such unorganized baseball teams [as perceived by the White establishment] as the Baltimore Elite Giants and Newark Eagles."[31]

And Gaines continued to toil away. On August 8, when Bob Romby faltered in the first inning, Gaines came on in relief. He entered the game with two outs. Romby's four walks had allowed the Grays to take a 2-0 first-inning lead. Gaines stopped the bleeding, striking out nine, as the Elites came back to win, 9-4. Against the Grays on August 22, Gaines once again was the victor, scattering eight hits in a complete-game 4-2 win. His start a week later produced similar results. Against the New York Black Yankees, he allowed five hits in an 8-1 win.

After the 1947 season, the Elites barnstormed, and in a game at Baltimore opposed a team of White minor leaguers. The opposition, led by Howie Moss, who had slugged 53 homers for the minor-league Baltimore Orioles (International League) that season, included four players from the Orioles. Gaines struck out 15 batters in a 2-0 win on October 3.[32]

Gaines returned to the Elites in 1948, and his season got off to a good start with a 9-4 win over the Grays on May 28. He won nine games and lost five during the season. His best performance of the year came in a seven-inning game against the Black Yankees. He allowed only two hits in a 4-0 shutout. At the end of the season, the Elites played the Grays for the right to advance to the Negro League World Series. The Elite Giants came up on the short end. In his only appearance in the series against the Grays, on September 14, Gaines faltered. He came out of the game in the fourth inning with his team trailing 5-0. They lost 6-0.

The Negro Leagues reorganized in 1949 and the Elite Giants were in the five-team Eastern Division of the Negro American League. They won both halves of the season and triumphed in the Negro League World Series, winning four straight games from the Chicago American Giants.

But Gaines was not part of the picture for the Elites in 1949. In April he was traded to the Houston (formerly the Newark) Eagles for Leon Day. The transplanted Eagles were not particularly competitive. They and other league teams played many of their games at neutral sites. On May 30 the Eagles and Philadelphia Stars played at Chester, Pennsylvania. Gaines pitched the entire game, yielding only five hits, but two of those hits were home runs, and Philadelphia won, 4-3.[33]

Not long thereafter, Gaines moved to the Philadelphia Stars. Statistics for 1949 were as of 2024 not complete, and little specific is known of Gaines's performance in 1949, beyond the one game with Houston. Per the Howe News Bureau, he appeared in seven games and went 0-4 for Philadelphia.

After the 1949 season, Gaines played with Vargas in the Venezuelan Winter League.

In 1950 Gaines, then 35, was with Philadelphia and according to the Howe News Bureau, he appeared in nine games, pitched 39 innings and was 2-3 with a 3.46 ERA. With each passing year, coverage of Negro League games in the print media was on the decline, and the statistics were in question. Jonas Gaines and Willie Gaines each pitched for the Stars and there was confusion between the two when the statistics were compiled.

Gaines won at least four times in 1950. He won the May 14 Opening Day game against Indianapolis at Shibe Park, 2-1. Little in the way of specifics is known about the game. Two weeks later at Yankee Stadium, he defeated the Kansas City 3-0 in the first game of a three-team doubleheader.[34] Another win came at another big-league ballpark. He defeated Baltimore at Griffith Stadium, 8-3, on June 25, scattering seven hits.[35]

Satchel Paige hooked up with Philadelphia hoping for another shot at the major leagues. On a barnstorming trip, the Stars made stops in Brooklyn and Hartford. Gaines relieved Paige in each game and was charged with a pair of losses. In Brooklyn the stars lost 1-0 to the semipro Bushwicks. Gaines entered the game in the fourth inning and yielded the decisive run.[36] In Hartford, he pitched the middle innings against the semipro Hartford Indians, and absorbed the 7-3 loss.[37]

Gaines next won in 1950 at Baltimore on July 30. He entered the game in the fourth inning with his team trailing 4-0 and pitched six scoreless innings as the Stars came from behind to win, 10-4. In those six innings, he allowed only one hit, and he struck out seven batters.[38]

Gaines was again selected for the East team in the East-West Game, but first there was a trip to Toronto, where the Stars, with Paige starting, faced the Indianapolis Clowns. By the time Gaines entered the game, it was a lost cause as the Clowns won 9-4.[39]

In the East-West Game on August 20 (the last of his five East-West appearances), Gaines hurled scoreless ball in the sixth and seventh innings, but by then the West team had established a 5-2 lead and went on to win, 5-3.

In 1951 Gaines made his way to the Manitoba-Dakota League, a haven for Black players, and played with Minot. Statistics are not available for the 1951 Man-Dak League, but it is known that he was credited with a win on June 30 as Minot defeated Brandon, 12-4. Gaines pitched the entire game and scattered six hits.[40]

After the 1951 season, Gaines joined a barnstorming troupe led by Roy Campanella and took the field with Campanella, Willie Mays, Hank Thompson, Harry Simpson, and Don Newcombe as the team, with Gaines doing the pitching, defeated the Negro American League All-Stars, 6-3. Gaines pitched the seven-inning game (Newcombe played first base) and allowed seven hits while striking out six batters.[41]

In 1952 Gaines got a crack at White Organized Baseball with the Scranton Miners of the Eastern League, thanks to Bill Veeck. In 1951 Scranton, then affiliated with the Boston Red Sox, had no Black players. The next year, Scranton became affiliated with Veeck's St. Louis Browns. No fewer than six Black players went to spring training with the Double-A Miners. On April 14 at Thomasville, Georgia, in an exhibition game, Gaines entered the contest in the fifth inning and pitched five hitless innings. His team lost to Pine Bluff, 8-7, but writer Joe Butler of the *Scranton Times* wrote that Gaines would have a spot on the team's roster for the regular season.[42]

But as the team broke training, Gaines returned home to Baton Rouge and stayed there, nursing a wrenched left ankle and a bruised right knee.[43] Gaines did not pitch for Scranton in 1952. He returned to the Man-Dak League for another season with Minot.[44] He went 9-3[45] as Minot won the first of three consecutive league championships. And again, after the season he barnstormed with Roy Campanella.[46] In Galveston on November 1, Gaines pitched the first seven innings in an 18-1 shellacking and received credit for the win.[47] He then went to the Cuban Winter League and appeared for Cienfuegos in five games, going 1-1.

In 1953 Gaines was off to Hankyu, Japan and a season in the Japanese Pacific League. He went 14-9 with an ERA of 2.53. He was second in the league with 142 strikeouts. He was quite welcome in Japan and pictures of the three Black players on the Hankyu team (Gaines, Larry Raines, and John Britton) were painted on a building in Osaka.[48] Owner Bill Veeck of the Browns had thought that playing in Japan would be a good learning experience for Gaines and Raines, who were contractually tied to the Browns organization. But by the time Gaines returned from Japan, Veeck was out of baseball, the Browns had become the Baltimore Orioles, and Gaines was on his own to find a new team. That search took him to Texas.

In 1954 Gaines was with Pampa in the Class-C West Texas-New Mexico League, where he went 16-7 and was named to the postseason all-league team. Pampa went 81-54 and finished in first place. Gaines had one shutout during the season. It came on July 24 against Albuquerque.[49] In the postseason playoffs, Pampa eliminated Abilene in the first round and went up against Clovis in the finals, Gaines, who had lost two close decisions in the playoffs (one against Abilene and the other against Clovis), was handed the ball one last time on September 23 and came through with a 3-2 win as Pampa won the best-of-seven series in six games.[50]

In 1955 Gaines was back in the Man-Dak League, this time with the Bismarck Barons. His first win of the season came on June 2 when Bismarck defeated Williston, 5-4. In the game, former Negro League catcher Bill Cash, who was Gaines's batterymate, hit a home run.[51] On July 17 Gaines cruised to a two-hit 2-0 shutout over Minot.[52] Bismarck, with Gaines posting an 8-3 record, went on to win the regular-season championship. However, the Barons could not get past the first round of the playoffs, losing the best-of-seven series in five games to Dickinson.

In 1956, at age 41, Gaines was still hurling, this time with the Carlsbad Potashers of the Class-B Southwestern League. He compiled a 9-7 record and returned to go 6-10 in 1957, his final season.

In the following decade, as the remaining Negro League teams were in their final decline, the names of Gaines and most of his fellow teammates were largely forgotten. But that was about to change. In his induction speech at Cooperstown, Ted Williams called for recognition and enshrinement of Negro League players. Although Gaines has not been inducted as of 2024, his name has consistently surfaced as former Negro League players and officials remembered the largely forgotten days of the Negro Leagues.

In 1985 former Elite Giants teammate Riley Stewart remembered Gaines as "the first pitcher to show me how to throw a change of pace."[53]

On June 28, 1997, Gaines was one of seven living Negro League players from Louisiana to be honored at a Braves game in Atlanta. On that day, Louisiana Governor Mike Foster proclaimed the day as Negro Leagues Baseball Players Day.[54]

After his playing days, Gaines worked in the alteration department at the D.H. Holmes department store in Baton Rouge. He never married. He died on August 6, 1998, in Baker, Louisiana. He is buried at Port Hudson National Cemetery in Zachary, Louisiana.[55]

Acknowledgments

The author is particularly grateful to Frederick Bush for finding sources for this story and to Cassidy Lent of the National Baseball Hall of Fame and Museum for articles and information from the Jonas Gaines file at the Giamatti Research Center.

SOURCES

In addition to the sources cites in the Notes, the author used Retrosheet.org, Seamheads.com, and Baseball-Reference.com.

Where won-lost records are available in Retrosheet.org, Retrosheet figures were used as they take into consideration all games. Seamheads uses only games for which box-score information is available.

Other sources used:

Glauber, Bill. "Elite Giants: Great Players, Even Greater Personalities," *Baltimore Sun*, April 30, 1990: 1C, 6C.

Johnson, Lloyd, and Miles Wolff, editors. *Encyclopedia of Minor League Baseball,* Third Edition (Durham, North Carolina: Baseball America, 2007).

Lester, Larry. *Black Baseball's National Showcase: The East-West All-Star Game 1933-1962,* Expanded Version (Kansas City: Noir-Tech Research, 2020).

Snider, Steve (United Press International). "Baseball Shrine Forgets Top Black League Stars," *Miami Herald*, August 13, 1972: 4-F.

Wiebusch, John. "Gilliam Recalls Tough Life in Negro Leagues," *Los Angeles Times,* March 12, 1969: III-1, 4.

NOTES

1   'Lefty" Gaines Hurls No-Hit No-Run Game," *Bogalusa* (Louisiana) *Enterprise and American*, July 21, 1933: 10.

2   "Valley City Wins," *Bismarck* (North Dakota) *Tribune*, May 14, 1934: 1.

3   John M. Coates, "Hancock Looks Back Some 50 Years at Negro Baseball," *Sioux City* (Iowa) *Journal*, February 25, 1973: C-3.

4   "Bismarck Conquers Valley City, 2 [*sic*] to 1," *Bismarck Tribune*, June 27, 1935: 8.

5   "Colored Tigers Win Debut from Baton Rouge '9,'" *Bogalusa* (Louisiana) *Enterprise and American*, April 17, 1936: 8.

6   "Bismarck Trounces Valley City, 12-4, Behind a 12-Hit Bat Attack," *Bismarck Tribune*, June 23, 1936: 6.

7   "Bismarck Nine Sweeps Four-Game Series with Astecas," *Bismarck Tribune*, July 6, 1936: 8.

8   "Chief Nusser Halts Bismarck's Win Streak at 21 Games," *Bismarck Tribune*, August 11, 1936: 6.

9   Not long into his career, he shaved three years off his age, claiming to have been born in 1918.

10   "Pirates Bow to Elites in Three-Hitter," *Red Bank* (New Jersey) *Standard*, August 31, 1938: 15.

11   R.S. Simmons, "Grays Beat Elites 14-2 at Toledo," *Chicago Defender*, June 25, 1938: 8.

12   Buster Miller, "15,000 See Newark and Elite Giants Win 4-Team Doubleheader at Stadium," *New York Age*, July 8, 1939: 8.

13   "Homesteaders in Pair with Bushwicks: Nashville Elites Down Dexter Parkers in Battle Under Arcs," *Brooklyn Eagle*, August 19, 1939: 11.

14   "Partlow Steals Show as Grays Top Nashville," *Brooklyn Eagle*, September 5, 1939: 15.

15   "Baltimore Bats Way to Titular Game with Grays," *Pittsburgh Courier*, September 23, 1939: 16.

16   Buster Miller, "Elite Giants Top Homestead Grays to Win Ruppert Trophy," *New York Age*, September 30, 1939: 8; "Elites Win, 2-0, in Colored Final," *New York Daily News*, September 25, 1939: 40.

17   "Elite Giants Batter Dexters in Opener, 7-4," *New York Daily News*, July 21, 1941: 34.

18 Russ Cowans, "Grays and Giants Split Two Games: Jonas Gaines Yields Four Hits in First to Blank Homestead Nine, 6-0," *Detroit Tribune*, August 9, 1941: 7; "28,000 See Negro 9's," *Detroit Times*, August 4, 1941: 11.

19 "Ban at Briggs Stadium Broken After 20 Years," *Baltimore Afro-American*, July 26, 1941: 19.

20 "Elite Southpaws Hurl No-Hitter," *Pittsburgh Courier*, April 25, 1942: 16.

21 "Barnhill has Edge in Fine Pitching Duel," *Michigan Chronicle* (Detroit), June 20, 1942: 21.

22 "20,000 See Cubans Take Twin Bill from Elite Giants," *Pittsburgh Courier*, June 20, 1942: 16.

23 "Grays Defeat Philadelphia Stars; Cuban(s) Down Elite Giants in Yankee Stadium Doubleheader," *New York Age*, June 27, 1942: 11.

24 Jonas "Lefty" Gaines Questionnaire, National Baseball Hall of Fame and Museum Giamatti Research Center.

25 Lester Rose, "Major Prospects," *New York Daily News*, August 16, 1942: 34.

26 Art Carter, "Jonas Gaines Displays Pitching Prowess in Army," *Baltimore Afro-American*, August 14, 1943: 22.

27 Jay Burrell, "Dix Gets Lefty Gaines, NNL Star," Unidentified publication donated to National Baseball Hall of Fame and Museum Library by Jonas Gaines in 1972.

28 "Gray, Elite Nines Meet," *Baltimore Evening Sun*, June 14, 1946: 37.

29 "Baltimore Takes NNL from Newark," *Pittsburgh Courier*, July 20, 1946: 16.

30 "Elites Capture Double-Header," *Baltimore Sun*, June 23, 1947: 16.

31 Marion E. Jackson, "Negro Major League Owners Worry About 'Unofficial' Status," *Alabama Tribune* (Montgomery), August 1, 1947.

32 "Elite Giants Defeat All-Star Nine by 2-0," *Baltimore Sun*, October 4, 1947: 14.

33 "2 Home Runs Enable Stars to Score Win," *Delaware County Daily Times* (Chester, Pennsylvania), May 31, 1949: 13.

34 "Philly Stars Take Two; Nip Kay See 3-0, Clowns 3-1, *New York Age*, June 3, 1950: 27.

35 "Philadelphia Stars Top Baltimore Giants Twice," *Washington Evening Star*, June 26, 1950: 11.

36 "Paige Sparkles but Dexters Glow," *Brooklyn Eagle*, July 20, 1950: 20.

37 Jimmy Cunavelis, "Satch Paige Weighs Offer from Majors," *Hartford Courant*, July 27, 1950: 13.

38 Thomas Skinner, "Satchel Paige and Philly Stars Win 10-4 Then Bow to Baltimore Elite Giants, 3-4," *Kansas City Call*, August 4, 1950: 9.

39 Joe Perlove, "Clowns Go to Town at Satch's Expense," *Toronto Star*, August 19, 1950: 13.

40 "Mallard Club Finds Range," *Regina* (Saskatchewan) *Leader-Post*, July 3, 1951: 17.

41 Kermit Westerholm, "Major Leaguers Defeat Minors in 6-3 Contest," *Austin* (Texas) *Statesman*, November 2, 1951: A-22.

42 Joe M. Butler, "Gaines Shows Class as Scranton Bows – Court Miners," *Scranton Times*, April 15, 1952: 20.

43 Butler, "Baseball Miners to Appear in York Tonight," *Scranton Times*, April 19, 1952: 13.

44 "Minot Mallards Nearing Title," *Saskatoon* (Saskatchewan) *Star-Phoenix*, September 3, 1952: 15.

45 Wendell Smith, "Tan Aces Head for Japan," *Pittsburgh Courier*, March 14, 1953: 6.

46 Marion E. Jackson, "Campanella All-Stars Open Tour Friday; Play Atlanta Monday Night," *Alabama Tribune*, October 10, 1952: 8.

47 "Roy Campanella Nine Wins, 18-1," *Shreveport Times*, November 3, 1952: 17.

48 Wendell Smith, "An American Reports on Japanese Baseball," *Pittsburgh Courier*, September 19, 1953: 14.

49 "Santos Hurls Hubber Finale," *Albuquerque Tribune*, July 26, 1954: 16.

50 "Pampa Grabs League Title," *Abilene* (Texas) *Reporter News*, September 24, 1954: 8.

51 "Barons Edge Oilers, 5-4," *Mandan* (North Dakota) *Morning Pioneer*, June 3, 1955: 12.

52 "Man-Dak League, *Mandan Morning Pioneer*, July 18, 1955: 8.

53 Bill McIntyre, "Former Player Riley Stewart High on Black Baseball Leagues' Talent," *Shreveport Times*, February 28, 1985: 6-C.

54 "Negro Leagues Players to be Honored in State Today," *Shreveport Times*, June 28, 1997: 1-C.

55 Jonas Gaines Obituary, *Baton Rouge Advocate*, August 11, 1998: 6.

TOM "LEFTY" GLOVER

BY GARY CIERADKOWSKI

Lefty Glover was one of the players who followed the Elite Giants when they relocated from Washington to Baltimore in 1938. Though he pitched for the Elites for over seven seasons, until recently Glover's background and even his real name were clouded in mystery. However, the discovery of his death certificate in 2020 uncovered his real name as Thomas Glover Moss.[1]

The document further reveals that Glover was born on February 11, 1911, in Montgomery County, Alabama. His mother was Luvelia Moss, born in Montgomery, and his father was listed as Willie Glover, birthplace unknown.[2] It appears that Lefty used "Moss" for the early part of his life and career. A box score from August 1, 1932, has "Lefty" Moss pitching for the semipro Atlanta Shops team against the Montgomery Grey Sox.[3] However, the April 16, 1933, *Montgomery Advertiser* lists Tom "Lefty" Glover as a pitcher for the Montgomery Grey Sox of the Negro Southern League.[4]

Glover did fairly well with Montgomery, pitching a three-hitter against the Birmingham Black Barons in July and a four-hitter against the Detroit Stars in August.[5] He next surfaces in late May of 1934, when Birmingham played a series of spring-training games with a tall, lanky newcomer on the mound. Called "Walter Glover" by the Birmingham press, this was actually Tom Glover, and he made an impression right out of the gate. Facing the Atlanta Black Crackers, Glover three-hit them and won 8-0.[6] The southpaw then threw another shutout against the Cleveland Cubs, followed by a six-hit, 5-2 win over the Kansas City Monarchs.[7] By the time the 1934 Negro Southern League season opened, Tom "Lefty" Glover was Birmingham's best pitcher and was given the honor of being the team's Opening Day hurler. Facing the Memphis Red Sox in the first game of a doubleheader, Glover relinquished only six hits while striking out seven to win 5-4. Two weeks into the season, Birmingham's ace disappeared, making a beeline north to join the Cleveland Red Sox of the Negro National League.[8]

In the spring of 1935, the *Pittsburgh Courier* reported that Allan Page, owner of the New Orleans Black Pelicans, had gone to great expense to create a good ballclub and that Lefty Glover was their ace.[9] Once again, Glover jumped clubs, this time to the Columbus Elite Giants of the Negro National League. However, because the Elites already had a solid rotation, Glover left the team in June of 1936 and rejoined the Montgomery Grey Sox before jumping to the Birmingham Black Barons in July. He returned to the Elites in 1937 when they relocated to Washington and remained with the club when it finally settled down in Baltimore in 1938.[10]

By the time he rejoined the Elites, they had an above-average pitching staff anchored by Bill Byrd, Pullman Porter, and Schoolboy Griffith. Since the Negro Leagues played a short "official" season of between 40 and 60 games, three top-tier starters were a luxury. The bulk of an average Negro League team's games were exhibitions against White semipros or other Black teams that did not count in the standings. For those games, Negro League clubs carried a couple of second-tier pitchers, and this is the role Lefty Glover filled on the Elites.

Newspaper stories described him as a speedball pitcher and curveball artist.[11] For many of his games, box scores show a pitcher who recorded few strikeouts but many groundouts or fly outs, validating his mastery of a good curveball. The box scores also revealed that he typically ran out of steam around the seventh inning and sometimes had a problem with his control. The Elites apparently recognized Glover's weakness and often

Lefty Glover. Courtesy of Gary Cieradkowski.

pitched him in the second game of doubleheaders, which at the time were seven-inning affairs.

Because the Elites had Byrd, Porter, and Griffith, Glover's official Negro National League record is modest; six wins and six losses for 1937-1939. His nonleague and exhibition games were not recorded.

The year 1939 marked a major milestone in Lefty Glover's career. That summer, the Elites finished the season with a record of 21-23, good enough to be one of the four teams invited to play for the Ruppert Memorial Trophy, a championship tournament played at New York's Yankee Stadium and named after the Yankees' recently deceased owner, Jacob Ruppert. The Elites wound up winning the trophy, defeating the Homestead Grays, winners of the regular-season pennant that year. Winning the Ruppert Cup gave the Elites the title of "Champions," though the Grays believed their winning the pennant gave them rights to the title. Four teams then played a postseason tournament (Elites vs. Eagles, Grays vs. Stars) with Baltimore defeating the Grays 3-1-1 to claim the season title.[12]

After going 1-2 in seven league games for the "Champion" Elites in 1939, Glover was invited to join an exclusive group of Blackball players in the California Winter League. This loosely organized league had been in existence since the 1920s and typically featured a couple of all-White teams made up of Los Angeles-based major and minor leaguers and one all-Black team. Over the years, the Black team boasted such future Hall of Famers as Satchel Paige, Turkey Stearnes, and Bullet Joe Rogan, along with many of Blackball's greatest stars. Because the money was good, to be invited to play in the California Winter League meant you were deemed among the best, and in 1939 Lefty Glover made the grade.

That winter the all-Black team was called the "Philadelphia Royal Giants," and they fielded a good cross-section of stars.[13] Besides Glover, the pitching staff included Elites teammate Bill Harvey and New York Black Yankees ace Terris McDuffie. The rest of the club included Jim West at first, Jake Dunn at second, Marlin Carter at short, Hoss Walker at third, Wild Bill Wright, Mule Suttles, and Bill Hoskins in the outfield and Pepper Bassett behind the plate.[14] The all-Black entry was the smart pick for winning the short season, with former Brooklyn Dodgers star Babe Herman's White Kings team expected to come in a close second.[15]

On November 6, 1939, the White Kings met the Royal Giants in a doubleheader at Hollywood's Gilmore Field. When it was over, Glover had pitched a no-hitter and gained immortality for himself in Blackball lore. True to form, he recorded just four punchouts, but his curveball allowed only three balls to leave the infield. His control stayed true as he issued just two bases on balls.[16] The Royal Giants won the 1939-40 championship with a 10-6 record. Besides his no-hit masterpiece, Glover led the league with a .750 winning percentage and a 3-1 record.[17] It's at this point that Lefty Glover decided to capitalize on his fame and follow the money. In 1940 this meant south of the border.

While baseball had been played in Mexico since the 1840s, the country's first functioning league did not start up until 1925. By 1940 the league's leading benefactor was Jorge Pasquel, a rich importer-exporter from Monterrey and a baseball fiend. Pasquel knew that to have a thriving league he needed to import established stars to both attract fans and help native players elevate their game. Inducing the better-paid White players to come to Mexico was not feasible, but Negro League and Cuban-based players, who drew less pay and faced racial discrimination up north, was easier. Glover's no-hit masterpiece was reported in most sports pages, making him a known commodity and ripe for Mexican League recruitment.

However, if Glover thought Mexico was going to be easier than the California Winter League, he was very wrong. Besides the best Latin players of the day, the 1940 Liga Mexicana was a veritable who's who of Negro League superstars, including future Hall of Famers Josh Gibson, Leon Day, Martin Dihigo, Cool Papa Bell, Ray Dandridge, and Willard Brown, plus almost all of Glover's Royal Giants teammates. Against this star-studded "outsider baseball" congregation, Lefty went 8-13 in 36 games with an ERA over 5.00. He also bounced around throughout the season, playing for La Junta de Nuevo Laredo, Unión Laguna de Torreón, and Gallos de Santa Rosa, teams that finished fifth, sixth, and seventh in the seven-team league. Glover stayed in Mexico the following year, winning four and losing six for the last-place Carta Blanca de Monterrey.

Just when the Liga Mexicana was shaping up to be a haven for Negro Leaguers, World War II stepped in. Ballplayers in Mexico were instructed to return to the States to make themselves easier for their draft boards to reach and persuade to take jobs in a war-related industry. Glover returned to Baltimore and rejoined the Elite Giants.[18]

Throughout the summer of '42, the Elites battled the Homestead Grays for first place in the Negro National League II, but eventually came up short. During a crucial point in the season, Baltimore lost catcher Roy Campanella to Mexico and, lacking his bat in the lineup, lost the pennant to the Grays on the last game of the season.[19] Glover was the team's third starter and had gone 5-3 with a 3.38 ERA.

The next year, 1943, both the Elite Giants and Lefty Glover underachieved, with the team falling to a distant fifth place and Glover delivering a disappointing 3-5 record. Off the field, Lefty did find success, getting married in June of that year to a woman named Gertrude.[20]

Despite threatening to stay out of baseball in 1944 and remain in his steel plant job, Glover stayed with the Elites but managed only a 1-2 record.[21] Glover was expected to take a bigger role in the team's rotation, with the *Baltimore Afro-American* reporting, "[I]ndications point to Tom Glover as the North Carolina port-sider appears to be the farthest advanced of the Elite flingers in the matter of conditioning."[22]

The next season, 1945, turned out to be Lefty Glover's Negro League swan song. Though he finished the season 4-3, the fans thought enough of Baltimore's left-hander to vote him onto that year's East-West All-Star Game. Glover was picked to start the game but was sent to the showers in the second inning after giving up four runs to the West team. He was charged with the loss in the West's 9-6 win.[23]

According to the August 11, 1945 *Afro-American*, Glover gave the Negro National League the big "to-ell-with-you" and rejoined the Carta Blanca de Monterrey, going 5-1 for the remainder of the season.[24] He moved farther south in 1946, first playing winter ball in Panama, where he made the Pro League all-star team and pitched against the visiting New York Yankees, then summered in Venezuela with the Pastora club.[25]

Glover's jumping of his Elite Giants contract led to the Negro National League officially banishing him for five years.[26] He was absent from American baseball circles until this heart-breaking item in the March 13, 1948, edition of the *Baltimore Afro-American*:

Glover at Henryton

Tom Glover, former Baltimore Elite Giants pitcher, is at Henryton Health Sanitarium and anxious to see his old Baltimore friends and fans.[27]

Henryton was a segregated tuberculosis sanitarium in Marriottsville, 30 miles outside Baltimore. Though called a hospital, Henryton was basically a place of exile for TB patients rather than a treatment center.[28]

Inevitably, a few months later, he died, on June 7 at age 35. His obituary appeared in the *Afro-American*:

Ex-Baltimore Elite Giants Hurler Dead

BALTIMORE. Death closed the career of Thomas (Tom) Glover, former southpaw pitching star of the Baltimore Elite Giants, here Monday morning.

Glover, who joined the Elites in 1935, saw service in the Negro National League and also performed in the leagues of Mexico, Cuba, Panama and South America. He was said to be 36 years of age.

His most notable achievement was a no-hit, no-run game he pitched against an all-star major and minor league team on the West Coast in 1939.

Glover is survived by his wife Gertrude. His death occurred at Henryton Sanitarium.[29]

SOURCES

This biography was modified from the author's original article "Lefty Glover: Requiem for a Southpaw" published in *21: The Illustrated Journal of Outsider Baseball, Volume 2* that can also be accessed online at https://studiogaryc.com/2021/04/04/lefty-glover-requiem-for-a-southpaw/.

Unless noted, Negro League and Mexican League statistics and final standings referenced are from the Seamheads Negro League Database.

NOTES

1 Glover's death certificate obtained through the Maryland State Archives.

2 It has been very difficult to learn more details about Glover's parents. Several families with the surname Moss resided in the Montgomery County, Alabama, region during the 1920 and 1930 censuses, but none appear to have been Thomas Glover's family. The 1930 census shows a Will Glover with his wife, Flora, 20-year-old daughter, Rosa, and 19-year-old son, Tom residing in Scott, Arkansas. All four are recorded as having been born in Alabama. Will Glover's occupation is listed as a cotton farmer and Tom Glover as a teamster in the cotton farming industry. Back in the late 1980s, some of his teammates told this author that he had grown up with different relatives, but that is unsubstantiated.

3 "Grey Sox Mill Win, 7-1; 1,200 Fans See Tilt," *Montgomery Advertiser*, August 1, 1932: 6.

4 "Grey Sox Mill Battle Nashville Nine Today," *Montgomery Advertiser*, April 16, 1933: 6.

5 "Glover Hurls Sox to Win Over Foxes," *Montgomery Advertiser*, July 31, 1933: 6; "Grey Sox, Detroit Divide Twin Bill," *Montgomery Advertiser*, August 14, 1933: 6.

6 William J. Plott, *The Negro Southern League: A Baseball History, 1920-1951* (Jefferson, North Carolina: McFarland & Company, 2015), 116-117.

7 Plott, 117.

8 Plott, 117.

9 "New Orleans Sees Two Major Nines This Week," *Chicago Defender*, April 27, 1935: 16.

10 There are no known interviews with Glover, nor do any newspaper articles yet uncovered suggest why he seems to have moved switched teams so frequently.

11 "No Hit No Run Game," *Bakersfield Californian*, November 6, 1939: 14; "Bob Feller to Hurl Tonight for All-Stars Against Giants," *Los Angeles Times*, October 11, 1939: 14.

12 See Richard J. Puerzer, "The 1939 Negro National League Championship Series: Baltimore Elite Giants vs. Homestead Grays," in this volume.

13 "Doubleheader Marks Opening of Winter Baseball," *Van Nuys* (California) *News*, October 5, 1939: 6.

14 "Negro Southpaw Blanks Kings," *Los Angeles Times*, November 6, 1939: 30.

15 "Doubleheader Marks Opening of Winter Baseball."

16 "Negro Southpaw Blanks Kings," *Los Angeles Times*, November 6, 1939: 30.

17 William McNeil, *The California Winter League: America's First Integrated Professional Baseball League* (Jefferson, North Carolina: McFarland & Company, 2002), 200.

18 "Stars Here Sunday in NNL Opener," *Baltimore Afro-American*, May 5, 1942: 21.

19 One looking at the final league standings as reported on Seamheads in early 2024 sees the Elite Giants (38-27) a full 13 games behind Homestead (54-17), but *Baltimore Afro-American* coverage of games in the final week of the season consistently expressed a dramatic fight for the pennant. After the Elites split a doubleheader on Sunday, September 6, the newspaper wrote, "The result of the day's

activities left the Elites still a game behind the league-leading Washington Homestead Grays, with only the Labor Day twin bill remaining on the schedule." Art Carter, "Divide Sunday Twin Bill," *Baltimore Afro-American*, September 8, 1942: 19. The full-page eight-column headline on the same page proclaimed, "Grays Clinch Flag; Open World Series in D.C.," *Baltimore Afro-American*, September 8, 1942: 19.

20   Art Carter "Elites Must Patch Cracking Infield," *Baltimore Afro-American*, June 12, 1943: 25.

21   "Elite Giants May Lose Key Men," *Pittsburgh Courier*, March 27, 1943: 18.

22   "Elites Break Even; Stage Set for Sunday Opening," *Baltimore Afro-American*, May 5, 1945: 23.

23   Larry Lester, *Black Baseball's National Showcase: The East-West All-Star Game, 1933-1953* (Lincoln: University of Nebraska Press, 2001), 455.

24   "Defi!," *Baltimore Afro-American*, August 11, 1945: 26.

25   "Yanks Flash Sock When Badly Needed," *Brooklyn Daily Eagle*, February 28, 1946: 15.

26   "Bids for 2 Berths Refused," *Pittsburgh Courier*, March 23, 1946: 16.

27   "Glover at Henryton," *Baltimore Afro-American*, March 13, 1948: 24.

28   Kelcie Pegher, "The Little World Series of the West," *Carroll County Times* (Westminster, Maryland), June 25, 2013. https://archive.ph/20131105015410/http://www.carrollcountytimes.com/news/local/demolition-begins-at-former-henryton.

29   "Ex-Baltimore Elite Giants Hurler Dead," *Baltimore Afro-American*, June 12, 1948: 9.

DAVID WILLIAM "BILL" HARVEY

BY MATT CLEVER

Bill Harvey was a left-handed pitcher and outfielder who played parts of up to 21 years in the Negro Leagues, Mexico, and Puerto Rico. Though unimposing both physically (5-feet-8, 175 pounds) and statistically (31-52, 5.68 ERA in 140 official Negro League games), Harvey had a long and colorful career that was not without its share of memorable moments. Known as "a dapper dresser and an acknowledged ladies' man who was frequently fined for violating curfew,"[1] he was also a pretty fair hitter, and once hit three home runs in a game at Yankee Stadium.[2]

David William Harvey was born on March 23, 1908, in Clarksdale, Mississippi. At the time of the 1910 census, his parents, Lewis and Sarah Harvey, were living in the home of her parents, Price and Jennie Donaldson. The Donaldsons were farmers; Lewis Harvey was listed as a laborer who did street work. Two of Sarah's sisters, both laundresses for private families, lived there as well.

After "learning baseball on the sandlots of Mississippi and Memphis, Harvey had his first taste of professional ball with the Memphis Red Sox ... when they were in the Negro Southern League."[3] Though some sources claim he may have debuted as early as 1926, no reliable records exist for the NSL prior to 1932. On April 16 of that year, in Memphis, Harvey pitched a six-hit, 3-0 shutout for the Red Sox against Rube Foster's Chicago American Giants that completed a sweep of a three-game exhibition series between the two teams.[4] In May Harvey garnered two more wins, a 14-6 triumph over the Cleveland Cubs and a 5-4 victory over the Nashville Elite Giants in which "he won his own game ... when he clouted a home run with two runners on bases in the seventh inning."[5] By the end of the season Harvey had posted a 3-2 record with Memphis and also was 0-1 in two appearances for the Monroe Monarchs, another member team of the NSL.

Harvey opened the 1933 season with Memphis and developed into a frontline hurler as the Red Sox captured the first-half championship in the NSL.[6] Harvey had already become so well-known that he received a nickname. The July 1, 1933, *Chicago Defender* reported that "Son Harvey showed Howard from across the river that it is very hard to secure enough hits while in the Red Sox park to take a victory from him" as it gave an account of Memphis's three-game sweep of Little Rock; Harvey won the middle game by a 4-1 score.[7] In mid-July Harvey pitched a no-hitter in the abbreviated (six-inning) second game of a doubleheader against Nashville. Not only did he baffle the

Left-hander Bill Harvey. *Courtesy of Robert D. Retort.*

opposition hitters, but it was his bat that drove in the only run in the 1-0 triumph. According to a news account of the game, in the bottom of the sixth and final inning, Memphis second baseman Marlin Carter "beat out a hit to the infield, [left fielder Harvey] Peterson laced a two-bagger to right field, Carter going to third; on the first ball pitched, Harvey laid down a perfect bunt and Carter crossed the plate with the only run needed for victory."[8]

Harvey's pitching gained notice and, later in the season, he debuted in the much stronger and more prominent Negro National League (NNL)– first, briefly, with Bingo DeMoss's Cleveland Giants, and then with the soon-to-be legendary Pittsburgh Crawfords. Early in his career Harvey developed a reputation both for wildness and for his willingness to knock a batter down. Among his repertoire of pitches was one that he called a "needleball." The needleball created what he called an "overload" which only Harvey could sense, and which he could somehow use to his advantage.[9] That advantage was not yet apparent in his short stint in the NNL in 1933, as he posted a 23.63 ERA in 2 2/3 innings with Cleveland and a 9.63 ERA in 5 2/3 innings with Pittsburgh.

Fortunately for the 1933 Crawfords, they did not require any contribution from Harvey to win the second half of the NNL's split-season format. The club featured five future Hall of Famers: catcher Josh Gibson, center fielder Cool Papa Bell, third baseman Judy Johnson, ace right-hander Satchel Paige, and manager-infielder Oscar Charleston. With a roster like that, it is no wonder that Harvey played sporadically for two years, unable to establish a full-time spot for himself until 1935. Charleston did whatever he could to help his young southpaw survive against some of the best hitters in the world. "Charleston could take a ball in his hands and loosen the cover. If you wanted to throw a cut ball, you just gave it to him," said Harvey years later.[10]

Harvey began the 1934 season back in Memphis; however, neither he nor the team fared as well as in the previous season. This is not to say that there were no highlights. On May 26, Harvey's arm and bat again served him well in a 5-3 victory over the Birmingham Black Barons. It was reported that "Bill Harvey, durable Red Sox hurler, had a swell day Saturday afternoon. ... On the mound he limited the invaders to six hits and at bat the lefthander got four hits out of four times up, knocked in a couple of runs and crossed the plate twice himself."[11] The very next day wasn't too shabby either: Harvey entered the nightcap of a doubleheader in relief and earned another win. Once more Harvey helped his own cause as he went 1-for-2 at the plate and scored a run in Memphis's seven-inning, 5-4 triumph.[12]

On June 3 Harvey struck out 12 Monroe Monarchs but his effort was not enough in a tough 8-7 loss in the first game of a doubleheader; Monroe also captured the second game, 4-2, as the Red Sox hit a rough patch in their season. Harvey was also inconsistent, as is evidenced by the report of a series that Memphis played against the 24th Infantry team from Fort Benning, Georgia. The press noted, "Bill Harvey fanned eight of the infantry boys in the nightcap [a 5-1 Memphis victory] even though he was somewhat careless in his mound work."[13]

Inconsistent or not, Harvey was a lefty, and southpaws have always been in demand in baseball. Thus, Harvey made his return to Pittsburgh for the 1935 season. The 1935 Crawfords are considered by many to be the greatest Negro League team ever assembled. Harvey's role was as a spot starter and long reliever, and he posted a 2-3 record with a 4.18 ERA in 51⅔ innings over 12 appearances (5 starts). He collected two hits as a relief pitcher in a 6-2 win over the Philadelphia Stars on May 27, then did so again as the starting pitcher on June 29 when he defeated the Newark Dodgers.

Harvey contributed less to the team's incredible victory on August 24 at Cole's Park in Chicago. He was hit hard by the Chicago American Giants and was no longer in the game when the Crawfords rallied from a 7-4 deficit in the ninth inning to tie the score. Pittsburgh went on to win the game in the 19th inning.

Four weeks later, on September 23, manager Charleston chose Harvey to start the seventh game of the NNL championship series against the New York Cubans, at Parkside Park in Philadelphia. The clincher was truly a team effort as Harvey pitched effectively, Charleston and Gibson each homered, right-hander Roosevelt Davis extinguished a New York rally in the ninth, and the Crawfords became the champions of the Negro National League.

However, the luster of that 1935 championship quickly wore off. The Crawfords' owner, influential Black businessman/racketeer/philanthropist Gus Greenlee, found himself in need of cash in 1936 to pay off a hit on a heavily played number in his gambling racket.[14] The ballpark he had built, Greenlee Field, was badly in need of maintenance (and ultimately was seized by the City of Pittsburgh to make way for a housing project).[15] Harvey stuck with the Crawfords through all this turmoil, and posted a 3-4 record in 1936 for a Crawfords team that won a second consecutive NNL championship, though this time by virtue of having the league's best record rather than via a championship series.

Harvey stuck with the Crawfords, though he continued to be used sparingly. Even after Greenlee saw a mass defection of his players to the Dominican Republic in 1937, Harvey's role on the team still did not expand. In fact, an early May news article stated, "(Pitcher Ernest 'Spoon' Carter) and Harvey, serving their third year in Crawfords' uniforms, will be forced to give better performances if they expect to remain in fast company."[16] Harvey struggled to a 1-3 record and 6.00 ERA in 1937, and went 3-3 with a 5.40 ERA in 1938; he pitched slightly more than 40 innings for the Crawfords in both campaigns. By 1938, the club was struggling both on the field and at the gate, with Charleston as its only remaining future Hall of Famer, and Greenlee's financial situation had become so bad that he had no choice but to sell the team. Under a new ownership team led by Hank Rigney, the Crawfords moved west to Toledo, Ohio, for the 1939 season.

Initially, Harvey did not rejoin the Crawfords in their new city. Instead, he began the early part of the year with the Baltimore Elite Giants. On April 9, 1939 Harvey started what turned out to be a slugfest at Atlanta's Booker T. Washington High School. The Elite Giants came from behind to win, 13-12. Harvey earned a save the following day when he tossed three scoreless innings to finish off another wild win, 11-10. After Harvey took over, the Atlanta Black Crackers batters, who "had been murdering the ball, were looking very silly at the plate, driving weak rollers back at (Harvey), producing lazy infield popups, or actually cutting arcs into just so much gentle air as third strikes breezed past," according to "Melancholy" Jones of the *Atlanta Daily World*.[17] Harvey turned in his best performance as a member of the Elite Giants in the second game of a Sunday doubleheader at Nashville on April 23 when he allowed only one hit – a single by Chicago American Giants first baseman Ed Young – in a seven-inning win.

Soon, Harvey sojourned to Toledo, where he rejoined the Crawfords. He made only five starts for the team, which moved from the NNL to the Negro American League (NAL) in midseason, and put up a 0-1 record, and he also started a few games in left field. The Crawfords played to a 4-5-1 record in the NNL and an 8-11-1 mark in the NAL in what can best be described as a lost season.

In the fall of 1939 Harvey reunited with the Baltimore Elite Giants when they traveled west to play in the California Winter League, the only organized league in which teams of Negro Leaguers could compete against teams composed of White major leaguers and minor leaguers. Before a crowd of 5,000 in Hollywood on October 11, Harvey started a game opposite Cleveland Indians fireballer Bob Feller, the American League's top pitcher that year. Harvey hit a triple and dueled Feller to a 2-2 tie into the late innings. Harvey's teammates broke through against Feller's relievers, and Harvey was credited with the win as the Elite Giants triumphed 5-3 over a squad called Pirrone's Major League All-Stars.[18]

In the spring of 1940 Harvey's best offer came from Los Industriales de Monterrey, so the 32-year-old headed south of the border to the Mexican League. Battling a sore arm for much of 1940, he went 7-9 with a 4.64 ERA between Monterrey, for which team he received all of his pitching decisions, and Los Alijadores de Tampico. The hot, dry air and high elevations made the league a notoriously tough one for pitchers. When Harvey registered for the World War II draft in October that year, he listed his occupation as "Unemployed Baseball Player Tampico [sic] Mex Team," perhaps indicating that his prospects of returning to the Mexican League seemed dim after his performance in 1940.

Return he did, however. Harvey pitched for Tampico in 1941, but with his arm still ailing, he posted a 2-7 record with a 7.60 ERA, and issued 44 walks in 58 innings. Nevertheless, Harvey, like many other veteran Negro Leaguers of the era, enjoyed playing in Mexico. Not only did they earn more money than they could in the States but, even more importantly, they did not have to live like second-class citizens because of their color. Quite the contrary, the players were treated like kings. "We live in the best hotels, we eat in the best restaurants, and go anyplace we care to. We are heroes here," observed Hall of Famer Willie Wells, who faced Harvey as a member of Los Azules de Veracruz.[19]

Harvey's struggles in Mexico did not deter the Elite Giants from bringing him back to Baltimore for the 1942 season. The Elites also lured pitcher Tom Glover and hard-hitting outfielder Burnis "Wild Bill" Wright out of the Mexican League that year, and they were poised to contend for the pennant after having finished second to the Homestead Grays the year before. On April 12, during the spring exhibition season, Harvey took part in his second career no-hitter, though this one was a combined effort rather than a solo job. The *New York Amsterdam News* reported on the no-no:

"A seven-inning, no hit, no run performance highlighted the twin victory the Baltimore Elite Giants scored over the Cuban stars at Pelican Stadium [in New Orleans], April 12. The scores were 4-0 and 4-3.

"Two lefthanders, Jonas Gaines and Bill Harvey, shared the 4-0 triumph. Gaines went four innings, Harvey three ..."[20]

Harvey pitched well enough that he made the Elite Giants' regular-season roster, and he entered Baltimore's Opening Day game in relief in the top of the 10th inning. On May 10, in front of a crowd of 5,500, the Elite Giants defeated the Philadelphia Stars, 9-8, in their home opener at Bugle Field. Catcher Roy Campanella, the future Brooklyn Dodgers Hall of Famer, hit a bases-loaded single in the 10th inning that "produced the winning tally for Tom Wilson's hirelings" as "Bill Harvey hurled the final inning for the Elites and was rewarded with the winning pitcher honors."[21]

The Elite Giants caught fire in the second half of the season, but the Grays, who had already won the first half, kept pace with them. Going into their Labor Day doubleheader at Philadelphia, the Elite Giants needed a sweep of the Stars and a loss by the Grays in order to win the second half and the right to play the Grays for the championship. Harvey started the first game of that doubleheader and rose to the occasion as he tossed a masterful one-hit shutout. But the Grays outslugged the Newark Eagles, 14-12, to clinch their third straight Negro National League championship.[22]

In 1943 Harvey's ERA+ of 109 showed him to be a roughly league-average pitcher in spite of his dismal 2-11 record for a Baltimore team that finished in fifth place in the NNL with an 18-26-3 league record (25-42-3 overall). As usual, Harvey also managed to get a few starts in the outfield and at first base, and he batted .231 with one home run. The reason for the Elite Giants' rapid decline was attrition. In late April, it was reported that "[t]he Baltimore Elite Giants began preparations for the coming Negro National League camping here at Bugle field, with a war-time squad of six players, and a new manager in the person of George 'Tubby' Scales."[23] Campanella, shortstop Pee Wee Butts, and outfielder Bill Wright had defected to the Mexican League while second baseman Sammy Hughes and pitcher Bill Barnes had been lost to military service. In a down season, one highlight for Harvey was his seven-inning, one-hit, 2-0 shutout of the Grays on June 4 at Bugle Field.[24] On August 1 Harvey made his only appearance in the annual East-West All-Star Game at Comiskey Park in Chicago. He entered in the sixth inning, tossed a scoreless frame for the East team in a 2-1 loss, and then was relieved by Hall of Famer Leon Day, who remained a close friend of Harvey's into old age.[25]

In 1944 Baltimore improved its record to 34-36 in the NNL (41-39 overall), but that was still only good enough for a fourth-place finish. Harvey had a 1-4 record with an inflated 7.24 ERA. On September 2, 1944, it was reported that Harvey was among the list of players who had been signed by Gus Greenlee for his second incarnation of the Pittsburgh Crawfords. This new Crawfords team competed in the United States League in 1945 and 1946. Greenlee helped to found the league to compete against the established NNL and NAL, and he was up to his old tricks of raiding other teams for talent. According to the news article, "Greenlee, who figures this winter to take his team to Cuba or South America for a full season of Winter League competition, will be one up on his competitors since he is giving his men year-round employment at high salary."[26]

Greenlee apparently took his new Crawfords to Mexico for Winter League play – rather than to Cuba as had been anticipated – because that is where the FBI eventually tracked Harvey down after he had been drafted into the Army and had not reported for service. The FBI escorted him back to the United States, and Harvey fulfilled his duty to his country.[27] He joined the Army on December 1, 1944, and served through August 13, 1945, when he was given a medical discharge. Since Harvey was stationed at Fort George G. Meade in the Baltimore area, he was still able to play for the Elite Giants at times during his enlistment, and he pitched to a 2-0 record with a 2.55 ERA in 17⅔ innings in three appearances.

By this time, Harvey had settled down enough to marry. His wife, Charlotte Cager, was a 1930 graduate of Frederick Douglass High School in Baltimore, the only high school in the city open to Black students at that time.[28] She recalled the experience of attending Negro League ballgames in Baltimore to watch her husband: "It was a nice crowd. That is, there were very few arguments among the fans. I would get a ride with someone, or take the old number 27 bus line. Vernon Green [owner of the Elite Giants] always had my ticket, which I think cost 25 cents, in an envelope, for a box seat right behind home plate."[29]

When Harvey attended spring training with the Elite Giants in 1946, it was noted that he had "established himself as something of a Peck's Bad Boy" – an early twentieth-century term for a prankster or rule-breaker – "and will have to mend his ways greatly if he hopes to stick."[30] For whatever reason, he failed to stick with Baltimore that spring. A brief appearance with the New York Black Yankees later in 1946 was Harvey's last hurrah as a professional ballplayer. His reputation for wildness and willingness to knock a batter down had not diminished over the decades.

At a Negro Leagues reunion in Kentucky in 1981, Harvey was kidded by Ted Page, whose arm Harvey had broken with a pitched ball in 1935. It was the first time the two men had seen each other in more than 40 years. It was also remembered that Harvey had broken two of Vic Harris's ribs in a game against the Crawfords' crosstown rivals, the Grays.[31]

Bill and Charlotte Harvey lived the rest of their lives in a predominantly Black neighborhood in West Baltimore, not far from Leon Day's house. "Harvey is older than a New Guinea coconut tree," said Day in 1987. "And they have to be a hundred years old before they bear coconuts!"[32]

Bill Harvey died in his adopted hometown of Baltimore on March 3, 1989, a few weeks shy of his 81st birthday, and was buried in Maryland National Memorial Park in Laurel.

Acknowledgment

Thanks to Frederick C. Bush, co-editor of this volume, for providing genealogical research as well as numerous articles about Bill Harvey's early years with Memphis, his later years with Baltimore, and his extremely brief stint with the second iteration of Gus Greenlee's Pittsburgh Crawfords.

SOURCES

In addition to the sources cited in the Notes, the author also consulted the following:

Holway, John. *The Complete Book of Baseball's Negro Leagues: The Other Half of Baseball History* (Fern Park, Florida: Hastings House, 2001).

Ancestry.com, used to determine Harvey's genealogy and for his military draft and enlistment records.

Unless otherwise indicated, all statistical data and team records were taken from the Seamheads Negro League Player Database:

seamheads.com/NegroLgs/player.php?playerID=harve01bil

NOTES

1   James A. Riley, *The Biographical Encyclopedia of the Negro Baseball League* (New York: Carroll & Graf, 1994), 367. The question of how many years Harvey played revolves around the 1926-31 seasons. Riley

states that he played those seasons, but there has been no confirmation of that in other sources.

2   Riley, *Biographical Encyclopedia,* 366.

3   Riley, *Biographical Encyclopedia,* 366.

4   "Memphis Tops Jim Brown's Team, 5 to 0," *Chicago Defender,* April 23, 1932: 8; "Memphis Red Sox and Birmingham Barons Open Today," *Atlanta Daily World,* April 21, 1932: 5.

5   "Memphis Takes 3 Straight from Cleveland," *Chicago Defender,* May 21, 1932: 9; "Memphis Drops Nashville from League Lead; Wins Three Games," *Chicago Defender,* May 28, 1932: 9.

6   For 1933 NSL standings, see negrosouthernleaguemuseumresearch-center.org/Portals/0/Negro%20Southern%20League/Negro%20Southern%20League%20%20(1920-1951)STANDINGS.pdf.

7   "Memphis Wins Three in Arkansas/Sox Increase Lead in Southern Loop," *Chicago Defender,* July 1, 1933: 9.

8   "Harvey in No-Hit No-Run Win," *Pittsburgh Courier,* July 15, 1933: 15.

9   Riley, *Biographical Encyclopedia,* 367.

10   Bruce Anderson, "Time Worth Remembering," *Sports Illustrated,* July 6, 1981: 51-52.

11   "Memphis Cops Birmingham Series/Harvey Stars for Victorious Nine," *Chicago Defender,* June 2, 1934: 15.

12   "Memphis Cops Birmingham Series."

13   "Memphis Red Sox Whip the Ft. Benning 9," *Chicago Defender,* June 16, 1934: 17.

14   Riley, *Biographical Encyclopedia,* 339.

15   See Jeb Stewart, "Greenlee Field," in the present volume.

16   "Crawfords Send Out SOS and Get Brewer," *Chicago Defender,* May 1, 1937: 14.

17   "Melancholy" Jones, "Black Crax Again Nosed Out by Baltimore, 11-10," *Atlanta Daily World,* April 11, 1939: 5.

18   William F. McNeil, *The California Winter League: America's First Integrated Professional Baseball League* (Jefferson, North Carolina: McFarland & Company, 2002), 181.

19   James A. Riley, *Dandy, Day, and the Devil* (Cocoa, Florida: TK Publishers, 1987), 109.

20   "Elites Score No Hit-Run Win/Cubans Lose Exhibitions, 4-0 and 4-3," *New York Amsterdam News,* April 25, 1942: 12.

21   "Campanella's Homer Beats Phillies, 9 to 8," *Chicago Defender,* May 16, 1942: 20.

22   David E. Hubler and Joshua H. Drazen, *The Nats and the Grays: How Baseball in the Nation's Capital Survived WWII and Changed the Game Forever* (Lanham, Maryland: Rowman & Littlefield, 2015), 82.

23   Dick Powell, "Baltimore Gets Ready/Loss of Snow, Butts, and Campanella Hurts," *Chicago Defender,* April 24, 1943: 21.

24   "Baltimore Wins Couple from Grays," *Chicago Defender,* June 5, 1943: 20.

25   Riley, *Dandy, Day, and the Devil,* 109.

26   "Greenlee Raids Black Yanks in War on NNL/Takes Players from Grays, Elites, Chicago for Crawfords; Will Play in Cuba Winter Loop," *New York Amsterdam News,* September 2, 1944: 6.

27   Riley, *Biographical Encyclopedia,* 367.

28   "National Register Information System," *National Register of Historic Places,* National Park Service, March 13, 2009.

29   Bob Luke, *The Baltimore Elite Giants: Sport and Society in the Age of Negro League Baseball* (Baltimore: Johns Hopkins University Press, 2009), 31.

30   "Elite Pitching Is No Problem; 11 Seek Berths," *New York Amsterdam News*, April 13, 1946: 12.

31   Anderson, 51.

32   Riley, *Dandy, Day, and the Devil*, 57.

CRUSH HOLLOWAY

BY DAVE WILKIE

"He was what could be classified as a crazy ball player. You could never defense him well or pitch him certain kinds of pitches because he was so unpredictable. If you were nine runs down, Holloway might try to steal home if he thought it might help to motivate the team in their comeback effort."
–Clint Thomas[1]

Crush Holloway was an all-around ballplayer, often hitting leadoff for some of the most storied teams in Negro League history where he had a knack for getting on base and wreaking havoc on the base paths, doing anything needed to guide his team to victory. Holloway learned his aggressive baserunning style by emulating his idol, Ty Cobb. Holloway explained this unlikely connection. "His picture used to come in Bull Durham tobacco. Showed the way he'd slide. That was my hero. I said, 'I want to slide like Ty Cobb. I want to run the bases like him.'"[2] Holloway also played for a lot of teams and had a penchant for jumping from one to another. So much so that while playing for manager and future Hall of Famer Pete Hill in Baltimore, Holloway was nicknamed "The Frog" due to his constant hopping from team to team.[3]

Crush Christopher Columbus Holloway, when talking about his early life and unique moniker, told this to baseball historian John Holway in 1969:

Crush, that's my real name, that ain't no nickname. And I'll tell you how I got it. The day I was born, September 16, 1896, down in Hillsboro, Texas, my father was fixing to go see a "crash," a collision.[4] They'd take two old locomotive engines and crash them together for excitement, sort of a fair, and my father was going to see it. Before he got on the train, somebody pulled him off and said, "Your wife is about to have a child." And when I turned out to be a boy, he named me "Crush." That's how I got my name. Oh, I've got some middle names, Crush Christopher Columbus Holloway, but I don't use those other names. I just use Crush,'cause I like Crush better.[5]

Holloway's father, Thomas Holloway, was born on August 10, 1866, in South Carolina and his mother, Dora Criner, was born October 1, 1869, in Texas.[6] The couple had eight children and life couldn't have been easy on the family farm, where Thomas and his oldest son, Crush, toiled endlessly in the fields

Crush Holloway with the Baltimore Black Sox. Courtesy National Baseball Hall of Fame and Library.

producing cotton, corn, and wheat. The Holloway family owned the farm and Thomas was also a schoolteacher, although his son didn't make it past the fourth grade.[7] Holloway explained how difficult his early life was:

I was the oldest boy, see. Had five sisters, but they couldn't do nothing on the farm. I was the only boy he could depend on, you know what I mean? I had brothers, but they were so young, ten to twelve years younger than me. They couldn't do anything. That's why Pop would depend on me. I was his man, had to do everything. That's what I did until I got grown.[8]

Four of Holloway's sisters, Verna (1898), Zelma (1902), Ruth (1909), and Tommie (1916), were all younger than him; only Olga (1894) was older. Holloway also had two much younger brothers, Richard (1904) and Tyree (1905).

Holloway so badly wanted to escape the labors of the family farm that he attempted to enlist in the US Army during World War I, but quotas kept him out until his chances faded with the ending of the conflict. Finally, at the age of 21, Holloway left with his father's blessing to pursue a career in baseball. Holloway recalled his parting conversation with his father like this: "My father said, 'You're a grown man, you can do what you want to do, but I want you to stay here with me.' I said, 'No! I'm going to play baseball. That's the end of it, Pop. I got to go.' He was a good father, didn't try to hold me. He knew I did my chores right. So he let me go."[9]

As a kid Holloway snuck off on Sundays to play sandlot ball with his friends until the sun went down. Back on the farm, he hit pebbles with a broomstick and imagined he was his favorite hitter, Frank "Home Run" Baker, smashing homers into the distance.[10] Holloway's dream became a reality in 1919 when he suited up for his first professional team, the Waco Black Navigators. The team struggled mightily for the first three months of the season until it was sold to a man named L.W. Moore and moved to San Antonio to become the formidable Black Aces.[11]

The 1919 San Antonio Black Aces were a loaded squad with talent that included such Negro League stalwarts as Hall of Famer Biz Mackey, Steel Arm Davis, Robert "Highpockets" Hudspeth, Johnny Jones, and Namon Washington. The *San Antonio Evening News* compared second baseman Holloway to Eddie Collins and praised him in a September 19, 1919, column, writing, "He covers about as much ground as a big top at the circus, and they never come down there too hot for him."[12] Black and White fans alike rallied around the team, causing the *San Antonio Evening News* to also exclaim, "The Black Aces would give any Negro club in the country a battle."[13]

By season's end it was determined that the San Antonio Black Aces would face off against the Dallas Black Marines to determine the Texas Negro League champion and collect a cash prize of $1,000. The Black Aces sported a record of 45-10 and the Black Marines were right on their tails at 51-17.[14] This ferociously fought series came down to a deciding fifth game when the hometown Black Aces quickly fell into a five-run deficit. Clawing back, the Aces managed to tie it up, 5-5, going into the ninth inning when Steel Arm Davis smashed a double to drive in the winning run.[15] The win soon turned bittersweet, though, as 1919 turned out to be the only season of existence for the champion San Antonio Black Aces.

C.I. Taylor, owner of the Indianapolis ABCs, knew talent when he saw it and he quickly pounced and offered contracts to six of the Black Aces' best players. Holloway, Henry Blackmon, Highpockets Hudspeth, Biz Mackey, Morris Williams, and Namon Washington were all set to join the ABCs in the inaugural season of the newly formed Negro National League, but Holloway balked.[16] Holloway described to Holway the dismantling of his beloved Black Aces and why he refused to join his teammates in Indianapolis: "It broke our club all to pieces. I didn't go that year. I didn't want to go 'cause I was mad. I was so mad I didn't know what to do." Holloway cooled down enough to join the ABCs the following season, in 1921, and later called the 1922 ABCs the greatest team he ever played on.[17]

The *Indianapolis News* welcomed Holloway to the team with this glowing mention: "Crush Holloway, who will take care of the keystone sack, hails from Texas. He is a big fellow, handles himself with ease around second and gets the ball away in good form. A reputation as a hitter precedes him and some of the players who have seen him slam the ball are loud in their praises of him. He bats from the left side of the plate, and hits them far and often."[18]

Holloway was one of many great Black ballplayers from the Lone Star state that included Cyclone Joe Williams, Willie Wells, Hilton Smith, Rube and Bill Foster, Jesse Hubbard, and fellow Black Ace and ABC teammate Biz Mackey. He was especially fond of Mackey, of whom he said, "And he was funny. He was jolly, especially with those fast men who said they were

gonna steal on him. When he'd throw them out, he'd get such a kick out of it, he'd fall down laughing."[19]

Holloway was never shy about heaping praise on his fellow teammates and the man standing to his right in the ABCs outfield was no exception. Holloway considered Oscar Charleston to be the greatest defensive outfielder he'd ever witnessed and said that if Charleston "had time to get under a fly ball, he'd walk, he had it timed, he'd walk fast. And he'd do acrobatics. People used to come out and see him do his stunts in the outfield."[20] Holloway also credited ABCs owner and manager C.I. Taylor with helping him convert to the outfield and refining his base-running skills.[21]

While Holloway was a consistent .300 hitter and above-average right fielder in his three years with the ABCs, the team never quite reached its potential, playing second fiddle to the powerhouse Chicago American Giants and Kansas City Monarchs.

The California Winter League was a Southern California league that presented the perfect destination for the best Black baseball stars to showcase their talents. Beginning with Rube Foster's 1910 Leland Giants until the integration of White major-league baseball, Black superstars like Cyclone Joe Williams, Bullet Rogan, Cool Papa Bell, Pop Lloyd, and Satchel Paige were fixtures in the circuit.[22] These players dominated their White counterparts, winning more than 60 percent of their matchups, including an incredible 13 of 16 championships between 1924 and 1939.[23]

Holloway's first appearance in the CWL took place in 1922-23 with the St. Louis All-Stars, but he shined most brightly with the CWL champion Philadelphia Royal Giants in 1925-26. Featuring a stacked lineup consisting of old friend Biz Mackey, Rap Dixon, Bullet Rogan, and Newt Allen, Holloway and his band easily outdistanced the White King Soapsters to capture the title.[24] Holloway led his team with a .371 batting average, swiped 10 bases, and led the league with 59 hits in 41 games. Overall, in six winter seasons played on the West Coast, Holloway batted .303 in 476 at-bats.[25]

After the 1923 season the Indianapolis ABCs were raided of some of their best players, including Oscar Charleston and Holloway. Holloway signed with the team he would be most associated with, the Baltimore Black Sox, citing money as his motivation for moving east. Holloway was making $150 a month with the ABCs and $350 to $375 with the Black Sox. Of his jump to the Black Sox, he said: "Man, you know we were going to come here."[26] Holloway had a stellar first season with the Black Sox, hitting .324 with 18 stolen bases, and he credited manager Pete Hill for his improvement at the plate. "He's the man taught me how to hit to left field," Holloway explained. "I was pulling the ball. Ball on the outside, I was pulling to right. He gave me a bigger bat [and said,] 'Now knock that third baseman down. Just step up in front of the plate, hit the ball out in front, see?' "Oh he was a great hitter."[27]

Baltimore's march toward the pennant ended abruptly with the sudden passing of third baseman Henry Blackmon. This, coupled with an unbalanced schedule in which Hilldale lost and played more games than the Black Sox, allowed Hilldale to capture the flag and earn a spot in the first-ever Negro League World Series against the Kansas City Monarchs, denying the Black Sox their chance at immortality.[28]

When not taking advantage of the warm California sunshine, Holloway was found tearing around the bases and outfields of the Cuban Winter League. The 1924-25 winter season was Holloway's first venture to the island and he was in good hands with the Habana team and legendary Cuban Hall of Fame manager Miguel González. There wasn't a shortage of star power on the Habana team: Holloway shared the field with Cristóbal Torriente, Martín Dihigo, and Rats Henderson, but the team finished a distant second place to the Almendares team despite Holloway's .311 average. Holloway returned to Cuba just once more, in 1928-29, and seemed to prefer spending his winters playing ball in California.[29]

For the next four seasons, 1925 to 1928, Holloway patrolled the outfield for the perennial bridesmaids the Baltimore Black Sox. The team was never able to fire on all cylinders during Holloway's tenure, but it featured a powerful lineup that included a group referred to as the "Four Horsemen," a quartet that consisted of Jud Wilson, John Beckwith, Heavy Johnson, and Holloway.[30] Holloway also was often singled out for his spectacular displays of fielding and in 1926 he was regarded as the second best Eastern League fielder after Oscar Charleston and lauded as a "Ball Hawk" by the *Baltimore Afro-American*.[31] His personal highlights with the Black Sox were many, but a few stood out. In a late July 1927 doubleheader sweep of the Brooklyn Royal Giants, which saw the Black Sox score 20 runs and collect 28 hits, Holloway smashed four safeties, scored four runs, and stole home against fireballer Dick "Cannonball" Redding.[32] In another doubleheader sweep, this time of the Bacharach Giants on May 10, 1928, Holloway lit up the scoresheet with four hits, including a double, triple, home run and a stolen base.[33]

Holloway was a phenomenal basestealer and certainly ranked among the all-time greats. Intimidation may have played a large role in his success. Cool Papa Bell, perhaps the greatest basestealer of them all, explained: "Some guys even sharpened their spikes with a file. Crush Holloway was one. I suppose he wanted to be like Ty Cobb."[34] In an incident on July 8, 1926, Holloway spiked mild-mannered Judy Johnson so badly that Johnson went after him with a bat.[35] On July 25, 1931, Holloway almost caused a riot when he once again took out Johnson, this time almost tearing the third basemen's pants off. Holloway was ejected from the game for unnecessary roughness as the fans swarmed the field.[36]

Double Duty Radcliffe described another Holloway run-in: "One guy cut me, gave me five stitches. His name was Crush Holloway. He came sliding home and cut open my leg. Two nights later I pitched against him and threw one behind his head about 100 miles an hour. He said, 'Ain't no use doin' that, Duty. You could'a killed me!' I said, "Man, look where you cut me!" He said, 'I'm sorry. I beg my pardon.' He bought me beer all night."[37] Holloway had a chance to defend himself in his 1969

interview with John Holway: "Stealing? Oh, I was pretty good. That's what they say anyway. Yeah, I made them jump down there on second base. They were scared of me 'cause I'd say, I'm gonna jump on you. I wouldn't really jump on them, just try to scare them. I didn't want to hurt anybody. But I filed my spikes, that's true. Most fast men used to do that. We didn't intend to hurt anybody, though, just scare them, that's all. Naw, I wouldn't hurt anybody for anything in the world. Unless it's necessary."[38]

In late January of 1929, in a blockbuster deal, Holloway was traded to Ed Bolden's Hilldale Club, also known as the Daisies, along with second baseman Dick Jackson for Merven "Red" Ryan and Frank Warfield. The *Philadelphia Tribune* commented, "Crush will fit in as a lead-off man that is gifted with the knack of getting on the sacks and in turn can sock the apple at a lively clip."[39] *Pittsburgh Courier* columnist W. Rollo Wilson sympathized with the Black Sox for losing Holloway, writing, "By my faith, replacing him with a fly-chaser of equal ability isn't a job you can leave to the janitor. While there are a few who are the peer of the talented Crush none of them is on the mart for sale or barter."[40]

Crush Holloway depicted with the 1924 Baltimore Black Sox. Artwork by Graig Kreindler 5"x7" oils on linen mounted to panel. From the collection of Jay Caldwell, Baseball Art LLC

In an unfortunate twist of fate, Holloway's former team, the Black Sox finally reached their potential in 1929 and ran away with the American Negro League crown, winning both the first and second halves to claim the title without him. Holloway's new team finished a distant third. despite the presence of four future Hall of Famers – Biz Mackey, Judy Johnson, Martín Dihigo, and Oscar Charleston. One has to wonder if team chemistry was an issue with Holloway and Judy Johnson sharing the same field after their previous heated altercation. For his part, Holloway had a stellar season, hitting .296 and leading the league in stolen bases with 29 as reported by the secretary's office of the American Negro League.[41] Holloway's Hilldale stint was short and he bolted to the Detroit Stars in 1930 to fill the vacant spot in center field.[42] (He briefly returned to Hilldale in 1932 to witness the demise of the once-proud club.)

Holloway spent the entirety of the 1930 season manning the outfield for the second-half champions of the Negro National League, the Detroit Stars, but despite playing alongside the great Turkey Stearnes, the Stars faded losing an exciting seven-game series to Cool Papa Bell and his St. Louis Stars. Holloway played all seven games, scored eight runs, struck nine hits for a .310 average and had a sparkling .412 on-base average. Instead of reloading for another shot with Detroit, Holloway jumped back to an old favorite, the Baltimore Black Sox, for the 1931 season. Without him, the Stars suffered through a miserable final season, which turned out to be the last of their existence.

Holloway was 34 years old but showing no signs of slowing down. After a mid-July doubleheader against the Homestead Grays, the *Afro-American* commented that Holloway's "fielding in both games was little short of sensational."[43] Charley Walker, president of the Grays, heaped more praise on Holloway, stating, "Crush Holloway is one of the most powerful men on the offense in the game because of his hitting, base running and ability to get on."[44]

Holloway's services were never in more demand than in 1932, when he would display his penchant for hopping from team to team. He began the year with the Black Sox, but on May 24 he was released to the Hilldale Club to play left field.[45] His time with Hilldale was short and by early July he was suiting up for the New York Black Yankees. At this time "jumping" in search of a bigger paycheck was becoming a huge problem for Negro League baseball; even the mighty Homestead Grays had a difficult time fielding a team when five of their players bolted.[46] Holloway was on the field and batting third in a July 16 matchup with Satchel Paige and his Pittsburgh Crawfords. Paige no-hit the Black Yankees that day, winning 6-0 at Greenlee Field in the Steel City.[47]

Holloway was still with the Black Yankees in early March of 1933 when they took three of four games against a Cuban team in Puerto Rico as a spring-training warm-up.[48] Holloway sprained his ankle and missed some playing time.[49] He next turned up in 1933 back in Baltimore, but this time for the Baltimore Sox. The team lost the right to use the name Black Sox after failing to pay their taxes in 1930.[50] While the Sox were a mediocre team

all year, Holloway's season was packed with highlights. On May 30, in a doubleheader sweep of the Detroit Stars, he smacked a three-run homer and stole a base while covering center field and batting second for the Sox.[51] On June 18, in a twin-bill split with the Chicago American Giants, Holloway's brilliant play in the outfield was pointed out by the *Baltimore Afro-American:* "Crush Holloway proved a thorn in the side of the Giants, accepting five chances without an error, two of which were difficult running catches and one of which he took off the centerfield fence."[52] In a three-game sweep of the Detroit Stars at the end of June, Holloway was once again praised for his fielding, but also made his presence known with the lumber with six hits, including a double and two triples.[53] On July 23 the Sox clobbered the Bacharach Giants, outscoring them 28-11 and outhitting them 36-22 in a doubleheader massacre that featured six hits and five runs from Holloway.[54] The dog days of summer certainly didn't slow him down as he swatted five hits in six at-bats in a 17-13 loss to the Philadelphia Stars on July 30.[55]

Holloway, by now 37 years old, labored through a disastrous 1934 season with the next-to-last-place Philadelphia Bacharach Giants. He hit a meager .141 in 17 games. The next season he was relegated to backup status, splitting the season between the New York Black Yankees and the Brooklyn Eagles. As luck would have it, Holloway enjoyed one last hurrah when in 1936 he latched on with the New York Crusaders, one of the leading black traveling clubs in the East.[56] The Crusaders were a rag-tag bunch led by manager-pitcher Connie "Broadway" Rector, a 22-year veteran of the Negro Leagues. Besides Holloway, this fascinating team featured Dick Lundy, George Britt, Johnny "Schoolboy" Taylor, and Henry Spearman.[57] This is most likely the team Holloway was referring to when he told John Holway, "I retired in 1937. I was playing up in Albany, New York, then. We had one colored team in the league and all the rest were white, but we won the championship."[58]

Holloway seemed to be sipping from the fountain of youth while playing for the Brooklyn Royal Giants, also in 1936, when, in a doubleheader on June 21 against Bay Ridge, he swatted six hits in 10 at-bats with five runs and two stolen bases.[59] Even more unlikely, in early September, once again in a doubleheader against Bay Ridge, Holloway stroked four hits, but this time with an amazing three stolen bases on tired, 39-year-old legs.[60]

Holloway didn't hang up his spikes for good in 1937 as he claimed. He showed up in a box score for a team mysteriously called the Baltimore Black Sox in an early July 1939 16-1 loss to a New Jersey-based team, the Long Branch Greys. Baltimore's lone run is mentioned as "a prodigious circuit clout by Crush Holloway, Baltimore's touted slugger in the third round."[61] Oddly, there is, no known record of a Baltimore Black Sox team existing in 1939 outside of this newspaper reference. Holloway finally called it quits after what appears to be an emergency start for the Baltimore Elite Giants in a doubleheader played against the New York Cubans on August 27, 1939. In a game that was scheduled on the same day as the East-West All-Star contest, the 42-year-old Baltimore native Holloway filled in for all-star-bound Wild Bill Wright in right field for the Elites. Holloway proved to still have some thump left in his bat as he banged out at least two run-scoring flies, including a 400-foot drive that took a spectacular grab by center fielder José Vargas to rob him of a hit.[62] The Elite Giants upset the heavily favored Homestead Grays to win the championship that year, but Holloway was not around to enjoy it.

After his playing days were through, Holloway stayed in the game by umpiring for the Baltimore Elite Giants, but threats from players and shamefully low pay led him to be disillusioned with the profession quickly enough to state, "To umpire in the Negro National League is not a life's ambition of mine." Umpires' jobs were also subject to the whims of team owners who could easily let go of an umpire who ruled a close play against his team.[63] In June of 1947 the NNL requested that the Elite Giants stop using Holloway as an umpire effectively ending his career. NNL Vice President Alex Pompez accused Holloway of "action detrimental to the best interests of the game" in explaining his actions.[64]

Holloway was always regarded as a sharp dresser, and in April 1951 he was recognized as the "best dressed man" at an Easter parade in Baltimore.[65] Holloway and his wife, Buelah, settled down in Baltimore and ran a tailor shop together. They were married in 1921, but don't appear to have had any children.[66]

Crush Holloway died on June 24, 1972, from cancer and is buried at the Mount Calvary Cemetery in Baltimore, Maryland. When standout Negro League first baseman Dave "Showboat" Thomas was asked in 1944 to fill out his all-time team, he chose Holloway as his right fielder.[67] Sportswriter Marion Jackson, writing for the *Atlanta Daily World* in 1971, listed Holloway, along with familiar names like Josh Gibson, Cool Papa Bell, Buck Leonard, Ray Dandridge, Vic Harris, and Cannonball Redding as players he thought should be enshrined in Cooperstown.[68] There is no doubt that Holloway was one of the top outfielders of his era and undeniably one of the all-time greats on the basepaths.

When speaking about his time in the Negro Leagues just two months before his death in 1972, Holloway told John Holway: "Those were great players back then. But nobody knows about us anymore. If you put all these stories in the sporting pages, they could read all about it and understand how it was. But that's lost history, see? It's just past, that's all. Nobody's going to dig it up."[69] Thankfully, Mr. Holloway was wrong about that. One just wishes he could have been around to see it.

SOURCES

All statistics, unless otherwise noted, are from Seamheads.com.

NOTES

1   Phil Dixon, *The Negro Baseball Leagues: A Photographic History* (Mattituck, New York: Amereon Ltd., 1992), 145.

2   Richard Bak, *Turkey Stearnes and the Detroit Stars: The Negro Leagues in Detroit, 1919-1933* (Detroit: Wayne State University Press, 1995), 189.

3   Bob Luke, *Pete Hill: Black Baseball's First Superstar* (Jefferson, North Carolina: McFarland & Company Inc., 2023), 146.

4   Most sources list Holloway's birthdate as September 15 although there are some discrepancies regarding the year. On his World War I draft registration card, it's listed as 1896, but on his World War II draft card it's listed as 1899.

5   John Holway, *Voices From the Great Black Baseball Leagues* (New York: Da Capo Press Inc., 1992), 62. Hereafter: *Voices*.

6   Ancestry.com.

7   *Voices*, 63.

8   *Voices*, 63.

9   *Voices*, 64.

10 *Voices*, 62-63.

11 *Voices*, 64.

12 "A Dozen Black Aces Sure Make a Winning Hand," *San Antonio Evening News*, September 12, 1919: 11.

13 "Black Aces and Marines Split Games," *San Antonio Evening News*, July 5, 1919: 11.

14 Edwin Ocasio-Lopez, "*San Antonio Black Aces*" (San Antonio: Texas A&M University-San Antonio, 2020), 14.

15 Ocasio-Lopez, 15-16.

16 Paul Debono, *The Indianapolis ABCs: History of a Premier Team in the Negro Leagues* (Jefferson, North Carolina: McFarland & Company Inc., 1997), 87-89.

17 *Voices*, 66.

18 "A.B.C. Team Has Two New Infielders for 1921 Club," *Indianapolis News*, April 11, 1921: 18.

19 John Holway, *Blackball Stars: Negro League Pioneers* (Westport, Connecticut: Meckler Books, 1988), 221.

20 Jeremy Beer, *Oscar Charleston: The Life and Legend of Baseball's Greatest Forgotten Player* (Lincoln: University of Nebraska Press, 2019), 133.

21 Debono, *The Indianapolis ABCs*, 141.

22 William F. McNeil, *The California Winter League: America's First Integrated Professional Baseball League* (Jefferson, North Carolina: McFarland & Company Inc., 2002), 12.

23 McNeil, 237.

24 McNeil, 14.

25 McNeil, 112.

26 Neil Lanctot, *Fair Dealing & Clean Playing: The Hilldale Club and the Development of Black Professional Baseball, 1910-1932* (Syracuse, New York: Syracuse University Press, 1994), 107.

27 *Voices*, 67.

28 Bernard McKenna, *The Baltimore Black Sox: A Negro Leagues History, 1913-1936* (Jefferson, North Carolina: McFarland & Company Inc., 2020), 108-109.

29 Jorge S. Figueredo, *Who's Who in Cuban Baseball* (Jefferson, North Carolina: McFarland & Company Inc., 2003), 44, 45, 75, 353.

30 McKenna, *The Baltimore Black Sox*, 110.

31 "Second Best," *Baltimore Afro-American,* July 24, 1926: 6; "Three Additions Would Give Sox Greatest Team in Loop," *Baltimore Afro-American,* March 27, 1926: 7.

32 "The Charleston Deal Is Off," *Baltimore Afro-American,* July 30, 1927: 15.

33 "Black Sox Win Double Header," *Pittsburgh Courier,* May 12, 1928: A6.

34 Jim Bankes, *The Pittsburgh Crawfords* (Jefferson, North Carolina: McFarland & Company Inc., 2001), 86.

35 Lanctot, *Fair Dealing & Clean Playing,* 150.

36 "Hilldale Defeats Baltimore Black Sox," *New York Age,* August 1, 1931: 6.

37 Kyle P. McNary, *Ted "Double Duty" Radcliffe: 36 Years of Pitching & Catching in Baseball's Negro Leagues* (St. Louis Park, Minnesota: McNary Publishing, 1994), 152-153.

38 *Voices,* 60.

39 "The Stamp of Approval Awaits Warfield at Balto.," *Philadelphia Tribune,* March 14, 1929: 10.

40 W. Rollo Wilson, "Sport Shots: Popular Kid Chocolate," *Pittsburgh Courier,* March 16, 1929: A4.

41 "Smith Heads American Negro League in Final Averages," *New York Amsterdam News,* September 25, 1929: 12.

42 "DeMoss Takes His Detroit Stars to Balmy Nashville," *Chicago Defender,* April 12, 1930: 8.

43 "Sox and Grays Split Bill," *Baltimore Afro-American,* July 18, 1931: 12.

44 W. Rollo Wilson, "Sport Shots," *Pittsburgh Courier,* July 18, 1931: A4.

45 "Black Sox in League Lead," *New York Amsterdam News,* May 25, 1932: 13.

46 "Johnson, Tolan, Dues Score in Olympic Tests," *Baltimore Afro-American,* July 9, 1932: 15.

47 John B. Holway, *Josh and Satch: The Life and Times of Josh Gibson and Satchel Paige* (New York, New York: Carroll & Graf Publishers, Inc., 1991), 50.

48 "Black Yankees Win Series," *Baltimore Afro-American,* March 11, 1933: 16.

49 William F. McNeil, *Black Baseball Out of Season: Pay for Play Outside of the Negro Leagues* (Jefferson, North Carolina: McFarland & Company Inc., 2007), 114.

50 McKenna, *The Baltimore Black Sox,* 152.

51 "Sox Enter Win Column, Beat Detroit Twice," *Baltimore Afro-American,* June 10, 1933: 16.

52 "Sox Take Chicago," *Baltimore Afro-American,* June 24, 1933: 17.

53 "Sox Move Up by Taking Series From Detroit," *Baltimore Afro-American,* July 1, 1933: 16.

54 "Sox Pound Four Bacharach Hurlers to Win Twin Bill," *Baltimore Afro-American,* July 29, 1933: 16.

55 "Stars Win From Sox Both Ends of Double Bill," *Baltimore Afro-American.* August 5, 1933: 21.

56 "Pilot Drops Nolan Vamps,'" *Mount Vernon* (New York) *Argus,* May 28, 1936: 23.

57 "Allendale A's Play New York Crusaders," *Allentown* (Pennsylvania) *Morning Call,* May 22, 1936: 28.

58 *Voices,* 68.

59 "Bay Ridge Has Faith in Team Despite Losses," *Brooklyn Times Union,* June 22, 1936: 11.

60 "Bay Ridge Wins Double-Header," *Brooklyn Daily Eagle,* September 9, 1936: 40.

61 "Long Branch Nine Drives Out 17 Blows to Crush Black Sox for Third Straight Victory," *Asbury Park Press,* July 7, 1939: 13.

62 Ralph F. Boyd, "Elites and Cubans Split Twin Bill," *Baltimore Afro-American,* September 2, 1939: 23.

63 "Dan Burley's 'Confidentially Yours,'" *New York Amsterdam News,* October 27, 1945: 14.

64 "Washington's Bat Gives Locals Win," *Baltimore Afro-American,* June 7, 1947: 17.

65 "On the Avenue," *Baltimore Afro-American,* April 14, 1951: 9.

66 *Voices,* 60.

67 "Dan Burley's 'Confidentially Yours,'" *New York Amsterdam News,* May 27, 1944: 6B.

68 "Views Sports of the World," *Atlanta Daily World,* July 1, 1971: 12.

69 *Voices,* 69.

WILLIAM "BIG BILL" HOSKINS

BY THOMAS KERN

"One of the hardest hitters in baseball"
– *Atlanta Daily World*[1]

As is the case with so many Negro League ballplayers who were born before the twentieth century or just after it began, details of William Hoskins' birth and early years are wanting. His draft registration card, issued in 1940, offers as much clarity as is available about his origins, including his reported birth on March 14, 1914, in Tallahatchie County in north central Mississippi.[2]

In 1940 when he registered for the draft, Hoskins was well into his tour with the Baltimore Elite Giants, but the address on the registration card is listed as 749 Bey Street in Memphis, Tennessee. The residence could be explained by Hoskins' time with the Memphis Red Sox before he joined Baltimore. His wife is listed on the registration card, but only as Mrs. William Charles Hoskins; no first or maiden name is identified. It is possible that he married while in Tennessee and the address is his wife's family home. Penciled in on the registration card are two additional addresses, one at 31 Rutland Avenue, Baltimore, probably Hoskins' residence while playing for the Elite Giants. Scribbled above the Bey Street address is 144 E. Main Street in Charleston, Mississippi, the county seat of Tallahatchie County.

The Tallahatchie connection helps refine a search for records that offer further insight on Hoskins' origins. A 1920 Census record identifies a 6-year-old William Hoskins living with his family in Quitman County, Mississippi, not far from Charleston in neighboring Tallahatchie County.[3] This connection is further substantiated by newspaper reports in the mid-1930s identifying fledgling ballplayer Hoskins as a Charleston resident making his way into the baseball world.[4]

In 1936, at the age of 23, Bill Hoskins' initiation into Black professional baseball surfaced in newspaper stories placing him that season with the Claybrook Tigers[5] and the Cincinnati Tigers.[6] A common denominator for those teams was Ted "Double Duty" Radcliffe, whom John Claybrook, owner of the Claybrook Tigers (based across the Mississippi River from Memphis in Arkansas), hired as player-manager. Radcliffe noted in his autobiography that Claybrook enticed him to play for the Tigers after seeing him in action for Bismarck the year before.[7] After a time with Claybrook, Radcliffe jumped to the Cincinnati Tigers before moving on to the Memphis Red Sox, each time in search of a bigger paycheck.[8] No records have yet been unearthed of Hoskins on the Cincinnati squad, but the Radcliffe connection may have played a part in his movement among these three clubs.

Hoskins surfaced again in early 1937 when he joined the first of his Negro League teams of which we are certain: the St. Louis Stars (later the Detroit Stars). Hoskins' arrival in St. Louis was captured by the *Birmingham News*, noting that at the instigation of Stars manager Dizzy Dismukes, "Hoskins was purchased from Charleston" the prior winter. The Charleston connection speaks to Hoskins' hometown.[9]

By the mid-1930s, Dizzy Dismukes' Negro League playing career was long over, but he remained as a manager. He had managed the Columbus Bluebirds in 1933, a team on which Ted Radcliffe played. The Dismukes/Radcliffe tie may have contributed to Dismukes' recruiting of Hoskins for the Stars.

The *Pittsburgh Courier* affirmed Hoskins' presence on the team in early May,[10] but by the end of June, after only a half-dozen recorded games with St. Louis, he was in Detroit. "The Stars will have their latest acquisition Billy Hopkins [*sic*] in right field," the *Detroit Tribune* reported. "Hoskins, a young Mississippian has seen service with the Cincinnati Tigers and St. Louis Stars. He displayed rare hitting ability on the recent road trip of the Stars and as result has been placed fifth in the batting order."[11] It is not known why Hoskins moved teams, but the player he replaced in left field in Detroit, Eli Underwood, hit only .167 that year and Hoskins' bat was clearly an upgrade.

Hoskins starred against his former team in a five-game series in Detroit in July, swept by the hosts. "Bill Hoskins, the young pumpkin who had been placed in leftfield by the Stars, paced the onslaught on the Mound City pitchers with eight hits in 16 official times at the plate. Yes sir, Mississippi Bill was pounding the ball with a gusto that provoked smiles on the face of owner Jim Titus."[12] If ever a newspaper story captured the essence of Hoskins' gift to the game – his pure hitting ability – the *Detroit Tribune* did. This second coming of the Detroit Stars formed in 1937 by Jim Titus, was disbanded later that year, and Hoskins had to find another home in 1938 for his emerging talents.

That home was the Memphis Red Sox, managed by none other than Double Duty Radcliffe. Multiple news stories lauded the formation of a strong squad shaped by the Martin brothers, owners of the team, and helped by Radcliffe's prior connections, including those with the Cincinnati Tigers. "In the outer garden are the hard-hitting William Hoskins, last year with Detroit," and Lloyd Davenport, who played for Radcliffe in Cincinnati the year before,[13] and Nat Rogers.[14] "The Memphis Red Sox will have the strongest outfield in the Negro American League this year," the *Atlanta Daily World* declared. Alongside Davenport and Rogers would be "William Hoskins, one of the hardest hitters in baseball from Charleston, Miss."[15] The hype about the 6-foot-2, solidly-built left-handed batter was no doubt informed as much as anything by Hoskins' 1937 exploits.

But Hoskins' time with Memphis[16] was short; he was pirated along with two other Red Sox by the Buffalo Aces, a short-lived affiliate member of the NNL despite the expressed intent of the Negro American and National Leagues to respect each other's team contracts. Cumberland Posey in the *Pittsburgh Courier* wrote, "[Leonard] Henderson, the manager of the Buffalo Club, came to the conclusion that his club needed considerable strengthening if they wished to compete with other clubs of the N.N.L., so he made a trip to Memphis and signed up three players of the Memphis Red Sox of the Negro American League. This violated a verbal agreement between the two Leagues."[17] However, the players were not returned to Memphis because although "the Negro National League have agreed not to touch players of the Negro American League" it has "not received the reciprocal agreement from the N.A.L."[18]

Upon Hoskins' arrival in Buffalo, the *Buffalo Evening News* wrote, "Buffalo Aces, the first team in history to represent Buffalo in the Negro National League, will open its home season Sunday

Left fielder Bill Hoskins with Baltimore. Courtesy SABR Rucker Archive.

afternoon at 3 o'clock against the Newark Eagles in Offerman stadium. … Outstanding players in their lineup include … Bill Hoskins, left field, who hit .360 and connected for 32 home runs with the Detroit Stars in 1937 [Seamheads statistics tell a different story for Hoskins that year: 1 home run, 8 RBIs, and a .324 batting average]."[19] Clearly though, Henderson did not do enough to shore up Buffalo's deficiencies; the club collapsed in the first half of the season and another NNL team swooped in. "The Washington Black Senators have been bolstered for their weekend games at Griffith Stadium with the Newark Eagles and Philadelphia Stars by the addition of five new players. Returning from Buffalo, where the Stars[20] [*sic*, Aces] disbanded, Secretary Roy Sparrow had the signed contracts of Jimmy Ford, second baseman; Bang Long, third baseman; "One Shot" Hoskins, outfielder; and pitchers "Doc" Hayeslett and Slim Johnson."[21]

The Black Senators did not do much better than Buffalo and compiled a record of 2-20 in 1938, not even finishing the second half of the season. In the two recorded games for the Black Senators, Hoskins did what he did well: hit. He went 5-for-9 with two doubles and a triple. With the Black Senators' demise, Hoskins opportunistically moved to his fourth team in 1938, less than 50 miles up the road to Baltimore where he began to make a name for himself for nearly a decade as a linchpin in the outfield.

In his first year with Baltimore during the second half of the 1938 season, in 12 games for which box scores are available, Hoskins' average sagged to .244. He more than made amends in future seasons and the Elite Giants, now firmly entrenched in Baltimore after its nomadic existence beginning in Nashville nearly 20 years before. The Elite Giants had in Hoskins a key piece that helped elevate them to the Negro National League championship a year later. Managed by George Scales, Baltimore finished in third place in 1938, behind the perennial champion Homestead Grays and equally talented Philadelphia.

Hoskins contributed significantly to the success of Baltimore's championship team in 1939, and continued to in all or parts of nine seasons for the Elite Giants, where he ended his Negro League career, save for a cup of coffee with the Black Yankees in 1946. He was a career left fielder, a constant outfield presence for Baltimore in at least 349 documented games with the team over nearly a decade playing for Tom Wilson.

The road to the 1939 championship was paved by solid play from a range of Baltimore players. Bill Byrd, Wild Bill Wright, Sammy Hughes, Henry Kimbro, Jonas Gaines, Willie Hubert, 17-year-old Roy Campanella, and their teammates played well enough to squeeze into the four-team playoff that marked how the 1939 NNL champion was crowned. And then there was Bill Hoskins. He led the team in batting at .382, drew a walk whenever he could, had an OPS of .961, and was considered a good fielder with plenty of speed.

In the deciding game of the championship against the Grays, Hoskins drove in the first run of the game in the seventh and later scored, accounting for both runs in the 2-0 Elites victory. His performance as described by the *Baltimore Afro-American* is worth recounting. "In the lucky seventh … [against Grays hurler Roy Partlow], the Elites crashed the scoring column with the winning tallies. Bill Wright, hero of many Elite games throughout the season, doubled to start the Grays's downfall. Wright romped home with the initial run of the game a few seconds later as Bill Hoskins walloped a single to left. … [After one out] Hoss Walker … beat out a dribble to third, as Spearman threw wide to the bag, pulling Leonard off. Hoskins pulled up at second on the play, then scored as Leroy [sic] Campanella, young Elite catcher, smashed a single through the box."[22]

On the heels of their first championship, the Elite Giants began the 1940 season without three of their players: Bill Byrd went to Venezuela and Wild Bill Wright and Tom Glover took their talents to Mexico. The money was better. The Elites traded for George Scales to return as a player (he had gone to the Black Yankees as player-manager in 1939).[23] Two new pitchers were signed. The season began well: Baltimore was in first place until the end of June. But a losing streak had them finish second to the Grays at the end of the first half. The second half of the season ended in the same way, with Baltimore trailing the Grays.

At the age of 26, Hoskins hit a stellar .343 and had an OPS of .996. With Wright in Mexico, George Scales filled in at right and the outfield tandem of Hoskins, Kimbro, and Scales managed batting averages of .343, .260, and .352 respectively. Baltimore's season might have been summed up by its late July series with the Philadelphia Stars. The Elites swept a doubleheader on a Saturday on the Stars' home ground but lost to them in Oriole Park the next day, 6-5 in 10 innings, the kind of game Baltimore needed to win to keep pace with the Grays. Hoskins did his best, though, going 3-for-5 and "in the fifth, hit a homer into the rightfield bleachers to score Hughes and Tom Butts ahead of him."[24]

In 1941 Baltimore overhauled its team significantly via two trades with the Black Yankees. Baltimore sent Bill Perkins, Harry Kimbro, Bud Barbee, Red Moore, Tom Parker, and Everett Marshall to New York, receiving Charlie Biot, Robert Clarke, Roy Williams, Henry Spearman, and Johnny Washington. The rebuild did not hurt the Elites; in fact, they were only 2½ games behind Homestead over a full season's play. Wrote Bob Luke, "The Elites kept up the pace [in the first half, behind the Grays] by winning six out of seven behind the heavy hitting of Hoskins, Homer "Goose" Curry, and Charlie Biot. Unfortunately … the Grays played even better, taking first place in the first-half race.[25] Meanwhile, the Cubans got hot and won the second half, falling to Homestead in the championship round."[26]

The 1941 season was very good for Hoskins: He garnered the fourth-highest number of votes among outfielders and was selected to play in his only East-West All-Star Classic. Hoskins contributed to the East's 8-3 shellacking of their West opponents, driving in a run in the East's six-run fourth inning. Hoskins, batting third, went 1-for-5 and was one of three Elite Giants who played that day,[27] alongside Roy Campanella behind the plate and Bill Byrd, who pitched a scoreless ninth to nail down the victory.[28]

The situation for the Elite Giants leading into 1942 could not have been better framed than what Bob Luke wrote in his history of the team: "The Elites had acquitted themselves well during the two years of disruption to their roster brought about by trades and defections of star players to Latin America. They looked for better things in 1942."[29]

Thanks to Kimbro's return from the Black Yankees, the league's best outfield was reassembled – Hoskins, Wright, and Kimbro. Wright had returned from Mexico as had Sammy Hughes, Andy Porter, and Tom Glover. The team played well in the first half of the season, outperforming the opposition. Somehow, there was no playoff between the first- and second-half champions and Baltimore lost the opportunity to play for a place in the World Series against the NAL's Monarchs.[30] Hoskins again was superb; he could always be relied on to bat over .300 and hit for extra bases and power and did not disappoint with a .314 batting average and 15 extra base hits in 159 at-bats.

In mid-June, when Baltimore was leading the league, the *Baltimore Afro-American* ran a story with photos of the Elite outfielders, writing that "this trio of fly chasers guard the outer pastures for the Baltimore Elites and rate as one of the best, if not the top-ranking outfield in the National League."[31] In the second half, the Grays built up steam and led Baltimore throughout. The Elites tried to catch up as the season neared an end, and swept the Black Yankees at Bugle Field in a three-game series, punctuated by Hoskins hitting in every game, driving in and scoring runs.[32] But the Grays prevented Baltimore's sweep of a Labor Day doubleheader with Homestead that had been necessary for the Elite Giants to claim the crown.

Entering the 1943 season, Baltimore had had a good run in the NNL – above .500 in its first year in the league in 1938, a championship in 1939 and successive second-place finishes to rival Homestead the following three years. But 1943 was different, and in league play the team finished a distant fifth despite the acquisition of solid left-handers Bill Burns and James Carter. It did not help that Baltimore lost Campanella, Wright, and Butts to Mexico. Scales replaced Felton Snow as manager and despite Tom Wilson shoring up the club with players from his Nashville Cubs, the team struggled out of the gate and never recovered.[33]

Hoskins registered for the draft in 1940 and, although he did not serve in the military, he and fellow Elite Giants worked locally on defense jobs during the war. The *Afro-American* noted in January: "Jim Kimbro, Bill Harvey, Bill Hoskins, and Tom Glover, all members of the Elite Giants, are working in a Baltimore steel plant."[34] In March the newspaper wrote, "In Baltimore, four key players of the Baltimore Elite Giants have threatened to stay on their defense jobs, giving up baseball for the duration. The men, all of whom are employed in the city, are Bill Hoskins and Henry Kimbro, regular outfielders, and two of last season's pitching mainstays, lefthanders Tom Glover and Bill Harvey."[35] This may have been a ploy by the players to leverage better pay from owner Wilson. Eventually, the players quit their jobs in time for the regular season.[36] The May 29 *Afro-American* reported that "Jim Kimbro, Bill Hoskins, and rookie, Biggie Williams … are the outfielders."[37] Hoskins played in fewer games that season than most of his Baltimore teammates; his 36 appearances represented half of the Elite Giants' regular-season total of 69. Early in the season the *Afro-American* noted his absence due to illness: "Bill Hoskins, Elites outfielder, was in Baltimore ill, necessitating the use of Byrd and Bill Harvey, pitchers, as an outfielder at alternate turns."[38] Whether one or more ailments that year contributed significantly to Hoskins' reduced play and his career-low batting average of .275 is uncertain.

In 1944 Hoskins had one of his best years, albeit for a fourth-place team – .388 batting, a .441 on-base percentage, .621 slugging percentage, and a mammoth 1.062 OPS. The core of the team remained from previous years and Hoskins played alongside Kimbro, Snow, Campanella, Butts, and Scales in a fearsome lineup that was otherwise let down by the rotation of Byrd, Gaines, Glover, and Harvey, who could not match their previous accomplishments. Box scores routinely noted Hoskins' ongoing contributions. A game in June in Detroit against the Cubans delighted the locals. "Bill Hoskins, playing before his former hometown fans, shoved the Elites to the front in the first inning when he pelted one of Dave Barnhill's fast balls high into the right field tier [of Briggs Stadium]."[39] Against the Cubans later in the season, the *Afro-American* wrote, "Bill Hoskins, Elites leftfielder, poled a homer in the eighth with two on."[40]

In 1945 the Elites finished no better than the middle of the pack. Hoskins did not match his 1944 numbers, but they were not to be sneezed at: He batted .315 over .300 continuing to show power and speed with 19 extra-base hits. One bright spot for the team was its veteran presence – Hoskins, Kimbro, and Wright continued to patrol the outfield; Campanella, although only 23, was himself a veteran, having played for the team since its Washington Elite Giants edition in 1937; Doc Dennis, Harry Williams, Butts, and Snow in the infield all contributed serviceably. However, the aging pitching staff let the team down with a composite ERA of 4.72; the team simply could not compete against the Grays and Eagles and came in third. Hoskins did his best, as captured by a June storyline in the *Baltimore Afro-American*: "The big bat of Bill Hoskins and the trusty right arm of Archie Hinton, rookie pitcher, combined to set the New York Cubans back on their heels here last Tuesday night, 9-2. Hoskins connected for a home run and a triple to account for five runs."[41]

The 1946 season marked the beginning of a youth movement for Baltimore. Three rookies drew the attention of the team, but for the time being Hoskins was still in the plans. The *Afro-American* noted, "The whole squad, with the exception of Bill Hoskins who is expected to report from Panama this weekend, and Jonas Gaines … are gradually rounding into shape."[42] The reference to Panama implied Winter League play for Hoskins in Central America, but no details so far have been found. The season then began for Hoskins as most others did; in May, in a rain-shortened game against the Grays in Washington. Hoskins produced, hitting a 410-foot run-scoring triple in cavernous Griffith Stadium to ensure a Baltimore victory.[43]

Hoskins' long run with Baltimore came to an end in June 1946. "The Baltimore Elite Giants on Monday announced a deal which sent Bill Hoskins, veteran outfielder, to the New York Black Yankees in exchange for Johnny Hayes, a catcher who formerly played with the Newark Eagles. Hoskins, however, had not reported to the Yankees late Monday night, there being a strong hint that he could not reach salary terms with the Harlemites."[44] The Black Yankees and Hoskins did reach a deal and Hoskins' career continued in New York for the remainder of the 1946 season. Records show Hoskins playing in nine games with the Black Yankees, having already played in 44 that season with Baltimore. His batting average for the combined season was .287, the lowest of his career except for his .275 average in 1943. It was his lowest OPS (.762), well under his career average of .906, due primarily to recording no home runs.

In early 1947, *Afro-American* columnist Sam Lacy reported that the "[r]ebuilding Balto. Elites are hanging out the names of Bill Hoskins … Andy Porter [and others] as trade bait."[45] This came after the Elites' trade of Hoskins to the Black Yankees a year before; perhaps Hoskins had returned to Baltimore to offer his talents in his adopted hometown, only for the Elites to prefer the continuing youth movement. There were no takers. Two months later Lacy wrote, "Bill Hoskins, veteran Elite outfielder, reports that he's been offered $500 per month by the Mexican League."[46] His obituary in 1968 also suggested he played for the Mexico City Reds for several years, but this has not yet been substantiated.[47]

Hoskins continued to play baseball, and in 1948 and 1949 was with the Richmond Giants, a Negro American Association team. The NAA was formed to complement the still-existing NAL and maintain Black baseball in some form in the face of slow integration of the American and National Leagues. Hoskins was only 32, but his prospects for playing in either the White majors or their minor-league systems was dim. Richmond had to suffice. Multiple reports in 1948 in the *Richmond Times-Dispatch* affirmed that he could still hit.[48] However, 1949 was the beginning of the end. In April the paper wrote that the "biggest disappointment to date has been the hitting of Big Bill Hoskins, the team's top batter with .339 and 27 homeruns last season." The Giants folded at the end of the 1949 season and Hoskins' further play in organized baseball of any form has not yet been substantiated.[49]

Along with his Negro League play, Hoskins also participated in the California Winter League. He first appeared for the Philadelphia Royal Giants, in the winter of 1939-1940 after Baltimore's championship season. The Royal Giants won the league going away and Hoskins, with a .303 batting average in nine games, teamed with fellow Elite Giants Bill Wright, Jim West, Bill Harvey, and Tom Glover, as well as Mule Suttles, Pepper Bassett, and Jake Dunn, to win the title. Although a squad under the name of the Baltimore Elite Giants, managed by Felton Snow, participated in the League, Hoskins did not join it.[50]

In 1945 and 1946, Hoskins returned to the California Winter League, this time with the Kansas City Royals, managed by Chet Brewer. Hoskins reprised his time out west with Elite Giants teammates Bill Wright and Andy Porter, but Brewer, Satchel Paige, and a young shortstop by the name of Jackie Robinson were the more prominent names on the Royals. Hoskins still had it, though, and led the league in batting (.444) and home runs (2).[51]

In 1947 there was no Winter League per se, but two teams led by Bob Feller and Satchel Paige more than made up for it by a series of exhibitions that autumn. Hoskins played on the Royals again alongside Piper Davis, Jesse Williams, and Paige. Feller's All-Stars. Who included Feller, Peanuts Lowrey, Bob Lemon, Roy Partee, and Cliff Mapes, bested the Royals in their head-to-head play, but KC redeemed itself by defeating another team, led by Ewell Blackwell.[52]

Having played in Baltimore for nearly a decade, Hoskins' roots in the city were well established. The 1950 Census had him in Baltimore working for a department store as a warehouseman. Sam Lacey, in a 1958 column in the *Baltimore Afro-American*, confirmed this, writing, "Bill Hoskins, ex-Elite outfielder, is a department store employee in Baltimore."[53] The Census does not refer to his wife or any offspring, nor does his obituary in the *Afro-American* 10 years later.

Hoskins died on February 9, 1968, in Baltimore. According to the *Afro-American*, Hoskins "had a history of heart difficulty."[54]

With more research about Negro League taking place, players like Bill Hoskins begin to get their due. Hoskins was not a Hall of Famer, but he was a solid outfielder who could hit for both average and power. He might have won a roster spot on an American or National League team of the day, and who knows, more fans would have known about him and celebrated his game.

SOURCES

All statistics are from Seamheads and Baseball Reference, unless otherwise noted. Special thanks to Rich Bogovich for his insights into Big Bill.

NOTES

1   Memphis Red Sox Line up for Practice," *Atlanta Daily World*, March 4, 1938: 5.

2   William C. Hoskins 1940 draft registration card.

3   1920 Federal Census.

4   One additional layer meriting future research relates to Hoskins' relationship to Ben and Dave Hoskins – Cousins of his – who also played baseball, including, in the case of Dave, time in both the Negro Leagues and then the Cleveland Indians in the 1950s.

5   "St. Louis Stars' Notes," *St. Louis Argus*, April 30, 1937: 6.

6   "Chicago-Star Series Sharpened by Rivalry," *Detroit Tribune*, June 26, 1937: 3.

7   Kyle P. McNary, *Ted "Double Duty" Radcliffe, 36 Years of Pitching and Catching in Baseball's Negro Leagues* (Minneapolis: McNary Publishing, 1994), 129-131.

8   McNary, 138-140.

9   Untitled, *Birmingham News*, May 14, 1937: 8.

10   "St. Louis Stars Ready for Season," *Pittsburgh Courier*, May 8, 1937: 17.

11   "Chicago-Stars Series Sharpened by Rivalry."

12   "Visitors Are Shoddy with Play Afield: Pitching and Batting of St. Louis Club Also Weak," *Detroit Tribune*, July 10, 1937: 6.

13   "Memphis to Strengthen Out Garden: Fastest Fly Chaser in League Is What the Margins Want," *Chicago Defender*, March 5, 1938: 10.

14   "Memphis Gets in Shape for N.N. Leaguers," *Chicago Defender*, March 26, 1938: 9.

15   Memphis Red Sox Line Up for Practice," *Atlanta Daily World*, March 4, 1938: 5.

16   When Hoskins left Memphis, Cowan Hyde replaced him to team up with Davenport and Rogers in the outfield for a team that would win the 1938 Negro American League over strong competition from Kansas City, Chicago, and Atlanta.

17   Cum Posey, "Posey's Points," *Pittsburgh Courier*, May 7, 1938: 16.

18   "Posey's Points."

19   "Negro Nine to Open," *Buffalo Evening News*, May 26, 1938: 12.

20   Did the Stars reference mean there was a connection between the Detroit team's demise the year before and the formation of a new Negro League team in Buffalo in 1938?

21   "D.C. Colored '9' Adds 5 Players," *Washington Times*, June 30, 1938: 32.

22   "Elite Giants Win National League Championship: Baltimore Nine Tops Grays in Series, 10-5 and 2-0 to Gain Rupert Trophy; Gaines Hurls Shutout Over Homestead Team," *Baltimore Afro-American*, September 30, 1939: 21.

23   George Scales – Society for American Baseball Research (sabr.org).

24   "Elites Jolted by Philly Stars in 10 Innings, 6-5," *Baltimore Afro-American*, July 27, 1940: 21.

25   Bob Luke, *The Baltimore Elite Giants: Sport and Society in the Age of Negro League Baseball* (Baltimore: The Johns Hopkins University Press, 2009), 65.

26   New York Cubans – 1941 Season Recap – RetroSeasons.com.

27   "Three Elites Named to Play on East Team," *Baltimore Afro-American*, July 26, 1941: 21.

28   Larry Lester, *Black Baseball's National Showcase: The East-West All-Star Game, 1933-1953* (Lincoln: University of Nebraska Press, 2001), 152-155.

29   Luke, 67.

30   Luke, 72-73.

31   "3 Reasons Why Elites Hold Loop Lead," *Baltimore Afro-American*, June 13, 1942: 22.

32   "Gain on Grays in Hot Race," *Baltimore Afro-American*, September 5, 1942: 23.

33   Luke, 81-83.

34   Art Carter, "From the Bench: Philly Stars, Newark Eagles Are Hit Hardest by the Draft," *Baltimore Afro-American*, January 30, 1943: 18.

35   "Baseball Bits," *Baltimore Afro-American*, March 27, 1943: 23.

36   No information is available about the terms of the players' employment in the defense industry and their eligibility to be called up. Hoskins was 28 in 1943.

37   "Mayor to Throw Out Ball as Elites Play Grays on Sunday," *Baltimore Afro-American*, May 29, 1943: 23.

38   Art Carter, "Gibson Hits 2 Homers; Grays Sweep Philly Series: Eagles, St. Louis Divide Cubans Take Twin Win from Elites to Stay Unbeaten," *Baltimore Afro-American*, May 29, 1943: 23.

39   Russ Cowans, "26,000 See Elites, N.Y. Cubans Split," *Baltimore Afro-American*, June 17, 1944: 18.

40   "Elites Top Cubans Twice in Series, Drop Exhibition," *Baltimore Afro-American*, August 26, 1944: 18.

41   "Hoskins Bat Beats Cubans," *Baltimore Afro-American*, June 2, 1945: 23.

42   "2 Puerto Ricans Impress Elites," *Baltimore Afro-American*, April 13, 1946: 18.

43   "Hoskins's Triple Spoils Grays' Bow," *Baltimore Afro-American*, May 18, 1946: 15.

44   "Elites Trade Hoskins, Farm Out Infielder," *Baltimore Afro-American*, June 29, 1946: 19.

45   Sam Lacy, "A to Z Sports," *Baltimore Afro-American*, February 1, 1947: 17.

46   Sam Lacy, "From A to Z," *Baltimore Afro-American*, March 29, 1947: 13.

47   Neither Baseballreference.com nor Pedro Tetro Cisneros's excellent compilation of statistics from the Mexican League in *The Mexican League / La Liga Mexicana: Comprehensive Player Statistics, 1937-2001 bilingual edition* records Hoskins' presence in the league.

48   The newspaper diligently covered the Giants, and Hoskins' power was often featured. See *Richmond Times-Dispatch*, May 10, June 13, July 19, August 30, 1948.

49   "Giants Ready Before Long, Says Manager," *Richmond Times-Dispatch*, April 15, 1949: 33.

50   William F. McNeil, *The California Winter League: America's First Integrated Professional Baseball League* (Jefferson, North Carolina: McFarland & Company, 2002), 201-205. Over the next several years, teams named the Baltimore Colored or Elite Giants played in the league, but these were all-star squads of Negro League players and not the Baltimore team itself.

51   McNeil, 223-232.

52   McNeil, 232-235.

53   Sam Lacy, "A to Z Sports," *Baltimore Afro-American*, August 23, 1958: 13.

54   "Ex-Elite Bill Hoskins Is Buried," *Baltimore Afro-American*, February 20, 1968: 14.

WILLIE "BUBBER" HUBERT

BY DARREN GIBSON

Rookie sensation Willie "Bubber" Hubert hurled the final pitch of the 1939 Negro National League championship, completing a four-out save for the victorious Baltimore Elite Giants over the Homestead Grays. Hubert, plucked into the NNL from the barnstorming Miami Ethiopians Clowns a year earlier, became a frontline starter for the Elite Giants the next season and later bounced around various Negro League organizations throughout the mid-1940s.

William Henry Hubert was born on January 19, 1913, in Ocala, Florida, to William H. and Cora (Wilson) Hubert.[1] As of the 1920 US Census, young Willie resided in Dade County, Florida, with his mother and Bahamian-born grandmother Anna Wilson, along with younger siblings Thomas and Lillian. Cora was listed as a cook for a private family. By the 1930 Census, 17-year-old Willie was listed as a laborer in Miami and living with his grandmother and brother.

The first found listing of Hubert playing any level of baseball was in training camp of the Newark Dodgers, managed by Dick Lundy, in the spring of 1935 in High Point, North Carolina.[2] In September 1936 Hubert pitched for the Miami Red Sox barnstorming squad.[3] He soon joined the Ethiopian Clowns, arguably the most famous Negro barnstorming team in baseball history, also based in Miami. Against his former Red Sox squad, "Bubber" (Hubert, who relieved in the third inning), and starting pitcher "Smoky" were each knocked around for seven hits in an October loss.[4]

Willie Hubert.

Hubert spent the 1937 campaign back with the Clowns, which presented a lineup utilizing African monikers such as Gohari, King Tut (moniker for Richard King), Limpopo (Buck O'Neil), Wahoo, Tana, Takoloo, Aussa, and Sardo.[5] Actual names of other Clowns pitchers during this time included Dave Barnhill (Impo), Melvin Coleman (Macan), Rogers Pierre (Askari), Eddie "Peanuts" Davis (Nyasses), and Willie Burns (Kaliharri).[6] In an April victory over the Jacksonville Red Caps, Hubert "had plenty of stuff on the ball but was inclined to hurt himself by getting angry and fighting with the Jacksonville ribbers, some of whom were experts."[7] It was reported that the Clowns won 125 of their 141 contests of the season.[8]

For 1938, Hubert, a 5-foot-11, 173-pound right-hander, returned to the Clowns, captained by catcher Thad Christopher (Tarzan).[9] Hubert lost twice to the Jacksonville Red Caps

on consecutive days in late October as Jacksonville claimed the colored state championship honors.[10] By December 1938, "Bubber" had re-signed with his former Miami Red Sox, the Clowns' intracity rivals.[11]

Dick Lundy, still manager of the Newark Eagles, "took heed and squinted at some young fellers cavorting for the Ethiopian Clowns, away down thar."[12] Lundy remembered Hubert, and picked him up, along with pitcher Jimmy Hill and outfielder Frank "Freddie" Wilson, signing the trio from the Clowns to contracts and inviting them to the Eagles' 1939 spring training in Daytona Beach, Florida. The early reports were that "Wilbur [sic] 'Bubber' Hubert ... has been doing well in camp."[13] Hubert beat his former team the Clowns, 6-4, on April 9 in an exhibition in Miami.[14] Newark led the NNL as of late June, boasting a lineup including first baseman Mule Suttles, second baseman Dick Seay, third baseman Monte Irvin, and pitcher Leon Day.[15]

However, by July 8, Hubert first appeared with the Baltimore Elite Giants, also in the NNL.[16] The Giants has just lost star first baseman Jim West to the Philadelphia Stars and catcher Biz Mackey to the Newark Eagles. The Elites finished third in the NNL in the first half, so manager Felton Snow had added Hubert, and, from the Atlanta Black Crackers, shortstop Tommy Butts, first baseman Red Moore, and young catcher Oscar Boone.[17] Snow also inserted 17-year-old catcher Roy Campanella into the starting lineup. Hubert wore number 1 on his Elite Giants jersey in 1939.[18]

Hubert was at times referred to as "Hank" in the *Baltimore Afro-American*.[19] On July 23 he threw a two-hitter over six innings in besting his former Newark team, 4-1.[20] He beat the Memphis Red Sox 14-1 in a seven-inning contest in the nightcap of a doubleheader on August 6.[21] By the time the Elite Giants traveled to Birmingham, Alabama, to play the New York Black Yankees later in August, their reinforced roster had won its last eight contests.[22] "Buffer" Hubert flummoxed the New York Cuban Stars, 11-1, on August 13 with a complete-game six-hitter in the opener of a four-team doubleheader at Yankee Stadium that also included the Homestead Grays and New York Black Yankees.[23]

The *New York Age* commented that Hubert, "who hitch-hiked here from Georgia, (is) doing alright on the mound for league leading Baltimore Elite Giants. But (he) won't stand up to the plate when it's his turn to bat."[24] By September, "Bubbles" Hubert was labeled by the *Afro-American* as the "rookie sensation of the Baltimore Elites."[25] The *Age* later dubbed him "the sensational 'Bubbles' Hubert who has developed into one of the greatest pitchers in the game in his first year in the league."[26] Regardless of which nickname was used, the 26-year-old rookie Hubert was very effective.

Hubert beat Newark again, 5-2, on September 10 in the NNL Divisional Series in Baltimore with a complete-game (six innings) victory, allowing just two runs and two hits.[27]

This sent the Elite Giants to face off against the Homestead Grays in the Negro National League championship series. In the deciding game, on September 24 in front of 10,000 at Yankee Stadium, Baltimore starter Jonas Gaines carried a 2-0 lead until the top of the eighth inning. After two were out in the frame, Gaines walked Grays player-manager Vic Harris, slugging catcher Josh Gibson, and first baseman Buck Leonard.[28] Then "Bill Hubert, Georgia rookie, came in as relief hurler and retired the side by making (Henry) Spearman pop to Snow."[29] The rookie "Hubert held the Grays hitless the rest of the game."[30] With the 2-0 victory, Baltimore became the 1939 Negro National League champion.

Hubert is listed as living in Chicago as of the 1940 Census, with his in-laws; his wife, Mary, seven years Willie's junior and born in Arkansas; and their two-year-old daughter, Bernice, and nine-month-old son, Westley Lee. The listing also stated that Willie was born in Georgia and was a park project laborer.

During his time with the Elite Giants, Hubert was described as "an accomplished pitcher who was known for cutting the ball to compensate for his lack of other legitimate pitches," but he was also "difficult to handle both on and off the field."[31] Nonetheless, Hubert returned to Baltimore for the 1940 season, becoming one of its two best pitchers, behind ace Emery Adams. The Giants trained in New Orleans that spring, then barnstormed their way north to Maryland.

On May 18 Hubert pitched eight innings to earn the win over the Grays, 9-8, with two homers by Roy Campanella supplying the power.[32] A week later, in a four-way doubleheader at Yankee Stadium which also included the Grays and Stars, Hubert beat the New York Black Yankees, 8-1,[33] where "it was Hubert all the way."[34]

Four days later, on May 30, Hubert threw the final 3⅔ innings in relief of Ross "Satchel" Davis in a combined 5-0, seven-inning no-hitter in the second game of a doubleheader in Newark against the Eagles.[35] The next time out, Hubert again beat the Black Yankees, 7-2, improving the Elite Giants' early-season record to 10-1.[36] By late June, Hubert "right now (was) considered one of the league's top-notchers."[37]

On June 21 the Elite Giants beat the New York Cubans 5-4 in 16 innings in Yankee Stadium, with Hubert pitching the first eight innings and newcomer Nate Moreland tossing shutout ball for the final eight.[38] On June 25 Hubert and Moreland combined to beat the Kansas City Monarchs, 11-10 in 11 innings.[39] The *Brooklyn Daily Eagle* reported that "'Buffer' Hubert, a right-hander, has earned recognition for this assignment by the consistent form he has shown in Negro National League games. He was especially effective at Yankee Stadium in the Ruppert Cup Memorial series, where he won two games in as many starts with impressive twirling."[40]

However, Hubert began to lose his shine. On July 24 he allowed 16 hits but still was victorious, 6-4 in 11 innings, over the Cuban Stars.[41] On August 1, the Newark Eagles smacked Bill "Bud" Barnes and Hubert around for 20 hits in a 13-9 victory.[42] Maybe it was the new ineffectiveness, or possibly the addition of new Elite Giants pitcher Jimmy Reese, but Hubert did not see much action down the stretch. Baltimore came up short by 3½ games to the Homestead Grays for the 1940 NNL title.

In January 1941, Hubert, still property of the Elite Giants, was part of a massive 11-player trade, sent by Baltimore owner Tom Wilson (also NNL president) to the New York Black Yankees.[43] The Black Yankees reportedly were to send Johnny Washington, Charley Biot, Roy Williams, and Robert Clarke to the Elite Giants for Hubert, Red Moore, Tom Parker, Everett "Ziggy" Marcell, Bud Barbee, Henry Kimbro, Bill Perkins, and cash.[44] However, Hubert, along with Specs Roberts, Bob Griffith, and Tom Parker, had been given a three-year NNL ban for jumping and playing in Mexico.[45] Rather than pay a $100 fine to settle the issue, Hubert chose to ply his trade with the newly formed Miami Stars against the Pepsi-Cola Giants of Tampa.[46] It was said that Hubert dropped out of the league for independent ball.[47]

Hubert began the 1942 campaign in New Orleans for spring training with the Cincinnati Buckeyes of the Negro American League. He shined against the Birmingham Black Barons on April 26 in an exhibition in Oklahoma City, and "just about had the number for the Black Barons but threw his arm out in the first part of the fifth inning and had to be relieved."[48] In a May 10 loss to the Memphis Red Sox, Hubert surrendered eight runs in the fourth inning before being replaced.[49]

By June 1942, Hubert joined the Baltimore Grays of the upstart Negro Major League.[50] On June 28 newcomer Hubert tossed a seven-inning one-hitter in a 2-1 win over the 1301st Service Unit team of New Cumberland, Pennsylvania.[51] Hubert and Baltimore lost 7-4 to the Cincinnati Ethiopian Clowns on July 5.[52]

Hubert pitched five games for the Homestead Grays in 1944, after his three-year Negro National League ban expired. He beat his old Baltimore Elite Giants 3-1, on May 13, with seven innings of seven-hit ball.[53] He shut out the New York Cubans, 3-0, on June 4 on three hits over his former Clown teammate Dave "Impo" Barnhill.[54] He tossed 6⅔ relief innings on June 19 in a 9-2 loss to Don Newcombe and Newark.[55] The Grays won the Negro World Series.

In 1945 Hubert attended the spring-training camp of the Indianapolis Cardinals in the reconfigured Negro Southern League, where it was reported that his "curve ball has puzzled Negro league players for six years."[56] By late April, he signed with the Pittsburgh Crawfords of the United States Negro League. The Crawfords won the first half of the U.S. League. Hubert beat the Brooklyn Brown Dodgers 8-4 in seven innings on August 27 in Montreal,[57] and again beat them on September 9.[58]

Hubert started 1946 back with the Crawfords. On April 28 the "tall gangling right-hander" earned the win with four relief innings of one-run ball in a 12-7 victory over Hoosier Beer in South Bend, Indiana.[59] However, Hubert was released in May, and lost to the Crawfords later in the month as a member of the new Brooklyn Brown Dodgers.[60] Both teams were part of the United States Negro Baseball League.[61] Records indicate he later joined the Cincinnati Buckeyes and later rejoined his former Baltimore Elite Giants squad, but saw no league action. Lastly, he pitched and lost for the Philadelphia Stars on September 1 against the New York Cubans.

In 1948 Hubert pitched in five games in Canada, in the independent and integrated Quebec Provincial League for the Farnham Pirates.

By the 1950 Census, Hubert lived in Chicago with Mary and children Bernice, Westley, Donald, William J., Rita, and Evann, and was a steel mill chipper. Not much is available on Hubert after this time.

Willie Hubert died on May 19, 2000,[62] at the age of 87 in the Bronx, New York, and is buried at George Washington Memorial Park in Paramus, New Jersey.

SOURCES

In addition to the sources shown in the Notes, the author consulted Baseball-Reference.com, Seamheads.com, and MyHeritage.com.

NOTES

1   The 1920 census, however, lists Hubert as being born in Georgia.
2   "Newark Displays Savvy in Training Camp," *Negro Star* (Wichita, Kansas) April 5, 1935: 6.
3   "Miami Red Sox Whip Fort Pierce Negro 9," *Miami News*, September 28, 1936: 11.
4   "Miami Red Sox Triumph over Ethiopian Clowns," *Miami News*, October 26, 1936: 11.
5   "Ethiopians to Play Pirates Tomorrow Night," *Red Bank* (New Jersey) *Register*, July 7, 1938: 18.
6   "Blues, Clowns Play Here Tonight," *Wisconsin State Journal* (Madison), August 13, 1939: 25.
7   "Clowns Beat Jacksonville," *Miami News*, April 19, 1937: 14.
8   "Norwalk Squad Plays Tonight," *Sandusky* (Ohio) *Register*, July 13, 1938: 8.
9   "Ethiopian Clowns Play at Norwalk Wednesday," *Sandusky Register*, July 12, 1938: 6.
10 "Win Florida Baseball Championship," *Chicago Defender*, October 29, 1938: 9.
11 "Clowns and Red Sox to Play Again Sunday," *Miami News*, December 8, 1938: 17.
12 "Dugout Doings," *New York Amsterdam News*, March 25, 1939: 19.
13 "Dick Seay's Return from S.A. Hailed," *New York Amsterdam News*, April 29, 1939: 19. In the headline, S.A. stands for South America.
14 "Clowns Lose to Eagles, 6-4," *Miami News*, April 10, 1939: 15.
15 "Yankees, Eagles to Play 2 Games," *Winston-Salem* (North Carolina) *Sentinel*, June 20, 1939: 6.
16 "Giants Beat Stars Twice," *Philadelphia Inquirer*, July 9, 1939: 33.
17 William E. Clark, "The Sports Parade," *New York Age*, July 22, 1939: 8.
18 "So You'll Know Them," *Warren* (Pennsylvania) *Times Mirror*, August 23, 1939: 8.
19 "Elites Clash with Eagles," *Baltimore Afro-American*, July 22, 1939: 23.
20 "Baltimore and Newark Split Double-Header," *Washington Evening Star*, July 24, 1939: 12; "Elites Divide 2 with Newark," *Baltimore Afro-American*, July 29, 1939: 22.
21 "Negro Teams Halve Bill," *Birmingham Post*, August 7, 1939: 8.
22 "Black Yanks Meet Giants Tuesday, 8:15," *Birmingham News*, July 30, 1939: 16.
23 "Homestead Grays Take Black Yankee Team," *Phoenix* (Arizona) *Index*, August 19, 1939: 4.
24 Buster Miller, "The Sports Parade," *New York Age*, August 19, 1939: 8.
25 "Stars, Eagles, Giants, Grays, in Twin Bill," *Baltimore Afro-American*, September 2, 1939: 22.
26 "20,000 to See Four Team Doubleheader at Ruppert Stadium," *New York Age*, September 2, 1939: 8.
27 Ralph Boyd, "Elites Whip Eagles to Gain Championship Series," *Baltimore Afro-American*, September 15, 1939: 23.
28 "Elite Giants Win National League Championship," *Baltimore Afro-American*, September 30, 1939: 21.
29 Buster Miller, "Elite Giants Top Homestead Grays to Win Ruppert Trophy," *New York Age*, September 30, 1939: 8.
30 "Elites Win, 2-0, in Colored Final," *New York Daily News*, September 25, 1939: 224.
31 Bob Luke, *The Baltimore Elite Giants* (Baltimore: Johns Hopkins University Press, 2009), 50. Quote is from James A. Riley, *The Biographical Encyclopedia of the Negro Baseball Leagues* (New York: Carroll & Graf, 1994), 399.
32 "2,500 See Elite Giants Win Here," *Harrisburg* (Pennsylvania) *Sunday Courier*, May 19, 1940: 2.
33 "Elites, Grays Win in Twin Bill," *Baltimore Afro-American*, June 1, 1940: 20.
34 William E. Clark, "Homestead Grays and Elite Giants Victorious in First 4-Team Double-header in N.Y.," *New York Age*, June 1, 1940: 5.
35 "Elites Clip Eagles in Twin Bill," *Baltimore Afro-American*, June 8, 1940: 20.
36 "Elites Increase N.N. League Lead," *Baltimore Afro-American*, June 4, 1940: 18.
37 "Play Series Tilt Here Tomorrow," *Harrisburg Evening News*, June 21, 1940: 15.
38 Morgen S. Jensen, "10,000 See Game in Yankee Stadium; Yanks Beats Tars," *Pittsburgh Courier*, June 22, 1940: 17.
39 "Elites Nip K.C. Monarchs, Face Eagles," *Baltimore Afro-American*, June 29, 1940: 22.
40 "Elite Giants Tangle with Bushwicks," *Brooklyn Daily Eagle*, June 28, 1940: 14.

41   "Elites Defeat Cuban Tossers," *Baltimore Evening Sun*, July 25, 1940: 33.

42   "Eagles Top Elites on Homers," *Jersey Journal* (Jersey City), August 2, 1940: 13.

43   See *Baltimore Afro-American*, January 11, 1941: 19.

44   Hayward Jackson, "Black Yanks, Elites Complete Ten Player Deal," *Pittsburgh Courier*, April 12, 1941: 17.

45   Luke, 78.

46   "Schoolboy Impo to Pitch for Clowns," *Philadelphia Tribune*, March 20, 1941: 11.

47   Art Carter, "Rival Grays Opponents in Debut," *Baltimore Afro-American*, May 6, 1941: 18.

48   "Cincinnati Win Close Game from Birmingham in Season Opener Sunday 4 to 3," *Cincinnati Black Dispatch*, May 2, 1942: 12.

49   Sam Brown, "Memphis in Double Win over Cincy," *Chicago Defender*, May 16, 1942: 20.

50   "Baltimore Grays Meet Richmond Hillsdales," *Baltimore Sun*, June 7, 1942: 30; "Baltimore Grays Play Port of Richmond Nine," *Baltimore Sun*, June 21, 1942: 27.

51   "Twin Bill Lost by Service Unit," *Harrisburg Evening News*, June 29, 1942: 6.

52   "Clowns Retain Lead," *Cincinnati Enquirer*, July 6, 1942: 24.

53   "Homestead Grays Beat Baltimore in Opener, 3-1," *Philadelphia Inquirer*, May 14, 1944: 31; "Grays Hand Jolt to Elite Giants," *Harrisburg Evening News*, May 15, 1944: 15.

54   "Grays, Cubans Split; Giants Lose Twin Bill," *Pittsburgh Courier*, June 10, 1944: 12.

55   "Homestead and Penbrook Lose," *Harrisburg Evening News*, June 20, 1944: 13.

56   "Three Twirlers Join Indianapolis Cardinals," *Indianapolis Star*, April 1, 1945: 38.

57   "Pitt Team Tops Dark Dodgers," *Montreal Star*, August 28, 1945: 16.

58   "Crawfords Too Good for Foes at Ebbets Field," *Brooklyn Daily Eagle*, September 10, 1945: 12.

59   Bob Towner, "Hoosier Beer Loses Opener to Crawfords," *South Bend* (Indiana) *Tribune*, April 29, 1946: 12.

60   "Pittsburgh Topples Brooklyn Nine, 14-7," *York* (Pennsylvania) *Dispatch*, May 23, 1946: 26.

61   "Pittsburgh Opposes Brooklyn Ball Club," *York Dispatch*, May 22, 1946: 16.

62   MyHeritage.com listed Hubert's date of death as May 21, 2000.

SAMMY HUGHES

BY CHRIS BETSCH

Sammy Hughes's name will almost certainly appear on any list of the top players of the Negro Leagues in the 1930s and 1940s. Hughes didn't draw the attention of some of the bigger personalities of the day like Satchel Paige and Josh Gibson, but it is generally agreed that he was one of the most talented and well-rounded players in the leagues. Former stars Monte Irvin, Cool Papa Bell, and Buck Leonard were among several Negro League greats who listed Hughes as their top second baseman when asked to compile their personal all-time teams.[1]

The Seamheads.com database recorded Hughes's career batting average in the Negro Leagues as .316, with a high of .372 in the 1939 title season. And though fielding statistics for Negro Leagues may not be absolute, what is available shows that Hughes was among the top fielders at second base year after year. He led the league in Range Factor/Game three times and finished in the top five in fielding percentage in five seasons. In the 2001 edition of his *Historical Baseball Abstract*, Bill James described Hughes as "a smart player who did everything well" and compared him to Hall of Famers Barry Larkin and Ryne Sandberg.[2]

There is no question that Hughes was one of the top infielders of his time, and possibly the top second baseman. The question could instead be whether he should join his fellow Blackball stars in the National Baseball Hall of Fame.

He preferred to keep a low profile and stay clear of some of the excitement that came from being a professional baseball player. Contemporary player and fellow second baseman Dick Seay recalled, "Hughes was a nice fellow. He wasn't one of those drinking guys. ... I'd be in one of those taverns talking to the guys, but he'd stay in the hotel or go out and get his girl and go to her house."[3] That may be part of the reason he never garnered as much attention for the Hall of Fame as other stars of his generation.

Samuel Thomas Hughes was born on October 20, 1910, in Louisville. He was the last of 12 children born to Susie Hughes (née Cowherd). There is some uncertainty as to the identity of his father. On his player questionnaire sheet, he listed Henry

Sammy Hughes working out.

Hughes as his father, and Henry and Susie had been married, but the 1910 US Census has Susie listed as a widow when she would have been expecting Sammy. It could be that Henry died just before Sammy's birth. The Hughes family resided in downtown Louisville, and after Henry's death Susie supported them as a laundress and housekeeper.

Sammy went to school through the eighth grade, then presumably went to work in either the coal mines or tobacco fields, where he had older brothers working. Sammy found time to play baseball in the city, though; when he was 18, he was deemed good enough to join one of the top Black teams of the area, the Black Caps. By that time, he may have already had some experience as a semipro player. A player named Hughes, conceivably Sammy, played second base for Black teams in Kentucky in 1926, first in Maysville and then in Lexington.[4] Then as a 16-year-old in 1927, Sammy appeared in a team photo with one of the other top teams in Louisville, the White Sox, but it is uncertain whether he played in any of their games.

The Louisville Black Caps were members of the Southern Negro League in 1929 when Hughes debuted. Then in 1930 the team moved up to the Negro National League; thus, Hughes became a major leaguer at the age of 19.[5] Toward the end of the 1930 season, the Black Caps were incorporated with the White Sox. The combined team kept the White Sox name for the 1931 season and kept Hughes on the roster.

After the 1931 season, in which he batted .337 in league games, Hughes was recruited to join the Washington entry in Cum Posey's new East-West League for 1932. He initially played second base for Louisville, but the team wanted to try another player there, so he was moved to first base. The Washington Pilots thus recruited Hughes as a first baseman; the keystone belonged to Frank Warfield, the Pilots' manager and the heart of the team. In a sad turn of events, Warfield unexpectedly died in July after a hemorrhage, and Hughes inherited the regular second-base role.

While playing in Washington, it was likely that Hughes was married. A 1932 article mentions that he temporarily left the team to tend to his sick wife in Louisville.[6] However, US Census records from 1930 and 1940 do not indicate that he was married in those years.

In many of his pictures, Sammy can be seen with a grin on his face. Outside of giving umpires the occasional hard time, he was mild-mannered and possessed a friendly disposition – but if his grin didn't help pinpoint him in a photo, then his height usually gave him away. Standing 6-feet-3, he was tall for about any position player in the league those days, let alone a second baseman. His stature not only helped him reach up to snag more line drives but also, when combined with his graceful footwork and mobility, increased his range and helped Hughes become one of the top defenders at the position. And Sammy T., as he was often called, was just as adept with his offense. He hit for high average and decent power, and his skills on the basepaths would later be considered equal to Jackie Robinson's.[7]

The Pilots ceased operations after the 1932 season (and the East-West League dissolved soon after), leaving Hughes to look for a new team. Many of his former Louisville team-mates, including Felton Snow, Poindexter Williams, and Willie Gisentaner, had joined the Nashville Elite Giants of the Negro National League, and Hughes reunited with them in Tennessee for the 1933 season. It was with the Elite Giants that the baseball world, including the White major leagues, started to recognize Hughes as a standout second baseman.

In August 1934 he was elected to play in his first East-West Classic, the Negro League equivalent of the White major leagues' All-Star Game. He eventually was chosen for eight East-West games in his career (and played in six of them). But Hughes always considered his first appearance in the classic to be his favorite baseball moment.[8]

October 1934 marked Hughes's first appearance in the California Winter League. Many baseball players in those days, Black and White, stayed busy nearly year-round playing in exhibition games and tournaments, winter leagues, semipro leagues, and barnstorming tours, and Hughes was no exception. The California Winter League was regarded as one of the prime showcases for Hughes and other Negro League players to demonstrate their talents against competitive teams of White players. The Elite Giants owner, Tom Wilson, annually brought a team out to the league, and they could normally be found atop league standings, with Hughes often in a prominent role. Over his seven seasons in the league, he was consistently one of its top players, ranking fifth all-time in the circuit in career batting average (for a minimum 70 at-bats) and seventh overall in home runs.[9]

In 1935 Hughes followed the Elite Giants from Nashville to Columbus, Ohio (after a failed move to Detroit). He then returned to Washington when the team moved there in 1936. He played in the East-West Classic both years and was also selected to join in various all-star tournaments outside of the Negro National League.

Hughes participated in the highly advertised fall exhibition games in 1934 and 1935 played between teams led by Dizzy Dean and Satchel Paige. In August 1936 he had the opportunity to really put his talents on display on a national stage. Tom Wilson took his Elite Giants team, enhanced with select players from the rival Homestead Grays, and sent them out west to take part in the popular Denver Post Tournament for semipro teams not associated with Organized Baseball. The tourney was sometimes referred to as the "Little World Series of the West."[10]

The Negro League teams were not connected to Organized Baseball (not by their choice, of course). Thus, Wilson's "National Negro All Stars" were eligible to take part in the event. The talent on the team was head and shoulders above the rest of the competition, and they dominated the field. Hughes hit .379 in the tournament as the All-Stars won all seven of their games and earned the cash prize of $5,000.[11]

Afterward much of the team stayed intact and took part in a tour formed by sports promoter Ray Doan. Among other things, Doan was known for his work with the traveling House of David team. Doan teamed up with Rogers Hornsby in October to stage a tour through Colorado and Iowa that would pit the team of Negro All-Stars against players from the White major leagues.

A team highlighted by Hughes, Satchel Paige, Cool Papa Bell, Oscar Charleston, and Newt Allen took on a squad led by Hornsby that featured Johnny Mize, Harlond Clift, and Ival Goodman, among others. The Negro All-Stars won four out of the five games, much to Hornsby's dismay.[12] Hughes stood out for the Negro All-Stars, hitting .571 for the series, which topped Bell's .421 and Charleston's .364.

The only stretch when the Negro All-Stars seemed concerned was when 17-year-old Bob Feller started one game in his home state of Iowa and faced Paige for three innings. Feller was dominant, striking out 8 of the 10 batters he faced over the three innings he pitched. (Paige just about matched Feller, striking out 7 of 11.) Hughes got the only hit off the teenage fireballer, an infield single that first baseman Mize fielded, but on which Feller didn't get to the bag fast enough to make the putout. After Feller left the game, the All-Stars' bats came to life, and they won, 4-2.

By 1937 Hughes was generally recognized as one of the top players in the Negro Leagues. He was selected that year to play in his fourth consecutive East-West All-Star Game, but he was one of many notable players who did not take part in the game. Several league stars, including Paige and Gibson, also skipped it, instead joining a touring club assembled under the aegis of the Dominican Republic's dictator, Rafael Trujillo.

Hughes did not join that team, but he was included among a group of players whose owners kept them out of the East-West Game in protest of how Pittsburgh Crawfords owner Gus Greenlee managed the annual contest.[13] Hughes instead joined a different team of all-stars that faced off against Paige and the "Dominican" team in a series of exhibition games.

He followed up the NNL season with an outstanding performance in the California Winter League, hitting .435 to help Wilson's Philadelphia Royal Giants easily take the league pennant.

In December 1937 Homestead Grays owner Cum Posey put out list of his All-Time All-Americans of the Negro Leagues in the *Pittsburgh Courier* newspaper and selected Hughes as his second baseman. That honor came one week after a column in the paper opined how the Pittsburgh Pirates and just about any major-league team could be improved by signing some of the top Negro League players, with Hughes specifically being mentioned.[14]

The Elites moved to Baltimore for the 1938 season, where they finally settled for good. Amid all the team's moves, Hughes was a steady performer for the Giants. He was the only Giant selected to represent the team in the East-West Game from all four of the cities that it called home.

Hughes was the overwhelming leader in votes received for second base in 1938, making his fourth East-West classic. He again represented Baltimore in both games of a two-game all-star set in 1939.

The 1939 Baltimore Elite Giants, managed by Hughes's longtime teammate Felton Snow, finished fourth in league standings but made the postseason when the league used a Shaughnessy playoff format that year.[15] Hughes helped lead the way all season for the Giants with a .378 batting average and a .500 slugging percentage.

After a surprising 3-1 series win over the Newark Eagles in the first round of the playoffs, Hughes and the Giants upset Josh Gibson and the powerful Homestead Grays to claim the Negro National League championship.

After the close of the 1939 season, Hughes made his only appearance in the Cuban Winter League. He started the season with Habana before joining Snow and Willie Wells with the Almendares team, but he did not fare well in Cuba. He hit an uncharacteristic .246 there (while teammate Wells won league MVP honors).[16]

The less-than-stellar performance by Hughes in Cuba didn't slow him down; he had another solid year in 1940. His average

Sammy Hughes chats with catcher Roy Campanella. Courtesy SABR Rucker Archive.

dipped to .267, but he led the league in doubles with 13. In June, Hughes was again mentioned as a player who could contribute in the top all-White leagues. *Baltimore Afro-American* columnist Sam Lacy wrote that Hughes and other Black players "might bear watching" by AL and NL teams.[17]

Hughes was again the leading vote-getter at second base for the 1940 East-West game (and fifth in overall voting).[18] However, he did not get to play in the showcase after being beaned in a game a week before.

The 1940 season was the last chance that Hughes would have to play in the all-star event. He likely would have earned one more bid in 1941, but he left the Elite Giants and took an offer to jump to the Mexican League for the season. He joined several stars who played south of the border that year, including Josh Gibson, Cool Papa Bell, and Willie Wells.

Hughes played much better with Algodoneros de Unión Laguna in Mexico than he did in Cuba, batting .324 in support of manager Martín Dihigo. He played only the one season in Mexico, then returned to the United States in time for one more season in the California Winter League.

However, he played only two games in the California Winter League that winter, focusing instead on various exhibition games, including an October series in Los Angeles against a team including several AL and NL players. Jimmie Foxx and Ted Williams were the headliners of that series, but Slamming Sammy Hughes was advertised in the *Los Angeles Times* as the top hitter for the Eastern Colored Giants.[19] Hughes had two hits in the main game and scored two runs in a 9-6 loss to the White major leaguers. While playing in the California Winter League and various exhibition tournaments in the state, Hughes must have taken a liking to Los Angeles – he made the city his home as early as 1940.[20]

Over the course of Hughes's years in baseball, some momentum started building toward allowing Black players to integrate the White major leagues. Several players and managers from the AL and NL – among them Dizzy Dean, Johnny Vander Meer, and Bill McKechnie – came out in favor of Negro League players being accepted.[21] At that time, though, no one team wanted to take the first step.

Lester Rodney, the sports editor of the *Daily Worker*, spearheaded a 1941 campaign titled "Can You Read, Judge Landis" that was directed to Commissioner Kenesaw Landis, imploring the AL and NL to bring in Negro Leaguers. With White players being pulled into military service in World War II, there was no valid reason for talented Black ballplayers to still be kept from helping at least to fill out AL and NL rosters, or even hold starting jobs. Several other newspapers and a number of union organizations joined Rodney in the campaign to integrate the top White circuits. The pinnacle of the effort was an open letter to Landis penned by Rodney that was posted in the May 6 edition of the *Daily Worker*, demanding that the commissioner take action.

Following the bustle that Rodney's letter stirred, and possibly as a result of it, the Pittsburgh Pirates looked like the team willing to make the move to integrate. Hughes was one of the players the Pirates invited to a tryout in 1942, along with one of his Baltimore teammates, rising star Roy Campanella, and New York Cubans pitcher Dave Barnhill. According to news releases, the tryout was initially set to take place on August 4, but after several weeks, the tryout had still not taken place. Some references claim the tryout was dropped with no official explanation from the Pirates.[22] Yet it is also highly likely that the Pirates were never seriously considering a tryout and that the story was blown out of proportion by news media.

After the widespread news of the Pirates tryout, Hughes, Campanella, and Barnhill were invited to play with the Negro American League's Cleveland Buckeyes in an exhibition game in August. Teammates Hughes and Campanella requested permission from owner Wilson to play in the game, but with the Giants getting ready to face the rival Grays in the middle of a heated pennant race, the request was denied. Both players joined the Buckeyes anyway for $200 each (and maybe for a good cause – Campanella said the game was being played to raise funds for a ball field in Cleveland).[23] Wilson then fined each man $250 for deserting the team and suspended them, denying both a chance to take part in that year's East-West Game.[24] Both players returned to the Giants, but Campanella soon left and played out the year in Mexico, and the Elites finished in second place.

Heading into 1943, Hughes was 32 years old and would have been preparing for his 15th season in pro ball. He likely had a few good seasons left, but in January he was drafted into the US Army. He spent three years serving in the Pacific Theater.

Many professional ballplayers serving in the military during the war were assigned duties to be morale boosters and to play ball in front of troops around the world. Hughes, however, saw action as part of the 196th Support Battalion, notably taking part in an invasion task force in New Guinea.[25]

When the war ended, Hughes rejoined the Elite Giants for the 1946 season. By his own admission, he was no longer in playing shape. "I was heavy, I couldn't move so well, and I thought, 'Well, maybe I can get that weight off, get back into shape, and maybe not.'"[26]

Newspaper reports stated that Hughes held out from signing until June to get a better contract offer, but it was also possible that he was planning to retire until the Giants persuaded him to come back and prepare his replacement. Baltimore was grooming young infielder Jim Gilliam to play second base alongside shortstop Pee Wee Butts but decided Gilliam wasn't ready yet defensively.

The team worked with Gilliam, and Hughes, especially, helped guide him on his defense, until the day the veteran was ready to hand over the position. Hughes said, "I told Felton Snow, our manager, 'Just let Gilliam and Butts, that combination, stay in there.'"[27]

The 1946 season, when Jackie Robinson broke the color line in Organized Baseball playing for the Brooklyn Dodgers' Montreal Royals Triple-A team, was Hughes's last as a player.

After retiring, Hughes worked in the warehouse at a Pillsbury Mills plant in Los Angeles, then later as a janitor (coincidentally at the Hughes Aviation company). He was remarried in 1956, to Thelma Novella Smith, and became a father to her daughter, Barbara. (In 1941 he had married Mildred Dandridge, but according to census records they were divorced before 1950.)

In 1972 Hughes was tracked down and interviewed by author John Holway for a piece that later appeared in Holway's book, *Black Giants*. Holway noted that Hughes was very welcoming for the interview, but that he also chain-smoked throughout their meeting. During his career, Hughes had stayed clear of trouble with alcohol, unlike many of his past teammates, but for years he was indeed a heavy smoker. In 1981 he was diagnosed with lung cancer. Then, within months of the diagnosis, he suffered a fatal heart attack.[28] He left behind his wife and stepdaughter.

Today, Hughes is buried in an unmarked grave next to two sisters, Bessie and Treacy, at Louisville Cemetery, located a few miles from where he was born and raised. In 2022, the Pee Wee Reese chapter of SABR identified providing a grave marker for Hughes as a future project.

Nearly 25 years after Holway's interview, Hughes's career was given some well-deserved attention when he was listed on the final ballot for the 2006 Special Committee on Negro Leagues election to the National Baseball Hall of Fame, but he was not selected. He was not on the Early Baseball Era ballot (which included both Negro Leaguers and White players) in 2021.

The years that Hughes lost to service in World War II likely hindered his case for election. Like so many players from his era, Hughes lost multiple years to the war that otherwise would have bolstered his career statistics. He came back to baseball just as Jackie Robinson was breaking the color barrier, and Hughes himself was still being suggested as one of the top candidates to make the leap into Organized Baseball. But as was the case with other Black stars of his time, he was born just a few years too early, and integration arrived much too late.

When the Baseball Hall of Fame again considers Negro League players for enshrinement, one might hope that Hughes will be one of the names at the top of the list. As baseball researcher Gary Cieradkowski professed in his popular *Infinite Baseball Card Set* online series, "The biggest problem with the Hall of Fame in Cooperstown is that Sammy T. Hughes isn't in it."[29]

Acknowledgments

Gary Cieradkowski sparked the idea for a Hughes bio during a discussion at the Pee Wee Reese Chapter SABR Day 2022 in Louisville.

The Louisville Public Library provided access to the digital archives of the *Louisville Leader* newspaper.

Statistics for Hughes in the Negro Leagues are taken from the Seamheads.com Negro League data base.

The National Baseball Hall of Fame provided Hughes's player questionnaire card from 1972.

This article was vetted by Howard Rosenberg and Rory Costello, fact-checked by James Forr, and copy-edited by Len Levin.

SOURCES

In addition to the sources cited in the Notes, the author used Baseball-Reference.com, SABR.org, Newspapers.com, Newspaperarchive.com, Ancestry.com, Seamheads.com, and the following:

Greenes, Steven R. *Negro Leaguers and the Hall of Fame: The Case for Inducting 24 Overlooked Ballplayers* (Jefferson, North Carolina: McFarland & Company, 2020).

Riley, James A. *The Biographical Encyclopedia of the Negro Baseball Leagues* (New York: Carroll & Graf Publishers, 1994).

NOTES

1   Larry Lester, *Black Baseball's National Showcase: The East-West All-Star Game, 1933-1953* (Lincoln: University of Nebraska Press, 2001), 480.

2   Bill James, *The New Bill James Historical Abstract* (New York: The Free Press, 2001), 183.

3   John B. Holway, *Black Giants* (Fairfax, Virginia: Lord Fairfax Press, 2010), 141.

4   "Standard Team Has Powerful Reputation," *Lexington* (Kentucky) *Herald*, July 29, 1926: 11.

5   The Negro National League was one of the leagues designated as a major league by MLB in December 2020.

6   W. Rollo Wilson, "Sports Spots," *Pittsburgh Courier*, August 20, 1932: 14.

7   Timothy M. Gay, *Satch, Dizzy & Rapid Robert: The Wild Saga of Interracial Baseball Before Jackie Robinson* (New York: Simon & Schuster, 2010), 145.

8   Holway, 142.

9   William McNeil, *The California Winter League: America's First Integrated Professional Baseball League* (Jefferson, North Carolina: McFarland & Company, 2002), 245.

10 Jason Hanson, "The Little World Series of the West," History Colorado, https://www.historycolorado.org/story/2021/07/07/little-world-series-west.

11 W. Rollo Wilson, "National Sports Shots," *Pittsburgh Courier*, August 22, 1936: 14.

12 Gay, 166.

13 Russ J. Cowans, "Easter Star Out of All-Star Game," *Detroit Tribune*, August 7, 1937: 7.

14 "Challenge Hurled at Pittsburgh Pirates on Sepia Players Issue," *Pittsburgh Courier*, December 11, 1937: 17.

15 Baseball-Reference.com shows that the Toledo Crawfords finished with the fourth-best record in the league, but the team had switched to the Negro American League before the end of the season.

16 Jorge S. Figueredo, *Who's Who in Cuban Baseball: 1878-1961* (Jefferson, North Carolina: McFarland & Company, 2007), 378.

17 Sam Lacy, "Looking 'Em Over," *Baltimore Afro-American*, June 1, 1940: 21.

18   Lester, 152.

19   "Ted Williams Heads All-Stars in Tussle," *Los Angeles Times*, October 8, 1941: 25.

20   Hughes listed a home address in Los Angeles on his World War II draft card, dated October 16, 1940.

21   Larry Lester, "Can You Read, Judge Landis?" SABR Journal Articles, https://sabr.org/journal/article/can-you-read-judge-landis/.

22   Larry Lester, "Can You Read, Judge Landis?"

23   Roy Campanella. *It's Good to Be Alive* (Lincoln: University of Nebraska Press, 1995), 89.

24   "Campanella, Hughes Cited for Fine, Suspension," *Baltimore Afro-American*, August 15, 1942: 26.

25   "Negro Leagues Players Played Major Role In World War II," Negro Leagues Players Played Major Role In World War II | by MLB.com/blogs | Monarchs to Grays to Crawfords (mlblogs.com).

26   Holway, 144.

27   Holway, 144.

28   Hughes' death certificate provided by the State of California Department of Public Health.

29   Gary Cieradkowski, "Sammy T. Hughes: The Problem with the Hall of Fame," StudioGaryC.com, https://studiogaryc.com/2020/12/20/sammy-t-hughes.

JOHNNY JOHNSON

BY JAY HURD

John Arthur "Long John" Johnson played briefly with the 1939 Baltimore Elite Giants. He had a professional baseball career, in the second Negro National League, that spanned nine seasons from 1938 to 1946. A pitcher – starting and relief – he threw right-handed and batted left-handed; he stood 6-feet-3 and weighed 182 pounds.

Johnson's career began in 1938 with the Newark Eagles, and possibly with the New York Black Yankees.[1] A fine pitcher – noted as an "ace"[2] in some newspaper reports – he played with numerous teams before joining the Eagles. In the NNL2 he played for the Eagles, the Elite Giants, the Homestead Grays, and the Black Yankees. According to James A. Riley, in his *Biographical Encyclopedia of the Negro Leagues*, Johnson also played with the Birmingham Black Barons in 1941-1942.

Born on September 26, 1915, in Louisiana,[3] Johnson was one of seven children. His father, Columbus Johnson, was born in Jefferson, Texas, on February 24, 1884. Columbus, who worked as a laborer and yardman for a sawmill company, married Minnie Shaw on July 7, 1903. Minnie is identified as a homemaker. Their first four children, Venolia (born 1905), Lula (1910), Jennie (1912), and Fannie (1914) were born in Jefferson. Their next three children, John Arthur (1915), Minnie (1917), and Eddie (1920), were born in Caddo Parish, Louisiana.[4] Columbus died on April 14, 1953, and Minnie died on February 20, 1961.

It appears that Johnson's baseball career began in Louisiana, and possibly continued in Arkansas, with local amateur or semipro teams. From Monroe, Louisiana, to Buffalo, New York, Johnson's name appeared on rosters for several teams before he played in the Negro National League. One of the earlier references (1935) to Johnson while with the Monroe Monarchs notes him as "Arthur Johnson." It said: "The team will probably be on the road for three months. … Players making the trip were Manager Frank Johnson; Catchers Harry Else and Ernest Smith; Infielders Johnny Washington, Andrew Henderson, Clarence Lamar, Jiggs Maxwell; Outfielders Otis Henry, Jack Moore, Booker Harmon; Pitchers Hilton Smith, Barney Morris, J.B. Griffin, [John] Arthur Johnson, Leland Foster, Hugh Little and Homer Allen."[5] Another 1935 article refers to Johnson: "John Arthur Johnson of Cedar Grove [Louisiana], who won many games for the Monarchs in their recent tour is scheduled to pitch one of the games against the [Shreveport] Tigers."[6]

By 1936, Johnson received additional attention, including a somewhat biographical newspaper piece:

In an effort to be at their best for the three-game series with the New Orleans Black Pelicans, the Shreveport Tigers yesterday signed John Arthur Johnson, former Monroe Monarchs ace hurler. The slim six-foot-three inch negro will oppose the Pelicans at Dixie Park Sunday. … Johnson travelled with the Monroe Monarchs last. season and this year started with a Cincinnati team and later went to Nashville. He was obtained by the Washington Elites of Washington, D.C., and remained with that team until last week. Johnson's home is in Cedar Grove."[7] He began the 1937 season with the Shreveport Tigers: "The Shreveport Tigers will line up as follows: Floyd, 1b; Doyle, 2b; Chapman, ss; Williams, 3b; Dawson, c; Guillard, lf; Johnson,[8] cf; Young, rf; and Gibson, John Johnson, Percy Dudlow and Lefty Crumberley to do the pitching.[9]

In 1938 Johnson made the trip from Louisiana to Buffalo, New York, and there played for the Buffalo Aces, an associate member of the 1938 Negro National League.[10] The Aces had a strong connection with Arkansas, and specifically with the Claybrook Tigers and the city of Marianna, Arkansas hosted Negro League spring training in 1938 for the Aces.[11] Regarding the Buffalo Aces, Johnson achieved some notoriety: "John Arthur Johnson, a pitcher with the Buffalo Aces, local Negro National League entrant, is one of the twirlers who holds a decision over the great Satchel Paige, fireball pitcher deluxe."[12] Not yet a member of the Newark Eagles, Johnson earned some not flattering reference in the press: "The Eagles pounded Dunbar and Johnson for 12 safeties."[13] And when the "Black Senators Defeat Buffalo, "J. Johnson" is noted as the pitcher.[14]

Also in 1938, Johnson joined the Newark Eagles under managers Abe Manley and Dick Lundy. Seamheads records that Johnson appeared in one game as the starting pitcher; he pitched nine innings and won the game. However, if the relief pitcher Johnson, referenced in an August 25, 1938, article, is indeed Johnny Johnson, then it can be inferred that he appeared in more than one game: "Ace Parker went the entire 16 innings for the Grays while John Johnson, relieving Bob Evans in the 4th, matched him stride for stride until being removed for a pinch hitter in the 15th inning."[15]

As will be noted, due to brief playing times with the NNL2 clubs, Johnson likely played on other teams during each of the seasons. For example, he played in only three known games with the NNL2 champion Baltimore Elite Giants, pitching 6⅔ innings and having no wins under manager Felton Snow. The team, however, played under other names and Johnson appeared with the Nashville Elite Giants vs. the Chevrolet Red Sox: "On page 24, the June 21 *Philadelphia Inquirer* listed a 6:00 P.M. game for that evening at Paterson, New Jersey between the Nashville Elite

Giants and Jamieson's Red Sox. Jack Eelman was the pitcher for the Red Sox (who had a second baseman named Paterson). He held the Elite Giants to eight base hits and allowed just one run in the sixth and another in the ninth. Johnny Johnson pitched for the Giants and surrendered two in the bottom of the first inning – on a single, double, infield out, and another single. A walk and a triple by the local centerfielder scored the third run. How the Elite Giants scored was not documented in the *Paterson Evening News*, though it was reported that West and Wright each drove in a run."[16]

Between 1940 and 1943, Johnson's story becomes cloudier. James Riley mentions that he may have played with the Birmingham Black Barons in 1941 and 1942.[17] Johnson did register for the military draft on October 16, 1940. Although the 1940 US Census notes his occupation as "Ball Player," his employer indicated on his draft card is W.E. Wheless, associated with the Allen Mfg. Co. in Shreveport, Caddo [Parish], Louisiana. Also of interest on the draft card is his cited place of birth as Jefferson, Texas – further confusing his actual birthplace.

In 1944 the Homestead Grays were champions of the NNL2. Johnson was a member of this team and appeared in 13 games under manager Candy Jim Taylor. Johnson did not compile a noteworthy record – he started six games and pitched 63⅓ innings but won only one game and lost six. However, he was part of a very noteworthy rotation that included Ray Brown, Edsall Walker, and Spoon Carter.

In 1945 and 1946, Johnson pitched for the New York Black Yankees. These seasons were not good ones for the team. Under managers George Scales (5-20), Willie Wells (4-9), and Marvin Barker (7-16), the team posted a 16-45 overall record, and a record in the NNL2 of 11-28 Marvin Barker did well with a .289 batting average, but the top pitcher Neck Stanley saw a 5-7 record. Johnson started three games, pitched 29⅓ total innings, and compiled a record of 1-2. The next season the Black Yankees, managed by Barker, were 17-53 overall and 9-45 in the NNL2. The top pitcher that season was Alex Newkirk, with a 4-5 record. In 15 games, Johnson had seven starts, pitched 55⅔ innings, and had a won-lost record of 0-5.

Sometime in the mid-1940s, Johnson married Alice – her surname is not known. The US City Directories from 1946 forward show that Johnson and Alice were married, and the 1950 US Census noted that he worked in sales for an ice company, Alice's occupation was housework, and they lived in a private home in Shreveport. Neither Johnny nor Alice date and place of death is known. It is possible that Alice is buried in Plainview Cemetery, Livingston Parish, Louisiana. Possibly Johnny is buried in the same cemetery. Records of his siblings' lives – marriages, children, death, etc. – are available, but they have not led to determination of Johnson's and his wife's death information.

John Arthur Johnson played professional baseball for several years, starting as early as 1935 when he was 20 years old. Only

speculation can determine the number of teams he played for. Evidence is strong that his role on each team was as a pitcher. He played with many great ballplayers – Mule Suttles, Hilton Smith, Jimmie Crutchfield, Monte Irvin, and Leon Day, to name a few. He appeared in 37 known games with four teams in the NNL2. A pitcher, he started 18 games, pitched 164 innings, and compiled a 3-14 record with a 6.15 ERA. Although these statistics may be unimpressive, his talent and perseverance cannot be overlooked.

NOTES

1   James Riley. *The Biographical Encyclopedia of the Negro Leagues* (New York: Carroll & Graf Publishers, 1994), 438.

2   "Former Monroe Monarchs Ace Will Be on Hill Here Sunday," *Shreveport* (Louisiana) *Times*, September 3, 1936: 11.

3   As of December 2023, Seamheads.com said that Johnson was born in Jefferson, Texas. His parents and four siblings were born there, but US Census records indicate that he was born in Louisiana.

4   Venolia married Albert Johnson, who died in 1924, leaving her a widow with two children, Mary (b.1923), and Zula Mae (1924). The two children (Columbus and Minnie's grandchildren) grew up with their mother in the same home that she had with her own parents and siblings. A third grandchild, Waddell, was born in 1933. The census record does not indicate who Waddell's parents were, and he is identified only as "grandson" to Columbus and Minnie.

5   "Monroe Monarchs Off on Long Road Jaunt," *Monroe* (Louisiana) *Morning World*, May 26, 1935: 10.

6   "Negro Team That Plays Here Sunday Has 68 Victories," *Shreveport Times*, September 18, 1935: 10.

7   "Local Negro Nine Adds Hurler for Games with Pels," *Shreveport Times*, September 3, 1936: 11.

8   Many Johnsons appear on these rosters, but John Arthur Johnson is a pitcher – he may have played other positions, but as seen here, he is a pitcher.

9   "Little Rock Negro Team Will Tackle Local Club Today," *Shreveport Times*, April 4, 1937: 34.

10   "Buffalo Aces," *Arkansas Baseball Encyclopedia,* https://arkbaseball.com/tiki-index.php?page=Buffalo+Aces.

11   "Negro League Spring Training in Marianna, AR," *Arkansas Baseball Encyclopedia,* https://www.arkbaseball.com/tiki-index.php?page=Negro+League+Spring+Training+in+Marianna%2C+AR.

12   Bob Stedler, "Sport Comment," *Buffalo Evening News*, May 13, 1938: 5.

13   "Abe Manley's Newark Eagles Move Up in League History," *New York Amsterdam News*, July 2, 1938: A5.

14   "Black Senators Defeat Buffalo," *New York Amsterdam News*, May 21,1938: 15.

15   "Eagles Take 16 Innings to Beat Grays," *Philadelphia Tribune*, August 25, 1938: 9. It is unclear who this Ace Parker was.

16   "Today's Sports Card," *Philadelphia Inquirer*, June 21, 1938: 24. "Elite Giants Bow to Eelman by 3-2 Decision," *Paterson* (New Jersey) *Evening News*, June 22, 1939: 29.

17   Riley, 438.

HENRY KIMBRO

BY CHRIS RAINEY

Henry Kimbro was a stocky speedster who earned his living slap-hitting baseballs between third base and shortstop or into the outfield gaps. He served as the leadoff hitter for the Baltimore Elite Giants for 13 of his 18 seasons in the Negro Leagues. Kimbro was not known for power, but his 5-foot-8 and 175- pound frame could generate quite a punch when he chose. He is one of the few players ever to launch a home run over the roof of Briggs Stadium in Detroit. A fine defensive outfielder, he started in five East-West Games from 1941 to 1947 and was a late substitute in another. He added three more all-star appearances in the 1950s, although the Negro Leagues were losing their luster by then.

Henry Allen Kimbro was born on February 10, 1912, in Nashville, Tennessee. He was the fifth child born to Will and Sallie (King) Kimbro. Both were Tennessee natives and resided in West Nashville. Will is listed as a cemetery groundskeeper in census reports and also raised crops for Walden College.[1] Sallie tended the children and took in laundry when the need arose. Kimbro attended school near home through the sixth grade, but the Black junior high was a 10- to 12-mile trek to the other side of town and that discouraged him from further schooling.

Kimbro took a job at a gas station where he worked into his early twenties. There he learned how to repair cars, keep them running, and even give them extra power. He earned a reputation as a top-notch driver and was rumored to have run moonshine in Western Tennessee. During his baseball career, his knowledge of cars came in handy as he helped to repair the team buses (Chevrolet and Buick) and served as a backup driver.

Kimbro met and fell in love with Nellie Bridges. They married and a son, Larry, was born March 10, 1936. That April, Kimbro departed home for the baseball season, leaving Nellie alone with Larry for over five months. The marriage was a struggle and the long separations made life even more difficult. Their volatile marriage eventually ended in divorce. In the mid-1940's, Kimbro had a relationship with a woman in Baltimore that produced a daughter, Geraldine. Kimbro included her as

Center fielder Henry Kimbro. Courtesy SABR Rucker Archive.

best he could in his life, but the family eventually lost track of her. She was his only child that did not complete college.

Tom Wilson had been sponsoring teams in Nashville for more than a decade when he became aware of Kimbro's talents on the amateur diamonds. He approached the speedster about joining the Nashville Elite Giants, but Kimbro turned him down at first. Then, in the fall of 1935, Kimbro joined a barnstorming troupe on a southern swing. He must have enjoyed the pay-for-play lifestyle because he signed with Wilson's Elite Giants in 1936 and went with the team when it transferred to Columbus, Ohio. In 1937 the franchise shifted to Washington, D.C., and joined the Negro National League. That fall, Kimbro joined a group of all-stars managed by Oscar Charleston. The highlight of the squad's short tour was playing Satchel Paige's team before 35,000 fans at Yankee Stadium.

In 1938 the Elite Giants made Baltimore their home and installed Kimbro as the leadoff hitter and center fielder. Nicknames were very common in baseball, and Kimbro was frequently called "Jimbo" or "Kimmie." In 1939 the Elite Giants barely earned a spot in the playoffs. They beat Newark in the first round of the NNL2 playoffs and then defeated the Homestead Grays in the league's championship series. Kimbro batted .235 (8 for 34) in nine playoff games, but he had hit .319 in league games to help get them to the playoffs. His defense earned raves, especially in Game Two when he made two spectacular catches. One came in the third inning when "he raced from deep centerfield to haul in Vic Harris' terrific clout near the right-field fence."[2]

Kimbro made his first trip to Cuba that fall with a group sponsored by Grays owner Cum Posey. They won all six games in the series. Kimbro remained in Cuba after the series and played for the winter-league champion Almendares ballclub.

After the Homestead Grays earned the Negro National League title in 1940, Wilson decided the Elite Giants needed a shake-up. In April 1941 he put together a two-part swap with the New York Black Yankees. When all the wheeling and dealing was done, the Black Yankees had Kimbro, three pitchers, two catchers, first baseman Red Moore and cash. Baltimore added first baseman Johnny Washington, center fielder Charlie Biot, plus a pitcher and a catcher.[3]

New York manager Tex Burnett tried to get Kimbro to drop his slap-hitting style and go for the long ball. He even installed Kimbro in the third spot of the lineup. The experiment did not last long. Kimbro had a .300 average for the season, but failed to hit a single home run. He was back in the leadoff position by late June. Kimbro was named a second-team outfielder on the *Pittsburgh Courier's* "Dream Team for '41." The team was selected by Cum Posey and included players from the American and National Negro Leagues as well as the Mexican League.[4]

In February 1942, Wilson made another deal with New York, this time returning Kimbro to Baltimore for Biot and pitcher Schoolboy Griffith. The Giants and Grays staged a hard-fought pennant chase. On August 9, Giants catcher Roy Campanella and infielder Sammy Hughes chose to play in an exhibition game against a White all-star team and missed a crucial game with the Grays. Unsurprisingly, the players were suspended. Campanella responded by going to Mexico for the remainder of the season, and Baltimore finished just behind Homestead in the second-half pennant race. That winter, as he had in 1941, Kimbro went with the Elite Giants to the California Winter League. The next couple of winters he stayed in Baltimore and worked on defense jobs.

The Elite Giants fell to fifth place in 1943 and struggled to a second-place finish in 1944. Kimbro's game kept improving, and his average was well over .300 in 1944. He duplicated his strong stats in 1945 and 1946 but the team never reached the championship. In the winter of 1946, he played for Havana. There he met Erbia de la Candida Del Rosario Mendoza, who was a student at a Havana teacher's college. Neither spoke the other's language, but, with friends and family acting as translators, they fell in love. Kimbro followed the traditional Cuban rules on courtship. The couple was able to date only if escorted by chaperones. Often, they simply sat together in the family home. He wooed the family with trips to the movies and chocolate.[5] After the 1947 season he returned to Cuba and won the batting title with a .346 average. It was initially reported that he earned a $1000 bonus for his efforts, but that was lowered to $600 in later reports.[6] In addition to the title, Kimbro set an all-time Cuban winter mark with 104 base hits, was named an all-star, and anchored Havana's championship team.[7]

Jackie Robinson and Larry Doby broke the major-league color barrier

Kimbro on the field.

in 1947, but Kimbro got very little attention as a potential big-leaguer. He had a reputation as a loner, his age (35) was working against him, and, by his own admission, "if somebody did something to me, I'd have been up at 'em. No way in the world I wouldn't have fought back."[8] When spring training opened in 1948, manager Candy Jim Taylor was hospitalized in Chicago and Kimbro was put in charge. When Taylor passed away, Jesse "Hoss" Walker was hired as manager. The Elite Giants won the first half pennant in 1948 but dropped the playoff series to the Grays in three straight games.

That winter, Kimbro returned to Cuba, where he led the league in walks. Patience at the plate was an integral part of his game. Teammate Butch McCord claimed, "I never saw him swing at a first pitch." After that season, Kimbro returned to the island to continue the courtship of Erbia, but he did not play baseball. Their daughter, Harriet, thinks he made only one trip a year until he finally earned permission to wed Erbia. He brought his fiancée back to Nashville where they were married on September 5, 1952.[9] Over the course of their marriage, the couple welcomed two daughters and a son and enjoyed their lives together in Nashville; the children remember taking trips back to Cuba in the 1950s.

In 1949 the Elite Giants ran the table and defeated the Chicago American Giants to win the Negro American League championship, 4-0. In September, the *Baltimore Afro-American* credited Kimbro with a .332 average; the Howe News Bureau credited Kimbro with a final season batting average of .360, but this figure likely also included his performances in exhibition games.[10] The Negro Leagues were winding down, but the 1950 Elite Giants were still going strong. Kimbro, now 38, was still a force at leadoff and in the field. On July 17, he added the title of manager to his resume when skipper Lennie Pearson was sold to Milwaukee of the American Association. The Giants won his first game, 5-4, over the Birmingham Black Barons but finished behind the New York Cubans and missed the playoffs. When the Elite Giants disbanded after the 1951 season, Kimbro moved to the Birmingham Black Barons and played for the team through 1953. By that time, the Negro Leagues had shrunk to four teams and Kimbro was 41 years old. He retired from baseball and took up family life as well as an arduous seven-days-a-week work schedule.

After a few years as a cab driver, Kimbro purchased a gas station and eventually started Bill's Cab Company in Nashville. Both endeavors proved to be successful and provided the family with steady income for over two decades. Kimbro was able to afford college for Larry (Tennessee State), Harriet (Fisk), Philip (Fisk), and Maria (Florida A&M). More importantly, "Daddy taught us how to live, how to triumph over any odds, how to succeed," his daughter Harriet later told the *Tennessean*.[11] After retirement Kimbro often met with fellow Negro Leaguers at a Nashville sports shop called the "Old Negro League Sports Shop." The "loner" image from his early days was a thing of the past.

When the National and American leagues chose to honor the Negro Leagues at events during the 1990s, Kimbro was a frequent invitee, including an appearance at the 1993 All-Star Game at Camden Yards. He was inducted posthumously into the Tennessee Sports Hall of Fame in 2003.

In his final years he struggled with a heart condition. After repeated hospitalizations in 1999, he opted to return home rather than to try experimental surgery. He died at his Nashville home on July 11, 1999, of congestive heart failure. After funeral services at the Patterson Memorial United Methodist Church, he was laid to rest in Greenwood Cemetery not far from where he grew up.

Henry Kimbro. Courtesy John W. Mosley Photograph Collection, Charles L. Blockson Afro-American Collection, Temple University Libraries.

SOURCES

All Negro League statistics and team records were taken from the Seamheads.com Negro League Database, unless otherwise indicated.

In addition to the sources cited in the Notes, the author consulted a number of other publications including:

Clark, Dick & Larry Lester. eds. *The Negro Leagues Book* (Cleveland, Ohio: SABR, 1994).

Heaphy, Leslie A. *The Negro Leagues, 1869-1960* (Jefferson, North Carolina: McFarland & Company, 2003).

Kelley, Brent. *Voices from the Negro Leagues* (Jefferson, North Carolina: McFarland & Company, Inc., 1998).

Luke, Bob. *The Baltimore Elite Giants* (Baltimore: Johns Hopkins University Press, 2009).

NOTES

1   Harriet Kimbro-Hamilton, *"Daddy's Notebook"* (Huntsville, Alabama: In Due Season Publishing: 2015); 15-16.

2   "Baltimore Bats Way to Titular Battle with Grays." *Pittsburgh Courier*, September 23, 1939: 16.

3   Hayward Jackson, "Elites get Johnny Washington in Big Swap with Yankees," *Pittsburgh Courier*, April 12, 1941: 16.

4   Cum Posey, "Posey's 18th All American Baseball Team," *Pittsburgh Courier*, October 25, 1941: 16.

5   Tasneem Ansariyah-Grace, "In a League of his Own," *Tennessean* (Nashville), March 4, 2000: 30. Also, information from Harriet Kimbro-Hamilton in email exchanges in May 2016.

6   *Afro-American* (Baltimore), March 20, 1948 and April 17, 1948.

7   Jorge S. Figueredo, *Cuban Baseball: A Statistical History, 1878-1961* (Jefferson, North Carolina: McFarland & Company, Inc., 2007).

8   Randy Horvick, "They Might Have Been Heroes," www.nashville-scene.com, May 2, 1996.

9   Kimbro's Hall of Fame questionnaire lists it as 1951. His daughter's book and various newspaper sources use the 1952 date.

10   "Negro American League (1949) League Leaders," Center for Negro League Baseball Research, http://www.cnlbr.org/Portals/0/Stats/NAL%201949/NAL1949.pdf, accessed January 29, 2023.

11   Harriet Kimbro-Hamilton, *Tennessean*, March 4, 2000: 30.

BIZ MACKEY

BY CHRIS RAINEY

In the summer of 1946, *Pittsburgh Courier* columnist Wendell Smith gave Newark Eagles manager Biz Mackey all the credit for molding "together the best all-around pitching staff in Negro baseball."[1]Assembling talent is one thing, using it wisely and coping with obstacles that arise is a totally different talent. Mackey's ace, Leon Day, opened the season with a no-hitter and led the team in wins. But he struggled with a sore arm and was of little use in the World Series. Mackey used his staff effectively, especially young Rufus Lewis, to capture a championship. His shortstop, Monte Irvin, simply said of Mackey, "As a player, as a manager, and as a personality, he was in a class by himself."[2]

Capturing the Negro League banner in 1946 was the final jewel of Mackey's brilliant career. Generally regarded as the finest defensive catcher in Negro League history, he was no slouch at the plate. The switch-hitter batted .411 in 1922 and .406 in 1930. He captured two World Series crowns in the Negro Leagues, one as a player and one as manager. He also won a championship in his only season in Cuba. In 2006 his life and talent were recognized with his selection to the National Baseball Hall of Fame in Cooperstown.

The journey to the top of his baseball world was not an easy one for Mackey. He was born the son of Texas sharecroppers. The absence of a birth certificate has led to speculation about his birthplace. In the past 30 years various researchers and writers have placed Mackey's birth in Eagle Pass, Texas, as well as Seguin, Kingsbury, Luling, and Eagle Lake, all in Texas.[3] Most current sources (Seamheads.com is a notable exception) accept the Eagle Pass location. Mackey listed his birthplace as Caldwell County (near Luling) on his World War I and World War II draft registrations.[4]

We do know that James Raleigh Mackey was one of six children born to John Dee (known as Dee to family and friends) and Beulah (Wright) Mackey, joining the family on July 27, 1897. His parents had wed in 1886 in Caldwell County and farmed there. In the 1900 census, Beulah listed herself as married but Dee was not living under the same roof. She was remarried in 1903 to Montgomery Meriwether, a farmer in a neighboring county. The 1910 census lists them in Guadalupe County between Seguin and Kingsbury. This blended family included Meriwether's three daughters along with Beulah's five surviving offspring.

The town of Luling, Texas, claims Mackey as its native son. He was wed there on October 20, 1917, to Ora Lee Dorn.[5] It is uncertain if Mackey and Ora ever had children. Mackey did have a daughter named Narcissus. She was born in 1914 and later married George H. Odoms. They took up residence in Caldwell County and raised at least three children. Her oldest son, Riley Mackey Odoms, had a long and successful football career with the Denver Broncos.[6]

Biz and Ora Lee moved to Dallas, where he played baseball and worked as a laborer in 1918. They separated in 1919 and divorced a few years later. Ora Lee remarried in 1924. She and her husband, Will Elam, lived in California. Late in his life, Mackey reconnected with Ora Lee and she is listed on his death certificate as "Informant" and appears to have handled his funeral arrangements.[7]

Mackey received his schooling in nearby Prairie Lea, Texas, through the 10th grade. It was common in rural America for students to take an exam when their schooling ended. They would earn the equivalent of today's high-school diploma with a good performance on the "Common Exam." Mackey met the requirements when he completed the test.

The 1910 census noted that Mackey worked as a farm laborer when not in school. A few years later he took a job as a clerk in a railroad warehouse. At age 16 he reportedly joined his brothers Earnest and Ray playing on the Luling Oilers, the local semipro team. Mackey caught and pitched. Most sources claim he joined the San Antonio Black Aces in 1918. It is more likely that he played for the Dallas Black Giants that season.

Before Mackey earned his nickname, he was known to fans and writers as Riley, Rollie, or Raleigh. He appears in box scores sometimes as Mackey and sometimes by his first name.[8] Based upon that information, it is likely that the Dallas catcher/ pitcher in 1918 shown as Riley was in fact Mackey.[9] He opened the 1919 season with the Giants but soon joined the Waco Black Navigators. His time with them was short-lived; he joined five other Waco players in jumping to the San Antonio Black Aces in early June.[10]

The addition of six starters to the Black Aces made them into a juggernaut. League standings showed them with a 45-10 record at the end of the Texas Colored League campaign in 1919. The Waco squad, which had started the season as the strongest team, disbanded shortly after the player defections. Dallas finished with a 51-17 mark and took on San Antonio in a postseason five-game championship.

After tight matches decided by a single run, the series came down to the nightcap of a doubleheader. The Aces sent Walter "Steel Arm" Davis to the mound, but he was pounded for three runs in the first. Mackey took the hill and allowed two more runs the rest of the way. In typical Hollywood fashion, Davis (who moved to center field) came to the plate in the eighth with two men on and lashed a double to give San Antonio a 7-5 victory and the title.

In December the leader of the Black Aces, L.W. Moore, announced his hopes of creating a Colorado-Texas-Oklahoma League. He also announced the signing of two catchers "who will fill the vacancy" created when Riley Mackey became a pitcher exclusively.[11] The new league did not materialize, and the Black Aces remained in the Texas Colored League. Mackey took the hill as planned but when one of the catchers left the team, Mackey was returned to occasional catching duties. He highlighted his return with a 5-for-5 performance against the Black Giants on June 11.

A month later Mackey was enticed to leave Texas. On July 13 he and Aces teammate Henry Blackmoan (mistakenly called Blackburn in the box score) debuted for the Negro National League Indianapolis ABC's against the Cuban Stars. Mackey smacked a double in four trips in the 5-2 victory.[12] Behind the plate he "worked in first-class style." When the Cubans' shortstop Matias Rios tried to steal second, "Mackey got the ball there so far ahead of him" that the second baseman walked up the line to tag Rios.[13] Many authors have said Mackey's contract was sold

Biz Mackey, with the Newark Eagles later in his career. Courtesy SABR Rucker Archive.

to the ABC's, but an article in the *San Antonio Evening News* mentioned that Aces leadership was contemplating a lawsuit because the players had jumped their contracts.[14]

The ABC's finished in fourth place. Mackey's work at bat and behind the plate earned him a contract for 1921. He wintered in Texas and played ball there before returning to Indiana for spring training in early April. Indianapolis opened the season with two wins over the Cuban Stars, but quickly fell off the pace after that. Mackey was even forced to take the mound and took three losses during the campaign. At the plate he hit .304, tied for the team lead in triples, and punched three home runs.

The ABC's stayed together after the season and did some barnstorming. Mackey played third base late in the year and during the fall. Russell Powell handled the catching during the regular season. In the fall, Mack Eggleston was recruited to catch. The team also welcomed back Oscar Charleston, who had spent the season with St. Louis.

Charleston remained with the ABC's in 1922 and the team finished second, tied with the Monarchs but trailing the Chicago American Giants. Charleston batted .395 and slammed 14 doubles, 9 triples, and 11 home runs. Not to be outdone, Mackey also mashed 14 doubles and hit a robust .411 while playing some shortstop and outfield along with catching.

In 1923 Ed Bolden, owner of the Hilldale Daisies (also called Giants and Darbys), led the formation of the Eastern Colored League (ECOL). A talent war ensued between the ECOL and the NNL that resulted in Mackey being signed by Hilldale. There he joined future Hall of Famers Judy Johnson, Pop Lloyd, and Louis Santop. Mackey was now 25 years old and had reached his full stature of 6 feet tall and probably 210 pounds.

The ECOL season opener was staged before 17,000 fans in Hilldale's new park. Mackey caught and batted fifth in the lineup behind Lloyd. The game was called because of rain in the sixth with Hilldale up 4-2 over the Bacharach Giants.[15] Mackey split the catching duties that season with Santop and spelled the 39-year-old Lloyd at shortstop. He is credited with leading the team in batting and RBIs. Hilldale posted a league-leading 32-17 record.

The nickname "Biz" first started to appear in 1923. Both the *Philadelphia Inquirer* and *Pittsburgh Courier* were using it by the end of the season. Mackey was a friendly, loquacious fellow with a competitive streak. He was known for giving the batter an earful when at the plate, hoping to break their concentration and focus. This "giving them the business" earned him the nickname of "Biz." It should be noted that he was not the first "Biz" Mackey to make the sports pages. A featherweight boxer who twice had world-championship matches against Abe Attell – yes, that Attell of Black Sox infamy – had appeared in headlines for two decades as the catcher grew up.

Hilldale was the dominant ECOL team again in 1924, posting a 47-22 mark. Mackey led the team in batting and handled the pitching staff of Nip Winters, Red Ryan, and Phil Cockrell expertly. The two Black leagues staged a world series after the regular season and the Kansas City Monarchs captured five of the nine games.

After the season Mackey went to Cuba to play for Almendares. He joined Lloyd, Charleston, Wilbur "Bullet" Rogan, and Adolfo Luque on a team that proved to be a juggernaut. The season was ended early because of Almendares' dominance. Mackey batted .309 with a team-leading 11 doubles.[16]

Because the regular season closed early, a postseason series was staged between an all-Cuban team and the "All Yankees" team made up of Negro League players. The All Yankees posted a 5-2-1 record. Mackey faced Cuban pitchers Jose Mendez and Martin Dihigo in the series and reportedly batted .333. Interestingly, Baseball Commissioner Kenesaw Landis attended one of the games.[17]

Unlike many of his contemporaries who played winter ball in the Caribbean and Mexico, this was Mackey's sole trip to the islands. He chose to spend his winters playing in the California Winter League, which featured a mix of Black and White teams. Mackey played 18 seasons on the West Coast and eventually made his permanent home in California. He is credited with a .366 batting average and 28 home runs in those seasons.[18]

The Hilldale squad ran away with the title again in 1925, posting a 52-15 record. The players did prove to be human during a week in June when they dropped three to the Harrisburg Giants and then lost a doubleheader to the Baltimore Black Sox. Mackey, who batted cleanup, produced only four hits in the games.[19] Hilldale was knocked out of first place by the losses but regained the lead in mid-July and never looked back.

Hilldale earned a rematch with the Monarchs in an October series. Mackey struggled early in the series. He was 2-for-17 in the first four games and even dropped a ball in a home-plate collision. Baseball takes a team effort and his teammates picked him up as Hilldale captured three of the first four matches. In the final games, in Philadelphia, Mackey's bat came alive and he had three hits, including a home run and double. Hilldale took five of six to capture the crown.[20]

Hilldale returned their core in 1926, and even added John Beckwith but its record dropped to 34-24 and the team finished in third place. In the offseason Mackey joined a barnstorming squad called the Philadelphia Royal Giants. They went to California and played in the winter league, posting a 26-11-1 record to win the crown. The team split up and some players returned to their teams for the regular season.

Mackey, along with Rap Dixon, Andy Cooper, and others, traveled to Japan and played a 48-game tour, the first tour by a Black entourage. The Americans entertained the locals with their brand of baseball, which included a pregame "shadow ball" routine. Years of experience in barnstorming had taught Mackey and his teammates the importance of keeping the local fans interested and entertained. Winning 20-0 would dampen enthusiasm and lessen the gate. It was to their advantage to keep the games close. In doing this they "played to the Japanese sense of honor and dignity."[21]

Mackey established himself as a fan favorite. He launched a massive home run at the new Meiji Shrine Stadium in Tokyo. He fascinated and amazed the crowds with his ability to throw from the crouch. He was quick with a smile and genuine sincerity toward opponents and fans alike. After hitting him with a pitch, a Japanese hurler bowed to apologize, as is the style in the country. Mackey returned the gesture and bowed in return.[22]

Biz returned to Japan for a second tour five years later. On this tour he did some pitching and led the American contingent with a .388 batting average.[23] The Japanese Baseball League would begin in 1936. Japanese baseball historian Kazuo Sayama credits the Royal Giants and Mackey with hastening the adoption of the game in his country. Babe Ruth's visit in 1934 certainly created a countrywide sensation, but without the groundwork laid by the Negro Leaguers the game would not have reached its level of influence and popularity.

The lengthy tour in 1927 caused Mackey and his mates to miss the first half of the ECOL season. Hilldale was experiencing a poor first half. Joe Lewis handled the catching, but three players were suspended indefinitely in early June because of their indifferent play. Mackey was threatened with a five-year suspension after his return to the United States in early July. The suspension proved to be a hollow threat and he was in the lineup on July 28 for a 5-3 win over the Bacharach Giants.[24]

The Daisies finished third in the second half after being in fifth at the close of the first half. Mackey batted .284. He was recruited by Cum Posey in the fall and traveled with the Homestead Grays on their extensive barnstorming trip.

Hilldale added Oscar Charleston to the roster but dropped out of the league in March 1928. Playing an independent schedule against all comers, the team covered the East with appearances. Mackey found himself playing shortstop on numerous occasions. In late September he and second baseman Frank Warfield were added to the roster of the Baltimore Black Sox.

Hilldale moved into the American Negro League in 1929 and Mackey returned to the team. He stayed with it through 1931 after they went independent. In 1932 he declined a contract and stayed in California until promoter Lonnie Goodwin left for the Orient with his tour. The team played nine games in Honolulu, then crossed the Pacific to play in Japan. They also had 10 games scheduled in China and 30 in the Philippines.

From 1933 to 1935 Mackey played with the Philadelphia Stars. He was selected by fan vote as the starting catcher in the inaugural East-West All-Star Game, played before 19,000 fans in Comiskey Park in Chicago. He split time with Josh Gibson at catcher in the 11-7 loss by his East team. In 1936 he was traded to the Columbus Elite Giants, but that franchise moved to Washington. Mackey had his first taste as manager when he filled in for Candy Jim Taylor. He also earned a starting spot in the All-Star Game.

The consensus among fans and scholars of the Negro Leagues was that Gibson was the better hitter, but Mackey was by far his defensive superior. Author James Riley said it best: "Considered the master of defense, (Mackey) possessed all the tools necessary behind the plate. … An expert handler of pitchers, he studied people. … [H]e was a master at … framing and funneling pitches. Pitchers recognized his generalship and liked to pitch" to Mackey. His surprising agility for a big man enabled him to play the infield.[25]

In 1937 Mackey took over as Washington manager when Taylor moved on. Mackey was selected by the fans as the manager for the East-West All Star Game. His East squad emerged with a 7-2 victory. He was tipped off about the talent of a teenager named Roy Campanella. Washington signed Campanella for $60 a month and Mackey began the task of turning him into a professional catcher. When Mackey left the Elite Giants, Campanella was ready to step into his shoes. Campanella recalled, "Biz Mackey was the master of defense of all catchers." Campanella always was quick to give Mackey credit for his development.[26]

Mackey was sold to the Newark Eagles in 1939. He took over as manager from Dick Lundy partway through the 1940 season. Despite a growing waistline and aching knees, Mackey continued to be an asset on the field. In 1942 he had a falling-out with the owners, Abe and Effa Manley, over salary and was replaced by Willie Wells.

Mackey returned to his California home. He supported the war effort by working at North American Aviation in Los Angeles and played baseball with the San Francisco Sea Lions. When the Manleys had a dispute with Wells, Mackey returned to Newark in 1945. He continued to play occasionally, mostly at first base.

The Eagles captured the first-half championship in 1946 with a record of 25-9. They weathered some hard times in the second half, including the demise of the team bus which forced players to drive their own cars to games at one point.

Mackey was renowned for his levelheadedness and emotional control on the field throughout his managerial career. He uncharacteristically lost his cool in a game against the Cleveland Buckeyes in late July of 1946 and pulled the Eagles from the field in protest. The Black press took him to task for being unsportsmanlike. Effa Manley came to his defense with a letter to the *Pittsburgh Courier* and the issue blew over.

The Eagles took the second half with a 22-7 mark and met the Kansas City Monarchs in the World Series. Led by Monte Irvin's bat and the pitching of Rufus Lewis, Newark captured the pennant, a triumph that earned each player a diamond ring.

Mackey managed the Eagles again in 1947. The Eagles sold Larry Doby to the Cleveland Indians that year. Mackey recommended moving the youngster from second base to the outfield, which the Indians did. Mackey was named manager of the East squad for the All-Star Game. The game was played on his 50th birthday and Mackey rewarded himself by pinch-hitting in the eighth inning. He had seen very little action that season, and his waistline had grown to where writer Wendell Smith called

him paunchy. His girth did not affect his batting eye; he walked. He immediately replaced himself with Vic Harris.

Mackey retired to California, where he continued to play with the Sea Lions and other teams. Fate has an odd way of impacting our lives. When Mackey made his first trip to Japan, he was intrigued to find a large contingent of Afro-Asians living in Tokyo. He met a young woman of mixed ancestry named Lucille and they became friendly. On later trips to Japan he made it a point to contact her. The pair understandably lost contact during the war.

According to Mackey's great-nephew Ray, Lucille and her family came to the United States in the late 1940s or early 1950s. She and Mackey were reunited in San Francisco. They spent the rest of their lives together. Mackey's reputation in baseball was that of a jovial, trash-talker but in his private life he was very reserved. He bordered on reclusive and did very little to publicize his baseball life.

That changed, for one day at least, on the evening of May 7, 1959. A reported 93,000 fans attended an exhibition game in the Los Angeles Coliseum between the Dodgers and the Yankees. The occasion was to pay tribute to Roy Campanella, the longtime Dodgers catcher, who had been paralyzed in a traffic accident the previous year. In the crowd were Mackey and his nephew Ray. In his thank-you speech to the throng, Campy called for Mackey to join him on the field and made sure that everyone there realized how important Biz had been in his development.[27]

After the Campanella tribute, Mackey lived quietly in Los Angeles and worked as a forklift driver for the Stauffer Chemical Company. In those days before the publication of *Only the Ball Was White*,[28] it was commonplace for a former Negro League player to live in anonymity. Lucille, called "Aunt Lucy" by the family, died a few months before Biz. The family wondered if the loss of the love of his life hastened Mackey's demise. Biz died on September 22, 1965, in Los Angeles. He was buried in that city's Evergreen Cemetery. His death received no coverage in *The Sporting News* nor did it appear in the Necrology of the *1966 Sporting News Official Baseball Guide*. In the 1970s and beyond, Mackey's name would make newspapers as a Negro League player who deserved Hall of Fame consideration. His time to enter Cooperstown finally came in 2006.

SOURCES

Statistics come from Baseball-Reference.com unless otherwise noted. Standings of teams come from *The Negro League Book* published by SABR in 1994. A big thank-you to Ray Mackey III for his tremendous wealth of information about Biz and the Mackey family. I would also like to extend my gratitude to renowned Negro League historian Larry Lester for his support and guidance in this research. Finally, a tip of the hat to the Allen County Library in Fort Wayne, Indiana, where a researcher named Cristella searched the *Los Angeles Sentinel* for Mackey info.

NOTES

1   Wendell Smith, "The Sports Beat," *Pittsburgh Courier*, July 13, 1946: 16.

2   templepress.wordpress.com/2018/01/24/biz-mackey-a-giant-behind-the-plate/.

3   John Holway listed the birthplace as Seguin in his 1988 book *Blackball Stars*; other sources found in Mackey's Hall of Fame file suggest Kingsbury, which is east of Seguin and Luling; in a correspondence from 2000 there was mention of Eagle Lake.

4   ancestry.com/interactive/6482/005152930_01688?pid=16453080&backurl=https://search. Last accessed February 26, 2019. search.ancestry.com/cgi-bin/sse.dll?db=YMDraftCardsWWII&indiv=try&h=17975243. Last accessed March 11, 2019.

5   search.ancestry.com/cgi-bin/sse.dll?dbid=60183&h=66427&indiv=try&o_vc=Record:OtherRecord&rhSource=8842.

6   Brad Gray, "Biz's Big Day," *Austin American-Statesman*, July 31, 2006: 20.

7   Gary Krause, email exchange from February 2000 found in Mackey's Hall of Fame file. Krause was researching Mackey's personal information and corresponding with a Hall of Fame library researcher, Eric Enders.

8   An example would be the box scores in the *Dallas Express* from August 23, 1919: 11, in which he was listed as Riley in the first game and Releigh (*sic*) in game two.

9   "Dallas Black Giants Win," *Dallas Morning News*, August 12, 1918: 7. He was also residing in Dallas in August when he signed up for the draft. See Note 4.

10 Gary Ashwill, "Steel Arm Davis," Agate Type, November 3, 2014. agatetype.typepad.com/agate_type/2014/11/steel-arm-davis.html. Last accessed February 26, 2019.

11 *San Antonio Evening News*, December 13, 1919: 10.

12 "New Players Show Class," *Indianapolis Star*, July 14, 1920: 10.

13 "New Players Show Class."

14 "Suit May be Filed for Taking Players from Black Aces," *San Antonio Evening News*, August 2, 1920: 7.

15 "Hilldale Opens New Park with Victory," *Philadelphia Inquirer*, April 29, 1923: 20.

16 Jorge S. Figueredo, *Cuban Baseball: A Statistical History, 1878-1961* (Jefferson, North Carolina: McFarland, 2003), 157-59.

17 Figueredo, 162.

18 Geri Strecker, "Winter Baseball in California: Separate Opportunities, Equal Talent," *The National Pastime* (SABR, 2011), accessed on February 28, 2019 at sabr.org/research/winter-baseball-california-separate-opportunities-equal-talent.

19 "Harrisburg Sweeps Three-Game Series with Hilldale; Leads Eastern League," *Pittsburgh Courier*, June 27, 1925: 12.

20 Game coverage from the *Pittsburgh Courier* of October 10 and 17.

21 Gary Joseph Cieradkowski, "Biz Mackey: International Man of Clout," Infinite Card Set blog October 2013. Last accessed on February 28, 2019 at infinitecardset.blogspot.com/2013/10/160-biz-mackey-international-man-of.html.

22 Kazuo Sayama and Bill Staples Jr., *Gentle Black Giants: A History of Negro Leaguers in Japan* (Fresno, California: NBRP Press, 2019), 121.

23 William F. McNeil, *Black Baseball Out of Season: Pay for Play Outside the Negro Leagues* (Jefferson, North Carolina: McFarland, 2012), 108.

24 "Mackey's 'Five-Years Suspension' Over, Aids Hilldale in Win Over Seasiders," *Pittsburgh Courier*, July 30, 1927: 16.

25 James A. Riley, *The Biographical Encyclopedia of the Negro Baseball Leagues* (New York: Carroll & Graf Publishers, 1994), 502-03.

26 Gray, "Biz's Big Day."

27 Telephone interviews with Ray Mackey III, March 6 and 11, 2019.

28 Robert Peterson, *Only the Ball Was White* (New York: Oxford University Press, 1992).

JAMES "RED" MOORE

BY LESLIE HEAPHY

James "Red" Moore had a long and distinguished career in the Negro Leagues, from 1936 to 1948. Best known for his fine fielding, Moore held his own at the plate as well. Playing primarily at first base, Moore anchored the infield for nearly two decades in Atlanta, Baltimore, Indianapolis, and Newark. Born on November 18, 1916, in Atlanta, Moore grew up around the game of baseball. His parents, James and Sadie, supported him playing baseball but also ensured that he attended Booker T. Washington High School. Moore got his start at 13 playing for the local Oakland City Cubs.[1] In the 1930 US Census, Sadie Moore was listed as a maid and her husband as a machinist.

Moore had to be innovative while he learned to play the game. As a young left-handed first baseman who had no money for a new glove, he turned a right-handed glove inside out and stitched it back together so he could play.[2] He and his friends would take old baseballs and tape them back together so they could play. This did not slow him down at all as he played with and against the many semipro teams around the Atlanta area. He finally got his chance at the big leagues when the Newark Eagles signed him after seeing him play with the Macon Peaches and Chattanooga Choo Choos.

James "Red" Moore at SABR convention in Atlanta, 2010, with Terry Sloope. Courtesy of Terry Sloope.

The 1936 Newark Eagles that Moore joined included four future Hall of Famers on their roster – Leon Day, Mule Suttles, Willie Wells, and Ray Dandridge. While Red played in only 13 games that first year, he learned a great deal from the team and came back in 1937 to play in 16 games and raise his average to .244. Moore recalled trying to hit against Satchel Paige with Josh Gibson catching. Paige struck out Moore on three straight pitches while Gibson heckled him as a rookie. Moore raised his average to .344 in 1938 with local businessman James Harden's Atlanta Black Crackers.[3] Moore helped the Atlanta club win the second-half pennant in the Negro American League though they lost to Memphis in the abbreviated playoffs. The series was cut short when ball fields could not be secured for all the games. Gabby Kemp managed the club and played second base while "Steel Arm" Eddie Dixon helped lead the pitching staff. Like Moore, most of the team came from the surrounding communities.[4]

Fans who came out to see Moore play were in for a treat. He became known as a flashy fielder who could make almost any play look easy. He would often make catches one-handed and flip the ball straight from his glove. He could dig out low throws and turn a mean 3-6-3 double play. Moore also warmed up before games by throwing a ball behind his back and through his legs just to entertain the fans. While he played with Atlanta in 1937, Moore's play was described as "scintillating escapades" and in a game against Chattanooga his fielding saved the game "as his frame sprawled forth on the greensward as he did a backhanded trap on the peg for a miraculous third out."[5] In 1940 a local news reporter referred to him as the "deluxe" first baseman.[6] Though Mule Suttles also played first base for the Newark Eagles, Moore was the better fielder, pushing Mule into the outfield when he played. Moore was part of what became known as the "Million Dollar infield" for the 1937 Eagles. He joined established stars Willie Wells, Dick Seay and Ray Dandridge to give the Eagles one of the best defensive clubs in the game.

Moore pioneered another innovation during his early playing days. In addition to his makeshift glove, he started wearing a batting glove to take the sting out of hitting. He took a leather winter glove and cut off the fingertips. He wore it for the rest of his career.[7]

By 1938 Moore's popularity in Atlanta was assured. The community thought so much of him that local businesses offered him a new glove, new shoes, a fancy chicken dinner, a new radio, and more. The fans were asked to bring their spare change to drop in the Red Moore pot at the ballpark. All this was happening because fans all over believed Moore to be the best first baseman ever. His own teammates said there was no jealousy over the accolades because "he is ... an unusually quiet and likeable chap with a minimum of 'mouth' and no lean toward rowdiness."[8] Moore would take this day in stride and not make a big deal out of it. He would just return to playing the game the best way he knew how. When he visited Kansas City to play the Monarchs, fans deemed him the best first baseman they had ever seen. "The way Moore scooped and speared the ball was a feature of every game and he left the fans singing his praises."[9]

In 1939 Moore signed with the Baltimore Elite Giants after the Indianapolis/Atlanta team folded, where he found himself rooming with 17-year-old rookie Roy Campanella. Moore and Campanella got along well as they had similar personalities. They were both quiet, unassuming, and well-liked by everyone. Moore and Campanella helped the Giants to a postseason championship series against the Homestead Grays. The Giants beat the Newark Eagles three games to one (with one tie) to make it to the final series. Moore was expected to be one to

contribute to the series, even as a newcomer. While most known for his fielding Moore was a good spray hitter who made good contact with the ball. He hit .214 in the five-game series with three hits and two walks.[10]

By mid-June of 1940, the city of Atlanta was looking to bring back the Black Crackers. One reporter said the only thing the team needed to ensure success was to bring back fan favorite Red Moore. The new owner, Mr. Greer, was told, "[S]ecure at whatever the cost the services of 'Red Moore,' Atlanta idol to play ball here. ... Baseball will pay in Atlanta, but if you want it resurrected and a moneymaker at the start make steps to secure Red Moore."[11]

After the 1940 season with Baltimore, Moore was in high demand. Double Duty Radcliffe tried to secure his services for Memphis while Syd Pollock also wanted Moore for the Ethiopian Clowns. Instead, Moore ended up being traded to the New York Black Yankees.[12]

Red Moore at Jackie Robinson Day event at Turner Field in April 2011 at Turner Field. Courtesy Atlanta Braves Archives.

Moore lost three years of playing time during World War II. He entered the US Army as a combat engineer in 1942, serving in England, Belgium, and France. After the war ended, Moore returned to play for the Atlanta Black Crackers for three more years, ending his career after the 1948 season. Moore then went to work for Colonial Warehouse in Atlanta, living in the area with his wife, Mary. He worked until his retirement in 1981. It would be many more years before Moore's accomplishments started to be remembered and recognized. The Georgia House of Representatives honored him with a resolution, and the local Mike Glenn Foundation presented him with a Pioneer Award. In 2006 his baseball achievements were further honored with his election to the Atlanta Sports Hall of Fame.[13]

In 2008 Major League Baseball held a special draft and Moore was selected by the Atlanta Braves. Moore had been a three-time all-star, played on championship teams, and was beloved by the fans. Moore died at the age of 99 on February 6, 2016. Services were held at Missionary Baptist Church, where Moore had served as a deacon. Moore loved the game of baseball and was lucky enough to live long enough to enjoy his many honors and accolades. Moore told a reporter, "It makes me feel real big to be honored. People can see history and not just read about it. That makes me feel real big."[14]

SOURCES

In addition to the sources cited in the Notes, the author consulted Seamheads and the National Baseball Hall of Fame player files.

NOTES

1   Oral history interview with James "Red" Moore, October 15, 1978. Living Atlanta oral history collection, Digital Library of Georgia; https://ohms.libs.uga.edu/viewer.php?cachefile=dlg/livatl/ahc-637-105-001.xml. Accessed February 5, 2024.

2   James A. Riley, "He Could Pick It," *2010 National Pastime: Baseball in the Peach State,* https://sabr.org/journal/article/red-moore-he-could-pick-it/.

3   Red Moore. https://www.baseball-reference.com/players/m/moore-re01.shtml.

4   James "Red" Moore interview, October 15, 1978.

5   Ric Roberts, "Red Moore, Tiloshi Howard Make Good in League," *Atlanta Daily World,* April 4, 1937: 7.

6   Lucius Jones, "Atlanta Fans Await Baseball Opener This Week," *Atlanta Daily World,* March 25, 1940: 5.

7   Riley, "He Could Pick It."

8   Ric Roberts, "Trammell Scott, Sou. League President, Honors Red Moore," *Atlanta Daily World,* July 22, 1938: 5; "Black Crackers Arrive Tonight," *Atlanta Daily World,* July 23, 1938: 5.

9   "Kansas City Fans Call Red Moore 'The Greatest to Ever Visit Kansas City,'" *Atlanta Daily World,* June 8, 1938: 5.

10   "Elites to Play Grays for Championship," *Baltimore Afro-American,* September 16, 1939: 23; https://www.baseball-reference.com/postseason/1939_NLC.shtml.

11   I.P. Reynolds, "'Red' Moore Still Lingers in Our Memory," *Atlanta Daily World,* June 21, 1940: 5.

12   Melancholy Jones, "Sports Slants," *Atlanta Daily World,* April 13 and 27, 1941: 8; "James (Red) Moore, Baltimore First Baseman, Traded to New York Outfit," *Atlanta Daily World,* April 12, 1941: 5.

13   James A. Riley, "He Could Pick It."

14   James "Red" Moore obituary, *Atlanta Journal Constitution,* February 7-12, 2016; Adena Andrews, Negro Leagues First Baseman James 'Red' Moore Still Living the Dream – ESPN, February 25, 2011.

JOHN "LEFTY" PHILLIPS

BY MARGARET M. GRIPSHOVER

The John William "Lefty" Phillips story begins with another ballplayer, his father, John "Hooty" Phillips.[1] Father and son played for their hometown Nashville Elite Giants, among other teams. Neither Hooty nor Lefty Phillips is especially well-known, although Hooty Phillips had a longer and more varied career than his son. And if baseball was all in the family for the Phillipses, it was also baseball that tore the family asunder and contributed to their unhappy endings.

John William "Lefty" Phillips was born in Nashville, Tennessee, on May 24, 1917. His parents, Hooty Phillips and Minnie Mae Kelly, married about three months before John Phillips's arrival. When they wed, Hooty Phillips was 19 years old, and Minnie Phillips was just a few months shy of her 16th birthday. Hooty Phillips was mostly an absentee father. When he wasn't on the road playing baseball, he worked alongside his father, William Phillips, at an East Nashville brickyard. It was likely a difficult marriage, and by 1925 Lefty Phillips's parents no longer shared the same Nashville address. One possible cause of the demise of the Phillipses' marriage was Hooty Phillips's long absences from home in pursuit of his baseball career.

Hooty Phillips started his professional baseball life in 1921 as a shortstop with the Nashville Elite Giants.[2] John "Lefty" Phillips was about 4 years old when his father had his championship season with the Elite Giants. Hooty Phillips was Nashville's starting shortstop and frequent leadoff man. Based on the published box scores for the Elite Giants, Hooty was known more for his fancy infield play than for any prowess at the plate. Throughout the spring and summer of 1921, he was lauded for taking "sensational chances without erring," and for his "great fielding at shortstop."[3] In September the Elite Giants vied for the Negro Southern League championship against the Montgomery Gray Sox at Athletic Park in Nashville.[4] Phillips's play was described as "brilliant," as he "cut off several prospective hits."[5] Phillips and his fellow Elite Giants took home the NSL championship and the trophy presented by NSL President Frank M. Perdue.[6] At the conclusion of the season, Hooty Phillips returned to his family's home on Sixth Avenue North in Nashville and headed back to work at the brickyard.[7]

Hooty Phillips, father of Lefty Phillips. Courtesy Nashville Metro Archives and Skip Nipper.

In the spring of 1922, Hooty Phillips briefly jumped from the Elite Giants to Fred Caulfield's New Orleans Black Pelicans, also known as "Caulfield's Ads," before boomeranging back to Nashville by June.[8] The Elite Giants were in New Orleans for a series with the Black Pelicans when owner Tom Wilson "pulled a deal" and "bought Square Moore, pitcher, and Phillips, shortstop, from Caulfield for a cash consideration."[9] Why Hooty Phillips skipped town and joined the New Orleans nine is unknown, but his return to Nashville helped to create a more "balanced and strengthened" team."[10] That summer Phillips had a few moments in the spotlight. On June 28, in a game against the Birmingham Black Barons, he stepped up and launched a three-run blast to deep center.[11] Against the Knoxville Giants on July 29, his "great fielding" and lively batting were among the highlights of a 13-inning marathon that ended in a 4-4 tie.[12] It was an unsatisfying day, with no winner declared and no light left by which to play. That was Phillips's last game with the Elite Giants – at least for 1922. At the end of July, the Elite Giants were in first place in the NSL, but this time around there would be no celebrations or trophies. The NSL collapsed before the season came to an official conclusion. In August the Elite Giants embarked on a barnstorming venture with the Knoxville Giants.[13] But it was back to Nashville and the brickyard for Phillips, and to his wife, Minnie, and young son and future Elites player, John William "Lefty" Phillips.

In the spring of 1923, Hooty Phillips once again left his wife and son behind to pursue his baseball career. But he did not return to the Nashville Elite Giants. Phillips was picked up by the Detroit Stars as their new second baseman, replacing Frank Warfield, who headed east to sign with Ed Bolden's Hilldale club of Darby, Pennsylvania.[14] Phillips's new boss was the Stars' player-manager and fellow Nashvillian, Bruce Petway. Hooty Phillips's tenure with the Detroit Stars was unremarkable and he was clearly heading toward the end of his baseball life expectancy. He played in at least four games for Detroit in May and June but produced no more than a handful of hits and about as many errors.[15] In early July, Phillips was offloaded to the hapless last-place Milwaukee Bears, only to continue his hitless and error-prone ways.[16] The newly constituted Milwaukee club was a hitless wonder and folded before end of the 1923 season.[17] Within a few weeks of his hibernation with the Bears, Phillips was back with the Stars where he sleepwalked through the remainder of the season, waking up only briefly to punch out the occasional single or bungle the ball. His final documented game with the Detroit Stars was on September 4, 1923.[18] Hooty Phillips's stint with the Stars ended that day in Detroit. He played third base and went 1-for-3 and scored a run in a 6-4 loss to the Chicago American Giants.[19]

After Hooty Phillips's brief turn with the Detroit Stars and Milwaukee Bears, he returned home to Minnie and John Phillips and their life in Nashville. The transition to domestic life was not easy and within a year Hooty and Minnie Phillips were no longer living at the same address. Phillips took a sabbatical from professional baseball and sat out the 1924 and 1925 seasons. It is unknown why he did not play during those years but marital problems may have contributed to his absence. Phillips returned to baseball in June 1926 when he signed, once again, with the Nashville Elite Giants.[20] He spent that summer primarily as Nashville's leadoff batter and as their man on the hot corner. Phillips's contributions to the Elite Giants in 1926 are difficult to gauge due to the lack of published game reports and/or box scores. But when results did appear in print, the outcomes for Phillips were mixed. In June he helped Nashville take down Montgomery 10-4 by swatting a double, scoring four runs, and stealing two bases.[21] In July Phillips exceeded his offensive expectations by going 3-for-5 at the plate and scoring three runs, albeit in a losing effort to the Chattanooga White Sox, who bested the Elite Giants, 12-8.[22] But the following day, Phillips chalked up two errors and went 1-for-5 in a poor effort against Chattanooga that saw Nashville fall by a score of 7-3.[23] As it turned out, 1926 was a mediocre year for both Phillips and the Elite Giants. Nashville finished the year in sixth place out of eight teams in the NSL standings.[24]

At the beginning of the 1927 season, Hooty Phillips left his family behind in Nashville and jumped to the Chattanooga Black Lookouts, formerly known as the Chattanooga White Sox.[25] He reclaimed his old familiar position at short, and joined a Chattanooga roster that included Satchel Paige – that is, at least until Paige jumped to the Birmingham Black Barons.[26] The change of scenery seems to have helped Phillips. In early May, his bat came alive just in time to help the Black Lookouts take three straight games from his old mates, the Elite Giants.[27] A week later, he swatted the pellet over the fence in Evansville, garnering three RBIs in the process, to seal a win for Chattanooga.[28] Phillips's renaissance in 1927 helped the Black Lookouts defeat the Elite Giants to win the first half of the NSL season. A dispute over league records later, however, resulted in Nashville being credited with the title.[29] Hooty Phillips's baseball career ended with the Black Lookouts in the summer of 1927. His final appearance in an NSL tilt was likely at Andrews Field in Chattanooga, when the Black Lookouts lost to Paige and the Black Barons, 7-2.[30] It was also the last game for Hooty Phillips in a professional baseball uniform.

After the curtain fell on his baseball career, Hooty Phillips returned to Nashville – but not to his family. His estranged wife, Minnie, and his son, John William Phillips, who was now 10 years old, lived at a different address. Hooty and Minnie Phillips never reconciled. Minnie and her son had not shared a home with Phillips since 1925. Hooty Phillips did not live long enough to see his son Lefty Phillips follow in his baseball footsteps. On November 16, 1935, Hooty was shot in the back during a dispute over a dice game and died four days later from a fatal gas gangrene infection. He was just 37 years old and his son was not yet a teenager. Hooty was buried in the Mount Ararat Cemetery in Nashville. His assailant, John McKinley, was given a 20-year sentence for second-degree murder.[31]

John "Lefty" Phillips likely pitched his first game for one of Nashville's sandlot teams in 1938, three years after the death of his father. It is unknown if Hooty Phillips had any influence in cultivating his son's baseball talents. Sandlot baseball leagues were organized for White players in Nashville as early as 1906.[32] By the 1930s, leagues for African American amateur nines were developed and teams participated in citywide tournaments held at Sulphur Dell.[33] Sandlot teams also played against some professional nines. In 1935, for example, the Elite Giants opened their home season by taking on the Old Hickory Black Caps, one of Nashville's "colored sandlot" teams.[34] Young Phillips made his baseball debut in the summer of 1938 with the Nashville Junior Elite Giants.[35] Although the Elite Giant Juniors played at least a dozen games that season, and upcoming games were announced in local newspapers, print coverage of the results was rare. Almost all the Junior Elite Giants' contests were doubleheaders played at Sulphur Dell against other sandlot aggregations. One notable exception was a contest between the Juniors and Phillips's father's former team, the Chattanooga Black Lookouts.[36] Lefty Phillips pitched in the opener and helped the Junior Elite Giants chew up Chattanooga, 13-4.[37]

With a season of amateur baseball under his belt, Phillips made the leap to the big time in the spring of 1939 when he graduated from the "Junior" leagues and was signed by his father's former employer, the Nashville Elite Giants, soon to be renamed the Washington Elite Giants and ultimately the Baltimore Elite Giants.[38] At the time, he was still living in Nashville with his mother, who worked as a cook. Phillips made his pitching debut for the newly relocated Baltimore Elite Giants on April 2, 1939, in a spring-training game against the Memphis Red Sox.[39] Phillips was the second of three hurlers used by the Elites in a 4-2 losing effort in Memphis.[40] A week later, Phillips was again the second hurler to take the slab for the Elites.[41] The quality of the pitching for that day was described as "alternately brilliant and lusterless," with Phillips's performance falling into the latter category.[42] Phillips was roughed up by the Atlanta Black Crackers and quickly replaced by Bill Harvey.[43] The winning pitcher for Atlanta that day was Eddie "Bullet" Dixon, who joined the Elite Giants later in the season after the Black Crackers crumbled in the summer of 1939.[44] Lucius Jones, who covered the Elite Giants-Black Crackers game for the *Atlanta Daily World*, was the first to refer to Phillips in print as Lefty Phillips.[45] Phillips had other nicknames in his brief career including Jack, Jake, and Johnnie, but Lefty, a good old-fashioned southpaw baseball moniker, stuck and for Phillips it was a good journalistic fit.[46]

During the Baltimore Elite Giants' 1939 championship year, Phillips was used sparingly in relief and rarely as a starter. One such rare occasion was on May 30, 1939, when Phillips was the starting hurler for Baltimore in the second game of a doubleheader against the New York Black Yankees at Dexter Park in Brooklyn.[47] He didn't last long. Lefty gave up six runs in the first inning and was sent to the showers.[48] Less than a week later, he was one and done again in a 14-1 victory over the Lloyd A.C., but this time it was in relief of Emory "Jim" Adams, and at the end of the one-sided affair.[49] Through June and July, Phillips was named as a possible pitcher for a number of tilts in Pennsylvania, Delaware, and New Jersey. Whether or not he made any appearances on the slab for the Elite Giants, however, is uncertain due to the absence of complete game reports and/or box scores.[50] The last time Phillips was listed as a member of the Elite Giants' pitching stable in 1939 was for a game against the Belmar Braves of Asbury Park, New Jersey, on July 18, which the Braves won 10-3.[51] His name did not appear in the box score for the Asbury Park game nor in any other press coverage of the Elite Giants for the remainder of the season.[52] Lefty Phillips did not play a role in Baltimore's 1939 championship series.

At the conclusion of the 1939 season, Minnie Phillips must have had déjà vu all over again when her son came back home to Nashville after his stint with the Elite Giants. Her late husband, Hooty, had a similar track record of bouncing back and forth between home plate on the road and his family's home base in Nashville during his baseball career, a pattern that likely contributed to their fractured marriage. Despite Lefty's poor showing on the hill for Baltimore in 1939, when the 1940 Census was conducted in Nashville on April 9, 1940, he listed his occupation as a professional baseball player, and his employer as Tom Wilson of the Elite Giants. He was definitely counting on playing in the coming season with Baltimore. When the Census was enumerated, Phillips lived with his mother in a house they rented for $2 per month on the northeast of downtown Nashville, that today is the site of Frederick Douglass Park. According to the Census, Minnie Phillips worked as a maid in a private home and earned $400 in 1939. For that same year, Lefty Phillips's income as a professional baseball player was $500.

When the 1940 spring-training season commenced for the Elite Giants, Phillips was not on the roster.[53] Baltimore's early-season slab staff consisted of veterans Willie Hubert, Emery Adams, Jonas Gaines, and Dixon; and newcomers including Cowboy Murray and Woody Williams.[54] But no Phillips. It was not until later in the 1940 season that he rejoined the Elite Giants. His first known appearance was in July in relief

of Baltimore's Bud Barbee in a 4-3 loss to the Bay Parkways in Brooklyn.[55] The next day, Phillips made one of his rare appearances on the mound as a starter for the Elite Giants in a losing effort against New Jersey's Belmar Braves.[56] Lefty gave up nine hits in 6⅔ innings, with two strikeouts to his credit and four walks charged to his account.[57] A few days later, he repeated his rescue of bullpen mate Barbee in an 11-10 win over the Bushwicks, although Phillips lasted only 1⅔ innings before he was relieved by Adams.[58]

The last time Phillips was named as a possible hurler for the Elite Giants was for a game that was played on August 8, 1940, against the Pirates of Red Bank, New Jersey.[59] At the time, the Baltimore nine was tied with the Homestead Grays for first-place honors in the Negro National League.[60] Phillips was slated to start the game but did not play. Barbee went the distance for Baltimore and was brilliant in a one-hitter, copping the win, 2-1.[61] It was back to Nashville for Phillips. His two-year tour with the Elite Giants was over, as was his career as a professional baseball player.

On October 16, 1940, Phillips registered for the US Army draft in Nashville. He was described as 5-feet-9½ and 182 pounds. He named his mother as the "person who will always know" his address but did not live with his mother, who had recently remarried. Phillips's residence was on Maury Street in Nashville, just a few blocks from the Napier neighborhood where Elite Giants owner Tom Wilson lived. Wilson was listed as Phillips's employer. Phillips did not serve in the Army; during the 1940s, he worked primarily as a truck driver at the Nashville Terminal rail yards and at a laundry and dry-cleaning shops. By the mid-1940s, Phillips had moved into the newly developed J.C. Napier Homes, a public housing project developed in Nashville in 1939.[62]

Details on Lefty Phillips's life after baseball are almost as scant as his stats and newspaper coverage of his game appearances. In 1955 he married Janie Mae Batey in Nashville, and for a time they operated a dry-cleaning establishment near the J.C. Napier Homes. By the late 1950s, however, Phillips was back on the road again as a truck driver, and life took a turn for the worse. In the summer of 1960, he was arrested in a bootlegging raid in Nashville and charged with possessing untaxed whiskey.[63] Nearly two years later, on October 11, 1962, Lefty died in Nashville from a massive gastrointestinal hemorrhage, caused by cirrhosis of the liver. He was 41 years old when he died; his father, Hooty, had died at age 37. Phillips's immediate survivors were his wife, son William Phillips, and his mother, Minnie Phillips Williams, who outlived her son by 10 years.[64] Lefty was buried in the Hills of Calvary Memorial Park in Nashville.

Acknowledgment
The author would like to express her heartfelt appreciation for the wisdom, good humor, generosity, encouragement, and expert editing of the late Frederick C. Bush, who assisted with the early research for this chapter.

SOURCES

Unless otherwise indicated, all Negro League statistics and records were sourced from Seamheads.com and baseball-reference.com. Ancestry.com was used to access census, birth, death, marriage, military, immigration, and other genealogical and public records.

NOTES

1   John Phillips's nickname appeared in various records as Hooty and/ or Hootie.

2   "Nashville Team Has Good Prospects," *Tennessean* (Nashville), February 26, 1921: 8.

3   "A Nashville Southern League Club Wins Game," *Tennessean*, April 26, 1921: 7; "Elite Giants Win First Game of Series," *Tennessean*, September 16, 1921: 8.

4   "Negro Title Series Open in the Dell," *Nashville Banner*, September 15, 1921: 10.

5   "Triple and Single Give Elite Giants Hard Game," *Tennessean*, September 19, 1921: 6.

6   "Giants Win Flag in Negro League," *Nashville Banner*, September 20, 1921: 9.

7   In 1921 the Phillipses' house was located about 1,000 feet from home plate of the present-day First Horizon Park, home to the Triple-A Nashville Sounds.

8   William J. Plott, *The Negro Southern League: A Baseball History, 1920-1951* (Jefferson, North Carolina: McFarland & Company, 2015), 34, 35.

9   "The Southern League," *Chicago Defender*, June 3, 1922: 10.

10 "Nashville Elite Giants Will Be Home Today," *Tennessean*, June 8, 1922: 8.

11 "Black Barons Drop Double-Header to Nashville Giants," *Birmingham* (Alabama) *News*, June 29, 1922: 17.

12 "Elite Giants and Knoxville Play Tie," *Tennessean*, July 29, 1922: 6.

13 Plott, 41; "Knoxville Giants Mop Up on Road," *Knoxville* (Tennessee) *Journal and Tribune*, August 5, 1922: 9.

14 Neil Lanctot, *Fair Dealing and Clean Playing: The Hilldale Club and the Development of Black Professional Baseball, 1910-1932* (Syracuse, New York: Syracuse University Press, 1994), 97.

15 "Monarchs Blank Detroit Stars, 6-0," *Detroit Free Press*, May 21, 1923: 14; "Detroit Stars Defeat A.B.C.'s," *Detroit Free Press*, June 11, 1923: 15; "Detroit Stars Lose," *Detroit Free Press*, June 14, 1923: 26; "Merchants Set for Fast Fray," *Port Huron* (Michigan) *Times Herald*, June 14, 1923: 13.

16 "Milwaukee Bears and A.B.C.'s Sunday," *Indianapolis News*, June 30, 1923: 20.

17 James A. Riley, *The Biographical Encyclopedia of the Negro Baseball Leagues* (New York: Carroll & Graf Publishers, Inc., 1994), 553.

18 "Giants Defeat Detroit Stars," *Detroit Free Press*, September 5, 1923: 13.

19 "Giants Defeat Detroit Stars."

20 "Negro Southern League Games Are Real Features with Ample Comedy," *Tennessean*, June 30, 1926: 11.

21 "Negro Southern League Games Are Real Features with Ample Comedy."

22 "Local Negroes Take Third in a Row," *Chattanooga Times*, July 6, 1926: 9.

23 "White Sox Outfit at Top Negro Loop," *Chattanooga Times*, July 7, 1926: 10.

24 Plott, 62.

25 "Want to Be Known as the Black Lookouts," *Chattanooga Times*, April 3, 1927: 15; "Black Lookouts to Meet Barons," *Chattanooga Times*, July 9, 1927: 8.

26 "Black Lookouts Play Giants Today," *Chattanooga Times*, April 22, 1927: 10.

27 "Black Lookouts Win Third in a Row," *Chattanooga Times*, May 11, 1927: 11.

28 "Evansville Outfit Meets Local Blacks," *Chattanooga Times*, May 13, 1927: 15.

29 "Black Lookouts Beat Nashville," *Chattanooga Times*, July 5, 1927: 11; Plott, 72.

30 "Black Barons Take Another from 'Nooga," *Birmingham Age-Herald*, July 11, 1927: 9.

31 "Negro Given Twenty Years for Murder," *Nashville Banner*, January 10, 1936: 14.

32 J.D. Langdale, "Negro Club House Boy Was Father of Amateurs Here," *Tennessean*, June 15, 1930: 15.

33 "Negro Amateurs Stage Meet in Dell Sunday," *Tennessean*, October 1, 1933: 28.

34 "Elite Giants Hold First Battle Here," *Tennessean*, April 7, 1935: 19.

35 "Elite Juniors Nab Two," *Tennessean*, July 25, 1938: 11.

36 "Giants in Action," *Nashville Banner*, July 22, 1938: 10.

37 "Elite Juniors Nab Two."

38 "Elites Train in Nashville," *Atlanta Daily World*, April 15, 1939: 5.

39 Sam R. Brown, "Memphis Red Sox in 4-2 Win Over Elites," *Atlanta Daily World*, April 4, 1939: 5.

40 "Memphis Red Sox in 4-2 Win Over Elites."

41 Lucius Jones, "Felix (Chin) Evans, Donald Reeves Star as Atlanta Nine Loses 13-12," *Atlanta Daily World*, April 10, 1939: 5.

42 Jones, April 10, 1939: 5.

43 Jones, April 10, 1939: 5.

44 Lucius Jones, "Slant on Sports," *Phoenix* (Arizona) *Index*, September 9, 1939: 6.

45 Jones, April 10, 1939: 5.

46 "Lloyd Tackles Elite Giants," *Chester* (Pennsylvania) *Times*, May 16, 1939: 11; "Baltimore Giants to Play Manheim," *Lancaster* (Pennsylvania) *Daily Intelligencer*, June 7, 1939: 12; "Five Elite Hurlers Ready to Face Star Batsmen in Bargain," *Baltimore Evening Sun*, July 7, 1939: 36.

47 "Black Yankees in Even Break," *Brooklyn Daily Eagle*, May 31, 1939: 18.

48 "Black Yankees in Even Break."

49 "Nashville-Baltimore Elite Giants Wallop Lloyd Tossers," *Chester Times*, June 3, 1939: 14.

50 "Nashville Colored Giants Scheduled for Pirates Park," *Long Branch* (New Jersey) *Daily Record*, June 22, 1939: 8; "Baltimore Giants to Play Manheim," *Lancaster Daily Intelligencer*, June 7, 1939: 12; "Five Elite Hurlers Ready to Face Star Batsmen in Bargain," *Baltimore Evening Sun*, July 7, 1939: 36; "Cubans to Meet Giants at Pennsy,"

Wilmington (Delaware) *Morning News,* July 15, 1939: 12; "Braves Import 2 New Hurlers," *Asbury Park* (New Jersey) *Evening Press,* July 18, 1939: 9.

51 "Braves Break Slump, Rout Nashville Elites, 10-3," *Asbury Park Evening Press,* July 19, 1939: 10, 14.

52 "Braves Break Slump, Rout Nashville Elites, 10-3."

53 Cum Posey, "Posey's Points," *Pittsburgh Courier,* April 13, 1940: 16.

54 Cum Posey, April 13, 1940: 16.

55 "Bay Parkways Beat Elites, 4-3 in Night Game," *Brooklyn Citizen,* July 26, 1940: 6.

56 "Belmar Braves Triumph, 6-5," *Long Branch Daily Record,* July 27, 1940: 8.

57 "Belmar Braves Triumph, 6-5."

58 "Parkways Battle House of David," *Brooklyn Daily Eagle,* August 3, 1940: 12.

59 "R.B. Pirates to Tackle Elite Giants Tonight," *Long Branch Daily Record,* August 9, 1940: 8.

60 "R.B. Pirates to Tackle Elite Giants Tonight."

61 "Pete Gray Spoils No Hit Tilt for Bud Barbee as Elite Giants Triumph," *Red Bank* (New Jersey) *Daily Standard,* August 10, 1940: 16.

62 "Housing Body Selects Names for Projects," *Tennessean,* August 19, 1939: 2.

63 "14 Arrested Here in Bootleg Raids," *Tennessean,* June 18, 1960: 3.

64 "Death Notices," *Tennessean,* October 11, 1962: 50.

CHARLIE RIVERA

BY JEB STEWART

Charlie Rivera was a third baseman, second baseman, and shortstop who played with several clubs in the Negro leagues for parts of five seasons, from 1939 to 1944. He was a right-handed hitter who stood 5-feet-9 and weighed 155 pounds.[1]

Carlos Manuel Lavezzari y Sierra was born to Manuel Lavezzari and Trinidad Sierra on September 6, 1912, in Santurce, Puerto Rico.[2] Little is known about his early years on the island. On September 28, 1918, he and his siblings boarded the *S.S. Philadelphia* with his mother and relocated to New York City.[3] Whatever happened to his father is a mystery.

At this point, his name was shortened to "Carlos M. Sierra."[4] However, by 1930, with his father not found in the US Census, his name was rendered as Carlos Lavezzary Revera; his surname was finally modified to "Rivera";[5] and his first name was later anglicized to "Charles."[6] Because his education was limited to grammar school, Rivera had few employment opportunities.[7] When he found work, it was as a helper in a laundry,[8] but he eventually became a carpenter's apprentice.[9]

Baseball historian James Riley concluded that Rivera broke into the Negro Leagues in 1933 as a member of the Cuban Stars.[10] However, contemporary newspaper accounts[11] and Seamheads.com[12] have determined that this player was not Carlos Rivera, but Nenene Rivera, a Puerto Rican who played shortstop for an independent team, Pollock's Cuban Stars.

Research has not uncovered how Charlie Rivera got interested in baseball. However, at some point, he returned to Puerto Rico and got his start in the game playing for $10 a day.[13] He played semiprofessionally for the Guayama baseball club in the Puerto Rican winter league in 1938-39.[14] While playing for Guayama, Rivera caught legendary pitcher Satchel Paige.[15]

Baseball historian Adrian Burgos interviewed Rivera in the mid-1990s, and Rivera related that he volunteered to catch Paige in 1938 when regular catcher Bill Perkins was injured and his backup declined to play.[16] Burgos was skeptical about the claim since Rivera was an infielder, not a catcher.[17] However, during a trip to Puerto Rico, he later verified the story by reviewing Guyama's official scorebook from that season. He identified Rivera as a catcher in Guayama's first game and concluded that the story was true. He described Rivera's memory of the game:

Charlie Rivera as depicted on his 1948-49 Toleteros baseball card.
Courtesy of Edwin Pérez.

Since he had grown up mostly in New York, Rivera communicated with Satchel Paige in English. Satchel jokingly called Rivera '*jamaiquino*' (Jamaican) because he spoke English without a Spanish accent. Paige's pinpoint control was legendary. Satchel just told Rivera to stick the catcher's mitt where he wanted the ball and not to worry about calling signals. He'll just throw whatever pitch he wanted, but to trust him, he will hit the mitt. So Rivera did exactly what Paige told him. Paige delivered as promised, hitting the catcher's mitt every time.[18]

By 1939, Rivera joined the Baltimore Elite Giants as a 26-year-old rookie, although the exact circumstances of his signing have been lost to history. The team included two future Hall of Famers at catcher, 41-year-old Biz Mackey and 17-year-old Roy Campanella. According to Seamheads, Rivera batted .256 in 11 games as a third baseman for the Elite Giants, primarily as player-manager Felton Snow's backup.[19]

Rivera's name first appeared in a box score on May 31, in a doubleheader split against the New York Black Yankees.[20] Rivera played well, contributing two hits and scoring a run in the opener and getting another hit in the second game before 7,000 fans.[21]

Rivera's season highlights included twice collecting two hits in wins over the Philadelphia Stars[22] and driving in the go-ahead run against the Manheim Barons.[23] He added two more hits against the Poughkeepsie All-Stars.[24] Perhaps Rivera's best moment of the season came in a loss to the Norristown Pros. He hit a "freak homer" in the second, "which cut over third base and then went behind the foul line."[25]

Baltimore finished in fourth place in the Negro National League II. Despite posting an uneven record of 21-23, the Elite Giants qualified for the NNL playoffs. They defeated the Newark Eagles in the first round, three games to one.[26] Baltimore then defeated the Homestead Grays, three games to one (with one tie) to capture the NNL title.[27] Whatever contributions Rivera made to the Elite Giants' championship run were not featured in the news reports of the postseason games, and are not documented by Seamheads. Baltimore released Rivera after the season.[28]

Rivera signed to play second base for the Brooklyn Royal Giants, which had previously been a top-tier Negro League team from 1905 to the mid-1930s. By 1940, the Royal Giants were a semipro outfit that barnstormed across the Northeast, the South, and the Midwest.[29] Midway through the campaign, Brooklyn reportedly had an improbable record of 40-5.[30] Most of the stories about the Royal Giants were previews of coming games, rather than game accounts. Whenever box scores did appear, Rivera's performance was often notable.

In a sweep of a doubleheader over the Bacharach Giants, he had two hits, two walks, and scored a run.[31] He followed up that performance with a hit and a run scored in a win over the Ethiopian Clowns.[32] In August, Rivera collected four hits in a doubleheader against the Mount Vernon Scarlets and turned three double plays.[33] And he had two hits, including a triple, and scored a run, in a late-season win over Jesse Owens' Toledo Crawfords.[34]

In 1941 Rivera joined another semipro barnstorming team, the Miami Ethiopian Clowns. The Clowns were known as much for entertaining fans with their comedy routines and unusual nicknames as they were for playing baseball, as historian Brian Carroll observed:

> Obscured by these vivid names and the vaudevillian antics that went with them is the fact that these entertainers also played first-rate baseball – as evidenced by the team's many Negro American League and semi-pro tournament titles – and did so for longer than any other Negro League team.[35]

Rivera played well in spring training for the Ethiopian Clowns. One report noted, "Charlie Rivera, Puerta [sic] Rican winter league star, is playing a bang-up of a game for the Clowns at shortstop and hitting the ball hard."[36]

Newspapers inevitably focused on the Clowns' performance at shadow ball, pepper, phantom fielding, and vaudevillian acts, rather than their baseball skills. One preview featured a photograph depicting Rivera and three other players wearing clown makeup.[37] However, he was better known for his on-field play. One story noted, "[t]he Clowns are more than a team of comedians; however, they are the champions of national Negro baseball and boast the services of Charlie Rivera of the Guayama, Puerto Rico, team, which won the international semi-pro title at San Juan last season."[38]

As with the Royal Giants the year before, newspapers probably exaggerated the ability of the Clowns. One article reported that the Clowns had a record of 58-6.[39] Another claimed that the team had not lost a series in five years.[40]

Rivera was one of the keys to the club's success. In June, his single drove in the winning run in a 1-0 victory in the first game of a doubleheader against the Kansas City Monarchs. Although the Clowns lost the second game, Rivera added two more hits and scored a run.[41] While box scores for the Clowns' games were not common, the ones that exist show Rivera had five other multihit games.[42] He also homered in a doubleheader sweep of the Victoria All-Stars in July.[43]

In another win over the Monarchs, his defense also shined. The game summary noted that "[s]hortstop Rivera of the Clowns pulled off two electrifying fielding plays, throwing out a runner from deepest short once and racing in behind the mound,

head down, to snap up a ground ball and beat a fast runner another time."[44]

After two years of barnstorming with independent squads, how Rivera spent the 1942 season is a mystery. His name did not appear in any stories about the Ethiopian Clowns or the Brooklyn Royal Giants. He also did not appear in games for any NNL or Negro American League franchises. Whether he played in 1942 has yet to be verified. In 1943, Rivera signed to return to the Clowns,[45] who had joined the NAL and rebranded as the Cincinnati Clowns.[46] However, his time with the Clowns was brief; he was traded to the New York Cubans for Buster Haywood during spring training.[47] With the Cubans, Rivera, who was now 30, filled a utility infielder role.[48]

Leading off for the team in a game against the Homestead Grays in June, Rivera had two hits and scored two runs in a wild 10-9 win played in front of 10,000 fans at Griffith Stadium in Washington.[49] Later that summer, the Cubans faced the Philadelphia Stars and the Kansas City Monarchs in a doubleheader before 20,000 patrons at Yankee Stadium.[50] Rivera had a hit in the first game and reached on an error against the Monarchs to help New York chase Satchel Paige from the second game.[51]

The Cubans had a record of 19-14-1 in 1943 but finished in a distant second place to the Homestead Grays, who ran away with the NNL pennant and later won the Negro League World Series. For his part, Rivera hit .250 with 12 RBIs and one home run for the Cubans.

The next year, 1944, was Rivera's final season in professional baseball. According to *The Biographical Encyclopedia of the Negro Baseball Leagues*, Rivera "split his playing time between the New York Cubans and New York Black Yankees."[52] However, no news stories or box scores have been located showing that Rivera played for the Cubans. According to Seamheads, he appeared only for the Black Yankees although the details of his signing have been lost to history. The Black Yankees had a terrible season, finishing in last place in the NNL with a forgettable 7-32 record.

Rivera played third base and batted .244. In probably his final appearance in a box score, he collected three hits while driving in three runs and scoring one in a doubleheader against the Brooklyn Bushwicks.[53]

On October 28, 1944, Rivera enlisted in the US Army and served for three years as a private.[54] In 1946 he married Amma Martinez in the Bronx, where the couple eventually settled.[55] Rivera then spent many years an elevator operator at Macy's department store in New York City,"[56] while his wife was a homemaker.[57]

In 1993 Rivera was honored with other former Negro League players at the Upper Deck Heroes of Baseball All-Star Game at Camden Yards in Baltimore.[58] He expressed his gratitude to the fans at the game in an interview with Bill Rabinowitz. He marveled at his baseball career, saying, "When I saw I could play for money, I was happy as a lark. I could play a game I loved, and they were going to pay me. Oh man." Although he missed out on playing in the major leagues, he added, "My wife told me that we were born too soon. ... I can't be mad at that because that's... the way it had to happen."

Rivera died on July 27, 2003, in the Bronx at the age of 90. His burial details are unknown.[59]

In 2020, Major League Baseball recognized seven professional Negro Leagues that operated from 1920 to 1948 as having major-league status.[60] Thus, Rivera has finally been recognized as a major leaguer for his play in the NNL.

SOURCES AND ACKNOWLEDGMENTS

Except where otherwise indicated, all player statistics and team records were taken from Seamheads.com.

The author is grateful to the late Rick Bush, who was always willing to cheerfully lend a hand to any researcher and take time to answer emails seeking his help. Charles Rivera does not have a player file with the National Baseball Hall of Fame Library, which added to the difficulty in researching his life. However, Rick provided crucial documents detailing Rivera's early life, military service, and family in an April 27, 2023, email to the author, which is indispensable to this biography. Sadly, Rick died suddenly on October 8, 2023. He will be missed by the author and anyone who was fortunate enough to get to know him, even if only through emails. The author also appreciates editor Bill Nowlin's usual patience and helpful suggestions.

NOTES

1   United States World War II Draft Cards Young Men, 1940-1947; https://www.seamheads.com/NegroLgs/player. php?playerID=rivero1cha.

2   Acta Nacimiento, Folio 88, Numero 1223, Registro Civil, San Juan, Puerto Rico. Thanks to Gary Ashwill.

3   United States, Departing Passenger and Crew Lists, 1914-1966, accessed at Ancestry.com.

4   United States, Departing Passenger and Crew Lists, 1914-1966, accessed at Ancestry.com.

5   New York. Manhattan. 1930 U.S. Census (Revera); United States, Departing Passenger and Crew Lists, 1914-1966, accessed at Ancestry.com (Rivera); United States World War II Draft Cards Young Men, 1940-1947; New York, New York, U.S., Marriage License Indexes, 1907-2018, accessed at Ancestry.com; Bronx, New York, 1940. U.S. Census.

6   New York, U.S., Arriving Passenger and Crew Lists (including Castle Garden and Ellis Island), 1820-1957, accessed at Ancestry.com.

7   United States, World War II Army Enlistment Records, 1938-1946, accessed at Ancestry.com.

8   New York. Manhattan. 1930 U.S. Census.

9   United States, World War II Army Enlistment Records, 1938-1946, accessed at Ancestry.com.

10 James A. Riley, *The Biographical Encyclopedia of the Negro Baseball Leagues* (New York: Carroll & Graf Publishers, 1994), 667.

11 "Cuban Stars Play Local Hornets Today," *Wilmington* (Delaware) *Morning News,* May 15, 1933: 11; "Cuban Stars Invade City Stadium For Clashes With Pats Sunday, Offering Real Test For Locals," *Paterson* (New Jersey) *News,* May 18, 1933: 26; "ALCOS Meet Famous Syd Pollock's Cubans Here In Night Game," *Dunkirk* (New York) *Evening Observer,* June 1, 1933: 14; "Cubans' Outlook Bright," *Pittsburgh Courier,* June 10, 1933: 15; "Nebraskans Win at Ute," *Sioux City* (Iowa) *Journal,* July 26, 1933: 9; "Cubans to Meet Bats Wednesday," *Mason City* (Iowa) *Globe-Gazette,* August 9, 1933: 9.

12 https://www.seamheads.com/NegroLgs/player. php?playerID=rivero1nen.

13 Bill Rabinowitz, "Charlie Rivera: A First-Class Act," *York* (Pennsylvania) *Daily Record,* July 13, 1993: 25; United States World War II Draft Cards Young Men, 1940-1947, accessed at Ancestry.com.

14 "Clown Nine Plans Show," *Cincinnati Post,* June 3, 1941: 13; Adrian Burgos Jr. "El Profe: 'I Caught Satchel Paige,'" lavidabasebell.com, June 18, 2018, accessed at https://www.lavidabaseball.com/el-profe-satchel-paige-charlie-rivera/.

15 "El Profe: 'I Caught Satchel Paige.'"

16 "El Profe: 'I Caught Satchel Paige.'"

17 "El Profe: 'I Caught Satchel Paige.'"

18 "El Profe: 'I Caught Satchel Paige.'"

19 https://www.seamheads.com/NegroLgs/team.php?-yearID=1939&teamID=BEG&LGOrd=1.

20 "Black Yankees in Even Break," *Brooklyn Daily Eagle,* May 31, 1939: 18. He sometimes appeared in box scores and newspaper stories as "Revere," "Riveria," and "Riberia."

21 "Black Yankees in Even Break."

22 "NNL League Dope," *New York Amsterdam News,* June 24, 1939: 15; "Philly Stars Win 2 Out of Three," *New York Amsterdam News,* July 15, 1939: 15.

23 "Manheim Lads Drop 4-3 Tilt to Baltimore," *Lancaster* (Pennsylvania) *Intelligencer Journal,* June 29, 1939: 16. The Barons were described as "the dark horse of the Lebanon Valley league." See "Baltimore Elite Giants Play Manheim Tonight," *Lancaster Intelligencer Journal,* June 28, 1939: 10.

24 "All-Stars Drop Hot Game To Elite Giants Team 7-1," *Poughkeepsie* (New York) *Eagle-News,* July 13, 1939: 8.

25 No Sheriff, "Norristown Sluggers Blast Three Hurlers for 19 Hits; Smith Gives Up Seven Blows," *Norristown* (Pennsylvania) *Times Herald,* July 17, 1939: 7.

26 Ralph Boyd, "Elites Whip Eagles to Gain Championship Series," *Baltimore Afro-American,* September 16, 1939: 22.

27 John H. Whoric, "Sportorials," *Connellsville* (Pennsylvania) *Daily Courier,* September 29, 1939: 16; "Baltimore Whips Homestead Grays for Title," *Chicago Defender,* September 30, 1939: 9; "Elite Giants Win National League Championship," *Baltimore Afro-American,* September 30, 1939: 21.

28 Riley, 667.

29 "Negro All-Stars Will Play Here," *Macon* (Georgia) *Evening News,* May 20, 1940: 1; "Wilkins Will Hurl Against Colored Aces," *Munster* (Indiana) *Times,* July 5, 1940: 17; "Brooklyn Royal Giants Face Puerto Rican All-Stars Here Wednesday," *Capital Times* (Madison, Wisconsin), July 9, 1940: 13; "Royal Giants, Stars Play Here Tonight," *Wisconsin State Journal* (Madison), July 10, 1940: 15; "Royal Giants to Meet Citizens Here Tonight," *Muncie Evening Press,* July 18, 1940: 16; "Jenkins Star of Bacharach Nine," *Harrisburg* (Pennsylvania) *Evening News,* July 20, 1940: 12; "Wilkins Will Hurl

Against Colored Aces," *Hammond* (Indiana) *Times,* July 5, 1940: 44; "One Six-Run Inning Beats Fraser Club," *Lynn* (Massachusetts) *Daily Evening Item,* July 29, 1940: 9; "Outfielder Hits Single in Tenth for Winning Run," *Kingston* (New York) *Daily Freeman,* August 10, 1940: 11; "Royal Giants Here Tonight," *Biddeford* (Maine) *Daily Journal,* August 20, 1940: 6.

30   "Citizens Meet Giants Tonight," *Muncie Star Press,* July 18, 1940: 8.

31   "Brooklyn Giants Sweep Twin Bill; Thomas Shines," *Harrisburg Evening News,* July 22, 1940: 13.

32   "Royals Row Way to 6-3 Win Over Ethiopians," *Sunbury* (Pennsylvania) *Daily Item,* June 25, 1940: 13.

33   "Adams' Hitting Streak Stopped At 40 Games," *White Plains* (New York) *Daily Argus,* August 12, 1940: 8.

34   "Brooklyn Defeats Toledo Nine, 6-2," *Harrisburg Telegraph,* August 26, 1940: 13.

35   Brian Carroll, "Black Baseball's 'Funmakers': Taking the Miami Ethiopian Clowns Seriously," *The National Pastime: Baseball in the Sunshine State* (Miami, 2016), accessed at https://sabr.org/journal/article/black-baseballs-funmakers-taking-the-miami-ethiopian-clowns-seriously/.

36   "Ethiopian Clowns in Four During Week," *Phoenix* (Arizona) *Index,* May 3, 1941: 4.

37   "Play Here Tomorrow," *Victoria* (British Columbia) *Times Colonist,* July 18, 1941: 11

38   "Clown Nine Plans Show."

39   "Satchel Paige Faces Clowns at Crosley Field Today," *Cincinnati Enquirer,* June 8, 1941: 33.

40   "Packer Club Drilling for Triple Bid," *Austin* (Minnesota) *Daily Herald,* June 20, 1941: 8.

41   "Negro Nines," *Cincinnati Enquirer,* June 9, 1941: 18.

42   "Locals Take Bad Beating From Clowns," *Bremerton* (Washington) *Daily News Searchlight,* July 16, 1941: 9 (two hits); "Clowns Lose to Boston, Bentley," *The Province* (Vancouver, British Columbia), July 19, 1941: 15 (two hits); "Ethiopians Top Cuban Stars by 6-0 Score," *Montana Standard* (Butte), July 28, 1941: 8 (two hits); Woody

Cannon, "Fans Agree Colorado Ball Clubs Could at Least Hit the Seed," *Salt Lake Telegram* (Salt Lake City, Utah), August 1, 1941: 18 (three hits); "Circuit Clout Climaxes 4-Run Rally," *Mansfield* (Ohio) *News-Journal,* September 6, 1941: 7 (two hits).

43   "Packed Stands Enjoy Clowns," *Victoria Times Colonist,* July 21, 1941: 10.

44   "Negro Nines Thrill Year's Best Crowd," *Winnipeg* (Manitoba) *Tribune,* June 26, 1941: 19.

45   "Clowns Hope To Win N.A.L. '43 Pennant," *St. Louis Argus,* April 2, 1943: 10.

46   Carroll.

47   "Clowns Sign Local Stars," *Cincinnati Post,* April 14, 1943: 14; "Clowns' Bassett Fine Comedian," *Birmingham* (Alabama) *Post,* April 16, 1943: 22.

48   "New York Cubans Send Probable Lineup for Tilt Tomorrow Night," *Lafayette* (Indiana) *Journal and Courier,* June 17, 1943: 18.

49   "Grays, Cubans Split Before 10,000 Fans," *Pittsburgh Courier,* June 19, 1943: 18.

50   "'Satch' is Blasted Before 20,000 Fans at Yankee Stadium," *Pittsburgh Courier,* August 14, 1943: 18.

51   "'Satch' is Blasted Before 20,000 Fans at Yankee Stadium."

52   Riley, 667.

53   "The Bushwick's Scores," *Brooklyn Citizen,* August 28, 1944: 6.

54   United States World War II Army Enlistment Records, 1938-1946; Bill Rabinowitz, "Charlie Rivera: A First-Class Act."

55   New York. Bronx County. 1950 US Census.

56   Rabinowitz.

57   New York. Bronx County. 1950 US Census.

58   Rabinowitz.

59   https://www.findagrave.com/memorial/99120409/carlos-rivera:

60   https://www.mlb.com/news/negro-leagues-given-major-league-status-for-baseball-records-stats.

FELTON SNOW

BY CHRIS BETSCH AND KEN DRAUT

The 1981 made-for-television movie *Don't Look Back: The Story of Leroy "Satchel" Paige*, opens with a scene at a game between the Dizzy Dean Major League All-Stars and the Satchel Paige Colored All-Stars.[1] The first name to be announced for the starting lineup is Felton Snow of the Baltimore Elite Giants. Many details from the movie are no doubt erroneous, but it was true that Snow played with Paige. In fact, Snow teamed with or managed almost every legend of the Negro Leagues who played during his two decades in baseball, from Paige, Oscar Charleston, and Josh Gibson to Jackie Robinson and Monte Irvin. The right-handed-hitting Snow played primarily as a third baseman, but he could be inserted nearly anywhere he was needed, whether it was the infield, outfield, or even on the pitching mound, and he often was slotted in by himself as a player-manager. For many years Snow had fallen into the dustbin of Negro League history, but in 2022 he was brought back into memory in his hometown of Louisville, Kentucky, and honored as one of the greats of the Negro Leagues.

Felton Snow was born on October 23, 1905, in Oxford, Alabama. His family had been in the town for generations; they likely obtained their name as slaves of the Snow family, one of the first White families to live in Oxford.[2] (There is a Snow Creek that runs through the town.) Felton's father, Jonah Snow, was born in post-Civil War Alabama, and in 1898 he married Claudia Johnson. Felton was the second of seven children for Jonah and Claudia, and the first son. After their last child was born in 1917, Jonah and Claudia separated, and Felton and two sisters moved with their mother to Louisville. The other siblings stayed with Jonah or other relatives in Alabama for a time but most eventually moved to Louisville. Jonah soon remarried and worked for years as a grocery deliveryman.

Felton quit school at age 14 and went to work to support his mother, who worked as a laundress in Louisville. When not working jobs as a porter or delivery boy, he found time to play baseball. He likely played for city teams in Louisville in his teens and into his 20s; his name began to appear in print in 1926.[3] He played parts of the next few years with one of the top Negro league teams in Louisville, the White Sox, and with other semipro and minor Negro-league teams around the city and across the Ohio River in Indiana. Various box scores show that Snow moved all over the infield and outfield. During the early part of his career, Snow married Elnora Calloway in 1927; however, according to Louisville city directories, they were divorced by 1933.

Snow joined the ranks of major leaguers when he suited up for the White Sox in 1931. By that season, the team was a member of the Negro National League, one of the circuits considered a major league by Major League Baseball as of 2020. He played with the Louisville Black Caps in 1932, but at the end of July, the team abruptly disbanded,[4] and Snow joined another team in Louisville, the Red Sox, to finish out the season.[5] As the Red Sox prepared for the 1933 campaign, they looked forward to having a strong team with Snow and other Louisville players like Sammy Hughes and Willie Gisentaner on the roster. Instead, before spring training started, those three players and others headed south to Nashville and joined Tom Wilson's Elite Giants of the Negro National League.

With the Elites, Snow blossomed into one of the top third basemen in the Negro Leagues. Standing 5-feet-10 and weighing 155 pounds, the freckle-faced Snow was not a showy player, but "he handled himself well and could make all the plays … had a rifle arm … and although not a baserunning threat, was a smart base runner."[6] He hit only .258 in his first season with the Giants, but he developed into a dependable hitter and was later considered to be "the most dangerous batter on the team in the clutch"[7] as he became one of the mainstays of Wilson's teams. Besides dragging the Giants between Nashville, Detroit, Columbus, Washington, and finally Baltimore, Wilson also took teams all over the country to play in barnstorming sessions between league games and then to winter leagues during offseasons. Tours included sessions in the famed California Winter League, where teams of Black players competed with teams of White players. Snow made his first appearance in the CWL in 1933 and handled himself well in the circuit, batting .322 in 43 games.[8]

Snow played in the popular East-West All-Star Game in 1935, representing the Elite Giants, now of Columbus, Ohio. He entered the game as a pinch-hitter in the 10th inning and drove in two runs with a single off Luis Tiant as the West team fought to an 11-8 victory in 11 innings. Leading up to the game, the *Chicago Defender* advised readers to keep an eye on Felton Snow: "Don't look for dash and flash when Snow walks out to third base. … But you'll be looking at a spread-eagle infielder who makes the hardest chances look easy. You'll be looking at a finished ball player."[9]

In addition to playing league games, it was customary for the Giants to barnstorm across the country as the team traveled west for the California Winter League and then returned home. In 1934, playing as the Philadelphia Royal Giants, Wilson's group swept a series from a team of minor-league all-stars headed by Frank Demaree. Wilson's squad participated in a much more celebrated game in 1935 – a matchup in Los Angeles on Halloween day that featured Dizzy Dean against Satchel Paige. Snow managed two hits in the game, but Dean's All-Stars won, 5-4.

After receiving over 7,000 votes for the 1936 East-West game, Snow switched sides to play for the East, since the Elite Giants had relocated to Washington, DC. He was again on the winning team as the East easily won, 10-2. Snow's votes were split between the third-base and shortstop positions, so Judy Johnson started the game at third, but Snow entered as a replacement and contributed to the East victory with a hit, a run scored, and a stolen base. Snow annually ranked near the top of East-West voting over his career, but 1935 and 1936 were the only years he played in the games.[10]

After the 1936 season, Wilson again took a team on the road. He assembled a squad from the Elite Giants, beefed up with stars including Gibson, Paige, and Cool Papa Bell, and took them to the Denver Post Tournament, known as the Little World Series of the West, for teams not associated with Organized Baseball. Since Negro League teams were not connected to Organized Baseball (not by their choosing, of course), Wilson's National Negro All-Stars were eligible to take part in the event. Snow played a limited role in the tournament after suffering a hand injury, but the team handily defeated all opponents and took home a $5,000 cash prize. The Denver Post Tournament was just one of the notable tournaments that Snow appeared in over the years. He also played in a 1936 tournament against the Rogers Hornsby All-Stars, as well as a series of North-South all-star games and an all-star tour of Cuba in 1938, among others.

After several years of instability, the Elite Giants found their permanent home when they moved to Baltimore in 1938, even though the press would still refer to them as the Nashville Elite Giants for the next few years. The team finished third in the Negro National League II (NNL2) standings that year. Wilson traded fiery team manager George Scales to the New York Black Yankees in February 1939 as he intended to bring former manager Candy Jim Taylor back to lead the team; however, when a deal with Taylor fell apart in March, Wilson was left scrambling to find a new manager before spring training began. The *Pittsburgh Courier* reported that Biz Mackey was to take over managerial duties,[11] but this was likely an assumption based on Mackey leading the team in 1937 before Scales arrived. Baltimore newspapers, however, referred to "Manager Felton Snow" in articles in April,[12] indicating that Wilson had instead given the role to Snow, which proved to be a wise choice.

After playing for the tempestuous Scales, the Elites welcomed the change to Snow, who was "calm and relaxed, able to get results without bullying or belittling his players,"[13] and he earned the nickname Skipper. An official announcement naming Snow as the manager was seemingly never posted, leaving some newspapers thinking that Mackey was running the club. Mackey was traded in July to make room for young catcher Roy Campanella as part of a youth movement that

Snow helped drive, leaving no question as to who was running the club. Baltimore had a sluggish start to the season, but came on strongly after the roster overhaul in July. The Elites made the playoffs and then surprised both the Newark Eagles and powerful Homestead Grays to claim the 1939 NNL2 championship. The title helped Felton reach the status of a local celebrity back in Louisville, to the point that the city's main paper, the *Courier-Journal*, made mention of him whenever his travels brought him back through the city.

Though he started managing at the age of 33, Snow became not just a team leader, but also a father figure to many of the younger players. He supported his players but also set curfews, disallowed cursing, and "would not tolerate any ball players two-timing their wives."[14] Snow helped to develop young Elite Giants like Campanella and Junior Gilliam. When Snow took

Manager/third baseman Felton Snow with the Elites. Courtesy John W. Mosley Photograph Collection, Charles L. Blockson Afro-American Collection, Temple University Libraries.

Felton Snow working out.

over as manager, Campanella was only 17, and overseeing him could sometimes present a challenge. Campanella's roommate on the road, William Barnes, later recalled in an interview how he and Campy would return to their hotel room and be in bed just before Snow's 11 o'clock curfew, fully dressed, then "no sooner than [Snow] left, we was out of the bed and gone."[15]

Some of Snow's dealings with his players influenced his thoughts on a popular topic of discussion: the integration of the White major leagues. When asked in 1939 about the possibility of Black players joining the majors, Snow was not sure it was the best idea at that time: "I don't know that it would be a good thing, we've got so many guys who just wouldn't act right. Some of these fellows who are pretty good on the diamond would give you a heartache elsewhere. ... We have good players, yes. And some of them would certainly qualify, but it is a task finding the right combination."[16] Snow's comment about finding the right combination was almost prophetic when Branch Rickey later signed Jackie Robinson to play for the Dodgers.

Even with additional managerial duties, Snow continued to play at a high level. In 1940 he hit .319 and slugged at a .414 rate for the Elites, his finest season statistically outside his 1934 campaign. The pinnacle of Snow's 1940 season was managing the East squad to an 11-0 victory in that year's East-West Game. Josh Gibson and other stars had jumped to Mexico to play and

were not in the game, but Buck Leonard still provided some fireworks with three hits, three RBIs, and two stolen bases.

Although known for his calm demeanor, Snow could get fired up when the situation dictated it. In 1942 he was fined $25 and suspended for three days after he made contact with umpire Fred McCrary following a called ball in a July game versus the New York Black Yankees. He reportedly had to be escorted off the field by police after letting his temper flare over the call. It is uncertain if the ruling was enforced, as Snow was back in action a few days later when he penciled himself in as the starting pitcher in the second game of a doubleheader against the Cuban Stars. The 1942 season overall was an eventful one for the Elites. It was rumored that stars Sammy Hughes and Roy Campanella had a tryout scheduled with the Pittsburgh Pirates, but the tryout may have been overblown by the media, and it never took place. Later that year, Campanella and Hughes were fined and suspended by Wilson after leaving the Giants in the middle of a pennant race to play in an exhibition game for another team. Campanella left the team to play in Mexico, and the Giants ended the season in second place in the NNL2. Snow's play suffered as well, and he hit only .222 for the year, one of his lowest season averages to date.

With fears of a possible World War II draft notice in 1943, Snow was given a break from managing duties.[17] Control of the team was handed back to George Scales, who had returned to play for the Elites in 1940. Losing Campanella, Pee Wee Butts, and Wild Bill Wright to Mexico, and then losing Sammy Hughes to the military draft severely weakened the Baltimore lineup. The draft also claimed members of the Elites' pitching staff,[18] and the depleted squad finished with a disappointing 18-26-3 league record that put them in fifth place in the seven-team NNL2. Snow returned to the managerial post in 1944 and rebounded with a .320 average, his best since 1940. The club improved, but still had a losing record of 34-38 for the year, and Baltimore fans were tiring of seeing their Elite Giants annually finish behind the Homestead Grays. Team business manager Vernon Green later explained, "Snow did the best he could with the material at hand and we can see no reason to change managers."[19]

Wilson and Green kept Snow as their captain, and he led Wilson's American All-Stars team that played in the Venezuelan league for the 1945-1946 winter season. Jackie Robinson was on the team, but he left early to join Branch Rickey and the Brooklyn Dodgers. In a February 1946 interview, Snow discussed how Robinson might perform in the majors. He appreciated Jackie's abilities but thought he would need experience and noted, "In time, he will probably develop into a top-notch ball player because he has all the makings, but he needs to know the brain work and strategy that goes into playing shortstop."[20]

Like everyone else, Snow knew the importance of Robinson's signing, but he still may have had reservations about how the experiment would work. In Roy Campanella's biography, Snow was quoted as observing, "I just don't know how it's gonna work. ... How's he gonna travel with them, and who's he gonna room with? And how about when they play exhibition games in the South or during the regular season in Baltimore?"[21]

The Elites got off to a fast start in 1946, and Snow was rewarded with coaching duties in that year's East-West Game. During his hiatus from the Elites for the game, however, a fight broke out in the Elites' clubhouse between Joe Black, rookie Gilliam, and three Puerto Rican team members.[22] The Hispanic players, Tite Figueroa, Luis Villodas, and Felix Guilbe, immediately quit the team (Villodas and Guilbe returned the next season.) Baltimore had already suffered the loss of Campanella, who had joined Robinson as a member of the Dodgers organization, and the Elites' season continued to go downhill. They finished in second place but were 12 games behind the champion Newark Eagles.

Wilson had stood by Snow for years, but he decided to shake things up for 1947. He reassigned Snow to manage the Elites' minor-league affiliate in the Negro Southern League, the Nashville Cubs, and selected Wesley Barrow as the new manager for the Giants. Wilson died that May, and Vernon Green took over the club. One of Green's first moves was to release Barrow in July and reinstate Snow. Although he had played regularly with the Cubs, Snow scaled back his playing time for the Giants and placed himself in only three league games. The team finished third, and Snow was again sent to Nashville for 1948. Snow had one last highlight as a player when he went 5-for-5 in an August 1947 game for the Cubs.

Snow joined a different organization for the first time in over 15 years when he piloted the New Orleans Creoles in 1950. Interestingly, one of the players on his team was Toni Stone, the groundbreaking female player of the Negro Leagues. He drew some attention from clubs looking for a manager after 1950 but did not manage again. Much is written about the legendary players of the Negro Leagues who never had a chance to play in the integrated White majors, and rightly so. What sometimes is forgotten is that, after the National and American Leagues finally admitted Black players, it took many more years before the teams hired Black managers and coaches. As the top players of Blackball began to jump to opportunities with major-league teams, Negro League teams started to fold, and the number of coaching positions dwindled. Snow could have been a boon to the coaching staff of any team in Organized Baseball, but, as he reflected on the situation, he acknowledged, "I guess I was born 30 or 35 years too early."[23]

Snow returned home to Louisville, where he joined the work force and helped to coach local teams. In 1958 he was cutting grass at a factory where he was employed and suffered a devastating injury when he fell into a ditch and the running lawn mower turned over on him.[24] He recovered from the injuries and returned to the working world, now cleaning up and performing maintenance at a barbershop and retail strip in St. Matthews, a city in the Louisville area. Snow became a respected and beloved member of the community. SABR member Ken Draut and Kentucky Sports Hall of Fame board member Bill Malone, among others, during their childhood in the area looked to "Mr. Snow" for advice on playing ball, and they intently listened whenever he brought out his scrapbook and described articles and mementos from his playing days. For many people he was more than a local personality. Greg Galiette, president of the International League's Louisville Bats in 2023, was one of those boys upon whom Snow had a special impact. Galiette related that, when his father was dying from cancer, Snow came around and helped with chores around the house and even played catch with the young boy.[25] To show appreciation for Snow, a St. Matthews Little League team was named for him for over 20 years.

In his retirement, Snow enjoyed watching games on TV and attending an occasional game near his home. He once related an amusing anecdote about attending a game when Louisville native Pee Wee Reese was coaching his son's Babe Ruth League team. Reese's team had men on first and second when the batter hit back to the pitcher, setting up an easy double play. Reese shouted from his position in the third-base coach's box for the opposing pitcher to throw to third base. The pitcher threw to third before realizing nobody was covering the base. Reese was ejected from the game, much to the entertainment of Snow and others in the stands.[26]

After more than three decades as a single man, Snow remarried in 1967 but enjoyed only seven years with his bride, Annie Mae Adams, before he died in 1974 from an apparent heart attack. Snow had a stepchild from each of his two marriages, but no children of his own. He was buried in an unmarked grave in Louisville's Eastern Cemetery for nearly 50 years until 2022, when SABR's Pee Wee Reese Chapter led an effort to honor him with a proper gravesite monument. Snow's life was also celebrated by the Louisville Bats in a ceremony before their game on September 2, 2022.[27] Several of Snow's family members were in attendance to see his jersey number 2 formally retired by the team.

Acknowledgments

The University of Louisville library provided access to archives of the *Louisville Leader* newspaper.

SOURCES

In addition to the sources cited in the Notes, the authors used SABR.org, Newspapers.com, and Newspaperarchive.com.

Snow's Negro League statistics were obtained from the Seamheads.com Negro League database.

Genealogical and family history was obtained from Ancestry.com.

Box scores for the East-West games were obtained from retrosheet.com.

The National Baseball Hall of Fame provided Snow's player questionnaire card.

California Winter League teams and standings were obtained from http://www.cnlbr.org/Portals/o/Standings/California%20Winter%20League%20Standings%20(1910%20-%201947).pdf.

Figueredo, Jorge S. *Who's Who in Cuban Baseball: 1878-1961* (Jefferson, North Carolina: McFarland & Company, 2007).

McNeil, William. *Black Baseball Out of Season: Pay for Play Outside of the Negro Leagues,* (Jefferson, North Carolina: McFarland & Company, 2007).

NOTES

1   https://www.youtube.com/watch?v=yWWOHIDIYws.

2   https://wc.rootsweb.com/trees/360650/I11479/-/individual.

3   "First Standards to Play Hustlers," *Lexington* (Kentucky) *Herald-Leader*, August 29, 1926: 6.

4   "Louisville Quits Southern League," *Chicago Defender*, July 30, 1932: 9.

5   There were reports of the Black Caps playing in August and September, but this appears to be the remnants of the Black Caps that joined another local outfit, the Louisville Red Birds. The team seems to have had game reports filed under both names. Both teams have manager Jim Brown mentioned in articles.

6   James A. Riley, *The Biographical Encyclopedia of The Negro Baseball Leagues* (New York: Carroll & Graf Publishers, Inc., 1994), 730.

7   Bob Luke, *The Baltimore Elite Giants* (Baltimore: Johns Hopkins University Press, 2009), 36.

8   William McNeil, *The California Winter League: America's First Integrated Professional Baseball League* (Jefferson, North Carolina: McFarland & Company, 2002), 260.

9   "Expect 30,000 at All-Star Game," *Chicago Defender*, August 10, 1935: 14.

10 Larry Lester's East-West book shows Snow in the East team picture for the 1942 game, but he was not listed in the box score for either of the two East-West games played that year. Larry Lester, *Black Baseball's National Showcase: The East-West All-Star Game: 1933: 1962, Expanded Edition* (Kansas City: Noir-Tech Research, 2020), 203.

11 Cum Posey, "Posey's Points," *Pittsburgh Courier*, March 25, 1939: 14.

12 "Elites Giants to Have Many New Players," *Baltimore Afro-American*, April 22, 1939: 22.

13 Neil Lanctot, *Campy: The Two Lives of Roy Campanella* (New York: Simon & Schuster, 2011), 55.

14 Belinda Cole-Schwartz, *An Inside View of Negro League Baseball: Told by Elite Giant, Don Troy* (Meadville, Pennsylvania: Fulton Books, 2022), 59.

15 Brent Kelley, *The Negro Leagues Revisited: Conversations with 60 More Baseball Heroes* (Jefferson, North Carolina: McFarland and Company, 2000), 90.

16 Sam Lacy, "Sepia Stars Only Lukewarm Toward Campaign to Break Down Baseball Barriers," *Baltimore Afro-American*, August 5, 1939: 19.

17 Art Carter, "Weather Adds to Elite's Problems as Camp Opens," *Baltimore Afro-American*, April 17, 1943: 24.

18 Pitchers Jonas Gaines and Bill Harvey were lost to the military draft. Joe Black was also drafted but was assigned to service in Baltimore and was able to pitch occasionally.

19 Lanctot, 104.

20 "Robinson Lacking Only in Experience, Says Snow," *Los Angeles Tribune*, February 9, 1946: 14.

21 Roy Campanella, *It's Good to Be Alive* (Lincoln: University of Nebraska Press, 1959), 117.

22 Sam Lacy, "3 Puerto Rican Stars Quit Elites in Huff," *Baltimore Afro-American*, August 24, 1946: 26.

23 Dean Eagle, "Press Box," *Louisville Courier-Journal*, February 15, 1969: 17.

24 "Felton Snow Severely Hurt on His Job," *Louisville Defender*, July 10, 1958: 1.

25 "Louisville Honors Former Infielder Felton Snow," Batsbaseball.com, https://www.milb.com/news/louisville-honors-former-infielder-felton-snow.

26 Dick Young, "Young Ideas," *Cincinnati Enquirer*, October 3, 1971: 35.

27 Batsbaseball.com.

JESSE "HOSS" WALKER

BY ADAM DAROWSKI AND BILL STAPLES JR.

Hoss Walker was a baseball lifer. He enjoyed a 20-year playing career in Black Baseball and then managed for nearly a decade. Prior to playing a single game in the major Negro Leagues, he was a teenage pioneer playing a small role in growing the game of baseball in the Far East. He played with some of Black Baseball's biggest stars on diamonds in Japan and Korea. Walker was born on September 10, 1911, in Austin, Texas. A "feisty infielder" and right-handed batter who was "clean cut and intellectual,"[1] Walker stood 5-feet-11 and weighed 190 pounds. His birth year has long been published as 1904, but newly discovered research places his birth in 1911.[2] Jesse's mother, Ollie Tinnin (a laundress), was married twice – first to Fred Guest (a porter) in 1902, then to John Walker (a laborer) in 1919. Genealogy records suggest that Guest may have been Jesse's biological father and that John Walker adopted Jesse after his marriage to Ollie in 1919.[3]

Hoss Walker with the 1944 Indianapolis Clowns. Courtesy of RMY Auctions.

Sometime in the early 1920s, Walker moved to California. In the July 17, 1921, issue of the *Austin American*, Ollie Walker stated that her husband, "Jake Walker," was killed. It's quite possible that Jake was indeed Ollie's husband John, and that this tragic event was the catalyst for the Walker family's move west.[4]

In 1925 at age 14, Walker joined the Los Angeles Railway Panthers, a team managed by Robert Fagan, former second baseman of the Kansas City Monarchs, St. Louis Stars, and the 25th Infantry Wreckers, an all-Black US Army team that featured Bullet Rogan, Heavy Johnson, and Dobie Moore.[5] By the following summer, Walker was playing third base with Fagan and O'Neal Pullen for the Los Angeles White Sox.[6]

The White Sox, managed by Lonnie Goodwin, were a top Black team that sometimes played in the integrated California Winter League (CWL). In the summer of 1926, the team barnstormed between CWL campaigns. In July, they played a highly publicized two-game series with the Fresno Athletic Club, managed by Japanese baseball pioneer Kenichi Zenimura. Fresno won both games, but Zenimura was impressed and recommended that Goodwin take the team to Japan for a tour.[7]

After the 1926-27 CWL season, Goodwin did just that, recruiting several players from his Philadelphia Royal Giants squad for a tour of the Pacific, years before Babe Ruth's All Americans went to the Far East. Negro League superstars Biz Mackey, Andy Cooper, Rap Dixon, and Frank Duncan, all members of the first-place Royal Giants, formed the team's nucleus. Walker was among the players Goodwin invited to fill out the lineup. Jesse was just 15 years old at the time but lied on his paperwork to make himself appear seven years older.

The Giants played 24 games in Japan, winning 23 (with one tie) from April through mid-May.[8] From there they went to Korea, winning all five contests they played.[9] They spent June in Hawaii, playing 11 games (winning nine). Walker played in every game in Hawaii, hitting .250 (10-for-40) with a pair of doubles.[10] He made just two errors.[11] Once back on the mainland, Walker joined Pullen on his Los Angeles Giants team.[12]

After the 1927-28 California Winter League season, the two Black clubs in the circuit, the Philadelphia Royal Giants and the Cleveland Stars, continued to barnstorm. Walker may not have played for either team during league play, but he appears to have played a part-time role for both during their exhibitions. For example, in mid-March Walker was the starting third baseman for the Cleveland All-Stars, managed by Pullen.[13] Just a week later, he was injured in a serious car accident with the Philadelphia Royal Giants when the team was traveling between venues. Walker, Mackey, Frank Warfield, Crush Holloway, Jesse Hubbard, and Pullen required hospitalization.[14]

In July Walker was again recruited by Pullen for a Hawaiian tour organized by Goodwin, this time with the Cleveland Giants. Mackey, Dixon, Cooper, and Duncan did not join this tour, opting to return to their Negro League clubs. The Hawaii papers noted that Walker was "back and he is very much improved," with his defense characterized as "nothing short of sensational."[15] The Giants returned to Los Angeles in September.[16]

The following spring, Jesse was back in Hawaii with the Pullen Giants (this time featuring Mackey, Dixon, George Carr, and Connie Day).[17] Walker hit .305 in 15 games on the tour and made just two errors in 67 chances.[18]

Upon returning to the mainland, Walker made his major Negro Leagues debut (in the American Negro League) with the Atlantic City Bacharach Giants. He was joined on the club by his Pullen Giants teammates Day, Carr, Ping Gardner, and Joe Cade. Starting at shortstop and third base, he hit .248 in games available on Seamheads. After the Bacharachs disbanded, Walker played with Pullen and Carr on the Milwaukee Giants in 1930.[19]

In 1931 Walker joined the Cleveland Cubs for their only season in the Negro National League. The team got a few appearances from a 24-year-old Satchel Paige but had an otherwise modest roster. Walker was the everyday shortstop and hit .235. During the season, Newspapers began using his "Hoss" nickname.[20] Nearly every reference to him in the press from then on used the moniker. That winter, he played in the California Winter League for the first time. As the Philadelphia Royal Giants' second baseman, he joined a star-studded lineup that featured Mule Suttles, Willie Wells, Cool Papa Bell, and Vic Harris. The rotation included Paige and Willie Foster. The team went 22-2.[21]

Walker joined the Nashville Elite Giants of the Negro Southern League in 1932, the only season in which the circuit is classified as a major league. Again the starting shortstop, he hit .273. After the season, Nashville (the second-half champion) squared off against the Chicago American Giants (the first-half champion) in the NSL Championship Series.[22] Chicago won the series four games to three.

Walker was back in the California Winter League after the season. His team was called the Nashville Elite Giants, but the roster was much different from the NSL squad (including Satchel Paige, Sam Bankhead, and Alex Radcliff in addition to his summer teammates Jim Willis and Felton Stratton). In 26 box scores collected by William McNeil, Walker hit .349 and tied for the league lead with 10 doubles.[23]

Nashville joined the second Negro National League in 1933 and Walker got the majority of starts at second base despite the presence of the 22-year-old Sam Bankhead. Among 37 box scores on Seamheads, Walker got into 20 games and hit just .169. The following season, Bankhead won the starting job for Nashville and Walker appeared in just 15 games among those on Seamheads (though he managed to hit .300).

The Elite Giants relocated to Columbus for the 1935 season. Hoss appeared in just five of 31 box scores for the team (hitting .176), and also appeared in two of 40 box scores for the Newark Dodgers (going 1-for-7). Despite the limited playing time, Walker played in the North-South All-Star Game in Memphis that September. He started and batted eighth for the North team (which featured Cool Papa Bell, Oscar Charleston, and Wild Bill Wright) and went 0-for-3.[24]

In 1936 Walker moved with the Elites to Washington, where he was again the starting shortstop. In 45 box scores, Walker appeared in 27 and hit .308. The Center for Negro League Research reports that Walker also managed the Nashville Black Vols of the NSL in 1936. Tom Wilson, owner of the Elite Giants, also served as the president of that league.[25] Walker spent the 1936-37 winter in the California Winter League with Wilson's Royal Giants, though he does not appear to have been a starter.[26]

Back with Washington in 1937, Walker appeared in all 37 known box scores and hit .238 as the starting shortstop. In the winter he played with the Philadelphia Royal Giants again in California. The stacked team featured Bell, Mackey, Suttles, Wright, Sammy Hughes, Leroy Matlock, and Chet Brewer. In 10 available game records, Walker hit .405 with three home runs (leading to an uncharacteristically high slugging percentage of .703).[27]

In 1938 the Elites went to Baltimore and Walker played a utility role (hitting .256 in 25 box scores). He also appeared for the Memphis Red Sox three times, going 1-for-11. Walker stayed with Memphis for the playoffs as they faced the Atlanta Black Crackers in the NAL Championship Series (by being first-half champions). The series was halted after just two games were played. Walker started both and went 2-for-8 with a pair of doubles.[28] In October Walker played in his second North-South All-Star Game, starting at shortstop for the South and going 0-for-3 with a sacrifice in the 3-1 victory over the North.[29]

Walker was again an All-Star in 1939 (starting at shortstop for the North and collecting two hits) and returned to the playoffs, this time with Baltimore. In the series against the Newark Eagles (won by Baltimore, three games to one), he appeared in one game, getting two hits in two at-bats. In the five-game Negro National League Championship Series, he appeared in three games and went 0-for-6 as Baltimore surprised the Homestead Grays to win the pennant. Back in California that winter, Hoss played second base for the Philadelphia Royal Giants.[30]

Walker spent the 1940 season with the New York Black Yankees (and also played a pair of games with Baltimore). Now 30 years old and the starting shortstop, he hit just .156 in 26 box scores found on Seamheads. He split the 1941 season between the Black Yankees and Birmingham Black Barons. Hoss was again the starting shortstop for Birmingham in both 1942 and 1943, returning to the postseason in 1943 as first-half champions. Birmingham faced the Chicago American Giants in the NAL Championship Series and won the five-game series three games to two. The Black Barons advanced to the Negro World Series against the mighty Homestead Grays, who prevailed by winning four of the eight games. (One was a tie.) Box scores are available for seven of the games. Walker played in six of them, going 3-for-20 (.150) with a double. In the winter, Hoss returned to the California Winter League with the Baltimore Elite Giants.

Before the 1944 season, Walker was traded to the Cincinnati-Indianapolis Clowns for John Britton.[31] He was named the team's manager and shared the starting shortstop duties with Henry Smith.[32] It was his first of many major-league managing roles. A "teacher and coach in the offseason," Walker was "loved and completely respected by his players."[33] The team still entertained fans with clowning in nonleague matches, but had done away with such hijinks in league contests.[34] The team improved from sixth place in the NAL to third under Walker's tutelage. Walker again played winter ball in California with Chet Brewer's Kansas City Royals.

In 1945, the Clowns slumped back to fifth place in the NAL. After the season Walker appeared in a handful of games in California for the Royals. Overall, in parts of nine CWL seasons recorded by William McNeil, Walker hit .328 and slugged .480 in 73 games – far above his Negro Leagues offensive performance.

The Clowns improved to second place in 1946, as Walker reduced his own playing time significantly (with Coco Ferrer and Gene Smith splitting most of the starts at shortstop). In August he was honored with "Hoss Walker Night" in Nashville as his Clowns faced the Nashville Cubs of the Negro Southern Association.[35]

Hoss was one of three Clowns managers in 1947, sharing the duties with Willie Wells and Reinaldo Drake. The team finished fifth, but was slightly better under Walker's guidance (17-23) than the others (23-49-2). Walker continued to back up the third base and shortstop positions.

Walker joined the Baltimore Elite Giants as manager for the 1948 season. The legendary manager Candy Jim Taylor was set to begin his first season leading the Elites in 1948, but died in April just before the season began. Walker was brought in to replace Taylor (with Henry Kimbro briefly acting as manager in the interim).[36] By this time, Walker had almost completely stepped back as a player, inserting himself into only three league games during the season. Baltimore had a very strong team with an exceptional rotation (headlined by Bill Byrd and Joe Black) and a robust lineup featuring Kimbro, Lester Lockett, Tommy Butts, and a young Jim Gilliam. The Elite Giants finished second in the league to a dominant Homestead squad led by Luke Easter. The two teams squared off in the League Championship Series and the Grays emerged as winners in controversial fashion. After Homestead won the first two games, the squads entered the ninth inning of the third match tied, 4-4. Homestead scored four times in the ninth to take an 8-4 lead, but the game was called before it reached completion (due to an 11:00 P.M. curfew). Baltimore won the fourth game 11-3, but when the league ruled that the third game would resume at the point at which it was halted (with the Grays up 8-4 rather than tied), Baltimore chose to forfeit and hand the series to the Grays.

In 1949 Walker was chosen to manage the East in the East-West All-Star Game.[37] His squad won 4-0 behind a combined two-hitter by Bob Griffith, Andy Porter, and Patricio Scantlebury.[38] Baltimore won the East Division (the Negro American League had split into Eastern and Western Divisions in 1949) with a 59-30 record and faced the Western Division's Chicago American Giants in the playoffs. (The Kansas City Monarchs had won the Eastern Division but did not participate in the playoffs because so many of its players had been signed by the American and National Leagues).[39] Baltimore swept Chicago to win the championship.[40] Walker was ejected from the deciding game for arguing with and shoving umpire Virgil Bluitt. He was handed a 10-game suspension.[41]

Hoss avoided the suspension by leaving the Negro American League, purchasing his hometown Nashville Cubs of the NSL, and naming himself the manager.[42] In December of 1950, Walker was announced as manager of the Raleigh Tigers.[43] However, by the time the Tigers NSA campaign kicked off, Fred Worthy was installed as skipper.[44] Instead, Walker returned to Baltimore one last time to manage the Elite Giants for the 1951 season.[45] Baltimore finished second in the East – but well below .500 and far behind the first-place Indianapolis Clowns.[46]

In 1953, Walker rejoined the Birmingham Black Barons as manager. Birmingham finished a distant second (of four teams) to the Kansas City Monarchs in the Negro American League.[47] He once again took part in the East-West All-Star Game as a coach for the East squad.[48] In all, he made four All-Star appearances in his career – two North-South games (both as a player) and two East-West games (one as a manager and another as a coach).

Willie Wells began the 1954 season as Birmingham's manager, but Walker replaced him in July.[49] Birmingham finished third in the expanded six-team circuit.[50] Despite already being announced as Birmingham's manager for 1955,[51] Walker started the season with the Detroit Stars of the Negro American League. He lasted until June before being replaced by Ed Steele.[52] His last managerial role came in 1956 with one last turn for the Black Barons.[53]

After his career in baseball, Walker worked as a janitor in Nashville and lived with his second wife, Gustavia. Walker had previously been married to Hattie Bush Walker, but they had split up by 1950.[54] Walker died suddenly on February 10, 1971, at just 59 years old, his cause of death not reported. In addition to Gustavia, he left behind six daughters (all of whom lived in Nashville) and two grandchildren.

SOURCES

In addition to the sources shown in the Notes, the authors used Baseball-Reference.com and the Seamheads Negro Leagues Database, as of December 13, 2023.

NOTES

1   Alan J. Pollack, *Barnstorming to Heaven: Syd Pollock and His Great Black Teams* (Tuscaloosa: University of Alabama Press, 2012), 150.

2   Bill Staples Jr., "The International Origins of Jesse 'Hoss' Walker's Storied Negro Leagues Baseball Career," International Pastime, http://billstaples.blogspot.com/2023/03/the-international-origins-of-jesse-hoss.html, accessed November 26, 2023.

3   Staples. The occupations of Fred Guest and John Walker are as reported respectively in the 1900 and 1920 US Censuses.

4   Staples.

5   "Farley Knocked Out of Box but the Panthers Win," *California Eagle* (Los Angeles), April 23, 1926: 7.

6   "Pirrone's Colts Easy for Sox Who Take Doubleheader," *California Eagle*, July 2, 1926: 7.

7   Coop Daley, "Breaking Barriers, Crossing Oceans: The History of Black Ballplayers in Japan, Part I," JapanBall, https://japanball.com/articles-features/japanese-baseball-historical-profiles/breaking-barriers-black-ballplayers-in-japan/, accessed December 11, 2023.

8   Kazuo Sayama and Bill Staples Jr., *Gentle Black Giants: A History of Negro Leaguers in Japan* (Fresno: Nisei Baseball Research Project Press, 2019), 27.

9   "Rogan's Giants Make Fine Record During Japan Tour," *Honolulu Star-Bulletin*, June 6, 1927: 27.

10   "Heavy Hitting by Giants," *Honolulu Star-Bulletin*, July 1, 1927: 36.

11   "Shortstop Pounds Out 18 Hits; Filipino Team Plays Errorless Ball," *Honolulu Star-Bulletin*, July 1, 1927: 16.

12   Staples, "The International Origins of Jesse 'Hoss' Walker's Storied Negro Leagues Baseball Career."

13   "Beavers Take 4 to 3 Decision in Fast Game," *Anaheim* (California) *Bulletin*, March 19, 1928: 6.

14   "Slippery Paving Injures Ten Men," *Bakersfield* (California) *Morning Echo*, March 24, 1928: 1.

15   "Collection of Best Negro Baseball Players To Be in Honolulu on Friday," *Honolulu Star-Bulletin*, July 14, 1928: 11.

16   "Royal Giants Win Two Games Over Weekend in Stadium," *Honolulu Star-Bulletin*, September 15, 1928: 29.

17   "Pullen Giants Play Between Loop Games; Impressive Opening Ceremonies Are Planned," *Honolulu Star-Bulletin*, March 23, 1929: 9.

18   "Giants' Records," *Honolulu Star-Bulletin*, May 17, 1929: 35.

19   "Colored Players," *Honolulu Star-Bulletin*, July 16, 1930: 24.

20   "Louisville Takes First from Cubs," *Pittsburgh Courier*, June 20, 1931: 14.

21   William F. McNeil, *The California Winter League: America's First Integrated Professional Baseball League* (Jefferson, North Carolina: McFarland & Company, 2002), 156.

22   Retrosheet, "1932 Negro League Postseason," https://www.retrosheet.org/NegroLeagues/1932PS.html, accessed November 26, 2023.

23   McNeil, 160.

24   Retrosheet, "North All Stars(N) (NAS) 6 South All Stars(S) (SAS) 4," https://retrosheet.org/NegroLeagues/boxesetc/1935/B09290SAS1935.htm, accessed November 26, 2023.

25   Dr. Layton Revel, "Forgotten Heroes: Henry Kimbro," Center for Negro Leagues Baseball Research, http://www.cnlbr.org/Portals/o/Hero/Henry_Kimbro%202019-10.pdf, accessed November 26, 2023.

26   McNeil, 262.

27   McNeil, 190.

28   Retrosheet, "1938 Negro League Postseason," https://www.retrosheet.org/NegroLeagues/1938PS.html, accessed November 26, 2023.

29   Retrosheet, "South All Stars(S) (SAS) 3 North All Stars(N) (NAS) 1," https://retrosheet.org/NegroLeagues/boxesetc/1938/B10020SAS1938.htm, accessed November 26, 2023.

30   McNeil, 200.

31   William J. Plott, *Black Baseball's Last Team Standing: The Birmingham Black Barons, 1919-1962* (Jefferson, North Carolina: McFarland & Company, 2019), 149.

32   "Leads Negro Club Here," *Muncie* (Indiana) *Evening Press*, June 27, 1945: 10.

33   *Barnstorming to Heaven: Syd Pollock and His Great Black Teams*, 150.

34   James A. Riley, *The Biographical Encyclopedia of the Negro Baseball Leagues* (New York: Carroll & Graf Publishers, 1994), 810.

35   "Hoss Walker Night," *Nashville Banner*, August 6, 1946: 15.

36   Riley, 810.

37   "Hoss Walker to Manage Giants," *Weekly Review* (Birmingham, Alabama), July 29, 1949: 5.

38   Retrosheet, "East All Stars(E) (ASE) 4 West All Stars(W) (ASW) 0," https://retrosheet.org/NegroLeagues/boxesetc/EW/B08140ASW1949.htm, accessed November 26, 2023.

39   Dr. Layton Revel, "Negro American League Standings (1937-1962)," Center for Negro Leagues Baseball Research, https://www.cnlbr.org/Portals/o/Standings/Negro%20American%20League%20(1937-1962)-2020.pdf, accessed November 26, 2023.

40   Riley, 50.

41   "Victorious Manager, 'Hoss' Walker, in Ten-Day Suspension in '50 for Dispute," *St. Louis Argus*, September 30, 1949: 21.

42   "Sports of the World," *Atlanta Daily World*, February 19, 1950: 7.

43   "Hoss Walker to Pilot Raleigh Tiger Nine," *Baltimore Afro-American*, December 16, 1950: 18.

44   "Raleigh Nips Stars, 9-7; Routs Sox," *New Journal and Guide* (Norfolk, Virginia), April 22, 1950: 19.

45   "Elites Here Tomorrow," *Baltimore Evening Sun*, August 4, 1951: 9.

46   "Negro American League Standings (1937-1962)."

47   "Negro American League Standings (1937-1962)."

48   "East-West Pilots, Coaches, Named," *Philadelphia Tribune*, July 11, 1953: 11.

49   "Jesse 'Hoss' Walker Replaces Wells as Birmingham Black Barons' Pilot," *Chicago Defender*, July 24, 1954: 24.

50   "Negro American League Standings (1937-1962)."

51   "Change of Pace," *Pittsburgh Courier*, January 1, 1955: 13.

52   "Steele Replaces Walker as Manager of the Stars," *Chicago Defender*, June 18, 1955: 10.

53   "Jesse 'Hoss' Walker Manager Black Barons," *Huntsville* (Alabama) *Mirror*, June 2, 1956: 7.

54   "The International Origins of Jesse 'Hoss' Walker's Storied Negro Leagues Baseball Career."

JIM WEST

BY JAY HURD

When and where someone happened upon a young infielder named Jim West is imprecise. It may very well have been in 1929, when he played for the Birmingham Negro Industrial League.[1] Although lacking details of West's early life and baseball career, his fine play at first base – perhaps noted by Bill Gatewood – prompted Clarence Smith, manager of the 1930 Negro National League Birmingham Black Barons, to invite him to spring training. The *Birmingham News* reported: "From the City League at home, the Barons will take with them James West who can field around first base with the best in any league. If he fails to make the grade, it will be because of his hitting."[2] Thus, the switch-hitting, 6-foot, 218-pound ballplayer began his career in professional baseball, and by 1931 his prowess at first base received attention: "West (when on the field is a ringer for Flournoy Miller[3] in black face) is a better first baseman than several whom I can name but won't name."[4]

James West was born to Andrew and Lydia West in Birmingham on April 23, 1905. According to the 1910 US Census, Jim, at 6 years old, was the sixth of six children. Andrew was 50 years old when he married 28-year-old Lydia. Lydia died on September 3, 1909. Andrew remarried on April 18, 1910. He married a woman identified on the marriage license as Mrs. Rena Wilson. In 1910, Jim's siblings ranged in age from 9 to 18. He had two brothers, Willie (18) and Eugene (17), and three sisters, Genella (12), Sendia (11), and Beatrice (9).[5] His father worked as a switchman for the steam railway and his mother worked at home. Andrew West died on May 11, 1918, making Rena a widow. She worked as a laundress and maid until her death on October 8, 1934. As is often the case, accurate information about Negro Leaguers and their families, can be sparse – and this certainly applies to Jim West and his family. Apparently in a previous marriage Rena gave birth to a son, Robert, surname Wilson; Robert was Jim's half-brother. A laborer for a steam railway company, Robert identifies as the "person who will always know address" of draftee on Jim's October 16, 1940, draft card. Jim shared accommodations with his family until his marriage, on June 26, 1930, to Christine (Chrstin) McLindan (McLendon). After his marriage, he and Christine lived in Birmingham with her parents, A. Charlie and Delia McLindan.[6] In the 1940 US Census he is identified as a "Base Ball Player," employed by a Philadelphia baseball team.

In 1930, West's first professional season, he played 12 games at first base and hit .243 for the Birmingham Black Barons, managed by Clarence Smith (34-29) and Bill Gatewood (12-19-2). By the end of June, West found himself playing for a different team at a different position. "In a trade negotiated between the Birmingham Black Barons and the Memphis Red Sox, five players changed uniforms. Harry Salmon, pitching ace of the Barons' staff; C [*sic*] West, a second baseman, and Andrews, veteran pitcher went to the Red Sox for William (Nathaniel) Rogers, former American Giant and hard-hitting outfielder, and Willie Cornelius."[7] West finished the season with another Negro National League club, the Memphis Red Sox, managed by Candy Jim Taylor. There, he appeared in 31 games, playing at first and second base, and finished the season with a .255 average.

In 1931 West signed with the Cleveland Cubs. The Cubs, a NNLI team, were owned by Tom Wilson, the original owner of the Nashville Standard Giants, a team that would be relocated and renamed five times between 1931 and 1938. Jim West played first base for each of Wilson's teams until 1939, when he was traded to the Philadelphia Stars from the Baltimore Elite Giants. With the Cubs, West appeared in 33 games for manager Joe Hewitt, all at first base, and hit .133. The Cubs finished the season with a 26-26 overall record. In 1931 sportswriters began to notice the talent of the 26-year-old: "West, shifty Cubs first sacker, is being rated in the class of McHaskell, formerly of the Memphis Red Sox, and McAlister [sp] (McAllister) of the Birmingham Black Barons for his splendid work at the initial sack. When he stopped C. Williams' grounder just inside the first sack in today's game the fans went wild with enthusiasm."[8]

West started the 1932 season with the Birmingham Black Barons, managed by Poindexter Williams, and played in only four games. As with his first season, 1930, West moved from the Barons to the Memphis Red Sox, now managed by Goose Curry. Whether or not this came from another trade is not clear. However, he drew attention in his first game with the Memphis Red Sox: "This West boy is the new first baseman, secured from Birmingham last Friday (May 6), where play was the feature of the whole series just closed."[9] The team finished with an overall record of 29-28, and he played in 32 games, hitting .248. With the demise of the Negro National League, both the Barons and Red Sox joined the Negro Southern League.

Gus Greenlee successfully created and introduced the second Negro National League in 1933. The Nashville Elite Giants, formerly the Cleveland Cubs, owned by Tom Wilson, joined the NNLII. West played on variants – in the Negro National League, I and II, and the California Winter League – of Tom Wilson's Giants from 1933-1939.

The 1933 Nashville Elite Giants were managed by Felton Stratton. He led the team to a 20-25-1 overall record. West, at first base, appeared in 37 games and hit .224. Candy Jim Taylor managed the 1934 Nashville Elite Giants. West hit .240 in 33 games for the Giants, who compiled a 22-32-1 overall record. As in previous years and seasons yet to come, he merited high praise: "Gilchrist, Redue [Redus] and C. Hughes played well for the visitors while West, Porter, Griffin, Hughes and Bankhead were the outstanding luminaries for the Giants."[10]

Tom Wilson, searching for a supportive financial population base,[11] moved his Giants from Nashville to Columbus, Ohio, in 1935. West traveled with the team, still managed by Candy Jim Taylor, to Ohio. Now 30 years old, he played first base in 31 games and hit .243. The Columbus Elite Giants posted an overall record of 30-25-2.

After the 1935 regular season, West appeared in the first of six seasons in the California Winter League (CWL). He traveled to Los Angeles with Tom Wilson's Royal Giants, managed by Candy Jim Taylor. His teammates included Turkey Stearnes, Biz Mackey, Mule Suttles, Sammy T. Hughes, and other excellent ballplayers. That team won the CWL championship, boasting a 23-6-2 record (.793), and West led all hitters with a .510 batting average. Here, he earned a new nickname: "Jim West dubbed 'One Wing' by west coast writers won the batting title with a scintillating .510 average."[12]

The 1936 regular season saw the Elite Giants find another new home – this time leaving Columbus and relocating to Washington, DC, as the Washington Elite Giants. Once again, Candy Jim Taylor managed the team and achieved an overall 30-34-1 mark. Leading up to the 1936 East-West All-Star Game, West received attention from the press after his stellar performance at first base and at the plate for the Elites. In 43 games, with 175 plate appearances the first baseman hit .344. "This youngster, who has developed into the most sensational fielding first baseman in the history of the game, is none other than Jim West of the Washington Elites."[13] West played in one game for the East All-Stars, managed by Oscar Charleston. In three plate appearances he had one hit an=d scored one run. After the East All-Stars defeated the West All-Stars, West headed for the West Coast, with the Royal Giants, for the 1936-1937 CWL. Candy Jim Taylor and his Giants were once again league champions, with a 21-7-1 record, and West, appearing in only three games, hit .273.

The 1937 Washington Elite Giants under Biz Mackey saw a 23-37-4 overall record. West played well, and in 37 games hit .394. He also appeared in three games for the NNL All- Stars that year, under Oscar Charleston. Although he uncharacteristically hit only .083 in this series, West did have a memorable game vs. the Santo Domingo Stars at the Polo Grounds. The Santo Domingo Stars fielded a team that included Satchel Paige, Sam Bankhead, Cool Papa Bell, and Chet Brewer. With Paige on the mound, "West came to the plate with two down in the eighth and found pinch hitter Kimbro on first as the result of a single to deep left center. With the count 1 and 2, Satchel sent up his high hard one which was just what Mr. West was looking for and he promptly poled high into the left field stands for a four-baser."[14]

Jim West, now 32, traveled to California for the 1937-1938 CWL, with the Royal Giants managed by Biz Mackey. This team won the CWL championship with a 21-3-1 record. And West, playing alongside Cool Papa Bell, Mule Suttles, Biz Mackey, Felton Snow, and Wild Bill Wright, appeared in nine games, hit .461, and won more praise. "It was not a bunch of amateur sandlotters on the San Diego Paris Inn team. ... West, sensational first baseman getting a homer and two-bagger."[15]

In 1938 Tom Wilson moved his Washington Elite Giants to Baltimore. "The Washington Elite Giants, formerly the Nashville Elite Giants, will move their franchise to Baltimore this year and will be known as the Baltimore Elite Giants. ... [The team] will start training on April 2. Most of last year's Washington squad will be with Tom Wilson's club."[16] Jim West returned to first base, and had another fine year – in 35 games, he hit .318 in

Jim West. Courtesy John W. Mosley Photograph Collection, Charles L. Blockson Afro-American Collection, Temple University Libraries.

150 plate appearances. He also garnered another nickname: "The Elites boast of the dean of receivers in Biz Mackey, Flat Foot Jim West at first, Sammy Hughes, second, and George Scales on third."[17] For the 1938-1939 CWL West, with the Philadelphia Royal Giants 11-2-1, West hit .364 in three games.

The 1939 regular season saw the Baltimore Elite Giants field a very talented nine, including Jim West, Roy Campanella, Sammy Hughes, Henry Kimbro, and Bill Hoskins. This was to be a different type of year for West, however. He appeared in 17 games and hit only .152. The team appeared to be on its way to a championship season and manager Felton Snow made some choices that impacted West. The sports pages noted that:

"Snow, a steady infielder for years, has the Elites moving at a rapid clip with new and younger charges and is out to gain the second half championship. Besides Mackey [to the Newark Eagles], the Elites traded the flashy first baseman, Jim West to the Philadelphia Stars, and Horse Walker, shortstop, made a free agent. ... With the release of the three veterans, the Giants bolstered the squad with a quintet of youngsters ... includ[ing] Jimmy (Red) Moore, who has been capably taking care of West's old post at first since joining the pennant contenders two weeks ago. ..."[18]

While the Elite Giants went on to win the NNLII Championship, West found a new home with the Philadelphia Stars, a team that finished below .500 under managers Jud Wilson (11-17-1) and Jake Dunn (13-12). He completed the 1939 season with the Stars, playing in 20 games and hitting .365. He played with the Philadelphia Royal Giants, managed by Wild Bill Wright, for the 1939-1940 CWL season. His five-game, .185 season was his final season in the CWL – World War II loomed.

West registered for the draft on October 16, 1940. While his residence was Birmingham, his place of employment was given as Philadelphia, and his employer as "Baseball Plant." Although Jim was married to Christine McLendon at the time, the "name of person who would always know" his address was his half-brother, Robert Wilson. Records of Jim West having served in the military during World War II if they exist, could not be found.

In addition to playing for the Philadelphia Stars for the 1940 season, West played in one game for Taylor's All-Stars in an Independent Clubs Series. He had no hits, and the team finished in third place in the series. The Philadelphia Stars, managed by Roy Parnell (5-7) and Jake Dunn (26-33), saw West play in 61 games and bat .338.

In 1941 West once again played for two teams – the New York Black Yankees, managed by Tex Burnett, and the Philadelphia Stars managed by Roy Parnell (3-14) and Oscar Charleston (14-39). He was 1-for-2 with the Black Yankees, and in 55 games with the Stars he hit .246.

The majority of the 1942 season saw West play with the Philadelphia Stars, now managed by Goose Curry (37-37-2). In 49 games, he hit .274 in 203 plate appearances. Under manager Vic Harris, West played in two games for the East All-Stars in the annual East-West Game and was 1-for-8.

In 1943 West hit .310 in 49 games for the Stars. In the North-South All-Star Game, which the South All-Stars won, 2-0, he was hitless.

In 1944, at 39 years old, West once again played under Curry for the Philadelphia Stars (38-29-1), and had a good season, hitting .358 in 51 games. With the Philadelphia Stars in 1945, he hit .269 in 51 games. Goose Curry, still the manager, completed the season with a 35-31-1 record. At some point between 1940 and 1945, Jim and Christine divorced, and by 1945 both had remarried. Jim married Geneva Brown, a button marker/trimmer for a wholesale blouse business, in Wilmington, Delaware, on February 2, 1945. They remained married until Geneva died on February 24, 1968.

In 1946 the 41-year-old West followed a new career path: "Jim West, veteran Philly Stars first sacker, has been named playing manager of the Oakland Club of the newly formed West Coast Baseball Association, it was learned this week. ... West made his last appearance on the coast as a member of the Birmingham Black Barons who barnstormed here last winter."[19] The West Coast Negro Baseball Association was formed on March 9, 1946. Abe Saperstein was named president and Jesse Owens was named vice president. The league played only one season[20]

In 1947 West played in one game with the Birmingham Black Barons managed by Tommy Sampson. That same year he appeared in seven games with the New York Black Yankees, under Marvin Barker, and batted .267. In his final professional season, 1948, at the age of 43, he played for managers Ramiro Ramirez (35-64-6) and Albert Elliott Buster Haywood (10-14-1) of the Indianapolis Clowns of the Negro American League and in three games went 2-for-7.

West's 18-year career included stints with multiple Negro National League (I and II) teams, a Negro American League team, independent clubs, All-Star teams, and West Coast teams. According to the Seamheads Negro League Data Base, he played in 708 games, mostly at first base. In 2,850 plate appearances he had 714 hits (.282). West was known as a "close student of the game."[21] If he dealt with injuries, they are not referenced in the sports pages. Perhaps this, from "The Sports Notepad" of June 1945, helps sum up West's ability and perseverance: "Big Jim West, the aging character who covers first base for the Philly Stars, was credited with 14 of the first 15 putouts in Sunday's game against the Elite Giants in Baltimore. And the youngsters were crying 'bout the heat."[22]

If numerous nicknames are a sign of respect for a ballplayer, then Jim West was well thought of. As with nicknames bestowed on other ballplayers, the origins and full context of his monikers are not always clear. However, the names certainly warrant attention – including and not limited to Big Jim West, Flashy Jim West, Colorful Jim West, Flat Foot, One Wing, Shifty Jim, and Hinkey Jim West. While many of these names came from newspaper writers, his peers added a few descriptive words – for example, in a conversation with Chester Washington from the *Pittsburgh Courier* in 1936, Candy Jim Taylor responded to a question about the greatest "showman of Taylor's generation, and the current game." Taylor named his Chicago American Giants teammate, Bill Monroe, and his current day picks were Satchel Paige and his current second baseman with the Elite Giants, Jim West."[23] Asked whether Buck Leonard was the "the first baseman," Albert Buster Haywood replied, "He was a good one, but you had Jim West. …"[24] And John Gibbons replied to a question about players he came across while playing: "On my team we had Big Shifty West, we had Chet Brewer. …"[25]

Documentation of West's life from 1949 to his death in 1969 is minimal. He was mentioned at least twice in columns that identified top Negro League players: in 1966, in the *Norfolk* (Virginia) *New Journal and Guide*[26] and in 1969 in the *New York Amsterdam News*.[27]

Geneva died of cardiac arrest on February 26, 1968. Jim was killed on September 2, 1969, while tending bar at the M and N Piccadilly Club in Philadelphia.

According to a newspaper account: "Big Jim West, 64, who 30 years ago was one of the best-known baseball stars, is dead, slain by three young men who had not even been born when Big Jim was thrilling fans with his exploits on the diamond. … Big Jim was shot to death.[28] West was buried in the Eden Cemetery, Collingdale, Pennsylvania, where Geneva had also been laid to rest.

In 1936 a newspaper wrote of West: "[W]ith his floppy old glove, his halting, stumbling slide and his Houdini touches [West] ranks head and shoulders above any man modern baseball has produced for color." Despite the "unbelievable feats of Jim West [his] color will always remain black; but [he] would be welcome to many a major league club."[29]

SOURCES

In addition to the sources cited in the Notes, the author consulted Seamheads.com and Retrosheet.org.

NOTES

1 "Black Barons Off for Spring Work at Fort Benning," *Birmingham News*, April 2, 1930: 14.

2 "Black Barons Leave Tuesday for Training Camp," *Birmingham Reporter*, March 29, 1930: 7.

3 Flournoy Miller collection 1928-1971 [bulk 1941-1951], New York Public Library Archives & Manuscripts, https://archives.nypl.org/scm/20858.

4 W. Rollo Wilson, "Sport Shots," *Pittsburgh Courier*, August 15, 1931: 14.

5 Spellings of names do vary in Ancestry.com.

6 Spelling of surname could be McLindon, McLendon,

7 "Memphis Red Sox and Black Barons Put Over Trade," *Chicago Defender*, June 28, 1930: 8. This was very possibly Jabbo Andrews, but he was a right fielder and not a pitcher.

8 "A.B.C.'s Drop 3-1 Encounter to Cleveland," *Chicago Defender*, June 13, 1931: 9.

9 "In Sportdom: Tuskegee Institute Alabama," "Red Sox Win Final," *Atlanta Daily World*, May 12, 1932: 5.

10 "Elite Giants Wallop Cleveland Crew Twice," *Nashville Tennessean*, May 28, 1934: 8.

11 "Baltimore Elite Giants," Negro League Baseball Museum eMuseum, https://nlbemuseum.com/history/teams/baltegiants.html.

12 William F. McNeil, *The California Winter League: America's First Integrated Professional Baseball League* (Jefferson, North Carolina: McFarland & Company, Inc., 2008), 178.

13 "Jim West, Gangling First Baseman of the Elites, Fields Like Grimm, Hits Like Gehrig," *Pittsburgh Courier*, August 22, 1936: A4.

14 Joe Bostic, "Taylor's No-Hitter Tops Satchel Paige," *Baltimore Afro-American*, September 25, 1937: 18.

15 "Winter League Ball Flourishes on Coast," *Baltimore Afro-American*, November 27, 1937: 17.

16 "Tom Wilson Takes Club to Baltimore," *Chicago Defender*, April 2, 1938: 8.

17 "Crawfords, Nashville Meet Here," *Greensburg* (Pennsylvania) *Daily Tribune*, August 18, 1938: 7. (This article still refers to the Nashville Elite Giants.)

18 "Elites Clash with Eagles," *Baltimore Afro-American*, July 22, 1939: 23.

19 "Jim West to Pilot Oakland," *Pittsburgh Courier*, March 9, 1946: 16.

20 Online Archive of California, Collection Guide, "Guide to the West Coast Negro Baseball Association," https://oac.cdlib.org/findaid/ark:/13030/c8125tf5/

21 "Jim West, Gangling First Baseman of the Elites Fields Like Grimm, Hits Like Gehrig."

22 "The Sports Notepad," *Baltimore Afro-American*, June 30, 1945: 18.

23 "Candy Jim Taylor Reminisces," *Baseball History Daily*, https://baseballhistorydaily.com/tag/jim-west.

24 Brent Kelley, *The Negro Leagues Revisited: Conversations with 66 More Baseball Heroes* (Jefferson, North Carolina: McFarland & Company, Inc., 2000), 111.

25 Kelley, 132.

26 Jacko Maxwell, "Old-Time Negro Baseball Players – A Major League Loss: Ol' Satch, Josh Gibson Symbols of Yesteryear," *New Journal and Guide* (Norfolk, Virginia), September 3, 1966: 26.

27 Joe Black, "On Sports," "Greatest Black Team," *New York Amsterdam News*, August 9, 1969: 38.

28 "Ex-Baseball Star Slain in Bar," *Louisville Defender*, September 18, 1969: A4.

29 "East-West Baseball Classic to Chicago," *Atlanta Daily Weekly*, August 18, 1936: 5.

JIM WILLIS

BY MARGARET M. GRIPSHOVER

Jim Willis began his baseball career with the New Orleans Black Pelicans in 1926 and ended it in 1949 as player-er-manager of the Evansville (Indiana) Dodgers. Over the 23-year arc of his life in baseball, Willis spent at least 12 seasons in an Elite Giants uniform. He made his last appearance on the mound for the Baltimore edition of the Elite Giants in 1939. He did not, however, pitch for the Elites during the 1939 Championship Series. He was a man in constant motion. He jumped from team to team with ease but not always without controversy. Willis was one of the best pitchers of his era that you likely have never heard of, mainly due to the long shadow cast by his sometime teammate, Satchel Paige.

In the early 1930s it was not unusual for Willis to notch double-digit strikeouts in a single game.[1] He hurled a wicked curveball with deceptive action often enhanced by a soda-bottle cap that he secretly used to rough up the ball.[2] Willis was also a man of mystery and of many names. He seems to have dropped into the baseball world from out of nowhere as a young pitcher in 1926, and then vanished into the gloaming in 1949 when he hung up his glove. He had just about as many nicknames as he did teams. Over his more than two-decade career, he was known as Smokey, Smoky, Wild Jim, Cannonball, Big Boy, Charley, Bullet, Big Jim, Speed, Vic, Sammy, and Eddie Willis.[3]

Who was Jim Willis, other than a man of many names? Little is known about his personal life and what leads do exist cannot be verified. His birth and death dates and locations are unknown. The lack of information about Willis's family background in government documents and published works, combined with his relatively common name, makes him an elusive target for the researcher. In fact, Jim Willis may not even have been his legal name. But what is known is that Willis had a career in baseball that lasted for more than two decades, and during that time, he pitched his way into baseball history.

Willis left behind few breadcrumbs regarding his life beyond the diamond. But what he did leave us with was a record of a long and winding baseball life that began as early as 1926 with the New Orleans Black Pelicans, also known as Caulfield's Ads, named for promoter Fred Caulfield.[4] By midseason Willis had the best won-lost record in the Negro Southern League.[5] Willis and the Black Pelicans traveled throughout the South, including stops in Nashville, where they tangled with the Elite Giants in September at Sulphur Dell.[6] Willis and the Black Pelicans lost, 5-3.[7] New Orleans absorbed that loss and went on to vie for the NSL title against the Black Barons, but it was Birmingham that wore the crown.[8] Willis ended his tenure with the Black Pelicans with a 17-9 record, the best in the NSL.[9] By then, Willis had

caught the attention of the Nashville management, and by the spring of 1928, he was plying his trade in an Elite Giants uniform. It would be the first of at least 11 seasons during which Willis drew a paycheck from various iterations of the Elite Giants.

Willis began his first go-round as an Elite Giant in the spring of 1927.[10] He won his first start for Nashville on April 20 with an impressive 6-0 thumping of the Milwaukee Giants, granting the visiting Wisconsinites just four hits.[11] He continued his good form throughout the NSL season and was known to Elite Giants fans as Wild Jim or Smokey Willis for his dominating and deceptive hurling.[12] But by midsummer, the NSL collapsed, leaving only the Dixie Series between Nashville and the Dallas Black Sox as the final defining moment for the Elite Giants.[13] Willis helped the Elites clinch the Dixie title when he downed the Black Sox 5-4 at Sulphur Dell.[14]

For Jim Willis, the grass was always greener on the other side of the outfield fence. He rarely played for one team for more than two years in a row and was prone to midseason migrations to greener pastures. So when the Dayton Independents reached out to Willis in February 1928 with an offer of employment, they must have known that he was in the mood for a change of scenery.[15] But Willis didn't head north to Ohio in early 1928; instead, he left Nashville and went south for spring training with the Birmingham Black Barons of the Negro National League.[16] Willis joined the Black Barons at their spring-training camp at Fort Benning, Georgia, and after 10 days was "rounded into form and ready to go."[17]

While Willis was able to manhandle the Twenty-Fourth Infantry nine of Fort Benning, once the competition stepped up in class, it was another story.[18] A week later, Willis and the Black Barons lost to the St. Louis Stars, 8-5, and a few days later, he failed as a reliever when the Stars swept a doubleheader against the Barons.[19] But Willis was not completely to blame for his losses. In May he lost a four-hitter to the Chicago American Giants 3-2, because of the Black Barons' four errors and their lack of offensive support.[20] The game was played under protest by Birmingham, which accused Chicago of using outfielder William "Nat" Rogers, who was "the property of the Memphis club," and for "having 17 players in Chicago uniforms when the league ruling calls for 16."[21] By early June, Willis had enough of the Magic City. He appeared in seven games for Birmingham, racking up a scratchy 2-4 record and a 6.06 ERA. The Black Barons went on to have a losing record of 46-53 for the 1928 season. On June 9 the president of the Birmingham club announced that two of their players were no longer with the Black Barons – outfielder Ruben Jones, who "felt there were some rules of the club that he did not feel he could obey," and Jim Willis, who was "displeased or dissatisfied because of his inability to win in this league, and decided to go where he could have an easy time and not work quite so hard."[22]

Where did Willis believe he could be more satisfied with his career? For Willis, the answer was Nashville. He jumped back to Nashville, where he regained his winning ways as a starter and reliever for the Elite Giants.[23] The Nashville Elite Giants played as an independent team in 1928, and since the NSL had collapsed, there was no end-of-season championship series.[24] Willis would have to wait for more satisfaction.

Willis was less of a rolling stone in 1929 and 1930 and stayed put in Nashville for two consecutive seasons – a rarity given his peripatetic ways. The Elite Giants were admitted as an associate member of the NNL in the spring of 1929 although they continued to compete in the NSL.[25] But the NSL operated only for the first half of the year; it collapsed in midsummer. Nashville was atop the standings and was declared the winner with a 9-3 record.[26] After the NSL lost its organizational structure, Willis and the Elite Giants spent the remainder of the 1929 season barnstorming against NNL teams including the Kansas City Monarchs, Memphis Red Sox, St. Louis Stars, and the Black Barons. And just as the NSL lost steam, so did Willis. His role as a starter was diminished to a handful of late-inning appearances and mostly in losing situations.[27] And things went from bad to worse. In mid-August he found himself tending the right-field garden for the Elites in a game against an East Chicago, Indiana, nine.[28] If that loss didn't sting Willis, less than two weeks later he was injured while sliding home in the 10th inning of a barnstorming game against the Indianapolis Lincoln Highways.[29] But Willis ended his year with the Elite Giants on a high note by tossing a gem of a one-hitter against the Miami Giants, a 3-0 victory for Nashville.[30]

In the spring of 1930, Willis returned to the Elite Giants, who were now full-fledged members of the NNL.[31] He chalked up a preseason win against the Louisville Black Caps in April by holding the visitors to four hits and fanning 12.[32] His pitching was described as "masterful … [F]our hits was the best they could do toward solving his slants."[33] The consolation prize for the Black Caps? They were given a guided tour of the city of Nashville by the Elite Giants players.[34] At the end of the 1930 season, it was the Elite Giants who were in need of some consolation. They finished the year deep in the basement of the NNL standings with a dismal 26-55-1 record. For Willis, however, there was some cause for celebration. He was Nashville's leading pitcher with a 3.99 ERA even though he posted an abysmal 3-12 record. As the Elites' top hurler, he was presented with a wristwatch by Harold L. Shyer, a local jeweler, vice president of the Nashville Vols, and one of the founding members of Nashville's Old Timers Club.[35] And Willis also gained a new nickname – Cannonball.[36]

Cannonball Willis earned his new sobriquet in 1930 during his first rotation with the Elite Giants/Royal Colored Giants in the California Winter League.[37] He pitched at least three seasons of winter ball in Los Angeles against such teams as the Pirrone All-Stars, the Metro-Goldwyn-Mayer studios nine, the El Paso Mexicans, and the San Luis Cubans, among others.[38] Among those with whom Willis shared the horsehide during winter ball were Cool Papa Bell, Turkey Stearnes, and Mule Suttles.[39] Willis also rubbed elbows with Hollywood celebrities like Buster Keaton and Joe E. Brown, who were on hand to promote their projects.[40] But when the curtain came down on the West Coast interlude in early 1931, it was back to Nashville for Willis and his chores on the mound for the Elite Giants. And it was truly drudgery. Willis and the Elite Giants lost all of their spring exhibition games.[41]

The Elites notched the first regular-season game win when Willis took to the hill and bested the Memphis Red Sox, 3-1.[42] But that was not enough to keep him satisfied. By early June, thoughts of greener pastures arose once more and he jumped to the newly minted Cleveland Cubs of the NNL.[43] While the city and uniforms changed, one thing remained the same: the team and Willis's boss. The Cleveland Cubs were essentially a reconstituted version of the Nashville Elite Giants and owned by Tom Wilson.[44] Willis was their leading pitcher with five wins and four losses and a wobbly 5.09 ERA, the highest of the starters with at least five appearances. Also on the Cubs' slab staff was Satchel Paige. Willis and Paige would later team up in the winter leagues and vie for top pitching honors. The Cleveland club was a one-year wonder and folded by the end of the 1931 season. They finished in second place in the NNL with a record of 23-22 in league play.

After his brief detour to Cleveland, in the spring of 1932 Willis was back with the Elite Giants in Nashville of the NSL. Willis was used mainly as a pitcher that year but did make an occasional appearance in the outfield.[45] He had a slow start with an early loss to the Louisville Black Caps, whom which he had so handily dismissed in 1930, but found his winning groove by the early summer and was rewarded with yet another nickname, Bullet Willis.[46] On June 25 Willis fanned 11 Red Sox batsmen for a solid 4-1 victory for Nashville over Memphis.[47]

Willis's sharpshooting on the mound helped the Elite Giants claim the second-half NSL championship and a date with the Chicago American Giants for the 1932 Dixie Series showdown. Alas, there was no happy ending for Willis and the Elites. They lost the series due to their error-prone defense and the timely and explosive offense posted by the American Giants led by Turkey Stearnes, Steel Arm Davis, and Sandy Thompson.[48] Willis ended the 1932 season as the best tosser on the Elite Giants staff, with a 4-5 record and a 2.54 ERA. His teammate Henry Wright was the club's top hurler, with six wins against three losses and a 2.62 ERA. But Willis didn't have much time to dwell on what could have been. In early October, Willis, and an aggregation that was first billed as Tom Wilson's "Philadelphia Elite Giants," but later named the "Royal Colored Giants," rolled into Union Station in Los Angeles to prepare for another California Winter League season.[49] Joining Willis and the Elites in Los Angeles for the first time was Satchel Paige, described to local fans simply as a "new man to the coast, who is also a catcher."[50]

In March 1933, for the fifth year in a row, Willis reported for spring training with the Elite Giants.[51] He seemed to be off to a good start. On June 8 his "masterful pitching" helped Nashville win the first half of a doubleheader against the Homestead Grays by a comfortable 7-1 score.[52] But a few weeks later, he was at the center of a firestorm when he jumped from the Elite Giants to the Philadelphia Stars.[53] Tom Wilson was "angry and choleric" over Willis's defection.[54] He demanded that his pitching ace be returned to his club, that no NNL club should play the Stars until Willis was back in Nashville, and that there was the matter of a $150 debt that Willis owed to Wilson that must be resolved.[55]

Wilson's fellow team owners voted to blacklist the Stars "until Willis is returned to Nashville and delinquent accounts" were paid.[56] Because of Willis's defection, the NNL ruled that "no league clubs would be permitted to play Philadelphia Stars on account of player Willis."[57] One team that ignored the ban was the Pittsburgh Crawfords. The Craws ignored the NNL prohibitions and not only played several games against the Stars in mid-August, but also one in which Willis was on the mound for Philadelphia.[58] When it came time for the East All-Star balloting for pitchers, at least 4,383 fans didn't seem to hold a grudge when they cast their votes for Willis.[59] Of course the stars did not align for Willis to be an All-Star in 1933. He was outshone by the top vote-getter, Sam Streeter, who garnered 29,989 tallies, and by Paige, who had an impressive 23,089 votes.[60] If Willis was affected by the controversy, it didn't show. He wore the Philadelphia uniform for the rest of the season.

In the end, in spite of all the drama and vitriol, it appears that Tom Wilson and Jim Willis reconciled their differences. By September, Willis was announced as a returning player on Wilson's Royal Giants of the California Winter League.[61] In Los Angeles Willis teamed up again with Paige; they shared the spotlight with Hollywood celebrities including George Raft and an actress named Constance Allen who was "the star of the recent nudist picture, 'Elysia.'"[62] Willis and Paige thrived in the California sunshine and dazzled crowds and baffled batters. Although just a few years earlier Paige was a relative unknown to the Los Angeles audience, by 1933 he was described as the "celebrated strike-out king."[63] But in truth, Willis was just as effective as Paige and grabbed headlines with sparkling performances. He even stole "some of Paige's thunder" when he struck out 13 batters to lead the Royal Giants to a 14-0, win over the White Kings.[64] Paige grabbed most of the headlines, but Willis was just as good. At the end of the season, the Royal Giants won their second straight Winter League championship.[65] Paige's record for the West Coast swing was 16-2 while Willis was credited with 14 wins against two losses.[66] But there was no rest for weary arms. After hoisting the pennant, Willis and his fellow Elite Giants headed back Nashville, playing exhibition and "spring training" games along the way to pay the freight.[67]

For Willis, the 1934 season was a mirror image of his working life in 1933 – spending the regular season with the Elite Giants and ringing in a new year in sunny Los Angeles in the Winter League. Willis crossed paths with Paige in May when the Pittsburgh Crawfords paid a visit to Nashville.[68] This time it was Bullet Willis who stole the spotlight, and thanks to some "sensational fielding" by Sam Bankhead, the Elites nipped Paige and the Crawfords, 2-1.[69] That moment may have been the highlight of the year for Willis. The Elites had a mediocre season and finished the year in fifth place in Negro National League II. Willis took the mound just six times for the Elites and posted a dismal 2-4 record but had the lowest ERA (2.65) among Nashville's top three hurlers. With the 1934 season in the books, Willis was westward bound for another Winter League swing and another reunion with Paige and the Royal Giants.

For the next few years, Willis continued to toss the pill for the Elite Giants as Wilson's team migrated from Nashville to Columbus, Detroit, and Washington, D.C., before finally settling down in for a stay in Baltimore in 1939. In 1935 Willis was touted as one of the "greatest stars of Negro baseball," and the "possessor of a good fast ball and a baffling change of pace," and as a "keen student of the game."[70] The changes in scenery did little to improve the Elites, and in 1935 they ended up in third place in the NNL2. Willis was the second-best pitcher on the squad with an improved 4-1 record and a 2.89 ERA, the lowest of the Elites' top slingers. In 1936 and 1937 the Elites settled in Washington. For Willis, the move was a capital idea. In 1936 he ended the year with a so-so 5-5 record but posted the lowest ERA (2.84) of any pitcher in the NNL2 with at least 10 appearances on the mound, including Paige, who went 8-2 with a 3.64 ERA. In 1937 Willis had a rough year with the Elites, though, and was relegated mainly to working in relief. Although he did have some success in a handful of nonleague tilts during the 1937 season, he was handed the ball for only two NNL2 games before racking up an eye-popping 15.19 ERA.[71] What caused Willis's rapid decline in 1937 is unknown but it was a harbinger of things to come. Cannonball Willis was misfiring and running low on ammunition.

The 1938 season marked the first time since 1928 that Willis did not start spring training in an Elite Giants jersey. He was now a member of the Evansville Morocco Stars, of Evansville, Indiana. The Morocco Stars were an independent barnstorming club whose roster included other castoffs from the NNL2 and NSL.[72] In May the "Theodore Acklen's" Stars and their marquee pitcher, "Big Jim Willis," described as a "former" big leaguer, were scheduled to make an appearance at Sulphur Dell in May in a game against the Cincinnati White Sox.[73] The Stars were described as a "local Negro" team, indicating that they had migrated from Indiana to Tennessee.[74] By August 1938, the Stars were rebranded as the Nashville Morocco Stars and claimed to have won 50 of their 60 games and boasted the services of such "outstanding stars" as Jim Willis.[75] The lack of newspaper coverage of the Morocco Stars' season makes it difficult to confirm their reported winning record or exactly how Willis contributed to that feat.

The Morocco Stars fell from the sky and did not field a team in 1939. Willis needed a job and the first offer came from the Baltimore Elite Giants. It was Jim Willis's last year in the NNL2. He appeared in two games for the Elite Giants during their championship season but did not play in the final series. Although he won one of his two starts for Baltimore, batters were no longer baffled by his curve and Willis quickly accrued a beefy 12.15 ERA. By early July, Willis was no longer in an Elites uniform. The Elite Giants were in the process of cleaning house and reinventing their lineup with more youthful talent, and Willis had to go.[76] He didn't have to leave town, but he did have to take a step down in class. He was signed by the Baltimore Black Sox, a Black minor-league team.[77] In one of his first outings with the Black Sox, Willis was planted out in left field and went 0-for-4 at the plate in a 16-1 drubbing by the Long Branch Greys.[78] The Black Sox used Willis more as a utility player than as a pitcher, and even then only as an occasional reliever.[79] When the 1939 Black Sox season was over, Willis did not play another game in Baltimore. In fact, he didn't play for another team until 1941.

During the 1940s, Willis's career was in steep decline. In the spring of 1941, he was picked up as player-manager by the Cincinnati White Sox, formerly known as the Cincinnati Tigers.[80] But that arrangement lasted less than two months and by June Willis's name no longer appeared in newspaper coverage of Cincinnati's games.[81] He resurfaced in 1942 as a player-coach for another team, Nashville's L.N-N.C. Railroaders.[82] In May it was reported that Willis had recently enlisted in the US Army but that his induction was "temporarily deferred."[83] No US Army records were found for a "Jim Willis" for that timeframe and location. Willis's name did not appear in any baseball game results for the remainder of 1942, or during the 1943 or 1944 seasons, leaving his whereabouts unknown.

The last four years of Jim Willis's baseball life were spent in Evansville, Indiana. In 1945 he took a turn with the Evansville Black Sox.[84] In 1946 and 1947, Willis found a home with the Evansville Reichert Giants, a team that was sponsored by the city's mayor, Manson L. Reichert, and managed in part by Charles "Dusty" Decker, an influential local businessman and politician who was formerly associated with the Indianapolis A.B.C.s, Memphis Red Sox, Detroit Stars, and the Louisville Black Colonels.[85] Willis experienced a bit of a renaissance and found himself back on the mound as a starting pitcher. Although he was described as a "Baltimore Giants' cast-off," he let his pitches do the talking in the summer of 1946 as he racked up a string of wins for the Reichert nine.[86] But it was nearly closing time for Willis. He came back to Evansville for the 1947 season but was ineffective.[87] Willis sat out the 1948 season and returned to Evansville in the summer of 1949 to put the final touches on his career as a manager and coach of the Evansville Dodgers of the NSL.

After Willis ended his baseball career in Evansville in 1949, he disappeared as mysteriously as he appeared with the New Orleans Black Pelicans in 1926. In more than two decades as a baseball player, no clues to his personal life appeared in newspapers. No obituaries about a former Negro League pitcher named Jim Willis have surfaced. What is known is that he had flashes of brilliance as a pitcher during the early 1930s that nearly equaled the flash and substance of Satchel Paige. And his peers recognized his brilliance. Negro Leagues historian John Holway quoted former Elite Giant Roy Campanella: "The Elites had five pitchers who could pitch in any league – any league. ... We had Robert Griffith, Andrew Porter, Bill Byrd, Jim Willis, and left-hander Tom Glover. I would take those five pitchers, put them right on the Dodgers, and all of those fellows would be starters in the big leagues."[88]

In a 1987 interview, Claude O'Neil, a Nashville Elite Giants fan, recalled that "Jim Willis had a great curve ball," and added, "They used to call Willis 'Black Gold.'"[89]

Acknowledgment

The author would like to express her heartfelt appreciation for the wisdom, good humor, generosity, encouragement, and expert editing of the late Frederick C. Bush, who assisted with the early research for this chapter.

SOURCES

Unless otherwise indicated, all Negro League statistics and records are from Seamheads.com and baseball-reference.com. Ancestry.com was used to access census, birth, death, marriage, military, immigration, and other genealogical and public records.

NOTES

1   "Elite Giants Capture Twice from Memphis," *Nashville Tennessean*, June 27, 1932: 7; "Giants Hand White Kings 14-0 Shutout," *Los Angeles Times*, December 25, 1933: 14.

2   Richard Schweid, "Club Built Against All Odds," *Nashville Tennessean*, September 2, 1987: 19, 22.

3   "Black Pelicans Try for Fourth in a Row," *New Orleans Item*, July 14, 1926: 20; "Nashville Elites Beat Black Barons," *St. Louis Argus*, August 12, 1927: 7; "Elite Giants Play Hopkinsville Sunday," *Nashville Tennessean*, April 11, 1930: 15; "Elite Giants Play Hopkinsville Today," *Nashville Tennessean*, April 13, 1930: 20; "'Babe' Herman on All Star Team," *Los Angeles Evening Express*, October 29, 1930: 18; "Elite Giants to Play Dixie Series Champs," *Nashville Banner*, June 4, 1932: 10; "Giants Win 1st Game in Winter League 8-2," *Indianapolis Recorder*, October 21, 1933: 2; "Tigers Add Trio of New Players," *Cincinnati Post*, May 15, 1934: 11; "Phila. Stars Cop Two from Nashville Nine," *Philadelphia Inquirer*, June 10, 1934: 29; "Philly Stars and Bushwicks in 1 to 1 Tie," *Brooklyn Eagle*, June 24, 1939: 7; "Baltimore Giants to Play Manheim," *Lancaster* (Pennsylvania) *Intelligencer Journal*, June 27, 1939: 12.

4   "Eight Cities Enter Negro Southern League," *New Orleans States*, April 7, 1920: 15; "Black Pelicans Open Season with Memphis Team Saturday," *New Orleans Item*, April 30, 1926: 19.

5   "Black Barons Meet Ads in Three Games," *Birmingham News*, July 18, 1926: 19.

6   "Black Pelicans Fall Before Elite Giants," *Nashville Banner*, August 9, 1926: 11.

7   "Elite Giants Defeat Black Pelicans, 5 to 3," *Nashville Tennessean*, August 9, 1926: 7.

8   "Black Barons Cop Final Go of Year from Ads," *Birmingham News*, September 9, 1926: 16.

9   William J. Plott, *The Negro Southern League, A Baseball History, 1920-1951* (Jefferson, North Carolina: McFarland & Co. Inc., 2015), 58.

10   "Elite Giants to Be Strong This Year," *Nashville Banner*, April 8, 1927: 19.

11   "Elite Giants Again Trounce Milwaukee," *Nashville Tennessean*, April 21, 1927: 11.

12   "Nashville Elites Beat Black Barons," *St. Louis Argus*, August 12, 1927: 7; "Black Barons Lose," *Birmingham Reporter*, August 13, 1927: 7.

13   Plott, 74-75.

14   "Elite Giants Capture Negro Dixie Title," *Nashville Banner*, September 12, 1927: 10.

15   "Dayton Seeks Stars," *Pittsburgh Courier*, February 18, 1928: 16.

16   "Black Barons to Train in Georgia," *Birmingham Post-Herald*, March 18, 1928: 22.

17   "Black Baron Pilot Working Team Hard," *Birmingham Post-Herald*, April 8, 1928: 26.

18   "Black Barons Win in Ninth Over Infantry," *Birmingham Post-Herald*, April 20, 1928: 12.

19   "St. Louis Stars Again Win from Birmingham Black Barons, 8 to 5," *St. Louis Globe-Democrat*, April 30, 1928: 9; "St. Louis Stars Win Double-Header from Birmingham, 5-0, 8-5," *St. Louis Globe-Democrat*, May 2, 1928: 13.

20   "Black Barons Lose to Chicago Giants Under Protest, 3-2," *Birmingham News*, May 6, 1928: 25.

21   "Black Barons Lose to Chicago Giants Under Protest, 3-2."

22   "Black Barons Release Jones; Add New Players," *Birmingham Reporter*, June 9, 1928: 7.

23   "Elite Giants Open with Chattanooga," *Nashville Banner*, June 21, 1928: 13; "Elite Giants Blank Lookouts," *Nashville Tennessean*, June 25, 1928: 9; "Squeeze Play Beats Majors in Last Frame," *Flint (Michigan) Sunday Journal*, August 19, 1928: 6.

24   Plott, 76.

25   "Elite Giants Are Ready for Work," *Nashville Banner*, April 7, 1929: 42; Plott, 78-79.

26   Plott, 78.

27   "Elite Giants Lose," *Nashville Banner*, June 17, 1929: 17; "Elite Giants Lost Twin Bill to Red Sox," *Nashville Banner*, July 29, 1929: 12; Dark Barons Take Two at Nashville," *Birmingham Post-Herald*, August 5, 1929: 11.

28   "Poindexter Stops Elites; Score 5 to 3," *Munster (Indiana) Times*, August 15, 1929: 14.

29   "Nashville Elites Divide Two with Lincoln Highways," *Chicago Defender*, August 24, 1929: 9.

30   "Elite Giants Divide with Florida Team," *Nashville Tennessean*, September 30, 1929: 9.

31   "Elite Giants Join the National Loop," *Nashville Tennessean*, March 25, 1930: 12.

32   "Black Caps Lose," *Louisville Courier-Journal*, April 20, 1930: 52.

33   "Elite Giants Win," *Nashville Banner*, April 20, 1930: 25.

34   "Elite Giants Win."

35   "Elite Giants Win and Tie with Black Barons," *Nashville Tennessean*, September 1, 1930: 6.

36   "'Babe' Herman on All Star Team," *Los Angeles Evening Express*, October 29, 1930: 18; "Harold L. Shyer Rites Tomorrow," *Nashville Tennessean*, October 19, 1971: 28.

37   "'Cannonball' Willis Will Twirl Sunday," *Los Angeles Daily News*, November 6, 1930: 15.

38   "'Babe' Herman on All Star Team; "'Cannonball' Willis Will Twirl Sunday"; "White Sox to See Nashville Giants, Mexicans and All-Stars Tilt," *California Eagle* (Los Angeles), November 14, 1930: 9; James Newton, "Winter Ball," *Chicago Defender*, February 7, 1931: 8.

39   "Elite Giants Cop Winter League Rag," *Nashville Banner*, February 4, 1934: 12.

40   "'Cannonball' Willis Will Twirl Sunday"; James Newton, "Winter Ball," *Chicago Defender*, February 21, 1931: 8.

41   "Elite Giants Defeated Twice Sunday Afternoon," *Nashville Banner*, April 20, 1931: 13; "Nashville Wins Season Opener," *Baltimore Afro-American*, May 16, 1931: 14.

42   "Nashville Wins Season Opener."

43   "Cubs to Meet Hoosiers Here," *Akron Beacon Journal*, June 3, 1931: 17.

44   James A. Riley, *The Biographical Encyclopedia of the Negro Baseball Leagues* (New York: Carroll & Graff Publishers, Inc., 1994), 178-179.

45   "Elite Giants Take Second from Crackers," *Nashville Tennessean*, May 15, 1932: 9.

46   "Black Caps Defeat Nashville Team, 7-4," *Louisville Courier-Journal*, June 14, 1932: 12; "Elite Giants to Play Dixie Series Champs," *Nashville Banner*, June 4, 1932: 10.

47   "Elite Giants Capture Twice from Memphis," *Nashville Tennessean*, June 27, 1932: 7.

48   "Five Homers Give Chicago Americans Win Over Elites," *Nashville Tennessean*, September 19, 1932: 7; "Elite Giants Lose in Playoff with Chicago for Southern Crown," *Nashville Tennessean*, October 3, 1932: 7; Al Monroe, "Giants Crush Nashville," *Chicago Defender*, October 8, 1932: 8.

49   "Winter League Ready for Greatest Season in History of Sox Park," *California Eagle*, October 2, 1932: 9; "Winter Ball to Start on Sunday," *Los Angeles Daily News*, October 5, 1932: 14.

50   "Winter League Ready for Greatest Season in History of Sox Park."

51   "Elite Giants Train in New Orleans, La.," *Nashville Banner*, April 2, 1932: 11; "Elite Giants Return from Spring Training," *Nashville Banner*, April 19, 1933: 10.

52   Fred D. McCrary, "Grays, Nashville Battle to Thrilling 10-10 Tie," *Pittsburgh Courier*, June 10, 1933: 15.

53   William G. Nunn, "Posey Refuses to Return Two Detroit Players," *Pittsburgh Courier*, July 1, 1933: 14.

54   Nunn.

55   Nunn.

56   Bill Gibson, "Pittsburgh's Grays Ousted from League," *Kansas City Call*, July 7, 1933: 12.

57   Cum Posey, "Pointed Paragraphs," *Pittsburgh Courier*, July 15, 1933: 14.

58 Russell J. Cowans, "Thru the Sport Mirror," *Detroit Tribune*, August 5, 1933: 7; "Crawfords Rally Local Stars Bow," *Philadelphia Inquirer*, August 13, 1933: 23; "5,000 Fans See Colored Teams at Eagle Park," *York* (Pennsylvania) *Gazette and Daily*, August 14, 1933: 12.

59 "The East-West Game Player Vote," *Pittsburgh Courier*, September 9, 1933: 15.

60 "The East-West Game Player Vote."

61 Harry Levette, "Winter League Opens October 14; To Be Greatest in History," *California Eagle*, September 22, 1933: 11.

62 "It's Newsom Day at Sox Park," *Los Angeles Times*, December 17, 1933: 61.

63 "It's Newsom Day at Sox Park."

64 "Giants Hand White Kings 14-0 Shutout," *Los Angeles Times*, December 25, 1933: 14.

65 "Elite Giants Cop Winter League Rag."

66 "Bell Bats .342 to Lead Coast Winter League," *Pittsburgh Courier*, February 24, 1934: 14; John Holway, *The Complete Book of Baseball's Negro Leagues: The Other Half of Baseball History* (Fern Park, Florida: Hastings House Publishers, 2001), 304.

67 "Elite Giants Cop Winter League Rag"; "Elite Giants Will Train in Longview," *Nashville Banner*, April 2, 1934: 10.

68 "Elite Giants Split Pair with Pittsburgh Club," *Nashville Tennessean*, May 7, 1934: 10.

69 "Elite Giants Split Pair with Pittsburgh Club."

70 "Craws to Vie with Cubans in Orleans," *Pittsburgh Courier*, April 27, 1935: 17; "Detroit Happy about Pitchers," *Baltimore Afro-American*, April 27, 1935: 19.

71 "Elite Giants Defeat Strand," *Vineland* (New Jersey) *Evening Times*, May 22, 1937; "Nashville Wins Over Congoleum," *Chester* (Pennsylvania) *Times*, July 22, 1937: 20.

72 "Fast Negro Club Organized Here," *Evansville* (Indiana) *Press*, April 22, 1938: 18.

73 Morocco Stars Play Cincinnati Sunday," *Nashville Banner*, May 27, 1938: 15

74 "Morocco Stars Play Cincinnati Sunday."

75 "Bombers Face Strong Foe," *Knoxville* (Tennessee) *News-Sentinel*, August 14, 1938: 14.

76 "Elites Clash with Eagles," *Baltimore Afro-American*, July 22, 1939: 23.

77 "Greys Defeat 'Black Sox,' 16-1," *Long Branch* (New Jersey) *Daily Record*, July 7, 1939: 7.

78 "Greys Defeat 'Black Sox,' 16-1."

79 "Lloyd Tossers and Baltimore Stage Thrilling Stalemate," *Chester Times*, August 12, 1939: 15; "Baltimore Sox in Week-End Games," *Chester Times*, August 19, 1939: 12.

80 "Black Colonels Book Cincy in Opener," *Louisville Courier-Journal*, April 9, 1939: 57; "Community League," *Cincinnati Enquirer*, April 26, 1941: 12.

81 Cincinnati White Sox, with Five Straight Triumphs, Face Grays Sunday," *Richmond* (Indiana) *Palladium-Item and Sun-Telegram*, June 27, 1941: 10.

82 Red O'Donnell, "Castleman May Forego [*sic*] Pro Career to Work, Play with DuPont," *Nashville Tennessean*, May 17, 1942: 39.

83 "Railroad Nine Meets Acitcos [*sic*] in Dell Today," *Nashville Tennessean*, May 24, 1942: 40.

84 "Black Sox Want to Book Games," *Evansville* (Indiana) *Courier*, May 21, 1945: 9.

85 "Reichert, City Mayor from 1943-'48, Dies," *Evansville Courier*, December 28, 1978: 1; Riley, 226-227.

86 "Giants Play Tomorrow," *Evansville Press*, April 20, 1946: 6; "Giants Win," *Evansville Press*, June 18, 1946: 12; "Giants Beat Owls," *Evansville Press*, June 18, 1946: 15; "Giants Win," *Evansville Press*, July 23, 1946: 12; "Giants Play Illinois Team," *Evansville Press*, September 17, 1946: 12.

87 "Wallace Field Promises to Be Haven for Home Runs," *Evansville Courier*, August 4, 1947: 8.

88 John Holway, "The Rube and Smokey Joe," *New York Amsterdam News*, September 24, 1977: 12.

89 Richard Schweid, "Club Built Against All Odds," *Nashville Tennessean*, September 2, 1987: 19, 22.

BURNIS "WILD BILL" WRIGHT

BY DOUG SKIPPER

Tall, powerful, and fleet-footed, Burnis "Wild Bill" Wright was one of the Negro Leagues' brightest stars for nearly a decade before embarking on a lengthy and successful Hall of Fame career in the Mexican Leagues.

A towering 6-foot-4, 220-pound switch-hitter who slashed for average and slugged with power, he bunted effectively, ran like the wind, fielded gracefully, and wielded a strong right arm from the outfield.

"Wright could circle the bases in 13.2 seconds," Negro League biographer James A. Riley wrote of the hulking but fleet fly chaser. "He was adept at pushing a bunt down the third-base line, and was a superior drag bunter, employing both in conjunction with his speed to avoid a prolonged batting slump by getting a leg hit when he needed one."[1]

His teammate and friend Roy Campanella called Wright "the biggest, strongest, fastest man that I've ever seen."[2]

Denied access to the segregated major leagues, Wright excelled with the Elite Giants during the heyday of the Negro Leagues, won a batting title, and helped lead Baltimore to the 1939 Negro National League (NNL2) championship.

He was a fixture in the East-West All-Star Game, the Negro Leagues' summer showcase, starting nine of the 10 times he was selected and batting .361. He also played in four North-South All-Star Games and five Negro National League vs. Negro American League showdowns. Wright's unique combination of size, strength, and speed drew comparison to the best all-around major-league players, and he was dubbed "the Black DiMaggio." "Yeah, except that I could run rings around him," Wright would laughingly recall.[3]

In 1939 the *Baltimore Afro-American* wrote, "Besides being the fastest man in the league, Bill Wright, the sensational outfielder of the Baltimore Elite Giants, is also the best hitter."[4]

By the time the next season started, Wright had moved to Mexico and joined several other Negro League stars who found greater opportunity – and bigger paychecks – south of the border. He returned to the United States twice over the next six years to enjoy successful Negro League seasons, and in between the two homecomings, won the 1943 Mexican League Triple Crown.

According to the Seamheads.com Negro League database, Wild Bill hit .326 over 10 Negro Leagues seasons. And according to the Outsiders.com database, he batted better than .300 in nine of 10 seasons in major-league Mexican League play.[5] But the Negro and Mexican League seasons were just a part of the story. Like most Black players of his time, Wright played nearly every day that weather allowed, and often more than one game in a day. He played hundreds of tournament, exhibition, and all-star games each year against Black players, starred for several seasons in the integrated California Winter League – winning 10 titles[6] – and in Winter League games in Mexico and Puerto Rico, and excelled in a number of games against White and mixed-race teams.

"Wright hit well against major-league pitchers, both in Mexico and in the California winter league, batting .371 in competition against major leaguers including Bob Feller, Dizzy Dean, Ewell Blackwell, Max Lanier, and Bobo Newsom," Riley wrote.[7]

Burnis Wright was born on June 6, 1914, near Milan (pronounced "My-lunn"), a small farming town in Gibson County in western Tennessee, located between Memphis (100 miles away) and Nashville (140 miles to the East).

He grew up in the home of his grandparents, Will and Mary Wright. At the time of the 1920 US census, there were 17 family members living in their farmhouse, including their son Theoda, daughter-in-law Ola and 6-year-old Burnis.[8]

"We made our own balls with rags, rosin and that good thread the shoe repair man gave us," Wright recalled at the age of 79. "Then we'd add the tongue from a pair of women's high-top leather shoes and make a pretty nice ball."[9]

He played for the Gibson County Training School in 1929.[10] By the time of the 1930 Census, the Great Depression was setting in, and the family had moved into a house in town. Grandfather Will was the only member of the household who was employed and was working on a farm; Burnis at 16 was no longer in school and not employed,[11] but he was playing baseball.

He started out as a pitcher and was saddled with the "Wild Bill" moniker when he struggled to throw strikes. According to legend, Wright injured his arm trying to throw hard in cold weather and was moved to the outfield.[12]

Wright made his professional debut in 1931 with his hometown Milan Buffaloes and before the 1932 season, earned a tryout with the Negro Southern League's Nashville Elite Giants as a 17-year-old. The NSL was designated as one of two Negro major leagues for 1932. Playing their home games at Wilson Park, named for team owner Tom Wilson, Nashville posted a 24-23 record for manager Joe Hewitt. The Elite Giants finished fourth overall but won the league's second-half title and met the first-half and pennant-winning Chicago American Giants in the league's championship playoff. Turkey Stearnes led the Second City team to a four-games-to-three victory.[13]

Wright turned 18 during the season and batted .256 in 26 NSL games, stroking a pair of doubles and a triple, along with 17 singles in 78 at-bats. The rookie right fielder stole three bases.[14]

After the season, he quarterbacked the Nashville Elite Giants to the "mythical professional championship."[15]

Wilson moved his Elite Giants franchise into the resurrected Negro National League (NNL2) in 1933. In his sophomore season, the 19-year-old Wright batted .321 in 36 games, scoring 18 runs and driving in 18.

Nashville finished fourth for manager Felton Stratton with a 19-22-1 record, 11½ games behind Gus Greenlee's Pittsburgh Crawfords, who fielded a lineup that included Josh Gibson, Judy Johnson, Cool Papa Bell, Ted Page, and Satchel Paige for player-manager Oscar Charleston.

After the season, Wright joined Paige's Philadelphia Royal Giants for a set of barnstorming exhibitions against a team of White major leaguers, then finished third behind teammates Bell and Wells in the integrated California Winter League batting race[16] as the Royal Giants posted a 34-8 record to win the loop's title.[17]

Wright struggled at the plate in 1934 as a 20-year-old, when he batted .252 for the Elite Giants, who finished fifth of eight NNL teams at 18-28-1 for manager Candy Jim Taylor. He was again superb in the California Winter League, batting a league-leading .481 over 17 games for league champion Nashville[18] and is said to have appeared in a classic 13-inning matchup of Paige and Dean at Wrigley Field in Los Angeles.[19]

In 1935 Wilson moved his franchise to Columbus, Ohio, where the Elite Giants posted a 29-24-2 mark to finish third behind the Crawfords and Martin Dihigo's New York Cubans. That season, the 21-year-old Wright moved from right field to center and emerged as a star. He batted .311 in 32 NNL games, clubbed 13 extra-base hits and stole 5 bases in league games.

He made his first appearance in the Negro League's showcase exhibition, the East-West All Star Game, in August at Comiskey Park in Chicago. Playing alongside Charleston, Gibson, Bell, and Buck Leonard for the West in a game that included more than a dozen players who would be inducted into Baseball's Hall of Fame, the youthful Wright flied out as a pinch-hitter in the eighth inning in his only at-bat.[20] He made his first North-South All-Star Game appearance in September in Memphis, collecting a hit, scoring a run, and driving in a run in a 6-4 North win. He also joined Paige against Dean in a Halloween exhibition,[21] batted a lofty .426, and slugged .639 for the California Winter League champion Royal Giants.[22]

Wilson moved the Elite Giants again in 1936, this time to share Washington's Griffith Stadium with the American League's Senators. The Elite Giants finished sixth among seven teams in the NNL standings with a 29-34-1 record but won the league's second-half championship. They swept the Philadelphia Stars in a two-game series in the first round of the playoffs but lost two of three to the Pittsburgh Crawfords in the NNL championship series.

The 22-year-old Wright batted .348 in 37 NNL games, with 15 extra-base hits and 37 runs scored.[23] Playing for the victorious East squad in the East-West All-Star Game at Comiskey Park,

Wright replaced Bell in center field and went hitless in two at-bats.[24]

In August Wild Bill joined Paige, Gibson, Bell, Leonard, and Ray Brown on Greenlee's Colored Stars team that swept seven games to win the prestigious Denver Post Tournament. Facing the flame-throwing Paige, the Borger, Texas, team was believed to be the first team to wear protective plastic helmets. Paige struck out 18 of them in the title game and won his third game of the tourney.[25]

In October, at Davenport, Iowa, on a barnstorming tour of Iowa and Colorado with Paige's team, he stroked a hit in four at-bats in an exhibition game against a team that included major-league stars Rogers Hornsby and Johnny Mize, and faced Feller, reaching base when he was hit by a pitch.[26]

Wright also starred in a two-games-to-one NNL All-Stars series win over Satchel Paige's Outlaws.[27] And he picked up four hits in 17 at-bats in a five-game series against a team of American and National League players and starred for the Elite Giants in the California Winter League.

Still just 23 years old, Wild Bill continued to develop into one of baseball's best players in 1937. He batted .381 (56-for-147), third best in the league, with an NNL-leading 11 triples, and slugged .728, third best in the league behind Gibson and Leonard. He started the East-West All Star Game for the first time, playing center field for Biz Mackey's East Squad. He collected two singles and a double in five trips, stole a base,[28] and "turned in the most dazzling catch of the day" on a game-saving snag of Newt Allen's line drive.[29]

He also collected a hit and a walk against Paige for the NNL All Stars in a 2-0 win over the Santo Domingo All Stars at the Polo Grounds in September. One week later, Paige set him down four times down in a 9-4 Santo Domingo win at Yankee Stadium.

Wright journeyed west with the Philadelphia Royal Giants in October and starred in an exhibition series against White Kings Soap,[30] a team anchored by American and National Leaguers including Brooklyn's Babe Herman. He then batted .378 for the Royal Giants during the California Winter League season.

Washington had finished fifth of six NNL teams in 1937 and Wilson was on the move again for the 1938 season. This time he found a home offering more financial stability, moving the Elite Giants to Baltimore, where they would play in the Negro Leagues until they ceased operations after the 1950 season.

Playing at Bugle Field for new manager George Scales, the Elite Giants climbed to third place, though Wright, at age 24, played in only about half of the team's league games, batting .300. Before the season ended, he played in a number of all-star games. He started for the East against the West in Chicago in August and was hitless in four at-bats.[31] He also led off and played left field against the Negro American League, collected three hits including a pair of doubles in six at-bats, scored four runs and drove in three in a 14-3 NNL win at Parkside Park in Philadelphia on September 24. A day later, he led off, played right field, and collected three hits including a double against the NAL at the Polo Grounds in a 5-4 NNL All Stars win. He started the North-South All-Star Game in October in Memphis, leading off and playing center field for the North. He was 1-for-3 with a walk and scored the only run for the North in a 3-1 loss. He also played again for the Philadelphia Royal Giants in the 1938-39 CWL.[32]

Wright enjoyed a spectacular 1939 season with the Elite Giants. He batted .365 in 25 league games, scored 23 runs, and drove in 24 runs. The Elite Giants played at Oriole Park (also

Right fielder Burnis "Wild Bill" Wright with Baltimore. Courtesy John W. Mosley Photograph Collection, Charles L. Blockson Afro-American Collection, Temple University Libraries.

known as Terrapin Park) and finished fourth in the NNL at 21-23, 9½ games behind the Homestead Grays. In a four-team competition, Baltimore dropped its first playoff game at Newark but battled back to win three straight against the Bears, the last two at home. Wright collected six hits in 16 trips to the plate, (.375) with a double, four runs scored, and two RBIs.

Wright, 17-year-old rookie catcher Roy Campanella, and first baseman Bill Hoskins led the Elite Giants into the finals against the Grays. Baltimore won three games against one loss and a tie, with the final win secured at Yankee Stadium, 2-0, when Wright started a two-run rally with a seventh-inning double.[33] Hoskins collected 9 hits, Wright 7, and Campanella 6. The trio drove in 13 and scored 12 of Baltimore's 21 runs in the series. Wright batted .412 over the five games, doubled three times, walked three times, and scored four runs as Baltimore captured the Jacob Ruppert Cup.[34]

Wild Bill appeared in both East-West games that year. After boxing champion Joe Louis threw out the first pitch, Wild Bill led off for the East and collected a single and a double in four at-bats at the traditional game at Comiskey Park, a 4-2 East win.[35] Three weeks later, Wright smacked a "smoking single" and a double in the East's 10-2 victory at Yankee Stadium in the summer's second East-West Game.[36] He batted third and collected two hits in five trips, scored a run and drove in one in North All-Stars' 10-1 victory over the South at Pelican Stadium in New Orleans on October 1, 1939. He starred in a postseason exhibition series with a 3-for-8 performance including a double off Feller in Los Angeles played in the California Winter League again for the champion Philadelphia Royal Giants.[37]

Before the 1940 season, Wright joined a number of high-profile Negro League stars who moved to Mexico to play in the Mexican League.[38] Negro League historians Dr. Layton Revel and Lewis Munoz wrote, "Mexico proved to be very desirable to Negro League players because they made higher salaries, traveling conditions were better, there were very few long road trips, teams generally only played games on Friday, Saturday and Sunday and there was significantly less racism."[39]

Baseball historian Lawrence D. Hogan wrote that it was a big step after Wright's successful Negro League career, "[y]et once this seven-time all-star saw that Mexicans adored him, he spent the rest of his career, from 1940 to 1951 in the country, and with a career .335 average and fistfuls of extra-base hits, it's not hard to see why. In Mexico, he was treated like the king of the diamonds he was."[40]

Wild Bill started the 1940 season with Gallos de Santa Rosa, then moved to Mexico City to join Los Diablos Rojos (Red Devils). In 87 Mexican League games, the 26-year-old Wright batted .360 with 126 hits, tied Wells for most doubles with 30, and stroked 10 triples and 8 home runs. He swiped 29 bases, second most in the league to Sammy Bankhead's 32. Playing at Parque Delta in Mexico City, Los Diablos Rojos went 50-30 to finish second behind Dihigo's Azules de Veracruz, led by Bell.

After the season, Wright rejoined the Elite Giants for California Winter League play. Wright batted .429 in limited action and teamed with Goose Curry, Sammy Hughes, Felton Snow, and Biz Mackey as Baltimore won the league title with an unofficial record of 9-4. On November 8, 1940, Wright registered for the military draft in Los Angeles, listed his address as 1200 East 49th Street, his next of kin as his wife, JT Wright, his birthdate as June 6, 1912, and his employer as Mexico City.[41]

Playing in 100 games in 1941, Wright posted a .390 batting average to win the Mexican League batting title ahead of Gibson (.374) and Ray Dandridge (.367). He tied for fourth in the league with 151 hits, tied for seventh with 25 doubles and tied for eighth with 9 triples. He was third in home runs with 17 (his career high) to Gibson's 33, tied for fifth with 85 RBIs, led the league with 26 stolen bases, with a .487 OBP edged Gibson's .484, and walked 72 times. Mexico City finished second again, this time at 52-47, 13½ games behind Azules. He served as player-manager for Senadores de San Juan in the Puerto Rican Winter League and batted .280 and hit a home run in game one of a two-game all-star series.

The United States entered World War II before the end of the year, and the African American players in Mexico were required to return to the States in case they were called up for service. Wright rejoined the Elite Giants at age 28 and collected 59 hits in 186 at-bats in 1942, a .317 mark. He also smacked 17 extra-base hits.

Baltimore posted a 45-33-1 record and finished fifth in the NNL with a 38-27-1 record. Wright tied Campanella for the team lead in RBIs with 34 and finished fourth in the league with 8 doubles.

In August Wright he reclaimed a spot in the East-West Game, started in right field and collected a pair of hits in five trips including a ninth-inning two-run single off Paige in a 5-2 East win at Comiskey Park.[42] Two days later, he started in right field again, collected two more hits in five at-bats, stroked a double, drove in a run, and scored one in a 9-2 East win at Municipal Stadium in Cleveland. After the season, he headed west for another campaign with the Royal Giants in the California Winter League.

Negro Leagues players were able to return to Mexico in 1943 and several did, though none played better than Wright in the Mexican League. The 29-year-old thrasher won the Triple Crown despite competition from some of the greatest players in the game.

Wright narrowly won the batting title over Dandridge (.366 to .354). He slugged 13 home runs, one more than Campanella and three others. And he drove in 70 runs, the same number as Dandridge and Alejandro Crespo. He finished first in the league in slugging percentage at .577 (his OPS was 1.002 and his OPS+ was 174, both tops in the league) and was second in the league in hits with 129 and in steals. He was named to the All-Mexican League team.[43]

Despite Wright's efforts, Diablos Rojos finished last among the six Mexican League teams with a 38-51 record, 14½ games behind Campanella's pennant-winning Industriales de Monterrey. After the season, Wright returned to the California Winter League, this time with the Kansas City Royals.

Wright enjoyed another great Liga del Mexico season in 1944 at age 30, posting a .335 average and earning All-Mexican League honors once more, but Los Diablos Rojos finished in the cellar again, 24½ games behind Azules de Vera Cruz. Wild Bill played 87 games in right field and ranked among the league leaders in batting average, hits, doubles, home runs, RBIs, and stolen bases.[44] After the season, Wright spent another season in California with Paige's Kansas City Royals.[45]

In 1945 Wright and other African American players returned to the States, where Wright rejoined his old team to lead the Giants to the NNL regular-season title in 1945 as a 31-year-old. He was superb again, hitting .362, and finished behind only Campanella and Frank Austin in the batting race. He finished in a six-way tie for second with five home runs (Gibson smashed eight) and finished second with 17 doubles, one behind Campanella. In 54 games and 213 at-bats, he collected 77 hits (second most in the league), 26 extra-base hits, 39 runs batted in (fourth in league), and 45 runs scored (second behind Campanella's 51). He stole 6 bases (fourth in league).

On July 29 in Chicago, Wright made his final appearance in the East-West All Star Game. He started in right field, went 0-for-2 and lost a pair of balls in right field. "The goat of the game was Bill Wright, veteran outfielder of Baltimore, who misjudged two drives that might have been caught if he had used his sunglasses," the Pittsburgh Courier reported. "Right field in Comiskey Park is one of the sunniest in the majors."[46]

After the season, Wright barnstormed with Satchel Paige's All-Stars and played center field for Paige's Kansas City Royals, starting for a California Winter League pennant-winner for the 10th time.[47]

Wright found himself at a crossroads in 1946. While integration of the national pastime was approaching slowly, it was evident that the doors to Organized Baseball would not be open for aging Black veterans like him. At the age of 31, Wright returned to Mexico, where he would spend the remainder of his career.

When Wright returned to Mexico, he found a changing landscape. Jorge Pasquel, a Mexican cigar-making entrepreneur and team owner, had become president of the Mexican League in 1943. He and his four brothers recruited a number of Black players and in 1946 set their sights on White major leaguers. They signed 18 players from Organized Baseball, including Sal Maglie and Max Lanier, despite threat of a lifetime ban from Organized Baseball. Black players from the United States and the Caribbean found themselves competing with emerging Mexican players like Bobby Avila and Bobby Estalella.

Though threatened with a five-year suspension by the NNL, Wright chose to return to Mexico and never returned to the Negro Leagues.

Negro League historian Gary Cieradkowski wrote, "In interviews he gave after his retirement, Wright stated that he preferred the absence of racial animosity in Mexico. South of the border he was an acknowledged star, while in his own country, no matter how good he was, he was only a marginal figure, known only by those who followed segregated baseball. Besides, life was easy for a ballplayer in Mexico. Unlike the Negro Leagues, where playing two games in different towns on the same day was not unheard of, the Liga Mexicana played only on Friday, Saturday, and Sundays. The travel was by train or airplane, a world apart from the bone-rattling bus rides that were the normal mode of transport in the Negro Leagues."[48]

Continued Cieradkowski: "Age also had something to do with Wright's decision to stay in Mexico. When Jackie Robinson integrated Organized Baseball in 1946, Wright was 32, too old to be seriously considered for a shot at the majors. This, combined with the quick collapse of the Negro Leagues after 1946, kept Wild Bill Wright in Mexico. The Mexican League had one last great season, 1946, when not only Negro League players, but also White big-leaguers, ventured south. In what can be called his last hurrah, Wild Bill outhit all the White major-league imports."[49]

Wright batted .301 in 85 games as a 32-year-old in 1946 for Los Diablos Rojos.[50] During the offseason, he played winter ball for Mazatlán in the Mexican Pacific Coast League. He hit .305 in 79 games for the Mexico City team in 1947 and earned All-Mexican League honors for the third time.[51] He spent the 1948 season with a new Mexican League team, Los Industriales de Monterrey, where he was a teammate of Cuban star Luis Tiant Sr. He hit .333 at age 34 but had no home runs and walked just 18 times in 66 games. In 1949 at age 35, Wright hit a combined .276 in 73 games for Los Diablos Rojos and Los Algodoneros de Union Laguna in the Mexican League.

In 1950 Wright rebounded and hit .302 in 63 games during his last full season with Los Diablos Rojos. "Sometimes called a dirty ballplayer," Riley wrote, "Wright could be temperamental and occasionally showed flashes of a mean streak, but in a game in Mexico in 1950 these attributes probably saved the life of his teammate Rufus Lewis."[52] Revel and Munoz explained that "Wright was involved in one of the most controversial plays in Mexican League history. With former Negro League pitcher Rufus Lewis on the mound and Lorenzo 'Chiquitin' Cabrera [a former New York Cuban player] batting, Lewis hit Cabrera with a fastball. Cabrera, who was known for his hot head and quick temper, took exception to the play, rushed the mound with bat in hand and hit Lewis with the bat, rendering him unconscious. Even though Lewis was unconscious and lying on the ground, Cabrera raised his bat to hit the fallen player again, but before he could do so, Wright ran out of the dugout with a bat of his own and hit Cabrera, knocking him unconscious. Accounts from spectators to the incident agree that Wright probably saved the life of Rufus Lewis; however, Wright remained under a dark cloud that most likely delayed his induction into the Mexican League baseball Hall of Fame."[53]

Wright's time in the Mexican League came to an end in 1951. He split time with Los Diablos Rojos (he is listed as one of the team's four managers in 1951) and Los Tecolotes de Nuevo Laredo. He hit .365 at the age of 37, the oldest player on either team.[54]

Wright played for Orizaba in the Vera Cruz Winter League after the 1952 season and compiled a .333 average. After the 1953 season, he played for the Jalapa Chileros in the Veracruz Winter League.

Wright batted .300 in 68 games in 1955 with Los Rieleros de Aguascalientes (Railroaders of Aguascalientes) in the Class-C Liga Central of Mexico, managed by Martin Dihigo. In 1956, at the age of 42, he collected 102 hits in 332 at-bats. He played in 77 of 79 games and finished second on the team in stolen bases. He remained in the game and served as one of four managers of Rojos de Fresnillo in the Mexico Central League Class-C circuit in 1956 and 1957.

Rather than return to the United States, Wright chose to move his permanent residence from California to Mexico in 1953. He retired from baseball to his home in Aguascalientes, where he opened a hamburger restaurant, Bill Wright's Dugout.[55] He made only infrequent visits to the United States during the remainder of his life.

In October 1958, months after Campanella was paralyzed in an automobile accident, the former catcher was featured on a televised episode of *This Is Your Life*. Wright, who had been his roommate when the 15-year-old Campanella made his NNL debut in 1937,[56] appeared as one of several surprise guests.[57] After that, Wright did not return to the United States for 32 years.

Wright was elected to the Mexican Baseball Hall of Fame in 1982. In 1986 Monte Irvin, a special assistant to Baseball Commissioner Bowie Kuhn and a former Negro Leagues and National League player, named Wright to the outfield for his all-time Negro League team. In an interview with historian Timothy Gay, "Irvin compared Wild Bill's hulking physique and playing style to that of Dave Parker, the 1970s-1980s star of the Pirates and Reds.[58]

Wright made his first journey to the United States in three decades to attend a 1990 reunion of Negro Leagues players.

In 1996 Negro Leagues legend Buck O'Neil named Wright to his all-time team, describing him as "a marvelous hitter."[59]

In March 1992 *Sports Illustrated*'s Shelley Smith reported that "Seventy-seven-year-old Bill Wright lives in a tiny, crumbling house in Aguascalientes, Mexico, barely able to walk because his feet are twisted with arthritis and he's unable to afford surgery. Things were different a half century ago, when he was a strapping young outfielder and gifted hitter for the Elite Giants of the Negro Leagues. In the 1930's, he dazzled the thousands of fans who crammed into parks to see him and teammates like Roy Campanella and hundreds of other black players.

"The fact is, Wright, and many like him, had almost as much to do with the integration of baseball as did (Jackie) Robinson. Yet Wright now lives in poverty and obscurity, as do so many other former Negro league ballplayers."[60]

Wright died on August 3, 1996, at age 82 in Aguascalientes. At the time, Paige, Gibson, Leonard, Irvin, Bell, Johnson, Charleston, Dihigo, Dandridge, Stearnes, and several other of his contemporaries had been elected to Cooperstown. In 2005 Wild Bill was one of 39 Negro League players considered for induction by the Special Committee on the Negro Leagues and the pre-Negro Leagues. Although 17 of the 39 were named to the Hall in 2006, Wright was not one of them. O'Neil and nineteenth-century standout Bud Fowler, both selected by the Veterans Committee in 2022, are the only Negro Leagues players inducted since.

In 2017 a restored bronze bust honoring Wright was unveiled in Aguascalientes at the site of Estadio Alberto Romo Chavez.

Wright was named to the Tennessee Sports Hall of Fame in 2017. Family members and supporters attended the ceremony in 2017, including his niece Mary Lillian Wright Allen of Ferguson, Missouri, and his adopted grandson, Burnis Bill Wright of Indianapolis.[61] His family also set up a Facebook tribute page with artwork and photos in Wild Bill's honor.[62]

SOURCES

In addition to the sources cited in the Notes, the author consulted Baseball-Reference.com, the Center for Negro League Baseball, Retrosheet.org, and Seamheads.com.

NOTES

1   James A. Riley, *The Biographical Encyclopedia of the Negro Leagues* (New York: Carroll & Graf Publishers, 1994), 880-882.

2   "Burnis 'Wild Bill' Wright," Tennessee Sports Hall of Fame, https://tshf.net/halloffame/burnis-wild-bill-wright.

3   https://www.facebook.com/BillWrightTribute. The quote is referenced several times on the tribute pages.

4   "Wright Gains NNL Batting Crown," *Baltimore Afro-American*, September 30, 1939: 21.

5   Darowski.com/outsider/wrighwi01.html.

6   Dr. Layton Revel and Luis Munoz, "Forgotten Heroes: Burnis 'Wild Bill' Wright," Center for Negro League Baseball Research, 2008, 17.

7   Riley, 880-882.

8   Fourteenth Census of the United States, 1920 – Population.

9   Steve Short, "Yesterday in Milan: Wild Bill Wright, Big League Baseball Great," undated article from *Milan* (Tennessee) *Mirror-Exchange* from circa 1993.

10 Short.

11 Fifteenth Census of the United States, 1930. The Census misspelled Wright's first name as "Bernice."

12 Riley, 880-882.

13 Seamheads.com.

14 Wild Bill Wright page on Seamheads.com: (https://seamheads.com/NegroLgs/player.php?playerID=wrigh01bil). Wright's page at Baseball-Reference.com (https://www.baseball-reference.com/players/w/wrighwi01.shtml) suggests that Wright actually batted .300 in league games. That the databases disagree is no surprise. Statistics for Negro League players are often inaccurate and almost always incomplete. Negro League players played nearly every day when the weather allowed, often played more than one game in a day, and many games were not documented or have been lost to history. They played against other African American teams, against White teams, and on occasion, against mixed-race teams. They played against amateur, semipro, and professional teams, and sometimes, against White major-league players. The surviving record primarily includes most Negro League games, notable all-star games and exhibition games that received media coverage. Both may be true, though drawn from a different set of records. The surviving record primarily includes most Negro League games, notable all-star games and exhibition games that received media coverage. Negro League season statistics for Wild Bill Wright are generally based on the Seamheads.com database. Mexican League and Winter League statistics are generally based on the Outsider.com database. Single-game statistics are generally based on the Retrosheet.org database.

15 "Nashville Elite Giants Claim National Pro Football Title," *Baltimore Afro-American*, December 24, 1932: 15. Wild Bill also played fullback for the Elite Giants football squad in 1933 and 1934. "Nashville Elites Swamp Bulldogs," *Pittsburgh Courier*, November 10, 1934: 4.

16 Timothy Gay, *Satch, Dizzy & Rapid Robert: The Wild Saga of Interracial Baseball Before Jackie Robinson* (New York: Simon & Schuster, 2010), 142-145; Darowski.com/outsider/wrighwi01.html.

17 Revel and Munoz, 1.

18 Revel and Munoz, 1

19 Gay, 105-107. Gay wrote that there were no contemporary media reports about the game, though it is very possible that local writers conspired to keep silent about the game in order to keep Dean from getting suspended for violating major-league barnstorming rules. "If the November '34 L.A. game was just an urban myth, then why were Dean, Paige, (Wally) Berger, (Bill) Veeck, and others not only adamant that the game was played, but in essential agreement over its details."

20 Larry Lester, *Black Baseball's National Showcase: The East-West National Showcase, 1933-1953* (Lincoln: University of Nebraska Press, 2001), 63-79

21 Gay, 132-134.

22 Gay, 147-148. According to Gay, before one CWL game, "the speedy Wright competed against entertainer Bill 'Bojangles' Robinson in a race in which Wright circled the bases and Robinson ran a shorter distance backward, a talent for which he held 'a world record.'"

23 According to Baseball-Reference, he hit .356 and led the league with 7 triples.

24 Lester, 80-63.

25 Mark Ribowsky, *Josh Gibson, The Power and the Darkness* (New York: First Illinois paperback, 2004), 152.

26 Gay, 160-165.

27 Lester, 100-101.

28 Several contemporary newspapers including the *Pittsburgh Courier*, *Philadelphia Tribune*, *Chicago Defender*, and *Kansas City Call*, credited Wright with a stolen base in the fourth inning. However, Retrosheet records: H(ilton) Smith replaced E(d) Mayweather (pitching); W. Wright singled to left field; B(uck) Leonard walked while W. Wright advanced to third on a wild pitch." Retrosheet charged Smith with a wild pitch.

29 Lester, 103-104. The *Pittsburgh Courier* missed on Wright's first name, referring to him as Ben. "Another stellar performer for the East was Ben Wright of Tom Wilson's Washington Elites. Wright led the Orient in batting, getting three hits, one of them a double and turned in the most dazzling catch of the day in snaring Allen's

Texas league into short center field. Ben came bounding in like an antelope until he saw that his only chance of catching the ball would be to plunge for it. Then he went into a swan dive, which would be a beautiful sight to behold. With his two hands stretch out far in front, he skidded along the grass … just far enough for his fingers to meet the fast-dropping horsehide. Then he squeezed it robbing (Newt) Allen of what looked like a sure hit on anybody's ball field. When big Ben came back to the dugout, the fans gave him a rousing round of applause."

30   The team was sponsored by White Kings Soap.

31   Lester, 107-119; https://www.retrosheet.org/NegroLeagues/boxe-setc/1938/B08210ASW1938.htm.

32   Gay, 178.

33   Ribowsky, 207-209.

34   The Jacob Ruppert Trophy was the namesake of the New York Yankees owner. Ribowsky, 209.

35   Lester, 120-132; Fay Young, "Gibson, Suttles and Leonard Held Hitless: Wilson's Homer Gives West Win Over East in Classic, 40,000 See Thriller, Robinson Starts Rally & West Wins 4 to 2," *Chicago Defender*, August 12, 1939, reprinted in Lester, 125-128.

36   Harry B. Webber, "East Swamps West in Revenge Game: Josh Gibson's Triple Scores Three Ahead," *Baltimore Afro-American*, September 2, 1939: 22; Lester, 133-139; Dan Burley, "NNL Power Crushes West 10-2: 17000 See Eastern Club Revenge East-West Defeat," *New York Amsterdam News*, September 2, 1939.

37   Gay, 178. Feller was pitching for the Pirrone All Stars.

38   Gay, 218: "This was the first step in Jorge Pasquel's master plan to bring major league baseball to Mexico. He believed if he attracted the best Negro League players with huge salaries, major leaguers would eventually follow, which would force the big leagues to sue for peace on terms that might give Mexico a big league franchise."

39   Revel and Munoz 4.

40   Lawrence D. Hogan, *Shades of Glory: The Negro Leagues and the Story of African-American Baseball* (Washington: National Geographic, 2006), 310-311.

41   U.S. World War II Draft Cards Young Men, 1940-47 for Burnis Wright. J.T. The 1940 census, taken earlier in the year, listed J.T. Wright, a native of Texas, as married and living at the same address, in the household of her parents, Fred and Bertha Monroe. Wild Bill wasn't listed in the 1940 Census, likely because he was playing baseball outside of the country. Notably, he listed his birthday as two years prior to the commonly accepted date and despite the fact that the 1920 Census listed his age as 6 years old and the 1930 Census listed his age as 16.

42   Lester, 172-206; Frank A, Young, "48,000 See East All-Stars Beat Paige and West; West Held to Four Hits as National Leaguers Triumph by 5-2 Score," *Chicago Defender*, August 22, 1942, reprinted in Lester, 194-195, and Ribowsky, 242.

43   Revel and Munoz, 17.

44   Rogers Hornsby managed Azules for 10 games before leaving the team in the hands of Ramón Bragaña.

45   Larry Tye, *Satchel: The Life and Times of an American Legend* (New York: Random House, 2009), 303; Darowski.com/outsider/wrighwi01.html.

46   Lester, 239-256; Wendell Smith, "The Sports Beat," *Pittsburgh Courier*, August 4, 1945, reprinted in Lester, 251-252; Wendell Smith

"Americans Too Good for Spiritless East: 31,714 See Classic; Davis, Robinson, Radcliffe and Ware Star as West Pours It on East in Annual All-Star Game," *Pittsburgh Courier*, August 4, 1945, reprinted in Lester, 248-251. Veteran sportswriter Smith pulled no punches: "Wright Blinded by Sun. The roof fell in on the East in the second inning when Neil Robinson of Memphis started off by beating out an infield hit. He promptly scampered to third when the veteran Alex Radcliff powered a drive to right field. Big Bill Wright, ace Baltimore outfielder, failed to get a line on the ball, and was unable to track it down because he was blinded by the sun. Had he started soon enough he could have caught the drive, but for some strange reason he did not have his sunglasses on and the ball got away from him, and rolled into deep right field. Archie Ware, colorful Cleveland first baseman, then drove the first two runs of the game in with a lazy slash over second base. Williams took a strike across the outside corner and then on the next pitch blasted a drive into right … in the direction of Bill Wright, the man without glasses. Again blinded by the sun, Wright was unable to judge the hit and it went for a rousing triple. Two more runs came in and the West held a commanding four-run lead. That was really the ball game."

47   The Kansas City Royals were also called (KC Chet) Brewer's Royals. Gay, 207.

48   Gary Cieradkowski, "Wild Bill Wright: The Neglected Negro League Star," https://sabr.org/latest/cieradkowski-wild-bill-wright-the-neglected-negro-leagues-star/.

49   Cieradkowski.

50   Revel and Munoz, 6. Eight players – Wright, Ray Brown, Ray Dandridge, Tom Glover, Bert Hunter, Terris McDuffie, Ed Stone, and Johnny Taylor – were suspended for five years by the NNL.

51   Revel and Munoz, 17.

52   Riley, 880-882.

53   Revel and Munoz, 7.

54   Riley, 880-882.

55   Wright knew his way around a restaurant. "Shangri-La Dining Room Under New Management," *Los Angeles Sentinel*, November 20, 1947: 5. Commented, "While resting on his laurels of being one of the country's finest athletes, Wright also possess a knowledge of the cuisine likened to an expert."

56   Neil Lanctot, *Campy: The Two Lives of Roy Campanella* (New York: Simon & Schuster, 2011), 42.

57   Lanctot, 385.

58   Gay, 145-147, said that "[Monte] Irvin compared Wild Bill's hulking physique and playing style to that of Dave Parker, the 1970s-80s star of the Pirates and Reds."

59   Buck O'Neil, with Steve Wulf and David Conrads, *I Was Right on Time* (New York: Simon & Schuster, 1996), 152.

60   Shelley Smith, "Baseball's Forgotten Pioneers: Former Negro League Players Gave Too Much to the Game to Be Left in Obscurity," *Sports Illustrated*, March 30, 1992.

61   Steve Short, "Milan Native Bill Wright Inducted into Tennessee Sports Hall of Fame," *Milan* (Tennessee) *Mirror-Exchange*, June 6, 2017: 1B.

62   https://www.facebook.com/BillWrightTribute.

TOM WILSON

BY SKIP NIPPER

A significant event in Nashville's Black community took place on Tuesday, February 19, 1907: a meeting held at the residence of J.W. White to organize the Standard Giants Base Ball club as reported in the February 22, 1907, edition of the *Nashville Globe*:

> Manager White called the house to order, and Mr. C.B. Reaves was made President: Mr. J.W. White, Manager, and W.G. Sublett, Secretary, and by unanimous voice of the house Mr. Howard Petway (brother of fellow Negro League player Bruce Petway), who did stunts for one of the professional teams of Chicago last season, was elected captain. "The Standards will travel extensively, having arranged games with Memphis, Hot Springs, Little Rock … playing all the leading teams, Chattanooga, Atlanta, Birmingham, Macon, New Orleans, and Beaumont, Texas. … One peculiarity is that every member claims Nashville as his home. It is composed exclusively of home talent, a characteristic no other team can boast of, and it is certain that every member will put up a fight for the glory of his home.[1]

The Standard Giants joined local teams in the Capital City League, which became the premier league for Nashville's African American teams playing their games at Greenwood Park and Athletic Park, later to become Sulphur Dell. The Black Sox, Nationals, Baptist Hill Swifts, Athletics, and Eclipse teams became established, and when others joined them, the community supported them all.[2]

One of those teams was the Maroons, and a young man named Thomas T. Wilson grew to love the game of baseball. Wilson, a native of Atlanta, had moved with his family to Nashville, where his parents, Thomas and Carrie, both physicians, studied medicine at Meharry Medical College. Wilson, born on November 29, 1889,[3] played on the sandlots of Nashville with the Maroons[4] as early as 1909, when he acquired the nickname Smiling Tom.[5]

Even though his highest school grade completed was the sixth grade[6] in elementary school, Wilson began accumulating wealth through his interests in entertainment. He soon became an entrepreneur, owning a local rail line, a nightclub, and an illegal numbers lottery. Notwithstanding his reputation in racketeering, the admiration afforded him by teammates, players, and business leaders was strong.

Author Harriet Kimbro-Hamilton, daughter of one of Wilson's brightest stars with the Elite Giants, Henry Kimbro, offered her view on why almost everyone admired Wilson for his success. "Back in the day, Black men could not go to the bank in those days," she says. "The numbers game allowed them to play the odds, borrow money when needed, and sometimes take home some cash. Daddy did not run a numbers business, but he admired Wilson's success and became a successful entrepreneur with a strong business sense like Tom Wilson."[7]

Wilson longed to own a professional baseball team, and on March 26, 1920, he and others formed a corporation with the State of Tennessee to set his acquisition of the Standard Giants in motion. The charter reads:

"Nashville Negro Baseball Association and Amusement Company, for the purpose of organizing base ball clubs and encouraging the art of playing the game of baseball according to high and honorable standards and of encouraging the establishment of a league of clubs in different section(s) of the state; and also of furnishing such amusements as usually accompanying base ball games and entertainments. Said corporation to be located in Nashville, Tennessee, and shall have an authorized capital stock of $5,000.00."[8]

T. Clay Moore, J.B. Boyd, Marshall Garrett, Walter Phillips, W.H. Pettis, J.L. Overton, and R.H. Tabor joined Wilson as investors. Garrett would become an essential cog in the new venture.

Wilson purchased the local semipro baseball club, the Standard Giants,[9] called them the White Sox, and, with Garrett at the helm, entered his team in the newly formed Negro Southern League. A 19-year-old future star born in Nashville who began his professional career with the club was Norman "Turkey" Stearnes, who was inducted into the National Baseball Hall of Fame in 2000.[10]

Seven teams made up the balance of the Negro Southern League, formed one month after the Negro National League formed: the Atlanta Black Crackers, Birmingham Black Barons, Jacksonville Stars, Knoxville Giants, Montgomery Grey Sox, New Orleans Caulfield Ads, and Pensacola Giants. Nashville finished the season 40-40.[11]

In 1921 Wilson changed the name of his club once again, giving them a name that would become synonymous with Negro Leagues baseball: Elite Giants. Nashville won the 1921 NSL pennant with a 72-46 record; but with erratic schedules over the next few years, it is difficult to pinpoint how Wilson's team fared between 1926 and 1929. The Elite Giants appear to have remained a member of the NSL but also had an associate membership in the NNL.

On April 17, 1929, a property deed transfer was recorded in Davidson County for the sale of 5 3/4 acres of land in Nashville from the estate of W.S. Whiteman, a Confederate veteran who owned real estate in the area and had died in 1926, to Tom Wilson for $10,000.

The property bordered Brown's Creek to the east, Factory Street to the north, the rail line of the Chattanooga, Nashville, and St. Louis Railway to the west, and south to a point ending at Culvert Street and Brown's Creek. The car tracks of the Nashville Railway and Light Company ended at an alley near Factory Street.[12] Many newspaper articles include the location as "at the end of the Radnor Car Line" or "Second Avenue, South."[13] It was a mile from the Tennessee State Fairgrounds.

Wilson built a ballpark on the site to hold 8,000 fans. It was one of two African American-owned professional ballparks, the other belonging to Gus Greenlee in Pittsburgh.

The 1930 Federal Census shows Wilson's occupation as "Proprietor – Ballpark." Wilson Park would not only host games but community events with no regard to race. Years later, Wilson demolished his ballpark and in its place built the Paradise Ballroom, which allowed him a lawful source of income to finance his ballclub.[14]

Wilson Park became the spring-training ground for the Elite Giants after Wilson moved his club to Columbus, to Washington, and then to Baltimore. When Sulphur Dell was

Elite Giants team owner Tom Wilson. Courtesy of Larry Lester.

too soggy for the Nashville Vols to practice and play, they often used the ballpark for preseason games. The Elite Giants often alternated home games between the two ballparks based on the out-of-town schedule of the Nashville Vols in the Southern Association.[15]

A local newspaper described the game to take place on the night of June 13, 1926, and emphasized that all fans – meaning both Blacks and Whites – would be welcome to view the marvel of night baseball. Wilson's advertisements and broadside announcements usually included the phrase "Special seats are reserved for white people."[16]

Wilson's mission had been to own a team exclusively in the Negro National League, formed by Rube Foster in Kansas City in 1920. The Nashville owner bided his time in the Negro Southern League until the opportunity came for a spot in the NNL in 1930. It was in that season when Nashville's Wilson Park was one of the earliest ballparks to employ the unique lighting system purchased by J.L. Wilkinson for his Kansas City Monarchs to play night games.[17] The Monarchs played a two-night-game series in Nashville on May 14 and 15.[18]

Nashville was unsuccessful in the NNL in 1930, finishing last with a 26-55-1 record.[19] The next season the Elites rejoined the NSL as the NNL collapsed in the midst of the Great Depression. With most teams from the North, Wilson learned it was expensive for his ballclub to travel from Nashville. He moved the team to Cleveland in 1931 after obtaining Satchel Paige from the cash-strapped Birmingham Black Barons and renamed it the Cubs, but returned to Nashville in midseason when attendance did not support the move. Paige left the ballclub to pitch for Cum Posey's Homestead Grays.[20]

Wilson placed a team in the California Winter League beginning with the 1931 season, naming it the Philadelphia Royal Giants. He signed stars Paige and Stearnes, Mule Suttles, Cool Papa Bell, and Willie Wells, among others.

In his book *The California Winter League*, author William McNeil calls Wilson's teams some of the best assembled, writing, "The 1934-35 Elite Giants, along with the 33-24 aggregation, may have been the greatest Negro League team ever to play in the California Winter League. It is impossible to differentiate between the two."[21]

Once again the Elite Giants returned to the disorganized NSL in 1932, becoming a barnstorming team for the most part. Nashville won the second half of the split season in 1932, earning a spot in the championship series against the Chicago American Giants. The team featured Stearnes as its star player.

"In 1932 with Joe Hewitt as manager, the Elite Giants were second half champions and played Chicago American Giants in the World Series," wrote Bill Plott in his book *The Negro Southern League*. "Postseason series would be a more accurate designation," Plott wrote.[22]

The NNL was reorganized in 1933, influenced by the leadership of the league president, Pittsburgh Crawfords owner Gus Greenlee, and the Elite Giants rejoined the league for two seasons. Greenlee and Wilson organized the first East-West

All-Star Game, played at Comiskey Park in Chicago before 19,568 fans.[23]

In 1934 Wilson was elected vice president of the league. He organized a best-of-three Negro League "North vs. South" all-star series at Sulphur Dell in Nashville in the fall of 1934.

The series opened with a doubleheader on October 7. The Monarchs' Stearnes hit a home run in the 12th inning to provide a 2-1 win for the North All-Stars. They also won the second game, 8-1. The South lineup came from Birmingham, Memphis, Monroe, and New Orleans; Nashville, Kansas City, Pittsburgh, and House of David stars represented the North. Felton Snow, Sammy Hughes, Tommie Dukes, Jim Willis, and Andy Porter represented the Nashville Elite Giants.

At the end of the year, Wilson was disappointed in hometown support, and by April of 1935 he announced Detroit to be his team's new home as long as there was a suitable field to play on. When plans for the move fell through, the Elites resumed the season with home games at Sulphur Dell before also playing at Columbus, Ohio, during the season.[24]

In 1936 Wilson moved his team to Washington, a city abandoned by the NNL when the Washington Black Senators failed to finish the season. He did not completely abandon his Nashville fans, organizing a team named the Black Vols to play in Nashville.[25]

In 1936 Wilson became treasurer of the NNL, returning as vice president in 1937. The league needed to be more solid in 1938, and there was division within its ranks.

SABR author Doron Goldman wrote that controversy pitted the Elite Giants, Philadelphia, and the Pittsburgh Crawfords against Newark, the New York Black Yankees, and the Homestead Grays.[26]

A three-member board consisting of Wilson, Greenlee, and Abe Manley was formed to overcome the rift, and they chose Cum Posey, owner-manager of the Homestead Grays, as league secretary-treasurer.

There were hopes that the NNL and the rival Negro American League (NAL), formed in 1937, would agree to a single commissioner. Wilson moved his franchise to Baltimore in 1938, a historic change that would give him the solid footing he wanted. Bugle Field, a mostly wooden 6,000-seat ballpark, became the home of the Elites.

Even before moving to Baltimore, Wilson needed someone to get the Black community behind his team. He hired Richard D. Powell to make it happen. Powell, a courier, a fight judge, and an employee of local bookies, talked about the Elite Giants to business leaders and community organizations. The team won the support of the sports editor of the *Baltimore Afro-American*, Leon Hardwick; Powell wrote articles promoting the Elite Giants and Hardwick published them.[27]

In 1939, their second season in Baltimore, the Elite Giants captured their first NNL championship, defeating the Homestead Grays in a playoff series three games to one with one tie. It was Felton Snow's first season as Wilson's manager. The ballclub received the Jacob Ruppert Trophy.[28] It was pre-

sented by Bill "Bojangles" Robinson, the entertainer who was a part-owner of the New York Black Yankees.[29]

Before the 1940 Opening Day doubleheader at Oriole Park against the Philadelphia Stars, Wilson presented wristwatches to members of the 1939 team. Then the Elites won both games, 6-1 and 5-2.[30]

Wilson would often travel with his team, but he maintained his suburban Nashville residence until he died. After moving to Baltimore, the team continued to hold spring training in Nashville,[31] and Wilson formed a minor-league team, the Cubs, to feed the Giants with players. On one occasion, on April 6, 1947, the Nashville Cubs beat their parent Elite Giants, 5-1, at Sulphur Dell. Local hero Clinton "Butch" McCord was the first baseman for the Cubs.[32]

Wilson's presidency of the NNL was sometimes the subject of controversy. In 1940 there was turmoil between Effa Manley, owner of the Newark Eagles, along with her husband, Abe, and Posey. Effa wanted Wilson removed from office, but failed to achieve her goal.

Wilson turned to the entertainment business by demolishing his ballpark in 1940 to build the Paradise Ballroom and forming a new enterprise to encompass all his ventures.

On April 29, 1941, Wilson and his wife chartered a new corporation, Elite Giants Baseball Club, Incorporated, with the State of Tennessee, to run his new facility.[33] The venue included a dance floor and often hosted basketball games and boxing matches, and appearances by jazz greats including Lena Horne, Lionel Hampton, Jimmy Lunceford, Sarah Vaughan, and Cab Calloway.[34]

Political connections of all colors often frequented in the nightclub and Wilson invited Whites to attend events on the balcony with seating for 1,000.[35] In 1945, he resurrected the Black Vols as a member of the Negro Southern League.[36] The *Louisville Courier-Journal* described them as "one of the best teams in the South." In December of 1945, the Paradise Ballroom hosted the Negro Southern Baseball League meetings.[37]

Effa Manley continued to pursue a replacement for Wilson in 1942. She believed that the NNL was poorly run by Wilson, needing an "efficient Chairman" because "we have never played the same number of games, our admission prices are all different, our umpire situation is pitiful, our contracts are not anything."[38]

Wilson helped maintain peace between the NNL and the Negro American League. A key issue through the World War II years was the possible raiding of Negro League players by Organized Baseball. Wilson and the NAL's president, Dr. J.B. Martin, met with Commissioner Happy Chandler, National League President Ford Frick, and American League President Will Harridge on January 17, 1946. According to Doron Goldman, Chandler proposed that when the Negro Leagues were better organized, there was an opportunity to become a part of a system of Organized Baseball. Once that occurred, all leagues, even amateur baseball, would fall under the authority of Commissioner Chandler.[39]

In a meeting in New York on January 5, 1947, Wilson was ousted after eight years as president of the NNL. John H. Johnson, a pastor and police chaplain, was elected to succeed him. Wilson was "advised to give up the job by his personal physician for reasons of poor health."[40]

Four months later, on May 15, 1947, Wilson died at his home in Nashville, survived by his wife, Bertha, his daughter, Christine Wilson Childs, and his son, Thomas T. Wilson Jr. (It was only a month after Jackie Robinson became the first Black player in a twentieth-century major-league game.)

The Paradise Ballroom continued to operate until it was sold to a private racing club in the 1950s.

There appears to be no record of Wilson's will. However, Thomas Jr. died two years later on August 9, 1949, and his will gives insight into the property acquired by his father, as it directed that his grandmother, Dr. Carrie L. Wilson, receive his house and lot on Sigler Street in Nashville, a Cadillac and Mercury Sedan, and two pistols "formerly the property of my deceased father."[41] In addition, he bequeathed to her a diamond ring in a white gold mounting that was his father owned, along with a watch and a Chevrolet pickup truck.

Thomas Jr. left the house on the Paradise Amusement Hall property to his "dear friend" Hattie Coleman, while he left his six motorcycles to two friends. Another friend was to receive the younger Wilson's Chevrolet truck, while all three were to share in the possession of all remaining guns and ammunition.

In 2003, with the assistance of Butch McCord, a Tennessee state historical marker was erected on the sidewalk near a Nashville public school, the Johnson School.[42] With confusion about the location several blocks away, the inscription reads:

Tom Wilson Park
1929-1946

Formerly located near this site was Tom Wilson Park. It opened in 1929 and was home to the Nashville Elite Giants baseball team of the Southern Negro League. Owned by Thomas T. Wilson, the facility was one of two African American-owned professional ballparks. Wilson Park also hosted spring training sessions for the Nashville Vols. a minor league team of the Southern Association. Spring training games brought such baseball greats as Babe Ruth, Lou Gehrig, and Roy Campanella to the park. In 1946, Tom Wilson resigned and discontinued all ball activities at Wilson Park."[43]

The entrepreneurial spirit of Tom Wilson includes a legacy of owning land in the city of Nashville and an estate in the middle Tennessee countryside, a successful nightclub, successful leadership in the Negro Leagues, a baseball team in several cities, and recognition as "The Father of Negro Leagues ball in Nashville."

Acknowledgments

The author wishes to thank the staff of Nashville Public Library/Metro Archives, Sarah Arntz, Kelley Sirko, Grace Hulme, and Ken Fieth, for their valuable assistance in locating public documents on Tom Wilson, and extends appreciation to Dr. Harriett Kimbro-Hamilton for reviewing and offering suggestions on this biography.

Much of Tom Wilson's career as an executive comes from Doron Goldman's article "1933-1962: The Business Meetings of Negro League Baseball," published in *From Rube to Robinson: SABR's Best Articles on Black Baseball*, https://sabr.org/journal/article/1933-1962-the-business-meetings-of-negro-league-baseball/, accessed November 18, 2023.

SOURCES

In addition to the sources credited in the Notes, the author consulted Ancestry.com, Findagrave.com, Newspapers.com, and Seamheads.com for information about Wilson and his family, and the following:

Lanctot, Neil. *Negro League Baseball: The Rise and Ruin of a Black Institution* (Philadelphia: University of Pennsylvania Press, 2004).

Wheeler, Lonnie. *Cool Papa Bell* (New York: Abrams Press, 2020).

NOTES

1   "The Standard Giants Base Ball Club Royally Entertained," *Nashville Globe*, February 22, 1907: 8.

2   "Capital City Baseball League Organized," *Nashville Globe*, May 2, 1913: 1.

3   Wilson's date of birth has been recorded as 1883, 1889, and 1890 in different places. However, his death certificate, signed by R.B. Jackson, shows his birth year as 1889.

4   James A. Riley, *The Biographical Encyclopedia of the Negro Baseball Leagues* (New York: Carroll & Graf Publishers, 1994), 875.

5   Negro League Baseball eMuseum, https://nlbemuseum.com/history/players/wilsont.html, accessed September 24, 2023.

6   1940 United States Federal Census.

7   Dr. Harriett Kimbro-Hamilton conversation with author, January 24, 2024.

8   Nashville Public Library/Metro Archives Special Collections/ Davidson County Charters of Incorporation.

9   Negro League Baseball eMuseum.

10   William J. Plott, *The Negro Southern League: A Baseball History, 1920-1951* (Jefferson, North Carolina: McFarland & Co., 2015), 21.

11   Plott, 9-10.

12   City of Nashville Deed Book 735: 545-546.

13   See, for instance, "Black Cats Arrive Today for 3 Games," *Nashville Tennessean*, July 29, 1929: 13.

14   Riley, 875.

15   "Elite Giants to Play Chicago Americans in Double-Header Today," *Nashville Tennessean*, June 24, 1934: 11.

16   "Nashville Elite Giants Lose to Black Barons," *Nashville Tennessean*, June 13, 1926: 10.

17   J.L. Wilkinson biography, National Baseball Hall of Fame, https://baseballhall.org/hall-of-famers/wilkinson-jl, accessed December 12, 2023.

18   "Elite Giants Bow to Monarchs in Second Night Tilt," *Nashville Tennessean*, May 16, 1930: 19.

19   https://www.seamheads.com/NegroLgs/year.php?yearID=1930.

20   Negro League Baseball eMuseum, accessed January 22, 2024.

21   William F. McNeil, *The California Winter League* (Jefferson, North Carolina: McFarland & Co., 2002), 70.

22   Skip Nipper, "Negro Leagues Are Part of Area's Story," *Nashville Tennessean*, April 13, 2015: C5.

23   Riley, 875.

24   "Colored Outfits Wrangle in Dell," *Nashville Banner*, July 2, 1935: 12.

25   "Black Vols," *Nashville Banner*, April 24, 1936: 11.

26   "1933-1962: The Business Meetings of Negro League Baseball," in John Graf, ed., *From Rube to Robinson: SABR's Best Articles on Black Baseball* (Phoenix: SABR, 2021).

27   Bob Luke, *The Baltimore Elite Giants* (Baltimore: The Johns Hopkins University Press, 2009), 23-24.

28   "Final Double Header of Season at Yankee Stadium Sunday," *New York Age*, September 23, 1939: 8.

29   Luke, 50.

30   "Elites Sweep Opening Series," *Baltimore Afro-American*, May 18, 1940: 20.

31   Luke, 39.

32   Clinton "Butch" McCord interview with author, June 12, 2009.

33   Nashville Public Library/Metro Archives Special Collections/ Davidson County Charters of Incorporation.

34   Richard Schweid, "Club Built Among All Odds," *Nashville Tennessean*, September 2, 1987: 19.

35   Paradise Ballroom Advertisement, *Nashville Banner*, May 15, 1941: 15.

36   Plott, 145.

37   "Negro Southern Drops 4 Cities," *Nashville Tennessean*, December 7, 1945: 46.

38   Letter, Effa Manley to Rufus "Sonnyman" Jackson, January 2, 1942; letter, Effa Manley to Joseph Rainey, January 26, 1942, Manley Papers, Charles F. Cummings New Jersey Information Center, Newark Public Library, https://newarkpubliclibrary.libraryhost.com/ repositories/3/resources/82, accessed February 5, 2024.

39   Doron Goldman, "1933-1962: The Business Meetings of Negro League Baseball," https://sabr.org/journal/article/1933-1962-the-business-meetings-of-negro-league-baseball, accessed January 3, 2024.

40   Goldman.

41   Nashville Public Library/Metro Archives Special Collections/ Davidson County Wills & Probates.

42   McCord interview.

43   The Historical Marker Database, https://www.hmdb.org/m.asp?m=147542, accessed December 12, 2023

TERRAPIN PARK/ ORIOLE PARK (V)

BY DAVID B. STINSON

Terrapin Park, also known as Oriole Park (V), was the home of the Federal League Baltimore Terrapins in 1914 and 1915, the International League Orioles from 1916 to 1944, and parttime home field to the Negro National League Baltimore Elite Giants from 1939 to 1942.[1] It was located at the northwest corner of what is now Greenmount Avenue (formerly York Road) and 29th Street, across the street from the site of Oriole Park (II) and (IV).[2] First base paralleled East 29th Street, right field paralleled Greenmount Avenue, left field paralleled East 30th Street, and third base paralleled Vineyard Lane.[3]

Ned Hanlon, the manager of the National League Orioles from 1892 to 1898, played an important role in bringing major-league baseball back to Baltimore in 1914. After the 1899 season, Baltimore lost its National League franchise when the league contracted from 12 teams to eight. An inaugural member of the American League in 1901, the Orioles played only two seasons in Baltimore. In December 1902, after the demise of the American League Orioles,[4] Hanlon purchased American League Park for $3,000.[5] In 1903 Hanlon acquired an Eastern League franchise from Montreal and moved it to Baltimore.[6] Hanlon renamed the team the Orioles and the team moved into the former American League Park, rebranded as Oriole Park,[7] installing former National League Oriole Wilbert Robinson as manager of the team.[8]

While owner of Baltimore's Eastern League Orioles, Hanlon was also manager of the National League Brooklyn Superbas from 1899 to 1905, and the National League Cincinnati Reds in 1906 and 1907.[9] His hopes of bringing a major-league team back to Baltimore at the former American League Park never materialized and, after the 1909 season, Hanlon sold the team, and the ballpark, to Jack Dunn, a former American League and Eastern League Oriole, as well as one of Hanlon's Brooklyn Superbas' star pitchers.[10]

In 1913 the Federal League was formed as an independent league with six teams located in the Midwest.[11] In October 1913 Baltimore was offered a franchise in the Federal League for the 1914 season.[12] As observed by the *Baltimore Sun*:

> This is considered the time to step into a new major league that has a chance to become as good as any. If Baltimore lets the chance slip, it may have to resign itself to being a minor league town for the balance of its day.[13]

On October 27, 1913, Baltimore filed its Federal League Articles of Incorporation, which called for issuance of both preferred and common stock.[14] As for the location of the team's ballpark, the *Sun* reported the likelihood of building on a tract of land owned by Hanlon just across the street from Oriole Park (IV):

> Those interested in the club have an option on a fine tract for a ball park, lying just northwest of the present Oriole Park, although it has not definitely been selected. The ground belongs to Edward Hanlon, former manager of the champion Orioles.
>
> The proposed ground is that upon which was situated the old Brady mansion for a time used as a school-house. It is said that not a great amount of grading will be necessary as the elevation is such that the bleachers could be built upon it without much excavation
>
> The ground is 90 feet west of York road and on the east extends from Twenty-ninth to Thirtieth street, a distance of about 400 feet. The land runs westward to Gilmer Lane, a distance of about 600 feet. Gilmer lane runs at an angle of about 45°, making the plot irregular.
>
> If the ground is selected, there will be a triangle used for automobiles. It is said that the grandstand may be placed along Gilmer lane and Twenty-ninth street and that the sun would thus never strike the patrons. The bleachers could be arranged so that the sun would strike them from the side.
>
> Mr. Hanlon's counsel has just completed arrangements for the purchase of a small piece of land at Gilmer lane and Twenty-ninth street, which thus gives Mr. Hanlon a field considered very desirable.
>
> Wherever the park is located, the plans are to build a better stand than Baltimore has ever had and to have a seating capacity on all stands of at least 15,000.[15]

Baltimore officially was admitted to the Federal League on November 1, 1913.[16] The team reviewed plans for the ballpark on November 7, 1913.[17] As reported in the *Baltimore Sun*:

> According to the plan as presented, the grandstand would be built near the southwest corner of the lot, curving behind the home plate. At either end pavilions are proposed and in right field a bleacher stand. If the grandstand is built with an upper

deck, a total seating capacity will be about 10,000. If a single decker is built, the seats will be 3,000 to 4,000 fewer.

Behind the grandstand is a space that it is proposed to make a parked place for automobiles.[18]

On November 12, 1913, Hanlon was elected a director of the Baltimore Federal League club and reportedly purchased "a considerable amount of the stock."[19] Hanlon told the *Baltimore Sun*:

"This is not the first time that I have tried to bring big league ball back to this city and I know something of the difficulties. If we make no effort to break the present monopoly in organized baseball, Baltimore seems permanently side-tracked in a league from which no matter how many stars we might develop they would promptly be taken away to strengthen teams in cities perhaps smaller than Baltimore."[20]

As a director of the Baltimore franchise, Hanlon insisted that the team sell $10 shares of the corporation to encourage fan participation in the club itself, giving each stock owner full voting power and a first lien on the club's property, plus 7 percent dividends.[21] At the end of December 1913, the team selected Hanlon's tract of land and Hanlon completed his purchase of additional land necessary to construct the new Baltimore Federal League ballpark:

The Feds have selected the lot just in the rear of Oriole Park, which is owned by Ned Hanlon. It was not until yesterday that the deal was put through for a small tract which was necessary to make a suitable ball ground.

Hanlon yesterday purchased from James Keelty and his wife a tract beginning at the southeast corner of Gilmer lane and Thirtieth street measuring 73.8 by 293 feet. The sale was made in fee simple and the title was examined by the Title Guarantee and Trust Company.

With all the necessary ground in their possession – for the directors of the local club have decided upon Hanlon's lot as the home of their team – it is probable that the work of grading and building the stands will begin in a very short time. The directors are not at all worried about having the grounds in tiptop shape for the opening of the championship season, for Hanlon has called their attention to the very short time required to transform old Union Park from a lot into a ball yard.[22]

The ballclub petitioned the First Branch City Council for an ordinance approving its plans for the ballpark at York Road on January 12, 1914.[23] The plans submitted by the team called for "a large wooden structure on steel supports in the triangle formed by the York road, Twenty-ninth street, Thirtieth street and Gilmer lane."[24] The ordnance specified additional details about the ballpark:

The ordinance authorizes the club to build a grandstand 110 feet long, 65 feet high and 69 feet wide within the triangle. It is

to extend east on Twenty-ninth street, a distance of 182 feet and 08 inches, and northeast on Gilmer lane 182 feet. There is to be a single deck stand on Twenty-ninth street, starting 20 feet east of the grandstand and extending parallel with Twenty-ninth street for a distance of 180 feet, and to be 85 feet high and 52 feet wide.

Provision is also made for a single deck stand on Gilmer lane, 84 feet northeast of the grandstand, and to be 115 feet long, 38 feet high and 59 feet wide.

The bleachers are to be on the York road, according to the plan filed with Building Inspector Stubbs by Architect Simonson, and they will be 145 feet long and 190 feet wide. There is to be another wooden stand for bleachers on Thirtieth Street.[25]

Construction of the new ballpark began on January 20, 1914, with a groundbreaking ceremony, featuring Baltimore Mayor James H. Preston and directors of the club.[26] Architect Otto G. Simonson submitted his plans and specifications for the ballpark on January 26, 1914, and bids for construction of the ballpark grandstand, two covered pavilions, and bleachers were set to be opened on January 31, 1914.[27] The architect's plans for the ballpark were as follows:

In round figures the seating capacity will be about 13,000 persons, divided thus: Grandstand, 7,000: pavilion A, 2,509; pavilion B, 1,400, and the bleachers, 2,100. Pavilions A and B will be covered. Directly in the rear of the grandstand will be parking space for motor and other vehicles.

The distance from home plate to the left-field fence is about 300 feet, to the right field fence about 335 feet and to the intersection of centre and left-field fences about 460 feet. Between home plate and the grandstand will be a distance of 76 feet.[28]

Joe Smith was named groundskeeper for the new ballpark, and in March 1914 he installed beneath the diamond "a network of passages in which will be put the tile for draining purposes."[29] The new team was named the Terrapins and its new home was named Terrapin Federal League Ball Park.[30] The team's uniform included a Terrapin emblem on the front of the shirt.[31] According to the *Baltimore Sun*, "[T]he words 'Terrapin Park' will be placed in large letters over the main entrance to the park and also above the other egresses."[32]

Construction of Terrapin Park neared completion by the end of March. A 12-foot fence was erected "from the right-field bleachers to the extreme point in centre field, and thence to the left field pavilion."[33] The dressing rooms and showers for the Terrapins, the visiting clubs, the club secretary, and the umpires were located beneath the right section of the grandstand, "only a few steps" from the field.[34] Five flagpoles were installed inside the park, with the largest placed in center field.[35]

Although the ballpark was built mainly of wood, the *Baltimore Sun* remarked, "[I]f patrons of the game will help keep big league ball here the concrete stand will replace the wooden ones and the park will be as imposing as any in the country."[36] The grandstand and the press gates were located at the intersection of Barclay and Twenty-ninth streets.[37] A press box sat atop the grandstand.[38] The ballpark included "12 turnstiles in all, four being placed at each of the three entrances."[39] Patrons entering the right-field pavilion walked "directly up a short flight of steps," while those in the left-field pavilion walked "beneath the grandstand, and along a cement walk."[40] The ballpark included "five large exits" to "permit the crowd to disperse quickly after the game."[41]

Opening Day at Terrapin Park was April 13, 1914, with Mayor Preston declaring the afternoon a municipal holiday to "enable the officials and employees to attend the opening game of the Federal League baseball season."[42] Before the game, the city held a parade in honor of both teams, with thousands lining the parade route "east on Baltimore street from Calvert, to Holliday, to Lexington, to St. Paul street, south on St. Paul street to Baltimore, to Charles, north on Charles to North avenue east to the York road to the grounds."[43] Paid admissions to the park totaled 27,692, with 12,000 spectators standing and several thousand outside the ballpark, unable to get in.[44] "The big grandstand, the right and left field pavilions, the bleachers were taxed to their capacity," with "hundreds of chairs on the field that were pressed into service."[45] According to the *Baltimore Sun*, "[E]verybody was happy, none more so apparently than the ticket scalpers who did a thriving business," with fans paying $3 for a $1 ticket.[46] The Terrapins defeated the Buffalo Buffeds 3–2, and "Baltimore was universally first in the standings."[47] According to the *Baltimore Sun*, "[t]he tremendous crowd, the wild enthusiasm and terrific rooting rivaled the glorious days of the old Oriole championship team 17 years ago."[48] Across from Terrapin Park on Twenty-Ninth Street, the International League Orioles lost an exhibition game to the National League New York Giants, 3–2, at Oriole Park (IV) before an audience of 3,000.[49]

More than 45,000 attended all three games of the opening series at Terrapin Park.[50] As noted by the *Baltimore Sun*, "[t]hat's going some for a city which has been considered a poor baseball town in the ranks of organized ball."[51] Ticket prices were: bleacher seats, 25 cents; pavilion seats, 50 cents; grandstand seats, 75 cents; and reserved grandstand seats and box seats, one dollar.[52] After the first homestand, the club built a higher fence in center field "in order to give batters a better view of the ball."[53] The club also added "a screen on the grandstand to shield the right fielders from the sun."[54]

The Terrapins were in first place on May 5, 1914, and remained there for over a month before dropping to third place.[55] In September they were in a tight pennant race with Chicago, Indianapolis, Brooklyn, and Buffalo.[56] The *Sun* noted:

> That the Federal teams are so evenly matched is wonderful when it is considered that managers were forced to search all the leagues in the country for players to fill out their rosters. A walkaway for any team in the Independent circuit would have caused interest in the third major to slacken, but the great fight

Oriole Park V in 1940. Baltimore Elite Giants pitchers at Oriole Park V, 1940. L to R: Emery Adams, Satchel Davis, Eddie Dixon, Woody Williams, Willie Hubert, and Bill Barnes. Courtesy David Stinson/ Bernard McKenna

which is now being waged, with Baltimore a very strong contender, makes the first real race of the invaders very attractive.[57]

The Terrapins ended the season in third place, 4½ games behind the pennant winner, Indianapolis.[58] During the season the ballpark hosted other baseball events. In June a local school league, sponsored in part by the Sun Newspapers, played a championship series at Terrapin Park in front of 2,000 students.[59] On June 30 Terrapin Park hosted a game between members of the Baltimore City Police and the *Baltimore Sun* and *Evening Sun*, for the benefit of the Babies' Milk and Ice Fund.[60] On July 14 the Terrapins "invited the inmates of Baltimore orphanages to witness the double-header between the Diamondbacks and the Buffeds."[61] In 1915 the use of Terrapin Park was expanded to include boxing matches and movies.[62]

Hope for the Terrapins seemed strong for Baltimore as the 1915 Federal League season began. In the offseason, the Terrapins had acquired future Hall of Fame pitcher Chief Bender, who it was thought could help bring a championship to Baltimore.[63] On Opening Day an impressive crowd of 18,391 watched the Terrapins lose 7-5 to the Newark Peppers (formerly the 1914 league champion Indianapolis Hoosiers).[64] The 1915 season did not turn out as Baltimore fans had hoped and attendance fell off drastically.[65] Bender won only four games and posted 16 losses.[66] By the end of the season, Baltimore was in last place, losing more than twice as many games as they won, with a record of 47-107, and 40 games behind the pennant-winning Chicago Whales.[67]

But in the end it really did not matter, as the Federal League folded after the season. Hanlon and other Terrapin Club officials continued in US District Court an action filed earlier by the Federal League, challenging Organized Baseball's hold on the national pastime, claiming it violated the Sherman Anti-Trust Act.[68] Ultimately, in 1922, the Supreme Court dismissed the Federal League challenge, holding that baseball was not subject to the Sherman Act because baseball was a state activity and did not qualify as interstate commerce.[69]

The major-league Baltimore Terrapins lasted just two seasons. It would not be until 1954 that what was then known as major-league baseball would return to Baltimore, when the city got its second American League franchise, the original 1901 Milwaukee franchise, which moved to St. Louis in 1902.[70]

The two years the Federals were in Baltimore proved most difficult for Dunn and his International League team. In 1914 Dunn signed, and then sold, Babe Ruth out of St. Mary's Industrial School for Boys to play for his International League Orioles.[71] As reported in the *Baltimore Sun*:

> The Oriole magnate signed another local player yesterday. The new Bird is George H. Ruth, a pitcher, who played with teams out the Frederick road. Ruth is six feet tall and fanned 22 men in an amateur game last season. He is regarded as a very hard hitter, so Dunn will try him out down South.[72]

Nicknamed Babe because of his youth, and as a reference early on to his being "Jack Dunn's Babe," Ruth was sold by Dunn to the Boston Red Sox, and assigned to the International League Providence Grays.[73] Dunn had received permission from the league to sell Ruth and other Orioles to help pay off the considerable debt he had incurred to run his team once the Terrapins took up residency across the street from him.[74] Before the 1915 season, unable to compete with the Federal League's hold on Baltimore baseball fans, Dunn moved his International League Orioles to Richmond, Virginia.[75] After the Federal League's demise, he purchased the Jersey City International League franchise and moved it to Baltimore.[76]

In March 1916, Dunn purchased Terrapin Park, which then became the fifth Baltimore ballpark known as Oriole Park. Wrote the *Sun*:

> It is believed that Dunn agreed to pay about $30,000 for the stands, which, with the improvement made upon the grounds,

cost the 600 Terrapin stockholders in the neighborhood of $90,000. Of course, Dunn got a bargain, for there never were more comfortable or more substantial wooden stands ever built than those put up for Baltimore's representative in the Baby Major.

> The lot, of course, was not included in the sale because that belongs to Ned Hanlon. Dunn will pay $4,000 a year rent for the lot, but has the privilege of buying it any time within the next eight years for $65,000.[77]

Hanlon sold Dunn the land on which the ballpark sat in January 1921.[78]

The Orioles played respectable ball during 1916 season, posting a record of 74-66, and placing fourth, eight games back of the league champion Buffalo Bisons.[79] The 1916 season saw the first of a dozen exhibition games that Babe Ruth would play at Oriole Park (V), with his final exhibition-game appearance there on May 1, 1930. On April 18, 1919, while with Boston, Ruth hit four home runs in an exhibition game against the Orioles, which the Red Sox won 12-3.[80] The next day he hit two more home runs, with five hit in a row (the last three at-bats of the first game and the first two at-bats of the second game).[81]

Dunn helped lead the charge to bring Sunday baseball to Baltimore. In 1918 he was arrested for violating Baltimore's blue laws, which restricted on Sundays the charging of admission to public events like baseball.[82] In 1910 Dunn built a ballpark in Baltimore County at Back River Park, to avoid the city's blue laws, and allow his Orioles to play baseball on Sundays.[83] By 1921 Dunn had won the right to stage baseball games on Sundays in Oriole Park (V).[84]

Beginning in 1919, Dunn built his Orioles into an International League powerhouse, winning over 100 games that year and the first of seven straight league championships.[85] In 1920 Dunn signed future Hall of Fame pitcher Robert Moses "Lefty" Grove. During his five seasons with the Orioles, Grove won 108 games and lost only 36.[86] Dunn sold Grove to the Philadelphia A's after the 1924 season for $100,600, the extra $600 added "to make it a sum greater than what the Yankees had paid Boston for Babe Ruth."[87] Grove would win 300 games in the major leagues.[88] Dunn died suddenly after the 1928 season.[89] During their final seasons at Oriole Park (V), 1926 until 1943, the International League Orioles never again won the league championship.[90]

In 1939, the Baltimore Elite Giants began playing their home games at Oriole Park (V),[91] once they were "finally accepted as occasional Sunday afternoon tenants of Oriole Park."[92] That season, the Elite Giants played 14 home games at Oriole Park (V) against Negro National League teams and two home games against Negro American League opponents (Cleveland Bears).[93] They also played four playoff games at the ballpark, including a September 10, 1939, doubleheader against the Newark Eagles, with the Elite Giants winning both games by scores of 7-3 and 5-2,[94] as well as a September 17, 1939, doubleheader against the Homestead Grays, with the Elite Giants winning the first game 7-5, and the teams playing to a 1-1 tie in the second game (five innings, game called because of a 6:00 P.M. curfew).[95] That season, the Elite Giants went on to win the Negro National League title, defeating the Homestead Grays at Yankee Stadium in the final game.[96]

In addition to games played at Oriole Park (V), beginning in 1938, the Elite Giants also played home games at Bugle Field, located in East Baltimore at the intersection of Federal Street and Edison Highway.[97] There currently are no recorded contests played at Bugle Field in 1939 between the Elite Giants and other major-league Black teams.[98] To the extent the Elite Giants played games against non-league (semipro, amateur) opponents at Bugle Field in 1939, those games appear to have been unrecorded in the press.[99]

The Elite Giants tenure at Oriole Park (V) came to an end on May 10, 1942, after a fight between fans caused minor damage to the ballpark and the owners of the ballpark decided to disallow any more Negro League games at Oriole Park (V).[100] The Elite Giants continued to play home games at Bugle Field through the 1949 season.[101] Bugle Field was demolished in October 1949,[102] and in 1950 and 1951, the Elite Giants played their final two seasons at Westport Stadium, a newly-constructed ballpark located on Annapolis Road in Westport, just south of the intersection of I-95 and I-295.[103]

On July 4, 1944, Oriole Park (V) was destroyed by a fire.[104] The *Baltimore Sun* reported on the destruction of the ballpark:

> Fire of undetermined origin razed the stands of famed Oriole Park, home of the Baltimore International League Club, today, causing a loss estimated by club officials at $150,000.
>
> The wooden stands burned so rapidly that within little more than an hour only charred and smoking timbers remained around the field where Jack Dunn once led his Orioles to seven straight league pennants, and where he developed such famous stars as Babe Ruth, Lefty Grove, Joe Boley, Tommy Thomas, Max Bishop and others.[105]

The International League Orioles won the pennant in 1944, beginning their season at Oriole Park (V),[106] and finishing their season (and subsequent seasons through 1953) at Baltimore Municipal Stadium, which later became Memorial Stadium.[107]

The site now is occupied by row houses, the Barclay Elementary School, and Peabody Heights Brewery.[108] In 2015 Peabody Heights Brewery hired the company that performed the original survey of Terrapin Park to help determine the exact, former location of home plate:

> Home plate, it turns out, stood in what is now a grass strip, midway up the east side of the 2900 block of Barclay St. The spot faces windows on the Barclay Elementary/Middle building. The pitcher's mound was not far from the south-facing wall of what is now the Peabody Heights Brewery, the former Royal Crown bottling plant.
>
> The surveyors relied upon a well-preserved 1914 original survey of the park created by the S.J. Martenet Co., a firm that

remains in business in Baltimore's Mount Vernon neighborhood. They found the coordinates to pinpoint where the base lines would have been.

> "We laid out the base lines, bleachers and grandstands in 1914," said Joel Leininger, an owner of Martenet. (It's his daughter who assisted in this week's resurvey.) He told me the outlines of the park property came into discussion recently when a neighboring building was sold. When land is transferred, it is customary for it to be resurveyed. It was this resurvey of the former DuPont warehouse that sparked the current conversation about the ballpark.[109]

Beginning in 2017, the SABR Baltimore Babe Ruth Chapter has held its annual SABR Day meetings at Peabody Heights Brewery, in an area of the brewery that was once the left-field pavilion of Terrapin Park and Oriole Park (V).[110] In 2021, the Baltimore SABR chapter placed an historic marker commemorating "Old Oriole Park" in the brewery's beer garden.

NOTES

1   Byron Bennett, "Baltimore's Other Major League Ballfield – Terrapin Park/Oriole Park," deadballbaseball.com, December 6, 2012, Baltimore's Other Major League Ballfield – Terrapin Park Oriole Park–Deadball Baseball (accessed January 29, 2024); Bob Luke, *The Baltimore Elite Giants* (Baltimore: Johns Hopkins Press University Press, 2009), 70, 81.

2   Byron Bennett, "The Six Different Ballparks Known as Oriole Park," deadballbaseball.com, December 30, 2013. The Six Different Ballparks Known As Oriole Park–Deadball Baseball (accessed January 29, 2024).

3   Byron Bennett, "The Six Different Ballparks Known as Oriole Park."

4   The future owners of the New York Highlanders/Yankees bought the Baltimore franchise and moved it to New York.

5   "Will Old League Buy? Receivers Appointed to Sell the Stands at New Baseball Park," *Baltimore Sun*, October 21, 1902: 6.

6   "Promise a Good Team: Hanlon to Have One in the Eastern League, Gets the Baseball Park," *Baltimore Sun*, January 30, 1903: 9.

7   In the succession of ballparks by this name, it has come to be known as Oriole Park (IV).

8   "Promise a Good Team."

9   baseball-reference.com/bullpen/Ned_Hanlon (accessed January 2, 2020).

10   James H. Bready, *Baseball in Baltimore, The First 100 Years* (Baltimore: Johns Hopkins Press University Press, 1977), 116-117; "Dunn as Team Owner: Jack Wants to Buy Local Club's Franchise, Hanlon Says He Will Sell, but the Manager Declares He Must Get 'Proper Price,'" *Baltimore Sun*, October 8, 1909: 10; "Hanlon Is Sole Owner: He Buys Up All the Stock Of Baltimore Baseball Club/Frank And Winternitz Sell, Hughey Jennings Also Lets His Bit Go and Jack Dunn May Become Real Oriole Magnate," *Baltimore Sun*, November 11, 1909: 10; "Jack Dunn Buys Orioles: Former Manager Is Sole Owner of Baltimore Baseball Club, Old Robbie Is a Director, Charles H. Knapp Is Third Director and Secretary and Treasurer -New Faces to Be Seen," *Baltimore Sun*, November 17, 1909: 10.

11 "Federal League Is Formed in The West," *Baltimore Sun*, March 9, 1913: A1.

12 "Major League Ball Offered Baltimore: Federal League, After One Season, Intends to Invade the East, This City Can Get Franchise, Independent Organization Said to Have Ample Financial Backing, and the Intention to Make Itself Second to None – Plenty of Players to Pick From," *Baltimore Sun*, October 21, 1913: 6.

13 "Major League Ball Offered Baltimore."

14 "Big League Plan Launched: Articles of Incorporation of Federal Club," *Baltimore Sun*, October 28, 1913: 16.

15 "Big League Plan Launched."

16 "Baltimore Is Admitted to Federal League," *Baltimore Sun*, November 2, 1913: S1.

17 "Ball Park Plans Scanned," *Baltimore Sun*, November 8, 1913: 7.

18 "Ball Park Plans Scanned."

19 "Hanlon With Federals: Famous Old Baseball Manager Enthusiastic for New League, Elected Director of Club," *Baltimore Sun*, November 13, 1913: 12.

20 "Hanlon With Federals."

21 "Club Stock for 'Fans' Federal League Preferred Will Be Sold at $10 a Share, Hanlon Demanded This Move," *Baltimore Sun*, November 20, 1013: 2.

22 "Hanlon Buys Ground for Feds' Ball Park, Deal Is Closed for Tract Required to Make Playing Field Sufficiently Large," *Baltimore Sun*, December 31, 1913: 5.

23 "New Ball Park Plans In, City Council Asked to Authorize Big Buildings at York Road and Twenty-Ninth Street," *Baltimore Sun*, January 13, 1914: 5.

24 "New Ball Park Plans In."

25 "New Ball Park Plans In."

26 "Russell Ford, Edgar Willet and Howard Camnitz Sign With Federal League; to Break Ground Today; Mayor Preston Will Start Work at Federal League Park," *Baltimore Sun*, January 21, 1914: 11.

27 "Park Bids Are Open, Baltimore Feds Will Award Contract Saturday for New Home, to Seat Nearly 13,000 Fans," *Baltimore Sun*, January 27, 1914: 9.

28 "Park Bids Are Open."

29 "Schoolboys to Root, Friends Will Send a Squad Of 100 to Terrapins' Opening Game, Fans Inspect New Ball Park," *Baltimore Sun*, March 16, 1914: 8.

30 "It's 'Terrapin Park,' Baltimore Federal Magnates Decide Upon Name for Their Home; All Grandstand Seats Sold," *Baltimore Sun*, March 18, 1914: 8.

31 "It's 'Terrapin Park.'"

32 "It's 'Terrapin Park.'"

33 "Work Progressing at Terrapin Park," *Baltimore Sun*, March 29, 1914: S2.

34 "Work Progressing at Terrapin Park."

35 "Work Progressing at Terrapin Park."

36 "Terrapin Park Is Ready to Welcome Baltimore Fans," *Baltimore Sun*, April 12, 1914: S2.

37 "Terrapin Park Is Ready."

38 "Terrapin Park Is Ready."

39 "Terrapin Park Is Ready."

40 "Terrapin Park Is Ready."

41 "Terrapin Park Is Ready."

42 "Municipal Holiday Today," *Baltimore Sun*, April 10, 1914: 14.

43 "28,000 See Contest; Inspiring Sight at Terrapin Park as Federal League Season Opens," *Baltimore Sun*, April 14, 1914; 1.

44 "28,000 See Contest."

45 "28,000 See Contest."

46 "28,000 See Contest."

47 Bready, 127.

48 "Baseball Features of the Day," *Baltimore Sun*, April 14, 1914: 1.

49 "Baseball Features of the Day."

50 "More Than 45,000 Fans Attend the Terrapin Games," *Baltimore Sun*, April 19, 1914: SS1.

51 "More Than 45,000 Fans Attend."

52 Classified Ad 7, *Baltimore Sun*, April 18, 1914: 1.

53 "Zinn Will Be Out of Game Several Days," *Baltimore Sun*, April 25, 1914: 11.

54 "Zinn Will Be Out."

55 Bready, 127.

56 "Baseball Races Close, Federal, National and International Furnishing Thrills, Baltimore Strong Contender," *Baltimore Sun*, September 17, 1914: 5.

57 "Baseball Races Close."

58 Bready, 127.

59 "School No. 42 Victor: Defeats No. 48 in Initial Championship Ball Game; 2,000 Children See Struggle," *Baltimore Sun*, June 23, 1914: 14.

60 "Dare 'Cops' to Take It; Game of Ball with Newspaper Men to Be Red-Hot One, for Babies' Milk and Ice Fund," *Baltimore Sun*, June 18, 1914: 4.

61 C. Starr Mathews, "Orphans Will See Games at Terrapin Park Today," *Baltimore Sun*, July 14, 1914: 5.

62 "Kid Must Like the Air: Williams Won His Greatest Battles in Outdoor Rings, Scored Three Knockouts," *Baltimore Sun*, July 21, 1915: 5; "Taylor Badly Battered, New Yorker No Match for Kid Williams, King of Bantams, Knocked Down in Thirteenth," *Baltimore Sun*, July 25, 1915: 110; "Dunn Buys Terp Park, Will Take Possession of Federal League Plant April 1, Price Believed About $30,000," *Baltimore Sun*, March 4, 1916: 11.

63 "Bender Will Pitch for the Terrapins, Player Committee Decides Indian Is Needed to Bolster Up Twirling Staff, Signed Two-Year Contract," *Baltimore Sun*, December 8, 1914: 1.

64 "Terrapins Lose Opening Game, Newark Peppers Capture First Contest of Season Before 18,391," *Baltimore Sun*, April 11, 1915: 1.

65 "Now Is The Time to Assure Ourselves of a Permanent Place on the Baseball Map – And IF It Is Not Done Now, It Will Be Never," *Baltimore Sun*, June 7, 1915: 6; "Ten-Cent Ball Today, New Prices to Go Into Effect Here at Terrapin Park, Two Games for the One Price," *Baltimore Sun*, August 13, 1915: 12.

66 Bready, 128.

67 Bready, 128.

68 "Terrapins to Keep Up Fight, Baltimore Trying to Block Baseball Settlement, Says Report, Would Continue Anti-Trust Suit," *Baltimore Sun*, December 23, 1915; 14; "Terrapins May File $900,000 Suit Today, Case Against O.B. and Federal Pacifists Will Be

Fought in Philadelphia," *Baltimore Sun*, March 17, 1916: 10; "Terps Fire Opening Gun in Suit Against Organized Ball: Cost O.B. a Million to Put Out Federals, Terms of Peace Pact Out in Trial of Baltimoreans' $900,000 Suit, Terps Ignored, They Claim," *Baltimore Sun*, June 12, 1917: 8.

69   *Federal Baseball Club v. National League*, 259 U.S. 200 (1922).

70   It should be noted that on December 16, 2020, Baseball Commissioner Robert Manfred announced that Major League Baseball had officially elevated the Negro Leagues to major-league status for the period 1920–1948. MLB Press Release, December 16, 2020, www.mlb.com/press-release/press-release-mlb-officially-designates-the-negro-leagues-as-major-league (last accessed January 30, 2024). Accordingly, prior to the American League Orioles coming to Baltimore in 1954, the city had two other major-league teams – the Baltimore Black Sox and the Baltimore Elite Giants–who played during at least a portion of the period 1920 to 1948.

71   Bready, 134.

72   Dunn Now Trying to Bolster Club," *Baltimore Sun*, February 15, 1914: S3.

73   Bready, 134-135.

74   "3 More Orioles Sold, Ruth, Shore And Egan Purchased by the Boston Red Sox, They Leave the Nest Tonight," *Baltimore Sun*, July 10, 1914: 5; "None to Quit, He Says; International President Declares All His Clubs Will Stick, Approves Sales by Jack Dunn," *Baltimore Sun*, July 13, 1914: 5.

75   "Richmond Gets Orioles, Virginia League Accepts Offer to Let in International, Jack Dunn to Head Company," *Baltimore Sun*, January 13, 1915: 11.

76   Bready, 143.

77   "Dunn Buys Terp Park: Will Take Possession of Federal League Plant April 1, Price Believed About $30,000," *Baltimore Sun*, March 4, 1916: 11.

78   "Jack Dunn Lifts Option on Baseball Grounds," *Baltimore Sun*, January 3, 1924: 12.

79   baseball-reference.com/bullpen/1916_International_League_season (accessed January 4, 2020).

80   Bready, 139.

81   Bready, 139.

82   "Jack Dunn Under Fire, Charged with Violating Sunday Law at Oriole Park, Sold Admissions, Is Charged," *Baltimore Sun*, July 16, 1918: 5; "Birds Trim the Leafs, Sunday Baseball in City Inaugurated with Victory, About 9,000 Cheer Dunnmen," *Baltimore Sun*, June 17, 1918: 5.

83   "To Have Sunday Ball, Dunn Will Build Stand and Grounds Opposite Prospect Park; to Lease the Property Today," *Baltimore Sun*, March 11, 1910: 10; Bready, 118.

84   "Great Throng at Oriole Park Attests Popularity of Game: Largest Sunday Baseball Crowd Overflows Stands and Fields – Gates Are Closed Momentarily and Thousands Turn Away," *Baltimore Sun*, April 21, 1925: 8.

85   Bready, 145.

86   baseball-reference.com/register/player.fcgi?id=grove-002rob (accessed January 5, 2020).

87   Bready, 154.

88   Bready, 154.

89   Bready, 186.

90   James H. Bready, *The Home Team Our Orioles* (25th Anniversary Edition) (self-published, 1959), 44.

91   Email from Gary Ashwill, Co-Creator & Lead Researcher, Seamheads, December 19, 2022.

92   Bready, *Baseball in Baltimore*, 175; "Stars to Meet Giants in National Negro Loop at Oriole Park Today," *Baltimore Sun*, June 27, 1937: S3; "Elite Giants Play Homestead Grays Today," *Baltimore Sun*, July 25, 1937: SS7; "Elite Giants to Open Season Next Sunday," *Baltimore Sun*, May 3, 1942: S3.

93   Email from Gary Ashwill, Co-Creator & Lead Researcher, Seamheads, December 19, 2022.

94   Ralph Boyd, "Elites Whip Eagles to Gain Championship Series," *Afro-American*, September 16, 1939: 22.

95   Art Carter, "Elites, Grays Tied in National League Title Series," *Baltimore Afro-American*, September 23, 1939: 19.

96   Bready, *Baseball In Baltimore*, 175.

97   Luke, 32; Bready, *Baseball In Baltimore*, 174.

98   Email from Gary Ashwill, Co-Creator & Lead Researcher, Seamheads, December 19, 2022.

99   Email from Gary Ashwill, Co-Creator & Lead Researcher, Seamheads, December 19, 2022.

100   Luke, 70, 81.

101   Luke, 121.

102   Byron Bennett, "Bugle Field – Home of the Baltimore Elite Giants," deadballbaseball.com, October 6, 2013, Bugle Field – Home of the Baltimore Elite Giants–Deadball Baseball (accessed January 29, 2024).

103   Byron Bennett, "Westport Stadium – Baltimore's Last Negro League Ballpark," deadballbaseball.com, October 28, 2013, Westport Stadium – Baltimore's Last Negro League Ballpark–Deadball Baseball (accessed January 29, 2024).

104   "Oriole Ball Park Destroyed by Fire: Baltimore Team Loses Uniforms and Trophies," *Baltimore Sun*, July 5, 1944: 19.

105   Oriole Ball Park Destroyed by Fire: Baltimore Team Loses Uniforms and Trophies."

106   Bready, *The Home Team*, 45.

107   Bready, *Baseball In Baltimore*, 204-208; Jesse A. Linthicum, "Sunlight on Sports," *Baltimore Sun*, July 5, 1944: 15.

108   Byron Bennett, "Baltimore's Other Major League Ballfield – Terrapin Park/Oriole Park"; Byron Bennett, "The Six Different Ballparks Known as Oriole Park."

109   Kelly Jacques, "Surveyors Find Home in a City Neighborhood: Documents Show Layout of Oriole Park, Which Burned In '44," *Baltimore Sun*, May 2, 2015: A3; David B. Stinson "Surveying Site of Old Oriole Park at Peabody Heights Brewery" (May 2, 2015), surveying-site-of-old-oriole-park-at-peabody-heights-brewery.

110   David B. Stinson, "Drinking Beer in The Left Field Tasting Room at Old Oriole Park," davidbstinsonauthor.com, July 31, 2015, drinking-beer-in-the-left-field-tasting-room-at-old-oriole-park (accessed January 29, 2024).

1939 BALTIMORE ELITE GIANTS TIMELINE

BY BILL NOWLIN

In 1938 the Baltimore Elite Giants had taken part in the Negro National League II playoffs and were looking forward to the 1939 season under a new manager. George Scales had led the team in 1938, when the Elite Giants finished third in the seven-team league, with a NNL II record of 26-23 but winning both the playoffs three games to one and the Championship Series, also three games to one. Bob Luke, author of 2009 book *The Baltimore Elite Giants*, writes in 2023, "From what I can tell now [Gus] Greenlee and [Cum] Posey, lacking any statement of hard evidence, simply published a letter anointing the Grays as winners of the second half that combined with their uncontested first place standing gave them the championship without any playoff games needed or played."[1]

Scales was named manager of the New York Black Yankees for 1939, and Felton Snow was named the new manager. Snow had been the team's shortstop in 1938, batting .254 with 22 RBIs in 36 league games.

A later report in the *Pittsburgh Courier* said that Biz Mackey would manage Baltimore.[2] That said, the *Chicago Defender* had cited "Manager Snow" as reporting that all but three players had reported to camp; one of the ones who had not yet reported was Biz Mackey.[3] The *Baltimore Afro-American* cited Snow as manager in an April 22 story emanating from Atlanta.[4]

Douglass Smith, "publicity man for the club," announced that the Elite Giants would have Oriole Park as their home field in 1939.[5] Bugle Field had been the home ballpark in 1938.

In 1939, despite having a losing league record (20-24), the Elite Giants repeated as champions. How did this come about? Thomas Kern notes that it was often the case in league play that the first- and second-half champions would meet in a playoff to determine the season champion. The Grays won the first half and Baltimore, reinforced by the acquisition of better players during the season, won the second half. However, in 1939 the Negro National League, according to the *Delaware County Daily Times*, adopted the Shaughnessy System, by which the top four teams participated in a playoff. The origins of the system date from athlete and executive Frank Shaughnessy, who designed a four-team playoff for Organized Baseball's International League in the late 1930s. Some argued that the approach should be applied in the American and National Leagues to facilitate a breakup of the New York Yankees dynasty.

Whether or not the Negro National League had the same thing in mind when it came to the dominance of the Homestead Grays, it applied the four-team playoff in 1939. As a consequence of taking the top four teams in the League, the Elite Giants' composite record for the season, due to a poor first half showing, was below .500. The first-place Grays drew the fourth-place Philadelphia Stars, who had narrowly edged the Black Yankees at the end of the regular season. The second-place Newark Eagles played third-place Baltimore. And Baltimore prevailed.[6]

One could, in fact, ask the question as well regarding the prior year: "Who were the NNL champions in 1938?" After the 1939 season was over, *Afro-American* columnist Art Carter did allow that "the Baltimore Elite Giants dethroned the two-time league champions, the Homestead Grays[,]" though he noted that the Grays had been seen as holding the two earlier championships "whether they won them by fair or foul means."[7] Indeed, he had written of the Elite Giants, "Actually, they have as much claim to the 1938 championship as the Homestead Grays, who are recognized as the league titleholders of last year, because last year's title series ended in a state of confusion. The Elites held the edge in the deciding game, when the Grays walked off the field, and the now-resigned president, Gus Greenlee, never did anything about it."[8]

There had been "playoffs" and on Sunday, September 11, the Elites played two games at Oriole Park, beating the Pittsburgh Crawfords, 10-1, in the first game.[9] In the second, at some point in the fourth inning, the Grays "were on the short end … when they started to pull the stall act." The umpire forfeited the game to the Elites, but the *Afro-American* explained that the win over the Crawfords would count in the playoffs but the forfeit would not.[10] No rationale was provided.

Carter continued: "Consequently, the Grays, who held the championship the previous year, continued to parade as title-holders. And the incumbent league prexy, Tom Wilson, never attempted to take the matter into his hands inasmuch as one of the involved clubs (the Elites) is owned by him, and any decision would naturally invite tales of favoritism."[11]

They were a team that had relocated from city to city. Bob Luke summarized some of their travels that brought them to Baltimore in 1938:

"Newspapers often referred to Smiling Tom Wilson's squad as 'the well-traveled Elite Giants.' They played their first game in 1921 in Nashville, Tennessee, and joined the Negro National League in 1929. The Great Depression caused the league to disband in 1932. The Elites rejoined the league when it reappeared in 1933. When he discovered that the East Coast teams found getting to and from Nashville a financial hardship, Wilson moved the franchise to Detroit, and they started the 1935 season there. But the Elites left Detroit after several weeks – they could not find a stadium to rent – and went to Columbus, Ohio, for the rest of the '35 season. There the city's modest black population (32,774 in 1930) could not muster sufficient support for the team, so Wilson again pulled up stakes, moving the Elites to Washington, D.C., for the 1936 and '37 season. In May 1938 he moved the team to Baltimore, where he at last found adequate community support."[12]

Preseason

A Negro National League meeting was held at the Harlem Chamber of Commerce in New York City on January 2. The six league teams from 1938 were represented, with Tom Wilson and Vunn (Vernon) Green there for the Elite Giants. It was reported that "[l]eague finances were found to be in better shape than at any time since the league was formed."[13] In the only player transaction mentioned in the *Courier*, Wilson announced that he had traded the team's 1938 manager, George Scales, along with pitcher Bob Griffith, to the New York Black Yankees for left-handed pitcher Barney Brown. Scales did manage the Black Yankees in 1939, but neither Brown nor Griffith pitched that year for any team in the league. Griffith, with his name spelled as Griffin, signed to play baseball in Mexico for Vera Cruz.[14]

The league season was set to begin on May 14 and run until Labor Day.[15]

Boxing and basketball dominated the sports page of the *Baltimore Afro-American*. Even cricket got mention, but there was disappointingly little about the Elite Giants through the end of April other than a brief mention of the April 23 game, brief enough that it didn't even mention the starting pitcher in

Spring training 1939 at Sulphur Dell, Nashville.

the first game or anyone on offense.[16] The team first played in Baltimore on May 14. Only the day before did the paper accord any significant coverage.

Gus Greenlee resigned as president of the league and at the February 18 league meeting in Philadelphia, Tom Wilson was elected league president.[17]

April 2, 1939: Memphis Red Sox 4, Baltimore Elite Giants 2, at Martin Park, Memphis

The Elite Giants had been training in Nashville, then traveled to Memphis for a 2:30 Sunday afternoon game in front of a "fair sized crowd" at Martin Park against the Memphis Red Sox.[18] Getting in a few innings apiece pitching for Baltimore were "Rogers," Lefty Phillips, and Emery Adams. The Red Sox scored two runs in the first inning and two in the third, yielding single runs in the fifth and seventh. Roy Campanella caught.[19] The *Memphis Commercial Appeal* had one sentence about the game, reassuringly understanding that the team had relocated to Maryland: "The Memphis Red Sox won their first exhibition game yesterday by defeating the Baltimore Elite Giants, 4 to 2, on the Martin's Park diamond."[20]

April 9, 1939: Baltimore Elite Giants 13, Atlanta Black Crackers 12, at Booker T. Washington High School field, Atlanta

The game was played in Easter Sunday. With Mackey managing, Baltimore and Atlanta squared off for "nine ding-dong, smash-bang frames" before the Elite Giants came from behind and scored three times in the top of the ninth, and then held the one-run lead. Atlanta outhit Baltimore 19-15 and overall there were 15 extra-base hits. Felix "Chin" Evans of Atlanta and Henry Kimbro of Baltimore each homered. All three triples were by Crackers. Sammy Hughes doubled twice for Baltimore, while West, Walker, Campanella, and Wild Bill Wright each hit a double. Bill Harvey, Lefty Phillips, and Bill Byrd were the three pitchers for the Elite Giants. In the ninth, with Baltimore down by two runs, Byrd led off with a walk. Mackey had himself pinch-hit for Campanella and grounded out. Kimbro hit a two-run inside-the-park home run to deep left-center. That tied the score, 12-12. Snow flied out. (The *Atlanta Daily World* called him "Mammy" Snow.)[21] Hughes hit his second double. Wright walked. James West beat out an infield hit to short. The bases were loaded with two outs. Hoskins came to bat.[22] He battled Dixon for 10 pitches, fouling off five and finally earning a base on balls on Dixon's 11th pitch. That forced in the go-ahead run for the Elite Giants.

April 10, 1939: Baltimore Elite Giants 11, Atlanta Black Crackers 10, at Booker T. Washington High School field, Atlanta

The Monday afternoon game was another high-scoring game decided by one run, though in this game all the scoring was done in the first six innings and neither team put one across in the seventh, eighth, or ninth. The line score read:

Baltimore	001 541 000	11 11 4
Atlanta	212 014 000	10 19 5

The *Atlanta Daily World* dubbed it "one of the weirdest exhibitions of professional baseball ever seen here in a number of years." For Atlanta, it was the second day in a row they had collected precisely 19 base hits. It wasn't enough. Yet again, they came up one run short of matching the Elite Giants. The "Black Crax" had held a 5-1 lead after three innings, and then came the middle innings, in which Baltimore scored 10 to Atlanta's five, before Lefty Glover and Chin Evans suddenly got in an "old-fashioned pitcher's battle" for the final three.[23]

Some dramatic defensive plays were detailed and some amateurish errors. Mitchell (charged with six runs) had started for Atlanta, relieved by Evans. Evans homered for the second day in a row, as did Kimbro, who also had two doubles. Hoskins, too, homered for the Giants. Willie Hubert (who had two hits) started for the Giants, relieved by Lefty Glover and Bill Harvey.

There may have been one or more other games played in Georgia. Researcher Rich Bogovich found a brief article in a Macon newspaper saying that the local Bibb Fast Blacks expected to play a number of preseason games before their own season opened on April 15, with teams including the Newark Eagles, Atlanta Black Crackers, and the "Washington Elite Giants."[24]

April 16, 1939: Baltimore Elite Giants 6, Atlanta Black Crackers 3, at Engel Stadium, Chattanooga

A reported 500 fans attended the game, but the *Chattanooga Daily Times* provided no other details than the score and the venue. It gave the team name as the Nashville Elite Giants.[25] The designation of the city name was seen as an ongoing matter, noted Randy Dixon in the *Pittsburgh Courier* when he described "Tom Wilson's Elite Giants [whose] precise geographical home hovers between Baltimore and Nashville as the whim strikes."[26]

The *Atlanta Daily World* offered a bit more information. Starting for the Black Crax was Eddie "Bullet" Dixon, who shut out the Baltimore Elite Giants (named as such) through the first seven innings, "only to have late rallies, aided by untimely errors, ruin the brilliant early season performance."[27]

The team stationery, at least well into May, was headed "Nashville Elite Giants Baseball Club," located at 84 Claiborne Street in Nashville.[28]

April 23, 1939: Nashville Elite Giants 5, Chicago American Giants 3 (first game); Nashville Elite Giants 5, Chicago American Giants 0 (second game); at Sulphur Dell Park, Nashville

Young, Hughes, Mackey, and Snow all hit doubles off Willie Cornelius in the first game, for five runs in all. Right-hander Bill Byrd gave up two runs to Chicago in the top of the first, but the Giants came back with one in the bottom of the first. They added one in the fifth, two in the sixth, and (after Chicago scored its second run) another in the sixth.

The second game was the standout game – "South Paw Harvey" (Bill Harvey) allowed just one base hit, a single by first baseman Ed Young, in the seven-inning game. Lefty Bowe was Chicago's pitcher. Succeeded by Rogers Pierre, the pair allowed four runs in the first and another in the fourth inning, allowing 10 hits in all. The only extra-base hit was a double by Felton Snow.[29]

April 24, 1939: Chicago American Giants 10, Baltimore Elite Giants 6, at Sulphur Dell Park, Nashville

The source provided is as presented by the *Chicago Tribune*. No other source of information has been found.[30]

April 30, 1939: Homestead Grays 6, Baltimore Elite Giants 2; Homestead Grays 5, Baltimore Elite Giants 2, at Rickwood Field, Birmingham

Details of the game are scarce, but the *Atlanta Daily World* said about 5,000 turned out, and that Roy Partlow "limited the Giants to four hits" in the first game "although his wildness in the seventh and eighth innings came near wrecking him. The Grays socked three twirlers for 14 hits."[31] The four starters were not named, but Partlow started the first game for Homestead and Lefty Phillips started the second for the Elite Giants. The games were also previewed in the *Birmingham News* in a fairly lengthy story on April 24 and again on the 29th, the latter article staying that "Willys" (Jim Willis) and Porter (Andy Porter) were expected to be the two pitchers for the Nashville Elite Giants.[32]

May 7, 1939: Baltimore Elite Giants 6, Kansas City Monarchs 4; Baltimore Elite Giants 17, Kansas City Monarchs 3, at Sulphur Dell Park, Nashville[33]

In a story datelined Nashville, the *Chicago Defender* reported that "the Nashville Elites" handed the Monarchs "a licking." It noted that the "first game was played in a drizzle of rain" but that 3,000 "braved the weather" to attend.[34] Byrd pitched the first game for the Elites. While it's likely that more than one pitcher worked the second game, there was no box score or other indication who the losing pitchers might have been nor why the second game was so lopsided.

May 13, 1939: The *Philadelphia Inquirer* listed a game for that afternoon at the 44th and Parkside ballpark – Parkside Athletic Field – between Bolden's Stars and the Baltimore Elite Giants, but if the game was actually played, no trace of it has been found.[35]

Regular season

The day before the season got underway, the *Baltimore Afro-American* devoted more than an inch or two of coverage for the first time, noting that the 1938 NNL championship team would open at Oriole Park (Twenty-Ninth and Greenmount) against the league's "next best team," the Homestead Grays.[36]

Manager (and third baseman) Felton Snow had "virtually the same combination doing chores for him that worked for

Tom Wilson's crew, last year" – naming catcher Biz Mackey, second baseman Sammy Hughes, shortstop Hoss Walker, first baseman Jim West, center fielder Henry Kimbro, and right fielder Wild Bill Wright. Bill Byrd had held the Monarchs to six hits and was expected as starting pitcher. Bill Hoskins had played a bit at the end of the 1939 season but was seen as a relatively new face, playing left field as the closest the team had to a newcomer (new enough that he was called "Jimmie" Hoskins in the newspaper).

Taking on the Grays would be a challenging way to kick off the new season. Homestead had topped the league in 1937, and then won the "world's championship" from the Chicago American Giants. In 1938 they had been runners-up to the Elites.

There was to be a pregame "ceremony" in which "sports editors from the local papers, daily and weekly, will engage in a pitch, catch, bat and umpire scene."[37]

May 14, 1939: Homestead Grays 7, Baltimore Elite Giants 1; Homestead Grays 11, Baltimore Elite Giants 0 (six innings), at Oriole Park, Baltimore

The first day of championship season play for the Elite Giants got off to a depressing start when they played two home games and managed to score only one run. As the *Chicago Defender* said, the Elites "took it on the chin twice."[38] They had been scheduled to play the first game of the regular season in Philadelphia against the Stars on May 13, but rain prevented that.

The lone run they scored came in the bottom of the first inning of the first game. They were already facing a two-run deficit, the Grays having scored twice off Byrd. Roy Partlow was pitching for Homestead. Felton Snow doubled off the wall in right field and Wild Bill Wright singled to bring him home. Pitching for Homestead was Ray Partlow. He allowed only five hits. Bill Byrd pitched for Baltimore and was no mystery, giving up 16 hits. First baseman Buck Leonard was 4-for-4 in the first game. Also hitting for the Grays was center fielder Benjamin Gray, 3-for-5 with a single, double, and triple.

Left-hander Edsall Walker pitched for the Grays in the six-inning second game, and threw a two-hit shutout, a single by Hoskins and a single off the bat of pitcher Emery Adams. Walker struck out eight. Leonard started the scoring, homering his first time up, hitting the ball over the wall and "on the housetops adjacent to right-field."[39] Josh Gibson had doubled and scored on Leonard's home run. In the fourth inning, Gibson hit a two-run homer over the wall in left, driving in Sam Bankhead. The Elites used four pitchers in the six innings – Johnny "Slim" Johnson, Adams, Tom Glover, and Lefty Phillips.

May 17, 1939: Lloyd A.C. 3, Nashville-Baltimore Elite Giants 1, at Lloyd Athletic Field, Chester, Pennsylvania

The Lloyd semipro club's Johnny Holstein gave up one run in the top of the first. Kimbro hit a slow roller to second and the fielder's throw went wild, resulting in Kimbro perched at second with nobody out. Felton Snow lined a ball over the right-field wall; it was scored a ground-rule double. There was no further

scoring in the game until the bottom of the sixth inning, with Lefty Glover pitching for the Elite Giants. Snow's triple in the third counted for naught, as the Lloyd men worked their way out of trouble. In the top of the sixth, the Giants got two singles and a double and failed to score. Bill Wright was picked off first after the first single. Sammy Hughes doubled but was thrown out at the plate after a player named Williams singled.[40] In the home seventh, Holstein walked. Their center fielder hit one off Glover's glove for a hit. The next batter walked and the bases were loaded with nobody out. Biz Mackey replaced Glover with right-hander Johnny Johnson. Lloyd's left fielder grounded out, second to first, and the tying run scored. First baseman Worm Wearshing got his third base hit of the game, singling to center and driving in two more. The local newspaper called it "one of the greatest baseball games ever played in this area."[41]

May 20, 1939: Scheduled Sunday 3:00 P.M. game against the Newark Eagles at Dunn Field, Trenton, New Jersey, rained out

One can draw one's own conclusions about the meaning behind the wording, but the next day's *Trenton Evening Times* article noting the rainout advised readers that rainchecks would be "good for any future Negro loop game here."[42]

May 21, 1939: Newark Eagles 4, Baltimore Elite Giants 0; Newark Eagles 4, Baltimore Elite Giants 3 (seven innings), at Ruppert Stadium, Newark

The Elites started their season 0-4 by dropping another doubleheader, this one on the road in Newark. Nineteen-year-old Jimmie Hill threw a two-hitter for the Eagles in the first game, and in the second "a late-inning rally upset the dope."[43] The game was scoreless through seven innings. Bill Byrd pitched for the Elite Giants and allowed only seven hits, but the Eagles bunched some together and, in part due to an error by Hughes, scored four runs in the bottom of the eighth. The first run came after Hill singled, was sacrificed to second, then reached third and home on successive errors.[44] The lone base hits for Baltimore were by Snow and Hughes. The game drew 5,000 fans. Byrd was said to have been pitching "under the evident pain of a sprained ankle [but] carried on like a Spartan and deserve a better fate."[45]

Falling behind 2-0 in the first inning of the second game, Eagles pitcher James Brown took over from Jesse Brown and held the Elites to one more run while Newark scored three times. Johnny Johnson started for Baltimore and Emery Adams took over at some point.[46] Newark scored twice in the bottom of the second, adding another run later on. The Giants tied the score in the top of the ninth on a triple by Bright and a single by Hoskins, but pinch-hitter Johnny Hayes doubled for the Eagles and Jesse Brown drove him in with the winning run. It is unclear who "Bright" may have been – presumably Bill Wright.[47]

It is interesting to see a breakdown of the attendance at the May 21 game, showing the number of seats sold in each price category, as reported by the Newark Baseball Club.[48]

The Elite Giants were supposed to play a game on May 22, also at Chester, against the Philadelphia Stars, according to that morning's edition of the *Chester Times*. See "League Game at Lloyd Tonight," on page 15, but the official NNL report indicates that the game was rained out.[49]

May 26, 1939: R.D. Wood club 9, Baltimore Elite Giants 8, at Florence Township, New Jersey

The Wood club, known as the Pipemakers, were losing 7-3 in the sixth inning but rallied to beat Phillips. Snow was 3-for-5. The newspaper informed readers that "Williams socked a homer for the Negroes."[50]

May 27, 1939: Baltimore Elite Giants 5, New York Black Yankees 1; Baltimore Elite Giants 2, New York Black Yankees 1, at Parkside Athletic Field, Philadelphia[51]

One would think it would be possible to find more information about a relatively high-profile doubleheader such as this one, but despite the combined efforts of a number of SABR researchers, we have been unable to do so.

May 28, 1939: New York Black Yankees 10, Baltimore Elite Giants 8; New York Black Yankees 3, Baltimore Elite Giants 1 (second game, five innings), at Oriole Park, Baltimore

The *Baltimore Evening Sun* had written on May 25 that the Elite Giants team – which it said was being managed by Felton Snow – would be joined by two new pitchers, Sam Woodrow from Nashville and Cliff Johnson from Memphis. Neither is listed on Seamheads.[52]

Starting pitchers in the first game were Bill Byrd for Baltimore and Roy K. Williams for the Black Yankees. The first inning saw New York score four times (three of them on a home run over the wall in right-center by left fielder Alex Brooks) and Baltimore score three. New York added two more unmatched runs in the top of the second. Brooks homered again in the fifth, a solo homer that increased their lead to 7-3. Baltimore scored once in the fifth. In the top of the seventh, Brooks doubled and right fielder Zollie Wright homered. The Elites got two more runs in the seventh on solo home runs by Bill Wright and Biz Mackey. Brooks drove in the Black Yankees' 10th run in the top of the ninth, singling in Goose Curry. The Elites scored twice in the bottom of the ninth, the third out coming with the potential tying runs on base.[53]

Alex Brooks was clearly New York's star in the first game with two homers, a double, and a triple in a 4-for-5 game.[54]

The second game saw the Elites score first, with one run off New York starter Neck Stanley in the bottom of the second. Campanella ("Campanelli" even in the hometown *Afro-American*) beat out an infield hit, stole second, and scored when Hoss Walker singled to center field. It was their only run of the game. Jim Holland took over from Stanley and allowed only three hits in the remaining five innings. Emery Adams started for Baltimore and lost, giving up two hits and one run in the third, fourth, and fifth innings. The only extra-base hit of the game was a fourth-inning double by Yankees catcher Bob Clarke.[55]

May 30, 1939: Baltimore Elite Giants 11, New York Black Yankees 3; New York Black Yankees 14, Baltimore Elite Giants 5, at Dexter Park, New York

The *Brooklyn Daily Eagle* was still referring to the out-of-towners as the Nashville Elite Giants. Some 7,000 came to the games. Glover started the first game, with Byrd coming in near the end and contributing a home run to the cause.[56] Each team scored once in the first. The Elites scored once more in the second and two in the seventh. The Black Yankees made it 4-2 with one run in the bottom of the eighth, but then the Elites exploded for seven runs in the top of the ninth, putting the game pretty much out of sight. New York scored a third run in the bottom of the ninth but that was it.[57] At some point during the first game, catcher Roy Campanella of the "Nashville E. Giants" was ejected and a 15-minute argument followed, with the "Nashville Club … almost threatening to leave."[58] Campanella did catch in the second game.

The Black Yankees turned the tables completely in the second game. Though the Elites scored once in the top of the first, the Black Yankees scored six times in their half of the first and added four more in the second. Pitching for the visitors were four men: Lefty Phillips, Johnny Johnson, Willis, and Emery Adams. New York took a 12-1 lead in the fourth. The Giants scored four runs in the top of the fifth, and the Black Yankees answered with two more of their own. Terris McDuffie pitched the full game for New York. Black Yankees first baseman John Washington was the star on offense, going 4-for-4 with three doubles.

June 2, 1939: Nashville-Baltimore Elite Giants 14, Lloyd A.C. 1, at Lloyd Athletic Field, Chester, Pennsylvania

In a sequel to the May 17 game, the Elite Giants (still bearing the two-city name in the Chester paper) exacted revenge on both Holstein and the Lloyd semipros. First up was Kimbro, and Holstein struck him out – but before the inning was over the Giants scored four times. Sammy Hughes led off with a double to center. Wright singled to left, scoring Hughes. West singled past second base, and Wright scored. The scoring had begun.[59]

After three innings and eight runs, Holstein gave way to a reliever. Three Lloyd pitchers gave up 17 hits and 14 runs. Eight of the hits were doubles, with Hughes doubling three times. Playing with ground rules that a ball hit over the right-field wall was a two-base hit, Hughes had hit two of his doubles out of the park. A ball hit over the wall in right-center, however, was a home run and Hoskins picked up one of each – the first out-of-the-park home run at the field in 1939 (a two-run homer in the fourth, as well as a double in the first and two singles later, finishing with four RBIs.)

Tom Glover pitched the first three innings for the Elites, with both Adams and Phillips getting in some work as well.

The lone Lloyd run came in the first, off Glover, on a single, a stolen base, and a double off the left-field fence by Wearshing.

June 4, 1939: Baltimore Elite Giants 7, New York Cubans 3, at Yankee Stadium, New York

There was a four-team doubleheader at Yankee Stadium planned at Yankee Stadium, with New York Lieutenant Governor Charles Poletti scheduled to throw out the first pitch.[60] The games were meant to be the first of a series of 10 games for the Jake Ruppert Trophy. The doubleheader drew a reported 12,500.

In the first game. the Elites looked to be letting the game get away from them early on, Byrd giving up one run in the second and two more in the third. Then Byrd clamped down and saw his teammates score one in the fourth, one in the seventh, three in the eighth (a three-run homer by Byrd himself in the eighth, off Luis Tiant), and another two runs in the top of the ninth. Hoskins was 4-for-5 in the game, all doubles.[61] The *New York Age* reporting varied, saying that right fielder "Babe" Hoskins had three doubles and a triple, that "Dick" Byrd and Kimbro had homered for the two runs in the ninth.[62] The *Pittsburgh Courier* provided what might be deemed the most reliable account. It agreed that Byrd and Kimbro had homered in the ninth, both drives into the right-field stands. It ascribed the three-run rally in the eighth to a double by Snow, a single by Wright, a double by Hoskins, and a single by Jim West. It accorded Hoskins two doubles and a 405-foot triple.[63]

The *Baltimore Afro-American* shows a score of 7-3 with the box score in agreement. The June 5 *Philadelphia Inquirer*, in a simple listing of independent game scores on page 18, reported the score as 7-2. The *New York Daily News* reported the score as 8-4 on page 42 of the June 5 edition, showing an entirely different line score and stating that the pitching matchup was Byrd vs. Diaz (not Tiant). Seamheads shows no Diaz on the 1939 Cubans roster. No one by that name appears in any of the other newspaper accounts. There is a good chance that "Diaz" in the *Daily News* is a simple mistake for "Tiant" – perhaps a name that was misheard. The line score in the *Daily News* showed:

Baltimore Elites 001 203 020 8 13 1

New York Cubans 120 000 010 4 11 1

The *New York Amsterdam News* gives the Cubans four runs, but describes only the scoring of three runs – and its account of the scoring gives two runs scored to Casey and one to Vargas, but the box score gives one run scored each to Vargas, Caraballo, Casey, and Rodríguez.[64] Dan Burley's reporting was the most detailed. His game story also agreed that both Byrd and Kimbro had homered in the ninth – but the newspaper's box score may have come up short. It credited Byrd with a homer but not Kimbro. The box score did credit Hoskins with three doubles and a triple. All in all, the reporting of this game – held in a high-profile ballpark – perhaps provides a lesson in the problem of researching and presenting reliable information on Negro Leagues games of the era.

The second game was to feature the Philadelphia Stars and the New York Black Yankees.

June 5, 1939: Baltimore Elite Giants vs. Norristown Pros, at Norristown, Pennsylvania

The morning's *Philadelphia Inquirer* announced a 6 P.M. game for that day at Norristown, Pennsylvania between the Elite Giants and the Norristown Pros.[65] No subsequent coverage has been found.

June 8, 1939: Baltimore Elite Giants 12, Philadelphia Stars 9, at Penmar Park, Philadelphia

Both teams used three pitchers in this high-scoring game. If we understand the box score to show the pitchers in sequence, Adams, then Gaines, and finally Byrd pitched for Baltimore while the Stars used Thompson, Ellis, and McDonald. The Elites outhit the Stars by what looks like 16-9. The big inning for Baltimore was the top of the third, in which they overcame the 2-0 lead the Stars had put up in the second. Baltimore scored six runs in the third, adding one in the fifth, three in the sixth, and two in the seventh. Hughes and Mackey both had four-hit games, while Wright got three hits. Hoskins, Rivera, and Adams each got two hits. The number of errors is not shown in the *New York Amsterdam News* box score nor is the number of walks, but one way or another Snow scored twice without benefit of a base hit.

The newspaper complained that it was unable to even report the scores of some league games "due to the fact that the teams are still dilatory about getting such information to the sports writers."[66]

Penmar Park was located at 44th and Parkside Avenue, Philadelphia. The *Philadelphia Inquirer* routinely referred to it as Parkside Athletic Field.

June 10, 1939: Baltimore Elite Giants 4, Homestead Grays 2; Homestead Grays 5, Baltimore Elite Giants 2 (six innings), at Forbes Field, Pittsburgh

Gaines pitched the first game for the Elites, allowing eight hits but only two runs, one in the second inning and one in the bottom of the ninth. Baltimore had scored first, with one in the top of the first. They added one in the fourth and two more in the top of the ninth – the two runs that made the difference. Felton Snow had three of the Giants' 10 base hits. Wright homered over the left-field wall for the Elites.

The second game was cut short by a thunderstorm after 5½ innings. Johnson pitched for Baltimore. The Grays scored three runs off Glover in the bottom of the first, and after the Elites scored two in the top of the second, Homestead added a fourth run off reliever Johnny Johnson for good measure in the bottom of the second. Their fifth run scored in the bottom of the fifth. For the Grays, Roy Partlow lost the first game and Specs Roberts won the second.[67]

June 11, 1939: Baltimore Elite Giants 4, Homestead Grays 3; Homestead Grays 13, Baltimore Elite Giants 8 (seven innings), at Red Bird Stadium, Columbus, Ohio

The *Columbus Evening Dispatch* wrote that "Bill Byrd, a Columbus boy, defeated the Grays in the opener, 4-3, and Ray Brown upset the Giants in the nightcap, 13-8."[68] The paper had said of his team, "The Elites formerly represented Columbus in league ball."[69] The *Pittsburgh Post-Gazette* presented line scores showing Byrd and Mackey as the winning battery in the 4-3 first game. Neither team had scored through the first five. The Elites scored once off Homestead's Edsall Walker in the top of the sixth, but the Grays came right back with two in the bottom of the inning. Baltimore put up two more runs in the seventh, then added a fourth run in the top of the ninth. The Grays scored once in the bottom of the ninth.

The seven-inning second game was pretty much put out of sight right away in the bottom of the first inning as Homestead scored nine runs off pitcher "J. Graves" – perhaps Jonas Gaines. They added a 10th run in the second and two more in the third. The Elites are shown getting two runs in the second and one in the third, then scoring four in the top of the seventh. Ray Brown was pitching for the Grays. The final score would appear to be 13-7 per the line score, but the *Post-Gazette's* one-sentence summary of the doubleheader gave the final score as 13-8.[70]

June 12, 1939: Baltimore Elite Giants 7, Homestead Grays 3, at Perry Stadium, Indianapolis

"Like a ship at sea without the stellar services of Josh Gibson, the Grays floundered around in a sea of mud trying to stem the tide."[71] The Grays were without Josh Gibson in the lineup due to a bruised hip, and it may have cost them. Homestead's battery was left-hander Willie Ferrell pitching to Robert Gaston. Emery Adams pitched solid ball for the Giants, striking out 11. Biz Mackey worked behind the plate.

The weather was chilly and only a few hundred came out to Perry Stadium.

With this win, the *New Journal and Guide* wrote, "Baltimore came to life and defeated the preseason favorite Grays, 3 out of 5 games."[72]

June 13, 1939: The *Dayton* (Ohio) *Herald* said that the Homestead Grays and Baltimore Elite Giants would be playing at Wings Park at 8:15 that evening. Ray Brown, Dayton native, was to pitch for the Grays. Wet grounds caused cancellation of the game.

June 14, 1939: The *Bluefield* (West Virginia) *Daily Telegraph* on June 11 ran a note that the Homestead Garys would meet the Baltimore Elite Giants in what it said was a "National colored league baseball game" at Welch, West Virginia, on Wednesday the 14th at 8:15 P.M.[73] We could find no indication that the game ever occurred.

June 15, 1939: Baltimore Elite Giants 2, Homestead Grays 1, at Kanawha Park, Charleston, West Virginia

The game was a true pitchers' duel, with Gaines giving up just one run on three hits while Homestead's lefty Edsall Walker allowed but five. The Giants scored twice in the top of the first inning, the key hit a triple by Byrd. Campanella ("Campello" in the *Charleston Gazette*) was Gaines's catcher.[74] Both the *Gazette* and the *Charleston Daily Mail* offered line scores showing the Giants scoring two in the first and the Grays scoring one in the bottom of the second and one in the bottom of the third, agreeing that the score was, nevertheless, 2-1. One has to assume that the Grays scored in only one of those two innings, but we don't know which. Gaines struck out six and only walked one.[75]

June 18, 1939: Newark Eagles 8, Baltimore Elite Giants 1; Newark Eagles 2, Baltimore Elite Giants 0, at Oriole Park, Baltimore

As he had when the two teams had met in Newark back on May 21, Jim Hill pitched a very solid game for the Eagles, this one a nine-hitter for an 8-1 win. He even collected two hits at the plate, but the batting star was the Eagles' Monte Irvin, who was 5-for-5 with two doubles and three singles. In his Newark debut, Max Manning shut out the Elites, 2-0, on four hits. The two Newark runs came on a two-run homer over the right-field wall by Mule Suttles.[76] For the Elite Giants, swept again, Bill Byrd pitched the first game, and Emery Adams the second.[77]

June 19, 1939: Baltimore Elite Giants 17, Newark Eagles 6, at Mayo Island Park, Richmond, Virginia

For the 8:30 P.M. game at Mayo Island Park (also known as Tate Field), there was to be a "special section reserved for white spectators."[78]

Lefty Glover pitched for the Elites and had a "masterful" game going until he hit the ninth inning, when he gave up six runs and was relieved by Slim Johnson.[79]

The next day's *Richmond News-Leader* reported the score as 17-6. It said that Glover pitched for Baltimore and that someone named Stone, the Giants shortstop, hit a three-run homer over the left-field fence in the fifth. There were reportedly 37 hits in the game, 21 for Baltimore and 16 for Newark.[80]

The *Baltimore Afro-American* reported the score as 17-7 but also said that the Elites had lost two to the Eagles in Baltimore (even though the games were played in Newark).

The *Newark Evening News* also reported a score of 17-7, in a brief article datelined Baltimore. It said the Giants had 21 base hits and had jumped out to an 8-0 lead in the very first inning. Five of Newark's runs came in the ninth.[81]

Lastly, the *Norfolk* (Virginia) *New Journal and Guide* reported the score as 17-6. (With the two Virginia newspapers agreeing on that score, it is the one we have used here.) It agreed on the eight runs scored (on six hits) by the Giants in the first inning. The Eagles got one run in the third, but the Giants responded, adding five more runs in the bottom of the third, the last three on a homer by Snow. They added a 14th run on the fourth on a hit, error, walk, and fielder's choice, and then added two more runs in the fifth inning on three hits and two walks. The 17th run came in the seventh on another walk and three base hits. The Eagles scored one in the eighth, finally putting together six base hits for four runs in the top of the ninth.[82]

June 20, 1939: The June 20 *Philadelphia Inquirer* reported that the Homestead Grays would play the Baltimore Elite Giants that evening at 9:00 at Parkside Athletic Field. It said that another game featuring a team called the All-Phillies would be rescheduled "to allow the Elites and Grays to play this affair while they are both in the East before the League's first half schedule is completed on July 4."[83] Three days earlier, the *Norfolk New Journal and Guide* reported that the Newark Eagles and Elite Giants would be playing in Baltimore on June 20 and 21.[84] Did Baltimore actually play either team – or maybe someone else – on June 20? We have been unable to answer the question.

June 21, 1939: Chevrolet Red Sox 3, Elite Giants 2, at Eastside Park, Paterson, New Jersey

On page 24, the June 21 *Philadelphia Inquirer* listed a 6:00 P.M. game for that evening at Paterson, New Jersey, between the Nashville Elite Giants and Jamieson's Red Sox. Jack Eelman was the pitcher for the Red Sox (who had a second baseman named Paterson). He held the Elite Giants to eight hits and allowed just one run in the sixth and another in the ninth. Johnny Johnson pitched for the Giants and surrendered two in the bottom of the first inning – on a single, double, infield out, and another single. A walk and a triple by the local center fielder scored the third run. How the Elite Giants scored was not documented in the *Paterson Evening News*, though it was reported that West and Wright each drove in a run.[85]

June 22: On page 31, the *Philadelphia Inquirer* listed a 9:00 P.M. game for that evening between the Baltimore Elite Giants and the Philadelphia Stars, at Parkside Athletic Field. This is, however, another one of the games which we have been unable to determine whether it was ever played. In each such case, we tracked weather reports to see if rain might have been a reason for such an announced game not to have been played. It was not.

June 23, 1939: Nashville Elite Giants 6, Red Bank Pirates 4, at Pirate Park, Red Bank, New Jersey

The June 22 *Red Bank Daily Standard* reported that the Nashville Elite Giants would be playing the Red Bank Pirates (a team of White semipros) the following evening at Pirate field on Newman Springs Road. The Pirates – apparently also known as the Bay Parkways – were going for their eighth straight win. The Elite Giants was to be their "first colored team of the season."[86]

Neither team scored for the first four innings. Pitching for the Elite Giants was "Burd." They took a 1-0 lead in the fourth when Snow walked, "Revere" (Rivera) sacrificed, and "Capanilla" (Campanella) singled. Three hits in the fifth gave them another

run. The Pirates got one back. The visitors scored one more run in the sixth and four in the seventh, then held on to win.[87]

The team was apparently not hitting that well. The June 24 *Michigan Chronicle* reported a team batting average of .174, led by Bill Hoskins at .280 and B. Wright at .250. The only other two with averages of over .200 were Byrd at .222 and Snow at .207.[88]

June 25, 1939: Bushwicks 4, Nashville Elite Giants 3; Bushwicks 9, Nashville Elite Giants 8 (13 innings), at Dexter Park, Brooklyn

The 11,000 fans who came to the Sunday doubleheader at Dexter Park were treated to two very close games. In the first game, the Elite Giants scored all three of their runs in the first inning, and though Big Jim Peterson allowed 14 hits in all, "the powerful Negro hitters were unable to register after the first frame."[89] All the hits were singles except a double by Snow. Gaines started for the Giants, with Adams and Byrd pitching later. It is unclear whom the Bushwicks victimized in the bottom of the sixth when they scored all four of their runs, for a come-from-behind 4-3 victory built on a single, double, three walks, and a single. Notable in the first game was Wright, who singled three times in succession on bunts.

The second game saw the lead go back and forth a bit. The Bushwicks scored one in the bottom of the first. The Giants scored three in the top of the third. In the fourth, the home team scored seven times, but the Giants scored four runs in the seventh. (A bases-clearing triple by Hughes was the big hit.) There was controversy on a close play during the big inning, disputed by Bushwicks first baseman Mack West, who was ejected for "profane language." Angered fans spilled onto the field as did "pop bottles, beer bottles and milk bottles." It was a "near riot" that held up the game for 10 or 15 minutes before police quieted things down.[90]

The Elites tied it, 8-8, with a run in the top of the ninth. Neither team scored until the bottom of the 13th when a single, sacrifice, and single did the visitors in.[91] Pitching for the Elites had been Glover, and then appearances by both Adams and, for the last few innings, Gaines. Gaines actually walked the bases loaded in the bottom of the 10th but bore down. In the 13th, a single, sacrifice, and two-out single won the game.

June 26, 1939: Nashville Elite Giants 6, Springfield Greys 4, at Sherwood Oval, Springfield Gardens, Long Island, New York

A night game saw Springfield starter Freddy Swift hold the Elite Giants (listed as Nashville in both the *Mount Vernon Argus* and the *Long Island Daily Press*) to single runs in the second and third innings – and both of those were unearned runs. Greys players committed five errors in all, three by outfielders. Tom Glover started for the Giants. He gave up two runs in the third and the game remained tied 2-2 through six. Though Swift struck out nine, the Giants took a 6-2 lead with three in the seventh and another in the eighth, but the Greys made it close in the bottom of the ninth. A double and an RBI single scored one. A pinch-hit Texas Leaguer put runners on second and third. Emery Adams relieved Glover. He struck out the first batter he faced, then secured a second out on an infield play that allowed another run to score from third. He then walked the next two Greys, loading the bases with two outs and the potential tying run on second. Jonas Gaines took over from Adams – the third Giants pitcher of the inning. A groundout to second base ended the game.[92]

June 27, 1939: Baltimore Elite Giants 12, Cleveland Bears 0; Baltimore Elite Giants 6, Cleveland Bears 1, at Oriole Park, Baltimore

One might think that sweeping a doubleheader at home would prompt at least a mention in the *Baltimore Afro-American*, there was no mention at all. The paper did, however, print league standings for the first time, showing the Elite Giants in fourth place with a record of 9-11.[93] A previous issue of the paper had included American League standings (Negro American League) but not the NNL. The reporting of these results came originally from the Negro League Researchers & Authors Group, but with no sources attached. We could find no source for this doubleheader, nor could Seamheads. It's possible there was a mixup and it came from some other part of the season or even a different season entirely.

June 27, 1939: Philadelphia Stars 11, Baltimore Elite Giants 4, at Forty-fourth and Parkside, Philadelphia

Three games in one day? The *Chicago Defender* said the Elites had played another game that same night, Tuesday June 27, at Forty-fourth and Parkside in Philadelphia, that "Byrd was on the mound for the losers and allowed 14 hits. Wellmark, Ellis and Thompson hurled for the Stars."[94]

The starters were left-hander Roy Welmaker for the Stars and Bill Byrd for the Elites. Baltimore scored one in the first inning and once in the second, then saw the Stars tie it, 2-2, in the bottom of the second. Neither team scored in the third or fourth but the Elites got two more in the fifth, the Stars responding with just one. After a scoreless sixth, it was the seventh inning when Baltimore blew the game open with six runs. Relieving for the Stars were both Rocky Ellis and Sam Thompson. The Elites added an 11th run in the top of the ninth, and the Stars got their fourth and final run off Byrd in the bottom of the ninth. Baltimore outhit Philadelphia, but only by 14 to 9. It looked as though Byrd was keeping the ball in the infield. First baseman Wright recorded 11 putouts, with catcher Mackey only three. Elites outfielders recorded only five putouts total. Wright was 3-for-5 and Hughes 3-for-5. Kimbro, Rivera, and Byrd each had a pair of base hits.[95] Both Mackey and West appeared in the game, in what was perhaps the last appearance for both with the team. (See July 9 entry.)

June 28, 1939: Baltimore Elite Giants 4, Manheim Barons 3, at Fruitville Pike diamond, Lancaster, Pennsylvania

Johnson pitched for the Elites. A three-run third inning gave Manheim a one-run lead, but the Elites' Hughes got on and Jim West drove him in with a double to left-center, then scored himself on a single by Rivera, giving them back the lead, which they held. The game drew about 900.[96]

June 29, 1939: Alcyon All-Stars, at Alcyon Park, Pitman, New Jersey

A planned game was announced in the *Bridgeton* (New Jersey) *Evening News* but neither the Gloucester County Historical Society, the Pitman Memorabilia Museum, nor two local libraries were able to find any trace of the game being played.

June 30, 1939: An announced night game to be held at Queens Park between the Nashville Elite Giants and the Queens Club was washed out by rain.[97]

July 1, 1939: Baltimore Elite Giants 8, Newark Eagles 4, at Newark, New Jersey

The *New Jersey Herald News* reported that the Elites had come to town on Saturday and knocked Newark out of first place with an 8-4 win. They had held a 4-0 lead until two homers by Eagles Monte Irvin and Ed Stone evened the score at 4-4, but the Elites scored three in the seventh and another in the eighth, and earned the win. The papers provided no further information, such as the venue and who pitched for either team.[98]

July 2, 1939: Baltimore Elite Giants 4, New York Black Yankees 0, at Yankee Stadium, New York

Some 15,000 fans turned out for another doubleheader at Yankee Stadium. The league's first-place Newark Eagles easily beat the Philadelphia Stars, 8-1, in the first game. Jonas "Slim" Gaines shut out the New York Black Yankees in the second game, 4-0. He was in trouble a few times, with Black Yankees runners on the basepaths in five different innings, but held the line and kept them scoreless. Sammy Hughes doubled twice in the game and Felton Snow tripled.[99]

In the same day's *Afro-American*, skipper Felton Snow predicted that his team, which placed third in the first-half standings, had started to "hit its stride" – with the batters showing better at the plate – and looked to get off to a fast start in the second half.[100] There was no mention at all of splitting the doubleheader with the Homestead Grays four days before the publication date. Just to confuse matters, there was another Black baseball team called the Baltimore Giants (without the Elite moniker), a semipro team.[101]

July 3, 1939: Baltimore Elite Giants 9, Belmar Braves 5, at Memorial Field, Asbury Park, New Jersey

The July 3 *Asbury Park Press* reported on page 10 that the Belmar Braves would host the "Nashville Elite Giants" at 9:00 P.M. at Memorial Field with Byrd pitching for the Elites.[102] Two days later, the paper described them as "the Elite Giants, formerly of Nashville but now representing Baltimore."[103] The Giants collected 14 hits; their pitcher was actually Johnny Johnson, who surrendered nine. Byrd played right field. They scored one run in the first, two in the second, and three in the third, but then the progression stopped. They scored only one in the fourth.

Kimbro led off with a double off the right-field fence, then scored on Byrd's single. In the second inning, West and Snow both walked. Johnson singled, loading the bases. Two more walks, to Kimbro and Hughes, each forced in a run. With two down in the third, Snow singled. Rivera walked. Campanella "scorched" one off the third baseman's glove, driving in Snow. Johnson walked. Kimbro hit a two-run Texas Leaguer. The Braves came back with three in the bottom of the third. The Giants scored once in the fourth (Hoskins singled and Snow doubled), and then twice more in the top of the seventh – Snow singled, Campanella hit a ground-rule double, Johnson walked to load the bases, and Hughes singled in two. Campanella was 3-for-4 with two doubles.

July 4, 1939: Philadelphia Stars 6, Baltimore Elite Giants 1; Philadelphia Stars 6, Baltimore Elite Giants 3, at Parkside Athletic Field, Philadelphia

This was a 1:30 P.M. doubleheader at Parkside Athletic Field. The next day's *Philadelphia Inquirer* reported the Stars winning 6-1 and then 6-3 in the second game.[104]

The *Chicago Defender* reported a July 4 doubleheader but in reverse order, with the Stars beating the Elite Giants 6-3 and 6-1, with the winning pitchers being Henry McHenry and Jim Missouri over Emery Adams and Willie Hubert.[105]

The season's halfway point

July 4 was the end of the NNL's first half. The Elites were in third place with a 12-13 record, despite losing seven consecutive games at one point. The standings were:

Homestead Grays (23-7)
Newark Eagles (18-6)
Baltimore Elite Giants (12-13)
New York Black Yankees (9-11)
Philadelphia Stars (15-20)
Toledo Crawfords (3-11)
New York Cubans (3-15)[106]

July 5, 1939: game at Chester, Pennsylvania, postponed

The visitors returned to play Lloyd a third time. With 1,500 fans present, impending threatening weather resulted in cancellation at the game at 5:00, only for the weather to suddenly become sunny half an hour after it was called off.[107]

BASEBALL TONIGHT
RED BANK PIRATES
Vs.
NASHVILLE ELITE GIANTS
Game Called 9 P. M.
Bleachers 35c   Boxes 66c   Grandstand 40c
Newman Springs Road   Red Bank
FOR RESERVATIONS CALL R. B. 2009

Advertisement from July 7 *Daily Record* (Long Branch, New Jersey).

July 7, 1939: Nashville Elite Giants 6, Red Bank Pirates 0, at Pirate Park, Red Bank, New Jersey

It was back to Red Bank once more for a 9:00 P.M. game on Friday, July 7. The semipro Pirates suffered their first shutout of the season. Johnny Johnson went the distance for the "strong colored team," allowing just six hits.[108] "Burd" played right field. The Elites scored two in the first and two in the second, then two more in the seventh. Kimbro walked leading off both the first and the second. Hoskins singled in the first run, and West's fly out produced the second run. Bird drove in both second-inning runs with a double. The Elites got only five hits. The runs in the seventh scored on an error, a hit-by-pitch, a passed ball, a walk, and a run-scoring double play. It was a rough day for Hughes, who was hit twice by pitches and also was spiked while fielding at second base. One of the players for the Pirates was one-armed outfielder Pete Gray, who played for the 1945 St. Louis Browns. Mal Allen notes, "Not only did Pete Gray play, he was the only opponent with an extra-base hit or more than one hit. Batting second and playing CF, he went 2-for-4 with a double. His third-inning drive hit the CF fence and he was thrown out trying for a triple. The Red Bank Pirates played in the Metropolitan League."[109]

July 8, 1939: Baltimore Elite Giants 10, Philadelphia Stars 2; Baltimore Elite Giants 5, Philadelphia Stars 4, at Penmar Park, Philadelphia

The visitors won the first game with ease. The Stars scored first with one run in the bottom of the first. In the top of the fourth, however, according to the *Philadelphia Inquirer*, "Buzz Mackery" hit a three-run homer. The Stars made it 3-2 with a second run in the bottom of the fourth, but the Giants kept scoring, with two in the sixth, another in the seventh, and then four runs (largely due to a three-run homer by West) in the top of the ninth. It was not indicated in the *Inquirer* who pitched for either team.[110] Fortunately, the *Chicago Defender* offered a box score and one can see that the pitchers were Byrd for the Giants and Jim Missouri for the Stars.[111] The *Norfolk New Journal and Guide* of July 15 says the scores were 6-2 and 5-4 – but a guess is that they were simply just wrong as to the first-game score.

In the second game, again the Stars scored once in the first. Glover and Willie Hubert both pitched for the Giants. They tied it in the third, but the Stars took a 3-1 lead in the fourth. In the sixth, the Giants scored twice, tying the game. It was a seven-inning second game. In the top of the final inning, the Giants scored twice, first on an RBI single by West (Kimbro and Hoskins had apparently both singled before him), and then on a fly ball by third baseman "Don Riberia" – who we can safely guess was Charlie Rivera. The Stars got one run back in the bottom of the inning, but still came up one run short.[112]

July 9, 1939: Baltimore Elite Giants 24, Philadelphia Stars 6; Baltimore Elite Giants 9, Philadelphia Stars 0 (forfeit), at Oriole Park, Baltimore

The Elite Giants had executed a major trade before this twin bill, and four of five new players took part in this doubleheader win. The team had shed (or was reported in the process of shedding) Biz Mackey, Hoss Walker, and Jim West. They thought they were picking up Chester Williams from the Stars, though that didn't happen. West did wind up with the Stars. Mackey was said to be becoming a free agent (the following week's paper said he was traded to the Newark Eagles). What would happen to Walker was a "matter of conjecture … as no club had indicated a willingness to purchase the infielder."[113] Two players were coming from the Atlanta Black Crackers: James "Red" Moore to play first base and Tommy "Pee Wee" Butts to play shortstop. Snow played shortstop until Butts was ready.

Hughes had been out with a spike wound, was expected back in the second half, and Snow himself was going to resume playing third base in place of Charlie Rivera at third base. Replacing Mackey as catcher was young Leroy Campanella with Oscar Boone as backup catcher.[114] Two new pitchers were said to be joining the team: Ed Dixon and Felix Evans.[115]

The first game was something of a slaughter, with the Giants banging out 30 base hits off seven Philadelphia pitchers: Henry McHenry, Rocky Ellis, Webster McDonald, Purnell Mincy, Henry Miller, Jim Missouri, and first baseman Curtis "Popeye" Harris. Jonas Gaines pitched for Baltimore, holding the Stars to "eight well scattered blows."[116] Both Mackey and Wild Bill Wright homered for the Elites. West was 3-for-3 with two doubles. Kimbro and Wright were both said to have five hits apiece.

The score in the second game was 7-4 in favor of the Elite Giants when halted. Pitcher Felix Evans ("another newcomer to the Elite roster") was said to have started but been "shelled from the mound" by the Stars in the first inning, replaced by Emery Adams (called "Jimmie Adams" in the *Defender*).[117] Evans, Red Moore, and Pee Wee Butts were said to have all come over from the Atlanta Black Crackers. This may have been Evans's only appearance for the team. One sees Dixon pitching in a July 17 exhibition game.

In the game, the Elites scored four runs in the second inning. Felton Snow hit a solo homer in the third inning, and three singles combined led to two more runs in the fourth inning.[118]

There had apparently been a lot of complaining by the Stars regarding the ball-and-strike calls of umpire Fred McCrary in the first game. At the beginning of the fifth inning in the second game, with the Stars down 7-4, manager Jake Dunn "refused to permit his players to continue the fray, and injected every stalling ruse possible to delay the game." Dunn was hoping not to see the game become official (five innings), but McCrary "ruled the nightcap a forfeit."[119]

July 10, 1939: Baltimore Elite Giants 10, Trenton Senators 4, at Dunn Field, Trenton

The 9:00 P.M. exhibition game was played against the Class-C Inter-State League Trenton Senators (managed by Goose Goslin). It kicked off with an inside-the-park home run by Giants right fielder Bill Wright in the top of the first inning, giving Baltimore a 2-0 lead. Wright had three RBIs in the game. Someone named Davis (perhaps a local player, in order to spare the Giants the use of a starter in a nonchampionship game) pitched for Baltimore, which fell behind 3-2 in the bottom of the fifth inning, but rallied for five runs in the top of the sixth. They added one in the seventh and two more in the eighth. Snow, Hoskins, and Campanella all had doubles.[120]

July 12, 1939: Nashville Elite Giants 7, Poughkeepsie All-Stars 1, at Riverview Park, Poughkeepsie, New York

"Stars to Play Negroes Tonight" – so read a headline in the *Poughkeepsie Eagle-News*.[121] The game was to be a night game at Riverview Park between the Nashville Elite Giants. In the prior two years, they had beaten the local Poughkeepsie All-Stars 12-3 and 8-5. After beating the New York Black Yankees twice, the Elite Giants had "climbed into the position of being the top colored outfit in the country." The newspaper apparently did not figure out that the team was now from Baltimore.

It was an efficient 1 hour 27-minute game, remarked upon for its brevity, that in part due to Lefty Glover's three-hit pitching.[122] Boone caught Glover. The Elites scored three runs in the top of the first and two each in the sixth and seventh. Kimbro homered in the game.

July 13, 1939: Nashville Elite Giants 3, Farmers 2, at Freeport, Long Island

Emery Adams pitched most of the game, Gaines coming in near the end. All the scoring was done early – one in the second and two in the third by the Elites and single runs in the third and fifth by the Farmers. The *Brooklyn Daily Eagle* rendered Campanella as "Campbell."[123] One wonders if anyone remembered this when he was a three-time MVP with the Brooklyn Dodgers in 1951-55.

July 14, 1939: Springfield Greys 11, Baltimore Elite Giants 10, at Sherwood Oval, Springfield Gardens, New York

The *New York Times* said there would be a night game at the Oval on Merrick Road in Springfield Gardens, Long Island, between the Nashville Giants and the Springfield Greys.[124] The box score in the *Brooklyn Daily Eagle* described the Elite Giants as "Nashville." The Elites scored first, with one run in the top of the second. The Greys responded with two off starter Johnny Johnson. "Nashville" took the lead with two runs in the third, but the Greys promptly tied it with one. The Elites again scored two in the fourth, the Greys coming back with one. Down 5-4, the Greys took a 6-5 lead in the sixth. The Elites used a number of pitchers; Johnson walked four and hit a batter, Greys catcher Duay. After 4⅔ innings, someone named Barry Dixon relieved Johnson. Glover took over from Dixon for the eighth and Jonas Gaines pitched the ninth.

The Elites tied the game 6-6 in the eighth, then scored four runs in the top of the ninth. Springfield, however – with their backs to the wall – came back with five runs and walked off with an 11-10 victory.[125]

Gaines gave up a single to the first batter he faced, Eddie Boland, then walked the next two. He struck out the Greys' shortstop, but then hit catcher Duay, which produced the first run. Gaines then struck out a pinch-hitter, but walked the next batter, forcing in a second run. A single to right scored two more and tied the game. Another base on balls loaded the bases again. This brought up Boland for the second time in the inning. He walked, too, which forced in the winning run.[126]

The nine runs in the ninth were ascribed by one newspaper reader to "the rawest kind of umpiring ever perpetrated on any diamond."[127] The letter to the editor noted that the Giants didn't commit even one error and simply excoriated the pitch calling of plate umpire Bill Heck.

There had apparently been quite an uproar as "everything from pop bottles to seat cushions came flying onto the field. … At one time a number of fans took to the field, but when they saw the police, they were back to their seats. Some stayed and abused the umpires and several Greys ballplayers."[128]

July 15. 1939: Baltimore Elite Giants 12, New York Cubans 2, at Pennsy Field, Wilmington, Delaware

"The Nashville Elite Giants representing Baltimore in the National Negro Baseball League, scored a 12-2 win over the Cuban Stars in their loop game played at Pennsy Field on Saturday afternoon."[129] Thus read the complete coverage of the game in the *Wilmington Morning News*. It had been a 3:30 P.M. start, according to the previous day's paper, which said, "If today's game is well attended, several National Negro League games will be played here the remainder of the season."[130] One more Elite Giants game was played the following week.

A letter sent by Edward Gottlieb on August 5 under what passed for Negro National League stationery (the league name as typed at the top of the page) said that this game was – at least temporarily – taken out of league standings, per a protest by Alex Pompez of the Cubans that the two teams had agreed beforehand it was to be an exhibition game.[131]

July 16, 1939: New York Cubans 5, Baltimore Elite Giants 1; Baltimore Elite Giants 8, New York Cubans 3 (seven innings), at Oriole Park, Baltimore

Though the scores weren't particularly close, the two games in this Sunday doubleheader were described as "bitterly fought contests."[132] Though the visiting Cubans had won the opener, 5-1, they perhaps lost a chance to win the second game when

their second baseman, Antonio Rodriguez, was ejected from the game during the third inning. Baltimore's Bill Wright had been hit by a pitch thrown by Luis Tiant and knocked "groaning to the ground with a painful injury" but recovered and took first base. After Hoskins flied out to the catcher, Red Moore hit a "looping grounder" to second. Rodriguez leapt for the ball, snagged it, and believed he had tagged Wright, who was running toward second. Umpire Charles Cromwell ruled Wright safe. Rodriguez "lost his head and rushed straight to the arbiter with outstretched hands." Teammate Fermin Valdez, the shortstop, blocked Rodriguez and protected Cromwell, but umpire Pops Turner ejected Rodriguez.

Pitcher Bill Byrd drove in five runs and scored two in the game, in which he homered, doubled, and singled, going 3-for-3. In the third the Cubans had been ahead 2-0 when Moore and Snow singled and Byrd doubled to center to drove them both in and tie the score. In the fourth, his RBI single to left drove in Campanella with the go-ahead run. In the sixth, he homered over the wall in right field, scoring Rivera ahead of him. The ball cleared the bleachers and the wall behind by about four feet. Kimbro followed with a single and scored on a triple over third base by Hughes, who scored on an infield out by Adams.

The doubleheader drew 2,000. The visitors won the first game behind the six-hit pitching (all singles) of Luis Ruiz. Jonas Gaines started for the Giants. Hughes – back for his first game after a spike wound – misplayed a grounder from the Cubans' leadoff batter, Valdez. Four singles followed and the "islanders" had a quick 4-1 lead. Willie Hubert – called "Hank" by the *Baltimore Afro-American*, took over from Gaines and pitched scoreless ball until the eighth inning, when the Cubans got their fifth run on a home run into the right-field stands by third baseman Ramon Heredia. The only run the Elites got off Ruiz came in the bottom of the first. Hughes walked. Wright reached on a force play that retired Hughes, and then scored when Heredia committed an error on a ball hit by Hoskins.

In the fifth inning. Kimbro was caught off base on "the old hidden ball trick."[133] In the eighth, Kimbro hit a ball to deep center but was out trying to get two bases out of it.

July 17, 1939: Norristown Profs 10, Baltimore Elite Giants 3, at Roosevelt Field, Norristown, Pennsylvania

The *Philadelphia Inquirer* said that the Elite Giants would play the Norristown Pros that evening.[134] The team, though, was called the Profs, according to a lengthy game summary in the *Norristown Times Herald*. The Elites scored one run in the top of the first, but surrendered two in the bottom of the inning. In the second, they scored one more run, but this time gave up four. Said to have started for the Elites was Eddie Dixon, who was chased from the game in the second – as was Lefty Gaines.[135] They were both gone before the second inning was over, replaced by Johnny Johnson. The bombardment in all resulted in 19 base hits for the Profs – and the embarrassment of the Elites pitchers was suggested to have been so great that the *Times Herald* reported that Johnson "tried to enter the game under the fancy nom de plume of Joe Dunk so he could escape the shame."[136] Every batter in the Profs lineup had at least one base hit; all but two of them had multiple hits. They scored three more runs in the seventh.

The Elites got seven hits in all, two by Hughes. Snow singled and Hoskins doubled, and thus scored their first run. Charlie Rivera hit a "freak homer" in the second, "which cut over third base and then went behind the foul line."[137]

July 18, 1939: Belmar Braves 10, Nashville Elite Giants 3, at Memorial Field, Asbury Park, New Jersey

Belmar got off to a strong start, scoring once in the first inning, six in the second inning, and two in the third. Emery Adams had been the starter for the Elite Giants but was gone after 1⅓ innings, charged with three walks, six hits, and six runs. Hubert pitched the rest of the game. Already down 7-0 after just two innings. Kimbro doubled and Hughes singled in the top of the third, but it was for just one run. They scored twice more in the sixth, then had not a hit in the final three innings.[138]

July 19, 1939: Easton 9, Baltimore Elite Giants 7, at Easton, Pennsylvania

Adams was given another start the very next evening but gave way in midgame to Johnny Johnson. (They each had two at-bats, Johnson getting one hit.) Easton scored twice in the first inning, but the Elite Giants tied it in the top of the second and took a 5-2 lead in the third. Easton then scored four runs in the bottom of the third. The Giants tied it in the top of the fourth, but Easton came right back with two more to take an 8-6 lead. Neither team scored again until Baltimore put across one run in the top of the ninth, falling just short. Wright had three of Baltimore's nine hits.[139]

July 20, 1939: The *Philadelphia Inquirer*'s daily listing said the Elite Giants would play Bolden's Philadelphia Stars at Parkside and 44th.[140] It was to be a 9:00 P.M. makeup of a rained-out game from the last week of June.[141] Did it happen? We are unable to pin down whether this game and that of July 21 ever occurred.

July 21, 1939: "Newark Eagles, first-half champions of the Negro National League" were to play the Baltimore Elite Giants at 8:30 P.M. on Mayo's Island per the *Richmond Times-Dispatch*, July 21, 1939: 14.

July 22, 1939: Newark Eagles 8, Baltimore Elite Giants 5, at Pennsy Field, Wilmington, Delaware

Clower (presumably Tom Glover) pitched for the Elite Giants, Boone catching. For Newark, it was left fielder Fred Wilson, in his only pitching start of the season. Wilson gave up 15 base hits to Glover's 10 but won the game. In the top of the first, the Eagles scored four runs and never looked back. Baltimore got one. After Newark scored two more in the top of the third, Baltimore got another one. The three runs the Elites scored in the fifth still left them one short, and Newark added two more insurance runs in the seventh. Kimbro, Moore, Wright, and Hoskins all had three-hit games.[142]

July 23, 1939: Newark Eagles 4, Baltimore Elite Giants 2 (first game); Baltimore Elite Giants 4, Newark Eagles 1 (second game, six innings), at Griffith Stadium, Washington

General admission was 55 cents, but box seats set back those who splurged an extra 30 cents per ticket. Before some 3,700 fans at Griffith Stadium, Newark scored single runs off Jonas Gaines in the second, fourth, sixth, and ninth innings. The only two runs achieved off Eagles pitcher Leon Day ("masterly pitching," wrote the *Washington Post*) in the first game were in the bottom of the ninth.[143] One of the two runs was driven in by Bill Byrd, pinch-hitting for shortstop Pee Wee Butts. Hoskins and Snow were both on base. Byrd singled to right field and drove in Hoskins. Another pinch-hitter followed; Oscar Boone drove in Snow. Day retired Kimbro on a fly ball, though, ending the game. Leon Day was the star of the game. He not only struck out 10 batters but also hit two triples.[144]

In the second game, a six-inning affair, Willie Hubert threw two wild pitches in the game and gave up one run in the first inning but "held Newark to two hits in the final, and never was in trouble after the first inning."[145] One of the two hits was by Biz Mackey, who had started the season with the Elites. The Elites scored once in the third, twice in the fourth, and once in the fifth. Wright and Hughes both doubled; the team had eight hits in all. Pitching for Newark was Max Manning, charged with six of the hits and with five bases on balls, and then James Brown, Manning taking the loss.

July 24, 1939: Newark Eagles 12, Baltimore Elite Giants 3, at Pennsy Field, Wilmington, Delaware

A 6 o'clock game was deemed an exhibition game, even though both teams were in the same league. The batteries were Bob Evans and Biz Mackey for Newark and Henry Kimbro and Oscar Boone for Baltimore. It's not clear how long Kimbro pitched; even though he had been given a one-run lead, the Eagles scored six runs in the bottom of the first inning and six more runs in the bottom of the second inning. At some point, Glover took over. The Elites scored two more runs in the top of the third, but that was it. It was a seven-inning game.[146] Kimbro is not shown as pitching any other game throughout his career.

July 25, 1939: Newark Eagles 8, Baltimore Elite Giants 5, at Federal Park, Easton, Pennsylvania

The star of this game was outfielder Ed Stone of the Newark Eagles, who hit for the cycle, 5-for-5 with two singles, a double, a triple, and a home run. His first-inning double drove in the first run and his two-run homer drove in the final two in the eighth inning. Newark's Big Train Cozart gave up 12 hits, but the Eagles collected 15 off an unnamed Elite Giants pitcher.[147]

July 26, 1939: Baltimore Elite Giants 9, Newark Eagles 6, at Gordy Park, Salisbury, Maryland

The *Newark Evening News* devoted three sentences to this game, while managing to misspell the city as Salisburg in the dateline. The Giants outhit the Eagles, 16 to 12. There was no indication who pitched for Baltimore or how they scored their runs, but it was said to have been a five-run rally in the eighth that made the difference in the game.[148]

July 27, 1939: Once again, the *Inquirer* announced a scheduled game, which we have yet to locate. It was to be at 44th and Parkside on July 27 against the Newark Eagles.[149]

July 30, 1939: Baltimore Elite Giants 2, New York Black Yankees 1; New York Black Yankees 5, Baltimore Elite Giants 2, at Victory Field, Indianapolis

The team headed out on what was dubbed a "barnstorming tour" planned to take them to Indianapolis, Nashville, Birmingham, and Louisville.[150] The Elites and Black Yankees split a doubleheader on Sunday the 30th, at a venue known as both Perry Field and Victory Field. Seamheads calls it Victory Field; the *Baltimore Afro-American* says Perry Field. Byrd allowed a scattered seven hits. Terris McDuffie allowed only six, "but the Elites' blows were bunched."[151] New York scored its one run in the first inning; Baltimore scored both of its runs in the eighth inning. Adams and Hubert pitched in the second game.

July 31, 1939: The *Nashville Banner* of July 26 said there would be an 8:15 game at Sulphur Dell against the New York Black Yankees on this date. The July 31 paper said there would be a game that night. Did a game ever happen? Researchers were unable to find one.

August 1, 1939: Baltimore Elite Giants 4, New York Black Yankees 3, at Rickwood Field, Birmingham

There had been an article in the Sunday *Birmingham News-Age-Herald* two days earlier, advancing the 8:15 P.M. game at Rickwood and another the following evening. This time it identified the Elites as from Baltimore and noted that it was their second 1939 visit to Birmingham, having lost to Homestead the time before. "Since that time, however, the Baltimore management unleashed the purse strings from the bankroll, purchased new players, and at the moment they are the talk of the Negro National League."[152] It said they had won eight consecutive games. Lefty Gaines was said to have "tamed the Black Yankees" on this date.[153]

An accompanying story offered more detail. Baltimore won the first visit to "Dixie" of the "Dark Yankees" and helped draw 2,000 fans "to the Wood." Baltimore pitching held the New Yorkers to six hits, while the batters got eight, committing just one error to New York's two. Confusingly, after a sentence in which the *News* praised Gaines, the following sentence mentioned Glover: "Lefty Gaines, of the Elite Giants, certainly gave them an eyeful as he went about the business of hooking and fast-balling the fast-stepping Yankees to death. Glover was never in finer fettle than when he tamed the idols of Harlem in their initial battle on Southern soil."[154]

The New York team was not used to playing under the lights, said manager George Scales. "The lights are something new to us as we don't have any night baseball in New York. I think my boys became accustomed to the floods last night, however, and we are going gunning for the Elites with a real artillery attack tonight."[155]

For Baltimore, the August 1 game was said to be their 10th consecutive win. The *Birmingham News* article also noted that both right fielders were named Wright – though not named in the article, they were Wild Bill Wright for Baltimore and Zollie Wright for New York.

August 2, 1939: There were to have been two games at between the Black Yankees and the Elite Giants at Rickwood, the second one on Wednesday, August 2. Despite all the advance attention and the coverage of the first game in the *News*, there is no indication that the second one occurred.

August 3, 1939: New York Black Yankees 4, Baltimore Elite Giants 2, at Cramton Bowl, Montgomery, Alabama

The *Montgomery Advertiser* had announced games on August 3 and 4 the week before and suggested they would present "a chance to see some real baseball as much of the diamond's game talents lies in the negro field."[156] The first game drew 2,000 and was dubbed "thrilling" with "sensational plays and great running catches … numerous on both sides." Both Adams for Baltimore and McDuffie for New York pitched complete games. If he saw the August 4 *Advertiser*, catcher Oscar Boone may have been amused – or not. He was listed as "Goon." There was little detail other than to say that "George" Washington (the paper used the quotation marks) – first baseman Johnny Washington – had three base hits. New York was the home team and scored once in the second, gave up two runs in the fourth, tied it with one in the fifth, and took the lead with two more in the sixth.[157]

Standings as of August 5, 1939

Per Ed Gottlieb's letter to the owners of this date, the NNL standings at the time were:

	W	L
Baltimore Elite Giants	12	4
Homestead Grays	6	6
Newark Eagles	7	7
New York Black Yanks	3	5
Philadelphia Stars	6	10
Cuban Stars	1	3

August 6, 1939: Memphis Red Sox 7, Baltimore Elite Giants 3 (first game); Baltimore Elite Giants 14, Memphis Red Sox 1 (second game, seven innings), at Rickwood Field, Birmingham

The Frisco Railroad was to bring Red Sox fans on a special excursion train from Memphis for a 2:15 P.M. doubleheader at Rickwood Field.[158] The game drew 3,000 to see the Negro American League Memphis Red Sox play the Elite Giants. The first inning of each game spelled the difference in the two games. Roosevelt Davis pitched for Memphis in the first game and held Baltimore to three runs, benefiting from five runs his team scored in the top of the first. It was an inning that apparently featured the novelty of an umpire being ejected. The *Birmingham News* wrote that the first inning had taken half an hour to play, in part because of "a prolonged argument that ended only after Umpire Putnom had been ejected. The Giants claimed Umpire Putnom missed a strike. It was probably the first time an umpire ever got the worst of an argument with the players at Rickwood."[159] Baltimore actually outhit Memphis, 14 to 9, in the first game, but came up short in runs scored. Jonas Gaines bore the loss.

The seven-inning second game was sparked by a nine-run first inning by Baltimore. Memphis starter Porter Moss was gone after a third of an inning in which the Giants sent 14 men to the plate and collected nine hits and a walk with one batter hit by a pitch. They added five more runs in the second. Hubert held Memphis to six hits, scoreless through six, allowing just one run in the top of the seventh.[160] The fans were spirited as well, the *News* reporting that "several fights enlivened the evening for both ballplayers and fans. The game was halted for a few minutes once when fans began fighting back of the dugout used by the Birmingham Barons."[161] Hubert won the game for Baltimore.

On this same date, August 6, the East-West Game was played at Comiskey Park in Chicago.

Three Baltimore players were among the top vote-getters for the East team: pitcher Bill Byrd, second baseman Sammy Hughes, and outfielder Bill Wright all placed first in the voting at their respective positions.[162] Wright led off and played center for the East, and had two of his team's five hits. (One of his hits was a double.) Byrd pitched three innings. The West won, 4-2.

August 7, 1939: the *Greenville* (Mississippi) *Delta Democrat-Times* of August 6 ran an ad for an 8:15 P.M. game at Recreation Park between the Baltimore Elite Giants and the Memphis Red Sox. The ticket prices were 44 cents for men and 33 cents for women. The advertisement indicated that even ticket sale venues were different by race. Black fans could buy tickets at Red's Place on Nelson, Lawrence Barber Shop, and at Cook's Service Station, adding "Reserve Seats for Whites Sold by Winn Johnson at Nelms and Blum."[163]

August 9, 1939: Memphis Red Sox 5, Baltimore Elite Giants 4, at Martin Park, Memphis

Memphis scored twice in the first, saw Baltimore tie it in the third and take a 4-2 lead in the fourth, but came back with one in the first and two in the seventh. Lefty Howard and Double Duty Radcliffe limited the Giants to six hits. The account does not say who pitched for the Elite Giants.[164]

August 10, 1939: The *Nashville Banner* of August 5 said the Elite Giants would play the Memphis Red Sox at Sulphur Dell on this date. The August 9 issue had said the same. Was there a game? As with the announced July 31 game, there is no indication we could find that the game ever occurred, but that does mean it did not. Skip Nipper, SABR's leading authority on Sulphur Dell, was unable to find either game. The weather

doesn't seem to have been adverse. Skip noted, "It was not unusual for Nashville newspapers to omit reports of Negro League games. It appears, at least to me, that information was published only if the team(s) provided it; if someone from the ball club did not call the report in, it was left out."[165]

SABR member Keith Wood reported that in the *Memphis Press-Scimitar*, "the more progressive afternoon paper," there is nothing on games that may have involved the Red Sox and Elite Giants during this time span, nor had there been for April 3. The Black newspaper, the *Memphis World*, does not include 1939 "because of a fire in the archive at the newspaper, and neither the Memphis Public Library nor the Library of Congress has microfilm from 1939."[166]

August 13, 1939: Baltimore Elite Giants 11, Cuban All-Stars 1, at Yankee Stadium, New York

In the first game of a four-team doubleheader at Yankee Stadium, the Giants' Hubert held the All-Stars to six base hits, while a combination of Silvino Ruiz, Luis Tiant, and Connie Rector gave up 11 runs on 15 hits – hampered by six Cubans errors. Sammy Hughes was 4-for-6 with two singles, a double, and a triple. Hoskins also had a triple and scored three times.[167] The Homestead Grays beat the New York Black Yankees in the second game. The Elite Giants' win in this game earned them the coveted Jacob Ruppert Cup.

Keeping busy, the Elites also had scheduled a game against the local ballclub at Municipal Stadium in Cedarhurst for the evening of August 13, but that game was rained out.[168]

August 14, 1939: Schwartz A.A. 3, Baltimore Elite Giants 2, at Yorston Field, New Brunswick, New Jersey

The victory was said to be the third of the season in which the Schwartz club had triumphed over "outstanding Negro ball clubs."[169] A month earlier, they had beaten the Philadelphia Stars and two weeks before this contact, they had beaten the Brooklyn Royal Giants.

Jonas Gaines pitched for the Elites, and Leon Revolinsky for Schwartz. Gaines was done in by a three-run third inning. Baltimore had scored first, in the top of the inning, on three straight singles by Oscar Boone, Gaines, and Sammy Hughes and a fly ball by Red Moore.

In the bottom of the inning, there was a Schwartz single, a sacrifice, and a bunt single. The next batter grounded to Felton Snow at third base, who threw home to catch the runner off third base. A rundown began, but Snow dropped the ball and the runner was able to score as the other two runners moved up to second and third. A single scored one of them. Gaines struck out the next batter, but the one after that hit the ball back to Gaines "who leaped high to stop the apple, but was off balance and could not complete the play to first base" as the third run scored.[170]

In the top of the seventh, Kimbro hit a two-out double and Hughes hit a ball off the second baseman's glove. The eight-inning game was played in front of just 200 or 300 spectators.

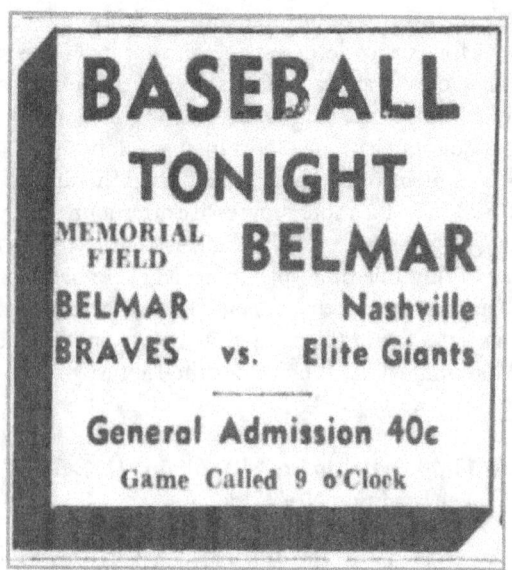

Advertisement from the August 15 *Asbury Park Press* (Asbury Park, New Jersey).

August 15, 1939: Belmar Braves 6, Baltimore Elite Giants 2, at Memorial Field, Asbury Park, New Jersey

In their third matchup, the Belmar Braves beat the Elite Giants 6-2. They had lost the first of the three, 9-5, but then beat Baltimore, 10-3, on July 18. Pitching for Belmar was left-hander Jim McCloskey, who had pitched in four games for the Boston Braves (without a win or loss but an 11.25 earned-run average). McCloskey gave up five hits and a pair of runs over the first two innings, but then allowed just "three scattered hits" for the duration.[171] In the fourth inning, and again in the fifth, he struck out the side.

The two Baltimore runs came in the second. Tom Butts walked on four pitches but was picked off first. Snow singled to left. So did Campanella, Snow going to third. Pitcher Johnny Johnson ("the string-bean Elite flinger") reached first on a fielder's choice, the throw going to the plate but Snow safely scoring. Kimbro hit into a force play at second base, Campanella scoring. McCloskey doubled and drove in Belmar's first run, in the bottom of the second, then scored himself on a subsequent double. The Braves scored one run in the third, one in the fourth, one more in the fifth, and yet one more in the sixth.

August 17, 1939: Baltimore Elite Giants 4, Alcyon Park 3, at Camden, New Jersey

Lefty Glover, pitching for Baltimore, yielded seven hits – just half the 14 his teammates made. He and batterymate Campanella were the only Elite Giants held hitless. Moore and Wright each had three hits, one of Wright's being a home run. The game was scoreless through three, then the Giants scored two, saw Alcyon Park come back with three. They tied the game, 3-3, in the top of the fifth. In the top of the ninth, Kimbro walked,

was sacrificed to second by Hughes, and scored the go-ahead run on a single up the middle by Moore.[172]

August 18, 1939: Nashville Elite Giants 9, Bushwicks 0, at Dexter Park, Brooklyn

The Elites were to play the Bushwicks, according to the August 14 *Daily Eagle*. The paper was still calling them the Nashville Elite Giants, as did the *Brooklyn Citizen*, though the *Citizen* did say they "are now representing Baltimore in the colored circuit."[173] The *Citizen* story and box score, however, called them Nashville.

Gaines threw a three-hit shutout. The Elites had 16 hits, including a double and a triple by "Campinello," who was 4-for-5, and they scored in every inning but the third, seventh, and eighth.[174] Both Wright and Hughes had three base hits.

August 19, 1939: Per the *Philadelphia Inquirer* that morning, there was a 1:30 P.M. doubleheader scheduled at Philadelphia's Parkside Athletic Field (44th and Parkside) between the Elite Giants and the Philadelphia Stars. Did these games get played? Inquiring minds want to know, but no trace of them has yet been uncovered.

August 20, 1939: New York Black Yankees 4, Baltimore Elite Giants 3; New York Black Yankees 2, Baltimore Elite Giants 1, at Oriole Park, Baltimore

It had been tough to win games at home. Even though the team was in the league lead, it lost two more home games on the 20th. We have been unable to find any details on these games.

August 22, 1939: The *Philadelphia Inquirer* announced a game that evening between the Newark Eagles and the Baltimore Elite Giants. This proved to be another announced game that may not have been played, or wasn't reported, despite seemingly being a game of potential real interest.

August 23, 1939: Lloyd A.C. 4, Baltimore Elite Giants 1, at Lloyd Athletic Field, Chester, Pennsylvania

In the third matchup between the two teams, Bill Martini pitched for the Lloyd Athletic Club. Johnny Johnson worked for the "Nashville-Baltimore Elite Giants."[175] On May 17 Lloyd prevailed, 3-1. On June 2, the Elite Giants slaughtered Lloyd, 14-1. Johnson worked the first five innings, giving up four runs, all in the bottom of the third. Byrd took over and pitched the final three. The one run scored by the Elites was in the top of the sixth.[176] Sammy Hughes reached and pulled up at second base on a throwing error by the shortstop. Red Moore singled to short, Hughes advancing to third. Bill Wright singled off Martini's glove, Hughes scoring.

Bill Byrd threw three hitless innings, the sixth through the eighth. Moore led off the eighth with a base hit and Hoskins led off the ninth with another, but both times a double play squelched any threat.[177]

Uniform numbers

Players come and go throughout a season and the Baltimore Elite Giants were no exception. Just after mid-August, the *Warren* (Pennsylvania) *Times-Mirror* published a list of the players who were on the team before the August 24 game against the Homestead Grays.[178]

The players, with their names spelled as printed in the newspaper, are listed here as presented:

No.	Player	Position
12	Kimbro	Center Field
2	Hughes	Second Base
21	Wright	Right Field
8	Hoskins	Left Field
10	Moore	First Base
15	Snow	Third Base
6	Butts	Shortstop
19	Campinello	Catcher
22	Byrd	Pitcher
23	Johnson	Pitcher
1	Hubert	Pitcher
16	Glover	Pitcher
18	Adams	Pitcher
31	Gaines	Pitcher
14	Dixon	Pitcher
11	Boon	Catcher
9	Riveria	Utility

Were the Giants giant?

The *Chester Times* dubbed them "the well-named Giants" and declared that they had "proved popular in two previous appearances here, with the local fans being amazed at their size." It cited Kimbro, Wright, Hoskins, and Snow, but particularly called out Sammy Hughes, 6-feet-4 and over 200 pounds, as "one of the greatest baseball players in the game," adding, "This second sacker is a symphony of grace on the field and is as fast as light as lean sprinter [*sic*]. Pairing as the keystone combination with Hughes is the even larger Jessie Walker, who is an inch taller than Sammy."[179]

August 24, 1939: Homestead Grays 7, Baltimore Elite Giants 4, at Russell Field, Warren, Pennsylvania

This 5:30 P.M. regular-season game featured the first-half champion Homestead Grays against the Elite Giants, who were leading in the season's second half, and foreshadowed

the NNL championship series, which began on September 16. The game was sponsored by the North Warren Civic Club and drew 1,000 fans.[180]

Baltimore's Jonas "Curley" Gaines came into the contest riding an eight-game winning streak. Pitching for the Grays was right-hander Ray Brown, in his eighth season for the team. Baltimore scored first with single runs (both unearned) in the first and third innings, and was bailed out in one three-hit inning from a possible worse fate by a double play. In between, Homestead put up a pair of runs in the second. Baltimore added a third run in the top of the sixth and a fourth in the top of the eighth, giving the Elite Giants a 4-2 lead. But Homestead struck back with five runs in the bottom of the eighth. Snow, playing third base, booted a ball hit his way and Grays left fielder Vic Harris reached. Bankhead singled. Josh Gibson singled to right, scoring Harris. Buck Leonard sacrificed both baserunners into scoring position so Gaines intentionally walked Henry Spearman (who already had three hits in the game), loading the bases. Country Davis singled, driving in two runs. Jelly Jackson sacrificed to advance the runners. Brown walked, loading the bases once more. Campanella let a pitch get by him – a passed ball – and another run scored. Right fielder David Whatley singled in the fifth run of the inning. Baltimore was held scoreless in the ninth.

August 27, 1939: New York Cubans 5, Baltimore Elite Giants 1; Baltimore Elite Giants 8, New York Cubans 4 (seven innings), at Oriole Park, Baltimore

The Elite Giants were missing three regulars – Bill Wright, Sammy Hughes, and Bill Byrd, but nonetheless managed a split in a doubleheader at Oriole Park against the visiting Cuban Stars. Willie Hubert pitched the first game, opposing the Cubans' Silvino Ruiz. The Cubans scored unearned runs in the first and in the second, the Giants scoring their lone run in the bottom of the second. The game remained a tight one until the top of the eighth, when Hubert was hit for a double, single, walk, and double, producing three runs which went unanswered.

In the second game, the Giants jumped out to a 4-0 lead in the first inning. Kimbro singled to lead off, then stole second. Snow singled to drive him in, then took second on a sacrifice by Red Moore. Hoskins walked. Pee Wee Butts singled to left, driving in Snow. Holloway flied out to deep center field, around 400 feet, in a ball caught by Jose Vargas with "one of the most sensational catches seen in the park."[181] Walker then doubled "off the top of the left-field wall" to drive in both Hoskins and Butts. They added a fifth run in the second inning, then saw the

Advertisement from *Warren Times-Mirror* (Warren, Pennsylvania).

Cubans get three in the top of the third. In the fourth inning, the Giants got one more. Snow walked, stole second, and came home on Moore's double to in front of the right-field bleachers.

Snow got another base hit in the sixth and Moore sacrificed him again. Jim Hoskins then homered over the wall in left field. Emery Adams was the winning pitcher in seven innings.

August 28, 1939: The *Philadelphia Inquirer* listed a game for 9:00 P.M. to be played at Parkside Athletic Field between Bolden's Philadelphia Stars and the Baltimore Elite Giants. No subsequent coverage has been found.

August 30, 1939: The *Camden* (New Jersey) *Morning Post* announced a 6:00 P.M. game against the R.D. Wood club to be held at the local park (R.D. Wood Park) in Florence, New Jersey. We could find no trace of the game having been played.

August 31, 1939: The Baltimore Elite Giants were to play an opposing team that was not named at 6 P.M. at Rutherford, New Jersey.[182] The *Bergen* (New Jersey) *Evening Record* said the opponent was to be the Laird-Johnson club of Rutherford.[183] There had been an article – albeit one dated 17 days earlier – in the *New York Amsterdam News* – saying that the Newark Eagles and the Elites were scheduled to play this day at an unnamed location; those plans, of course, may well have changed.[184] And the August 30 *Nassau Daily Review-Star* (Freeport, New York) had previewed "an arc-light struggle" against the Cedarhurst ballclub to be played at Cedarhurst Municipal Stadium.[185] Whatever games may have been planned, apparently rain prevented the contest.

September 1, 1939: Baltimore Elite Giants 6, Cedarhurst Baseball Club 3, at Municipal Stadium, Cedarhurst, New York

Tom Glover pitched for the Elites; Wally Holborrow and Eddie Baratta pitched for the Long Island club. The Elites scored one run in each of six different innings – the first, fifth, sixth, seventh, eighth, and ninth. Cedarhurst got all three of its runs in the bottom of the sixth, tying the game at the time, but then the Elites pulled away a run at a time. Readers of the *Long Island Daily Press* (Jamaica, New York) were informed that "a feature of the fracas was a home run by Barney Wright of the invading team," but not whether it might have been the run in the top of the seventh that won the game.[186]

September 2, 1939: a game that did not happen

Lloyd Field was to host an afternoon game between the "Nashville-Baltimore Elite Giants" and the Philadelphia Stars, per the September 1 *Chester Times*, but the next day's edition reported that the "Homestead Grays, instead of the Nashville-Baltimore Elite Giants, will provide the opposition for Bolden's Philadelphia Stars."[187]

September 3, 1939: Baltimore Elite Giants 10, Philadelphia Stars 2, at Ruppert Stadium, Newark, New Jersey

The "Second Annual Four Team Doubleheader" was held at Ruppert Stadium. In the first game, the Elite Giants beat the Philadelphia Stars, 10-2. In the second, the Homestead Grays beat the Newark Eagles, 7-4. Hughes and Butts both doubled in the sixth inning, and Snow followed with a homer. Wright tripled and doubled in the game, and Walker doubled as well. Byrd pitched and got the win.[188]

September 4, 1939: Homestead Grays 5, Nashville Elite Giants 3, at Dexter Park, New York

In the second inning of the second game of a four-team doubleheader that drew 6,000 (*Brooklyn Citizen*) to 10,000 (*Brooklyn Eagle*), Homestead Grays pitcher Roy Partlow hit a Jonas Gaines pitch over the right-field fence for a grand slam as part of a five-run rally that won the game. The Elite Giants scored one in the second and two in the fifth.[189]

Final season standings
SECOND HALF
Elites 13-8
Grays 10-7
Stars 16-12
Eagles 11-14
Black Yankees 6-10
OVERALL
Grays 33-14
Eagles 29-20
Elites 25-21
Stars 31-32
Black Yankees 15-21
Toledo 3-11 (only played first half)
Cuban Stars 5-22[190]

Looking ahead to the playoffs, columnist Art Carter of the *Baltimore Afro-American* lamented how Baltimoreans had not turned out in bigger numbers to support their "hustling, never-say-die team." He acknowledged, "At the outset of the season, it is true that the Elites failed to live up to early expectations – losing the first four contests played at home and returning a few weeks later to drop another game." There followed, though, "a brilliant spurt … in the later stages of the first half race which saw the hustling aggregation move from fifth to second place in the loop standings, and the heads-up ball that has kept them on top from start to finish during the second half campaign."[191]

Baltimore fans, however, had not been turning out the way one might have expected. "It is no weak team," he continued, "that Owner Tom Wilson and Road Secretary Vernon Green have given Baltimore fans, either. Only a few names, Bill Wright, Bill Byrd, Sammy Hughes and Manager Felton Snow, which smack of long-time experience and brilliance, dot the line-up, but Wilson has given Snow a hustling bunch of youngsters who balance the club with the right amount of spirit and clever performances. This combination, along with a well-balanced hurling staff, has put the Elites in the running for the championship."[192] It was the second year in a row the Elites had "been on the brink" of the title.

Playoffs

September 6, 1939: Newark Eagles 8, Baltimore Elite Giants 6, at Ruppert Stadium, Newark

In the first game of the best-of-five league playoffs, the Elites scored one in the third inning and four in the fourth inning to build up a nice 5-0 lead for starter Adams. The Eagles, though, chipped away by scoring two runs in the bottom of the fourth on a Mule Suttles home run, four more in the fifth (one on a solo homer by Suttles), and two more runs in the sixth. Byrd relieved Adams. Bob Evans had started for Newark, relieved by Max Manning. Coverage in the Newark newspaper did not report who did what for the opposing team.[193]

September 8, 1939: game postponed

It wasn't a playoff game, but the Elite Giants attempted to stay in shape (and rake in some more money) by taking on the Bushwicks at Dexter Park. The game, however, was not held due to the field being too soggy.[194]

September 9, 1939: Baltimore Elite Giants 11, Newark Eagles 3, at Penmar Park, Philadelphia

In the second playoff game, the Elite Giants evened things up with an 11-3 win. Leon Day started for Newark, relieved by Bob Evans. Gaines pitched for the Giants and allowed just seven base hits. Baltimore jumped off to an early start and just kept scoring. They got two runs in the top of the first, on back-to-back leadoff walks, a sacrifice, another walk, and then a two-run double by Felton Snow. They added one run per inning in the second, third, and fourth. They were held scoreless in the fifth, but then added four more runs in the sixth (in part due to three Eagles errors) and a final two in the top of the eighth. Hughes homered for the Giants – a solo homer to center field accounting for their run in the second inning – and joined four others in hitting a double: Snow, Moore, Kimbro, and Hoskins.

The Eagles committed four errors to just one by Baltimore. Suttles hit another home run for Newark, a two-run shot over the left-field wall in the seventh – the first runs off Gaines in the game.[195]

September 10, 1939: Baltimore Elite Giants 7, Newark Eagles 3; Baltimore Elite Giants 5, Newark Eagles 2 (six innings), at Oriole Park, Baltimore

The Elites finally earned a full-page headline in the *Afro-American* by taking two from the Eagles in a home doubleheader at Oriole Park, winning the first round of the playoffs: "Elites Whip Eagles to Gain Championship Series."[196] They were thus due to face the winner of the Homestead Grays-Philadelphia Stars series for the ultimate Negro National League championship.

Bill Byrd pitched the first game, a 7-3 victory. Though he allowed 13 hits, he gave up only three runs. The Elites scored twice in the third and twice again in the fourth. The first of the third-inning runs was on Byrd's "tremendous drive over the right centerfield wall." Kimbro doubled down the left-field line and scored on Hughes's hit over third base. In the top of the fifth, the Eagles scored once and, by adding two more in the sixth, came within a run.

Hubert pitched the second game, called after six innings due to a 6:00 P.M. curfew. Hubert allowed just two base hits. One was a fifth-inning home run by right fielder Ed Stone of the Eagles, who had also homered in the first game. Newark had scored its other run in the first on a walk and two Baltimore errors. The Elites scored twice in the top of the first on a single by Hughes, a double by Wright, and a single by Snow. Wright was 3-for-7 in the doubleheader and was credited with several defensive gems.[197]

League Championship Games

September 16, 1939: Homestead Grays 2, Baltimore Elite Giants 1, at Penmar Park, Philadelphia

Roy Partlow pitched for the Pittsburghers and Bill Byrd for the Giants. The Grays got to Byrd right away in the first inning, with singles by David Whatley and Vic Harris, and an RBI single by Sam Bankhead. Harris took third base when Josh Gibson grounded into a force play. Buck Leonard then "knocked an easy one to [shortstop] Butts who juggled the ball long enough for Harris to bring in the Grays' second run."[198] Byrd shut them out the rest of the way, but Partlow allowed only one run, when Hughes doubled to right in the fourth inning, advanced to third on Moore's out, and scored on a "slow roller" hit by Bill Wright to third baseman Henry Spearman.

September 17, 1939: Baltimore Elite Giants 7, Homestead Grays 5; Baltimore Elite Giants 1, Homestead Grays 1 (tie, five innings), at Oriole Park, Baltimore

Some 3,000 fans turned out at Oriole Park to see a Sunday doubleheader in the best-of-seven championship series. The Homestead Grays had won the first game, 2-1, in Philadelphia the day before. Jonas Gaines started for the Elites. He retired the first two batters, but Sam Bankhead singled and Josh Gibson followed with a home run over the wall in left field. A great catch by Kimbro prevented at least one more run from scoring later in the inning. Baltimore got one back in the bottom of the second. Wright's liner off Tom Parker eluded Harris in left field and wright wound up on second. Snow singled and drove in Wright. The Eagles made it 3-1 in the top of the fourth. The Elites' Moore led off the bottom of the fourth by drawing a base on balls. Wright doubled, then Snow doubled. Hoskins singled, scoring Snow. There was still nobody out, but no further runs scored that frame. It was 4-3, Elites.

The Grays promptly retied the game with another run in the fifth. In the bottom of the sixth, Snow singled – his third hit of the game. There was an error by the shortstop, and then a passed ball as Campanella struck out followed by a wild throw to second base by Gibson that was wild enough to allow Snow to score. The Elites took the lead, then added a sixth run in the seventh on Kimbro's single, sacrifices by Hughes and then Moore, and a single by Wright. And another run in the eighth on a Hoskins single, a bunt by Butts, an infield out by Campanella, and a fielding error by Bankhead. Newark got a runner on in the ninth but a double play and a strikeout by Gaines ended the game.

Lefty Glover pitched the second game for the Elites and held the Eagles to just three hits and one run. The one run they scored was in the second inning due to a baserunner going from first to third on a stolen base and a throwing error by Campanella, and then a passed ball also charged to the Baltimore catcher. The Elites scored their lone run in the bottom of the third. Edsall Walker was pitching for Newark. Campanella reached on an error by the left fielder. Glover sacrificed him to second and Hughes singled him home. They loaded the bases, but Snow struck out. The Elites almost scored in the fifth, as it was the clear the 6:00 P.M. curfew was impending. With one out, Hughes walked. A strikeout followed and then Wright hit the ball to right field, which could have been a game-winning double, but trying to go from first to home, Hughes was – just barely – out at the plate.[199]

September 20, 1939: Bushwicks 3, Elite Giants 1, at Dexter Park, Brooklyn

Two titleholders were to meet in the final games under the lights at Dexter Park. The Bushwicks had won the Metropolitan Baseball Association crown and the Elite Giants were the second-half winners in the Negro National League. The *Brooklyn Citizen* wrote, "For several seasons the Nashvilles have attempted to gain a place in the colored league playoff but were unsuccessful. They changed their home city representation in moving to Baltimore and the new scenery has worked wonders with the outfit."[200]

The game had Adams (the first six innings) and Hubert pitching for the visitors. Someone named Childress served as catcher. The Bushwicks outhit the Elites, six hits to five, and played errorless ball while the Elites committed three errors.[201] The only run they scored was by bunching three singles in the fourth inning.

September 23, 1939: Baltimore Elite Giants 10, Homestead Grays 5, at Penmar Park, Philadelphia

Roy Campanella – still being called Leroy by the *Baltimore Afro-American* – was the star of the game, going 4-for-5 with a home run, a double, and two singles, and accounting for five of the 10 runs the Elites scored. Baltimore scored two in the second inning, but the Grays – playing as the home team –tied it with one in the second and one in the third. They then scored two in the fourth to take a 4-2 lead. With single runs in the fifth and sixth, the Elites tied it again, 4-4, heading into the seventh.

It was Specs Roberts for Homestead and Bill Byrd for Baltimore. Hughes singled, moving to second on Moore's sacrifice. Wright received an intentional walk. Snow hit the ball to shortstop, fielded by Bankhead who had taken over after Jelly Jackson had been thrown out of the game for fighting with Kimbro. Bankhead "juggled" the ball, and everyone was safe. Hoskins singled to center field, driving in two runs. Butts singled, loading the bases again. Campanella singled and two more runs scored. Byrd hit a fly ball to right for the fifth run of the inning. It was 9-4, Baltimore. Each team scored one run in the ninth; there remained a five-run spread and the Elite Giants had won the game.[202]

September 24, 1939: Baltimore Elite Giants 2, Homestead Grays 0, at Yankee Stadium, New York

This was the game that won the Elite Giants the Negro National League championship, held at Yankee Stadium and drawing perhaps 15,000 patrons.[203] Baltimore had to play without star second baseman Sammy Hughes, who was stricken with a stomach ailment so severe he was taken to Harlem Hospital. (He was released after the game.[204]) Felton Snow played second.

It was an exceptionally well-pitched game, with left-hander Jonas Gaines pitching three-hit ball for the Elite Giants and Roy Partlow pitching for the Grays. There were no runs scored at all for the first seven innings.

In the top of the eighth, Bill Wright doubled. Hoskins then singled to right field, Wright scoring. After an out, Walker beat out a single on a dribbler to third base. Hoskins held at second, but scored when Campanella shot a single up the middle. It was 2-0, a thin lead that the Grays threatened when they loaded the bases in the bottom of the eighth on three consecutive two-out walks by Gaines, who had already lost his control. Snow called on Hubert to relieve Gaines. Third baseman Henry Spearman was due up. He hit three foul balls and then flied out to Snow at second base. Threat over. Neither Partlow nor Hubert allowed a run in the ninth.

In ceremonies after the game, Tom Wilson was presented the Jacob Ruppert Trophy.

In a moment that may have seemed one of anticlimax, there was a second, seven-inning exhibition game in which "a picked team from the Elites and Grays played a 1-1 tie with a combination of minor league players."[205] The minor leaguers were from the Piedmont League. That game lasted seven innings and was called on account of darkness.[206]

After the season

After winning the championship, the Elites gathered at the York Hotel in Baltimore and then headed to Nashville, home to owner Tom Wilson. Wright, Walker, and Glover were joined by several other NNL stars to play at a North-South game in New Orleans on Sunday, October 1.[207]

Art Carter of the *Baltimore Afro-American* offered a postscript to the season: "The Elites' win should serve as a shot in the arm to the National League popularity, which fortunately took an upward turn this year, despite the continued shortcomings of the loop's operation, because except for a few isolated periods, the Pittsburgh crowd had begun to dominate the championships – whether they won them by fair or foul means. First it was the Grays, then the Pittsburgh Crawfords, now defunct, and again the Grays.

"And yet, the Pittsburgh hometown crowd gave the teams little support. But with the title dangling from the shoulders of a club in the seaboard sector, where the attendance at the loop games is high, support for the organization should go up by leaps and bounds."[208]

Regarding the future prospects of the Elite Giants, Carter continued, "the roster of the victorious Elite Club is by no means dotted with a galaxy of aging veterans, who totter around solely on experience. Manager Felton Snow, who deserves plenty of praise for piloting the Elites to the crown, Bill Wright, and Sammy Hughes, perhaps qualify as seasoned veterans, but otherwise, the roster of the Elites is made up of hustling, ambitious youngsters." He added, "Owner Tom Wilson, his club secretary, Vernon Green, and Manager Snow have been equally fair in giving the youngsters a chance, and the winning of the championship is doubtless the reward."[209]

In the October 17 Pittsburgh Courier, columnist Randy Dixon praised both Felton Snow and the Elite Giants. After Snow had been badly beaned a couple of years earlier it was thought he might never play again. But he had shown "guts and gusto plus a generous portion of acumen as manager of the Elites."[210]

The Detroit Tribune wrote that the 1939 season was "the best financial season ever enjoyed by the Negro National League." Among the reasons were better weather and receipts from all-star games, "but mainly from the desire of the owners to pull together instead of against one another." The paper added, "Not since 1934 [citing that year's Homestead Grays] has so many raw newcomers showed on a team, as the Baltimore Elites flashed during the second half of the 1939 season. It was the inspired work of these newcomers which captured the Ruppert Cup for the Elites." The paper cited the addition of the left-handed Gaines and Wright in particular and declared that Bill Wright "hitting almost .500 in league games, had the best season ever enjoyed by any player of league. Bill is one player who is a major leaguer."[211]

After the season, the Elite Giants were to make their "annual trek to the Pacific coast."[212]

October 8, 1939: Major and Minor League All-Stars 3, Negro National League All-Stars 1, at Oriole Park, Baltimore

Of note, there was a game played at Oriole Park on October 8. The game featured a number of major-league and minor-league ballplayers against a strong team of Negro Leaguers. The two teams were described in the Afro-American box score as the "White All-Stars" and the "Colored All-Stars." The text described them as they are listed above – the "white Major and Minor League All-Stars and the Negro National League

All-Stars."[213] The NNL players featured four from the Elite Giants: Webster McDonald, Biz Mackey, Roy Campanella, and Mickey Casey. The team of White ballplayers were all from the American League, five from the Philadelphia Athletics, with starting pitcher Pete Appleton and Mickey Vernon from the Washington Senators, and one player each from the Boston Red Sox and the St. Louis Browns.

The 2,000 fans who turned out saw the White players score twice in the first inning (Dee Miles homered after Doc Cramer reached base) and once in the second, off pitcher Cain. In the second, Cain gave up three successive singles and then misplayed a ball hit to him by Appleton.[214] With nobody out, McDonald – the team's manager – took over and threw seven innings of no-hit ball. The only run the NNL All-Stars scored came in the fifth when Jelly Jackson singled, stole second, reached third on an error by Appleton, and scored on a passed ball charged to catcher Hal Wagner.

October 11, 1939: Baltimore Elite Giants 5, Pirrone's Major League All-Stars 2, at Gilmore Field, Hollywood

The team – or much of it – had headed west and on Wednesday night, October 11, beat Pirrone's Major League All-Stars, 5-2, in Los Angeles despite Bob Feller striking out 14. Elite Giants in the game included Bill Harvey pitching, Hoskins, Wright, and West. Hoskins doubled off Feller and Wright and Harvey both hit triples.[215] The Atlanta Daily World printed an Associated Negro Press dispatch reporting the score as 5-3, with Feller striking out 15 in front of an audience of 5,000 which included "many movie stars." It said that Feller's team had been ahead 3-0 but the Giants tied the game in the seventh on hits by Dunn, Wright, and Hoskins. Feller departed the game ("perhaps to save his face, the announcement was made that Feller would have to leave to catch a plane back east"), but from the dugout saw West and Walker drive in two more.[216]

In his SABR biography of Marlin Carter, Mal Allen provides information about the Baltimore Elite Giants' trip to the West Coast:

In late 1939, Carter was part of the Baltimore Elite Giants club that competed against major and minor-leaguers in the integrated California Winter League. "The team we had … was really an all-star team," he explained. "We had Pepper Bassett, Bill Wright, Jesse Walker, William Harvey, Mule Suttles, James West."[217] In their first league action, the Elite Giants were swept in a doubleheader by the [Joe] Pirrone's All-Stars squad, but Carter went 3-for-9 against Lee Stine and Julio Bonetti.[218] When the Elites hosted the same team on October 18 at Gilmore Field in Los Angeles, they faced a soon-to-be 21-year-old who'd won 24 games for the Cleveland Indians that season while leading the majors in strikeouts. "Despite the opposition of two major previews – "The Roaring Twenties" and "Disputed Passage" – Cleveland pitcher Bob Feller attracted a huge turnout of movie celebrities," reported Ed Sullivan.[219] Feller whiffed 14 in his seven innings, but the Elite Giants scored three times against the bullpen to prevail, 5-2.[220] On November 19,

Carter tripled in the victory that mathematically eliminated Pirrone's team.[221] He was at shortstop two weeks later when the Elite Giants clinched the championship."[222]

November 5, 1939: Elite Giants 4, White Kings 0; Elite Giants 3, White Kings 1 (five innings), at Gilmore Field, Hollywood

There was a particularly notable game on the trip – a no-hitter thrown by Lefty Glover in the first game of a doubleheader on Sunday, November 5. Only three of the White Kings reached base. Glover walked one. The other two reached on errors – one by Pepper Bassett and one by Glover himself, dropping the ball while taking a feed from first baseman West. The Giants had only six hits but made them count. Glover struck out four and faced a total of just 29 batters.

In the second game, Wright hit a two-run homer over the right-field fence in the third inning.[223]

The final day's games on the trip were won by the "Royal Giants" taking two from Pirrone's All-Stars, 5-3 and 4-0. Bill Harvey threw the second of the two games, a one-hitter with only one other batter reaching first base, on a walk. Players on the Royal Giants included Carter, Dunn, Wright, Hoskins, West, Summers, Walker, Bassett, and first-game winner McDuffie.[224]

SOURCES

Thanks to Mal Allen, Gary Ashwill, Rich Bogovich, Rick Bush, Thomas Kern, Bob Luke, and Tom Thress, with additional assistance from Joe DeLeonard, Bob Golon, Marc Magee, Brian Michaels, and Jeb Stewart. Thanks as well to Jennifer Knisley, Warren (Pennsylvania) Public Library; Barry Rauhauser, Historical Society of Montgomery County, Norristown, Pennsylvania; Bruce Bardarik, Paterson Free Public Library, Paterson, New Jersey.

NOTES

1   Bob Luke, *The Baltimore Elite Giants* (Baltimore: The Johns Hopkins University Press, 2009), 42. Luke notes, however, that "records for the second-half standings are non-existent." League President Gus Greenlee and Grays owner Cum Posey "filed a report" declaring that the Grays had finished first in the second half, but "[h]ow they arrived at the standings is not known. They did not provide a won-lost record for any of the teams in their report." Indeed, the two executives acknowledged, "sports writers of our weekly papers … did not receive league news and standings regularly because the various club secretaries did not send in the scores to the secretary of the league." See "NNL Turns in Report," *Baltimore Afro-American*, September 10, 1938: 23. This was further clarified as quoted in the text, per an email Bob Luke to author dated July 18, 2023.

2   Cum Posey, "Posey's Points," *Pittsburgh Courier*, March 25, 1939: 14. The April 1 *Atlanta Daily World* also reported Mackey as manager.

3   "Elites Train in Nashville," *Chicago Defender*, April 15, 1939: 9.

4   "Elite Giants to Have Many New Players," *Baltimore Afro-American*, April 22, 1939: 22.

5   "Elite Giants at Oriole Park for Home Games," *Baltimore Afro-American*, January 7, 1939: 19.

6   See Luke, 49, and "Negro League Game Tomorrow," *Delaware County Daily Times* (Chester, Pennsylvania), September 1, 1939: 14.

7   Art Carter, "From the Bench," *Baltimore Afro-American*, October 7, 1939: 21.

8   Art Carter, "From the Bench," *Baltimore Afro-American*, September 16, 1939: 23.

9   Among the newspapers declaring these as playoffs were the *Chicago Defender* and *Pittsburgh Courier*. See John L. Clark, "League Playoffs Start in Baltimore Sunday," *Pittsburgh Courier*, September 10, 1938: 16. Clark, in a different article, referred to the games as the "official playoff." John L. Clark, "Crawfords, Elites, Grays in 3-Game Twin Bill Sunday," *Chicago Defender*, September 10, 1938: 9.

10   "Elites Trounce Crawfords, 10-1," *Baltimore Afro-American*, September 17, 1938: 22.

11   Art Carter, "From the Bench," *Baltimore Afro-American*, September 16, 1939: 23.

12   Luke, 16.

13   "Protect Players Is Plea at Pow-Wow," *Pittsburgh Courier*, January 4, 1939: 17.

14   Cum Posey, "Posey's Points," *Pittsburgh Courier*, February 18, 1939: 14.

15   "Baseball League to Be Headed by Wilson; Greenlee Absent," *New York Age*, February 25, 1939: 8.

16   "Elites Win 2 from Giants," *Baltimore Afro-American*, April 29, 1939: 14. The Elites were the Baltimore team; the Giants were the Chicago American Giants.

17   "Wilson Elected Prexy; Cubans to Get Franchise," *Pittsburgh Courier*, February 25, 1939: 17.

18   Sam R. Brown, "Red Sox Chatter," *Atlanta Daily World*, April 4, 1939: 5.

19   "Red Sox in 4-2 Victory over Elites," *Chicago Defender*, April 8, 1939: 8.

20   "Red Sox Register," *Memphis Commercial Appeal*, April 3, 1939: 13.

21   The *Atlanta Daily World* presented a detailed game story. "Melancholy" Jones, "Felix 'Chin' Evans, Donald Reeves Star as Atlanta Nine Loses 13-12," *Atlanta Daily World*, April 10, 1939: 5.

22   For reasons unknown, the *Daily World* dubbed him Erskine Hoskins.

23   "Melancholy" Jones, "Black Crax Again Nosed Out by Baltimore, 11-10," *Atlanta Daily World*, April 11, 1939: 5.

24   "Baseball News," *Macon* (Georgia) *Telegraph*, March 25, 1939: 13. Rich was unable to find other coverage of the Fast Black from April 10 into early May.

25   "Elite Giants Win," *Chattanooga Daily Times*, April 17, 1939: 11.

26   Randy Dixon, "The Sports B-U-G-L-E," *Pittsburgh Courier*, May 13, 1939: 17. Dixon added, "In truth, the entire league is sorta whimsical." Foreshadowing an announced May 17 game at Chester, Pennsylvania, the *Chester Times* called the team "the Nashville-Baltimore Elite Giants, headed by the famous Biz Mackey." "Lloyd Tackles Elite Giants," *Chester Times*, May 16, 1939: 11. One doubts that league business records were unclear as to the name of the team. An article in the *Omaha Guide* newspaper said that three of the teams in the Negro Southern League that year (Memphis, Atlanta, and Jacksonville) "are operating on a plan of a twin home city. They have a Dixie home and a northern home. This follows the pattern of the Baltimore Elite Giants who also claim the title of the Nashville

Elite Giants." See "Talk Revival of Negro Southern League," *Omaha Guide*, May 27, 1939: 6.

27   Lucius "Melancholy" Jones, "Slants on Sports," *Atlanta Daily World*, April 18, 1939: 5.

28   https://archive.org/details/NewarkEagles1101005. Accessed December 5, 1939.

29   "Nashville Wins Two Games from Chicago," *Chicago Defender*, April 29, 1939: 10. The *Defender* shows a shortstop named Robinson playing shortstop in the second game. This may have been "Skin Down" Robinson – if so, perhaps appearing in his only Negro Leagues game in 1939. The *Nashville Banner* likewise presented the team as the Elite Giants (with no city name designated) in the two sentences it accorded the event. "Series Finale," *Nashville Banner*, April 24, 1939: 10. Two days later it briefly mentioned them as the Nashville Elite Giants as did the *Brooklyn Eagle* in a very brief mention. On May 6, the *Pittsburgh Courier* had them as the Baltimore Elite Giants.

30   "American Giants Win," *Chicago Tribune*, April 25, 1929: 25. No other source has been found regarding this game.

31   "Homestead Grays Win Couple from Elite Giants," *Atlanta Daily World*, May 2, 1939: 5.

32   "Elite Giants Battle Grays Here April 30," *Birmingham News*, April 24, 1939: 11; "Nashville Elites Meet Homestead Grays at Rickwood," *Birmingham News*, April 29, 1939: 9. See also "Negro Teams Meet Sunday at Rickwood; Homestead Grays Will Battle Nashville Elites in Double-Header," *Birmingham News-Age-Herald*, April 30, 1939: 7, which had a lengthy story naming the same two pitchers for the Elites on the morning of the game – but again, no coverage of the actual games.

33   "Elites Down K.C. Twice," *Pittsburgh Courier*, May 13, 1939: 16.

34   "Elites Beat Monarchs," *Chicago Defender*, May 13, 1939: 10.

35   "Today's Sport Card," *Philadelphia Inquirer*, May 13, 1939: 19.

36   "Elites to Open Against Grays," *Baltimore Afro-American*, May 13, 1939: 18.

37   "Elites to Open Against Grays."

38   "Homestead Grays Hand Double Beating to Baltimore," *Chicago Defender*, May 20, 1939: 9.

39   "Homestead Grays Grab 2 from Elite Giants," *Baltimore Afro-American*, May 20, 1939: 14.

40   This was probably Clarence "Geechie" Williams, who is listed on Seamheads as playing left field in one league game for the 1930 Elite Giants. The Williams who played against Lloyd was the team's left fielder in this exhibition game. The local newspaper called him Tom Williams.

41   "Wearshing Hits Two-Run Single for Lloyd Win," *Chester Times*, May 19, 1939: 26.

42   "Eagles Rained Out for Second Time," *Trenton Evening News*, May 21, 1939: 20.

43   "Elites on Edge for Black Yanks," *Baltimore Afro-American*, May 27, 1939: 21.

44   "Eagles Make It Four Straight," *Newark Evening News*, May 22, 1939.

45   "Eagles Snare Doubleheader," *New Jersey Herald News* (Newark), May 27, 1939: 8.

46   "Newark Wins Four Straights on Home Lot," *New York Amsterdam News*, June 3, 1939: 19.

47   "Newark Wins Four Straights on Home Lot." Wright did play center field in the first game; there was no box score provided for the second.

48   "Daily Statement of Attendance and Receipts," Newark International Base Ball Club, Inc., May 21, 1939. https://archive.org/details/NewarkEagles1101005. Accessed December 5, 2023.

49   See https://archive.org/details/NewarkEagles0809021. Accessed December 5, 2023.

50   "Baltimore Giants Lose to R.D. Wood," *Camden* (New Jersey) *Courier-Post*, May 27, 1939: 14.

51   "Elites Win Two and Lose Two," *New Journal and Guide* (Norfolk, Virginia), June 3, 1939: 18. See also "Yesterday's School, College, Independent Sports Results," *Philadelphia Inquirer*, May 28, 1939: S3.

52   "Elite Giants Sign Two New Pitchers for Yankee Jousts," *Baltimore Evening Sun*, May 25, 1939: 44.

53   "3 Homers Help Yankees Even Series with Elites," *Baltimore Afro-American*, June 3, 1939: 18.

54   "Elites Win Two and Lose Two."

55   "3 Homers Help Yankees Even Series with Elites."

56   The home run was mentioned in "Elite Giants Split with B. Yankees," *New York Daily News*, May 31, 1939: 57.

57   "Black Yankees in Even Break," *Brooklyn Eagle*, May 31, 1939: 18.

58   "Elite Giants Split with B. Yankees."

59   Full details are provided in the game writeup. See "Visitors Wreck Lloyd Hurlers in Revenge Tilt," *Chester Times*, June 3, 1939: 14.

60   "Poletti to Throw Out First Ball for Series," *Brooklyn Daily Eagle*, May 31, 1939: 16.

61   Peter Jackson, "Elites, Yankees Win in New York Doubleheader," *Baltimore Afro-American*, June 10, 1939: 22.

62   "10,000 See Black Yankees and Elite Giants Win in Four-team Doubleheader," *New York Age*, June 10, 1939: 8.

63   Randy Dixon, "15,000 See Four-Team Twin Bill in Yankee Stadium," *Pittsburgh Courier*, June 10, 1939: 16. One notes that the *Courier* added 5,000 to the attendance total proclaimed by the *Age*. Dixon also rendered Byrd's first name as Sam, not Bill.

64   Dan Burley, "Black Yankees Nose out Philadelphia, 5 to 4, in NNL Feature at Yankee Stadium; Cubans Bow to Baltimore," *New York Amsterdam News*, June 10, 1939: 14.

65   "Sports Card," *Philadelphia Inquirer*, June 5, 1939: 18.

66   "NNL League Dope," *New York Amsterdam News*, June 24, 1939: 15.

67   "Grays Divide with Baltimore," *Pittsburgh Press*, June 11, 1939: 22. See also "Homestead Grays and Baltimore Elite Giants Divide Double-Header at Forbes Field," *Pittsburgh Courier*, June 17, 1939: 17.

68   "Grays, Elites Even," *Columbus Evening Dispatch*, June 12, 1939: B-5. The *Dispatch* had described Gray as a "product of Columbus sandlots and a former East High student." See "Columbus Product is with Elite Giants," *Columbus* (Ohio) *Evening Dispatch*, June 10, 1939: 8.

69   "Hilton Snow at Helm of Baltimore Elites," *Columbus Evening Dispatch*, June 7, 1939: B-7.

70   "Grays, Elites Split," *Pittsburgh Post-Gazette*, June 12, 1939: 17.

71   "Grays Bow 7-3 to Baltimore With Gibson Out of Line-up," *Indianapolis Recorder*, June 17, 1939: 14.

72   "Royal Giants Take Doubleheader from Grays," *New Journal and Guide*, June 24, 1939: 17.

73 "Homestead Grays to play Baltimore team," *Bluefield* (West Virginia) *Daily Telegraph*, June 11, 1939: 10.

74 "Baltimore Elites Beat Grays, 2 to 1," *Charleston* (West Virginia) *Gazette*, June 16, 1939.

75 The *Daily Mail* article was "Elite Giants Beat Homestead Grays," *Charleston* (West Virginia) *Daily Mail*, June 16, 1939.

76 The New Jersey paper described the Eagles batter as Monte Irving. "Eagles Continue to Set Pace with Double Win over Elites," *New Jersey Herald News* (Passaic), June 24, 1939: 8. See also "Newark Eagles Take Twin Bill," *Newark Evening News*, June 19, 1939.

77 "Newark Eagles Take Twin Bill," *Newark Evening News*, June 19, 1939.

78 "Negro Nines Play Here Tonight," *Richmond Times-Dispatch*, June 19, 1939: 13.

79 "Elites Beat Eagles at Richmond, 17-7," *Baltimore Afro-American*, June 24, 1939: 23.

80 "Newark Eagles Lose to Elite Giants; Play Yankees Next," *Richmond News-Leader*, June 20, 1939: 20. Newark did have a player named Stone, but he was an outfielder.

81 "Newark Eagles Defeated by Baltimore Elites, 17-7," *Newark Evening News*, June 20, 1939.

82 "Elite Giants Hammer Eagles In 17-6 Win," *New Journal and Guide*, July 1, 1939: 18.

83 "Postponed Game Carded Tonight," *Philadelphia Inquirer*, June 20, 1939: 20.

84 "Eagles Still Hold Lead in League Race," *New Journal and Guide*, June 17, 1939: 17.

85 "Elite Giants Bow to Eelman by 3-2 Decision," *Paterson* (New Jersey) *Evening News*, June 22, 1939: 29.

86 "Pirates Will Meet Elite Giants Tomorrow Night," *Red Bank* (New Jersey) *Daily Standard*, June 22, 1939: 19.

87 "Elite Giants Break Pirate Win Streak; Down Red Bank, 6-4," *Red Bank Daily Standard*, June 24, 1939: 16.

88 The newspaper declared, "Baltimore Elites have always been noted for their batting are hitting as a club only .174, which accounts for their failure to be further up in the standing." See "Newark Batting .500; 3 Regulars Hit .400," *Michigan Chronicle* (Detroit), June 24, 1939: 9.

89 "Bushwicks Show Power Nosing Out Nashville Elite Giants Twice," *Brooklyn Eagle*, June 26, 1939: 16.

90 John G. Palmer, "Bushwicks Twice Beat Nashvilles as Bottle Fly at Dexter Park," *Brooklyn Citizen*, June 26, 1939: 6.

91 "Bushwicks Show Power Nosing Out Nashville Elite Giants Twice."

92 "Greys (sic) Halted by Giants, 6-4," *Long Island Daily Press* (Jamaica, New York), June 27, 1939: 12.

93 "Baseball Standings," *Baltimore Afro-American*, July 1, 1939: 22.

94 "Phillies 11, Elites 4," *Chicago Defender*, July 8, 1939: 17.

95 "Philly Stars Win 2 Out of Three," *New York Amsterdam News*, July 15, 1939: 15.

96 "Manheim Lads Drop 4-3 Tilt to Baltimore," *Lancaster* (Pennsylvania) *Intelligencer Journal* June 29, 1939: 16. The Barons were described as "the dark horse of the Lebanon Valley league." See "Baltimore Elite Giants Play Manheim Tonight," *Lancaster Intelligencer Journal*, June 28, 1939: 10.

97 "Baseball and Tennis Postponed by Rain," *Long Island City* (New York) *Star-Journal*, July 1, 1939: 10.

98 "Elite Giants Upset Eagles," *New Jersey Herald News*, July 8, 1939: 8.

99 Peter Jackson, "Elites Blank Yanks, Eagles Trounce Stars in Twin Bill," *Baltimore Afro-American*, July 8, 1939: 21.

100 "Elites to Play Philly Stars," *Baltimore Afro-American*, July 8, 1939: 21.

101 See, for instance, "Strong All-Star Team to Play Balto. Giants," *Baltimore Afro-American*, July 15, 1939: 21.

102 "Braves, Elites Clash Tonight," *Asbury Park* (New Jersey) *Press*, July 3, 1939: 10.

103 "Belmar Braves Drop Second Straight, Losing to Elites, 9 to 5," *Asbury Park Press*, July 5, 1939: 10. All game play detail comes from this account.

104 *Philadelphia Inquirer*, July 5, 1939: 31.

105 "Philadelphia Wins Two from Baltimore Elites," *Chicago Defender*, July 15, 1939: 8.

106 "Homestead Grays Win First Half," *Baltimore Afro-American*, July 15, 1939: 23.

107 "Famous Clowns Tackle Locals in Big Battle," *Chester Times*, July 6, 1939: 21.

108 "Red Bank Shut Out, 6-0," *Daily Standard*, July 6, 1939: 16.

109 Email from Mal Allen on March 8, 2023, citing "Pirates Trounced Again," *Red Bank Register*, July 13, 1939: 25.

110 "Giants Beat Stars Twice," *Philadelphia Inquirer*, July 9, 1939: 5.

111 "Elites Win a Doubleheader," *Chicago Defender*, July 15, 1939: 8.

112 "Giants Beat Stars Twice," *Philadelphia Inquirer*, July 9, 1939: 5. The *Defender* box score suggests that another batter after West must have reached base one way or another.

113 "Elites Bolster Team for Cuban Series Here," *Baltimore Afro-American*, July 15, 1939: 21. The following week's paper said he was the one made a free agent. See "Elites Clash with Eagles," *Baltimore Afro-American*, July 22, 1939: 23.

114 Roy Campanella was reported to be 18 in the July 15 edition, and 20 in the July 22 edition, apparently having aged two years in the course of one week. In fact, he was 17 years old at the time.

115 "Elites Bolster Team for Cuban Series Here."

116 "Elites Take Lead in Second Half," *Baltimore Afro-American*, July 15,1939: 21.

117 The "shelled from the mound" phrase comes from "Elite Giants Win Four as Second Half Opens," *New Journal and Guide*, July 15, 1939: 17.

118 "Elite Giants Win Four as Second Half Opens."

119 "Elites Take Lead in Second Half." The *Chicago Defender* agreed on the forfeit, pointing out that there was a 6:00 P.M. curfew and that the stalling had begun at 5:45 with the forfeit declared at 5:55. It said that McCrary had forfeited the game after instructing Stars manager Jake Dunn "to have the players begin the inning and watching the Philly outfit refuse." "Baltimore Elites Win Three from Philadelphia," *Chicago Defender*, July 15, 1939: 10.

120 "Senators Play Allentown Tonight; 'American Legion Night' Tomorrow," *Trenton* (New Jersey) *Evening Times*, July 11, 1939: 11. Likely a typo, the *Philadelphia Inquirer* said that the game began at 9:00 A.M. "Other Games," *Philadelphia Inquirer*, July 10, 1939: 18.

121 "Stars to Play Negroes Tonight," *Poughkeepsie* (New York) *Eagle-News*, July 12, 1939: 8.

122 If he was really pitching right-handed as the article said, his accomplishment would have been even more remarkable. It talked about his "fast, right-handed toss." "All-Stars Drop Hot Game to Elite Giants Team 7-1," *Poughkeepsie Eagle-News,* July 13, 1939: 8.

123 "Bushwick Club to Use Signer in Box Tonight," *Brooklyn Eagle,* July 14, 1939: 8.

124 "Games This Week," *New York Times,* July 10, 1939: 16.

125 "Bushwicks to Pitch 'No-Hit' Jim Tomorrow," *Brooklyn Daily Eagle,* July 15, 1939: 11.

126 John Staudt, "Greys Win, 11-10, on 5 in 9th," *Long Island Daily Press,* July 15, 1939: 8.

127 Charles A. Pichard, of Bellaire, New York, letter to the editor, *Long Island Daily Press,* July 20, 1939: 21.

128 Staudt.

129 "Nashville Giants Win," *Wilmington* (Delaware) *Morning News,* July 17, 1939: 15.

130 "Cubans to Meet Giants at Pennsy," *Wilmington Morning News,* July 15, 1939: 12.

131 Newark Eagles Records, MG Nwk Eagles. Charles F. Cummings New Jersey Information Center, Newark Public Library. https://archive.org/details/NewarkEagles080902I Accessed December 5, 2023.

132 Art Carter, "Player Ejected as Elites Split with Cubans," *Baltimore Afro-American,* July 22, 1939: 23.

133 "Player Ejected as Elites Split with Cubans."

134 "Sports Card," *Philadelphia Inquirer,* July 17, 1939: 18.

135 There was an Eddie Dixon listed by Seamheads as on the Indianapolis ABCs/Atlanta Black Crackers team in 1939. As noted, a week earlier he was said to have been joining the team and in late August a pitcher named Dixon was said to have been assigned uniform number 14.

136 Sheriff (no other name provided), "Norristown Sluggers Blast Three Hurlers for 19 Hits; Smith Gives Up Seven Blows," *Norristown* (Pennsylvania) *Times Herald,* July 17, 1939: 7.

137 Sheriff.

138 "Braves Shake Slump, Rout Nashville Elites, 10 to 3," *Asbury Park Press,* July 19, 1939: 10.

139 "Easton East Penn Club Beats Colored Team, 8-7," *Allentown* (Pennsylvania) *Morning Call,* July 20, 1939: 16.

140 "Sports Events for Today," *Philadelphia Inquirer,* July 20, 1939: 22.

141 *Woodbury* (New Jersey) *Daily Times,* July 11, 1939.

142 "Newark Eagles Defeat Baltimore Giants, 8-5," *Wilmington Morning News,* July 24, 1939: 16.

143 "Giants Split with Eagles in Twin Bill," *Washington Post,* July 24, 1939: 14.

144 The *Newark Evening News* said that Day had struck out eight. "Leon Day Stars as Eagle Split," *Newark Evening News,* July 24, 1939.

145 "Baltimore and Newark Split Double-Header," *Washington Evening Star,* July 24, 1939: A-12. The *Newark Evening News* account said the second game was a seven-inning game.

146 "Newark Eagles Swamp Baltimore Elite Giants," *Wilmington Morning Call,* July 25, 1939: 20.

147 "Fancy Clouting," *Newark Evening News,* July 26, 1939.

148 "Rally Beats Eagles," *Newark Evening News,* July 27, 1939.

149 "Today's Sports," *Philadelphia Inquirer,* July 27, 1939: 27.

150 "Elites Barnstorming with N.Y. Black Yanks," *Baltimore Afro-American,* July 29, 1939: 22.

151 "Yanks, Elites Divide Bill in Indianapolis," *Baltimore Afro-American,* August 5, 1939: 22.

152 "Black Yanks Meet Giants, Tuesday, 8:15; Crack Negro Teams to Clash in Pair of Games at Rickwood Field," *Birmingham News-Age-Herald,* July 30, 1939: 4. See also "Dark Yankees and Giants to Meet Tuesday," *Birmingham News,* July 31, 1939: 11, and "Baltimore to Play Yankees Here Tonight; Big League Clubs to Perform at Rickwood for Two Nights," *Birmingham News,* August 1, 1939: 10.

153 "Negro Teams to Play Pair Tilts Here on Sunday," *Birmingham News,* August 5, 1939: 8.

154 "Baltimore Is Winner from Dark Yankees," *Birmingham News,* August 2, 1939: 15. A one-run, 4-3 victory seemed like hardly the mastery indicated.

155 "Baltimore Is Winner from Dark Yankees."

156 "Black Yankees to Meet Elite Giants Here Soon," *Montgomery Advertiser,* July 28, 1939: 16.

157 "Black Yankees Top Giants Here, 4 To 2," *Montgomery Advertiser,* August 4, 1939: 14.

158 "Red Sox Meet Black Giants in Pair Games," *Birmingham News,* August 4, 1939: 13.

159 "Memphis Splits Pair of Battles With Baltimore," *Birmingham News,* August 7, 1939: 9.

160 SNS, "Red Sox and Giants Divide Twin Bill," *Phoenix* (Arizona) *Index,* August 12, 1939: 4.

161 "Memphis Splits Pair of Battles With Baltimore."

162 "Sluggers Dominate All-Star Teams," *Baltimore Afro-American,* August 5, 1939: 21.

163 Advertisement, *Delta* (Mississippi) *Democrat-Times,* August 6, 1939: 5.

164 "Negro Red Sox Ahead," *Memphis Commercial Appeal,* August 10, 1939: 14.

165 Email to author from Skip Nipper, June 8, 2023.

166 Email to author from Keith Wood, June 7, 2023.

167 SNS, "Homestead Grays Take Black Yankee Team," *Phoenix Index,* August 19, 1939: 5.

168 "M.B.A. Lead; Point for Cedarhurst," *Nassau Daily Review-Star,* August 14, 1939: 10.

169 "Schwartz Repulses Elite Giants, 3-2," *Central New Jersey Home News* (New Brunswick), August 15, 1939: 10.

170 "Schwartz Repulses Elite Giants, 3-2."

171 "Belmar Braves Conquer Elites, 6-2, With McCloskey on Mound," *Asbury Park Press,* August 16, 1939: 8.

172 "Baltimore Giants Beat Alcyon Park," *Camden Morning Post,* August 18, 1939: 29.

173 John G. Palmer, "Bushwicks and Nashville Will Play Tonight," *Brooklyn Citizen,* August 18, 1939: 6.

174 John G. Palmer, "New Bushwick Twirler Is Given Poor Support and Nashvilles Win, 9-0," *Brooklyn Citizen,* August 19, 1939: 6.

175 "Martini Again Pitches Great Ball to Win, 4-1," *Chester Times,* August 24, 1939: 20.

176 "Lloyd A.C. Beats Elite Giants," *Delaware County Daily Times*, August 24, 1939: 20.

177 "Martini Again Pitches Great Ball to Win, 4-1."

178 "So You'll Know Them," *Warren* (Pennsylvania) *Times-Mirror*, August 23, 1939: 8.

179 "Lloyd A.C. Meets League Leaders," *Chester Times*, September 2, 1939: 11.

180 "Homestead Grays Rally in Eighth to Defeat Baltimore," *Warren Times-Mirror*, August 25, 1939: 9.

181 Ralph F. Boyd, "Elites and Cubans Split Twin Bill," *Baltimore Afro-American*, September 2, 1939: 23.

182 "Today's Sports," *Philadelphia Inquirer*, August 31, 1939: 23.

183 "Little Ferry A.A. Ready for Series with Laird-Johnson," *Bergen* (New Jersey) *Evening Record*, August 29, 1939: 13.

184 "Newark and Grays Play," *New York Amsterdam News*, August 12, 1939: 15.

185 "Baltimore Team at Cedarhurst," *Nassau Daily Review-Star*, August 30, 1939: 12.

186 "Elites Win, 6-3, At Cedarhurst," *Long Island Daily Press*, September 2, 1939: 7. Wright was the right fielder, Burnis "Wild Bill" Wright.

187 "Sports Shorts," *Chester Times*, September 2, 1939: 12.

188 "Elites and Giants Win N.Y. Twin Bill," *Baltimore Afro-American*, September 9, 1939: 22.

189 "Partlow Steals Show as Grays Top Nashville," *Brooklyn Eagle*, September 5, 1939: 15. See also "Cuban Stars and Homestead Grays Victors," *Brooklyn Citizen*, September 5, 1939: 6.

190 "National League," *Baltimore Afro-American*, September 9, 1939: 23.

191 Art Carter, "From the Bench," *Baltimore Afro-American*, September 16, 1939: 23.

192 "From the Bench."

193 "Mule Suttles Slugs Hard," *Newark Evening News*, September 7, 1939.

194 John G. Palmer, "Bushwicks to Play Two Star Teams of Met," *Brooklyn Citizen*, September 9, 1939: 6.

195 "Red Moore Hits Three for Four," *Atlanta Daily World*, September 16, 1939: 5. See also "Newark Eagles and Elite Giants Even," *Newark Evening News*, September 10, 1939. The newspaper assigned Hughes the first name of Jack.

196 Ralph Boyd, "Elites Whip Eagles to Gain Championship Series," *Baltimore Afro-American*, September 16, 1939: 22.

197 "Elites Whip Eagles to Gain Championship Series."

198 "Partlow Bests Byrd as Grays Win Opener, 2-1," *Baltimore Afro-American*, September 23, 1939: 21.

199 Art Carter, "Elites, Grays Tied in National League Title Series," *Baltimore Afro-American*, September 23, 1939: 19.

200 John G. Palmer, "Champions Are to Clash at Dexter Park," *Brooklyn Citizen*, September 19, 1939: 6.

201 "Bushwicks Nip Elites in Arclight Finale," *Brooklyn Eagle*, September 21, 1939: 20.

202 "Campanella in Star's Role as Elites Score," *Baltimore Afro-American*, September 30, 1939: 21.

203 The *Chicago Defender* reported "nearly 10,000" but a typesetting error also declared the score to be 20-0. Fortunately, the game story and accompany box score were in agreement with the *Baltimore Afro-American* that it was a 2-0 game. "Baltimore Whips Homestead Grays for Title," *Chicago Defender*, September 30, 1939: 9.

204 "Elite Giants Win National League Championship," *Baltimore Afro-American*, September 30, 1939: 21. The *Defender* wrote that Hughes "collapsed on the bench" but "returned to the park near the end of the game." See also "Baltimore Whips Homestead Grays for Title."

205 "Elites Win Title," *Jersey Journal* (Jersey City), September 25, 1929: 11.

206 "Elites Drub Grays for Jacob Ruppert Trophy," *New Journal and Guide*, September 30, 1939: 17.

207 "Elite Stars to Play in Game," *Baltimore Afro-American*, September 30, 1939: 20.

208 Art Carter, "From the Bench," *Baltimore Afro-American*, October 7, 1939: 21.

209 Carter, "From the Bench," October 7, 1939: 21.

210 Randy Dixon, "The Sports Bugle," *Pittsburgh Courier*, October 7, 1939: 17.

211 "Owners of Teams in Negro National League Enjoyed Best Year in Campaign Just Closed," *Detroit Tribune*, October 21, 1939: 7.

212 "Owners of Teams in Negro National League Enjoyed Best Year in Campaign Just Closed."

213 "McDonald Hurls Shutout Ball, but All-Stars Lose," *Baltimore Afro-American*, October 14, 1939: 21.

214 Marion "Sugar" Cain is shown on Seamheads as 25 years old and having pitched for the Crawfords in 1937 and 1938. The *Baltimore Afro-American* said the pitcher was Robert Cain, age 23, from Philly. "McDonald Hurls Shutout Ball, but All-Stars Lose."

215 James Newton, "Bob Feller Fans 14, but Elites Win, 5-2," *Baltimore Afro-American*, October 21, 1939: 21.

216 "Negro Aces Defeat Bob Feller 5-3," *Atlanta Daily World*, October 23, 1939: 5.

217 Prentice Mills, *Black Ball News Revisited* (Middletown, Delaware: Red Opel Books, 2019), 109.

218 "Pirrone's All-Stars Stifle Giants Twice," *Los Angeles Times*, October 9, 1939: A12.

219 Ed Sullivan, "Hollywood," *New York Daily News*, October 22, 1939: 30.

220 James Newton, "Bob Feller Fans 14, But Elites Win, 5-2," *Baltimore Afro-American*, October 21, 1939: 21.

221 James Newton, "McDuffie, Harvey Hurl Winning Ball on Coast," *Chicago Defender*, November 25, 1939: 22.

222 James Newton, "Giants Win Winter League Title," *Chicago Defender*, December 9, 1939: 24.

223 James Newton, "Glover Hurls No-Hit, No-Run Game on Coast," *Chicago Defender*, November 19, 1939: 24. See also "Glover Twirls No-Hitter as Royal Giants Win," *Los Angeles Times*, November 6, 1939: A12.

224 Newton, "Giants Win Winter League Title."

LATE HOME RUNS LIFT WEST TO WIN IN NEGRO LEAGUE ALL STAR GAME

AUGUST 6, 1939: WEST ALL-STARS 4, EAST ALL-STARS 2, AT COMISKEY PARK, CHICAGO

BY NORM KING

As the *Cheers* resident know-it-all Cliff Clavin might have said, "It's a little-known fact …" that the first major-league All-Star Game held at Comiskey Park in 1933 was not the only inaugural All-Star competition held that year at the ballyard that Charles Comiskey built.

Following on the heels of the Comiskey classic, Pittsburgh Crawfords secretary Roy Sparrow and *Pittsburgh Courier* editor Bill Nunn discussed the idea of having a similar game pitting the best players from the newly constituted Negro National League against each other.[1] Their initial idea was to hold the game at Yankee Stadium, but after receiving a tepid response to that suggestion, Crawfords owner Gus Greenlee recommended that the game be held at Comiskey Park because it would appeal to the Windy City's large Black population. The West won the first game, 11-7, on September 10, 1933, in front of approximately 15,000 rain-soaked fans. The game was a success and a new tradition was born.

With the organization of the Negro American League in 1937, the game pitted the best players from the two circuits against each other. Because Negro National League teams were based in the East, and Negro American League teams played in the Midwest, it was easy to continue calling the event the East-West All-Star Game.

The game grew in popularity as the pressures of the Depression eased. It helped that neither league dominated, as the two sides split the first games evenly, with three wins apiece. The first six games set the stage for one of the classic matchups in the event's history. On August 6, 1939, the West used home-run power in the seventh and eighth innings to overcome a 2-0 East lead in front of 40,000 fans, a record attendance for the classic up to that time.

Fans voted for the players on each side from ballots available through America's three leading Black community newspapers, the *Pittsburgh Courier*, the *Kansas City Call*, and the *Chicago Defender*. Even though they were only voting for baseball all-stars, the right to do so was important to many African Americans because many were denied the right to exercise their franchise under existing Jim Crow laws.

"(D)uring the 1930s, voting was so difficult for blacks that many did not bother," wrote Bo Smolka in his history of the Negro Leagues. "So the chance to vote for the East-West All-Star Game players was a big deal. More than 17 million ballots were submitted for the 1939 East-West Game."[2]

"That was a pretty important thing for black people to do in those days, even if it was just for ballplayers," said Hall of Famer Buck O'Neil.[3]

Those votes resulted in a lot of talented players participating in the game, including future Hall of Famers Willie Wells, Josh Gibson, Mule Suttles, Leon Day, and Buck Leonard for the East squad, and Hilton Smith for the West.

The weather was perfect as heavyweight boxing champion Joe Louis arrived wearing a snazzy gabardine suit to throw out the first pitch to Greenlee. Once the game started, the favored Easterners scored two runs in the second inning off starter Theolic Smith of the Memphis Red Sox. The rally started when Leonard was safe on an error by shortstop Ted Strong. Leonard took third on Pat Patterson's single, and after Patterson stole second, both runners scored on a single by Sammy Hughes.

Both sides pitched well over the next several innings as the score remained 2-0. In fact, keeping East sluggers Gibson, Suttles, and Leonard hitless (the three went 0-for-10) allowed the West to mount their comeback.

"At this point (the second inning) the hopes of the thousands of Western rooters hit a new 'low,' but still the West's pitching continued on a high plane," wrote Chester L. Washington Jr. "Eastern base hits were as scarce as hen's teeth and soon the hopes of the West started to soar again."[4]

That soaring began in the seventh inning when Neil Robinson broke the East's shutout bid, blasting Roy Partlow's first offering 380 feet into the second tier of the left-field stands.

The West completed its comeback in the eighth. Ted "Double Duty" Radcliffe singled to center and was sacrificed to second by Parnell Woods. Dan Wilson followed that with a two-run homer that put the West in the lead to stay. After Bill Holland replaced Partlow, Double Duty's brother Alex greeted him with a base hit. Robinson then hit a fly ball that Suttles lost in the sun. Radcliffe reached third on the play while Robinson landed on second with a double. The West showed what small ball is about when Billy Horne hit a sacrifice that brought Double Duty home with an insurance run. Double Duty Radcliffe pitched a one-two-three ninth and earned the victory for the West while Partlow was tagged with the loss.[5]

"With one bold stroke of his bat, this artist of the diamond painted a picture before the astonished eyes of some 40,000 fans … a painting as dramatic in its highlights and shadows as Rembrandt's [*sic*] 'Blue Boy,'" wrote Bill Nunn about Wilson's homer.[6] "Dan Wilson today stole the thunder of the vaunted power-hitters of the East."[7]

The West's victory gave them a 4-3 lead in the series and helped them maintain a dominance they held for the duration of the series' existence. The East-West All-Star Game was held annually at Comiskey Park until 1960, with the West winning 16 of the 28 matchups. The last two Classics were held at Yankee Stadium in 1961 and at Kansas City's Municipal Stadium in 1962, with the West winning both contests, 7-1 in 1961 and 5-2 in 1962.

SOURCES

In addition to the sources in the Notes, the author also consulted:

Negro League Baseball E-museum.

Thenationalpastimemuseum.com.

Finder, Chuck. "Negro Leagues Converged in an East Meets West Powerball Summit," *Pittsburgh Post-Gazette*, July 9, 2006.

Kleinknecht, Merl F. "East Meets West in Negro All-Star Game," *SABR Baseball Research Journal*, 1972.

Lester, Larry. *Black Baseball's National Showcase* (Lincoln: University of Nebraska Press, 2001).

Newman, Roberta J, "Shadow Culture, Shadow Game: The Negro Leagues," in the *Legacy of Slavery* web module, New York University, 2007.

Sullivan, Floyd, editor. *Old Comiskey Park: Essays and Memories of the Historic Home of the Chicago White Sox, 1910-1991* (Jefferson, North Carolina: McFarland and Company, 2014).

NOTES

1   The first Negro National League, founded in 1920, could not survive the Great Depression and folded in 1931.

2   Bo Smolka, *The Story of the Negro Leagues* (Minneapolis: ABDO Publishing Company, 2013), 9.

3   Smolka, 9.

4   Chester L. Washington Jr., "Sun Rises in the West," *Pittsburgh Courier*, August 12, 1939: 17.

5   Partlow played briefly with the Montreal Royals in 1946, the same year Jackie Robinson broke the color barrier in Organized Baseball.

6   William G. Nunn, "Homers by Dan Wilson, Robinson Decide Battle," *Pittsburgh Courier*, August 12, 1939: 17. *Blue Boy* was painted by the Englishman Thomas Gainsborough.

7   Nunn.

BALTIMORE ELITE GIANTS DEFEAT NEWARK EAGLES IN NNL2 PLAYOFFS TO REACH CHAMPIONSHIP SERIES

BY MIKE HUBER

In 1939 both the Baltimore Elite Giants and the Newark Eagles were "resolved to improve on the results"[1] of the previous season. The 1938 season had been the maiden campaign for Baltimore in the Negro National League II (NNL2), as the franchise had moved up the road from Washington.[2] Under player-manager George Scales, the Elite Giants went 26-23-3 in that first season in Baltimore, good for third place in the NNL2 standings but 12½ games behind the first-place Homestead Grays. The Grays had started a string of nine consecutive seasons in which they topped the league standings in 1937. In fifth position in 1938 were the Eagles (17½ games back), guided by Dick Lundy, who was in his second season as their skipper.[3]

For the Elite Giants and Eagles, their resolutions for the 1939 season came true. Although Baltimore's overall record for 1939 was 29-25 (their NNL2 record was 21-23), the Elite Giants "ran away with the second half championship."[4] In fact, they had been in first place in early June, "a position they clung to until the last week of June, when their fortunes headed south,"[5] and the team finished the first half of the season in third place. However, the Elite Giants then posted the best mark in the NNL2's second half, which began in July.

The Newark Eagles had finished the 1939 season in second place with a record of 32-23-1. They played consistently; although they were not quite good enough to win either half of the season, they were strong enough to stay in the mix for the playoffs.

Before the 1939 season had begun, the New York Yankees had offered the Jacob Ruppert Memorial Trophy, named after their recently deceased team owner, to the Negro National League II team that won the most games at Yankee Stadium each year. Yankees President Edward Barrow now had established a tournament to honor Ruppert that consisted of five four-team doubleheaders to be played on Sundays at Yankee Stadium. After all the games had been played, the team with the best overall record would receive the trophy and $500.[6] It was hardly a selfless gesture since the Yankee organization was profiting from the games, too. They charged teams between $2,000 and $3,000 per date to play at Yankee Stadium.[7]

The second such doubleheader took place on July 2. The Eagles handily defeated the Philadelphia Stars 8-1, while the Elite Giants blanked the New York Black Yankees, 4-0. Baltimore's "three-run rally in the ninth clinched the outcome."[8] Before the games, the Negro National League paid tribute to its Hall of Fame. According to the *New York Times*, "Pioneers of the sport in Negro circles [were to] be guests of honor at the games."[9] The nominations for the Hall of Fame included Newark's first baseman Mule Suttles and shortstop Willie Wells.[10]

As the season progressed, a decision was made to award the trophy to the winner of the Negro National League II pennant. Normally, the winners of each half of the season competed in a two-team playoff series to determine the pennant winner. Under a new format introduced in 1939, the four teams (out of the six total) that had won the most games throughout the entire season would compete in a set of playoff series. From a revenue standpoint, more teams in the playoffs meant more games played, and "more games meant more gate receipts."[11] In any event, under the expanded playoff format, the top-seeded Homestead Grays faced the fourth-seeded Philadelphia Stars, while the second-seeded Newark Eagles took on the third-seeded Baltimore Elite Giants.[12] Both series were scheduled for early September.

The Newark Eagles came into the series against Baltimore having slugged 32 home runs in 56 games during the regular season. Mule Suttles and Ed Stone paced the team with seven homers each. The Elite Giants had played only 44 games but had swatted 12 homers, led by Henry Kimbro and pitcher Bill Byrd (three homers each). Additionally, each ballclub had stars who had played in the East-West All-Star Game on August 6 at Comiskey Park in Chicago.[13]

Game One: September 6, 1939: Newark Eagles 8, Baltimore Elite Giants 6, at Ruppert Stadium, Newark, New Jersey

Game One took place on September 6 at Ruppert Stadium in Newark. The contest was characterized, and eventually decided by, the long ball. Newark's Bob Evans and Baltimore's Emery Adams had the starting mound duties. Evans had been playing

197

in Newark since 1934, first for the Newark Dodgers and then, beginning in 1936, for the Eagles. The 6-foot-5 right-hander was a workhorse for his first five seasons, but in 1939 he had made just four appearances on the mound, pitching 19⅔ total innings. His 1.780 WHIP contributed to a 7.32 ERA. Conversely, this was Adams's first season with Baltimore. He was also a righty but stood only 5-feet-8, and he had pitched the previous three seasons for the Memphis Red Sox. In 1939 Adams had five appearances (two starts).[14] Although he sported a 2-0 record, his ERA was 5.85, and he had allowed more walks than strikeouts; his strikeout-to-walk ratio was 0.86.

Baltimore jumped ahead with a run in the top of the third, and then the Elite Giants exploded for four more runs in the fourth, sending Evans to the showers. Over the next three innings, the Eagles "pulled an almost certain defeat 'out of the fire.'"[15] In the bottom of the fourth, Newark rookie Freddie Wilson reached first with a hit. Suttles, already known as "one of the greatest power hitters in Negro League history,"[16] clouted a home run into the left-field stands. The *Newark Star Eagle* reported that the blast traveled 425 feet.[17]

Max Manning, a 20-year-old rookie, relieved Evans to start the fifth and "held the Giants effectively."[18] In the home half of the fifth, Wilson homered into the center-field stands with two men aboard to tie the game. Suttles followed him with a solo shot over the left-field wall, his second home run in as many innings. This gave the Eagles the lead, and now it was Baltimore's turn to make a pitching change. Byrd was summoned to the mound to relieve Adams.

Byrd pitched for the Baltimore Elite Giants from 1938 through 1948 (and for the Cleveland Red Sox and the Columbus and Washington Elite Giants before that).[19] The right-hander later led the league in wins three times (in 1942, 1945, and 1948)[20] and in ERA once (1941). His 1939 statistics included a 7-2 record and a 3.32 ERA in 76 innings pitched. As a member of the Baltimore teams, he appeared in seven different East-West All-Star Games; he started both All-Star Games in 1939 for the East squad.[21] Byrd is also known as "the last Negro league pitcher to legally throw the spitball."[22] On top of that, in 1939 he batted .378 and had an OPS of 1.086.

Newark padded its advantage in the bottom of the sixth after 42-year-old Biz Mackey singled and advanced a base on Manning's sacrifice. Mackey had begun the season with Baltimore but after 13 games with the Elite Giants, was sold to the Eagles.[23] Joe Eckles doubled, plating Mackey, and Eckles later scored on Dick Seay's single to make it an 8-5 game in favor of Newark.

Manning cruised through the rest of the game as he fanned two Baltimore batters and yielded only four hits, although the Elite Giants did get another run in the seventh. The Eagles battered Adams and Byrd for 11 hits that included three homers. Suttles added a double to his two round-trippers to lead the Eagles' assault, driving in three runs. Wilson, Seay, and Mackey each contributed two hits as well. Baltimore pounded out 13 hits

total, but most of them came off Evans in the first four frames. Newark's 8-6 victory was an exciting start to the playoff series.

Game Two: September 9, 1939: Baltimore Elite Giants 11, Newark Eagles 3, at 44th and Parkside, Philadelphia

The second game of the series was played three days later in Philadelphia, at the 44th and Parkside ballpark. The Eagles still played as the home team. Baltimore again outhit the Eagles, and this time, the Elite Giants prevailed. Jonas Gaines started for Baltimore and pitched a complete game, scattering seven hits. In six appearances during the regular season, he had made five starts and tossed four complete games. Future Hall of Famer Leon Day started for Newark. He had tied for the league lead in starts in 1939 (with Philadelphia's Jim Missouri – each had 11), winning seven of 10 decisions with seven complete games. However, in this playoff game, he was soon replaced by Evans, in part because he walked five batters during his brief time on the mound.[24]

Baltimore scored two runs in the top of the first. Felton Snow's two-out double drove in both Kimbro and Sammy Hughes. Hughes later blasted a solo home run for Baltimore in the second inning, and Baltimore added single tallies in each of the next two innings as well. In the sixth, the visitors scored four more times to put the game out of reach. Each team scored twice in the eighth inning. Suttles hit his third homer of the series, a two-run round-tripper, to prevent Newark from being shut out. The Eagles added a run in the bottom of the ninth on Mackey's single that scored Wilson.

The Newark defense made five errors in the game, which contributed to the rout.[25] Hughes and Red Moore led the Elite Giants with three hits each, and half of Baltimore's 12 hits went for extra bases; in addition to Hughes's homer, the Elite Giants hit five doubles. Newark's leadoff batter, future Hall of Famer Monte Irvin, had done his utmost for the losing team on this day and joined Wilson and Mackey as Newark batters who had two hits each.

Game Three: September 10, 1939: Baltimore Elite Giants 7, Newark Eagles 3 (first game of doubleheader), at Terrapin Park, Baltimore

With the series tied at one game apiece, the two ballclubs headed to Baltimore for a game to be played on Sunday, September 10, at Baltimore's Terrapin Park, as the first game of a scheduled doubleheader. Newark sent rookie Harry "Big Train" Cozart, its "six feet four-inch chucker,"[26] to the mound. Baltimore countered with Byrd. Each team hoped to "continue their campaign for a place in the finals of the Negro National League playoffs."[27]

Byrd held the visiting Eagles scoreless through the first four innings. Meanwhile, the Elite Giants tallied twice in the bottom of the third. Byrd helped his own cause with a solo home run while Kimbro doubled and was driven in by Hughes. Baltimore added two more runs in the fourth for a 4-0 lead. Newark responded by scoring once in the fifth and then twice in the sixth, with one run coming on Ed Stone's homer, to make it a one-run game.

Baltimore got both runs back in the bottom of the sixth and added a final run in the eighth to win the game, 7-3. In spite of heavy hitting by both sides, the two starters pitched complete games. For the third consecutive game, the Elite Giants put up double-digit hits (10), and the Eagles banged out 13 hits in the losing cause.

Game Four: September 10, 1939: Baltimore Elite Giants 5, Newark Eagles 2 (second game of doubleheader, six innings), at Terrapin Park, Baltimore

At some point, a decision was made to play a doubleheader, perhaps to expedite determining a winner of this series that was to go a maximum of five games. The third game had taken 2 hours and 35 minutes, so the two teams began to play Game Four in the late afternoon. Willie Hubert started for Baltimore while Manning, who had pitched in relief in Game One, started for the Eagles.

Wells led off the game for Newark and reached on an error by third baseman Snow. Wells used his speed to steal a base and came around to score on catcher Roy Campanella's subsequent throwing error. Two errors had led to a run. In 1939 future Hall of Famer Campanella was just 17 years old, but he already was playing in his third season with the Elite Giants. Campanella credited Mackey as his mentor and catching coach, saying, "He just asked me to sit beside him. He helped me to learn everything."[28] After Mackey was sold to Newark in midseason, Campanella became Baltimore's starting catcher.

In the bottom of the first, Hughes singled with one out and scored on Wild Bill Wright's double. Wright had finished 10th in the NNL2 in 1939 with a .365 batting average, and he scored next on Snow's single.

Both pitchers notched scoreless second and third innings, but Baltimore added a run in the fourth and two more in the fifth. Through five innings, Manning had allowed 11 hits and a walk. Meanwhile, Hubert had shut down the Eagles. Stone launched his second home run of the series in the top of the sixth, but that was one of only two Newark hits in the game.

After six innings, the contest was called due to darkness. The Eagles had batted in all six frames; thus, the Elite Giants were named champions of the series, which gave them the opportunity to play for the Ruppert Trophy. Baltimore scored 29 runs in 31 innings in the four games. Although the Eagles had outhomered the Elite Giants, six to two, Baltimore's team OPS of .843 bested Newark's .795. Further, in the four games, the Elites had 44 hits, 10 more than their opponents, while each team drew 14 walks. The Newark pitching staff's ERA was almost three runs higher than Baltimore's.

Bill Byrd was one of Baltimore's playoff stars. He won Game Three on the mound, putting Baltimore within a win of the series championship, and he also went 2-for-3 at the plate with a home run and two runs scored. For the series, Sammy Hughes banged out a team-high seven hits (in 15 at-bats), good for a

.467 batting average and 1.329 OPS. For Newark, Biz Mackey was 6-for-12 and Mule Suttles went 4-for-15 (.267) with three home runs, three runs scored, and five runs batted in.

With the first-round series victory under their belts, the Elite Giants went on to face the Homestead Grays, winner of the other playoff series. It had taken the Grays five games to defeat the Stars; the first game was played at Municipal Field in Homestead, Pennsylvania. Games Two and Three consisted of a doubleheader on September 10 in Cleveland, and then the final pair of games were contested in Philadelphia (at 44th and Parkside). In a five-game championship series, Baltimore captured the pennant with three wins over the Grays (there was also a tie). According to the *New York Times*, in the finale, "the Baltimore nine registered a brace of runs in the seventh inning and earned a shut-out triumph, 2 to 0."[29]

The Line Scores[30]
Game One
September 6, 1939, at Ruppert Stadium, Newark

Baltimore Elite Giants	0 0 1	4 0 0	1 0 0	–	6	13 0
Newark Eagles	0 0 0	2 4 2	0 0 x	–	8	11 0

WP: M. Manning, LP: E. Adams

Game Two
September 9, 1939, at 44th and Parkside, Philadelphia

Baltimore Elite Giants	2 1 1	1 0 4	0 2 0	–	11	12 0
Newark Eagles	0 0 0	0 0 0	0 2 1	–	3	7 5

WP: J. Gaines, LP: L. Day

Game Three
September 10, 1939, at Terrapin Park, Baltimore

Newark Eagles	0 0 0	0 1 2	0 0 0	–	3	13 2
Baltimore Elite Giants	0 0 2	2 0 2	0 1 x	–	7	10 1

WP: B. Byrd, LP: H. Cozart

Game Four
September 10, 1939, at Terrapin Park, Baltimore

Newark Eagles	1 0 0	0 0 1	–	2	2 0
Baltimore Elite Giants	2 0 0	1 2 x	–	5	11 2

WP: W. Hubert, LP: M. Manning

SOURCES

In addition to the sources mentioned in the Notes, the author consulted Baseball-Reference.com, Retrosheet.org, and SABR.org.

The author sincerely thanks Elizabeth Young Miller, social sciences librarian at the E.W. Fairchild-Martindale Library of Lehigh University, for her assistance with searching for sources.

In addition, I thank the team at the Charles F. Cummings New Jersey Information Center of the Newark Public Library for scans of Newark newspapers.

NOTES

1   Bob Luke, *The Baltimore Elite Giants* (Baltimore: The Johns Hopkins University Press, 2009), 43.

2   Founded in 1930 as the Nashville Elite Giants, the franchise moved to Columbus, Ohio, in 1935 and then to Washington, DC, the following year, staying for just two seasons. The Elite Giants spent the next 11 years (1938-1948) in Baltimore.

3   The Eagles had been in Newark since 1936, after spending their inaugural season (1935) in the Negro National League as the Brooklyn Eagles.

4   "Elites, Grays to Vie for Ruppert Trophy, Sunday," *Pittsburgh Courier*, September 23, 1939: 16.

5   Luke, 47.

6   Luke, 47.

7   James Overmyer, "Black Baseball at Yankee Stadium: The House That Ruth Built and Satchel Furnished (with Fans)," an article in John Graf. ed., *From Rube to Robinson: SABR's Best Articles on Black Baseball* (Phoenix: SABR, 2021), found online at https://sabr.org/journal/article/black-baseball-at-yankee-stadium-the-house-that-ruth-built-and-satchel-furnished-with-fans/. Accessed April 2023.

8   "Black Yankees Bow, 4-0: Baltimore Giants Win Feature of Twin Bill at Stadium," *New York Times*, July 3, 1939: 13.

9   "Negroes to Honor Stars: Baseball Pioneers to Be Guests at Doubleheader," *New York Times*, July 2, 1939: S2.

10 The nominations for the Negro Baseball Hall of Fame came from Joe Louis, world heavyweight champion; Bill Robinson, veteran tap dancer; and Cab Calloway, orchestra leader. The nominees were Suttles, Wells, outfielder Fats Jenkins, pitcher Satchel Paige, catcher Josh Gibson, third baseman Little Black Francis, pitcher Cannonball Dick Redding, first baseman Oscar Charleston, pitcher José Mendez, center fielder Sam West, pitcher Bullet Rogan, and catcher Frank Duncan. See "Negroes to Honor Stars: Baseball Pioneers to Be Guests at Doubleheader." Paige, Gibson, and Jenkins were the only players with multiple nominations.

11 Luke, 47.

12 It is difficult to reconcile this seeding with the won-lost records for each team. Using Baseball-Reference, Homestead won 36 games. Newark was second-best, with 32 wins. Philadelphia won 24 games, and Baltimore won 21 games. The author has not found evidence to support why Philadelphia and Baltimore were switched in the seedings. A possible explanation was to give the Elite Giants some weight for having won the second half, thus combining the old and new playoff systems.

13 Norm King, "August 6, 1939: Late Home Runs Lift West to Win in Negro League All-Star Game," SABR Games Project, sabr.org/gamesproj/game/august-6-1939-the-east-west-all-star-game-got-their-vote/. Accessed April 2023.

14 Adams also played two games in 1939 as an outfielder. In eight games at the plate, he batted .417 (5-for-12, all singles).

15 "Homers Give Eagles Victory," *Newark Star Eagle*, September 7, 1939: 16.

16 Stephen V. Rice, "Mule Suttles," SABR Biography Project.

17 "Homers Give Eagles Victory."

18 "Homers Give Eagles Victory."

19 Byrd also made three total appearances for the Philadelphia Stars in 1943 and 1944.

20 In 1942 Byrd tied for the league lead in wins with Ray Brown of the Homestead Grays. In 1945 Byrd tied for the league lead in wins with Homestead's Ray Welmaker.

21 Byrd appeared in seven East-West All-Star Games while pitching for Baltimore. In each of 1939 and 1946, Byrd played in two contests, while in 1941, 1944, and 1945, there was only one game.

22 Luke, 37.

23 To help them in the second half of the season, the Elites picked up five players from the Atlanta Black Crackers (first baseman James "Red" Moore, Tommy "Pee Wee" Butts, pitchers Ed Dixon and Felix Evans, and catcher Oscar Brown). The Black Crackers began the 1939 season playing in Indianapolis as the Indianapolis A.B.C.'s, but the team could not find a ballpark and broke up, allowing for the players to join Baltimore (see Luke). This meant that the Elite Giants had to make room for the new additions to the roster, so they sold Jim West to the Philadelphia Stars and Mackey to the Eagles.

24 For the regular season, Day had walked 25 batters in 87 innings pitched.

25 Retrosheet's box score of the game leaves one column blank: the number of earned runs. Newspaper clippings do not list the number of earned/unearned runs in the game, so we cannot assess the impact of Newark's errors.

26 "Newark Eagles Are Eliminated," *Newark Star Eagle*, September 11, 1939: 14.

27 "Diamond Chips," *Newark Sunday Call*, September 10, 1939: 22.

28 Luke, 34.

29 "Elite Giants Gain Title," *New York Times*, September 25, 1939: 26.

30 Line scores found at https://www.retrosheet.org/NegroLeagues/1939NNL1a.html. Accessed April 2023.

THE 1939 NEGRO NATIONAL LEAGUE CHAMPIONSHIP SERIES

BALTIMORE ELITE GIANTS VS. HOMESTEAD GRAYS

BY RICHARD J. PUERZER

The 1939 Negro National League Championship Series featured a matchup between the Homestead Grays, in pursuit of their third consecutive league championship, and the Baltimore Elite Giants. The Grays, led by their principal owner, future Hall of Fame member Cumberland Posey, and their player-manager, the veteran outfielder Vic Harris, finished atop the Negro National League for the third year in a row in 1939. The Elite Giants, owned by Tom Wilson and led by player-manager Felton Snow, finished fourth in the league, primarily on the basis of a strong second half of the season.

The powerhouse Homestead Grays featured three future Hall of Fame players: Ray Brown, who is in the Hall of Fame as a pitcher but who appeared in this series as an outfielder and first baseman; first baseman Buck Leonard; and catcher Josh Gibson. Leonard and Gibson were two of the most fearsome sluggers to ever grace a baseball diamond. In 1939 Gibson was 27 years old and Leonard was 31, and each was at the height of his ability. Other great players on the team included second baseman Sam Bankhead and pitcher Roy Partlow.

The Baltimore Elite Giants were also a talented team, with outfielders Bill Hoskins and Wild Bill Wright, and second baseman Sammy Hughes. They featured two future Hall of Famers, Biz Mackey, who did not appear in the Championship Series, and starting catcher Roy Campanella, who was only 17 years old. The matchup between Gibson and Campanella made this Series special in that it was a battle between two of the greatest catchers of all time.

Game One: September 16, 1939, Homestead Grays 2, Baltimore Elite Giants 1, at 44th and Parkside, Philadelphia

The best-of-five-games Championship Series began on the evening of Saturday, September 16, before approximately 3,000 spectators at the ballpark at 44th and Parkside in Philadelphia. The Homestead Grays played as the home team at this neutral location, selected to capitalize on the sizable Negro League fan base in Philadelphia. Bill Byrd got the start for the Elite Giants, facing lefty Roy Partlow of the Grays. In the bottom of the first inning, the Grays got off to a quick start when leadoff hitter David Whatley, Vic Harris, and Sam Bankhead singled, with singles, with Whatley scoring on Bankhead's hit. Josh Gibson

then came to the plate and grounded to Giants second baseman Sammy Hughes, who forced Bankhead out at second. Buck Leonard followed with runners on the corners and grounded the ball to shortstop Tommy "Pee Wee" Butts, who bobbled the ball long enough to allow Harris to score.

In the fourth inning, the Elite Giants tried to rally back. Sammy Hughes led off with a double to right field. He advanced to third on an out by Red Moore and scored when Bill Wright grounded out to third base. Although Byrd allowed 10 hits in the game, including doubles by Whatley, Bankhead, and Leonard, he kept the Grays from scoring after the first inning. Meanwhile Partlow was equally good, preventing any scoring aside from the Giants' fourth-inning run. Both pitchers threw complete games, with Partlow getting the victory and the Grays taking a 1-0 lead in the series.[1]

Baltimore	0	0	0	1	0	0	0	0	0		1	4	1
Homestead	2	0	0	0	0	0	0	0	x		2	10	1

Game Two: September 17, 1939 (Game One of a doubleheader), Baltimore Elite Giants 7, Homestead Grays 5, at Oriole Park, Baltimore

The second game of the Series was played as the first game of a doubleheader on Sunday, September 17. The game was played in Baltimore at Terrapin Park, also known as Oriole Park, one of the Elites Giants' two home fields, along with Bugle Field. An estimated 3,000 fans were in attendance for the afternoon doubleheader. Tom Parker was the starter for Homestead, up against Jonas Gaines, southpaw hurler for the Elite Giants. Unlike the low-scoring first game of the Series, this game featured offensive explosions from both teams.

The Grays got on the board in the top of the first with a two-out rally. Sam Bankhead reached base on a single. Josh Gibson followed and pulled a home run over the left-field wall to give the Grays a two-run lead. The Grays continued to threaten as Buck Leonard ripped a single up the middle and Henry Spearman reached on a dropped third strike. Country Davis then drove a ball to deepest center field, but center fielder

Henry Kimbro tracked it down with an impressive running catch to end the inning. The Elite Giants tallied their first run in the bottom of the second when Bill Wright drove a ball to left field for a double, and scored on a single by Felton Snow. In the top of the third, Kimbro made another athletic play in center field when he chased down a towering fly ball struck by Vic Harris.

In the top of the fourth, the Grays scored another run to extend their lead. Buck Leonard drew a leadoff walk, stole second, and scored on a two-out Texas Leaguer by Jelly Jackson. In the bottom of the frame, the Elite Giants had their biggest rally of the game. Red Moore walked to lead off the inning. Bill Wright's double scored Moore, and Felton Snow followed with another double, plating Wright. Next up, Bill Hoskins singled to score Snow for the Elite Giants' third run of the inning, giving Baltimore a 4-3 lead. The Grays answered back in the top of the fifth. Sam Bankhead singled, Josh Gibson walked, and Buck Leonard singled to drive in Bankhead and tie the game, 4-4. The Elite Giants were able to manufacture runs in the sixth and seventh innings. In the sixth, Felton Snow singled for his third hit of the game and took second on an error by Grays shortstop Jackson. Roy Campanella struck out, but Josh Gibson dropped the third strike and threw wildly to first, allowing Snow to score. In the seventh, Henry Kimbro singled, made his way to third on sacrifices by Hughes and Moore, and scored on a single by Wright. The score now stood 6-4 in favor of the Elite Giants.

In the top of the eighth, the Grays threatened once more. With one out, Henry Spearman singled. Country Davis followed with a single to center. Henry Kimbro fielded the ball and threw to third to try to cut down Spearman, who was attempting to take the extra base, but Kimbro's throw flew over third baseman Snow's head and into the Grays dugout, allowing Spearman to score and Davis to advance to third. The Elite Giants prevented more runs from scoring with two great defensive plays. First, Bill Wright made a strong throw from right field on Jelly Jackson's fly out, keeping the runner at third. Then with two outs, Red Moore made a great play at first on a hard-hit groundball off the bat of Sam Bankhead. The Elite Giants now led 7-5.

The Grays refused to go down without a fight in the ninth. Ray Brown, pinch-hitting for David Whatley, singled to lead off the inning. But the Elite Giants defense came through once more, turning a third-to-second-to-first double play. Gaines then struck out Sam Bankhead to end the game and give the Elite Giants the victory.

The Elite Giants were able to win despite the Grays collecting 10 hits and 9 walks. Buck Leonard reached base all five times he came to the plate. The Elite Giants defense quelled several Grays rallies, and Baltimore tied the Series at one game apiece.[2]

Homestead	2	0	0	1	1	0	0	1	0	5	10	4
Baltimore	0	1	0	3	0	1	1	1	x	7	10	1

Game Three: September 17, 1939 (Game Two of a doubleheader), Baltimore Elite Giants 1, Homestead Grays 1, at Oriole Park, Baltimore

The second game of the doubleheader pitted the Elite Giants starter, lefty Tom Glover, against the starting hurler for the Grays, Edsall Walker. The Grays struck first, scoring a run in the top of the second inning. Country Davis led off the inning with a walk but was cut down at second on a groundball hit by Jelly Jackson. Jackson proceeded to steal second, go to third on Roy Campanella's error, and score on another Campanella miscue, this time a passed ball. The Elite Giants scored in the bottom of the third. Campanella reached first on a muffed fly ball by Grays left fielder Vic Harris. Glover's sacrifice advanced Campanella to second and brought up the top of the order. Henry Kimbro grounded out for the second out of the inning, but Sammy Hughes followed with a single to score Campanella and tie the game. Red Moore then drew a walk and Bill Wright was intentionally walked to load the bases. Grays pitcher Walker worked his way out of the jam by striking out Felton Snow.

The game remained a 1-1 tie as the 6:00 P.M. Sunday curfew approached. In the bottom of the fifth, the Elite Giants came within inches of winning the game. With one out, Sammy Hughes reached base on a walk. Red Moore struck out for the second out of the inning. Bill Wright followed and drove a ball to right field. Hughes raced around the bases attempting to score, but the Grays defense was solid, with Harris firing to cutoff man Bankhead, who threw a bullet to Gibson to cut down Hughes on a close play at the plate. The curfew ended the game, tied 1-1.[3]

Homestead	0	1	0	0	0		1	3	1
Baltimore	0	0	1	0	0		1	5	1

Game Four: September 23, 1939, Baltimore Elite Giants 10, Homestead Grays 5, at 44th and Parkside, Philadelphia

The Series resumed at 3:00 P.M. on Saturday, September 23, back in Philadelphia at the ballpark at 44th and Parkside. The Grays were the home team once again and gave the start to Specs Roberts in his adopted hometown of Philadelphia. Baltimore manager Snow gave Bill Byrd the start, his second of the series. The umpire behind the plate was Cool Turner and covering the bases was Phil Cockrell.

Baltimore got the scoring started in the top of the second inning. Bill Hoskins slugged a triple and was driven home on a single to left by Roy Campanella, who then scored on a double off the bat of Byrd. Homestead came back in the bottom of the inning when Josh Gibson smashed a leadoff home run over the center-field wall. The Grays tacked on another run in the bottom of the third, and two more in the fourth to extend their lead to 4-2.

The fifth inning was rather tempestuous and demonstrated the competitive fire of both teams. Elite Giants center fielder

Henry Kimbro led off the top of the inning with a single. Sammy Hughes then grounded out to short for what seemed like a routine play. However, Kimbro broke for third on the play. Grays first baseman Buck Leonard fired the ball across the diamond to shortstop Jelly Jackson, who ended up on top of Kimbro as he slid into the base. Kimbro was called safe on the play but, taking exception to Jackson's physical play, hopped up and threw punches at him. Jackson readily took part in the fisticuffs himself until the players were pulled apart. Both Kimbro and Jackson were ejected from the game, but the rhubarb seemed to bring new energy to the Elite Giants. Hoss Walker replaced Kimbro on third base and was driven home by Red Moore to bring the Elite Giants within one run. In the sixth inning, Roy Campanella cracked a solo home run to left field to tie the game, 4-4.

In the seventh, the Elite Giants broke the game open. Hughes led off with a single and was sacrificed to second by Moore. The Grays took the bat out of the hands of Elite Giants cleanup hitter Bill Wright with an intentional walk. Felton Snow followed with a smash to shortstop, where Sam Bankhead was playing in place of Jackson. Bankhead bobbled the ball, and the bases were loaded. Bill Hoskins followed with a single, driving in two runs. Pee Wee Butts singled, loading the bases again, and Campanella continued the barrage with a single to drive two more runs home. The Elite Giants scored their fifth run of the inning when pitcher Bill Byrd's fly ball to right scored Butts from third. When the dust had settled for the inning, the Elite Giants were leading 9-4. Both teams scored a single run in the ninth inning and the Elite Giants walked away with a 10-5 victory.

Both pitchers gave up 15 hits in the game, but Elite Giants hurler Byrd was able to stay out of much trouble and earned the victory. Notably, both Josh Gibson and Roy Campanella homered and had four hits each. However, all of Gibson's at-bats came with the bases empty, while Campanella's hits drove in five runs in leading his team to victory. The victory gave the Elite Giants a two-games-to-one lead in the series.[4]

Baltimore	0	2	0	0	1	1	5	0	1		10	15	1
Homestead	0	1	1	2	0	0	0	0	1		5	15	1

Game Five: September 24, 1939, Baltimore Elite Giants 2, Homestead Grays 0, at Yankee Stadium, New York

Yankee Stadium was the location of the next game in the Series, played in the afternoon on Sunday, September 24. This was the fourth game the Elite Giants and the third game the Grays played in Yankee Stadium in 1939. Yankee Stadium being the location of this game allowed the Black press additional opportunities to market the game, and in turn to draw a much larger crowd and make for a significant payday for the teams. A crowd of 8,000 to 15,000 (depending on the game account) attended. The game also gave the teams the opportunity to vie

for the Ruppert Memorial Trophy, named after the recently deceased owner of the Yankees, Jacob Ruppert. Beginning in 1939, the trophy was given to the Negro National League team that won the most games at the Stadium that year. For 1939, the winner of this game would take home the trophy.[5]

Baltimore was the home team for the game and started Jonas Gaines, who had won Game Two. Homestead started its ace, Roy Partlow, the winner of Game One. Just before the start of the game Elite Giants second baseman Sammy Hughes passed out on the bench and was taken to Harlem Hospital. (He was able to return to the Stadium before the end of the game.) Felton Snow took Hughes's position at second for the game and Hoss Walker took Snow's regular spot at third.

The game was a tense affair. Gaines and Partlow were in control and the two teams remained in a scoreless tie through the first six innings. In the bottom of the seventh, the Elite Giants offense finally broke through. After Red Moore grounded out, Bill Wright doubled and advanced to third on an infield single by Hoskins. Tommy Butts bunted foul on strike three for the second out of the inning. Hoss Walker followed with a groundball to third. Walker was safe when Henry Spearman's throw pulled Buck Leonard off first base. Wright scored on the play and Hoskins went to second. Roy Campanella drove a ball to right field for a single, knocking in Hoskins with the second run of the inning. Partlow struck out Gaines for the third out, but the damage had been done, courtesy of two unearned runs. The Grays threatened in the eighth. With one out, Gaines walked Vic Harris, but got Bankhead for the second out. However, Gaines then walked Josh Gibson and Buck Leonard to load the bases. Elite Giants manager Snow went to his bullpen and brought in Willie Hubert in relief of Gaines. Hubert was the only reliever to pitch in the entire Series. Henry Spearman was up next for the Grays and battled, fouling off three pitches, before he was induced into hitting an infield popup to end the inning. Hubert finished off the Grays in the ninth inning, securing the victory for the Elite Giants. The Baltimore Elite Giants won the series three games to one and were the champions of the Negro National League.[6]

Homestead	0	0	0	0	0	0	0	0	0		0	3	1
Baltimore	0	0	0	0	0	0	2	0	x		2	7	1

Series Postscript

After the game, the entertainer Bill "Bojangles" Robinson presented the Ruppert Memorial Trophy to Elite Giants team owner Tom Wilson. Aside from Game Four, which the Elite Giants won 10-5, all the games were quite close, and the Grays played well. On offense, the Grays were led by their sluggers, with Josh Gibson slugging two home runs and sporting a slash line of .353/.476/.706 for the Series. Likewise, Buck Leonard had an impressive series slash line of .462/.588/.462. For the Elite Giants, Roy Campanella gave a glimpse of his future greatness, smacking the only home run of the Series for his team while leading them with six RBIs. Jonas Gaines led the Elite Giants pitchers with two wins and a 2.16 ERA in 16⅔ innings pitched. Felton Snow also received plaudits for his steady leadership in blending a team of young players and veterans to the Series win.[7]

The final game of the series was the first game of a double-header, taking advantage of the Yankee Stadium crowd. The second game of the twin bill was played between a team made up of a mix of players from the Elite Giants and the Grays against what was termed an "All-Star" team of White minor leaguers That game was ended in the seventh inning due to darkness with the game tied, 1-1.[8] After the Series, several players from both teams joined separate barnstorming tours, with the Elite Giants heading South toward New Orleans, and the Grays pairing with the New York Black Yankees and heading for North Carolina.[9]

SOURCES

In addition to the sources cited in the Notes, the author consulted:

Clark, Dick, and Larry Lester, eds. *The Negro Leagues Book* (Cleveland: Society for American Baseball Research, 1994).

Riley, James A. *The Biographical Encyclopedia of the Negro Baseball Leagues* (New York: Carroll & Graf Publishers, Inc., 1994).

Unless otherwise noted, Seamheads.com was used for all Negro League player statistics.

NOTES

1   "Grays, Elites Divide," *Chicago Defender*, September 23, 1939: 8; "Homestead Grays, Elites Divide Pair," *Chicago Defender*, September 23, 1939: 8; "Partlow Bests Byrd as Grays Win Opener, 2-1," *Baltimore Afro-American*, September 23, 1939: 21. The game details described are drawn primarily from the game stories provided in the *Baltimore Afro-American*. Different sources, including game box scores, often provided fewer details.

2   "Grays, Elites Divide," *Chicago Defender*, September 23, 1939: 8; "Elites, Grays Tied in National League Title Series," *Baltimore Afro-American*, September 23, 1939: 19.

3   "Grays, Elites Divide"; "Elites, Grays Tied in National League Title Series."

4   "Campanella in Star's Role as Elites Score," *Baltimore Afro-American*, September 30, 1939: 21. Neil Lanctot, *Campy: The Two Lives of Roy Campanella* (New York: Simon & Schuster, 2011), 58-60.

5   Jim Overmyer, "Black Baseball at Yankee Stadium: The House That Ruth Built and Satchel Furnished (With Fans)," *Black Ball: A Negro Leagues Journal*, Volume 7, 2014, 5-32. Going into this game, the Elite Giants had won three games in Yankee Stadium while the Grays had won two for the season. It was decided that the winner of this game would be awarded the Ruppert Memorial Trophy.

6   "Elite Giants Win National League Championship," *Baltimore Afro-American*, September 30, 1939: 21; "Baltimore Whips Homestead Grays for Title," *Chicago Defender*, September 30, 1939: 9; "Elites Drub Grays For Jacob Ruppert Trophy," *New Journal and Guide* (Norfolk, Virginia), September 30, 1939: 17; Dan Burley, "Baltimore Elites Cop NNL Title, Beat Grays 2-0," *New York Amsterdam News*, September 30, 1939: 14; "Elites Beat Grays for Title," *Pittsburgh Courier*, September 30, 1939: 16.

7   Randy Dixon, "The Sport Bugle," *Pittsburgh Courier*, October 7, 1939: 17.

8   "Baltimore Whips Homestead Grays for Title," *Chicago Defender*, September 30, 1939: 9; "Elites Drub Grays For Jacob Ruppert Trophy."

9   "Elite Stars to Play in Game," *Baltimore Afro-American*, September 30, 1939: 20; "Grays, Yanks Barnstorm Through South," *Baltimore Afro-American*, September 23, 1939: 20.

CONTRIBUTORS

Born in Baltimore, **MALCOLM ALLEN** grew up about five miles north of the former site of Oriole Park, where the 1939 Elite Giants played their home games. Now based in Brooklyn, New York, he manages an event production warehouse and enjoys spending time with his wife, Sara, and their two daughters.

CHRIS BETSCH lives in New Albany, Indiana, and has been a member of SABR since 2018, a member of the Pee Wee Reese Chapter of Louisville, Kentucky. He has written a number of articles for BioProject and Games Projects, and has also submitted articles for the newsletters of the Minor Leagues and Deadball Era Committees.

RICHARD BOGOVICH has authored three books: *Frank Grant: The Life of a Black Baseball Pioneer*, *Kid Nichols: A Biography of the Hall of Fame Pitcher*, and *The Who: A Who's Who*. In 2023 he solved the disappearance of Negro Leaguer Dave Brown with verification assistance from the late Frederick "Rick" Bush, Brown's SABR biographer. Richard has degrees from Northern Illinois University and is office manager of the Wendland Utz law firm in Rochester, Minnesota.

FREDERICK C. "RICK" BUSH joined SABR in March 2014. He wrote articles for over two dozen SABR books as well as the BioProject and Games Project. He co-edited seven SABR books about the Negro Leagues: *Bittersweet Goodbye: The Black Barons, the Grays, and the 1948 Negro League World Series* (2018); *The Newark Eagles Take Flight: The Story of the 1946 Negro League Champions* (2019); *Pride of Smoketown: The 1935 Pittsburgh Crawfords* (2020); *When the Monarchs Reigned: Kansas City's 1942 Negro League Champions* (2021); *The First Negro League Champion: The 1920 Chicago American Giants* (2022), *The Stars Shone on Philadelphia: The 1934 Negro National League Champions* (2023), and this volume. Before his passing in 2023, Rick lived with his wife, Michelle, their three sons – Michael, Andrew, and Daniel – and their border collie-mix, Bailey, in the greater Houston area, where he taught English at Wharton County Junior College's satellite campus in Sugar Land.

GARY JOSEPH CIERADKOWSKI is the artist and writer behind The Infinite Baseball Card Set at the StudioGaryC.com. He is an award-winning graphic artist and illustrator, and chances are you've visited or bought something he had a hand in designing: Bicycle Playing Cards, the music department of Barnes & Noble, the Folgers Coffee can, and the graphics for Oriole Park at Camden Yards, still regarded as the best designed ballpark in the majors. Gary's baseball writing, art, and research were recognized by the Baseball Reliquary in 2015 when he was named the recipient of the Tony Salin Award for Contributions to Baseball History. His book, which he wrote, illustrated, and designed, *The League of Outsider Baseball: An Illustrated History of Baseball's Forgotten Heroes*, was published in 2015 by Simon & Schuster. His latest book is *21: The Illustrated Journal of Outsider Baseball, Volume 2*. Growing up a Mets fan in the 1970s, Gary learned to live with pain and disappointment until he married his beautiful wife, Andrea. The two live happily in Northern Kentucky, unless they discuss the merits of the designated-hitter rule.

MATT CLEVER retired from the Air Force to become a land surveyor in his native Pennsylvania. A member of SABR since the 1990s, he has contributed to various publications including *The Glorious Beaneaters* (2019); *Whales, Terriers, and Terrapins* (2020); *The Pride of Smoketown* (2020); and *Baltimore Baseball* (2021). Matt lives with his teenage son Trey (who, sadly, cannot understand his father's obsession) and two old cats named Utley and Rollins.

ALAN COHEN chairs the BioProject fact-checking committee, serves as vice president-treasurer of the Connecticut Smoky Joe Wood Chapter, and is a datacaster (milb first pitch stringer) for the Hartford Yard Goats of the Double-A Eastern League. His biographies, game stories, and essays have appeared in more than 70 SABR publications. He is a proud contributor to SABR books on the Negro Leagues including *Bittersweet Goodbye*, *Pride of Smoketown*, *When the Monarchs Reigned*, and *The Stars Shone on Philadelphia*. His story "Josh Gibson Blazes a Trail," appeared in the Fall 2020 issue of the *Baseball Research Journal*. He is currently involved with the Retrosheet project on Negro League Games and serves on the SABR Negro Leagues Committee. He has four children, nine grandchildren, and one great-grandchild and resides in Connecticut with wife Frances, their cats, Zoe and Ava, and their dog Buddy.

ADAM DAROWSKI is the director of design and product management for Sports Reference, maker of Baseball Reference, Stathead, Immaculate Grid, and more. He lives with his family and trio of rescue dogs in Massachusetts. He has been a member of SABR since 2013 and shares his baseball research projects on darowski.com.

KEN DRAUT, a retired educational researcher and US Navy officer, is an active member of the Pee Wee Reese Chapter of

SABR in Louisville, Kentucky. As a child, Ken met Felton Snow in 1960 and they talked regularly until Mr. Snow's death in 1974. Prior to this article, Ken wrote a short Wikipedia article about Mr. Snow and has had a lifetime interest in the Negro League Baseball Era. Ken lives in St. Matthews, Kentucky, with his wife, Melissa, and his golden retriever, Loki.

DARREN GIBSON spent his Little League and high-school years in Lakewood, California, playing alongside multiple athletes who eventually made "The Show," but his baseball highlight was actually getting a "call-back" during walk-on tryouts at UCLA's Jackie Robinson Stadium in the late 1980s. Darren has been an avid baseball simulation player for decades and he still "bleeds Dodger blue." He has written over 35 SABR baseball player biographies, and is currently a math teacher, coach, and high-school football official in Aliso Viejo, California.

MARGARET M. "PEGGY" GRIPSHOVER is a professor of geography at Western Kentucky University. She earned her Ph.D. in Geography at the University of Tennessee and her M.S. and B.S. degrees in Geography from Marshall University. She has been a SABR member since 2006 and combines her love of baseball with her geographic research on race, ethnicity, urbanization, horse racing, and cultural landscapes. Peggy has published articles in the *Baseball Research Journal* and contributed a chapter on "Wrigleyville" for *Northsiders: Essays on the History and Culture of the Chicago Cubs*, edited by Gerald R. Wood and Andy Hazucha (McFarland, 2008). She has written biographies for numerous SABR publications including *Bittersweet Goodbye: The Black Barons, the Grays, and the 1948 Negro League World Series* (SABR 2017); *The Newark Eagles Take Flight: The Story of the 1946 Negro League Champions* (SABR 2019); *Pride of Smoketown: The 1935 Pittsburgh Crawfords* (SABR 2020), *When the Monarchs Reigned: Kansas City's 1942 Negro League Champions* (SABR 2021), *The First Negro League Champion: The 1920 Chicago American Giants* (SABR 2022), and *The Stars Shone on Philadelphia: The 1934 Negro National League Champions* (SABR 2023), all edited by Frederick C. Bush and Bill Nowlin. She is a native of Cincinnati and a lifelong Reds fan. She lives in Bowling Green, Kentucky, with her husband, Thomas L. Bell.

JOHN V. HAYNES II is a paramedic and student at Eastern Kentucky University who resides in Estill County, Kentucky, with his wife and three children. He joined SABR in 2023 and is making his first contribution to a baseball-related publication. A veteran of the US Navy, he served as a mass communication specialist and contributed to several news articles, photographs, and videos related to military operations published in news outlets around the world. John was born and raised in Cincinnati and is a lifelong Reds fan but will take in a baseball game anywhere he sees one. He is passionate about Black baseball history and aside from the occasional guest post on the blog "Home Plate Don't Move," he operates a website that attempts to catalog player uniforms and equipment at nlbuniforms.com.

LESLIE HEAPHY, associate professor of history at Kent State University at Stark, is vice president of SABR and president of the board for the IWBC (International Women's Baseball Center). She has written numerous articles, book chapters, and books on both the Negro Leagues and women's baseball.

MIKE HUBER grew up in Charm City and has been rooting for Baltimore's baseball teams (professional and college) for over 50 years. A professor of mathematics at Muhlenberg College, Mike enjoys regularly teaching a course titled Reasoning With Sabermetrics, mentoring students in sabermetrical research and writing for SABR's Games Project. He has contributed to more than 40 SABR book projects.

JAY HURD is a librarian, retired from Harvard University, and a museum educator. A member of the Society for American Baseball Research for more than 20 years, he contributes to the SABR Baseball Biography Project and presents on baseball-related topics including the Negro Leagues, baseball literature for children and young adults, and women in baseball. A longtime fan of the Boston Red Sox, Jay relocated from Medford, Massachusetts, to Bristol, Rhode Island, in 2016. He continues to research baseball in Rhode Island, with special attention given to Lizzie Murphy, from Warren, Rhode Island, who played professional baseball exclusively on men's teams. Jay was interviewed on Lizzie Murphy by Rhode Island PBS.

BILL JOHNSON has contributed over 40 biographies to SABR's BioProject and presented papers at the 2011 Cooperstown Symposium on Baseball and American Culture, the 2017 and 2023 Jerry Malloy Negro League Conferences, and the inaugural Southern Negro League Conference. He has published a biography of Hal Trosky (McFarland and Co., 2017) and most recently an article about Negro American League All-Star Art "Superman" Pennington in the journal *Black Ball*. Bill and his wife, Chris, currently reside in Georgia.

THOMAS KERN was born and raised in Southwest Pennsylvania. Listening to the mellifluous voices of Bob Prince and Jim Woods in his youth, how could one not become a lifelong Pirates fan? He now lives in Silver Spring, Maryland, and sees the Pirates, Nationals, and Orioles as often as possible. He is a SABR member dating back to the mid-1980s. With a love and appreciation for Negro League baseball in addition to the Pirates, he has written SABR bios for the 1979 Pirates and Clemente books and has completed bios for Leon Day, John Henry Lloyd, Willie Foster, Judy Johnson, Turkey Stearnes, Hilton Smith, Louis Santop, Andy Cooper, Double Duty Radcliffe, and others.

NORM KING (1957-2018) of Ottawa, Ontario, joined SABR in 2010 and became a prolific contributor to the SABR BioProject and Games Project until his untimely death from a rare form of bile duct cancer in 2018. He was the lead editor and author of *Au jeu/Play Ball: The 50 Greatest Games in the History of the Montreal*

Expos, published in 2016, and wrote chapters for a number of other SABR books, including *That's Joy in Braveland: The 1957 Milwaukee Braves, Winning on the North Side: The 1929 Chicago Cubs*, and *A Pennant for the Twin Cities: The 1965 Minnesota Twins*. He was an active member of SABR's Quebec Chapter and a friendly face at the SABR national convention each year.

LEN LEVIN is a longtime newspaper editor in New England, now retired. He lives in Providence with his wife, Linda, and an overachieving orange cat. He now (Len, not the cat) is the grammarian for the Rhode Island Supreme Court and edits its decisions. He also copy-edits many SABR books, including this one. He is just down the interstate from Fenway Park, where he has spent many happy (and some less happy) hours.

BOB LUKE took up writing baseball books after a 40-year career in human resource development. He holds a Ph.D. in Sociology from the University of Maryland. His most recent book is *Pete Hill: Baseball's First Black Superstar*, published by McFarland. Others include *The Most Famous Woman in Baseball: Effa Manley and the Negro Leagues* (Potomac Books), *The Baltimore Elite Giants: Sport and Society in the Age of Negro League Baseball* (John Hopkins University), *Integrating the Baltimore Orioles and Race in Baltimore* (McFarland), and *Willie Wells: "El Diablo" of the Negro Leagues* (University of Texas). He lives in Garrett Park, Maryland, with his wife, Judy.

SKIP NIPPER is a member of the Nashville Old Timers Baseball Association and the Grantland Rice-Fred Russell (Nashville) chapter of the Society for American Baseball Research. He is a contributing author to the Baseball Biography Project. Skip is the author of *Baseball in Nashville* (Arcadia Publishing, 2007). He shares his knowledge of local baseball history at https://baseballinnashville.com/. He assisted the Nashville Sounds in correctly identifying images and descriptions placed throughout First Horizon Park. He is a historical adviser for the initiative to bring major-league baseball to Nashville. Skip and his wife, Sheila, reside in Mt. Juliet, Tennessee. Together, they have seven children and 17 grandchildren, and along with their dogs, Sully Dell and Baseball Annie, they all love baseball.

BILL NOWLIN is from Cambridge, Massachusetts, born in Boston not far from Fenway Park. He is a co-founder of the Rounder Records music label and a former professor of political science. A lifelong Ted Williams fan, he has written or edited more than 100 books – mostly on baseball – and written more than 1,000 articles for SABR.

RICHARD J. PUERZER is the chairperson of the Department of Engineering at Hofstra University. His writing on baseball has appeared in numerous SABR books, as well as in *Nine: A Journal of Baseball History and Culture; Black Ball; The National Pastime; The Cooperstown Symposium on Baseball and American*

Culture proceedings; Zisk; and *Spitball*. He and his wife, Clare, have four children, Casey, Aaron, Josh, and Addie.

CHRIS RAINEY (1951-2020) was a SABR member since the late 1970s when he helped Eugene Murdock transcribe interviews of former players. In 2008 he wrapped up a 35-year teaching/coaching career in Yellow Springs, Ohio. He was a devoted Cleveland Indians fan, a dedicated historian, and an avid collector of baseball cards and Indians memorabilia. He was also deeply devoted to SABR, authoring over 80 biographies. After his death, his obituary declared that he had "stepped onto the Field of Dreams."

CARL RIECHERS retired from United Parcel Service in 2012 after 35 years of service. With more free time, he became a SABR member that same year. Born and raised in the suburbs of St. Louis, he became a big fan of the Cardinals. He and his wife, Janet, have three children and he is the proud grandpa of two.

DOUG SKIPPER has contributed to a number of SABR publications, presented research at national and regional conventions, and written more than two dozen player, manager, and game profiles for SABR's BioProject. A SABR member since 1982, he served as president of the Halsey Hall (Minneapolis) Chapter in 2014-2015, is a member of the Deadball Era Committee, and chairs the Lawrence Ritter Award Committee. He is interested in the history of Connie Mack's Philadelphia Athletics, the Boston Red Sox, the Minnesota Twins, and old ballparks. A market research consultant residing in Apple Valley, Minnesota, Doug is also a veteran of father-daughter dancing. Doug and his wife, Kathy, have two daughters, MacKenzie and Shannon.

BILL STAPLES JR. of Chandler, Arizona, has a passion for researching and telling the untold stories of the "international pastime." A SABR member since 2006, he counts among his areas of expertise Japanese American and Negro Leagues baseball history as a context for exploring the themes of civil rights, cross-cultural relations, and globalization. He is a board member of the Nisei Baseball Research Project and Japanese American Citizens League-Arizona Chapter, and chairman of the SABR Asian Baseball Committee. Staples is the author of *Kenichi Zenimura, Japanese American Baseball Pioneer* (McFarland, 2011), and co-authored *Gentle Black Giants: A History of Negro Leaguers in Japan* (NBRP Press, 2019) with Japanese baseball historian Kazuo Sayama. Staples has contributed to multiple SABR publications and received the SABR Baseball Research Award in 2012 for the Zenimura biography and in 2020 for the article, "Early Baseball Encounters in the West: The Yeddo Royal Japanese Troupe Play Ball in America, 1872." Learn more at zenimura.com.

JEB STEWART is a lawyer in Birmingham, Alabama, who is excited that MLB is coming to Rickwood Field in the summer of 2024. He has been a SABR member since 2012 and is co-president of the Rickwood Field SABR Chapter. He is an executive committee member on the Board of the Friends of Rickwood Field and is a regular contributor to the *Rickwood Times*. He also edits the Friends' quarterly newsletter, "Rickwood Tales." He has written several biographies for SABR's Biography Project.

DAVID B. STINSON is the administrator and photographer for the lost ballpark website deadballbaseball.com and posts blogs discussing Baltimore baseball history on his website, davidbstinsonauthor.com. He is the author of *Deadball, A Metaphysical Baseball Novel*, and co-author of *The College Baseball Primer: A Guide to College Baseball, Recruiting, Scholarships, and Summer Collegiate Wooden Bat Leagues*. David spent 10 years coaching youth baseball and is a former board member of the Cal Ripken Collegiate Baseball League (CRCBL), and former general manager of the Silver Spring-Takoma Thunderbolts of the CRCBL. David assisted Jane Leavy with historical research concerning Babe Ruth in Baltimore for Ms. Leavy's book, *The Big Fella: Babe Ruth and the World He Created*, and contributed several chapters about Baltimore's lost ballparks in SABR's 2021 publication *Baltimore Baseball*. He has consulted on Baltimore baseball history for Sagamore Development Company (now Weller Development Partners) and its redevelopment of Port Covington in Baltimore, and for the Peabody Heights Brewery in Baltimore, which sits on the former site of Terrapin Park and Oriole Park (V). He currently is assisting an effort to place a historical marker at the former site of Union Park and Oriole Park (III), and in 2020 helped place a marker at Peabody Heights Brewery recognizing the baseball history of that site. Still gainfully employed, he works as an administrative judge for the Department of Defense. He hopes someday to find photographs of the interior and exterior of John McGraw and Wilbert Robinson's Diamond Café, Baltimore's first sports bar, which from 1897 to 1915 was located at 519 North Howard Street.

RICK SWAINE is a semi-retired CPA who lives in the Tallahassee, Florida, area. He coaches and still competes in senior men's baseball leagues and tournaments. He is the author of *Beating the Breaks: Major League Ballplayers Who Overcame Disabilities* (McFarland 2004), *The Black Stars Who Made Baseball Whole: The Jackie Robinson Generation in the Major Leagues* (McFarland 2006), *The Integration of Major League Baseball* (McFarland 2009), *Baseball's Comeback Players* (McFarland 2014), and *Do It for Chappie: The Ray Chapman Tragedy* (Tucker Bay Publishing 2019). Rick is also a contributor to *The National Pastime* and the *Baseball Research Journal*. His latest book, *The Integration of Minor League Baseball: A History and Player Register 1946-1959 (*McFarland, co-authored with Gary Fink), was scheduled for release in spring 2024.

DAVE WILKIE grew up a third-generation San Francisco Giants fan in Western Canada idolizing Willie McCovey, Vida Blue, and Jack Clark. His obsession with Negro League baseball can be traced to a 1983 mail-order purchase of the book *The All-Time All-Stars of Black Baseball*, by SABR member James A. Riley. He has written SABR biographies on Negro League greats Sam Bankhead, Johnny Davis, Chester Williams, Cool Papa Bell, Frank Duncan, Judy Gans, and Rocky Ellis. He also contributed a chapter for the 2023 SABR publication *Nichibei Yakyu: US Tours of Japan*. Dave lives in Richmond, Virginia, with his son, Monte, and is currently working on his first book.

The Stars Shone on Philadelphia: The 1934 Phila. Stars

ISBN 978-1-960819-04-8 $9.99 ebook

ISBN 978-1-960819-05-5 $29.95 paperback

Biographies of Ed Bolden's 1934 Negro National League champions, including Biz Mackie and Jud Wilson.

When the Monarchs Reigned: KC's 1942 Champions

ISBN 978-1-970159-52-3 $9.99 ebook

ISBN 978-1-970159-53-0 $39.95 paperback

Featuring biographies of Hall of Famers Satchel Paige and Hilton Smith, the great Buck O'Neil, and Kansas City Call reporter Willa Bea Harmon.

The Newark Eagles Take Flight: The Story of the 1946 Negro Leagues Champions

ISBN 978-1-970159-06-6 $9.99 ebook

ISBN 978-1-970159-07-3 $29.95 paperback

The veterans of the Eagles are a veritable Who's Who including Larry Doby, Monte Irvin, Leon Day, "Biz" Mackie, and co-owner Effa Manley.

The First Negro League Champion: The 1920 Chicago American Giants

ISBN 978-1-970159-79-0 $9.99 ebook

ISBN 978-1-970159-80-6 $29.95 paperback

Rube Foster, founder of the Negro National League, Cristóbal Torriente, "Lefty" Brown, Bingo DeMoss.

Bittersweet Goodbye: The Black Barons, the Grays, and the 1948 Negro League World Series

ISBN 978-1-943816-54-5 $9.99 ebook

ISBN 978-1-943816-55-2 $44.95 paperback

Biographies of every player and coach on both teams, the Birmingham Black Barons and Homestead Grays.

Pride of Smoketown: The 1935 Pittsburgh Crawfords

ISBN 978-1-970159-24-0 $9.99 ebook

ISBN 978-1-970159-25-7 $34.95 paperback

Includes bios of James "Cool Papa" Bell, Oscar Charleston, Josh Gibson, and William "Judy" Johnson.

From Rube to Robinson: One-Win Wonders

ISBN 978-1-970159-40-0 $9.99 ebook

ISBN 978-1-970159-41-7 $34.95 paperback

A collection of the best Negro League baseball scholarship that SABR has produced, including work by the late Jerry Malloy, Jeremy Beer, & Larry Lester.

The Negro Leagues are Major Leagues

Co-published with Baseball Reference

ISBN 978-1-970159-62-2 $9.99 ebook

ISBN 978-1-970159-63-9 $12.95 paperback

An essential primer on Negro Leagues history and the integration of baseball's statistical records.

www.ingramcontent.com/pod-product-compliance
Lightning Source LLC
Chambersburg PA
CBHW080955120626
46546CB00010B/2906